Quest for Goodness

An Introduction to Ethics

Keith W. Krasemann

SIMON & SCHUSTER CUSTOM PUBLISHING

Copyright © 1998 by Keith Krasemann
All rights reserved.

This copyright covers material written expressly for this volume by the editor/s as well as the compilation itself. It does not cover the indi-vidual selections herein that first appeared elsewhere. Permission to reprint these has been obtained by Simon & Schuster Custom Publishing for this edition only. Further reproduction by any means, electronic or mechanical, including photocopying and recording, or by any information storage or retrieval system, must be arranged with the individual copyright holders noted.

Printed in the United States of America

10 9 8 7 6 5 4 3 2 1

ISBN 0-536-00604-0
BA 97419

SIMON & SCHUSTER CUSTOM PUBLISHING
160 Gould Street/Needham Heights, MA 02194
Simon & Schuster Education Group

Copyright Acknowledgments

Grateful acknowledgment is made to the following sources for permission to reprint material copyrighted or controlled by them:

Excerpt from *A Dream of Red Mansions*, by Cao Xueqin, 1994, translated by Huang Xinqu, Purple Bamboo Publishing.

"Candide, or Optimism," by Voltaire, reprinted from *Candide, or Optimism*, edited by Richard Ellis, translated by Richard Aldington, 1973, The George Macy Companies.

"Basic Doctrines - The First Sermon," by Buddha, reprinted from *The Life of Buddha as Legend and History*, by Edward J. Thomas, 1927, Routledge, Ltd.

"The Synopsis of Truth," by Buddha, reprinted from *Further Dialogues of the Buddha*, Vol. 6, translated by Lord Chalmers, 1927, Oxford University Press.

"Dependent Origination," by Henry Clarke Warren, reprinted from *Buddhism in Translations*, 1976, by permission of Harvard University Press.

"From Cruelty to Goodness," by Philip Hallie, Institute of Society, Ethics and the Life Sciences.

Excerpt from *Leviathan*, by Thomas Hobbes, 1651, reprinted from *Today's Moral Issues: Classic and Contemporary Perspectives*, edited by Daniel Bonevac, 1996, Mayfield Publishing Company.

"The Road Less Traveled," by M. Scott Peck, M.D., reprinted from *The Road Less Traveled*. Copyright ©1978 by M. Scott Peck, M.D. Reprinted by permission of Simon & Schuster.

"Moral Concern," by Rodger Beehler, reprinted from *Moral Life*, 1978, by permission of Rowan & Littlefield.

"Response," by Martin Buber, reprinted from *The Way of Response*, edited by Nahum N. Glatzer, 1966, Schocken Books, a division of Random House, Inc.

"The Story-Telling Animal," by Alasdair MacIntyre, reprinted from *After Virtue: A Study in Moral Theory*, 1981, University of Notre Dame Press.

"Kisagotami," by Peter D. Hershock, reprinted from *Liberating Intimacy: Enlightenment and Social Virtuosity in Chin Buddhism*, 1996, by permission of The State University of New York Press.

"The Good Samaritan," reprinted from *The New American Bible*, Confraternity of Christian Doctrine, 1970.

"Compassion," by Lawerence Blum, reprinted from *Explaining Emotions*, edited by Amelie O. Rorty. Copyright ©1980 by The Regents of the University of California. Reprinted by permission of University of California Press.

"The Practice of Reciprocity," by Confucius, reprinted from *Ethics of World Religions*, edited by Arnold Hunt, Marie T. Crotty, and Robert B. Crotty, 1991, by permission of Greenhaven Press.

"The Deep Beauty of the Golden Rule," by Robert M. MacIver, reprinted from *Moral Principles of Action*, edited by Ruth Anshen. Copyright ©1952 by Harper & Row Publishers, Inc. Reprinted by permission of HarperCollins Publishers, Inc.

"The Moral Insight," by Josiah Royce, reprinted from *The Religious Aspects of Philosophy*, 1885, Houghton Mifflin Company.

"Respect for Persons," by Immanuel Kant, reprinted from *Foundations of the Metaphysics of Morals*, Second Edition, translated by Lewis White Beck. Copyright ©1990 by Macmillan College Publishing Co. Reprinted by permission of Simon & Schuster.

"The Conscience of Huckleberry Finn," by Jonathan Bennett, reprinted from *Philosophy*, Vol. 49, 1974, by permission of Cambridge University Press.

"The Divine Imperative," by Emil Brunner, reprinted from *The Divine Imperative*, translated by Olive Wyon. Copyright ©1947 by W.L. Jenkins. Reprinted by permission of Westminster John Knox Press.

"The Chapter of the Night Journey," by Muhammad, reprinted from *The Koran*, translated by E.H. Palmer, 1900, Oxford University Press.

"Good Will, Duty and the Categorical Imperative," by Immanuel Kant, reprinted from *Fundamental Principles of the Metaphysics of Morals*, translated by T.K. Abbott, 1898.

"The Principle of Utility," by Jeremy Bentham, reprinted from *The Principles of Morals and Legislation*, 1789.

"Humans Are Always Selfish (The Ring of Gyges)," by Plato, reprinted from *The Republic of Plato*, translated by F.M. Cornford, 1941, Oxford University Press.

"Humans Are Not Always Selfish," by James Rachels, reprinted from *Egoism and Moral Scepticism*, 1972, Oxford University Press. Copyright ©1972 by James Rachels.

"Hindu Perspectives on Ethics," by Michael C. Brannigan, reprinted from *The Pulse of Wisdom: The Philosophies of India, China, and Japan*, 1995, by permission of Wadsworth Publishing Co.

"Individual Life in Harmony with the Tao: Taoist Perspectives on Ethics," by Lao-tzu and Chuang-tzu, reprinted from *The Texts of Taoism: Sacred Books of the East*, translated by James Legge, 1891, Oxford University Press.

"The Age of Relativism," by Luther Binkley, reprinted from *Conflict of Ideals*, 1969, Wadsworth Publishing Co.

"When in Rome . . .," by Burton F. Porter, reprinted from *Reasons for Living: A Basic Ethics*. Copyright ©1988 by Macmillan Publishing Co. Reprinted by permission of Prentice-Hall, Inc.

Excerpt from *Cultural Relativism*, by Melville Herskovits, 1972, Random House, Inc.

"Self-Assertion," by Friedrich Nietzsche, reprinted from *The Philosophy of Nietzsche*. Copyright ©1927 by Random House, Inc. Copyright © renewed 1955 by The Modern Library, Inc.

Excerpt from *Beyond Good and Evil*, by Friedrich Nietzsche, George Allen & Unwin, Ltd. (HarperCollins UK).

Excerpt from *The Genealogy of Morals*, by Friedrich Nietzsche, George Allen & Unwin, Ltd. (HarperCollins UK).

Excerpts from "Morality as Based on Sentiment," by David Hume, reprinted from *A Treatise of Human Nature*, 1740, Book III, Part I, Section I and *An Inquiry Concerning the Principles of Morals*, 1751, Appendix I.

"Ethics Are Relative," by William G. Sumner, reprinted from *Folkways*, 1907.

"Ethics Are Not Relative," by W.T. Stace, reprinted from *The Concept of Morals*. Copyright ©1937 by Macmillan Publishing Co. Copyright © renewed 1966 by Walter T. Stace. Reprinted by permission of Simon & Schuster.

"The Ethical Implications of Cultural Relativity," by Carl Wellman, reprinted from *Journal of Philosophy*, Vol. LX, No. 7, March 1963, Columbia University.

"Trying Out One's New Sword," by Mary Midgley, reprinted from *Heart and Mind*. Copyright ©1981 by St. Martin's Press, Inc. Reprinted by permission of St. Martin's Press.

"Japanese Ethical Perspectives," by Michael C. Brannigan, reprinted from *The Pulse of Wisdom: The Philosophies of India, China, and Japan*, 1995, by permission of Wadsworth Publishing Co.

"The Law of Human Nature," by C.S. Lewis, reprinted from *Mere Christianity*, 1952, by permission of HarperCollins Publishers, Ltd.

"Vice," by Plutarch, reprinted from *Moralia*, translated by Frank Cole Babbitt, 1928, 1956, 1962, by permission of Harvard University Press.

"The Depths of Vice," by St. Augustine, reprinted from *The Confessions of St. Augustine*, translated by John K. Ryan. Copyright ©1960 by Doubleday, a division of Bantam, Doubleday Dell Publishing Group, Inc. Reprinted by permission of Doubleday.

"Desire and Sin," by Peter Ableard, reprinted from *Abelard's Ethics*, translated by R. McCallum, Blackwell Publishers, Ltd.

"Jealousy, Envy, and Spite," by Immanuel Kant, reprinted from "Jealousy, Envy, and Grudge," in *Lectures on Ethics*, translated by Louis Enfield, 1963, Random House UK, Ltd.

"*Jen* as a Living Metaphor in the Confucian *Analects*," by Tu-Wei Ming, reprinted from *Confucian Thought: Selfhood as Creative Transformation*, 1985, by permission of The State University of New York Press.

"The Virtues of the Superior Man," by Confucius, reprinted from *Questions for the Soul: An Introduction to Philosophy*, edited by Keith W. Krasemann, 1996, Copley Publishing Group.

"The Virtues in Heroic Societies," by Alasdair MacIntyre, reprinted from *After Virtue: A Study in Moral Philosophy*, 1981, University of Notre Dame Press.

Excerpt from *Nicomachean Ethics*, by Aristotle, translated by Terence Irwin, 1985. Reprinted by permission of Hackett Publishing Co. All rights reserved.

"Courage," by Jean-Louis Servan-Schreiber, reprinted from *The Return of Courage*, translated by Frances Frenaye, 1987, Addison Wesley Longman.

"Thirteen Virtues," by Benjamin Franklin, reprinted from *The Autobiography of Benjamin Franklin,* 1706-1790, The World's Popular Classics Books, Inc.

"The Ethics of Virtue," by James Rachels, reprinted from *The Elements of Moral Philosophy*, Second Edition. Copyright ©1993 by McGraw-Hill Companies. Reprinted by permission of McGraw-Hill Companies.

"On the Decay of the Art of Lying," by Mark Twain, 1906, Harper Brothers.

"The Evil of Lying," by Charles Fried, reprinted from *Right and Wrong*, 1978, by permission of Harvard University Press.

"On a Supposed Right to Tell Lies from Benevolent Motives," by Immanuel Kant, reprinted from *Thirteen Questions in Ethics*, Harcourt Brace & Company.

"The Duty of Veracity," by Henry Sidgwick, reprinted from *Methods of Ethics*, Macmillan, Ltd. The following are reprinted from *Lying: Moral Choice in Public and Private Life* by Sissela Bok,1978, Vintage Books:

"Is the 'Whole Truth' Attainable?" and "Truthfulness, Deceit, and Trust."

"Sex, Lies, and Advertising," by Gloria Steinem, reprinted from *Ms. Magazine*, 1990. Reprinted by permission of the author.

"Upon Self-Deceit," by Bishop Butler, reprinted from *Fifteen Sermons Upon Human Nature*, 1726.

"Secrecy and Self-Deception," by Sissela Bok, reprinted from *Secrets: On the Ethics of Concealment and Revelation*, 1984, Vintage Books.

"Living Up to One's Word," by Roger Ames and David Hall, reprinted from *Thinking Through Confucius*, 1987, by permission of The State University of New York Press.

"Integrity: Wholeness of Standards and Actions," by Charles E. Watson, reprinted from *Managing with Integrity: Insights from America's CEO's*. Copyright ©1991 by Praeger Publishers, Inc., an imprint of Greenwood Publishing Group, Inc., Westport, CT. Reprinted by permission of Praeger Publishers, Inc.

Excerpt from *The Apology*, by Plato.

"Integrity," by Lynne McFall, reprinted from *Ethics* 98, 1987. Reprinted by permission of University of Chicago Press.

"Solitude," by Jean-Louis Servan-Schreiber, reprinted from *The Return of Courage*, 1987, Addison Wesley Longman.

"Of Friendship," by Bacon, reprinted from *Other Selves: Philosophers on Friendship*, by Michael Pakaluk, 1991, Hackett Publishing Co.

"On Philosophy and Friendship," by Seneca, reprinted from *Epistulae Morales*, 1917, Harvard University Press.

"Friendship," by Aristotle.

"Friendship," by Elizabeth Telfer, reprinted from *Proceedings of the Aristotelian Society for 1970*. Copyright ©1970 by the Aristotelian Society. Reprinted courtesy of the Editor of the Aristotelian Society.

"Friendship," by Ralph Waldo Emerson, Hackett Publishing Company.

"On Grief for Lost Friends," by Seneca, reprinted from *Epistulae Morales*, translated by R. M. Gummere, 1917, Harvard University Press.

"The Conditions of Female Friendship," by Janice Raymond, reprinted from *A Passion for Friends*. Copyright ©1986 by Janice G. Raymond. Reprinted by permission of Beacon Press, Boston, MA.

"Men and Friendship," by Stuart Miller, reprinted from *Men and Friendship*. Copyright ©1983 by Stuart Miller. Reprinted by permission of Houghton Mifflin Co. All rights reserved.

"What Love Is," by Robert C. Solomon, reprinted from *Love: Emotion, Myth and Metaphor*, edited by Bowie, Michaels, and Solomon, 1976, Harcourt Brace & Company.

"Universal Love," by Mo Tzu, reprinted from *Mo Tzu: Basic Writings*, by Burton Watson. Copyright ©1963 by Columbia University Press. Reprinted by permission of Columbia University Press.

"Love, the Answer to the Problem of Human Existence," by Erich Fromm, reprinted from *The Art of Loving*. Copyright ©1956 by Erich Fromm. Renewed 1984 by Annis Fromm. Reprinted by permission of HarperCollins Publishers, Inc.

"The Story of Solon and Croesus," by Herodotus, reprinted from *The Norton Book of Classical Literature*, translated by Aubrey de Selincourt, Penguin Books, Ltd.

"Virtue and Happiness," by Aristotle.

"Happiness Not the End," by Viktor E. Frankl, reprinted from *The Doctor and the Soul: From Psychotherapy to Logotherapy*, translated by Richard Winston and Clara Winston. Copyright ©1955, 1965 by Alfred A. Knopf, Inc. Reprinted by permission of Random House, Inc.

Excerpt "Happiness is Enjoying the Chief Good" from *Of the Morals of the Catholic Church*, by St. Augustine, reprinted from *The Works of Aurelius Augustine*, edited by M. Dods, 1892, T&T Clark, Edinburgh.

Excerpt from "The Encheiridion," by Epictetus, reprinted from *The Discourses*, Volume II, translated by W.A. Oldfather, 1978, by permission of Harvard University Press.

"Letter to Menoeceus," by Epicurus, reprinted from *Epicurus: The Extant Remains*, translated by Cyril Bailey, 1926, Oxford University Press.

"Enlightenment," by Heinrich Zimmer, reprinted from *Philosophies of India*, 1951, 1979, Princeton University Press.

"The Conflict Between Individual and Social Morality," by Reinhold Niebuhr, reprinted from *Moral Man and Immoral Society: A Study in Ethics and Politics*. Copyright ©1932 by Charles Scribner's and Sons (Macmillan). Reprinted by permission of Simon & Schuster.

Excerpt from "The Analects," by Confucius, reprinted from *World Philosophy: A Text with Readings*, edited by Solomon/Higgins, translated by Roger T. Ames. Copyright ©1995 by McGraw-Hill Companies. Reprinted by permission of McGraw-Hill Companies.

"The Ideal State," by Plato, reprinted from "The Republic," Book IV in *The Dialogues of Plato*, translated by Benjamin Jowett, 1892.

Excerpt from "On Liberty," by John Stuart Mill, 1859.

"The Enforcement of Morals," by Lord Patrick Devlin, reprinted from *The Enforcement of Morals*, 1965, Oxford University Press.

"Taking Rights Seriously," by Ronald Dworkin, reprinted from *Taking Rights Seriously*, 1977, by permission of Harvard University Press.

"Human Rights, Civil Rights," by Malcolm X, reprinted from *Speech at Militant Labor Reform* on "Prospects for Freedom in 1965." Copyright ©1965, 1990, Pathfinder Press and Betty Shabazz.

"Women's Rights as Human Rights: Toward a Re-Vision of Human Rights," by Charlotte Burch, reprinted from *Human Rights Quarterly*, Vol. 12, No. 4, November 1990, by permission of Johns Hopkins University Press.

"Justice as Fairness," by John Rawls, reprinted from *A Theory of Justice*, 1971, by permission of Harvard University Press.

"What Libertarianism Is," by John Hospers, reprinted from *The Libertarian Alternative*, edited by Tibor R. Machan, 1974, by permission of Nelson-Hall Publishers.

"Alienated Man," by Karl Marx, reprinted from *Economic and Philosophic Manuscripts of 1844*, translated by Martin Milligan, 1959, Progress Publishers, Moscow.

"Consciencism," by Kwame Nkumah, reprinted from *Consciencism: Philosophy and Ideology for Decolonization and Development with Particular Reference to the African Revolution*, 1964, Heinemann Educational Books.

"The Declaration of Independence," by Thomas Jefferson.

"I Have a Dream," by Martin Luther King, Jr. Copyright ©1963 by Martin Luther King, Jr. Renewed in 1991 by Coretta Scott King. Reprinted by permission of The Heirs to the Estate of Martin Luther King, Jr., c/o Writers House, Inc. as agent for the proprietor.

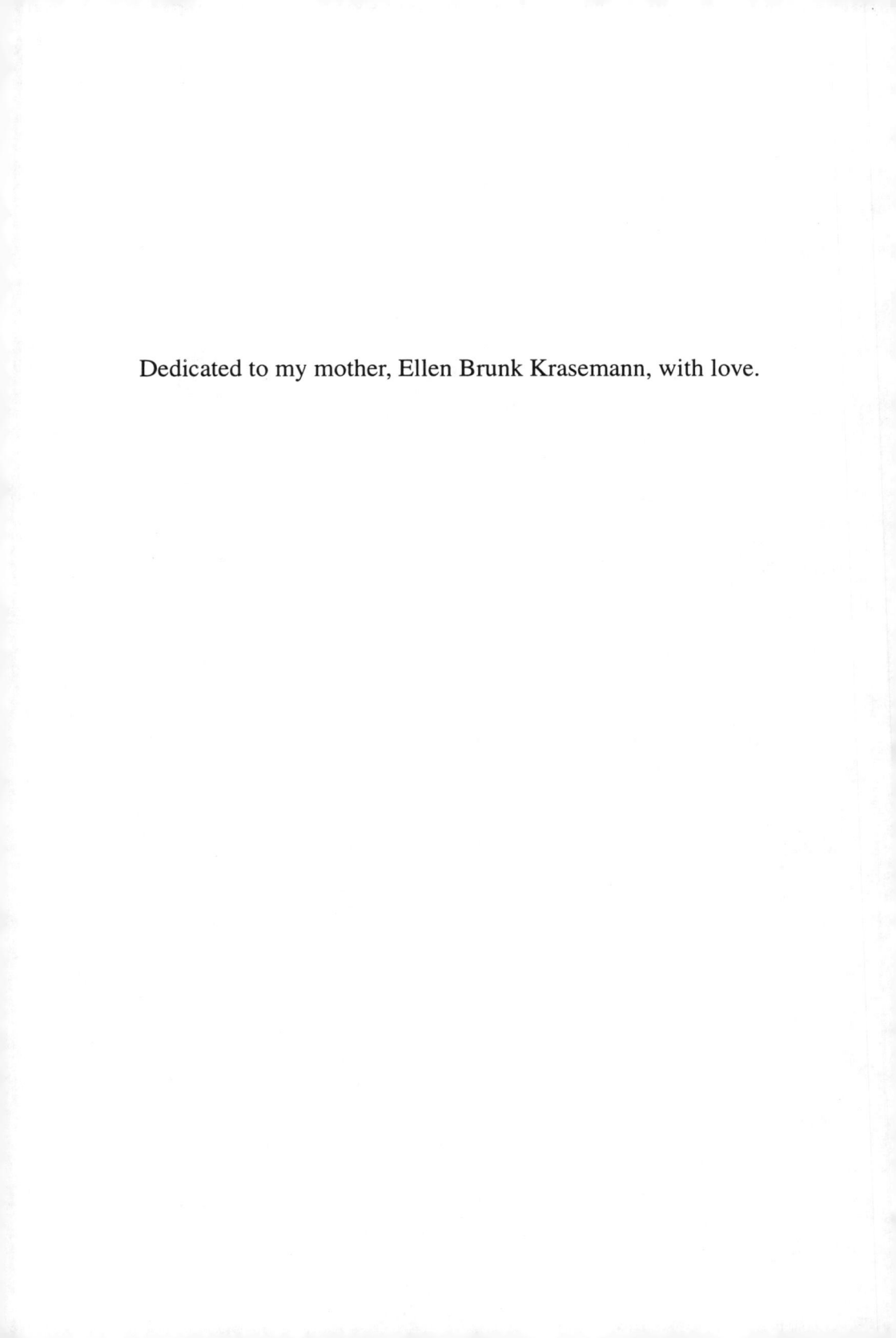

Dedicated to my mother, Ellen Brunk Krasemann, with love.

Contents

Preface xxi

Chapter I: Life in the World: Trouble 1

from A Dream of Red Mansions 5
    Cao Xueqin

from Macbeth 6
    Shakespeare

Candide, or Optimism 7
    Voltaire

Basic Doctrines 16
    Buddha

Creation, Fall, and the Promise of Redemption 21
    from Genesis

In the World Ye Shall Have Tribulation (Trouble) .. 26
    from The Gospel of John

From Cruelty to Goodness 27
    Philip Hallie

from Leviathan (1651) 40
    Thomas Hobbes

The Road Less Traveled 49
    M. Scott Peck

Moral Concern 63
    Rodger Beehler

Chapter II: Responding to Others 73

Response 76
  Martin Buber

The Story-Telling Animal 83
  Alasdair MacIntyre

Kisagotami 87
  Peter D. Hershock

The Good Samaritan 95
  from The Gospel of Luke

Compassion 96
  Lawrence Blum

The Practice of Reciprocity 105
  from Confucianism

The Deep Beauty of the Golden Rule 107
  R. M. MacIver

The Moral Insight 115
  Josiah Royce

Respect for Persons 118
  Immanuel Kant

The Conscience of Huckleberry Finn 122
  Jonathan Bennett

Chapter III: Moral Theories and Ethical Perspectives 135

The Divine Imperative 139
  Emil Brunner

The Ten Commandments and the Sermon on the Mount 143
  from The Holy Bible

from The Koran 148
  Muhammad

Good Will, Duty, and the Categorical Imperative 151
  Immanuel Kant

Intuition: A Foundation for Moral Principles 160
  Robert Lorek

The Principle of Utility 165
    Jeremy Bentham

Humans Are Always Selfish (The Ring of Gyges) 172
    Plato

Humans Are Not Always Selfish 175
    James Rachels

Hindu Perspectives on Ethics 185
    Michael C. Brannigan

Taoist Ethical Perspectives 193
    Lao-tzu and Chuang-tzu

Chapter IV: Relativism 201

The Age of Relativism 205
    Luther Binkley

When in Rome. 216
    Burton F. Porter

Cultural Relativism and Cultural Values 224
    Melville Herskovits

Self-Assertion 241
    Friedrich Nietzsche

Morality as Based on Sentiment 253
    David Hume

Ethics Are Relative 257
    William Sumner

Ethics Are Not Relative 270
    W. T. Stace

The Ethical Implications of Cultural Relativity 283
    Carl Wellman

Trying Out One's New Sword 296
    Mary Midgley

Japanese Ethical Perspectives 301
    Michael C. Brannigan

The Law of Human Nature 307
    C. S. Lewis

Chapter V: Vice and Virtue 311

Vice 316
  Plutarch

The Depths of Vice 319
  Saint Augustine

Desire and Sin 323
  Peter Abelard

Jealousy, Envy and Spite 330
  Immanuel Kant

Jen as a Living Metaphor in the Confucian *Analects* 337
  Tu-Wei Ming

The Virtues of the Superior Man 348
  Confucius

The Virtues in Heroic Societies 356
  Alasdair MacIntyre

Habit and Virtue 361
  Aristotle

Courage 367
  Jean-Louis Servan-Schreiber

Thirteen Virtues 371
  Benjamin Franklin

The Ethics of Virtue 373
  James Rachels

Chapter VI: Lying and Veracity 389

On the Decay of the Art of Lying 392
  Mark Twain

The Evil of Lying 397
  Charles Fried

On a Supposed Right to Tell Lies from Benevolent Motives 405
  Immanuel Kant

The Duty of Veracity 409
  Henry Sidgwick

Is the "Whole Truth" Attainable? 415
  Sissela Bok

Truthfulness, Deceit, and Trust 425
    Sissela Bok

Sex, Lies, and Advertising 436
    Gloria Steinem

Chapter VII: Self-Deception and Integrity 453

Upon Self-Deceit 457
    Bishop Butler

Secrecy and Self-Deception 463
    Sissela Bok

Living Up to One's Word (hsin* 信) 476
    Roger Ames

Integrity: Wholeness of Standards and Actions 482
    Charles E. Watson

The Apology 491
    Plato

Integrity 511
    Lynne McFall

Chapter VIII: Friendship and Love 519

Solitude 524
    Jean-Louis Servan-Schreiber

Of Friendship 530
    Bacon

On Philosophy and Friendship 535
    Seneca

Friendship 540
    Aristotle

Friendship 545
    Elizabeth Telfer

Friendship 560
    Emerson

On Grief for Lost Friends 571
    Seneca

The Conditions of Female Friendship 575
    Janice Raymond

Men and Friendship 581
    Stuart Miller

What Love Is 588
    Robert C. Solomon

Universal Love 593
    Mo Tzu

The Love of God 596
    from I Corinthians

Love, the Answer to the Problem of Human Existence 597
    Erich Fromm

Chapter IX: Happiness 605

True Happiness 608
    Psalm I

The Story of Solon and Croesus 609
    Herodotus

Virtue and Happiness 616
    Aristotle

Happiness Not the End 626
    Viktor E. Frankl

Happiness Is Enjoying the Chief Good 637
    Saint Augustine

The Encheiridion 641
    Epictetus

Letter to Menoeceus 656
    Epicurus

Enlightenment 660
    Heinrich Zimmer

Chapter X: The Individual and Society 677

The Conflict Between Individual and Social Morality 683
    Reinhold Niebuhr

from The Analects 695
    Confucius

The Ideal State 698
    Plato

from On Liberty (1859) 724
    John Stuart Mill

The Enforcement of Morals 737
    Lord Patrick Devlin

Taking Rights Seriously 743
    Ronald Dworkin

Human Rights, Civil Rights 754
    Malcolm X

Women's Rights as Human Rights:
Toward a Re-Vision of Human Rights 756
    Charlotte Bunch

Justice as Fairness 768
    John Rawls

What Libertarianism Is 774
    John Hospers

Alienated Man 785
    Karl Marx

Consciencism 796
    Kwame Nkrumah

The Declaration of Independence 801
    Thomas Jefferson

I Have a Dream 805
    Martin Luther King, Jr.

Preface

A quest begins with questions. The quest for goodness is a response to questions for the soul—those questions which most profoundly and deeply concern the life of a human being. These questions are properly philosophical in nature and issue forth from the very core of human existence and the human condition. The human condition is life in the world and this condition is troubling.

What is the nature of goodness and what does it mean to be a "good person"? What is the meaning of my existence? What makes life worth living? How can I lead a good life? What is the relationship of goodness to happiness? What does life require of me? How ought I to live in a world of good and evil? How can I make right choices?

The quest for goodness endeavors to find answers to the above questions. The quest for goodness involves coming to a deeper understanding of what the above questions ask. But, the quest for goodness seeks more than knowledge and understanding.

The quest for goodness is a practical quest. The quest for goodness is a personal quest. It is also a shared quest. The quest for goodness is a quest for moral worth. The quest for goodness is a quest, not merely to know the good, but to become good. The quest for goodness is the diligent pursuit of human excellence or virtue. The quest for goodness is the passion to live with integrity. It is the search for meaning and justification. The quest for goodness is noble and ennobling. It is noble because of its high purpose to seek moral truth for its own sake. The quest for goodness is ennobling to the end that one endeavors to live this truth because it is the truth. Yet it is the quest itself that discloses this truth. It is the journey, not the destination, that transforms an individual's life.

This book is an introduction to ethics. Normative thinking about how we, as human beings, are to dwell in this world constitutes that branch of philosophy known as ethics. Ethics is thinking philosophically about the moral dimension of human existence. Ethics is concerned to examine the nature of good and evil, the nature of right, and the essence of justice. Ethics deals with the character and conduct of life. It involves both human vice and virtue, reflections on the nature of friendship, love, human happiness and personal integrity. It is hoped that the reader appropriate to, and for, himself or herself, not so much the thinking of others concerning life's most fundamental questions, but, rather, the questions themselves. It is

Quest for Goodness: An Introduction to Ethics

further hoped that the reader authentically and personally take up the quest for goodness.

The approach to ethics taken in this book is thematic. I look first at the nature of life in the world and then consider, in order, responding to others, moral theories and ethical perspectives, relativism, vice and virtue, lying and veracity, self-deception and integrity, friendship and love, happiness, and the individual in relation to society.

I have included in this volume classic philosophical writings on ethics. I have also included recent philosophical essays, as well as literary pieces, that I felt were both interesting and relevant. I have included non-philosophical writings from inspired texts because these are indispensable to a comprehensive consideration of ethics. Finally, I have included many non-Western writings in order to expand the possible ways by which an individual might set upon the quest for goodness.

I am thankful for my family and friends who have shown me care and love, who have been exemplars, and who have guided and inspired me in my quest for goodness. I am grateful to my teachers and my students for all they have done to help me think and re-think life's great questions. I want to thank Ed Kies and Ed Storke for their unwavering support of my work. I wish also to acknowledge my colleagues in philosophy at College of DuPage for the many intangible contributions they have made to my life and to this book: Thomas Elkins, Fred Hombach, Werner Kriegelstein, Robert Lorek, John Modschiedler, Kent Richter and P. G. Sheehan.

Special thanks to Frank S. Burrows, Jr., Mary Choi, and Don Kilburn. I wish to acknowledge Frank for his help both in initiating this project and bringing it to fulfillment. I am grateful to Mary for many wonderful years of friendship, for her undying encouragement, and for her professional insight. I am thankful to Don for his support and belief in this venture.

The final form of this book is the result of the diligent work of Kristen Colman. With warmest thanks I applaud the work of Kristen and her associates.

Special recognition must go to Paula Kuntz for her extensive help in the preparation of this manuscript. Her work was greatly appreciated. Also, a word of appreciation must be given to Mario Reda for his initial input and vote of confidence concerning this project.

Finally, I also wish to recognize Eileen Brandt, Amanda Kirkwood, Nancy Ludeks, Ayoob Meah, Joyce Medows, Kathy Montana, Jenise Ronning, Susan Tisdale, Brian Viray and Yu Xiong for their assistance.

Sycamore, Illinois   K. W. K.
July, 1997

Chapter I
Life in the World: Trouble

Life in the world is troubling. The root of this trouble may be located in the very structure of existence. The fact that, as human beings, we are mortal is troubling. Human mortality is a condition of limitation. The individual, living in the world, is both time bound and death bound. In such a condition, trouble is inevitable. Can this condition be overcome? How can one make sense of his or her life in the midst of trouble? What makes life in such a world valuable? How is it possible to make right choices in a world of good and evil? Or, to echo the words of the Hebrew prophet, "How should we then live?"

In what is arguably the greatest work in Chinese vernacular fiction, *A Dream of Red Mansions (Hong Lou Meng),* the authors Cao Xueqin and Gao E present a comprehensive and penetrating view into the Chinese world during the 1700s. In this work the reader becomes a spectator to life: the rise and fall of dynasties and the changing fortunes of ruling class families, the folly of love, the destiny and fate of individual lives, the plight of the poor, and remembrances of past innocence in the garden. Alternatively called, *The Story of the Stone,* the work is written from the Stone's point of view upon entering the realm of "red dust." That is, on a more universal scale, the novel recounts life in the world. The novel was structured around poems written by Cao Xueqin. The selections of the poetry included in this volume eloquently summarize Xueqin's estimate of the human situation. The novel begins with the first stanza of poetry and closes with the last stanza. The remaining four stanzas are taken from the body of the text. Xueqin writes passionately about life: "Pages of absurd words soaked with bitter tears."

He concludes that human life in this world is folly. It is a "tale of bitterness . . . so absurd that it is more grief than joy."

Cao Xueqin's assessment of life parallels the reflections on the brevity of life found in Shakespeare's *Macbeth*. In this tragedy, a work which discloses evil and its systematic manifestations in consciousness and act,

Shakespeare speaks of life as "a tale told by an idiot, full of sound and fury, signifying nothing." Yet, even though the world is troubling, the above conclusions are less than comforting and, at best, evoke only pity. All of us sense, at some level, that this state of affairs ought not to be.

In Voltaire's *Candide,* or *Optimism,* the hero is expelled from the "noblest and most agreeable of all possible castles" and journeys through a world of trouble. In spite of numerous extreme circumstances which reveal the worst elements of inhumanity, Candide, as naive as he is optimistic, clings to the belief that "everything is for the best." Doctor Pangloss, "the greatest philosopher of the whole world," had taught Candide that "Leibniz could not be in the wrong and pre-established harmony is the finest thing imaginable," and, thus, events, of necessity, always work out for the best in this world. Voltaire's novel is literary satire. Rather than attack the views of Leibniz (and Alexander Pope), both of whom maintained the world was created in ideal form, Voltaire utilized a *reductio ad absurdum* approach in which he illustrated that human experience in the world contradicts the notion that all works out for the best.

In order to live rightly in the world, Buddha claimed that "the noble truth of suffering must be comprehended." This truth, namely that life is suffering (*dukkha:* trouble, pain), is fundamental to a right understanding of life. Furthermore, this understanding is necessary in order for the individual to overcome a finite existence which is both troubling and painful. The world is held within the sway of the fivefold grip on existence which are all sufferings.

But, in the midst of trouble there is hope. The first Noble Truth discloses the world as suffering, trouble, and pain. The second Noble Truth reveals the cause of this condition. It is craving (*tanha:* desire, selfish desire that attaches the individual to the world). The third Noble Truth declares that cessation of suffering is possible and the fourth Noble Truth shows the way to escape the human condition.

The way is the Noble Eightfold Path, namely: right view, right intention, right speech, right action, right livelihood, right effort, right mindfulness, and right concentration. The four Noble Truths and the Noble Eightfold Path comprise the core teachings of Buddhism and are the foundation of Buddhist ethics.

The Bible makes it abundantly clear that the human condition is a "fallen" condition. As a result of disobedience, humankind has become separated and estranged from God. Human beings in the world are alienated from the source of their being. The well-known narrative of the temptation, fall, and promise of redemption is recorded in the opening chapters of "Genesis." Eve was beguiled by the serpent and Adam knowingly disobeyed God's command. They both ate of the fruit of the tree of the knowledge of good and evil. Shame, fear, and rationalization followed this act. Adam and Eve were driven from Eden and sorrow, toil, and death were among the major consequences of disobedience—that is, of individuals placing their own will above God's. Yet, in the midst of this trouble, God gave them hope and a promise of redemption.

Genesis 3:15 was both a promise and prophecy. It foretold of a coming redeemer, one born of a woman, who would be bruised by the evil one but would, in turn, utterly destroy that evil one and his schemes.

For the Christian, the promised redemption was accomplished in the person of Jesus Christ. In the Gospel of John, shortly before his crucifixion and resurrection, Jesus disclosed the nature of the world. "In the world," he stated, "ye shall [absolutely, without question] have tribulation." The word "tribulation" is from the Greek, *thlipsis*. *Thlipsis* is also translated as "trouble" or "affliction." It refers to mental pressure, turbulence, and confusion which is caused by the oppression of evil in the world. However, Jesus taught that even in the midst of a world of trouble and affliction, it was possible to have peace. Even in a world of trouble, Jesus exhorted his followers: "Be of good cheer; I have overcome the world." Jesus taught that it was possible to overcome the human condition.

In "From Cruelty to Goodness," Philip Hallie shows the reader extremes of evil and goodness. On the one hand, he examines the institutionalized cruelties perpetrated by the Nazis upon death camp inmates and, on the other hand, the unconditional love, goodness and hospitality manifested in the lives of the people in the French village of Le Chambon. "Cruelty," says Hallie, "involves the maiming of a person's dignity, the crushing of a person's self-respect." Cruelty is maintained through a power imbalance and Hallie concludes that institutionalized cruelty is the subtlest kind of cruelty. Why? Because in this relationship both the victim and the victimizer find ways of obscuring the actual harm being done.

Hallie participated in the conflict he described. He enlisted in World War II because, as a matter of duty, he felt he must stop Hitler and the Nazis from committing more atrocities. But, in the performance of his "moral duties," Hallie himself became a perpetrator of destruction and killing. He has referred to himself, apart from his essay, as a "decent killer." That is, he believed it was his moral duty to stop Hitler, but at what cost?

Yet, in the midst of the storm of war and institutionalized cruelty, the people of the small French village of Le Chambon were the living manifestation of goodness and active love and hospitality. They followed, from a pure heart, the positive Biblical injunctions, "Defend the fatherless" and "Be your brother's keeper," as well as the negative moral injunction, "Thou shalt not murder or betray." At risk to their lives, these Christians saved 6,000 Jews, mostly children, from the Nazis. Hallie concludes that their success in throwing back the evil was that they never lost sight of the point of view of the victim. They even attempted to save the Nazis from themselves.

Thomas Hobbes, *Leviathan,* argues for absolute sovereignty in the state and defends the social contract theory. He postulates a state of nature (i.e., the state of human beings in the world free of the laws and conventions of the state) and maintains that life in this natural state would be a condition of war. It would be "a war as is of every man against every man."

M. Scott Peck is direct in his assessment of the human condition. He says plainly, "Life is difficult." But, he continues:

> This is a great truth, one of the greatest truths. It is a great truth because once we truly see this truth we transcend it. Once we truly know that life is difficult—once we truly understand and accept it—then life is no longer difficult. Because once it is accepted, the fact that life is difficult no longer matters.

Life in the world presents us with problems on a daily basis. It is naive to think that life will not be difficult or that it should be easy or problem free. The problematic nature of life in the world offers possibilities for personal growth and evolution to a higher self. Problems call forth courage and wisdom. As individuals, when we actively engage life, in all of its difficulty, we realize ourselves, our potential to overcome, and discover meaning in suffering and mortality.

In order to confront life authentically and to deal constructively with pain Peck insists that discipline is essential. By discipline he means an interrelated system of techniques: delaying gratification, assumption of responsibility, dedication to truth or reality, and balancing. This ongoing process of self-discipline is, in effect, a series of deaths and rebirths. As such it is a self-enlarging process.

Rodger Beehler's "Moral Concern," both concludes Chapter I, "Life in the World: Trouble," and serves as a bridge to Chapter II, "Responding to Others." Here we consider, for example, the instance of Tralala and her thugs "lushing" and brutally beating the young soldier. Beehler asks us to reflect on precisely what we mean when we maintain that acts such as brutal beatings are morally wrong. Are we not saying that acts such as this "ought not to be done?"

Our moral concern for others, Beehler holds, is grounded in care. But, it depends on why one cares for another. It matters whether one *cares about* the other or has *regard* for the other. If, for example, my care that the soldier not be beaten stems from my concern to pry information from him, then my concern is not a moral concern. I have no regard for the person but my concern is to use him for my purposes. If I genuinely care about the soldier my concern is a moral concern. Beehler claims: "It is ultimately this regard or caring for other persons which gives our moral language its sense." Caring is a form of life "which makes possible, and gives sense to, moral practices." The fact that we care about one another allows for the possibility of agreement in moral judgments.

from *A Dream of Red Mansions*

Cao Xueqin

Pages full of absurd words
Soaked with bitter tears:
All say he is a fool in love,
But who his message hears!

All men know it's nice to be immortal,
Yet to rank and fame each one scrambles:
Where are the rich and mighty now?
Their graves are but a mass of brambles.

All men know it's nice to be immortal,
Yet silver and gold they all prize.
Each day they grumble they've not made enough,
When they've enough, death seals their eyes.

All men know it's nice to be immortal,
Yet dote on the loving wives they've wed,
Who swear to love their husbands ever more,
But they're off with another, once you're dead.

All men know it's nice to be immortal,
Yet with their darling heirs they won't have done.
Although there's no shortage of fond parents,
Who ever really saw a grateful son?

Now a tale of bitterness is told,
So absurd that it's more grief than joy.
Since all of us live in a dream,
Why should we laugh at other's folly?

from Macbeth

Shakespeare

Tomorrow, and tomorrow, and tomorrow
Creeps in this petty pace from day to day,
To the last syllable of recorded time;
And all our yesterdays have lighted fools
The way to dusty death. Out, out, brief candle!
Life's but a walking shadow, a poor player
That struts and frets his hour upon the stage
And then is heard no more. It is a tale
Told by an idiot, full of sound and fury
Signifying nothing.

Macbeth, V, v, 19.

Candide, or Optimism

Voltaire

How Candide was brought up in a Noble Castle, and how he was expelled from the same.

In the castle of Baron Thunder-ten-tronckh in Westphalia there lived a youth, endowed by Nature with the most gentle character. His face was the expression of his soul. His judgment was quite honest and he was extremely simple-minded; and this was the reason, I think, that he was named Candide. Old servants in the house suspected that he was the son of the Baron's sister and a decent honest gentleman of the neighbourhood, whom this young lady would never marry because he could only prove seventy-one quarterings, and the rest of his genealogical tree was lost, owing to the injuries of time.

The Baron was one of the most powerful lords in Westphalia, for his castle possessed a door and windows. His Great Hall was even decorated with a piece of tapestry. The dogs in his stable-yards formed a pack of hounds when necessary; his grooms were his huntsmen; the village curate was his Grand Almoner. They all called him "My Lord," and laughed heartily at his stories.

The Baroness weighed about three hundred and fifty pounds, was therefore greatly respected, and did the honours of the house with a dignity which rendered her still more respectable. Her daughter Cunegonde, aged seventeen, was rosy-cheeked, fresh, plump and tempting. The Baron's son appeared in every respect worthy of his father. The tutor Pangloss was the oracle of the house, and little Candide followed his lessons with all the candour of his age and character.

Pangloss taught metaphysico-theologo-cosmolonigology. He proved admirably that there is no effect without a cause and that in this best of all possible worlds, My Lord the Baron's castle was the best of castles and his wife the best of all possible Baronesses.

"'Tis demonstrated," said he, "that things cannot be otherwise; for, since everything is made for an end, everything is necessarily for the best end. Observe that noses were made to wear spectacles; and so we have spectacles. Legs were visibly instituted to be breeched, and we have breeches. Stones were formed to be quarried and to build castles; and My Lord has a very noble castle; the greatest Baron in the province should have the best house; and as pigs were made to be eaten, we eat pork all the year round; consequently, those who have asserted that all is well[1] talk nonsense; they ought to have said that all is for the best."

Candide listened attentively and believed innocently; for he thought Miss Cunegonde extremely beautiful, although he was never bold enough to tell her so. He decided that after the happiness of being born Baron of Thunder-ten-tronckh, the second degree of happiness was to be Miss Cunegonde; the third, to see her every day; and the fourth, to listen to Doctor Pangloss, the greatest philosopher of the province and therefore of the whole world.

One day when Cunegonde was walking near the castle, in a little wood which was called The Park, she observed Doctor Pangloss in the bushes, giving a lesson in experimental physics to her mother's waiting-maid, a very pretty and docile brunette. Miss Cunegonde had a great inclination for science and watched breathlessly the reiterated experiments she witnessed; she observed clearly the doctor's sufficient reason, the effects and the causes, and returned home very much excited, pensive, filled with the desire of learning, reflecting that she might be the sufficient reason of young Candide and that he might be hers.

On her way back to the castle she met Candide and blushed; Candide also blushed. She bade him good-morning in a hesitating voice; Candide replied without knowing what he was saying. Next day, when they left the table after dinner, Cunegonde and Candide found themselves behind a screen; Cunegonde dropped her handkerchief, Candide picked it up; she innocently held his hand; the young man innocently kissed the young lady's hand with remarkable vivacity, tenderness and grace; their lips met, their eyes sparkled, their knees trembled, their hands wandered. Baron Thunder-ten-tronckh passed near the screen, and, observing this cause and effect, expelled Candide from the castle by kicking him in the backside frequently and hard. Cunegonde swooned; when she recovered her senses, the Baroness slapped her in the face; and all was in consternation in the noblest and most agreeable of all possible castles.

What happened to Candide among the Bulgarians.

Candide, expelled from the earthly paradise, wandered for a long time without knowing where he was going, weeping, turning up his eyes to

Chapter I: Life in the World: Trouble

Heaven, gazing back frequently at the noblest of castles which held the most beautiful of young Baronesses; he lay down to sleep supperless between two furrows in the open fields; it snowed heavily in large flakes. The next morning the shivering Candide, penniless, dying of cold and exhaustion, dragged himself towards the neighbouring town, which was called Wald-berghoff-trarbk-dikdorff. He halted sadly at the door of an inn. Two men dressed in blue noticed him.

"Comrade," said one, "There's a well-built young man of the right height."

They went up to Candide and very civilly invited him to dinner.

"Gentlemen," said Candide with charming modesty, "you do me a great honour, but I have no money to pay my share."

"Ah, sir," said one of the men in blue, "persons of your figure and merit never pay anything; are you not five feet five tall?"

"Yes, gentlemen," said he, bowing, "that is my height."

"Ah, sir, come to table; we will not only pay your expenses, we will never allow a man like you to be short of money; men were only made to help each other."

"You are in the right," said Candide, "that is what Doctor Pangloss was always telling me, and I see that everything is for the best."

They begged him to accept a few crowns, he took them and wished to give them an IOU; they refused to take it and all sat down to table.

"Do you not love tenderly. . . ."

"Oh, yes," said he. "I love Miss Cunegonde tenderly."

"No," said one of the gentlemen. "We were asking if you do not tenderly love the King of the Bulgarians."

"Not a bit;" said he, "for I have never seen him."

"What! He is the most charming of Kings, and you must drink his health."

"Oh, gladly, gentlemen."

And he drank.

"That is sufficient," he was told. "You are now the support, the aid, the defender, the hero of the Bulgarians; your fortune is made and your glory assured."

They immediately put irons on his legs and took him to a regiment. He was made to turn to right and left, to raise the ramrod and return the ramrod, to take aim, to fire, to double up, and he was given thirty strokes with a stick; the next day he drilled not quite so badly, and received only twenty strokes; the day after, he only had ten and was looked on as a prodigy by his comrades.

Candide was completely mystified and could not make out how he was a hero. One fine spring day he thought he would take a walk, going straight ahead, in the belief that to use his legs as he pleased was a privilege of the human species as well as of animals. He had not gone two leagues when four other heroes, each six feet tall, fell upon him, bound him and dragged him back to a cell. He was asked by his judges whether he would rather be thrashed thirty-six times by the whole regiment or receive a dozen lead bullets at once in his brain. Although he protested that men's wills are free and that he wanted neither one nor the other, he had to make a choice; by virtue of that gift of God which is called *liberty*, he determined to run the gauntlet thirty-six times and actually did so twice. There were two thousand men in the regiment. That made four thousand strokes which laid bare the muscles and nerves from his neck to his backside. As they were about to proceed to a third turn, Candide, utterly exhausted, begged as a favour that they would be so kind as to smash his head; he obtained this favour; they bound his eyes and he was made to kneel down. At that moment the King of the Bulgarians came by and inquired the victim's crime; and as this King was possessed of a vast genius, he perceived from what he learned about Candide that he was a young metaphysician very ignorant in worldly matters, and therefore pardoned him with a clemency which will be praised in all newspapers and all ages. An honest surgeon healed Candide in three weeks with the ointments recommended by Dioscorides.[2] He had already regained a little skin and could walk when the King of the Bulgarians went to war with the King of the Abares.[3]

How a splendid auto-da-fe was held to prevent earthquakes, and how Candide was flogged.

After the earthquake which destroyed three-quarters of Lisbon, the wise men of that country could discover no more efficacious way of preventing a total ruin than by giving the people a splendid *auto-da-fé* It was decided by the university of Coimbra that the sight of several persons being slowly burned in great ceremony is an infallible secret for preventing earthquakes.

Consequently they had arrested a Biscayan convicted of having married his fellow-godmother, and two Portuguese who, when eating a chicken, had thrown away the bacon; after dinner they came and bound Dr Pangloss and his disciple Candide, one because he had spoken and the other because he had listened with an air of approbation; they were both carried separately to extremely cool apartments, where there was never any discomfort from the sun; a week afterwards each was dressed in a sanbenito and their heads were ornamented with paper mitres; Candide's mitre and sanbenito were painted with flames upside down and with devils who had neither tails nor claws; but Pangloss's devils had claws and tails, and his flames were upright.

Chapter I: Life in the World: Trouble

Dressed in this manner they marched in procession and listened to a most pathetic sermon, followed by lovely plain-song music. Candide was flogged in time to the music, while the singing went on: the Biscayan and the two men who had not wanted to eat bacon were burned, and Pangloss was hanged, although this is not the custom. The very same day, the earth shook again with a terrible clamour.

Candide, terrified, dumbfounded, bewildered and covered with blood, quivering from head to foot, said to himself:

"If this is the best of all possible worlds, what are the others? Let it pass that I was flogged, for I was flogged by the Bulgarians, but, O my dear Pangloss! The greatest of philosophers! Must I see you hanged without knowing why! O my dear Anabaptist! The best of men! Was it necessary that you should be drowned in port! O Miss Cunegonde! The pearl of women! Was it necessary that your belly should be slit!"

He was returning, scarcely able to support himself, preached at, flogged, absolved and blessed, when an old woman accosted him and said:

"Courage, my son, follow me."

Cunegonde's Story

"I was fast asleep in bed when it pleased Heaven to send the Bulgarians to our noble castle of Thunder-ten-tronckh; they murdered my father and brother and cut my mother to pieces. A large Bulgarian six feet tall, seeing that I had swooned at the spectacle, began to rape me; this brought me to, I recovered my senses, I screamed, I struggled, I bit, I scratched, I tried to tear out the big Bulgarian's eyes, not knowing that what was happening in my father's castle was a matter of custom; the brute stabbed me with a knife in the left side where I still have the scar."

"Alas! I hope I shall see it," said the naive Candide.

"You shall see it," said Cunegonde, "but let me go on."

"Go on," said Candide.

She took up the thread of her story as follows:

"A Bulgarian captain came in, saw me covered with blood, and the soldier did not disturb himself. The captain was angry at the brute's lack of respect to him, and killed him on my body. Afterwards, he had me bandaged and took me to his billet as a prisoner of war. I washed the few shirts he had and did the cooking; I must admit he thought me very pretty; and I will not deny that he was very well built and that his skin was white and soft; otherwise he had little wit and little philosophy; it was plain that he had not been brought up by Dr Pangloss. At the end of three months he lost all his money and got tired of me; he sold me to a Jew named Don

11

Issachar, who traded in Holland and Portugal and had a passion for women. This Jew devoted himself to my person, but he could not triumph over it; I resisted him better than the Bulgarian soldier; a lady of honour may be raped once, but it strengthens her virtue. In order to subdue me, the Jew brought me to this country house. Up till then I believed that there was nothing on earth so splendid as the castle of Thunder-ten-tronckh; I was undeceived.

"One day the Grand Inquisitor noticed me at Mass; he ogled me continually and sent a message that he wished to speak to me on secret affairs. I was taken to his palace; I informed him of my birth; he pointed out how much it was beneath my rank to belong to an Israelite. A proposition was made on his behalf to Don Issachar to give me up to His Lordship. Don Issachar, who is the court banker and a man of influence, would not agree. The Inquisitor threatened him with an *auto-da-fé*. At last the Jew was frightened and made a bargain whereby the house and I belong to both in common. The Jew has Mondays, Wednesdays, and the Sabbath day, and the Inquisitor has the other days of the week. This arrangement has lasted for six months. It has not been without quarrels; for it has often been debated whether the night between Saturday and Sunday belonged to the old law or the new. For my part, I have hitherto resisted them both; and I think that is the reason why they still love me.

"At last My Lord the Inquisitor was pleased to arrange an *auto-da-fé* to remove the scourge of earthquakes and to intimidate Don Issachar. He honoured me with an invitation. I had an excellent seat; and refreshments were served to the ladies between the Mass and the execution. I was indeed horror-stricken when I saw the burning of the two Jews and the honest Biscayan who had married his fellow-godmother; but what was my surprise, my terror, my anguish, when I saw in a sanbenito and under a mitre a face which resembled Pangloss's! I rubbed my eyes, I looked carefully, I saw him hanged; and I fainted. I had scarcely recovered my senses when I saw you stripped naked; that was the height of horror, of consternation, of grief and despair. I will frankly tell you that your skin is even whiter and of a more perfect tint than that of my Bulgarian captain. This spectacle redoubled all the feelings which crushed and devoured me. I exclaimed, I tried to say: 'Stop, barbarians!' but my voice failed and my cries would have been useless. When you had been well flogged, I said to myself: 'How does it happen that the charming Candide and the wise Pangloss are in Lisbon, the one to receive a hundred lashes, and the other to be hanged, by order of My Lord the Inquisitor, whose darling I am? Pangloss deceived me cruelly when he said that all is for the best in the world.'

"I was agitated, distracted, sometimes beside myself and sometimes ready to die of faintness, and my head was filled with the massacre of my father, of my mother, of my brother, the insolence of my horrid Bulgarian soldier, the gash he gave me, my slavery, my life as a kitchen-wench, my

Bulgarian captain, my horrid Don Issachar, my abominable Inquisitor, the hanging of Dr Pangloss, that long plain-song *miserere* during which you were flogged, and above all the kiss I gave you behind the screen that day when I saw you for the last time. I praised God for bringing you back to me through so many trials, I ordered my old woman to take care of you and to bring you here as soon as she could. She has carried out my commission very well; I have enjoyed the inexpressible pleasure of seeing you again, of listening to you, and of speaking to you. You must be very hungry; I have a good appetite; let us begin by having supper."

Both sat down to supper; and after supper they returned to the handsome sofa we have already mentioned; they were still there when Signor Don Issachar, one of the masters of the house, arrived. It was the day of the Sabbath. He came to enjoy his rights and to express his tender love.

What happened to Candide, to Cunegonde, to Pangloss, to Martin, & c.

Pardon once more," said Candide to the Baron, "pardon me, reverend father, for having thrust my sword through your body."

"Let us say no more about it," said the Baron. "I admit I was a little too sharp; but since you wish to know how it was you saw me in the galley, I must tell you that after my wound was healed by the brother apothecary of the college, I was attacked and carried off by a Spanish raiding party; I was imprisoned in Buenos Ayres at the time when my sister had just left. I asked to return to the Father-General in Rome. I was ordered to Constantinople to act as almoner to the Ambassador of France. A week after I had taken up my office I met towards evening a very handsome young page of the Sultan. It was very hot; the young man wished to bathe; I took the opportunity to bathe also. I did not now that it was a most serious crime for a Christian to be found naked with a young Mahometan. A cadi sentenced me to a hundred strokes on the soles of my feet and condemned me to the galley. I do not think a more horrible injustice has ever been committed. But I should very much like to know why my sister is in the kitchen of a Transylvanian sovereign living in exile among the Turks."

"But, my dear Pangloss," said Candide, "how does it happen that I see you once more?"

"It is true," said Pangloss, "that you saw me hanged; and in the natural course of events I should have been burned. But you remember, it poured with rain when they were going to roast me; the storm was so violent that they despaired of lighting the fire; I was hanged because they could do nothing better; a surgeon bought my body, carried me home and dissected me. He first made a crucial incision in me from the navel to the collarbone. Nobody could have been worse hanged than I was. The executioner of the holy Inquisition, who was a sub-deacon, was marvelously skillful in burning people, but he was not accustomed to hang them; the rope was wet and did not slide easily, and it was knotted; in short, I still breathed. The crucial incision caused me to utter so loud a scream that the surgeon fell over backwards and, thinking he was dissecting the devil, fled away in terror and fell down the staircase in his flight. His wife ran in at the noise from another room; she saw me stretched out on the table with my crucial incision; she was still more frightened than her husband, fled, and fell on top of him. When they had recovered themselves a little, I heard the surgeon's wife say to the surgeon:

"'My dear, what are you thinking of, to dissect a heretic? Don't you know the devil always possesses them? I will go and get a priest at once to exorcise him.'

"At this I shuddered and collected the little strength I had left to shout:

"'Have pity on me!'

"At last the Portuguese barber grew bolder; he sewed up my skin; his wife even took care of me, and at the end of a fortnight I was able to walk again. The barber found me a situation and made me lackey to a Knight of Malta who was going to Venice; but, as my master had no money to pay me wages, I entered the service of a Venetian merchant and followed him to Constantinople.

"One day I took it into my head to enter a mosque; there was nobody there except an old Imam and a very pretty young devotee who was reciting her prayers; her breasts were entirely uncovered; between them she wore a bunch of tulips, roses, anemones, ranunculus, hyacinths and auriculas; she dropped her bunch of flowers; I picked it up and returned it to her with a most respectful alacrity. I was so long putting them back that the Imam grew angry and, seeing I was a Christian, called for help. I was taken to the cadi, who sentenced me to receive a hundred strokes on the soles of my feet and sent me to the galleys. I was chained on the same seat and in the same galley as My Lord the Baron. In this galley there were four young men from Marseilles, five Neapolitan priests and two monks from Corfu, who assured us that similar accidents occurred every day. His Lordship the Baron claimed that he had suffered a greater injustice than I; and I claimed that it was much more permissible to replace a bunch of flowers between a woman's breasts than to be naked with one of the Sultan's pages. We argued continually, and every day received twenty strokes of the bull's pizzle, when the chain of events of this universe led you to our galley and you ransomed us."

"Well! my dear Pangloss," said Candide, "when you were hanged, dissected, stunned with blows and made to row in the galleys, did you always think that everything was for the best in this world?"

Chapter I: Life in the World: Trouble

"I am still of my first opinion," replied Pangloss, "for after all I am a philosopher; and it would be unbecoming for me to recant, since Leibnitz could not be in the wrong and pre-established harmony is the finest thing imaginable, like the plenum and subtle matter."

Endnotes

1. "*Tout est bien* (all is well)," said Rousseau in his famous attack on Voltaire's poem about the Lisbon earthquake.
2. A Greek author of the time of Nero.
3. The Bulgarians are the Prussians and the Abares the French. The King of vast genius is Frederick the Great, whose recruiting methods are glanced at in this chapter.

Basic Doctrines

Buddha

The First Sermon[1]

These two extremes, O monks, are not to be practiced by one who has gone forth from the world. What are the two? That conjoined with the passions, low, vulgar, common, ignoble, and useless, and that conjoined with self-torture, painful, ignoble, and useless. Avoiding these two extremes the Tathāgata has gained the knowledge of the Middle Way, which gives sight and knowledge, and tends to calm, to insight, enlightenment, Nirvāna.

What, O monks, is the Middle Way, which gives sight . . . ? It is the noble Eightfold Path, namely, right views, right intention, right speech, right action, right livelihood, right effort, right mindfulness, right concentration. This, O monks, is the Middle Way. . . .

(1) Now this, O monks, is the noble truth of suffering[2]: birth is painful, old age is painful, sickness is painful, death is painful, sorrow, lamentation, dejection, and despair are painful. Contact with unpleasant things is painful, not getting what one wishes is painful. . . .

(2) Now this, O monks, is the noble truth of the cause of suffering: that craving, which leads to rebirth, combined with pleasure and lust, finding pleasure here and there, namely the craving for passion, the craving for existence, the craving for nonexistence.

(3) Now this, O monks, is the noble truth of the cessation of suffering: the cessation without a remainder of the craving, abandonment, forsaking, release, nonattachment.

(4) Now this, O monks, is the noble truth of the way that leads to the cessation of suffering: this is the noble Eightfold Path, namely, right views, right intention, right speech, right action, right livelihood, right effort, right mindfulness, right concentration. "This is the noble truth of suffering."

Chapter I: Life in the World: Trouble

Thus, O monks, among doctrines unheard before, in me sight and knowledge arose, wisdom, knowledge, light arose. "This noble truth of suffering must be comprehended." Thus, O monks, among doctrines heard before, by me was this truth comprehended. And thus, O monks, among doctrines unheard before, in me sight and knowledge arose. . . .

As long as in these noble truths my threefold knowledge and insight . . . was not well purified, even so long, O monks, in the world with its gods, Māra, Brahmā, with ascetics, brahmins, gods and men, I had not attained the highest complete enlightenment. Thus I knew.

But when in these noble truths my threefold knowledge and insight duly with its twelve divisions was well purified, then, O monks, in the world . . . I had attained the highest complete enlightenment. Thus I knew. Knowledge arose in me, insight arose that the release of my mind is unshakeable; this is my last existence; now there is no rebirth. . . .

The Synopsis of Truth[3]

Thus have I heard. Once when the Lord was staying at Benares in the Isipatana deerpark, he addressed the Almsmen as follows: It was here in this very deerpark at Benares that the Truth-finder, Arahat all-enlightened, set a-rolling the supreme Wheel of the Doctrine—which shall not be turned back from its onward course by recluse or brahmin, god or Māra or Brahmā or by anyone in the universe,—the announcement of the Four Noble Truths, the teaching, declaration, and establishment of those Four Truths, with their unfolding, exposition and manifestation.

What are these four?—The announcement, teaching . . . and manifestation of the Noble Truth of Suffering—of the origin of Suffering[4]—of the cessation of Suffering—of the path that leads to the cessation of Suffering.

Follow Sāriputta and Moggallāna and be guided by them; they are wise helpers unto their fellows in the higher life. . . .

Having thus spoken, the Blessed One arose and went into his own cell.

The Lord had not been gone long when the reverend Sāriputta proceeded to the exposition of the Truth-finder's Four Noble Truths, as follows:

What, reverend sirs, is the Noble Truth of Suffering?—Birth is Suffering; decay is Suffering; death is Suffering; grief and lamentation, pain, misery and tribulation are Sufferings; it is Suffering not to get what is desired;—in brief all the factors of the fivefold grip on existence are Sufferings.

Birth is, for living creatures of each several class, the being born or produced, the issue, the arising or the re-arising, the appearance of the plastic forces, the growth of faculties.

Decay, for living creatures of each several class, is the decay decaying, loss of teeth, gray hair, wrinkles, a dwindling term of life, sere faculties.

Death, for living creatures of each several class, is the passage and passing hence, the dissolution, disappearance, dying, death, decease, the dissolution of the plastic forces, the discarding of the dead body.

Grief is the grief, grieving and grievousness, the inward grief and inward anguish of anyone who suffers under some misfortune or is in the grip of some type of Suffering.

Lamentation is the lament and lamentation the wailing and the lamenting of anyone who suffers under some misfortune or is in the grip of some type of Suffering.

Pain is any bodily Suffering or bodily evil, any Suffering bred of bodily contact, any evil feeling.

Misery is mental Suffering and evil, any evil feeling of the mind.

Tribulation is the tribulation of heart and mind, the state to which tribulation brings them, in anyone who suffers under some misfortune or is in the grip of some type of Suffering.

There remains not to get what is desired. In creatures subject to birth—or decay—or death—or grief and lamentation, pain, misery and tribulation—the desire arises not to be subject thereto but to escape them. But escape is not to be won merely by desiring it; and failure to win it is another suffering.

What are in brief all the factors of the fivefold grip on existence which are Sufferings?—They are: The factors of form, feeling, perception, plastic forces, and consciousness.

The foregoing, sirs, constitutes the Noble Truth of Suffering.

What now is the Noble Truth of the Origin of Suffering? It is any craving that makes for rebirth and is tied up with passion's delights and culls satisfaction now here now there;—such as the craving for sensual pleasure, the craving for continuing existence, and the craving for annihilation.

Next, what is the Noble Truth of the Cessation of Suffering?—It is the utter and passionless cessation of this same craving,—the abandonment and rejection of craving, Deliverance from craving, and aversion from craving.

Lastly, what is the Noble Truth of the Path that leads to the Cessation of Suffering?—It is just the Noble Eightfold Path, consisting of—right outlook, right resolves, right speech, right acts, right livelihood, right endeavor, right mindfulness and right rapture of concentration.

Right [views are] to know Suffering, the origin of Suffering, the cessation of Suffering, and the path that leads to the cessation of Suffering.

Right [intention is] the resolve to renounce the world and to do no hurt or harm.

Right speech is to abstain from lies and slander; from reviling, and from tattle.

Right acts are to abstain from taking life, from stealing and from lechery.

Right livelihood is that by which the disciple of the Noble One supports himself, to the exclusion of wrong modes of livelihood.

Right [effort] is when an Almsman brings his will to bear, puts forth endeavor and energy, struggles and strives with all his heart, to stop bad and wrong qualities which have not yet arisen from ever arising, to renounce those which have already arisen, to foster good qualities which have not yet arisen, and, finally, to establish, clarify, multiply, enlarge, develop, and perfect those good qualities which are there already.

Right mindfulness is when realizing what the body is,—what feelings are—what the heart is—and what the mental states are,—an Almsman dwells ardent, alert and mindful, in freedom from the wants and discontents attendant on any of these things.

Right . . . concentration is when, divested of lusts and divested of wrong dispositions, an Almsman develops, and dwells in, the First Ecstasy with all its zest and satisfaction, a state bred of aloofness and not divorced from observation and reflection. By laying to rest observation and reflection, he develops and dwells in inward serenity in focusing of heart, in the zest and satisfaction of the Second Ecstasy, which is divorced from observation and reflection and is bred of concentration,—passing thence to the Third and Fourth Ecstasies.

This, sirs, constitutes the Noble Truth of the Path that leads to the Cessation of Suffering.

Such, reverend sirs, is the announcement . . . and manifestation of the Four Noble Truths,—the supreme Wheel of the Doctrine set a-rolling in the deerpark at Benares by the Truth-finder, Arahat all-enlightened, that Wheel which shall not be turned back from its onward course by recluse or brahmin, god, Māra or Brahmā, or by anyone in the whole universe.

Thus spoke the reverend Sāriputta. Glad at heart, those Almsmen rejoiced in what the reverend Sāriputta had said.

Dependent Origination[5]

That things have being, O Kaccāna, constitutes one extreme of doctrine; that things have no being is the other extreme. These extremes, O Kaccāna, have been avoided by the Tathāgata, and it is a middle doctrine he teaches:

On ignorance depends karma;
On karma depends consciousness;
On consciousness depend name and form;
On name and form depend the six organs of sense;
On the six organs of sense depends contact;

Quest for Goodness: An Introduction to Ethics

On contact depends sensation;
On sensation depends desire;
On desire depends attachment;
On attachment depends existence;
On existence depends birth;
On birth depend old age and death, sorrow, lamentation, misery, grief, and despair: Thus does this entire aggregation of misery arise.

But on the complete fading out and cessation of ignorance ceases karma;
On the cessation of karma ceases consciousness;
On the cessation of consciousness cease name and form;
On the cessation of name and form cease the six organs of sense;
On the cessation of the six organs of sense ceases contact;
On the cessation of contact ceases sensation;
On the cessation of sensation ceases desire;
On the cessation of desire ceases attachment;
On the cessation of attachment ceases existence;
On the cessation of existence ceases birth;
On the cessation of birth cease old age and death, sorrow, lamentation, misery, grief, and despair. Thus does this entire aggregation of misery cease. . . .

Endnotes

1. Edward J. Thomas, *The Life of Buddha as Legend and History* (New York: Alfred A. Knopf, 1927), pp. 87–88.
2. Editor's note: The term *pain* in this section has been replaced by *suffering* for the sake of consistency.
3. *Further Dialogues of the Buddha*, translated by Lord Chalmers, *Sacred Books of the Buddhists*, vol.6 (London: Oxford University Press, 1927), pp. 296–299.
4. Editor's note: The term *Ill* in this section has been a placed by *Suffering*, for the sake of consistency.
5. Henry Clark Warren, *Buddhism in Translations* (New York: Atheneum, 1976; originally published by Harvard University Press, 1896), pp. 213–233. Reprinted by permission of Harvard University Press. © Harvard University Press.

Creation, Fall, and the Promise of Redemption

from Genesis

Chapter 1

In the beginning God created the heaven and the earth.

2 And the earth was without form, and void; and darkness *was* upon the face of the deep. And the Spirit of God moved upon the face of the waters.

3 And God said, Let there be light: and there was light.

4 And God saw the light, that *it was* good: and God divided the light from the darkness.

5 And God called the light Day, and the darkness he called Night. And the evening and the morning were the first day.

6 ¶ And God said, Let there be a firmament in the midst of the waters, and let it divide the waters from the waters.

7 And God made the firmament, and divided the waters which *were* under the firmament from the waters which *were* above the firmament: and it was so.

8 And God called the firmament Heaven. And the evening and the morning were the second day.

9 ¶And God said, Let the waters under the heaven be gathered together unto one place and let the dry *land* appear: and it was so.

10 And God called the dry *land* Earth; and the gathering together of the waters called he Seas: and God saw that *it was* good.

11 And God said, Let the earth bring forth grass, the herb yielding seed, *and* the fruit tree yielding fruit after his kind, whose seed *is* in itself, upon the earth: and it was so.

12 And the earth brought forth grass, *and* herb yielding seed after his kind, and the tree yielding fruit, whose seed *was* in itself, after his kind: and God saw that *it was* good.

13 And the evening and the morning were the third day.

14 ¶ And God said, Let there be lights in the firmament of the heaven to divide the day from the night; and let them be for signs, and for seasons, and for days, and years:

15 And let them be for lights in the firmament of the heaven to give light upon the earth: and it was so.

16 And God made two great lights; the greater light to rule the day, and the lesser light to rule the night: *he made* the stars also.

17 And God set them in the firmament of the heaven to give light upon the earth,

18 And to rule over the day and over the night, and to divide the light from the darkness: and God saw that *it was* good.

19 And the evening and the morning were the fourth day.

20 And God said, Let the waters bring forth abundantly the moving creature that hath life, and fowl *that* may fly above the earth in the open firmament of heaven.

21 And God created great whales, and every living creature that moveth, which the waters brought forth abundantly, after their kind, and every winged fowl after his kind: and God saw that *it was* good.

22 And God blessed them, saying, Be fruitful, and multiply, and fill the waters in the seas, and let fowl multiply in the earth.

23 And the evening and the morning were the fifth day.

24 ¶ And God said, Let the earth bring forth the living creature after his kind, cattle, and creeping thing, and beast of the earth after his kind: and it was so.

25 And God made the beast of the earth after his kind, and cattle after their kind, and every thing that creepeth upon the earth after his kind: and God saw that *it was* good.

26 ¶ And God said, Let us make man in our image, after our likeness: and let them have dominion over the fish of the sea, and over the fowl of the air, and over the cattle, and over all the earth, and over every creeping thing that creepeth upon the earth.

27 So God created man in his *own* image, in the image of God created he him; male and female created he them.

28 And God blessed them, and God said unto them, Be fruitful, and multiply, and replenish the earth, and subdue it: and have dominion over the fish of the sea, and over the fowl of the air, and over every living thing that moveth upon the earth.

29 ¶ And God said, Behold, I have given you every herb bearing seed, which *is* upon the face of all the earth, and every tree, in the which *is* the fruit of a tree yielding seed; to you, it shall be for meat.

30 And to every beast of the earth, and to every fowl of the air, and to every thing that creepeth upon the earth, wherein *there is* life, *I have given* every green herb for meat: and it was so.

31 And God saw every thing that he had made, and, behold, *it was* very good. And the evening and the morning were the sixth day.

Chapter 2

Thus the heavens and the earth were finished, and all the host of them.

2 And on the seventh day God ended his work which he had made; and he rested on the seventh day from all his work which he had made.

3 And God blessed the seventh day, and sanctified it: because that in it he had rested from all his work which God created and made.

4 ¶ These *are* the generations of the heavens and of the earth when they were created, in the day that the LORD God made the earth and the heavens,

5 And every plant of the field before it was in the earth, and every herb of the field before it grew: for the LORD God had not caused it to rain upon the earth, and *there was* not a man to till the ground.

6 But there went up a mist from the earth, and watered the whole face of the ground.

7 And the LORD God formed man of the dust of the ground, and breathed into his nostrils the breath of life; and man became a living soul.

8 ¶ And the LORD God planted a garden eastward in Eden; and there he put the man whom he had formed.

9 And out of the ground made the LORD God to grow every tree that is pleasant to the sight, and good for food; the tree of life also in the midst of the garden, and the tree of knowledge of good and evil.

10 And a river went out of Eden to water the garden; and from thence it was parted, and became into four heads.

11 The name, of the first *is* Pison: that *is* it which compasseth the whole land of Havilah, where *there is* gold;

12 And the gold of that land *is* good: there *is* bdellium and the onyx stone.

13 And the name of the second river *is* Gihon: the same *is* it that compasseth the whole land of Ethiopia.

14 And the name of the third river *is* Hiddekel: that *is* it which goeth toward the east of Assyria. And the fourth river *is* Euphrates.

15 And the LORD God took the man, and put him into the garden of Eden to dress it and to keep it.

16 And the LORD God commanded the man, saying, Of every tree of the garden thou mayest freely eat:

17 But of the tree of the knowledge of good and evil, thou shalt not eat of it: for in the day that thou eatest thereof thou shalt surely die.

18 ¶ And the LORD God said, *It is* not good that the man should be alone; I will make him an help meet for him.

19 And out of the ground the LORD God formed every beast of the field, and every fowl of the air; and brought *them* unto Adam to see what he would call them: and whatsoever Adam called every living creature, that was the name thereof.

20 And Adam gave names to all cattle, and to the fowl of the air, and to every beast of the field; but for Adam there was not found an help meet for him.

21 And the LORD God caused a deep sleep to fall upon Adam, and he slept: and he took one of his ribs, and closed up the flesh instead thereof;

22 And the rib, which the LORD God had taken from man, made he a woman, and brought her unto the man.

23 And Adam, said, This *is* now bone of my bones, and flesh of my flesh: she shall be called Woman, because she was taken out of Man.

24 Therefore shall a man leave his father and his mother, and shall cleave unto his wife: and they shall be one flesh.

25 And they, were both naked, the man and his wife, and were not ashamed.

Chapter 3

Now the serpent was more subtil than any beast of the field which the LORD God had made. And he said unto the woman, Yea, hath God said, Ye shall not eat of every tree of the garden?

2 And the woman said unto the serpent, We may eat of the fruit of the trees of the garden:

3 But of the fruit of the tree which *is* in the midst of the garden, God hath said, Ye shall not eat of it, neither shall ye touch it, lest ye die.

4 And the serpent said unto the woman, Ye shall not surely die:

5 For God doth know that in the day ye eat thereof, then your eyes shall be opened, and ye shall be as the gods, knowing good and evil.

6 And when the woman saw that the tree *was* good for food, and that it *was* pleasant to the eyes, and a tree to be desired to make *one* wise, she took of the fruit thereof, and did eat, and gave also unto her husband with her; and he did eat.

7 And the eyes of them both were opened, and they knew that they *were* naked; and they sewed fig leaves together, and made themselves aprons.

8 And they heard the voice of the LORD God walking in the garden in the cool of the day: and Adam and his wife hid themselves from the presence of the LORD God amongst the trees of the garden.

9 And the LORD God called unto Adam, and said unto him, Where *art* thou?

10 And he said, I heard thy voice in the garden, and I was afraid, because I was naked; and I hid myself.

11 And he said, Who told thee that thou *wast* naked? Hast thou eaten of the tree, whereof I commanded thee that thou shouldest not eat?

12 And the man said, The woman whom thou gavest *to be* with me, she gave me of the tree, and I did eat.

13 And the LORD God said unto the woman, What *is* this *that* thou hast done? And the woman said, The serpent beguiled me, and I did eat.

14 And the LORD God said unto the serpent, Because thou hast done this, thou *art* cursed above all cattle, and above every beast of the field; upon thy belly shalt thou go, and dust shalt thou eat all the days of thy life:

15 And I will put enmity between thee and the woman, and between thy seed and her seed; it shall bruise thy head, and thou shalt bruise his heel.

16 Unto the woman he said, I will greatly multiply thy sorrow and thy conception; in sorrow thou shalt bring forth children; and thy desire *shall be* to thy husband, and he shall rule over thee.

17 And unto Adam he said, Because thou hast hearkened unto the voice of thy wife, and hast eaten of the tree, of which I commanded thee, saying, Thou shalt not eat of it: cursed *is* the ground for thy sake; in sorrow shalt thou eat *of* it all the days of thy life;

18 Thorns also, and thistles shall it bring forth to thee; and thou shalt eat the herb of the field;

19 In the sweat of thy face shalt thou eat bread, till thou return unto the ground; for out of it wast thou taken: for dust thou *art*, and unto dust shalt thou return.

20 And Adam called his wife's name Eve; because she was the mother of all living.

21 Unto Adam also and to his wife did the LORD God make coats of skins, and clothed them.

22 ¶ And the LORD God said, Behold, the man is become as one of us, to know good and evil: and now, lest he put forth his hand, and take also of the tree of life, and eat, and live for ever:

23 Therefore the LORD God sent him forth from the garden of Eden, to till the ground from whence he was taken.

24 So he drove out the man; and he placed at the east of the garden of Eden Cherubims, and a flaming sword which turned every way, to keep the way of the tree of life.

In the World Ye Shall Have Tribulation (Trouble)

from The Gospel of John

33 These things I have spoken unto you, that in me ye might have peace. In the world ye shall have tribulation: but be of good cheer; I have overcome the world.

From Cruelty to Goodness

Philip Hallie

I am a student of ethics, of good and evil; but my approach to these two rather melodramatic terms is skeptical. I am in the tradition of the ancient Greek *skeptikoi*, whose name means "inquirers" or "investigators." And what we investigate is relationships among particular facts. What we put into doubt are the intricate webs of high-level abstractions that passed for philosophizing in the ancient world, and that still pass for philosophizing. My approach to good and evil emphasizes not abstract common nouns like "justice," but proper names and verbs. Names and verbs keep us close to the facts better than do our highfalutin common nouns. Names refer to particular people, and verbs connect subjects with predicates *in time*, while common nouns are above all this.

One of the words that is important to me is my own name. For me, philosophy is personal; it is closer to literature and history than it is to the exact sciences, closer to the passions, actions, and common sense of individual persons than to a dispassionate technical science. It has to do with the personal matter of wisdom. And so ethics for me is personal—my story, and not necessarily (though possibly) yours. It concerns particular people at particular times.

But ethics is more than such particulars. It involves abstractions, that is, rules, laws, ideals. When you look at the ethical magnates of history you see in their words and deeds two sorts of ethical rules: negative and positive. The negative rules are scattered throughout the Bible, but Moses brought down from Mount Sinai the main negative ethical rules of the West: Thou shalt not murder; thou shalt not betray. . . . The positive injunctions are similarly spread throughout the Bible. In the first chapter of the book of Isaiah we are told to ". . . defend the fatherless, plead for the widow . . ." The negative ethic forbids certain actions; the positive ethic demands certain actions. To follow the negative ethic is to be decent, to have clean hands. But to follow the positive ethic, to be one's brother's keeper; is to be more than decent—it is to be active, even aggressive. If the negative ethic is one of decency, the positive one is the ethic of riskful, strenuous nobility.

In my early studies of particularized ethical terms, I found myself dwelling upon negative ethics, upon prohibitions. And among the most conspicuous prohibitions I found embodied in history was the prohibition against deliberate harmdoing, against cruelty. "Thou shalt not be cruel" had as much to do with the nightmare of history as did the prohibitions against murder and betrayal. In fact, many of the Ten Commandments—especially those against murder, adultery, stealing, and betrayal—were ways of prohibiting cruelty.

Early in my research it became clear that there are various approaches to cruelty, as the different commandments suggest. For instance, there is the way reflected in the origins of the word "cruel." The Latin *crudus* is related to still older words standing for bloodshed, or raw flesh. According to the etymology of the, word, cruelty involves the spilling of blood.

But modern dictionaries give the word a different meaning. They define it as "disposed to giving pain." They emphasize awareness, not simply bloodshed. After all, they seem to say, you cannot be cruel to a dead body. There is no cruelty without consciousness.

And so I found myself studying the kinds of awareness associated with the hurting of human beings. It is certainly true that for millennia in history and literature people have been torturing each other not only with hard weapons but also with hard words.

Still, the word "pain" seemed to be a simplistic and superficial way of describing the many different sorts of cruelty. In Reska Weiss's *Journey Through Hell* (London, 1961) there is a brief passage of one of the deepest cruelties that Nazis perpetrated upon extermination camp inmates. On a march

> Urine and excreta poured down the prisoners' legs, and by nightfall the excrement, which had frozen to our limbs, gave off its stench. . . .

And Weiss goes on to talk not in terms of "pain" or bloodshed, but in other terms:

> . . . We were really no longer human beings in the accepted sense. Not even animals, but putrefying corpses moving on two legs. . . .

There is one factor that the idea of pain and the simpler idea of bloodshed do not touch: cruelty, not playful, quotidian teasing or ragging, but cruelty (what the anti-cruelty societies usually call "substantial cruelty") involves the maiming of a person's dignity, the crushing of a person's self-respect. Bloodshed, the idea of pain (which is usually something involving a localizable occurrence, localizable in a tooth, in a head, in short, in the body), these are superficial ideas of cruelty. A whip, bleeding flesh, these are what the journalists of cruelty emphasize, following the etymology and dictionary meaning of the word. But the depths of an understanding of cruelty lie in the depths of an understanding of human dignity and of how you can maim it without bloodshed, and often without localizable bodily pain.

In excremental assault, in the process of keeping camp inmates from wiping themselves or from going to the latrine, and in making them drink water from a toilet bowl full of excreta (and the excreta of the guards at that) localizable pain is nothing. Deep humiliation is everything. We human beings believe in hierarchies, whether we are skeptics or not about human value. There is a hierarchical gap between shit and me. We are even above using the word. We are "above" walking around besmirched with feces. Our dignity, whatever the origins of that dignity may be, does not permit it. In order to be able to want to live, in order to be able to walk erect, we must respect ourselves as beings "higher" than our feces. When we feel that we are not "higher" than dirt or filth, then our lives are maimed at the very center; in the very depths, not merely in some localizable portion of our bodies. And when our lives are so maimed we become things, slaves, instruments. From ancient times until this moment, and as long as there will be human beings on this planet, there are those who know this and will use it, just as the Roman slave owners and the Southern American slave owners knew it when—one time a year—they encouraged the slaves to drink all the alcohol they could drink so that they could get bestially drunk and then even more bestially sick afterwards, under the eyes of their generous owners. The self-hatred, the loss of self-respect that the Saturnalia created in ancient Rome, say, made it possible to continue using the slaves as things, since they themselves came to think of themselves as things, as subhuman tools of the owners and the overseers.

Institutionalized cruelty, I learned, is the subtlest kind of cruelty. In episodic cruelty the victim knows he is being hurt, and his victimizer knows it too. But in a persistent pattern of humiliation that endures for years in a community, both the victim and the victimizer find ways of obscuring the harm that is being done. Blacks come to think of themselves as inferior; even aesthetically inferior (black is "dirty"); and Jews come to think of themselves as inferior, even aesthetically (dark hair and aquiline noses are "ugly"), so that the way they are being treated is justified by their "actual" inferiority, by the inferiority they themselves feel.

A similar process happens in the minds of the victimizers in institutionalized cruelty. They feel that since they are superior, even aesthetically ("to be blonde is to be beautiful"), they deserve to do what they wish, deserve to have these lower creatures under their control. The words of Heinrich Himmler, head of the Nazi SS, in Posen in the year 1943 in a speech to his SS subordinates in a closed session, show how institutionalized cruelty can obscure harmdoing:

> ... the words come so easily. "The Jewish people will be exterminated," says every party member, "of course. It's in our program ... extermination. We'll take care of it." And then they come, these nice 80 million Germans, and every one of them has his decent Jew. Sure the others are swine, but his one is a fine Jew ... Most of you will know what it means to have seen 100 corpses together, or 500 to 1000. To have made one's way through that, and ... to have remained a decent person throughout, that is what has made us hard. That is a page of glory in our history. ...

In this speech he was making a sharp distinction between the program of crushing the Jews and the personal sentiments of individual Germans. The program stretched over years; personal sentiments were momentary. He was pleading for the program, for institutionalized destruction.

But one of the most interesting parts of the speech occurs toward the end of it:

> ... in sum, we can say that we fulfilled the heaviest of tasks [destroying the Jews] in love to our people. And we suffered no harm in our essence, in our soul, in our character. ...

Commitment that overrides all sentimentality transforms cruelty and destruction into moral nobility, and commitment is the lifeblood of an institution.

Cruelty and the Power Relationships

But when I studied all these ways that we have used the word "cruelty," I was nagged by the feeling that I had not penetrated into its inner structure. I was classifying, sorting out symptoms; but symptoms are signals, and what were the symptoms signals *of*? I felt like a person who had been studying cancer by sorting out brief pains from persistent pains, pains in the belly from pains in the head. I was being superficial, and I was not asking the question, "What are the forces behind these kinds of cruelty?" I felt that there were such forces, but as yet I had not touched them.

Then one day I was reading in one of the great autobiographies of western civilization, Frederick Douglass's *Life and Times*. The passage I was reading was about Douglass's thoughts on the origins of slavery. He was asking himself: "How could these whites keep us enslaved?" And he suddenly realized:

> My faculties and powers of body and soul are not my own, but are the property of a fellow-mortal in no sense superior to me, except that he has the physical power to compel me to be owned and controlled by him. By the combined physical force of the community I am his slave—a slave for life.

Chapter I: Life in the World: Trouble

And then I saw that a disparity in power lay at the center of the dynamism of cruelty. If it was institutional cruelty it was in all likelihood a difference involving both verbal and physical power that kept the cruelty going. The power of the majority and the weakness of a minority were at the center of the institutional cruelty of slavery and of Nazi anti-Semitism. The whites not only outnumbered the blacks in America, but had economic and political ascendancy over them. But just as important as these "physical" powers was the power that words like "nigger" and "slave" gave the white majority. Their language sanctified if it did not create their power ascendancy over the blacks, and one of the most important projects of the slaveholders and their allies was that of seeing to it that the blacks themselves thought of themselves in just these powerless terms. They utilized the language to convince not only the whites but the blacks themselves that blacks were weak in mind, in will power, and in worth. These words were like the excremental assault in the killing camps of the Nazis: they diminished both the respect the victimizers might have for their victims and the respect the victims might have for themselves.

It occurred to me that if a power differential is crucial to the idea of cruelty, then when that power differential is maintained, cruelty will tend to be maintained, and when that power differential is eliminated, cruelty will tend to be eliminated. And this seemed to work. In all kinds of cruelty, violent and polite, episodic and institutional, when the victim arms himself with the appropriate strength, the cruelty diminishes or disappears. When Jews joined the Bush Warriors of France, the Maquis, and became powerful enough to strike at Vichy or the Nazis, they stopped being victims of French and Nazi cruelty. When Frederick Douglass learned to use the language with great skill and expressiveness, and when he learned to use his physical strength against his masters, the power differential between him and his masters diminished, and so did their cruelty to him. In his autobiography he wrote:

> A man without force is without the essential dignity of humanity. Human nature is so constituted that it cannot honor a helpless man, though it can pity him, and even this it cannot do long if signs of power do not arise.

When I looked back at my own childhood in Chicago, I remembered that the physical and mental cruelties that I suffered in the slums of the southwest side when I was about ten years old sharply diminished and finally disappeared when I learned how to defend myself physically and verbally. It is exactly this lesson that Douglass learned while growing up in the cruel institution of slavery.

Cruelty then, whatever else it is, is a kind of power relationship, an imbalance of power wherein the stronger party becomes the victimizer and the weaker becomes the victim. And since many general terms are most swiftly understood in relationship with their opposites (just as "heavy" can be understood most handily in relationship with what we mean by "light") the opposite of cruelty lay in a situation where there is no imbalance of power. The opposite of cruelty, I learned, was freedom from that unbalanced power relationship. Either the victim should get stronger and stand up to the victimizer, and thereby bring about a balance of their powers, or the victim should free himself from the whole relationship by flight.

In pursuing this line of thought, I came to believe that, again, dictionaries are misleading: many of them give "kindness" as the antonym for "cruelty." In studying slavery in America and the concentration camps of central Europe I found that kindness could be the ultimate cruelty, especially when it was given within that unbalanced power relationship. A kind overseer or a kind camp guard can exacerbate cruelty, can remind his victim that there are other relationships than the relationship of cruelty, and can make the victim deeply bitter, especially when he sees the self-satisfied smile of his victimizer. He is being cruelly treated when he is given a penny or a bun after having endured the crushing and grinding of his mental and bodily well-being. As Frederick Douglass put it:

> The kindness of the slave-master only gilded the chain. It detracted nothing from its weight or strength. The thought that men are for other and better uses than slavery throve best under the gentle treatment of a kind master.

No, I learned, the opposite of cruelty is not kindness. The opposite of the cruelty of the overseer in American slavery was not the kindness of that overseer for a moment or for a day. An episodic kindness is not the opposite of an institutionalized cruelty. The opposite of institutionalized cruelty is freedom from the cruel relationship.

It is important to see how perspectival the whole meaning of cruelty is. From the perspective of the SS guard or the southern overseer, a bit of bread, a smile is indeed a diminution of cruelty. But in the relationship of cruelty, the point of view of the victimizer is of only minor importance; it is the point of view of the victim that is authoritative. The victim feels the suffering in his own mind and body, whereas the victimizer, like Himmler's "hard" and "decent" Nazi, can be quite unaware of that suffering. The sword does not feel the pain that it inflicts. Do not ask it about suffering.

Goodness Personified in Le Chambon

All these considerations drove me to write my book *The Paradox of Cruelty*. But with the book behind me, I felt a deep discontent. I saw cruelty as an embodiment, a particular case of evil. But if cruelty is one of the main evils of human history, why is the opposite of cruelty not one of the key goods of human history? Freedom from the cruel relationship, either by

Chapter I: Life in the World: Trouble

escaping it or by redressing the imbalance of power, was not essential to what western philosophers and theologians have thought of as goodness. Escape is a negative affair. Goodness has something positive in it, something triumphantly affirmative.

Hoping for a hint of goodness in the very center of evil, I started looking closely at the so-called "medical experiments" of the Nazis upon children, usually Jewish and Gypsy children, in the death camps. Here were the weakest of the weak. Not only were they despised minorities, but they were, as individuals, still in their nonage. They were dependents. Here the power imbalance between the cruel experimenters and their victims was at its greatest. But instead of seeing light or finding insight by going down into this hell, into the deepest depth of cruelty, I found myself unwillingly becoming part of the world I was studying. I found myself either yearning to be viciously cruel to the victimizers of the children, or I found myself feeling compassion for the children, feeling their despair and pain as they looked up at the men and women in white coats cutting off their fingertips one at a time, or breaking their slender bones, or wounding their internal organs. Either I became a would-be victimizer or one more Jewish victim, and in either case I was not achieving insight, only misery, like so many other students of the Holocaust. And when I was trying to be "objective" about my studies, when I was succeeding at being indifferent to both the victimizers and the victims of these cruel relationships, I became cold; I became another monster who could look upon the maiming of a child with an indifferent eye.

To relieve this unending suffering, from time to time I would turn to the literature of the French resistance to the Nazis. I had been trained by the U.S. Army to understand it. The resistance was a way of trying to redress the power imbalance between Hitler's Fortress Europe and Hitler's victims, and so I saw it as an enemy of cruelty. Still, its methods were often cruel like the methods of most power struggles, and I had little hope of finding goodness here. We soldiers violated the negative ethic forbidding killing in order, we thought, to follow the positive ethic of being our brothers' keepers.

And then one gray April afternoon I found a brief article on the French village of Le Chambon-sur-Lignon. I shall not analyze here the tears of amazement and gladness and release from despair—in short, of joy—that I shed when I first read that story. Tears themselves interest me greatly—but not the tears of melancholy hindsight and existential despair; rather the tears of awe you experience when the realization of an ideal suddenly appears before your very eyes or thunders inside your mind; these tears interest me.

And one of the reasons I wept at first reading about Le Chambon in those brief, inaccurate pages was that at last I had discovered an embodiment of goodness in opposition to cruelty. I had discovered in the flesh and blood of history, in people with definite names in a definite place at a definite time in the nightmare of history, what no classical or religious ethicist could deny was goodness.

The French Protestant village of Le Chambon, located in the Cévennes Mountains of southeastern France, and with a population of about 3,500, saved the lives of about 6,000 people, most of them Jewish children whose parents had been murdered in the killing camps of central Europe. Under a national government which was not only collaborating with the Nazi conquerors of France but frequently trying to outdo the Germans in anti-Semitism in order to please their conquerors, and later under the day-to-day threat of destruction by the German Armed SS, they started to save children in the winter of 1940, the winter after the fall of France, and they continued to do so until the war in France was over. They sheltered the refugees in their own homes and in various houses they established especially for them; and they took many of them across the terrible mountains to neutral Geneva, Switzerland, in the teeth of French and German police and military power. The people of Le Chambon are poor, and the Huguenot faith to which they belong is a diminishing faith in Catholic and atheist France; but their spiritual power, their capacity to act in unison against the victimizers who surrounded them, was immense, and more than a match for the military power of those victimizers.

But for me as an ethicist the heart of the matter was not only their special power. What interested me was that they obeyed *both* the negative and the positive injunctions of ethics; they were good not only in the sense of trying to be their brothers' keepers, protecting the victim, "defending the fatherless," to use the language of Isaiah; they were also good in the sense that they obeyed the negative injunctions against killing and betraying. While those around them—including myself—were murdering in order presumably, to help mankind in some way or other, they murdered nobody, and betrayed not a single child in those long and dangerous four years. For me as an ethicist they were the embodiment of unambiguous goodness.

But for me as a student of cruelty they were something more: they were an embodiment of the opposite of cruelty. And so, somehow, at last, I had found goodness in opposition to cruelty. In studying their story, and in telling it in *Lest Innocent Blood Be Shed*, I learned that the opposite of cruelty is not simply freedom from the cruel relationship; it is *hospitality*. It lies not only in something negative, an absence of cruelty or of imbalance; it lies in unsentimental, efficacious love. The opposite of the cruelties of the camps was not the liberation of the camps, the cleaning out of the barracks and the cessation of the horrors. All of this was the end of the cruelty relationship, not the opposite of that relationship. And it was not even the end of it, because the victims would never forget and would remain in agony as long as they remembered their humiliation and suffering. No, the opposite of cruelty was not the liberation of the camps, not freedom; it was the hospitality of the people of Le Chambon, and of very

Chapter I: Life in the World: Trouble

few others during the Holocaust. The opposite of cruelty was the kind of goodness that happened in Le Chambon.

Let me explain the difference between liberation and hospitality by telling you about a letter I received a year ago from a woman who had been saved by the people of Le Chambon when she was a young girl. She wrote:

> Never was there a question that the Chambonnais would not share all they had with us, meager as it was. One Chambonnais once told me that even if there was less, they still would want more for us.

And she goes on:

> It was indeed a very different attitude from the one in Switzerland, which while saving us also resented us so much.
>
> If today we are not bitter people like most survivors it can only be due to the fact that we met people like the people of Le Chambon, who showed to us simply that life can be different, that there are people who care, that people can live together and even risk their own lives for their fellow man.

The Swiss liberated refugees and removed them from the cruel relationship; the people of Le Chambon did more. They taught them that goodness could conquer cruelty, that loving hospitality could remove them from the cruel relationship. And they taught me this, too.

It is important to emphasize that cruelty is not simply an episodic, momentary matter, especially institutional cruelty like that of Nazism or slavery. As we have seen throughout this essay, not only does it persist while it is being exerted upon the weak; *it can persist in the survivors* after they have escaped the power relationship. The survivors torture themselves, continue to suffer, continue to maim their own lives long after the actual torture is finished. The self-hatred and rage of the blacks and the despair of the native Americans and the Jews who have suffered under institutional crushing and maiming are continuations of original cruelties. And these continuations exist because only a superficial liberation from torture has occurred. The sword has stopped falling on their flesh in the old obvious ways, but the wounds still bleed. I am not saying that the village of Le Chambon healed these wounds—they go too deep. What I am saying is that the people I have talked to who were once children in Le Chambon have more hope for their species and more respect for themselves as human beings than most other survivors I have met. The enduring hospitality they met in Le Chambon helped them find realistic hope in a world of persisting cruelty.

What was the nature of this hospitality that saved and deeply changed so many lives? It is hard to summarize briefly what the Chambonnais did, and above all how they did it. The morning after a new refugee family came to town they would find on their front door, a wreath with

35

"*Bienvenue!*" "Welcome!" painted on a piece of cardboard attached to the wreath. Nobody knew who had brought the wreath; in effect, the whole town had brought it.

It was mainly the women of Le Chambon who gave so much more than shelter to these, the most hated enemies of the Nazis. There was Madame Barraud, a tiny Alsatian, who cared for the refugee boys in her house with all the love such a tiny body could hold, and who cared for the way they felt day and night. And there were others.

But there was one person without whom Le Chambon could not have become the safest place in Europe for Jews: the Huguenot minister of the village, André Trocmé. Trocmé was a passionately religious man. He was massive, more than six feet tall, blonde, with a quick temper. Once long after the war, while he was lecturing on the main project of his life, the promotion of the idea of nonviolence in international relations, one of the members of his audience started to whisper a few words to his neighbor. Trocmé let this go on for a few moments, then interrupted his speech, walked up to the astonished whisperer, raised his massive arm, pointed toward the door, and yelled, "Out! Out! Get out!" And the lecture was on nonviolence.

The center of his thought was the belief that God showed how important man was by becoming Himself a human being, and by becoming a particular sort of human being who was the embodiment of sacrificially generous love. For Trocmé, every human being was like Jesus, had God in him or her, and was just as precious as God Himself. And when Trocmé with the help of the Quakers and others organized his village into the most efficient rescue machine in Europe, he did so not only to save the Jews, but also to save the Nazis and their collaborators. He wanted to keep them from blackening their souls with more evil—he wanted to save them, the victimizers, from evil.

One of the reasons he was successful was that the Huguenots had been themselves persecuted for hundreds of years by the kings of France, and they knew what persecution was. In fact, when the people of Le Chambon took Jewish children and whole families across the mountains of southeastern France into neutral Switzerland, they often followed pathways that had been taken by Huguenots in their flight from the Dragoons of the French kings.

A particular incident from the story of Le Chambon during the Nazi occupation of France will explain succinctly why he was successful in making the village a village of refuge. But before I relate the story, I must point out that the people of the village did not think of themselves as "successful," let alone as "good." From their point of view, they did not do anything that required elaborate explanation. When I asked them why they helped these dangerous guests, they invariably answered, "What do you mean, 'Why'? Where else could they go? How could you turn them away? What is so special about being ready to help (*prête à servir*)? There was nothing else to do." And some of them laughed in amazement when I told them that I thought they were "good people." They saw no alternative to their actions and to the way they acted, and therefore they saw what they did as necessary, not something to be picked out for praise. Helping these guests was for them as natural as breathing or eating—one does not think of alternatives to these functions; they did not think of alternatives to sheltering people who were endangering not only the lives of their hosts but the lives of all the people of the village.

And now the story: One afternoon a refugee woman knocked on the door of a farmhouse outside the village. The farmers around the village proper were Protestants like most of the others in Le Chambon, but with one difference: they were mostly "Darbystes," followers of a strange Scot named Darby, who taught their ancestors in the nineteenth century to believe every word of the Bible, and indeed, who had them memorize the Bible. They were literal fundamentalists. The farm-woman opened the door to the refugee and invited her into the kitchen where it was warm. Standing in the middle of the floor the refugee, in heavily accented French, asked for eggs for her children. In those days of very short supplies, people with children often went to the farmers in the "gray market" (neither black nor exactly legal) to get necessary food. This was early in 1941, and the farmers were not yet accustomed to the refugees. The farm-woman looked into the eyes of the shawled refugee and asked, "Are you Jewish?" The woman started to tremble, but she could not lie, even though that question was usually the beginning of the end of life for Jews in Hitler's Fortress Europe. She answered, "Yes."

The woman ran from the kitchen to the staircase nearby, and while the refugee trembled with terror in the kitchen, she called up the stairs, "Husband, children, come down, come down! We have in our house at this very moment a representative of the Chosen People!"

Not all the Protestants in Le Chambon were Darbyste fundamentalists; but almost all were convinced that people are the children of God, and are as precious as God Himself. Their leaders were Huguenot preachers and their following of the negative and positive commandments of the Bible came in part from their personal generosity and courage, but also in part from the depths of their religious conviction that we are all children of God, and we must take care of each other lovingly. This combined with the ancient and deep historical ties between the Huguenots and the Jews of France and their own centuries of persecution by the Dragoons and kings of France helped make them what they were, "always ready to help," as the Chambonnais saying goes.

A Choice of Perspectives

We have come a long way from cruelty to the people of Le Chambon, just as I have come a long way in my research from concrete evil to concrete goodness. Let me conclude with a point that has been alternately hinted at and stressed in the course of this essay.

A few months after *Lest Innocent Blood Be Shed* was published I received a letter from Massachusetts that opened as follows:

> I have read your book, and I believe that you mushy-minded moralists should be awakened to the facts. Nothing happened in Le Chambon, nothing of any importance whatsoever.
>
> The Holocaust, dear Professor, was like a geological event, like an earthquake. No person could start it; no person could change it; and no person could end it. And no small group of persons could do so either. It was the armies and the nations that performed actions that counted. Individuals did nothing. You sentimentalists have got to learn that the great masses and big political ideas make the difference. Your people and the people they saved simply do not exist . . .

Now between this position and mine there is an abyss that no amount of shouted arguments or facts can cross. And so I shall not answer this letter with a tightly organized reply. I shall answer it only by telling you that one of the reasons institutional cruelty exists and persists is that people believe that individuals can do nothing, that only vast ideologies and armies can act meaningfully. Every act of institutional cruelty—Nazism, slavery, and all the others—lives not with people in the concrete, but with abstractions that blind people to individuals. Himmler's speech to the SS leadership in 1943 is full of phrases like "exterminating a bacillus," and "The Jewish people will be exterminated." And in that speech he attacks any German who believes in "his decent Jew." Institutional cruelty, like other misleading approaches to ethics, blinds us to the victim's point of view; and when we are blind to that point of view we can countenance and perpetrate cruelty with impunity.

I have told you that I cannot and will not try to refute the letter from Massachusetts. I shall only summarize the point of view of this essay with another story.

I was lecturing a few months ago in Minneapolis, and when I finished talking about the Holocaust and the village of Le Chambon, a woman stood up and asked me if the village of Le Chambon was in the Department of Haute-Loire, the high sources of the Loire River. Obviously she was French, with her accent; and all French people know that there are many villages called "Le Chambon" in France, just as any American knows that there are many "Main Streets" in the United States. I said that Le Chambon was indeed in the Haute-Loire.

Chapter I: Life in the World: Trouble

She said, "Then you have been speaking about the village that saved all three of my children. I want to thank you for writing this book, not only because the story will now be permanent, but also because I shall be able to talk about those terrible days with Americans now for they will understand those days better than they have. You see, you Americans, though you sometimes cross the oceans, live on an island here as far as war is concerned . . ."

Then she asked to come up and say one sentence. There was not a sound, not even breathing, to be heard in the room. She came to the front of the room and said, "The Holocaust was storm, lightning, thunder, wind, rain, yes. And Le Chambon was the rainbow."

Only from her perspective can you understand the cruelty and the goodness I have been talking about, not from the point of view of the gentleman from Massachusetts. You must choose which perspective is best, and your choice will have much to do with your feelings about the preciousness of life, and not only the preciousness of other people's lives. If the lives of others are precious to you, your life will become more precious to you.

FROM CRUELTY TO GOODNESS © Institute of Society, Ethics and the Life Sciences, 360 Broadway, Hastings-on-Hudson, NY 10706. Reprinted by permission of the copyright holder.

from Leviathan (1651)

Thomas Hobbes

Part I, Chapter XIII/Of The Natural Condition Of Mankind As Concerning Their Felicity And Misery

Nature has made men so equal in the faculties of body and mind, as that though there be found one man sometimes manifestly stronger in body, or of quicker mind than another; yet when all is reckoned together, the difference between man and man is not so considerable, as that one man can thereupon claim to himself any benefit to which another may not pretend as well as he. For as to the strength of body, the weakest has strength enough to kill the strongest, either by secret machination or by confederacy with others, that are in the same danger with himself.

And as to the faculties of the mind (setting aside the arts grounded upon words, and especially that skill of proceeding upon general and infallible rules, called science; which very few have, and but in few things; as being not a native faculty, born with us; nor attained, [as prudence] while we look after somewhat else), I find yet a greater equality amongst men than that of strength. For prudence is but experience; which equal time equally bestows on all men in those things they equally apply themselves unto. That which may perhaps make such equality incredible is but a vain conceit of one's own wisdom which almost all men think they have in a greater degree than the vulgar; that is, than all men but themselves and a few others, whom by fame, or for concurring with themselves, they approve. For such is the nature of men, that howsoever they may acknowledge many others to be more witty, or more eloquent, or more learned; Yet they will hardly believe there be many so wise as themselves: For they see their own wit at hand, and other men's at a distance. But this proves rather that men are in that point equal, than unequal. For there is not ordinarily a greater sign of the equal distribution of anything, than that every man is contented with his share.

From this equality of ability, arises equality of hope in the attaining of our ends. And therefore if any two men desire the same thing, which nevertheless they cannot both enjoy, they become enemies; and in the way to their end (which is principally their own conservation, and sometimes their delectation only) endeavour to destroy or subdue one another. And from hence it comes to pass, that where an invader has no more to fear than another man's single power; if one plant, sow, build, or possess a convenient seat, others may probably be expected to come prepared with forces united to dispossess and deprive him not only of the fruit of his labour, but also of his life or liberty: And the invader again is in the like danger of another.

And from this diffidence of one another, there is no way for any man to secure himself, so reasonable, as anticipation; that is, by force or wiles to master the persons of all men he can, so long, till he see no other power great enough to endanger him: And this is no more than his own conservation requires and is generally allowed. Also because there be some, that taking pleasure in contemplating their own power in the acts of conquest, which they pursue farther than their security requires; if others, that otherwise would be glad to be at ease within modest bounds, should not by invasion increase their power, they would not be able, long time, by standing only on their defence, to subsist. And by consequence, such augmentation of dominion over men, being necessary to a man's conservation . . . ought to be allowed him.

Again, men have no pleasure (but on the contrary a great deal of grief) in keeping company where there is no power able to over-awe them all. For every man looks that his companion should value him at the same rate he sets upon himself: And upon all signs of contempt or undervaluing naturally endeavours, as far as he dares (which amongst them that have no common power to keep them in quite is far enough to make them destroy each other) to extort a greater value from his contemners, by dommage; and from others, by the example.

So that in the nature of man, we find three principal causes of quarrel. First, competition; secondly, diffidence; thirdly, glory.

The first makes men invade for gain; the second, for safety; and the third, for reputation. The first use violence to make themselves masters of other men's persons, wives, children, and cattle; the second, to defend them; the third, for trifles, as a word, a smile, a different opinion, and any other sign of undervalue, either direct in their persons, or by reflexion in their kindred, their friends, their nation, their profession, or their name.

Hereby it is manifest that during the time men live without a common power to keep them all in awe, they are in that condition which is called war; and such a war as is of every man against every man. For war consists not in battle only, or the act of fighting; but in a tract of time, wherein the will to contend by battle is sufficiently known: and therefore the notion of *time* is to be considered in the nature of war, as it is in the nature of weather. For as the nature of foul weather lies not in a shower or two of rain, but in an inclination thereto of many days together; So the nature of war consisteth not in actual fighting, but in the known disposition thereto during all the time there is no assurance to the contrary. All other time is peace.

Whatsoever therefore is consequent to a time of war, where every man is enemy to every man; the same is consequent to the time wherein men live without other security than what their own strength and their own invention shall furnish them withall. In such condition, there is no place for industry; because the fruit thereof is uncertain: and consequently no culture of the earth, no navigation, nor use of the commodities that may be imported by sea; no commodious building; no instruments of moving, and removing such things as require much force; no knowledge of the face of the earth; no account of time; no arts; no letters; no society; and which is worst of all, continual fear and danger of violent death; And the life of man, solitary, poor, nasty; brutish, and short.

It may seem strange to some man that has not well weighed these things that nature should thus dissociate and render man apt to invade and destroy one another: and he may therefore, not trusting to this inference made from the passions, desire perhaps to have the same confirmed by experience. Let him therefore consider with himself, when taking a journey he arms himself and seeks to go well accompanied; when going to sleep, he locks his doors; when even in his house he locks his chests; and this when he knows there be laws and public officers armed to revenge all injuries shall be done him; what opinion he has of his fellow subjects, when he rides armed; of his fellow citizens, when he locks his doors; and of his children and servants when he locks his chests. Does he not there as much accuse mankind by his actions, as I do by my words? But neither of us accuse man's nature in it. The desires, and other passions of man, are in themselves no sin. No more are the actions, that proceed from those passions, till they know a law that forbids them: which till laws be made they cannot know: nor can any law be made, till they have agreed upon the person that shall make it.

It may peradventure be thought, there was never such a time, nor condition of war as this; and I believe it was never generally so, over all the world; but there are many places, where they live so now: For the savage people in many places of *America*, except the government of small families, that concord whereof depends on natural lust, have no government at all; and live at this day in that brutish manner; as I said before. Howsoever, it may be perceived what manner of life there would be where there were no common power to fear; by the manner of life, which men that have formerly lived under a peaceful government, use to degenerate into, in a civil war.

But though there had never been any time wherein particular men were in a condition of war one against another, yet in all times kings, and persons of sovereign authority, because of their Independence, are in continual jealousies and in the state and posture of gladiators, having their weapons pointing and their eyes fixed on one another; that is, their forts, garrisons, and guns, upon the frontiers of their kingdoms and continual spies upon their neighbours; which is a posture of war. But because they uphold thereby the industry of their subjects, there does not follow it that misery which accompanies the liberty of particular men.

To this war of every man against every man, this also is consequent; that nothing can be unjust. The notions of right and wrong, justice and injustice have no place. Where there is no common power, there is no law: where no law, no injustice. Force, and fraud are in war, and two cardinal virtues. Justice and injustice are none of the faculties neither of the body nor mind. If they were, they might be in a man that were alone in the world, as well as his senses and passions. They are qualities that relate to men in society, not in solitude. It is consequent also to the same condition, that there be no propriety, no dominion, no *mine* and *thine* distinct; but only that to be every man's, that he can get; and for so long as he can keep it. And thus much for the ill condition, which man by mere nature is actually placed in; though with a possibility to come out of it, consisting partly in the passions, partly in his reason.

The passions that incline men to peace are fear of death, desire of such things as are necessary to commodious living, and a hope by their industry to obtain them. And reason suggests convenient articles of peace, upon which men may be drawn to agreement. These articles are they, which otherwise are called the laws of nature, whereof I shall speak more particularly in the following chapters.

Chapter XIV / Of The First And Second Natural Laws And Of Contracts

The right of nature, which writers commonly call *jus naturale*, is the liberty each man has to use his own power, as he wills himself, for the preservation of his own nature; that is to say, of his own life; and consequently, of doing anything which in his own judgment and reasons he shall conceive to be the aptest means thereunto.

By liberty is understood, according to the proper signification of the word, the absence of external impediments: which impediments may oft take away part of a man's power to do what he would but cannot hinder him from using the power left him, according as his judgment and reason shall dictate to him.

A law of nature (*lex naturalis*) is a precept, or general rule, found out by reason, by which a man is forbidden to do that which is destructive of his life or takes away the means of preserving the same and to omit that by which he thinks it may be best preserved. For though they that speak of this subject used to confound *jus*, and *lex*, *right* and *law*; yet they ought to be distinguished, because right, consists in liberty to do or to forbear, whereas law determines and binds to one of them: so that law and right differ as much as obligation and liberty; which in one and the same matter are inconsistent.

And because the condition of man (as has been declared in the precedent chapter) is a condition of war of everyone against everyone, in which case everyone is governed by his own reason; and there is nothing he can make use of that may not be a help unto him in preserving his life against his enemies; it follows that in such a condition, every man has a right to everything; even to one another's body. And therefore, as long as this natural right of every man to every thing endures, there can be no security to any man (how strong or wise soever he be) of living out the time which nature ordinarily allows men to live. And consequently it is a precept or general rule of reason, *That every man ought to endeavour peace, as far as he has hope of obtaining it; and when he cannot obtain it, that he may seek, and use, all helps and advantages of war.* The first branch of which rule contains the first and fundamental law of nature; which is *to seek peace and follow it*. The second, the sum of the right of nature, which is *by all means we can, to defend ourselves*.

From this fundamental law of nature, by which men are commanded to endeavour peace, is derived this second law; *That a man be willing, when others are so too, as far-forth, as for peace and defence of himself he shall think it necessary to lay down this right to all things and be contented with so much liberty against other men as he would allow other men against himself.* For as long as every man holds this right of doing any thing he likes, so long are all men in the condition of war. But if other men will not lay down their right, as well as he, then there is no reason for anyone to devest himself of his: For that were to expose himself to prey (which no man is bound to) rather than to dispose himself to peace. This is that law of the gospel: *Whatsoever you require that others should do to you, that do ye to them.* And that law of all men, *Quod tibi fieri non vis, alteri ne feceris*.[1]

To *lay down* a man's *right* to any thing is to divest himself of the *liberty* of hindering another of the benefit of his own right to the same. For he that renounces or passes away his right gives not to any other man a right which he had not before; because there is nothing to which every man had not right by nature; but only stands out of his way, that he may enjoy his own original right without hindrance from him; not without hindrance from another. So that the effect which redounds to one man by another man's defect of right is but so much diminution of impediments to the use of his own right original.

Right is laid aside, either by simply renouncing it or by transferring it to another. By *simply* renouncing when he cares not to whom the benefit thereof redounds. By transferring when he intends the benefit thereof to some certain person or persons. And when a man has in either manner abandoned or granted away his right, then is he said to be obliged, or bound, not to hinder those to whom such right is granted or abandoned from the benefit of it; and that he *ought*, and it is his duty, not to make void that voluntary act of *his* own; and that such hindrance is injustice and injury as being *sine jure*, the right being before renounced or transferred. So that *injury* or *injustice*, in the controversies of the world, is somewhat like to that which in the disputations of scholars is called *absurdity*. For as it is there called an absurdity to contradict what one maintained in the beginning: so in the world, it is called injustice and injury voluntarily to undo that which from the beginning he had voluntarily done. The way by which a man either simply renounces or transfers his right is a declaration or signification by some voluntary and sufficient sign or signs that he does so renounce or transfer, or has so renounced or transferred the same to him that accepts it. And these signs are either words only, or actions only, or (as it happens most often) both words and actions. And the same are the bonds by which men are bound and obliged: bonds that have their strength, not from their own nature (for nothing is more easily broken than a man's word), but from fear of some evil consequence upon the rupture.

Whensoever a man transfers his right or renounces it, it is either in consideration of some right reciprocally transferred to himself or for some other good he hopes for thereby For it is a voluntary act: and of the voluntary acts of every man, the object is some *good to himself*. And therefore there be some rights which no man can be understood by any words, or other signs, to have abandoned or transferred. As first a man cannot lay down the right of resisting them, that assault him by force or take away his life, because he cannot be understood to aim thereby at any good to himself. The same may be said of wounds and chains and imprisonment, both because there is no benefit consequent to such patience, as there is to the patience of suffering another to be wounded or imprisoned, as also because a man cannot tell, when he sees men proceed against him by violence whether they intend his death or not. And lastly the motive, and end for which this renouncing and transferring of Right is introduced, is nothing else but the security of a man's person in his life and in the means of so preserving life as not to be weary of it. And therefore if a man by words, or other signs, seems to despoil himself of the End for which those signs were intended, he is not to be understood as if he meant it or that it was his will, but that he was ignorant of how such words and actions were to be interpreted.

The mutual transferring of right is that which men call contract.

There is difference between transferring of right to the thing and transferring, or tradition, that is, delivery of the thing itself. For the thing may be delivered together with the translation of the right, as in buying and selling with ready money or exchange of goods or lands, and it may be delivered some time after.

Again, one of the contractors may deliver the thing contracted for on his part and leave the other to perform his part at some determinate time after and in the meantime be trusted; and then the contract on his part, is called pact or covenant: Or both parts may contract now to perform hereafter, in which cases he that is to perform in time to come, being trusted, his performance is called *keeping of promise*, or faith; and the failing of performance (if it be voluntary) *violation of faith*.

When the transferring of right is not mutual, but one of the parties transfers in hope to gain thereby friendship or service from another or from his friends; or in hope to gain the reputation of charity, or magnanimity; or to deliver his mind from the pain of compassion; or in hope of reward in heaven, this is not contract, but gift, free-gift, grace: which words signify one and the same thing.

Signs of contract are either *express* or by *inference*. Express are words spoken with understanding of what they signify: And such words are either of the time *present*, or *past*; as, *I give, I grant, I have given, I have granted, I will that this be yours*: Or of the future; as, *I will give, I will grant*: which words of the future, are called promise.

Signs by inference are sometimes the consequence of words; sometimes the consequence of silence; sometimes the consequence of actions; sometimes the consequence of forbearing an action: and generally a sign by inference, of any contract, is whatsoever sufficiently argues the will of the contractor. . . .

In contracts, the right passes not only where the words are of the time present or past, but also where they are of the future, because all contract is mutual translation, or change of right; and therefore he that promises only because he has already received the benefit for which he promises is to be understood as if he intended the right should pass: for unless he had been content to have his words so understood, the other would not have performed his part first. And for that cause, in buying, and selling, and other acts of contract, a promise is equivalent to a covenant; and therefore obligatory. . . .

If a covenant be made wherein neither of the parties perform presently but trust one another in the condition of mere nature (which is a condition of war of every man against every man) upon any reasonable suspicion, it is void: But if there be a common power set over them both, with right and force sufficient to compel performance, it is not void. For he that performs first has no assurance the other will perform after; because the bonds of words are too weak to bridle men's ambition, avarice, anger, and other passions without the fear of some coercive power; which in the condition of mere nature, where all men are equal and judges of the justness of their own fears, cannot possibly be supposed. And therefore he which performs first does but betray himself to his enemy; contrary to the right (he can never abandon) of defending his life, and means of living.

But in a civil estate, where there is a power set up to constrain those that would otherwise violate their faith, that fear is no more reasonable; and for that cause, he which by the covenant is to perform first is obliged so to do. . . .

Covenants entered into by fear; in the condition of mere nature, are obligatory. For example, if I covenant to pay a ransom or service for my life to an enemy I am bound by it. For it is a contract, wherein one receives the benefit of life; the other is to receive money or service for it; and consequently, where no other law (as in the condition, of mere nature) forbids the performance, the covenant is valid. Therefore prisoners of war, if trusted with the payment of their ransom, are obliged to pay it: And if a weaker prince make a disadvantageous peace with a stronger for fear, he is bound to keep it, unless (as has been said before) there arises some new and just cause of fear to renew the war. And even in commonwealths, if I be forced to redeem myself from a thief by promising him money, I am bound to pay it till the civil law discharge me. For whatsoever I may lawfully do without obligation, the same I may lawfully covenant to do through fear; and what I lawfully covenant, I cannot lawfully break.

A former covenant makes void a later. For a man that has passed away his right to one man today has it not to pass tomorrow to another: and therefore the later promise passes no right, but is null.

A covenant not to defend myself from force, by force, is always void. For (as I have shown before) no man can transfer or lay down his right to save himself from death, wounds, and imprisonment (the avoiding whereof is the only end of laying down any right) and therefore the promise of not resisting force in no covenant transfers any right nor is obliging. For though a man may covenant thus, *Unless I do so, or so, kill me*; he cannot covenant thus, *Unless I do so, or so, I will not resist you, when you come to kill me*. For man by nature chooses the lesser evil, which is danger of death in resisting; rather than the greater; which is certain and present death in not resisting. And this is granted to be true by all men, in that they lead criminals to execution and prison with armed men, notwithstanding that such criminals have consented to the law by which they are condemned.

A covenant to accuse oneself without assurance or pardon is likewise invalid. For in the condition of nature, where every man is judge, there is no place for accusation; and in the civil state, the accusation is followed with punishment, which, being Force, a man is not obliged not to resist. The same is also true of the accusation of those by whose condemnation a man falls into misery; as of a father, wife, or benefactor. For the testimony of such an accuser, if it be not willingly given, is presumed to be corrupted by nature and therefore not to be received: and where a man's testimony is not to be credited, he is not bound to give it. Also accusations upon torture are not to be reputed as testimonies. For torture is to be used but as means of conjecture, and light, in the further examination and search of truth; and what is in that case confessed tends to the ease of him that is tortured, not to the informing of the torturers, and therefore ought not to have the credit of a sufficient testimony; for whether he deliver himself by true or false accusation, he does it by the right of preserving his own life. . . .

Endnote

1. "What you do not want done to yourself, do not do to others."—ED.

The Road Less Traveled

M. Scott Peck

Problems and Pain

Life is difficult.

This is a great truth, one of the greatest truths.[1] It is a great truth because once we truly see this truth, we transcend it. Once we truly know that life is difficult—once we truly understand and accept it—then life is no longer difficult. Because once it is accepted, the fact that life is difficult no longer matters.

Most do not fully see this truth that life is difficult. Instead they moan more or less incessantly, noisily or subtly, about the enormity of their problems, their burdens, and their difficulties as if life were generally easy, as if life *should* be easy. They voice their belief, noisily or subtly, that their difficulties represent a unique kind of affliction that should not be and that has somehow been especially visited upon them, or upon their families, their tribe, their class, their nation, their race or even their species, and not upon others. I know about this moaning because I have done my share.

Life is a series of problems. Do we want to moan about them or solve them? Do we want to teach our children to solve them?

Discipline is the basic set of tools we require to solve life's problems. Without discipline we can solve nothing. With only some discipline we can solve only some problems. With total discipline we can solve all problems.

What makes life difficult is that the process of confronting and solving problems is a painful one. Problems, depending upon their nature, evoke in us frustration or grief or sadness or loneliness or guilt or regret or anger or fear or anxiety or anguish or despair. These are uncomfortable feelings, often very uncomfortable, often as painful as any kind of physical pain, sometimes equaling the very worst kind of physical pain. Indeed, it is *because* of the pain that events or conflicts engender in us that we call them problems. And since life poses an endless series of problems, life is always difficult and is full of pain as well as joy.

Yet it is in this whole process of meeting and solving problems that life has its meaning. Problems are the cutting edge that distinguishes between success and failure. Problems call forth our courage and our wisdom; indeed, they create our courage and our wisdom. It is only because of problems that we grow mentally and spiritually. When we desire to encourage the growth of the human spirit, we challenge and encourage the human capacity to solve problems, just as in school we deliberately set problems for our children to solve. It is through the pain of confronting and resolving problems that we learn. As Benjamin Franklin said. "Those things that hurt, instruct." It is for this reason that wise people learn not to dread but actually to welcome problems and actually to welcome the pain of problems.

Most of us are not so wise. Fearing the pain involved, almost all of us, to a greater or lesser degree, attempt to avoid problems. We procrastinate, hoping that they will go away. We ignore them, forget them, pretend they do not exist. We even take drugs to assist us in ignoring them, so that by deadening ourselves to the pain we can forget the problems that cause the pain. We attempt to skirt around problems rather than meet them head on. We attempt to get out of them rather than suffer through them.

This tendency to avoid problems and the emotional suffering inherent in them is the primary basis of all human mental illness. Since most of us have this tendency to a greater or lesser degree, most of us are mentally ill to a greater or lesser degree, lacking complete mental health. Some of us will go to quite extraordinary lengths to avoid our problems and the suffering they cause, proceeding far afield from all that is clearly good and sensible in order to try to find an easy way out, building the most elaborate fantasies in which to live, sometimes to the total exclusion of reality. In the succinctly elegant words of Carl Jung, "Neurosis is always a substitute for legitimate suffering."[2]

But the substitute itself ultimately becomes more painful than the legitimate suffering it was designed to avoid. The neurosis itself becomes the biggest problem. True to form, many will then attempt to avoid this pain and this problem in turn, building layer upon layer of neurosis. Fortunately, however, some possess the courage to face their neuroses and begin—usually with the help of psychotherapy—to learn how to experience legitimate suffering. In any case, when we avoid the legitimate suffering that results from dealing with problems, we also avoid the growth that problems demand from us. It is for this reason that in chronic mental illness we stop growing, we become stuck. And without healing, the human spirit begins to shrivel.

Therefore let us inculcate in ourselves and in our children the means of achieving mental and spiritual health. By this I mean let us teach ourselves and our children the necessity for suffering and the value thereof; the need to face problems directly and to experience the pain involved. I have stated that discipline is the basic set of tools we require to solve life's problems. It will become clear that these tools are techniques of suffering, means by which we experience the pain of problems in such a way as to work them through and solve them successfully, learning and growing in the process. When we teach ourselves and our children discipline, we are teaching them and ourselves how to suffer and also how to grow.

What are these tools, these techniques of suffering, these means of experiencing the pain of problems constructively that I call discipline? There are, four: delaying of gratification, acceptance of responsibility, dedication to truth, and balancing. As will be evident, these are not complex tools whose application demands extensive training. To the contrary, they are simple tools, and almost all children are adept in their use by the age of ten. Yet presidents and kings will often forget to use them to their own downfall. The problem lies not in the complexity of these tools but in the will to use them. For they are tools with which pain is confronted rather than avoided, and if one seeks to avoid legitimate suffering, then one will avoid the use of these tools. Therefore, after analyzing each of these tools, we shall in the next section examine the will to use them, which is love.

Delaying Gratification

. . . . In summary, for children to develop the capacity to delay gratification, it is necessary for them to have self-disciplined role models, a sense of self-worth, and a degree of trust in the safety of their existence. These "possessions" are ideally acquired through the self-discipline and consistent, genuine caring of their parents; they are the most precious gifts of themselves that mothers and fathers can bequeath. When these gifts have not been proffered by one's parents, it is possible to acquire them from other sources, but in that case the process of their acquisition is invariably an uphill struggle, often of lifelong duration and often unsuccessful.

Responsibility

We cannot solve life's problems except by solving them. This statement may seem idiotically tautological or self-evident, yet it is seemingly beyond the comprehension of much of the human race. This is because we must accept responsibility for a problem before we can solve it. We cannot solve a problem by saying "It's not my problem." We cannot solve a problem by hoping that someone else will solve it for us. I can solve a problem only when I say "This is *my* problem and it's up to me to solve it." But many, so many, seek to avoid the pain of their problems by saying to themselves: "This problem was caused me by other people, or by social circumstances beyond my control, and therefore it is up to other people or society to solve this problem for me. It is not really my personal problem."

Neuroses and Character Disorders

Most people who come to see a psychiatrist are suffering from what is called either a neurosis or a character disorder. Put most simply, these two conditions are disorders of responsibility, and as such they are opposite styles of relating to the world and its problems. The neurotic assumes too much responsibility; the person with a character disorder not enough. When neurotics are in conflict with the world they automatically assume that they are at fault. When those with character disorders are in conflict with the world they automatically assume that the world is at fault.

Even the speech patterns of neurotics and those with character disorders are different. The speech of the neurotic is notable for such expressions as "I ought to," "I should," and "I shouldn't," indicating the individual's self-image as an inferior man or woman, always falling short of the mark, always making the wrong choices. The speech of a person with a character disorder, however, relies heavily on "I can't," "I couldn't," "I have to," and "I had to," demonstrating a self-image of a being who has no power of choice, whose behavior is completely directed by external forces totally beyond his or her control. As might be imagined, neurotics, compared with character-disordered people, are easy to work with in psychotherapy because they assume responsibility for their difficulties and therefore see themselves as having problems. Those with character disorders are much more difficult, if not impossible, to work with because they don't see themselves as the source of their problems; they see the world rather than themselves as being in need of change and therefore fail to recognize the necessity for self-examination. In actuality, many individuals have both a neurosis and a character disorder and are referred to as "character neurotics," indicating that in some areas of their lives they are guilt-ridden by virtue of having assumed responsibility that is not really theirs, while in other areas of their lives they fail to take realistic responsibility for themselves. Fortunately, once having established the faith and trust of such individuals in the psychotherapy process through helping them with the neurotic part of their personalities, it is often possible then to engage them in examining and correcting their unwillingness to assume responsibility where appropriate.

Few of us can escape being neurotic or character disordered to at least some degree (which is why essentially everyone can benefit from psychotherapy if he or she is seriously willing to participate in the process). The reason for this is that the problem of distinguishing what we are and what we are not responsible for in this life is one of the greatest problems of human existence. It is never completely solved; for the entirety of our lives we must continually assess and reassess where our responsibilities lie in the ever-changing course of events. Nor is this assessment and reassessment painless if performed adequately and conscientiously. To perform either process adequately we must possess the willingness and the capacity to suffer continual self-examination. And such capacity or willingness is not inherent in any of us. In a sense all children have character disorders, in that their instinctual tendency is to deny their responsibility for many conflicts in which they find themselves. Thus two siblings fighting will always blame each other for initiating the fight and each will totally deny that he or she may have been the culprit. Similarly, all children have neuroses, in that they will instinctually assume responsibility for certain deprivations that they experience but do not yet understand. Thus the child who is not loved by his parents will always assume himself or herself to be unlovable rather than see the parents as deficient in their capacity to love. Or early adolescents who are not yet successful at dating or at sports will see themselves as seriously deficient human beings rather than the late or even average but perfectly adequate bloomers they usually are. It is only through a vast amount of experience and a lengthy and successful maturation that we gain the capacity to see the world and our place in it realistically, and thus are enabled to realistically assess our responsibility for ourselves and the world.

Escape from Freedom

When a psychiatrist makes the diagnosis of a character disorder, it is because the pattern of avoidance of responsibility is relatively gross in the diagnosed individual. Yet almost all of us from time to time seek to avoid—in ways that can be quite subtle—the pain of assuming responsibility for our own problems. Whenever we seek to avoid the responsibility for our own behavior, we do so by attempting to give that responsibility to some other individual or organization or entity. But this means we then give away our power to that entity, be it "fate" or "society" or the government or the corporation or our boss. It is for this reason that Erich Fromm so aptly titled his study of Nazism and authoritarianism *Escape from Freedom*. In attempting to avoid the pain of responsibility, millions and even billions daily attempt to escape from freedom.

One of the roots of this "sense of impotence" in the majority of patients is some desire to partially or totally escape the pain of freedom, and, therefore, some failure, partial or total, to accept responsibility for their problems and their lives. They fell impotent because they have, in fact, given their power away. Sooner or later, if they are to be healed, they must learn that the entirety of one's adult life is a series of personal choices, decisions. If they can accept this totally, then they become free people. To the extent that they do not accept this they will forever feel themselves victims.

Dedication to Reality

The third tool of discipline or technique of dealing with the pain of problem-solving, which must continually be employed if our lives are to be healthy and our spirits are to grow, is dedication to the truth. Superficially, this should be obvious. For truth is reality. That which is false is unreal. The more clearly we see the reality of the world, the better equipped we are to deal with the world. The less clearly we see the reality of the world—the more our minds are befuddled by falsehood, misperceptions and illusions—the less able we will be to determine correct courses of action and make wise decisions. Our view of reality is like a map with which to negotiate the terrain of life. If the map is true and accurate, we will generally know where we are, and if we have decided where we want to go, we will generally know how to get there. If the map is false and inaccurate, we generally will be lost.

While this is obvious, it is something that most people to a greater or lesser degree choose to ignore. They ignore it because our route to reality is not easy. First of all, we are not born with maps; we have to make them, and the making requires effort. The more effort we make to appreciate and perceive reality, the larger and more accurate our maps will be. But many do not want to make this effort. Some stop making it by the end of adolescence. Their maps are small and sketchy, their views of the world narrow and misleading. By the end of middle age most people have given up the effort. They feel certain that their maps are complete and their Weltanschauung is correct (indeed, even sacrosanct), and they are no longer interested in new information. It is as if they are tired. Only a relative and fortunate few continue until the moment of death exploring the mystery of reality, ever enlarging and refining and redefining their understanding of the world and what is true.

But the biggest problem of map-making is not that we have to start from scratch, but that if our maps are to be accurate we have to continually revise them. The world itself is constantly changing. Glaciers come, glaciers go. Cultures come, cultures go. There is too little technology, there is too much technology. Even more dramatically, the vantage point from which we view the world is constantly and quite rapidly changing. When we are children we are dependent, powerless. As adults we may be powerful. Yet in illness or an infirm old age we may become powerless and dependent again. When we have children to care for, the world looks different from when we have none; when we are raising infants, the world seems different from when we are raising adolescents. When we are poor, the world looks different from when we are rich. We are daily bombarded with new information as to the nature of reality. If we are to incorporate this information, we must continually revise our maps, and sometimes when enough new information has accumulated, we must make very major revisions. The process of making revisions, particularly major revisions, is painful, sometimes excruciatingly painful. And herein lies the major source of many of the ills of mankind.

What happens when one has striven long and hard to develop a working view of the world, a seemingly useful, workable map, and then is confronted with new information suggesting that that view is wrong and the map needs to be largely redrawn? The painful effort required seems frightening, almost overwhelming. What we do more often than not, and, usually unconsciously, is to ignore the new information. Often this act of ignoring is much more than passive. We may denounce the new information as false, dangerous, heretical, the work of the devil. We may actually crusade against it, and even attempt to manipulate the world so as to make it conform to our view of reality. Rather than try to change the map, an individual may try to destroy the new reality. Sadly, such a person may expend much more energy ultimately in defending an outmoded view of the world than would have been required to revise and correct it in the first place. . . .

Openness to Challenge

What does a life of total dedication to the truth mean? It means, first of all, a life of continuous and never-ending stringent self-examination. We know the world only through our relationship to it. Therefore, to know the world, we must not only examine it but we must simultaneously examine the examiner. . . .

※ ※ ※

A life of total dedication to the truth also means a life of willingness to be personally challenged. The only way that we can be certain that our map of reality is valid is to expose it to the criticism and challenge of other map-makers. Otherwise we live in a closed system—within a bell jar, to use Sylvia Plath's analogy, rebreathing only our own fetid air, more and more subject to delusion. Yet, because of the pain inherent in the process of revising our map of reality, we mostly seek to avoid or ward off any challenges to its validity. To our children we say, "Don't talk back to me, I'm your parent." To our spouse we give the message, "Let's live and let live. If you criticize me, I'll be a bitch to live with, and you'll regret it." To their families and the world the elderly give the message, "I am old and fragile. If you challenge me I may die or at least you will bear upon your head the responsibility for making my last days on earth miserable." To our employees we communicate, "If you are bold enough to challenge me at all, you had best do so very circumspectly indeed or else you'll find yourself looking for another job."

The tendency to avoid challenge is so omnipresent in human beings that it can properly be considered a characteristic of human nature. But calling it natural does not mean it is essential or beneficial or unchangeable behavior. It is also natural to defecate in our pants and never brush our teeth. Yet we teach ourselves to do the unnatural until the unnatural becomes itself second nature. Indeed, all self-discipline might be defined as teaching ourselves to do the unnatural. Another characteristic of human nature—perhaps the one that makes us most human—is our capacity to do the unnatural, to transcend and hence transform our own nature.

※ ※ ※

We lie, of course, not only to others but also to ourselves. The challenges to our adjustment—our maps—from our own consciences and our own realistic perceptions may be every bit as legitimate and painful as any challenge from the public. Of the myriad lies that people often tell themselves, two of the most common, potent and destructive are "We really love our children" and "Our parents really loved us." It may be that our parents did love us and we do love our children, but when it is not the case, people often go to extraordinary lengths to avoid the realization. I frequently refer to psychotherapy as the "truth game" or the "honesty game" because its business is among other things to help patients confront such lies. One of the roots of mental illness is invariably an interlocking system of lies we have been told and lies we have told ourselves. These roots can be uncovered and excised only in an atmosphere of utter honesty. To create this atmosphere it is essential for therapists to bring to their relationships with patients a total capacity for openness and truthfulness. How can a patient be expected to endure the pain of confronting reality unless we bear the same pain? We can lead only insofar as we go before.

※ ※ ※

What rules, then, can one follow if one is dedicated to the truth? First, never speak falsehood. Second, bear in mind that the act of withholding the truth is always potentially a lie, and that in each instance in which the truth is withheld a significant moral decision is required. Third, the decision to withhold the truth should never be based on personal needs, such as a need for power, a need to be liked or a need to protect one's map from challenge. Fourth, and conversely, the decision to withhold the truth must always be based entirely upon the needs of the person or people from whom the truth is being withheld. Fifth, the assessment of another's needs is an act of responsibility which is so complex that it can only be executed wisely when one operates with genuine love for the other. Sixth, the primary factor in the assessment of another's needs is the assessment of that person's capacity to utilize the truth for his or her own spiritual growth. Finally, in assessing the capacity of another to utilize the truth for personal spiritual growth, it should be borne in mind that our tendency is generally to underestimate rather than overestimate this capacity.

All this might seem like an extraordinary task, impossible to ever perfectly complete, a chronic and never-ending burden, a real drag. And it is indeed a never-ending burden of self-discipline, which is why most people opt for a life of very limited honesty and openness and relative closedness, hiding themselves and their maps from the world. It is easier that way. Yet the rewards of the difficult life of honesty and dedication to the truth are more than commensurate with the demands. By virtue of the fact that their maps are continually being challenged, open people are continually growing people. Through their openness they can establish and maintain intimate relationships far more effectively than more closed people. Because they never speak falsely they can be secure and proud in the knowledge that they have done nothing to contribute to the confusion of the world, but have served as sources of illumination and clarification. Finally, they are totally free to be. They are not burdened by any need to hide. They do not have to slink around in the shadows. They do not have to construct new lies to hide old ones. They need waste no effort covering tracks or maintaining disguises. And ultimately they find that the energy required for the self-discipline of honesty is far less than the energy required for secretiveness. The more honest one is, the easier it is to continue being honest, just as the more lies one has told, the more necessary it is to lie again. By their openness, people dedicated to the truth live in the open, and through the exercise of their courage to live in the open, they become free from fear.

Balancing

By this time I hope it is becoming clear that the exercise of discipline is not only a demanding but also a complex task, requiring both flexibility and judgment. Courageous people must continually push themselves to be completely honest, yet must also possess the capacity to withhold the whole truth when appropriate. To be free people we must assume total responsibility for ourselves, but in doing so must possess the capacity to reject responsibility that is not truly ours. To be organized and efficient, to live wisely, we must daily delay gratification and keep an eye on the future; yet to live joyously we must also possess the capacity, when it is not destructive, to live in the present and act spontaneously. In other words, discipline itself must be disciplined. The type of discipline required to discipline discipline is what I call balancing, and it is the fourth and final type that I would like to discuss here.

Balancing is the discipline that gives us flexibility. Extraordinary flexibility is required for successful living in all spheres of activity. . . .

※ ※ ※

Mature mental health demands, then, an extraordinary capacity to flexibly strike and continually restrike a delicate balance between conflicting needs, goals, duties, responsibilities, directions, et cetera. The essence of this discipline of balancing is "giving up." I remember first being taught this one summer morning in my ninth year. I had recently learned to ride a bike and was joyously exploring the dimensions of my new skill. About a mile from our house the road went down a steep hill and turned sharply at the bottom. Coasting down the hill on my bike that morning I felt my gathering speed to be ecstatic. To give up this ecstacy by the application of brakes seemed an absurd self-punishment. So I resolved to simultaneously retain my speed and negotiate the corner at the bottom. My ecstasy ended seconds later when I was propelled a dozen feet off the road into the woods. I was badly scratched and bleeding and the front wheel of my new bike was twisted beyond use from its impact against a tree. I had lost my balance.

Balancing is a discipline precisely because the act of giving something up is painful. In this instance I had been unwilling to suffer the pain of giving up my ecstatic speed in the interest of maintaining my balance around the corner. I learned, however, that the loss of balance is ultimately more painful than the giving up required to maintain balance. In one way or another it is a lesson I have continually had to relearn throughout my life. As must everyone, for as we negotiate the curves and corners of our lives, we must continually give up parts of ourselves. The only alternative to this giving up is not to travel at all on the journey of life.

※ ※ ※

Although an entire book could be written about each one, let me simply list, roughly in order of their occurrence, some of the major conditions, desires and attitudes that must be given up in the course of a wholly successful evolving lifetime:

    The state of infancy, in which no external demands need be responded to
    The fantasy of omnipotence
    The desire for total (including sexual) possession of one's parent(s)
    The dependency of childhood
    Distorted images of one's parents
    The omnipotentiality of adolescence

The "freedom" of uncommitment
The agility of youth
The sexual attractiveness and/or potency of youth
The fantasy of immortality
Authority over one's children
Various forms of temporal power
The independence of physical health
And, ultimately, the self and life itself.

Renunciation and Rebirth

In regard to the last of the above, it may seem to many that the ultimate requirement—to give up one's self and one's life—represents a kind of cruelty on the part of God or fate, which makes our existence a sort of bad joke and which can never be completely accepted. This attitude is particularly true in present-day Western culture, in which the self is held sacred and death is considered an unspeakable insult. Yet the exact opposite is the reality. It is in the giving up of self that human beings can find the most ecstatic and lasting, solid, durable joy of life. And it is death that provides life with all its meaning. This "secret" is the central wisdom of religion.

The process of giving up the self (which is related to the phenomenon of love, as will be discussed in the next section of this book) is for most of us a gradual process which we get into by a series of fits and starts. One form of temporary giving up of the self deserves special mention because its practice is an absolute requirement for significant learning during adulthood, and therefore for significant growth of the human spirit. I am referring to a subtype of the discipline of balancing which I call "bracketing." Bracketing is essentially the act of balancing the need for stability and assertion of the self with the need for new knowledge and greater understanding by temporarily giving up one's self—putting one's self aside, so to speak—so as to make room for the incorporation of new material into the self. . . .

The discipline of bracketing illustrates the most consequential fact of giving up and of discipline in general: namely, that for all that is given up even more is gained. Self-discipline is a self-enlarging process. The pain of giving up is the pain of death, but death of the old is birth of the new. The pain of death is the pain of birth, and the pain of birth is the pain of death. For us to develop a new and better idea, concept, theory or understanding means that an old idea, concept, theory or understanding must die. . . .

Since birth and death seem to be but different sides of the same coin, it is really not at all unreasonable to pay closer heed than we usually do in the West to the concept of reincarnation. But whether or not we are willing to entertain seriously the possibility of some kind of rebirth occurring simultaneously with our physical death, it is abundantly clear that *this* lifetime is a series of simultaneous deaths and births. "Throughout the whole of life one must continue to learn to live," said Senaca two millennia ago, "and what will amaze you even more, throughout life one must learn to die."[3] It is also clear that the farther one travels on the journey of life, the more births one will experience, and therefore the more deaths—the more joy and the more pain.

This raises the question of whether it is ever possible to become free from emotional pain in this life. Or, putting it more mildly, is it possible to spiritually evolve to a level of consciousness at which the pain of living is at least diminished? The answer is yes and no. The answer is yes, because once suffering is completely accepted, it ceases in a sense to be suffering. It is also yes because the unceasing practice of discipline leads to mastery, and the spiritually evolved person is masterful in the same sense that the adult is masterful in relation to the child. Matters that present great problems for the child and cause it great pain may be of no consequence to the adult at all. Finally, the answer is yes because the spiritually evolved individual is, as will be elaborated in the next section, an extraordinarily loving individual, and with his or her extraordinary love comes extraordinary joy.

The answer is no, however, because there is a vacuum of competence in the world which must be filled. In a world crying out in desperate need for competence, an extraordinarily competent and loving person can no more withhold his or her competence than such a person could deny food to a hungry infant. Spiritually evolved people, by virtue of their discipline, mastery and love, are people of extraordinary competence, and in their competence they are called on to serve the world, and in their love they answer the call. They are inevitably, therefore, people of great power, although the world may generally behold them as quite ordinary people, since more often than not they will exercise their power in quiet or even hidden ways. Nonetheless, exercise power they do, and in this exercise they suffer greatly, even dreadfully. For to exercise power is to make decisions, and the process of making decisions with total awareness is often infinitely more painful than making decisions with limited or blunted awareness (which is the way most decisions are made and why they are ultimately proved wrong). Imagine two generals, each having to decide whether or not to commit a division of ten thousand men to battle. To one the division is but a thing, a unit of personnel, an instrument of strategy and nothing more. To the other it is these things, but he is also aware of each and every one of the ten thousand lives and the lives of the families of each of the ten thousand. For whom is the decision easier? It is easier for the general who has blunted his awareness precisely because he cannot tolerate the pain of a more nearly complete awareness: It may be tempting to say, "Ah, but a spiritually evolved man would never become a general in the first place." But the same issue is involved in being a corporation president, a physician, a teacher, a parent. Decisions affecting the lives of others must always be made. The best decision-makers are those who are willing to suffer the most over their decisions but still retain their ability to be decisive. One measure—and perhaps the best measure—of a person's greatness is the capacity for suffering. Yet the great are also joyful. This, then, is the paradox. Buddhists tend to ignore the Buddha's suffering and Christians forget Christ's joy. Buddha and Christ were not different men. The suffering of Christ letting go on the cross and the joy of Buddha letting go under the bo tree are one.

So if your goal is to avoid pain and escape suffering, I would not advise you to seek higher levels of consciousness or spiritual evolution. First, you cannot achieve them without suffering, and second, insofar as you do achieve them, you are likely to be called on to serve in ways more painful to you, or at least demanding of you, than you can now imagine. Then why desire to evolve at all, you may ask. If you ask this question, perhaps you do not know enough of joy. Perhaps you may find an answer in the remainder of this book; perhaps you will not.

A final word on the discipline of balancing and its essence of giving up: you must have something in order to give it up. You cannot give up anything you have not already gotten. If you give up winning without ever having won, you are where you were at the beginning: a loser. You must forge for yourself an identity before you can give it up. You must develop an ego before you can lose it. This may seem incredibly elementary, but I think it is necessary to say it, since there are many people I know who possess a vision of evolution yet seem to lack the will for it. They want, and believe it is possible, to skip over the discipline, to find an easy shortcut to sainthood. Often they attempt to attain it by simply imitating the superficialities of saints, retiring to the desert or taking up carpentry. Some even believe that by such imitation they have really become saints and prophets, and are unable to acknowledge that they are still children and face the painful fact that they must start at the beginning and go through the middle.

Discipline has been defined as a system of techniques of dealing constructively with the pain of problem-solving—instead of avoiding that pain—in such a way that all of life's problems can be solved. Four basic techniques have been distinguished and elaborated: delaying gratification, assumption of responsibility, dedication to the truth or reality, and balancing. Discipline is a *system* of techniques, because these techniques are very much interrelated. In a single act one may utilize two, three or even all of the techniques at the same time and in such a way that they may be indistinguishable from each other. The strength, energy and willingness to use these techniques are provided by love, as will be elaborated in the next section. This analysis of discipline has not been intended to be exhaustive, and it is possible that I have neglected one or more additional basic techniques, although I suspect not. It is also reasonable to ask whether such processes as biofeedback, meditation, yoga, and psychotherapy itself are not techniques of discipline, but to this I would reply that, to my way of thinking, they are technical aids rather than basic techniques. As such they may be very useful but are not essential. On the other hand, the basic techniques herein described, if practiced unceasingly and genuinely, are alone sufficient to enable the practitioner of discipline, or "disciple," to evolve to spiritually higher levels.

Endnotes

1 The first of the "Four Noble Truths" that Buddha taught was "Life is suffering."
2 *Collected Works of C. G. Jung*, Bollengen Ser., No. 20, 2d ed. (Princeton, NJ.: Princeton Univ. Press, 1973), trans. R. F. C. Hull, Vol. II, *Psychology and Religion: West and East*, 75.
3 Quoted in Erich Fromm, *The Same Society* (New York: Rinehart, 1955).

The Road Less Traveled, copyright © 1978 by M. Scott Peck, M.D. Reprinted by permission of Simon & Schuster, Inc.

Moral Concern

Rodger Beehler

> *I shall not surely be contradicted in granting to man the only natural virtue which the most passionate detractor of human virtues could not deny him, I mean that of pity, a disposition suitable to creatures weak as we are, and liable to so many evils; a virtue so much the more universal, and withal useful to man, as it takes place in him before all manner of reflection; and so natural that the beasts themselves sometimes give evident signs of it.*
>
> Rousseau

> *[R]emember that it is a primitive reaction to tend, to treat, the part that hurts when someone else is in pain . . .*
>
> *But what is the word 'primitive' meant to say here? Presumably that this sort of behaviour is* pre-linguistic: *that a language game is based on it. . .*
>
> Wittgenstein

One need not look outside one's own city or village for examples of physical assault. I shall take my example from a work of fiction, because this will enable me later to connect the discussion of this chapter to a consideration of moral understanding. This cannot, I think, be judged in any way to affect the validity of the discussion; for in these matters truth is at least as terrible as fiction.* Consider, then, from Hubert Selby's *Last Exit to Brooklyn*, the following human encounter:

> They got in a cab and drove to a downtown hotel. He bought a bottle of whiskey and they sat and drank and he talked. She kept filling his glass. He kept talking.

---

* Four years ago in a North American city two robberies were performed, one on a Saturday night, the other the following Sunday evening. The first was from a grocery store, the second from a garage. In both cases a small amount of money was taken. In both cases the eyes of the store-keeper and garage-attendant were put out to prevent their identifying the robber. From the reports of the victims, and examination of their wounds, authorities concluded that no weapon was used to accomplish this. The eyes of these men were put out by the bare hands of their assailant.

[Tralala] kept pouring but he wouldn't pass out. The bastard. He said he just wanted to be near her for a while . . . . She had been there over an hour.

The hell with it. She hit him over the head with the bottle. She emptied his pockets and left. She took the money out of his wallet and threw the wallet away. She counted it on the subway. 50 bucks.

They were sitting at the counter when the [soldier] came in. He was holding a bloodied handkerchief to his head and blood had caked on his wrist and cheek. He grabbed Tralala by the arm and pulled her from the stool. Give me my wallet you goddamn whore. She spit in his face [and] kicked him . . . . He grabbed her again. He was crying and bent over struggling to breathe from the pain of the kick. If I don't have the pass I cant get in the Base. I have to get back. They're going to fly me home tomorrow . . . . I've been all shot up. Please, PLEASE. Just the wallet . . . . The tears streaked the caked blood and he hung on Tony's and Al's grip and Tralala swung at his face, spitting, cursing and kicking. . .

Tony grabbed the doggie around the neck and Al shoved the bloodied handkerchief in his mouth and they dragged him outside in a darkened doorway. He was still crying and begging for his ID card when Tony pulled his head up by the hair and Al punched him a few times in the stomach and then in the face, then held him up while Tony hit him a few times; but they soon stopped, not afraid that the cops might come, but they knew he didn't have any money and they were tired from hitting the seaman they had lushed earlier, so they dropped him and he fell to the ground on his back. Before they left Tralala stomped on his face until both eyes were bleeding and his nose was split and broken then kicked him [.][1]

The acts of these young people against this soldier are a brutal instance of what it is morally wrong to do. What we are to seek to appreciate is what you, and I, and others, *are saying* when we say that these acts are morally wrong.

I take it we are saying: they ought not to be done. This obviously does not get us very far. But it is a beginning, since it identifies the crucial expression to be (as Hume saw) 'ought', rather than 'wrong'. Any act is wrong to do which is what you ought not to do. It is wrong *in being* what you ought not to do. If, for example, you are trying to fill the radiator of your automobile with water, what you are doing is wrong to do if you are pouring the water into the oil-fill pipe. It is wrong, because it is not what you ought to do to accomplish what you intend. (Thus when, as a young boy, I lean, watercan poised, under the hood, trying to recall the previous lesson, and touch hesitantly with my free hand first the generator cap, then the carburettor hood, then the oil-fill pipe, my watching father calls out at my elbow: 'Wrong . . . Wrong . . . Wrong. . .') Only if you wish to fill the engine with water is what you are doing the right thing—the thing you

Chapter I: Life in the World: Trouble

ought—to do. It is the same way in moral matters. That act is (morally) wrong to do which is what you ought not to do. It is the sense in which you, and I, and these young people, *ought not to do* what they are doing that we are after. . . .

✠ ✠ ✠

Let me return to the soldier being brutally beaten by the young people. Suppose I ask, straight out, what explains these acts *being* what ought not to be done? The only answer I can see to give is: their being the inflicting of harm and suffering. But why should the fact that they are acts of this kind matter? Why should inflicting harm and suffering on the soldier be something that *ought not* to be done?

Now someone has to answer these questions. And as I have tried to show in section I the answer you are able to give will depend ultimately upon your relation to the person against whom these acts are directed. If you are uncaring of whether the soldier is brutally beaten and injured, then the acts of these young people will not—cannot—be regarded by you as mattering. If on the other hand you do care that the soldier is not in pain and terror, or maimed, your response to these acts will be to care that they are not done. This caring that they are not done is what is expressed by the words "these things ought not to be done".

But we are not through yet, for everything will depend on *why* you care whether your concern that these acts not be done is a *moral concern* or not. In the words which (with philosophic license) I put into the Comte D'Argenson's mouth I deliberately gave an example of a concern that a man lives which is a completely self-interested concern. Similarly, if your concern that these acts not be done to this soldier proceeds from some use you have for him (from your desire, say, to pry out of him information about the war-zone he has just left), then as you watch from a window above the street and exclaim "They oughtn't to do that—they'll ruin everything!", your concern that these acts not be done is not a moral concern. You do not express with the words "They oughtn't to do that" that sense in which the young people's acts ought not to be done that we are seeking.

What sort of concern must inform these words for them to express that sense? A wonderfully ordinary example of the concern we are seeking is given in the following remembrance.

> It happened in Calgary some thirty years ago. I was rushing along the street to catch a train when a little girl walking in front of me dropped the bottle of milk she'd been sent to buy. The bottle broke, the milk spilled, the child started to weep. I went past and got my train. I have never forgotten that incident, never forgiven myself for my failure to stop and give the kid the price of another bottle. I should have known then what I know now: that there's always another train.[4]

65

What is remembered here is a moment when a man did not do what he should have done. The man did not stop to help the child, and I believe he would agree that he was wrong not to. The man now regrets his failure to stop. Why? Because the child was unhappy and afraid, and he did not help when he could have. He cannot forgive—or forget—his hurrying by. What this man's regret and shame reveal is a concern about the child, a caring that she was unhappy, and a wish to have helped her in her trouble. If the man could go back now and stop and help, he would do it, for the child. He would go back and give her the money because this would make a difference in her life which he wishes had been made, could be made, by him, or anyone, if this were possible. This regard for the child's happiness and suffering, this concern for how she is, is a paradigm of what we speak of as moral sensibility, moral concern. What does such concern or sensibility involve?

The man sees the milk fall and the child begin to weep. He responds to these things, and appreciates them, even as he hurries by. (For there is nothing in the remembrance as reported to suggest that it is only later that, he begins to feel remorse at what he has done. As the train pulls out of the station his regret may begin to form, and his sense of having done the wrong thing start to erode his peace of mind.) Why does this that he sees make this difference—where a crate of bottles standing idly on the sidewalk does not? Why is he affected by what he sees? This man himself knows what it is to break something that is wanted. He also knows something of the life of families, and the place of money there, and so of the possibilities there of exasperation and want. If the child were one of a family where money did not matter, would the broken bottle throw her into tears? It might, if it nevertheless mattered to her to perform this errand well. But to see this possibility requires an understanding of the importance to a person, even as a child, of achievement; of doing something well, or of being able to help someone who is loved and has given one a task to accomplish. Perhaps as, likely, what now awaits the child at home (what may have awaited her before) or perhaps what she mistakenly fears awaits her, is anger and resentment, a return to the store, with fear of dropping the milk again. Perhaps it is simply that now she will be late for school. It may be any one, or more, of these things which accounts for her sorrow. None of these possibilities needs to go through the mind of this man. We learn early that behind tears and fear and broken vessels there lies a human story. A child crying in the street over spilt milk is something we understand. Such distress and fear are appreciated from within an understanding of human concerns and relations and ways of living; from within a knowledge of how things are with people, and what makes us unhappy and afraid. This understanding is not something contingently connected to moral life, something which, while not necessary for, yet, if it exists, makes us 'better at', morality. Understanding of the kind I have sketched here is logically implied by the expressions 'moral concern'

Chapter I: Life in the World: Trouble

'moral life'. But it is not alone sufficient for moral concern, for moral life. It must be accompanied by just that relation to the child which I have described as *caring* about the child. In the chapters which follow I shall seek to establish further that this is so. For the remainder of this chapter I want to consider the implications of this view for an appreciation of the young people's acts against the soldier.

On the view I am proposing, *morally* to appreciate that the acts of these young people ought not to be done involves caring about the soldier against whom they are directed. This *caring about*, or *regard for*, another person is what in the eighteenth century was spoken of as 'natural affection', but which I shall prefer to characterize as a form of love. It is ultimately this regard, or caring, for other persons which gives our moral language its sense—contrary to the account given by Phillips and Mounce. At one point in their book *Moral Practices* Phillips and Mounce remark of Protagoras' claim that 'man is the measure of all things' that

> Precisely what Protagoras meant by this statement may be impossible to determine with certainty, but two interpretations seem plausible. According to the first interpretation, man is the measure of all things in the sense that each individual man, just in so far as he holds an opinion on morality or any other matter, is necessarily correct. Man is the measure of all things, on this interpretation, because each man's opinion is the measure of truth and goodness. According to the second interpretation however, truth and goodness are determined, not by the opinions of individual men, but by the conventions which they create. . . [T]he standards of truth and goodness lie not in the opinions of any particular man but in conventions; and yet man remains the measure of all things, for these conventions are nothing but a reflection of what the majority of men have decided to call bad or false.
>
> The first interpretation of Protagoras differs in obvious ways from the view we are presenting, for, in our view, it is not the individual who is the measure of what is morally right or wrong, but rather the individual's judgements on these matters derive their sense from the moral practice to which he belongs.[5]

Exactly what Phillips and Mounce mean by the last sentence in this passage is not altogether clear. It is clear that they reject the view that whatever each individual judges to be the case is the standard of truth or goodness. They assert that nevertheless *the sense* of each individual's judgment derives from—depends on—the human social practice to which he belongs. Do they mean by this that the *words* each individual uses *to express* his judgment derive their sense from social agreement—so that the word 'ought', say, like the word 'bottle', has the sense it has because of the precise use human beings have given to (their 'practice' with) this mark or sound? Or do Phillips and Mounce mean that the very *judgment* the individual expresses—WHAT he judges—derives its content (its meaning in *that* sense) from the social practice to which he belongs—so that it is the social practice which determines that something is morally right or wrong? These two are not the same and the second view is almost certainly false. A simple proof of this is the fact that I may use words (which have the meaning they do as a result of human agreement in their use) to say something which no one has ever said before. *What* I say, *what* I judge, *what* I express, by means of language, cannot therefore be determined by human agreement—by "a [social] practice to which [I] belong. . .". If it were, I should never be able to speak *for myself.*

Phillips and Mounce leave no room for doubt as to which of these two possible interpretations they mean. They go on directly to express their view as "it is the practice and not the individual which determines what is right or wrong"[6] (i.e., determines that such and such is right, such and such is wrong). In support of their view they invoke Wittgenstein quoting a remark from the *Investigations* at I:242:

> If language is to be a means of communication there must be agreement not only in definitions but also (queer as this may sound) in judgements.

Now this remark will (as Wittgenstein knew) sound queer, only if one thinks that all "judgment" *involves* using language. Mounce and Phillips' moral philosophy reveals an inclination to think exactly this. Their gloss on Wittgenstein's remark at I:242 reveals this inclination, and explains their own position.

> On Wittgenstein's view, we judge the truth of a statement by the criteria for verifying that statement. Whether it is true, for example, that an object is red, will depend on whether that object satisfies the criterion by which an object in given circumstances is judged to be red. If people did not agree in their application of this criterion it would be meaningless to speak of such a criterion, and meaningless, therefore, to speak of judging whether an object is red.[7]

Meaningless, because, on their view, without such a criterion whose existence requires that "people agree in their application of [it]"—there can be no "judging whether an object is red." But Wittgenstein's point is not that "If people did not agree in their application of the criterion, it would be meaningless to speak of such a criterion, and meaningless, therefore, to speak of judging whether an object is red." His point is that if people did not agree *in judging* the object to be red we could not *have* such a (public) criterion. If you and I and the next person did not agree *in what we see* when we regard the object, then indeed it would be meaningless—because impossible—to speak of "the criterion by which an object in given circumstances is judged to be red". For that criterion is: its looking red. How could I assess the truth or falsity of your judgment (and report) that the object is red, by appeal to "the criterion etc . . .", if we did not *agree* in our "(queer as this may sound) [colour] *judgments*"?

> It is, what human beings *say* that is true or false, and they agree in the *language* they use. That is not agreement in opinions but in *form of life*. [Lebensform][8]

We do ordinarily agree in the language we use to describe the colour of objects. But it is human agreement in what *is seen* that makes possible our (public) colour concepts such as 'red'—i.e. this *word*, this *bit of language*. Because we see the object to be red, we can agree in the language we use to describe its colour. Where we do not agree in the language we use (where you indifferently use 'blue' or 'green' of what I describe as 'red') this signals a difference in our primitive apprehension—"judgment"—of the colour. This agreement in seeing, which makes possible our colour vocabulary, and our mutual confirmation or disconfirmation of each other's colour ascriptions, is not "agreement in opinions" but agreement in primitive biological a-perception: in "form of life". Agreement in opinions is agreement in what we judge or believe—what we "want to say"—about something. But for there to be the possibility of agreement in our opinions, and the confirmation of these as true or false, there must first be agreement in form of life. Mounce and Phillips' talk of people agreeing in their application of the criterion by which an object in given circumstances is judged to be red obscures Wittgenstein's point, and delivers us to their own position. For the words "agree in their application" suggest that the criterion exists prior to each individual's "application" of it; and the word "application" itself suggests the consulting and following of a rule—the rule for the application of the word 'red', say. Now it is true that the criterion for the application of the word 'red' exists prior to each individual's application of it. The object is red before people see, and say, that it is. This is true even at the level of the origination of 'red' as the English word for this colour. (The initial stage of "definition".) But in another, and crucial sense, the criterion does not exist prior to each individual's "application" of it, since, as Wittgenstein is trying to show in these remarks, for the object's being red *to be* a criterion for *us* of the truth or falsity of what we each *say* about it, there must be agreement in our perceptual apprehension—"judgments"—of the world. This is not agreement in (i.e., not at the level of) "*definitions*", but in "*form of life*"—i.e. *experience*. (This is one reason why, as Wittgenstein remarks, "If a lion could talk, *we* [my emphasis] could not understand him."[9]) Mounce and Phillips' talk of "application" misleads, for it suggests that first there is the criterion, *and then* there is each individual's *application* of the criterion—all of which applications must for some (unexplained) reason agree for it to be possible to speak of such a criterion in the first place. Whereas it is our *agreeing*—in what we see—that constitutes (creates) the criterion in the first place. For a *criterion*, remember, is something that can function as a *public* test. There is a public criterion, which "people" can appeal to, here, by virtue of the fact that we agree in what we see.

Consider now the situation in morals. Phillips and Mounce are admiring of a remark by J. L. Stocks in which Stocks calls attention to some words by Browning:

> The moral attitude is essentially a concern for the rightness of action . . . morality requires that all means shall be justified in some other way and by some other standard than their value for this or any end: that however magnificent is the prospect opened out by the proposed course of action, and however incontestable the power of the means chosen to bring this prospect nearer, there is still always another question to be asked: not a question whether in achieving this you will not perhaps diminish your chances of achieving something still more important; but a question of another kind. 'There is a decency required,' as Browning said, and this demand of decency is prepared to sacrifice, in the given case, any purpose whatever.[10]

Now this requirement of decency of which Browning speaks is a function, surely, of agreement in *attitude*, not in practice. This is true for two reasons. The first is that the decency Browning speaks of is itself a kind of attitude. The second is that whatever requirement a social practice could make of one could at best be a logical and at worst, a physical (i.e. coercive), requirement. I shall try to illustrate what I mean here by recalling the example of the man who did not stop to help the child.

Consider a man to whom a similar incident occurred, and who now remembers it with regret, but with this difference. He regrets not doing then what he knows would have been the right thing to do, not because he is now, or was then, touched by the plight of the child, which might in fact mean nothing to him, but because he sees that here was a case where he did not do what (as society judges) it was right to do, and the awareness of this 'moral' failure is irksome to him. Now the man whose remembrance I quoted above also regrets his failure to stop. He is ashamed, and does not forgive himself, because the child was unhappy and afraid, and he did not help when he could have. This first man's remembrance reaches out to the child. The second man's remembrance reaches out to that *incident*, and then only, as it were, to return to himself. He regrets that he did not do what it was right to do (which he identifies by appeal to society's moral norms, and which it matters to him always to observe). But from this it does not follow that the man regrets the child's suffering and fear. Perhaps *these* things do not matter to him at all. (Perhaps he even resents the child, for being the occasion of his moral fault.) There is a kind of concern about one's actions which might be characterized as pharisaism. This is a concern always to do what it is right to do, because one wishes to be someone who does right, but where the importance one attaches to one's right actions is, so to speak, that one has done them. That is, it is possible to attach importance to doing what it is right to do, and yet to be indifferent to human suffering or happiness and so to be indifferent to what is done. As I remarked before—if the first man could go back now and stop and help, he would do it, for the child. But were the pharisee able to return, he would do so, not on the child's account, to restore her to untroubledness, but to perfect his record of uprightness. His act would be done, not for the child, but, as it were, for himself. This, I wish to claim, whatever it is, is not what Browning means by "decency", but something which one might want morally to condemn.

What I hope to have shown here are two things. First, that the expression "concern for the rightness of action" must include the pharisee as well as the good man, and therefore any attempt to characterize moral action, that is, action from moral considerations, must require more, than this or similar expressions to do it.—Unless, of course, action from moral considerations includes the pharisee's action; and this is a question about which one might wish to get clear. I have said enough to make plain that my own view is that where an action is called for by moral considerations, and the action called for is help or consideration of some sort to others, then any attempt to elucidate the *moral character* of this action cannot appeal solely to one's personal concern about some 'moral state' of oneself, for if this is the case it will be hard to see the connection between one's action and the persons with whom one is involved. These persons must seem to be simply occasions for 'moral' action, and the 'moral' concern must appear here to be a concern about the person who acts, rather than a concern about those toward whom one's actions are supposedly directed. I shall later try to show that the point of departure of moral action in such cases cannot *solely* be a concern to be a certain sort of person, since *this* concern can itself only be a *moral* concern if concern for other persons at its heart. Because one is concerned about others one is concerned not to be someone who treats them in certain ways.

Secondly: shame, remorse, and regret, are features of the moral life, and (for example) regret at not doing what one should have done for another, where this regret is a moral 'act', seems to involve a concern for or a caring about that other, rather than about oneself or some feature of oneself.

Now this last cannot itself proceed from a social practice. The only 'requirements' in respect of decency which society's "moral practices" can make of you (*qua* requirement) is either the logical requirement that you must do such and such if you are to be described as acting rightly, or the coercive requirement that you must do such and. such (what it is right to do) on pain of some discomfort if you fail to. Neither of these is what Browning refers to when he speaks of decency as being "required". These words "There is a decency *required*" are an expression of the claim upon Browning of his *regard* for other human beings, or, if you prefer, of his attitude toward human relationships. That attitude is what explains our "moral practices", not *vice versa*.

In brief, Wittgenstein's remarks do not support Mounce and Phillips' view, that the individual's moral judgment derives its sense from the moral practice to which he belongs. On the contrary, it is the "moral (social) practice" which derives its sense from individual "judgments". Or to put it less cryptically, it is agreement in that form of life I have called 'caring' which makes possible, and gives sense to, "moral practices". Just as in the case. of colour discrimination there is a public criterion of 'red' which we can appeal to by virtue of the fact that we agree in what we see, so too in the case of moral discrimination there is a moral concept (and specific criteria) of "decency" to which we can appeal by virtue of the fact (and to the extent) that we agree in caring about one another. The agreement here is not agreement in practice but agreement in attitude. It is not social but *psychological* agreement. Each responds as the others (not: each "applies" the 'socially dictated' response). Where there *is* among people a caring about one another there will arise—and there can be agreement in—moral judgments. You, and I, and another can see what these young people do, and agree that they ought not to do it. Failure of an individual to share in this "form of life" will have as its consequence the non-intelligibility of the moral.

Endnotes

1. Hurbert Selby, *Last Exit to Brooklyn* (New York: Grove Press, 1965) pp. 97–99.
2. Francois-Marie Arouet de Voltaire, *Alzaire, Discours Preliminaire.* (see *Oeuvres completes,* ed. L. Moland, 52 vols., Paris 1877–5)
3. *Emile,* Book III.
4. R. J. Needham, *A Writer's Notebook* (Toronto: MacMillan, 1969) p. 9.
5. Op. cit., pp. 61–2.
6. Ibid., p. 62.
7. Ibid., p. 63.
8. Ludwig Wittgenstein, *Philosophical Investigations,* Part I, s.241.
9. Whether Wittgenstein is right about this does not greatly matter; the point of the remark is what is important.
10. J. L. Stocks, *Morality and Purpose* (Routledge & Kegan Paul, 1969) p. 27. (Ed. D. Z. Phillips.) See *Moral Practices,* p. 39.

Chapter II
Responding to Others

As individuals we find ourselves in a world, which we neither made nor created, and in a life we did not request. Yet, even in this troubling world the individual man or woman is free and, therefore, he or she is responsible for that life. Furthermore, we, as individuals, also exist in this world with others. How we choose to respond to the other is one of the most fundamental issues in ethics. The nature and quality of one's response to the other is a manifestation of both an individual's humanness and goodness. How then is one to respond to life in a world with others?

Martin Buber claims: "This fragile life between birth and death can nevertheless be a fulfillment—if it is a dialogue." For Buber, "We practice responsibilities for that realm of life allotted and entrusted to us for which we are able to respond, that is, for which we have a relation of deeds which may count—in all our inadequacy—as a proper response." So, life then on Buber's account is a trust. It is lived in its concreteness and responsibility requires an "other." Ultimately Buber claims there must be One to whom we are responsible. He thus ties ethics to the response to and before God in the world with others. It is in response and relationships that truth, love and courage become real.

Alasdair MacIntyre's central thesis is that the human being is ". . . in his actions and practice, as well as in his fictions, essentially a story-telling animal. The human being . . . becomes through his history, a teller of stories that aspire to truth." MacIntyre says: "We live out our lives, both individually and in our relationships with each other, in light of certain conceptions of a possible shared future, a future in which some possibilities beckon us forward and others repel us." The narrative of our individual and social lives opens only to those possibilities consistent with the narrative. It is through stories that individuals, from childhood, learn how to respond to others in the world. The unity of an individual life is the unity of that narrative which a single life embodies. He states: "The unity of a human life is the unity of the narrative quest."

Peter D. Hershock is the author of *Liberating Intimacy: Enlightenment and Social Virtuosity in Ch'an Buddhism*. Hershock's reflections on the Buddhist story of Kisagotami show us that both suffering and healing occur in the context of a communally articulated life story. Hershock shows that the practical realization of the sociality of enlightenment and, indeed, social virtuosity occurs in the unfolding of self as narrator within a cultural matrix. According to Hershock, "Kisagotami's release from her debilitating grief does not occur, then, as an insight but with her welcoming the community back into herself and her inclusion of and inclusion by the Buddha in the intimacy of that healing narration."

In this famous passage from the Gospel of Luke, Jesus, in his role as a teacher, discloses by way of both question and answer, and narrative, that proper living in the world involves an ordering of one's relationships in a certain way and then comporting one's self in these relationships with the appropriate dispositions. He asks a lawyer what is written in the law, to which the other responds (correctly, according to Jesus): "You shall love the Lord your God with all your heart, with all your soul, with all your strength, and with all your mind; and your neighbor as yourself."

The question is then asked, "Who is my neighbor?" Jesus responds to this question by telling the story of the good Samaritan. Here again we see the power of narrative in disclosing moral truth. In the Samaritan's story we also see what modern ethics would call a "supererogatory response" to the other in need. Supererogatory actions are those acts which go above and beyond the call of duty. They are actions which aim at that which is best in a given situation as opposed to that which is merely required. Human motivations such as compassion and love are the realities which move individuals to aspire to that which is best. The story also points out that the other, to, and for, whom we are called to respond is often very different than ourselves or our ideal friends.

In "The Deep Beauty of the Golden Rule," R. M. MacIver observes:

> The greatest evils inflicted on man by man over the face of the earth, are wrought not by the self-seekers, the pleasure lovers, or the merely amoral, but by the fervent devotees of ethical principles. . . .

Ethical exclusivism has led to intolerance and manifold evil. MacIver holds that the golden rule, *Do unto others as you would have them do to you,* is the only rule that stands by itself in the "light of its own reason." It is ". . . the only rule that can stand by itself in the naked, warring universe, in the face of the contending values of men and groups." This supreme principle of reciprocity requires the individual to respond responsibly not only to the other but, more deeply, to self.

"The Practice of Reciprocity" sets forth the Confucian practice of *shu*, "reciprocity" or "mutual consideration." This is very much like the Western

Chapter II: Responding to Others

notion of the Golden Rule. Actually, it is often called the "Silver Rule:" *Never do to others what you would not like them to do to you.*

Traditional Chinese society is organized (metaphorically) as an extended family. There are Five (constant) Relationships which define and structure society. All are hierarchical. Reciprocity, ideally, should permeate all human relationships.

"Compassion," says Lawrence Blum, "is one of a number of attitudes, emotions, or virtues which can be called 'altruistic' in that they involve a regard for the good of other persons." Blum discusses the proper objects of compassion and concludes that compassion is both linked and connected to a rational and intelligent course of action.

Josiah Royce sees moral understanding as the key to correct moral action and response to others. Fellow feeling brings an individual to the place of "moral insight," namely: "Such as that is for me, so is it for him, nothing less." It is the realization that one's neighbor is a center or locus of experience and desire like ourselves. The neighbor is as real as our own future selves. Realizing this, one's duty is to treat him as we do ourselves.

Immanuel Kant, the eighteenth century German philosopher, has had a monumental impact on philosophy, in general, and on ethics in particular. Kant grounds his entire ethical enterprise in human reason. His supreme ethical principle is the categorical imperative. In this selection, entitled, "Respect for Persons," Kant gives his second formulation of the categorical imperative, sometimes called, "the principle of ends": *Act so you treat humanity whether in your own person or that of another, as an end and never as a means only.*

This principle claims that individuals have objective and unconditional duties not only to others but to self. The human being, for Kant, is a being of unconditional worth—an end in itself. In this essay Kant develops this thesis and discusses the nature of human dignity and respect.

Sometimes, as individuals, we are uncertain about how we ought to respond to others. That is, there are times when our understanding of the morality of our community is in conflict with our own deep sympathies and moral sentiments. What ought I do? Should I ignore my own understanding of morality and simply follow my feelings or should I discipline my feelings, by an act of will, to carry out the dictates of morality? Or, should I refuse to feel? Jonathan Bennett's, "The Conscience of Huckleberry Finn," discusses the above conflicts and various ways to deal with powerful moral dilemmas.

In fact, Bennett discusses three moral consciences: the conscience of Huckleberry Finn, the Nazi Heinrich Himmler, and the Calvinist theologian Jonathan Edwards. Furthermore, Bennett also calls the readers' attention to the fact that, at times, the official morality is a "bad morality." His purpose in writing this piece is "to illustrate different aspects of a single theme," namely the relationship between *sympathy* on the one hand and *bad morality* on the other.

Response

Martin Buber

Response

This fragile life between birth and death can nevertheless be a fulfillment—if it is a dialogue. In our life and experience we are addressed; by thought and speech and action, by producing and by influencing we are able to answer. For the most part we do not listen to the address, or we break into it with chatter. But if the word comes to us and the answer proceeds from us then human life exists, though brokenly, in the world. The kindling of the response in that "spark" of the soul, the blazing up of the response, which occurs time and again, to the unexpectedly approaching speech, we term responsibility. We practice responsibility for that realm of life allotted and entrusted to us for which we are able to respond, that is, for which we have a relation of deeds which may count—in all our inadequacy—as a proper response.

Responsibility

The idea of responsibility is to be brought back from the province of specialized ethics into that of lived life. Genuine responsibility exists only where there is real responding.

Responding to what?

To what happens to one, to what is to be seen and heard and felt. Each concrete hour allotted to the person, with its content drawn from the world and from destiny, is speech for the man who is attentive. Attentive, for no more than that is needed in order to make a beginning with the reading of the signs that are given to you.

Chapter II: Responding to Others

Ethics

Ethical life has entered into religious life, and cannot be extracted from it. There is no responsibility unless there is One to whom one is responsible, for there is no response where there is no address. In the last resort, religious life means concreteness itself, the whole concreteness of life without reduction, grasped dialogically, included in the dialogue.

Reality

With all deference to the world continuum of space and time I know as a living truth only concrete world reality which is constantly, in every moment, reached out to me. I can separate it into its component parts, I can compare them and distribute them into groups of similar phenomena, I can derive them from earlier and reduce them to simpler phenomena; and when I have done all this I have not touched my concrete world reality. Inseparable, incomparable, irreducible, now, happening once only, it gazes upon me with an awesome look.

Symbols

Dogmas and rules are merely the result, subject to change, of the human mind's attempt to make comprehensible, by a symbolic order of the knowable and doable, the working of the unconditional it experiences within itself. Primary reality is constituted by the effect of the unconditional upon the human mind which, sustained by the force of its own vision, unflinchingly faces the supreme power. Man's mind thus experiences the unconditional as that great something which is set over against it, as the Thou as such. By creating symbols, the mind comprehends what is in itself incomprehensible: thus, in symbol and adage, the illimitable God reveals Himself to the human mind, which gathers the flowing universal currents into the receptacle of an affirmation that declares the Lord reigns in this and in no other way. Or man's mind captures a flash of the original source of light in the mirror of some rule which declares that the Lord must be served in this and in no other way. But neither symbol nor adage makes man unworthy or untrue; they are rather forms the unconditional itself creates within man's mind which, at this particular time, has not yet developed into a more effective tool. "For the divine wishes to evolve within mankind." In mankind's great ages, the divine, in invisible becoming, outgrows old symbolisms and blossoms forth in new ones. The symbol becomes ever more internalized, moves ever closer to the heart, and is ever more deeply submerged in life itself; and the man who five thousand years ago saw it in the stars, sees it today in the eyes of a friend. It is not God who changes, only theophany—the manifestation of the divine in man's symbol-creating mind: until no symbol is adequate any longer, and none is needed, and life itself, in the miracle of man's being with man, becomes a symbol—until God is actually present when one man clasps the hand of another.

Dualism

We shall accomplish nothing at all if we divide our world and our life into two domains, one in which God's command is paramount, the other governed exclusively by the laws of economics, politics, and the "simple self-assertion" of the group. Such dualism is far more ominous than the naturalism I spoke of before. Stopping one's ears so as not to hear the voice from above is breaking the connection between existence and the meaning of existence. But he who hears the voice and sets a limit to the area beyond which its rule shall not extend is not merely moving away from God, like the person who refuses to listen; he is standing up directly against Him.

Imitatio

Man cannot "be like unto God," but with all the inadequacy of each of his days, he can follow God at all times, using the capacity he has on that particular day—and if he has used the capacity of that day to the full, he has done enough. This is not a mere act of faith; it is an entering into the life that has to be lived on that day with all the active fullness of a created person.

Limits

Human life and humanity come into being in genuine meetings. There man learns not merely that he is limited by man, cast upon his own finitude, partialness, need of completion, but his own relation to truth is heightened by the other's different relation to the same truth—different in accordance with his individuation, and destined to take seed and grow differently. Men need, and it is granted to them, to confirm one another in their individual being by means of genuine meetings. But beyond this they need, and it is granted to them, to see that the truth, which the soul gains by its struggle, is flashing up for the others, the brothers, in a different way, and equally confirmed.

The Primary Word

The primary word I-Thou can be spoken only with the whole being. Concentration and fusion into the whole being can never take place through my agency, nor can it ever take place without me. I become through my relation to the Thou; as I become I, I say Thou.

All real living is meeting.

Obstacles

The relation to the Thou is direct. No system of concepts, no foreknowledge, and no fancy intervene between I and Thou. The memory itself is transformed as it plunges out of its isolation into the unity of the whole. No set purpose, no greed, and no anticipation intervene between I and Thou. Desire itself is transformed as it plunges out of its dream into the appearance. Every means is an obstacle. Only when every means has collapsed does the meeting come about.

It–Thou

In all the seriousness of truth, hear this: without It man cannot live. But he who lives with It alone is not a man.

How powerful is the unbroken world of It, and how delicate are the appearances of the Thou!

Truth

Is there a truth we can possess? Can we appropriate it? There certainly is none we can pick up and put in our pocket. But the individual can have an honest and uncompromising attitude toward the truth; he can have a legitimate relationship to truth and hold and uphold it all his life. A man may serve Truth for seven years and yet another seven and still not win her, but his relationship has become more genuine and true, more and more truth itself. He cannot achieve this relationship to truth without breaking through his conditionality. He cannot shed it altogether; that is never within his power. But he can, at least, sense something of unconditionality—he can breathe its air. From that time on, this "something of" will quicken his relationship to the truth. Human truth becomes real when one tries to translate one's relationship to truth into the reality of one's life. And human truth can be communicated only if one throws one's self into the process and answers for it with one's self.

The Eternal Thou

The extended lines of relations meet in the eternal Thou.
    Every particular Thou is a glimpse through to the eternal Thou; by means of every particular Thou the primary word addresses the eternal Thou.

Thinking

If we are serious about thinking between I and Thou, then it is not enough to cast our thoughts toward the other subject of thought framed by thought. We should also, with the thinking, precisely with the thinking, live toward the other man, who is not framed by thought but bodily present before us; we should live toward his concrete life. We should live not toward another thinker of whom we wish to know nothing beyond his thinking but, even if the other is a thinker, toward his bodily life over and above his thinking—rather, toward his person, to which, to be sure, the activity of thinking also belongs.

Hope

The hope for this hour depends upon the renewal of dialogical immediacy between men. But let us look beyond the pressing need, the anxiety and care of this hour. Let us see this need in connection with the great human way. Then we shall recognize that immediacy is injured not only between man and man, but also between the being called man and the source of his existence. At its core the conflict between the mistrust and trust of man conceals the conflict between the mistrust and trust of eternity. If our mouths succeed in genuinely saying "thou," then, after long silence and stammering, we shall have addressed our eternal "Thou" anew. Reconciliation leads toward reconciliation.

Reciprocity

Philosophy errs in thinking of religion as founded in a noetic act, even if an inadequate one, and in therefore regarding the essence of religion as the knowledge of an object which is indifferent to being known. As a result, philosophy understands faith as an affirmation of truth lying somewhere between clear knowledge and confused opinion. Religion, on the other hand, insofar as it speaks of knowledge at all, does not understand it as a noetic relation of a thinking subject to a neutral object of thought, but rather as mutual contact, as the genuinely reciprocal meeting in the fullness of life between one active existence and another. Similarly, it understands faith as the entrance into this reciprocity, as binding oneself in relationship with an undemonstrable and unprovable, yet even so, in relationship, knowable Being, from whom all meaning comes.

Courage and Love

The relation of the spirit to the elemental forces and urges must not be interpreted from the point of view of pure thought. An attempt at interpretation must consider the influence of the spirit upon life. But—regardless of what it may call itself or be called at any given moment—the spirit which is not content in the area of thought and expresses itself in all of life becomes manifest as the power of faith. In the domain of the human soul, it appears as faithful courage and faithful love. Based on the power of faith, the spirit exerts its influence upon the world through its agents, courage and love. These constitute its power which may well govern the elemental forces because it has known them from the earliest times, and knows what is their due. Though in one historical era after another the spirit may seem dethroned and exiled, it does not lose its power. Again and again, unexpectedly and unpredictably, it causes what is intrinsic in the course of history through its agents, faithful courage and faithful love.

Education

The education I mean is a guiding toward reality and realization. That man alone is qualified to teach who knows how to distinguish between appearance and reality, between seeming realization and genuine realization, who rejects appearance and chooses and grasps reality, no matter what world-view he chooses. This education educates the adherents of all world-views to genuineness and to truth. It educates each of them to take his world-view seriously: to start from the genuineness of its ground and to move toward the truth of its goal.

The Story-Telling Animal

Alasdair MacIntyre

We live out our lives, both individually and in our relationships with each other, in the light of certain conceptions of a possible shared future, a future in which certain possibilities beckon us forward and other repel us, some seem already foreclosed and other perhaps inevitable. There is no present which is not informed by some image of some future and an image of the future which always presents itself in the form of a *telos*—or of a variety of ends or goals—towards which we are either moving or failing to move in the present. Unpredictability and teleology therefore coexist as part of our lives; like characters in a fictional narrative we do not know what will happen next, but none the less our lives have a certain form which projects itself towards our future. Thus the narratives which we live out have both an unpredictable and a partially teleological character. If the narrative of our individual and social lives is to continue intelligibly—and either type of narrative may lapse into unintelligibility—it is always both the case that there are constraints on how the story can continue *and* that within those constraints there are indefinitely many ways that it can continue.

A central thesis then begins to emerge: man is in his actions and practice, as well as in his fictions, essentially a story-telling animal. He is not essentially but becomes through his history, a teller of stories that aspire to truth. But the key question for men is not about their own authorship; I can only answer the question 'What am I to do?' if I can answer the prior question 'Of what story or stories do I find myself a part?' We enter human society, that is, with one or more imputed characters—roles into which we have been drafted—and we have to learn what they are in order to be able to understand how others respond to us and how our responses to them are apt to be construed. It is through hearing stories about wicked stepmothers, lost children, good but misguided kings, wolves that suckle twin boys, youngest sons who receive no inheritance but must make their own way in the world and eldest sons who waste their inheritance on riotous living and go into exile to live with the swine, that children learn or mislearn both what a child and what a parent is, what the cast of characters may be in the drama into which they have been born and what the ways of the world are. Deprive children of stories and you leave them unscripted, anxious stutterers in their actions as in their words. Hence there is no way to give us an understanding of any society, including our own, except through the stock of stories which constitute its initial dramatic resources. Mythology, in its original sense, is at the heart of things. Vico was right and so was Joyce. And so too of course is that moral tradition from heroic society to its medieval heirs according to which the telling of stories has a key part in educating us into the virtues.

I suggested earlier that 'an' action is always an episode in a possible history: I would now like to make a related suggestion about another concept, that of personal identity. Derek Parfit and others have recently drawn our attention to the contrast between the criteria of strict identity, which is an all-or-nothing matter (*either* the Tichborne claimant *is* the last Tichborne heir; *either* all the properties of the last heir belong to the claimant *or* the claimant is not the heir—Leibniz's Law applies) and the psychological continuities of personality which are a matter of more or less. (Am I the same man at fifty as I was at forty in respect of memory, intellectual powers, critical responses? More or less.) But what is crucial to human beings as characters in enacted narratives is that, possessing only the resources of psychological continuity, we have to be able to respond to the imputation of strict identity. I am forever whatever I have been at any time for others— and I may at any time be called upon to answer for it—no matter how changed I may be now. There is no way of *founding* my identity—or lack of it—on the psychological continuity or discontinuity of the self. The self inhabits a character whose unity is given as the unity of a character. Once again there is a crucial disagreement with empiricist or analytical philosophers on the one hand and with existentialists on the other.

Empiricists, such as Locke or Hume, tried to give an account of personal identity solely in terms of psychological states or events. Analytical philosophers, in so many ways their heirs as well as their critics, have wrestled with the connection between those states and events and strict identity understood in terms of Leibniz's Law. Both have failed to see that a background has been omitted, the lack of which makes the problems insoluble. That background is provided by the concept of a story and of that kind of unity of character which a story requires. Just as a history is not a sequence of actions, but the concept of an action is that of a moment in an actual or possible history abstracted for some purpose from that history, so the characters in a history are not a collection of persons, but the concept of a person is that of a character abstracted from a history.

What the narrative concept of selfhood requires is thus twofold. On the one hand, I am what I may justifiably be taken by others to be in the course of living out a story that runs from my birth to my death; I am the *subject* of a history that is my own and no one else's, that has its own peculiar meaning. When someone complains—as do some of those who attempt or commit suicide—that his or her life is meaningless, he or she is often and perhaps characteristically complaining that the narrative of their life has become unintelligible to them, that it lacks any point, any movement towards a climax of a *telos*. Hence the point of doing any one thing rather than another at crucial junctures in their lives seems to such a person to have been lost.

To be the subject of a narrative that runs from one's birth to one's death is, I remarked earlier, to be accountable for the actions and experiences which compose a narratable life. It is, that is, to be open to being asked to give a certain kind of account of what one did or what happened to one or what one witnessed at any earlier point in one's life than the time at which the question is posed. Of course someone may have forgotten or suffered brain damage or simply not attended sufficiently at the relevant times to be able to give the relevant account. But to say of someone under some one description ('The prisoner of the Chateau d'If') that he is the same person as someone characterised quite differently ('The Count of Monte Cristo') is precisely to say that it makes sense to ask him to give an intelligible narrative account enabling us to understand how he could at different times and different places be one and the same person and yet be so differently characterised. Thus personal identity is just that identity presupposed by the unity of the character which the unity of a narrative requires. Without such unity there would not be subjects of whom stories could be told.

The other aspect of narrative self-hood is correlative: I am not only accountable, I am one who can always ask others for an account, who can put others to the question. I am part of their story, as they are part of mine. The narrative of any one life is part of an interlocking set of narratives. Moreover this asking for and giving of accounts itself plays an important part in constituting narratives. Asking you what you did and why, saying what I did and why, pondering the differences between your account of what I did and my account of what I did, and *vice versa,* these are essential constituents of all but the very simplest and barest of narratives. Thus without the accountability of the self those trains of events that constitute all but the simplest and barest of narratives could not occur; and without that same accountability narratives would lack that continuity required to make both them and the actions that constitute them intelligible.

It is important to notice that I am not arguing that the concepts of narrative or of intelligibility or of accountability are *more* fundamental than that of personal identity. The concepts of narrative, intelligibility and accountability presuppose the applicability of the concept of personal identity, just as it presupposed their applicability and just as in deed each of these three presupposes the applicability of the two others. The relationship is one of mutual presupposition. It does follow of course that all attempts to elucidate the notion of personal identity independently of and in isolation from the notions of narrative, intelligibility and accountability are bound to fail. As all such attempts have.

It is now possible to return to the question from which this enquiry into the nature of human action and identity started: In what does the unity of an individual life consist? The answer is that its unity is the unity of a narrative embodied in a single life. To ask 'What is the good for me?' is to ask how best I might live out that unity and bring it to completion. To ask 'What is the good for man?' is to ask what all answers to the former question must have in common. But now it is important to emphasise that it is the systematic asking of these two questions and the attempt to answer them indeed as well as in word which provide the moral life with its unity. The unity of a human life is the unity of a narrative quest. Quests sometimes fail, are frustrated, abandoned or dissipated into distractions; and human lives may in all these ways also fail. But the only criteria for success or failure in a human life as a whole are the criteria of success or failure in a narrated or to-be-narrated quest.

Kisagotami

Peter D. Hershock

Narration and Personal Conduct: The Communality of Suffering and Its End

As a means of illustrating the direction in which I think it appropriate to move in coming to a contextually valid, Buddhist understanding of suffering, I would like to take a look at an extremely rich story present in the *Therigatta* (vv. 213–23). Once, there was a young woman named Kisagotami, the wife of a wealthy man, who had apparently lost her mind because of the death of her child. Carrying her dead child, she wandered from house to house in her village, begging her neighbors to give her some medicine that could revive the baby. Finally, someone referred her to the Buddha who was staying at Jevatana.

She approached the Buddha and, throwing herself at his feet, begged his assistance. He told her that to heal the child, he would have to have four or five mustard seeds from a house where no son, father, mother, daughter, or slave had died. Thanking the Buddha, Kisagotami set out, going from door to door in search of a house where death had never entered. Finally, she reached the very outskirts of town without having found a family that had not been visited by death. She returned to the Buddha and in his quiet presence her mind cleared. From that day on, she was one of his devoted followers.

According to our usual set of presuppositions, the point of this story is that suffering is universal. Kisagotami learns that grief is an experience common to all of us, one that is perhaps inevitable given the nature of sentient being. Among these presuppositions, however, is a more or less well-articulated belief in the objectivity of identity and hence in the reality of essences or universals—a belief which finds no purchase in the scheme of early Buddhism or the Ch'an tradition to which we shall later turn in some detail. In fact, for reasons which will hopefully become increasingly apparent, I would maintain that a consistently Buddhist interpretation of the story suggests that there are two alternative and profoundly practical implications of Kisagotami's trip through her village. First, she is made to realize that there is no free zone where impermanence and suffering do not reach. This is not to say that impermanence or suffering are everywhere the same, but only that there is no place in the world where one can go to avoid being confronted with changes and crises. Superficially, this means that no happiness can last indefinitely, that no good situation can be maintained forever. But more importantly for the Buddhist practitioner, the ubiquity of impermanence guarantees that no gridlock is intractable—that no matter how hopelessly stuck or stricken we feel, this bondage is also something arisen only in passing. All situations are negotiable.

Secondly, and for us most crucially, she learns that suffering always occurs in the context of a communally-articulated life-story. The Buddha does not simply tell her that everyone experiences such grief, but asks her to go from house to house inquiring of the inhabitants of each whether death has occurred there. It might be supposed that this is only a pedagogical device, a way of forcing a "hands-on" realization. But that hardly suffices. We have to recall that Kisagotami is not just "a woman," a faceless player in a generic tale, but someone known with greater or lesser intimacy by everyone in her village. When she knocks on a door, and asks if a death has occurred in the home, rather than being answered with a brusque yes or no, her own pain will call forth that of the person she meets.

In all likelihood, she is invited into the house and haltingly told or reminded how the eldest son—a boy named Sanjaya—was to have been married just a year ago. On a routine hunting trip, he had slipped down into a ravine and broken his back against a boulder lodged in the limbs of a fallen tree. He had died a month later in the very room in which they are speaking. She would be told about the bride-to-be—a teenage girl who is perhaps Kisagotami's own younger cousin or niece. She would hear about the effect the death has had on Sanjaya's brothers and sisters, about how his father still could not smile even though laughter had returned to the house among the youngest children, the ones with the shortest memories. All of these people would have names and birth dates, distinctive traits and dreams. They are friends and relatives whose life-stories include and are included in her own.

Hearing these stories and being drawn ineluctably back into the fabric of her neighbors' lives, their hopes and fears, their sorrows and joys, Kisagotami must have begun already to feel herself being healed. But it is only upon returning to the Buddha and reporting her failure to secure the mustard seeds that Kisagotami is said to have truly awakened. Relating the stories of her neighbors, Kisagotami actively understands that suffering is

Chapter II: Responding to Others

never merely objective or subjective, but profoundly and irreducibly interpersonal, shared. By entering the homes of her neighbors and asking about the intimate fortunes of their families, Kisagotami dissolves the barrier of grief-induced madness thrown up between herself and her life-companions. By relating those fortunes, including them now as part of her own, she opens herself to the unlimited reciprocity of true community. It is in that moment of profoundest narration that 'one' and 'many' dissolve. That is her awakening.

One of the implications of the personal nature of suffering is that its power is not a function of its being an *event*, but of its meaning-generating role in a person's life. *What* happens is decidedly less important than *how* it ramifies among all those whose stories are in even some very small way included in and inclusive of our own. The case studies of clinical psychologists amply testify to the truth of this—what proves traumatic for me and severely distorts the development of my character was for you an occurrence of no lasting effect or importance. Being empty, events have no essential nature or significance but are like all things and at all times in open transformation.

In actuality, whenever we speak of "my suffering" we are not merely making an assertion about a generic transformation of consciousness which we are at this point accidentally enduring. Rather, we are speaking the names of all our friends, relatives, and enemies and the relations established with them through the particular intentions we have formed, the karma we have created. In this sense, while suffering is irreducibly personal, unlike the pains which afflict us all from time to time, no suffering is in reality 'mine'—something I can possess or dispossess. And so, while suffering is always uniquely embedded in a history in which I am a principal player, it is never mine alone but always *ours*. The true locus of suffering is not the objective, so-called "natural" world of individual 'people' and 'things,' but the fathomless intimacy of *narration*. Thus, it is never merely my experience which is marked with distress and gone awry, but the entire drama—the world as a whole—from which both 'you' and 'I' are only artificially (even if relevantly) abstracted.

As persons, and consistent with the Buddha's denial of the existence of any beginning to the cycle of birth and death, we did not *come to be at* such and such a time and place, but rather are continually *coming about*. Rather than being seen as individuals, the truth of suffering leads to seeing each of us as the unfolding of a complex of relations not only between the members of a sometimes gradually and sometimes wildly articulating cast of characters—the primary of which is a nominally singular narrator—but between various times, places, actions, and levels of meaning as well. Contrary to the experience-biased intuitions of any centrist construction of both the person and of sociality, such a life-story is not the product of the narrator—the 'I' or ego referred to in Buddhism as "the self" (*atman*)—

who eventually *asserts* him/herself as the most important character in each of our tales and expends most of his/her efforts in commenting on and plotting the course of the narrative's unfolding. The subject to whose experiences we seem to be uniquely privileged is, in fact, but a single aspect of who we are as narration.

Just as a movie cannot be identified with or reduced to the musings of a voice-over narrator, but necessarily includes all the other characters developing in it as well as a unique group of settings and locales, a soundtrack, and so on, a person cannot be reduced to a thinking and acting individual. Instead, a person should be seen as an ambiguity-celebrating narration irreducible to even the sum of all its parts. The 'one' we usually refer to as "me" and the subnarratives he/she constructs in justification of a purported existence among but essentially apart from or independent of others are, in actuality, no more central (or for that matter, peripheral) than the neurotically self-reflective individualists that Woody Allen so frequently and brilliantly caricatured in films like *Annie Hall*.

There is necessarily, then, a tension involved in speaking about narration and our 'selves' in a single breath. In part, this is a function of the recursiveness of narration itself, and in part a consequence of our 'realistically' informed belief that stories are intentionally constructed out of logically and temporally prior facts or happenings. As a world, narration folds back on itself at many points, each typically identifying itself as an 'I' or 'me' apparently situated directly in the midst of things. Indeed, the very languages we speak are dialects of the 'self'—dialects wherein subject differs from object, where qualities adhere or inhere, where stories are told and listened to by storytellers and their audiences. We must, however, try bearing in mind that this tension between on the one hand the stories we tell about and in construction of our 'selves'—our identities as 'persons'—and on the other hand the narration or world/person of which 'you' and 'I' are simply abstract parts, is itself a function of the hubris and confusion that underlie existential objectification and the belief that we are self-identical individuals. And so, while there may be times when grammar and stylistic considerations insist that we speak of narration as if it were something 'we' do and not that out of which 'we' arise, in actuality the very distinction of whole and part, of creator and created, is—for the Buddhist—entirely spurious. Once again, all differences are made.

As indicated in the preface, narration should not, therefore, be understood primarily as telling, but as realizing intimate connection, as healing, making whole. Far from being a function of the storytelling ego who at times habitually and at times obsessively identifies him or herself as the *axis mundi* or center of the world through a juxtaposition with 'others' positioned at one or another level of circumference, narration is best seen as a dissolution of the selfish geometry of control and escape.

Chapter II: Responding to Others

In the context of a metaphysics in which value is seen as the origination of any 'being' and in which ambiguity is understood as, if not basic then at least pervasive, unlike the divisive telling practiced by the egoic 'self,' narration announces a healing creativity. While the stories 'we' tell settle or fix what is otherwise unsettling, they do so only through an original denial of our reciprocity with what is being told. That is, certainty is purchased at the price of ontological and so axiological isolation. And yet, even these tales must be recognized as features unavoidably derivative of the ever-burgeoning narration out of which 'you' and 'I' have been carefully, if not always consciously, abstracted. Thus, while our selfish telling may function as a primordial means of ascertaining or comprehending the world through its fixation in the 'self'-articulated forms of concretely told narrative, the narrative movement or conduct out of which we have chosen to identify our 'selves' as more or less discrete beings is by no means prohibited from blossoming in unabated creativity. The constant reference in the Mahayana texts favored by Chinese Buddhism to the interpenetration of myriad buddha-lands is in this sense a means of denying an ontological status for the difference among various places and articulating instead the realization that our 'world' is a single and limiting construal of the 'same' narration which a buddha constitutes as a realm in which everything without exception is continuously accomplishing the buddha-work of enlightenment. As such, conduct is the irrepressible unfolding of new worlds which our self-spoken and 'self'-articulating stories only imperfectly and obscurely mirror.

And so, while as selfish individuals we tell stories about who we are, selecting these or those events as useful and rejecting others as out of character for the constitution of our 'persons,' there is another level at which there is no 'one' telling the story, at which we are truly persons and not merely 'self'-articulating 'persons.' As a useful analogy, think of storytellers ('persons' or 'selves') as being like dots strung out along one side of a strip of paper and their narratives as wavy, often overlapping lines on the opposite side. A person—narration or a world in the fullest sense—is the folding of this paper into a mobius strip, a process by virtue of which the opposition of 'teller' and 'tale' is completely nullified—rendered a function of point of view. As the analogy suggests, whether we are the same or different from our narration is a matter of orientation.

As 'selves' we differ not only from each other, but from the lives we lead, the actions we undertake, the decisions we make. In the terminology of Ch'an, as 'selves' or 'persons,' we live *yu-wei*. Conversely, as persons we enjoy a liberating absence of all such horizons, living spontaneously, wholly without precedent or *wu-wei*. Thus, as terms of art, narrative—a thing told and hence which decides—will be associated with the doings of the self; and narration—what we will later and more fully describe as a mode of envaluation—will be allied with the harmony-realizing and yet suffering-occasioned improvisation of Buddhist personhood. Narratives distinguish 'selves' while narration fosters the timely—that is, dramatic—interpenetration (*t'ung*) of all things, the realization of what the Ch'an master Huang-po refers to as *i-hsin* or "one-mind."

If this is so, if suffering occurs in the dramatic context of a narration in which there can be no substitutions, in which no characters are generic, then the *experience* of suffering must have some relation to our expectations about how our narrative can and, should flow. That is, unlike the biologically explicable experience of pain, experienced suffering depends partially on who we take ourselves to be and partially on what we feel we have reason to expect of our life-experience. As such, suffering can be seen as a function of the collision of actuality and a set of ideals and expectations which inform our particular way of telling the story of our life—an undesired interruption, blockage, or diversion of the narrative out of which our 'selves' are born and nurtured. The extent to which this is a negative experience depends less on what happens than on how well we are able to meaningfully work this interruption into the flow of our narrative. Once again, suffering is not a thing or event, with specifiable and abiding characteristics, but a lacuna, the appearance of a diverting interstice or void. In the language of Buddhist metaphysics, suffering must be seen as having no marks *(laksana)*. That is, its nature is irreducibly axial, not ontic—a function of orientational stress and impedance.

Granted all of the above, the end of suffering is best construed neither as an escape nor as the attainment of unbreached control, but as the creative incorporation of what originally arises in our experience as a disruption of the order or timing of our life-narrative. A talented jazz musician will take an accidental or mistaken chord or note and improvise with and around it, creating in the process an entirely novel passage within the context of a perhaps quite familiarly ordered piece of music. And, in much the same way, the interruptions of suffering afford us the opportunity of conducting ourselves in an unprecedented and manifestly liberating fashion. It is through suffering that we first become aware of the karmic constraints both binding and continually bifurcating our narration. It is, however, and as numerous Ch'an masters have insisted, only by improvising with our karma that the dualisms and divisiveness it reinforces can be healed.

All this not withstanding, it remains the case that while actuality contributes a radically unique component to our suffering, the ideals and anticipations we entertain are in large part a function of the societal and cultural milieu into which we find ourselves born. This milieu does not only provide the original, raw conceptual material out of which we will fashion our sense of self, the experienced texture of our karma. It supplies us as well with a horizon of possibility within which we can expect our will to be more or less effective and beyond which we are led to believe our energies would be spent in vain.

Chapter II: Responding to Others

As implied by much of the recent research into the manner in which 'persons' are conceived in different cultures, we are not born of biological parents alone, but emerge as well from within a cultural matrix of which each of us is a uniquely creative articulation. Among the primary dimensions of this matrix are the linguistic, the mythic, the religious, and the technological orientations of the community under consideration. That is, what we take a person to be depends on how we speak, on the stories we have heard and tell about the archetypes of our communal experience, on the kinds of questions we pose for nature to answer, on the concrete mode of our listening, and on the tools we use in insuring our continued existence. Seen in this way, persons are neither natural nor inevitable. Rather, they are narrative creations emerging in conversation—literally "turning together"—at the highly charged, karmic nexus where the vector of individuality supplied by the genetic and psychodynamic uniqueness of one's parents and the vector of commonality supplied by the matrix of cultural dimensions intersect and interdepend.

Playing off the ideas forwarded by systems theorists like Ilya Prigogine (1980), we might suggest that suffering is a fundamentally personal form of chaos out of which it is possible for new narrative orders to evolve. In this sense, the ending of suffering is not a transcendence of the embodied, feeling self, but a transformation thereof. And since the 'self' or 'person' arises only in a cultural matrix, enlightenment must itself be seen as a process of both personal and cultural transformation.

Perhaps the single most significant ramification of seeing persons as narration—worlds presented in and as conduct—and of (at the same time) admitting the irreducibly personal nature of suffering is that the end of suffering cannot be understood as fundamentally experiential. The end of suffering is not realized as an achieved state of consciousness if by that is meant an internal, psychological state, but in responding with others—in conduct itself. Kisagotami's release from her debilitating grief does not occur, then, as an insight but with her welcoming her community back into herself and her inclusion of and inclusion by the Buddha in the intimacy of that healing narration.

Stripped of our egoic glosses, it becomes clear that even the narrative through which our 'selves' are engendered is not private. That is, our life-story does not have the form of an autobiography composed entirely after the fact from behind the closed doors of remembered perception. Rather, it reveals itself only in an always ongoing conversation in which there are many partners—some of them human, some not—all of whom are capable of making wholly unexpected contributions with which we must in one way or another respond.

One of the purposes of this work as a whole is to tell a convincing story in which a seminal and profoundly practical realization of the sociality of enlightenment occurred in T'ang-dynasty China. According to this story, one of the crucial conditions for this realization was the presence in China of radically different conceptions of both the nature of personhood and suffering than had traditionally obtained in India—differences in light of which the Buddha's teachings disclosed previously unsuspected ranges of meaning. As a means of establishing a context for regarding this story as plausible, I would like to contrast the broadly Indian and Chinese conceptions of suffering and personality through an examination of the implications of their disparate approaches, both ritually and philosophically, to the practice of ancestor worship. It is to that narrative-supporting task that we shall turn in the following chapter.

The Good Samaritan

from The Gospel of Luke

On one occasion a lawyer stood up to pose his problem: "Teacher, what must I do to inherit everlasting life?"

Jesus answered him: "What is written in the law? How do you read it?" He replied:

> "You shall love the Lord your God
> with all your heart,
> with all your soul,
> with all your strength,
> and with all your mind;
> and your neighbor as yourself."

Jesus said, "You have answered correctly. Do this and you shall live." But because he wished to justify himself he said to Jesus, "And who is my neighbor?" Jesus replied: "There was a man going down from Jerusalem to Jericho who fell prey to robbers. They stripped him, beat him, and then went off leaving him half-dead. A priest happened to be going down the same road; he saw him but continued on. Likewise there was a Levite who came the same way; he saw him and went on. But a Samaritan who was journeying along came on him and was moved to pity at the sight. He approached him and dressed his wounds, pouring in oil and wine. He then hoisted him on his own beast and brought him to an inn, where he cared for him. The next day he took out two silver pieces and gave them to the innkeeper with the request: 'Look after him, and if there is any further expense I will repay you on my way back.'

"Which of these three, in your opinion, was neighbor to the man who fell in with the robbers?" The answer came. "The one who treated him with compassion." Jesus said to him, "Then go and do the same."

Compassion

Lawrence Blum

This paper offers an account of compassion as a moral phenomenon. I regard compassion as a kind of emotion or emotional attitude; though it differs from paradigmatic emotions such as fear, anger, distress, love, it has, I will argue, an irreducible affective dimension.

Compassion is one among a number of attitudes, emotions, or virtues which can be called "altruistic" in that they involve a regard for the good of other persons. Some others are pity, helpfulness, well-wishing. Such phenomena and the distinctions between them have been given insufficient attention in current moral philosophy. By distinguishing compassion from some of these other altruistic phenomena I want to bring out compassion's particular moral value, as well as some of its limitations.[1]

My context for this inquiry is an interest in developing an alternative to Kantianism, in particular to its minimization of the role of emotion in morality and its exclusive emphasis on duty and rationality. I am influenced here by Schopenhauer's critique of Kant's ethics and by his view of compassion as central to morality.[2] But discussion of the specific views of these two philosophers will be peripheral to my task here.

The Objects of Compassion

How must a compassionate person view someone in order to have compassion for him?[3] Compassion seems restricted to beings capable of feeling or being harmed. Bypassing the question of compassion for plants, animals, institutions, I will focus on persons as objects of compassion. A person in a negative condition, suffering some harm, difficulty, danger (past, present, or future) is the appropriate object of compassion. But there are many negative conditions and not all are possible objects of compassion. The inconvenience and irritation of a short detour for a driver on his way to a casual visit are not compassion-grounding conditions.[4] The negative

Chapter II: Responding to Others

condition must be relatively central to a person's life and well-being, describable as pain, misery, hardship, suffering, affliction, and the like. Although it is the person and not merely the negative condition which is the object of compassion, the focus of compassion is the condition.

Compassion can be part of a complex attitude toward its object; it is possible to have compassion for someone in a difficult or miserable situation without judging his overall condition to be difficult or miserable. It is therefore necessary to distinguish the conditions for someone being an appropriate object of compassion from the conditions for compassion being the appropriate dominant response to the person. One might predominantly admire and take pleasure in the happiness of a blind person who has gotten through college, found a rewarding job, made close friends—someone whose life is generally happy and who does not dwell on what he misses by being blind. Nevertheless one can also feel compassion for him because his life is deficient and damaged by his blindness.

It is not necessary that the object of compassion be aware of his condition; he might be deceiving himself with regard to it. Nor, as in the case of the happy blind man, need he think of it as a substantial affliction, even if he is aware of it as a deficiency.

That compassion is limited to grave or serious negative conditions does not exclude other altruistic emotions from being entirely appropriate to less serious states. One can feel sorry for, commiserate with, or feel sympathy for a person's irritation, discomfort, inconvenience, displeasure. Nor are all altruistic attitudes primarily directed to particular persons: they can be directed to classes of persons (the blind) or to general conditions (poverty). In addition, there are altruistic virtues not so clearly involving emotions, which come into play in regard to less serious negative conditions: considerateness, thoughtfulness, helpfulness. It would be considerate or thoughtful to warn an acquaintance of an unexpected detour so that he could avoid needless inconvenience and irritation. Such virtues as these, while not necessarily involving emotion or feeling, do involve attention to another's situation and a genuine regard for the other's good, even when more self-regarding attitudes are conjointly brought into play.

Not all altruistic emotions are focused on negative states. Someone might take delight in giving pleasure to others. Though this altruistic attitude shares with compassion a regard for the good of others, compassion focuses on pain, suffering, and damage, whereas this other attitude focuses on pleasure. The capacity for one altruistic attitude is no assurance of the capacity for others. It is quite possible for a compassionate person to be insensitive to the pleasures of others. A focus on misery and suffering in the absence of regard for others' joys and pleasures constitutes a limitation in the moral consciousness of the merely compassionate person.[5]

The Emotional Attitude of Compassion

The compassionate person does not merely believe that the object suffers some serious harm or injury; such a belief is compatible with indifference, malicious delight in his suffering, or intense intellectual interest, for example of a novelist or psychologist for whom the suffering is primarily material for contemplation or investigation. Even a genuine interest in relieving someone's suffering can stem from meeting an intellectual or professional challenge rather than from compassion.

Compassion is not a simple feeling-state but a complex emotional attitude toward another, characteristically involving imaginative dwelling on the condition of the other person, an active regard for his good, a view of him as a fellow human being, and emotional responses of a certain degree of intensity.

Imaginatively reconstructing someone's condition is distinct from several sorts of "identification" with the other person. For instance, it does not involve an identity confusion in which the compassionate person fails to distinguish his feelings and situation from the other person's.[6] Such a pathological condition actually precludes genuine compassion because it blurs the distinction between subject and object.

In a second type of identification the subject "identifies" with the object because of having had an experience similar to his, the memory of which his experience evokes. ("I can identify with what you are going through, since I've suffered from the same problem myself.") Here no identity confusion is involved. While such identification can promote compassion and imaginative understanding it is not required for it. For compassion does not require even that its subject have experienced the sort of suffering that occasions it. We can commiserate with someone who has lost a child in a fire, even if we do not have a child or have never lost someone we love. The reason for this is that the imaginative reconstruction involved in compassion consists in imagining what the other person, given his character, beliefs, and values is undergoing, rather than what we ourselves would feel in his situation. For example I might regard my son's decision to work for the CIA with distress, while someone with different beliefs and values might regard such a decision with pride; yet this other person may well be able to understand my reaction and to feel compassion for me in regard to it.

The degree of imaginative reconstruction need not be great. The friend in the previous example might find it difficult to reconstruct for herself the outlook and set of values within which my son's decision is viewed with distress. But to have compassion she must at least dwell in her imagination on the fact that I am distressed. So some imaginative representation is a necessary condition for compassion, though the degree can be minimal.

Chapter II: Responding to Others

Certainly a detailed and rich understanding of another person's outlook and consciousness, of the sort available only to persons of exceptional powers of imagination, is not required for compassion.

Nevertheless, as a matter of empirical fact, we often do come to understand someone's condition by imagining what our own reactions would be. So expanding our powers of imagination expands our capacity for compassion. And conversely the limits of a person's capacities for imaginative reconstruction set limits on her capacity for compassion. Finding another person's experience opaque may well get in the way of compassion. Persons who are in general quite poor at imagining the experiences of others who are different from themselves, may well be less likely to have compassion for them. Yet this failure of imagination is typically not a purely intellectual or cognitive failure; for it can itself be part of a more general failure to regard the other as fully human, or to take that humanity sufficiently seriously. That a white colonialist in Africa does not imagine to himself the cares and sufferings of the blacks whom he rules cannot be separated from the fact that he does not see them as fully human.

A second constituent of compassion is concern for or regard for the object's good. It is not enough that we imaginatively reconstruct someone's suffering; for, like belief, such imagining is compatible with malice and mere intellectual curiosity. (In fact it is likely to be a component of them.) In addition we must care about that suffering and desire its alleviation. Suppose a neighbor's house burns down, though no one is hurt. Compassion would involve not only imagining what it is like for the neighbor to be homeless but also concerned responses such as the following: being upset, distressed, regretting the different aspects of his plight (his homelessness, his loss of prized possessions, his terror when inside the burning house, etc.); wishing the tragedy had not happened; giving thought to what might be done to alleviate the neighbor's situation; worrying whether he will be able to find another place to live; hoping that he will obtain a decent settlement from the insurance company; hoping and desiring that, in general, his suffering will be no greater than necessary.

The relation between concern for another person's good and these thoughts, feelings, hopes, desires is a necessary or conceptual one; compassionate concern would not be attributed to someone who lacked them (or at least most of them). This concern is not merely tacked on to the imaginative reconstruction as a totally independent component of compassion. Rather the manner in which we dwell on the other's plight expresses the concern for his good.

These concerned reactions must be directed toward the other's plight and not merely caused by it. The distress that is part of compassion cannot take as its focus the vivid realization that I might be afflicted with a like misfortune; for it would then be self-regarding rather than altruistic.

Compassion also involves viewing the other person and his suffering in a certain way. I can put this by saying that compassion involves a sense of shared humanity, of regarding the other as a fellow human being. This means that the other person's suffering (though not necessarily their particular afflicting condition) is seen as the kind of thing that could happen to anyone, including oneself insofar as one is a human being.[7]

This way of viewing the other person contrasts with the attitude characteristic of pity, in which one holds oneself apart from the afflicted person and from their suffering thinking of it as something that defines that person as fundamentally different from oneself. In this way the other person's condition is taken as given whereas in compassion the person's affliction is seen as deviating from the general conditions of human flourishing. That is why pity (unlike compassion) involves a kind of condescension, and why compassion is morally superior to pity.

Because compassion involves a sense of shared humanity, it promotes the *experience* of equality, even when accompanied by an acknowledgment of actual social inequality. Compassion forbids regarding social inequality as establishing human inequality. This is part of the moral force of compassion: by transcending the recognition of social inequality, it promotes the sensed experience of equality in common humanity.

Sometimes the reason we feel pity rather than compassion is that we feel that the object has in some way brought the suffering on himself or deserved it, or in any case that he has allowed himself to be humiliated or degraded by it. But such ways of regarding the objects do not necessarily undermine compassion, and they are not incompatible with it. It would be a mistake to see the essential difference between pity and compassion in such differing beliefs about the object's condition. No matter how pitiful or self-degraded one regards another human being, it is possible (and not necessarily unwarranted) to feel compassion and concern for him, simply because he is suffering.

Nietzsche's use of the term *Mitleid* does not distinguish between compassion and pity. Because Mitleid is focused on the negative states of others, Nietzsche saw it as life-denying and without positive value. But insofar as compassion involves a genuine concern for the good of others and a "living sense of another's worth,"[8] it is, unlike pity, fundamentally life-affirming and positive.

A fourth aspect of compassion is its strength and duration. If the distress, sorrow, hopes, and desires of an altruistic attitude were merely passing reactions or twinges of feeling, they would be insufficient for the level of concern, the imaginative reconstruction, and the disposition to beneficent action required for compassion. Though there are degrees of compassion, the threshold of emotional strength required from compassion (in contrast with other altruistic attitudes) is relatively high and enduring. Because well-wishing and pity can be more episodic and less action-guiding, they are morally inferior to compassion. As the etymology of the word suggests, compassion involves "feeling with" the other person, sharing his feelings. In one sense this means that the subject and the object have the same feeling-type: distress, sorrow, desire for relief. But in a more important sense the feelings are not the same; for the relation between their subjects and their objects are different. The focus of my neighbor's distress is *his own* homelessness; the focus of my distress in having compassion for him is *my neighbor's* homelessness (or his distress at his homelessness). This can partly be expressed as a matter of degree. My neighbor suffers; in "suffering with" him there is a sense in which I suffer too, but my suffering is much less than his.

Compassion and Beneficent Action

When it is possible for her to relieve another person's suffering without undue demands on her time, energy, and priorities, the compassionate person is disposed to attempt to help. We would hardly attribute compassion to X if she were to saunter by on a spring day and, seeing an elderly man fall on the sidewalk walk right by, perhaps with a sad shudder of dismay, leaving the old man lying alone.

Characteristically, then, compassion requires the disposition to perform beneficent actions, and to perform them because the agent has had a certain sort of imaginative reconstruction of someone's condition and has a concern for his good. The steps that the person takes to ameliorate the condition are guided by and prompted by that imaginative reconstruction and concern. So the beneficent action of a compassionate person has a specific sort of causal history, which distinguishes it from an equally beneficent action that might be prompted by other sorts of attitudes and emotions.

We saw that concern exists at different degrees of strength in different altruistic emotions and attitudes. Hence its corresponding disposition to beneficence exists at different levels of strength also. The stronger the disposition the more one is willing to go out of one's way, to act contrary to inclination and interest, in order to help the other person.[9] That compassion as a motive can and often does withstand contrary inclination begins to address the Kantian charge that emotions, including compassion, are unreliable as motives to beneficent action.[10] As a motive to beneficence, compassion can have the strength, stability, and reliability that Kant thought only the sense of duty could have. As a trait of character compassion can be as stable and consistent in its prompting of appropriate beneficent action as a conscientious adherence to principles of beneficence.

Though compassion is a type of emotion or emotional attitude, it is not like a Kantian "inclination." Acting from compassion does not typically involve doing what one is in the mood to do, or feels like doing. On the contrary the regard for the other's good which compassion implies means that one's compassionate acts often involve acting very much contrary to one's moods and inclinations. Compassion is fundamentally other-regarding rather than self-regarding; its affective nature in no way detracts from this.

Compassionate action may extinguish or diminish compassion itself, most obviously when its object is relieved of the negative condition by the action. But even merely *engaging* in action may involve a shift in the subject's consciousness from the imaginative reconstruction of the object's condition to a focus on the expected relief of that condition, thereby diminishing the compassion (though not the regard for the other's good and hence not the moral value of the attitude or state of mind).

Compassion, however, is not always linked so directly to the prompting of beneficent actions. For in many situations it is impossible (without extraordinary disruption of one's life and priorities) for the compassionate person herself to improve the sufferer's condition (for instance, when one is concerned for the welfare of distant flood victims). In other situations the beneficence might be inappropriate, as when intervention might jeopardize the sufferer's autonomy. Compassionate concern, in such cases, involves hope and desire for the relief of the condition by those in a position to provide it. It does not involve an active setting oneself in readiness to perform beneficent acts, once one firmly believes such acts to be impossible or inappropriate.

In the cases so far discussed a link exists between compassion and beneficent action, through the desire that action be taken by someone to relieve the sufferer's condition. But compassion is also appropriate in situations in which nothing whatever can be done to alleviate the affliction, as for instance when someone is suffering from incurable blindness or painful terminal cancer. In such situations compassionate concern involves sorrowing for the person, hoping that the condition might—all expectations to the contrary—be mitigated or compensated, being pleased or grateful if this occurs, and similar responses.

Because being compassionate involves actively giving thought to the relief of the sufferer's condition, a compassionate person may discover the possibility of beneficent action when it seemed unclear whether any existed. Compassion often involves resisting regarding situations as absolutely irremediable. On the other hand the compassionate person may for this reason fail to see and hence to face up to the hopelessness of the sufferer's situation.

That compassion is often appropriate when there is little or no scope for the subject's disposition to beneficence indicates that compassion's sole significance does not lie in its role as motive to beneficence. Even when nothing can be done by the compassionate person to improve the sufferer's condition, simply being aware that one is an object or recipient of compassion can be an important human good. The compassionate person's expression of concern and shared sorrow can be valuable to the sufferer for its own sake, independently of its instrumental value in improving his condition. Nor does the good of recognizing oneself to be an object of compassion depend on the compassionate person wanting to convey his attitude, though the recipient can in addition value the intention to communicate.

The compassionate attitude is a good to the recipient, not only because it signifies that the subject would help if she could but because we are glad to receive the concern of others, glad of the sense of equality that it promotes. Yet it is morally good to be compassionate even when—as often happens—the object of compassion is unaware of it. For any concern for the welfare of others, especially when it promotes the sense of equality, is *(ceteris paribus)* morally good. In this, compassion contrasts with attitudes and feelings such as infatuation or admiration which may convey goods to their recipients but which are without moral value because they do not essentially involve a regard for their recipient's good. The moral significance of compassion is not exhausted by the various types of goods it confers on its recipients.

Compassion can hurt its recipient. It may, for instance, cause him to concentrate too much on his plight, or to think that people around him see him primarily in terms of that plight. But these dangers and burdens of compassion can be mitigated to the extent that a person recognizes that compassion is not the sole or the dominant attitude with which one is regarded.

Compassion can also be misguided, grounded in superficial understanding of a situation. Compassion is not necessarily wise or appropriate. The compassionate person may even end up doing more harm than good. True compassion must be allied with knowledge and understanding if it is to serve adequately as a guide to action: there is nothing inherent in the character of compassion that would prevent—and much that would encourage—its alliance with rational calculation. Because compassion involves an active and objective interest in another person's welfare, it is characteristically a spur to a deeper understanding of a situation than rationality alone could ensure. A person who is compassionate by character is in principle committed to as rational and as intelligent a course of action as possible.

Endnotes

1. Compassion has a particular cultural history: its sources are Christian, it was further developed by Romanticism, especially by the German Romantics. Though I do not focus on this history explicitly, my emphasis on compassion as a particular moral emotion among others should leave room for the results of such a historical account.
2. Arthur Schopenhauer, *On the Basis of Morality* (New York: Bobbs-Merrill 1965).
3. In general I will use feminine pronouns to refer to the person having compassion (the "subject") and masculine pronouns to refer to the person for whom she has compassion (the "object").
4. I am making a conceptual rather than a moral point. The compassionate person cannot regard the object of her compassion as merely irritated or discomforted; but of course a genuinely compassionate person might mistakenly take an inconvenience to be a serious harm. To say that compassion is "appropriate" in this context is, then, simply to say that the object actually possesses the compassion-grounding feature which the subject takes him to possess. I do not discuss the further issue of when compassion is *morally* appropriate or inappropriate.
5. Nietzsche saw this focus on misery and suffering as a kind of morbidity in the compassionate consciousness; this view formed part of this critique of compassion.
6. Philip Mercer, *Sympathy and Ethics* (Oxford: Clarendon Press, 1972), and Max Scheler, *The Nature of Sympathy,* trans. Werner Stark (London: Routledge & Kegan Paul, 1965).
7. This way of viewing the other's plight differs from fundamentally self-regarding sentiment in which the person's plight is regarded as a symbol of what could happen to oneself. It is not actually necessary that one believe that the afflicting condition *could* happen to oneself: one might have compassion for someone suffering napalm burns without believing that there is any possibility of oneself being in that condition.
8. Nicolai Hartmann, *Ethics* (London: George Allen and Unwin, 1932), II, 273.
9. Aristotle recognizes differences in the strength of the disposition to beneficence in his discussion of *eunoia* ("well-wishing" or "good will" in Thompson's translation). Of persons who have eunoia toward others, Aristotle says, "All they wish is the good of those for whom they have a kindness; they would not actively help them to attain it, nor would they put themselves out for their sake." Aristotle, *Nichomachean Ethics,* b. IX (Baltimore: Penguin Books, 1955), 269.
10. For this Kandan view, see Kant, *Fundamental Principles of the Metaphysics of Morals,* trans. Beck (New York: Bobbs-Merrill, 1960), 6, 14, 28; and *Critique of Practical Reason,* trans. Beck (New York: Bobbs-Merrill, 1956), 75, 122.

From *Explaining Emotions*, ed. Amelie O. Rorty; pp. 507–17. Reprinted by permission of the publisher, University of California Press. © 1980 The Regents of the University of California.

The Practice of Reciprocity
from Confucianism

One obvious expression of goodness is the practice of *shu,* 'reciprocity or mutual consideration'. This is the golden rule for interpersonal relationships and it has a special relevance for rulers who have to deal with the affairs of their subjects.

> Tzu-kung asked, saying, Is there any single saying that one can act upon all day and every day? The Master said, Perhaps the saying about consideration. Never do to others what you would not like them to do to you.
> Analects 15: 23

> Jan Jung asked about Goodness. The Master said, Behave when away from home as though you were in the presence of an important guest. Deal with the common people as though you were officiating at an important sacrifice. Do not do to others what you would not like yourself. Then there will be no feelings of opposition to you, whether it is the affairs of a State that you are handling or the affairs of a family.
> Analects 12:2

The good man, in the teaching of the Analects, is enmeshed with his fellows in a network of duties and privileges. He can expect to receive from others; but he must also give. Mutual consideration should permeate all human relationships. This is the right way because it is the surest means of dispelling tension and fostering good will.

The Confucian emphasis on mutual consideration, on a 'give-and-receive' morality, was amplified in the description of Five Relationships. They constitute the essential structure of a person's life as a member of communities. It is doubtful whether the full-scale scheme of Five Relationships (and the attitudes which they involve) comes from Confucius himself. The scheme appears in the Book of Rites which, although it may contain early material, is dated two or three centuries after Confucius. It must be read in the context of a patriarchal society.

The Five Relationships and the attitudes they involve can be set out as follows:

Quest for Goodness: An Introduction to Ethics

Father	Is kind Gives protection Provides education	Shows respect Accepts father's guidance Cares for him in old age and performs the customary burial ceremonies	**Son**
Elder brother	Sets an example of refinement and good behaviour	Respects the character and experience of the elder	**Younger brother**
Husband	Carries out his family duties Is honourable and faithful Provides for his wife and family	Looks after the home Is obedient Diligently meets the needs of her husband and children	**Wife**
Elder	Gives encouragement Shows consideration towards younger people Sets a good example	Shows respect Defers to the advice of those with more experience Is eager to learn	**Junior**
Ruler	Acts justly Strives to improve the welfare of his people Is worthy of loyalty	Are loyal Serve their ruler Honour their ruler because of his position and character	**Subjects**

Three of these relationships belong to the family. Confucian teaching has, without question, had an enormous influence on Chinese family life. Both parents and children, young and old, had responsibilities to each other. The faithful fulfilment of these gave security, stability and continuity to the family. Beyond the family was the clan and beyond that the nation. Confucianism encouraged loyalty to the nation and sometimes likened it to a family of which the emperor was the father. But the main stress was on the virtues and attitudes that would enhance daily life. A man's loyalty to his family was seen in all his actions, his sacrifices at the ancestral shrine, his readiness to marry someone deemed suitable by his elders. A man accepted the wisdom taught by his father and in turn passed it on to his son.

A sense of order pervaded the Confucian family. Each member knew his or her place in relation to others and knew what that place involved. To belong to such a family might seem to us a very restrictive and stultifying experience. Whether it was felt to be so would depend on a person's expectations. . . .

The Deep Beauty of the Golden Rule

R. M. MacIver

The subject that learned men call ethics is a wasteland on the philosophical map. Thousands of books have been written on this matter, learned books and popular books, books that argue and books that exhort. Most of them are empty and nearly all are vain. Some claim that pleasure is *the* good; some prefer the elusive and more enticing name of happiness; others reject such principles and speak of equally elusive goals such as self-fulfillment. Others claim that *the* good is to be found in looking away from the self, in devotion to the whole—which whole? in the service of God—whose God?—even in the service of the State—who prescribes the service? Here indeed, if anywhere, after listening to the many words of many apostles, one goes out by the same door as one went in.

The reason is simple. You say: "This is the way you should behave." But I say: "No, that is not the way." You say: "This is right." But I say: "No, that is wrong, and this is right." You appeal to experience. I appeal to experience against you. You appeal to authority: it is not mine. What is left? If you are strong, you can punish me for behaving my way. But does that prove anything except that you are stronger than I? Does it prove the absurd dogma that might makes right? Is the slavemaster right because he owns the whip, or Torquemada because he can send his heretics to the flames?

From this impasse no system of ethical rules has been able to deliver itself. How can ethics lay down final principles of behavior that are not your values against mine, your group's values against my group's?

Which, by the way, does not mean that your rules are any less valid for you because they are not valid for me. Only a person of shallow nature and autocratic leanings would draw that conclusion. For the sake of your integrity you must hold to your own values, no matter how much others reject them. Without *your* values you are nothing. True, you should search them and test them and learn by *your* experience and gain wisdom where you can. Your values are your guides through life but you need to use your own eyes. If I have different guides I shall go another way. So far as we diverge, values are relative as between you and me. But your values cannot be relative for you or mine for me.

That is not here the issue. It is that the relativity of values between you and me, between your group and my group, your sect and my sect, makes futile nearly all learned disquisitions about the first principles of ethics.

By ethics I mean the philosophy of how men should behave in their relations to one another. I am talking about philosophy, not about religion. When you have a creed, you can derive from it principles of ethics. Philosophy cannot begin with a creed, but only with reasoning about the nature of things. It cannot therefore presume that the values of other men are less to be regarded than the values of the proponent. If it does, it is not philosophy but dogma, dogma that is the enemy of philosophy, the kind of dogma that has been the source of endless tyranny and repression.

Can it be a philosophy worth the name that makes a universal of your values and thus rules mine out of existence, where they differ from yours?

How can reasoning decide between my values and yours? Values do not claim truth in any scientific sense; instead they claim validity, rightness. They do not declare what is so but what *should* be so. I cling to my values, you to yours. Your values, some of them, do not hold for me; some of them may be repulsive to me; some of them may threaten me. What then? To what court of reason shall we appeal? To what court that you and I both accept is there any appeal?

The lack of any court is the final *fact* about final values. It is a fundamental fact. It is a terrifying fact. It is also a strangely challenging fact. It gives man his lonely autonomy, his true responsibility. If he has anything that partakes of the quality of a God it comes from this fact. Man has more than the choice to obey or disobey. If he accepts authority he also chooses the authority he accepts. He is responsible not only to others but, more deeply, to himself.

Does all this mean that a universal ethical principle, applicable alike to me and you, even where our values diverge, is impossible? That there is no rule to go by, based on reason itself, in this world of irreconcilable valuations?

There is no rule that can prescribe both my values and yours or decide between them. There is one universal rule, and one only, that can be laid down, on ethical grounds—that is, apart from the creeds of particular religions and apart from the ways of the tribe that falsely and arrogantly universalize themselves.

Do to others as you would have them do to you. This is the only rule that stands by itself in the light of its own reason, the only rule that can stand by itself in the naked, warring universe, in the face of the contending values of men and groups.

Chapter II: Responding to Others

What makes it so? Let us first observe that the universal herein laid down is one of procedure. It prescribes a mode of behaving, not a goal of action. On the level of goals, of *final* values, there is irreconcilable conflict. One rule prescribes humility, another pride; one prescribes abstinence, another commends the flesh-pots; and so forth through endless variations. All of us wish that *our* principle could be universal; most of us believe that it *should* be, that our *ought* ought to be all men's *ought*, but since we differ there can be, on this level, no possible agreement.

When we want to make our ethical principle prevail we try to persuade others, to "convert" them. Some may freely respond, if their deeper values are near enough to ours. Others will certainly resist and some will seek to persuade us in turn—why shouldn't they? Then we can go no further except by resort to force and fraud. We can, if we are strong, dominate some and we can bribe others. We compromise our own values in doing so and we do not in the end succeed; even if we were masters of the whole world we could never succeed in making our principle universal. We could only make it falsely tyrannous.

So if we look for a principle in the name of which we can appeal to all men, one to which their reason can respond in spite of their differences, we must follow another road. When we try to make our values prevail over those cherished by others, we attack their values, their dynamic of behavior, their living will. If we go far enough we assault their very being. For the will is simply valuation in action. Now the deep beauty of the golden rule is that instead of attacking the will that is in other men, it offers their will a new dimension. "Do as you *would* have others . . ." As *you* would will others to do. It bids you expand your vision, see yourself in new relationships. It bids you transcend your insulation, see yourself in the place of others, see others in your place. It bids you test your values or at least your way of pursuing them. If you would disapprove that another should treat you as you treat him, the situations being reversed, is not that a sign that, by the standard of your own values, you are mistreating him?

This principle obviously makes for a vastly greater harmony in the social scheme. At the same time it is the only universal of ethics that does not take sides with or contend with contending values. It contains no dogma. It bids everyone follow his own rule, as it would apply *apart* from the accident of his particular fortunes. It bids him enlarge his own rule, as it would apply whether he is up or whether he is down. It is an accident that you are up and I am down. In another situation you would be down and I would be up. That accident has nothing to do with my *final* values or with yours. You have numbers and force on your side. In another situation I would have the numbers and the force. All situations of power are temporary and precarious. Imagine then the situations reversed and that you had a more wonderful power than is at the command of the most powerful, the power to make the more powerful act toward you as you would want him to act. If power is your dream, then dream of a yet greater power—and act out the spirit of your dream.

But the conclusive argument is not in the terms of power. It goes far deeper, down to the great truth that power so often ignores and that so often in the end destroys it, the truth that when you maltreat others you detach yourself from them, from the understanding of them, from the understanding of yourself. You insulate yourself, you narrow your own values, you cut yourself off from that which you and they have in common. And this commonness is more enduring and more satisfying than what you possess in insulation. You separate yourself, and for all your power you weaken yourself. Which is why power and fear are such close companions.

This is the reason why the evil you do to another, you do also, in the end, to yourself. While if you and he refrain from doing evil, one to another—not to speak of the yet happier consequences, of doing positive good—this reciprocity of restraint from evil will redound to the good of both.

That makes a much longer story and we shall not here enter upon it. Our sole concern is to show that the golden rule is the *only* ethical principle, as already defined, that can have clear right of way everywhere in the kind of world we have inherited. It is the only principle that allows every man to follow his own intrinsic values while nevertheless it transforms the chaos of warring codes into a reasonably well-ordered universe.

Let us explain the last statement. What are a man's intrinsic values? Beyond his mere self-seeking every human being needs, and must find, some attachment to a large purpose. These attachments, in themselves and apart from the way he pursues them, are his intrinsic values. For some men they are centered in the family, the clan, the "class," the community, the nation, the "race." It is the warfare of their group-attachments that creates the deadliest disturbances of modern society. For some men the focus of attachment is found in the greater "cause," faith, the creed, the way of life. The conflict of these attachments also unlooses many evils on society and at some historical stages has brought about great devastation.

The greatest evils inflicted by man on man over the face of the earth are wrought not by the self-seekers, the pleasure lovers, or the merely amoral, but by the fervent devotees of ethical principles, those who are bound body and soul to some larger purpose, the nation, the "race," the "masses," the "brethren" whoever they may be. The faith they invoke, whatever it may be, is not large enough when it sets a frontier between the members and the non-members, the believers and the non-believers. In the heat of devotion to that larger but exclusive purpose there is bred the fanaticism that corrodes and finally destroys all that links man to the common humanity. In the name of the cause, they will torture and starve and trample under foot millions on millions of their fellowman. In its name they will cultivate the blackest treachery. And if their methods fail, as fail in

Chapter II: Responding to Others

the end they must, they will be ready, as was Hitler, to destroy their own cause or their own people, the chosen ones, rather than accept the reality their blinded purpose denied.

How then can we say that the golden rule does not disqualify the intrinsic values of such people—even of people like Hitler or, say, Torquemada? In the name of his values Torquemada burned at the stake many persons who differed from their fellows mainly by being more courageous, honest, and faithful to their faith. What then were Torquemada's values? He was a servant of the Church and the Church was presumptively a servant of Jesus Christ. It was not the intrinsic values of his creed that moved him and his masters to reject the Christian golden rule. Let us concede they had some kind of devotion to religion. It was the distorted, fanatical way in which they pursued the dimmed values they cherished, it was not the values themselves, to which their inhumanity can be charged.

Let us take the case of Hitler. Apart from his passion for Germany, or the German "folk," he would have been of no account, for evil or for good. That passion of itself, that in his view intrinsic value, might have inspired great constructive service instead of destruction. It was the method he used, and not the values he sought to promote thereby, that led to ruin, his blind trust in the efficacy of ruthless might. Belonging to a "folk" that had been reduced in defeat from strength to humiliation, fed on false notions of history and responsive to grotesque fallacies about a "master race," he conceived the resurgence of Germany in the distorted light of his vindictive imagination. Had Hitler been a member of some small "folk," no more numerous, say, than the population of his native Austria, he might have cherished the same values with no less passion, but his aspirations would have taken a different form and would never have expressed themselves in horror and tragedy.

The golden rule says nothing against Hitler's mystic adoration of the German "race," against any man's intrinsic values. By "intrinsic values" we signify the goals, beyond mere self-seeking, that animate a human being. If your group, your nation, your "race," your church, is for you a primary attachment, continue to cherish it—give it all you have, if you are so minded. But do not use means that are repugnant to the standards according to which you would have others conduct themselves to you and your values. If your nation were a small one, would you not seethe with indignation if some large neighbor destroyed its independence? Where, then, is your personal integrity if, belonging instead to the large nation, you act to destroy the independence of a small one? You falsify your own values, in the longer run you do them injury, when you pursue them in ways that cannot abide the test of the golden rule.

It follows that while this first principle attacks no intrinsic values, no primary attachments of men to goods that reach beyond themselves, it nevertheless purifies every attachment, every creed, of its accidents, its irrelevancies, its excesses, its false reliance on power. It saves every human value from the corruption that comes from the arrogance of detachment and exclusiveness, from the shell of the kind of absolutism that imprisons its vitality.

At this point a word of caution is in order. The golden rule does not solve for us our ethical problems but offers only a way of approach. It does not prescribe our treatment of others but only the spirit in which we should treat them. It has no simple mechanical application and often enough is hard to apply—what general principle is not? It certainly does not bid us treat others as others *want* us to treat them—that would be an absurdity. The convicted criminal wants the judge to set him free. If the judge acts in the spirit of the golden rule, within the limits of the discretion permitted, him as judge, he might instead reason somewhat as follows: "How would I feel the judge ought to treat *me* were I in this man's place? What could I—the man I am and yet somehow standing where this criminal stands—properly ask the judge to do for me, to me? In this spirit I shall assess his guilt and his punishment. In this spirit I shall give full consideration to the conditions under which he acted. I shall try to understand *him*, to do what I properly can for him, while at the same time I fulfill my judicial duty in protecting society against the dangers that arise if criminals such as he go free."

"Do to others as you would have others do to you." The disease to which all values are subject is the growth of a hard insulation. "I am right: I have the truth. If you differ from me, you are a heretic, you are in error. *Therefore* while you must allow me every liberty when you are in power I need not, in truth I ought not to, show any similar consideration for you." The barb of falsehood has already begun to vitiate the cherished value. While you are in power I advocate the equal rights of all creeds: when *I* am in power, I reject any such claim as ridiculous. This is the position taken by various brands of totalitarianism, and the communists in particular have made it a favorite technique in the process of gaining power, clamoring for rights they will use to destroy the rights of those who grant them. Religious groups have followed the same line. Roman Catholics, Calvinists, Lutherans, Presbyterians, and others have on occasion vociferously advocated religious liberty where they were in the minority, often to curb it where in turn they became dominant.

This gross inconsistency on the part of religious groups was flagrantly displayed in earlier centuries, but examples are still not infrequent. Here is one. *La Civilita Catholicâ*, a Jesuit organ published in Rome, has come out as follows:

"The Roman Catholic Church, convinced, through its divine prerogatives, of being the only true church, must demand the right for freedom for herself alone, because such a right can only be possessed by truth, never by error. As to other religions, the Church will certainly never draw the sword, but she will require that by legitimate means they shall not be allowed to propagate false doctrine. Consequently, in a state where the majority of the people are Catholic, the Church will require that legal existence be denied to error. . . . In some countries, Catholics will be obliged to ask full religious freedom for all, resigned at being forced to cohabitate where they alone should rightly be allowed to live. . . . The Church cannot blush for her own want of tolerance, as she asserts it in principle and applies it in practice."[1]

Since this statement has the merit of honesty it well illustrates the fundamental lack of rationality that lies behind all such violations of the golden rule. The argument runs: "Roman Catholics know they possess the truth; *therefore* they should not permit others to propagate error." By parity of reasoning why should not Protestants say—and indeed they have often said it—"We know we possess the truth; therefore we should not tolerate the errors of Roman Catholics." Why then should not atheists say: "We know we possess the truth; therefore we should not tolerate the errors of dogmatic religion."

No matter what we believe, we are equally convinced that *we* are right. We have to be. That is what belief means, and we must all believe something. The Roman Catholic Church is entitled to declare that all other religious groups are sunk in error. But what follows? That other groups have not the right to believe they are right? That you have the right to repress them while they have no right to repress you? That they should concede to you what you should not concede to them? Such reasoning is mere childishness. Beyond it lies the greater foolishness that truth is advanced by the forceful suppression of those who believe differently from you. Beyond that lies the pernicious distortion of meanings which claims that liberty is only "the liberty to do right"—the "liberty" for me to do what *you* think is right. This perversion of the meaning of liberty has been the delight of all totalitarians. And it might be well to reflect that it was the radical Rousseau who first introduced the doctrine that men could be "forced to be free."

How much do they have truth who think they must guard it within the fortress of their own might? How little that guarding has availed in the past! How often it has kept truth outside while superstition grew moldy within! How often has the false alliance of belief and force led to civil dissension and the futile ruin of war! But if history means nothing to those who call themselves "Christian" and still claim exclusive civil rights for their particular faith, at least they might blush before this word of one they call their Master: "All things therefore whatsoever ye would that men should do unto you, even so do ye also unto them; for this is the law and the prophets."

Endnote

1. Quoted in the *Christian Century* (June 1948).

Excerpt from *Moral Principles of Action* edited by Ruth Anshen. Copyright 1952 by Harper & Row, Publishers, Inc., renewed by Ruth Anshen. Reprinted by permission of HarperCollins Publishers.

The Moral Insight

Josiah Royce

... [The following] is our reflective account of the process that, in some form, must come to every one under the proper conditions. In this process we see the beginning of the real knowledge of duty to others. The process is one that any child can and does, under proper guidance, occasionally accomplish. It is the process by which we all are accustomed to try to teach humane behavior in concrete cases. We try to get people to realize what they are doing when they injure others. But to distinguish this process from the mere tender emotion of sympathy, with all its illusions, is what moralists have not carefully enough done. Our exposition [tries] to take this universally recognized process, to distinguish it from sympathy as such, and to set it up before the gates of ethical doctrine as the great producer of insight.

But when we say that to this insight common sense must come, under the given conditions, we do not mean to say: "So the man, once having attained insight, must act thenceforth." The realization of one's neighbor, in the full sense of the word realization, is indeed the resolution to treat him as if he were real, that is, to treat him unselfishly. But this resolution expresses and belongs to the moment of insight. Passion may cloud the insight in the very next moment. It always does cloud the insight after no very long time. It is as impossible for us to avoid the illusion of selfishness in our daily lives, as to escape seeing through the illusion at the moment of insight. We see the reality of our neighbor, that is, we determine to treat him as we do ourselves. But then we go back to daily action, and we feel the heat of hereditary passions, and we straightway forget what we have seen. Our neighbor becomes obscured. He is once more a foreign power. He is unreal. We are again deluded and selfish. This conflict goes on and will go on as long as we live after the manner of men. Moments of insight, with their accompanying resolutions; long stretches of delusion and selfishness: That is our life.

To bring home this view . . . to the reader, we ask him to consider carefully just what experience he has when he tries to realize his neighbor in the full sense that we have insisted upon. Not pity as such is what we desire him to feel. For whether or not pity happens to work in him as selfishly and blindly as we have found that it often does work, still not the emotion, but its consequences, must in the most favorable case give us what we seek. All the forms of sympathy are mere impulses. It is the insight to which they bring us that has moral value. And again, the realization of our neighbor's existence is not at all the discovery that he is more or less useful to us personally. All that would contribute to selfishness. In an entirely different way we must realize his existence, if we are to be really altruistic. What then is our neighbor?

We find that out by treating him in thought just as we do ourselves. What art thou? Thou art now just a present state, with its experiences, thoughts, and desires. But what is thy future Self? Simply future states, future experiences, future thoughts and desires, that, although not now existing for thee, are postulated by thee as certain to come, and as in some real relation to thy present Self. What then is thy neighbor? He too is a mass of states, of experiences, thoughts, and desires, just as real as thou art, no more but yet no less present to thy experience now than is thy future Self. He is not that face that frowns or smiles at thee, although often thou thinkest of him as only that. He is not the arm that strikes or defends thee, not the voice that speaks to thee, not that machine that gives thee what thou desirest when thou movest it with the offer of money. To be sure, thou dost often think of him as if he were that automaton yonder, that answers thee when thou speakest to it. But no, thy neighbor is as actual, as concrete, as thou art. Just as thy future is real, though not now thine, so thy neighbor is real, though his thoughts never are thy thoughts. Dost thou believe this? Art thou sure what it means? This is for thee the turning-point of thy whole conduct towards him. What we now ask of thee is no sentiment, no gush of pity, no tremulous weakness of sympathy, but a calm, clear insight. . . .

If he is real like thee, then is his life as bright a light, as warm a fire, to him, as thine to thee; his will is as full of struggling desires, of hard problems, of fateful decisions; his pains are as hateful, his joys as dear. Take whatever thou knowest of desire and of striving, of burning love and of fierce hatred, realize as fully as thou canst what that means, and then with clear certainty add: *Such as that is for me, so is it for him, nothing less.* If thou dost that, can he remain to thee what he has been, a picture, a plaything, a comedy, or a tragedy, in brief a mere Show? Behind all that show thou hast indeed dimly felt that there is something. Know that truth thoroughly. Thou hast regarded his thought, his feeling, as somehow different in sort from thine. Thou hast said: "A pain in him is not like a pain in me, but something far easier to bear." Thou hast made of him a ghost, as the imprudent man makes of his future self a ghost. Even when thou hast feared his scorn, his hate, his contempt, thou hast not fully made him for thee as real as thyself. His laughter at thee has made thy face feel hot, his frowns and clenched fists have cowed thee, his sneers have made thy throat feel choked. But that was only the social instinct in thee. It was not a full sense of his reality. Even so the little baby smiles back at one that smiles at it, but not because it realizes the approving joy of the other, only because it by instinct enjoys a smiling face; and even so the baby is frightened at harsh speech, but not because it realizes the other's anger. So, dimly and by instinct, thou hast lived with thy neighbor, and hast known him not, being blind. Thou hast even desired his pain, but thou hast not fully realized the pain that thou gavest. It has been to thee, not pain in itself, but the sight of his submission, of his tears, or of his pale terror. Of thy neighbor thou hast made a thing, no Self at all.

When thou hast loved, hast pitied, or hast reverenced thy neighbor, then thy feeling has possibly raised for a moment the veil of illusion. Then thou hast known what he truly is, a Self like thy present Self. But thy selfish feeling is too strong for thee. Thou hast forgotten soon again what thou hadst seen, and hast made even of thy beloved one only the instrument of thy own pleasure. Even out of thy power to pity thou hast made an object of thy vainglory. Thy reverence has turned again to pride. Thou hast accepted the illusion once more. No wonder that in his darkness thou findest selfishness the only rule of any meaning for thy conduct. Thou forgottest that without realization of thy future and as yet unreal self, even selfishness means nothing. Thou forgottest that if thou gavest thy present thought even so to the task of realizing thy neighbor's life, selfishness would seem no more plain to thee than the love of thy neighbor.

Have done then with this illusion that thy Self is all in all. Intuition tells thee no more about thy future Self than it tells thee about thy neighbors. Desire, bred in thee by generations of struggle for existence, emphasizes the expectation of thy own bodily future, the love for thy own bodily welfare, and makes thy body's life seem alone real. But simply try to know the truth. The truth is that all this world of life about thee is as real as thou art. All conscious life is conscious in its own measure. Pain is pain, joy is joy, everywhere even as in thee. The result of thy insight will be inevitable. The illusion vanishing, the glorious prospect opens before thy vision. Seeing the oneness of this life everywhere, the equal reality of all its moments, thou wilt be ready to treat it all with the reverence that prudence would have thee show to thy own little bit of future life. What prudence in its narrow respectability counseled, thou wilt be ready to do universally. As the prudent man, seeing the reality of his future self, inevitably works for it; so the enlightened man, seeing the reality of all conscious life, realizing that it is no shadow, but fact, at once and inevitably desires, if only for that one moment of insight, to enter into the service of the whole of it. . . . Lift up thy eyes, behold that life, and then turn away and forget it as thou canst; but if thou hast known that, thou hast begun to know thy duty.

THE MORAL INSIGHT From *The Religious Aspects of Philosophy* (Boston: Houghton Mifflin Co., 1885).

Respect for Persons

Immanuel Kant

[The Ultimate Worth of Persons]

... Suppose that there were something the existence of which in itself had absolute worth, something which, as an end in itself, could be a ground of definite laws. In it and only in it could lie the ground of a possible categorical imperative, i.e., of a practical law.

Now, I say, man and, in general, every rational being exists as an end in himself and not merely as a means to be arbitrarily used by this or that will. In all his actions, whether they are directed to himself or to other rational beings, he must always be regarded at the same time as an end. All objects of inclinations have only a conditional worth, for if the inclinations and the needs founded on them did not exist, their object would be without worth. The inclinations themselves as the sources of needs, however, are so lacking in absolute worth that the universal wish of every rational being must be indeed to free himself completely from them. Therefore, the worth of any objects to be obtained by our actions is at all times conditional. Beings whose existence does not depend on our will but on nature, if they are not rational beings, have only a relative worth as means and are therefore called "things"; on the other hand, rational beings are designated "persons" because their nature indicates that they are ends in themselves, i.e., things which may not be used merely as means. Such a being is thus an object of respect and, so far, restricts all [arbitrary] choice. Such beings are not merely subjective ends whose existence as a result of our action has a worth for us, but are objective ends, i.e., beings whose existence in itself is an end. Such an end is one for which no other end can be substituted, to which these beings should serve merely as means. For, without them, nothing of absolute worth could be found, and if all worth is conditional and thus contingent, no supreme practical principle for reason could be found anywhere.

Thus if there is to be a supreme practical principle and a categorical imperative for the human will, it must be one that forms an objective principle of the will from the conception of that which is necessarily an end for everyone because it is an end in itself. Hence this objective principle can serve as a universal practical law. The ground of this principle is: rational nature exists as an end in itself. Man necessarily thinks of his own existence in this way; thus far it is a subjective principle of human actions. Also every other rational being thinks of his existence by means of the same rational ground which holds also for myself; thus it is at the same time an objective principle from which, as a supreme practical ground, it must be possible to derive all laws of the will. The practical imperative, therefore, is the following: Act so that you treat humanity, whether in your own person or in that of another, always as an end and never as a means only. . . .

[Moral Agents as Law-Givers to Themselves]

If we now look back upon all previous attempts which have ever been undertaken to discover the principle of morality, it is not to be wondered at that they all had to fail. Man was seen to be bound to laws by his duty, but it was not seen that he is subject only to his own, yet universal, legislation, and that he is only bound to act in accordance with his own will, which is, however, designed by nature to be a will giving universal laws. For if one thought of him as subject only to a law (whatever it may be), this necessarily implied some interest as a stimulus or compulsion to obedience because the law did not arise from his will. Rather, his will was constrained by something else according to a law to act in a certain way. By this strictly necessary consequence, however, all the labor of finding a supreme ground for duty was irrevocably lost, and one never arrived at duty but only at the necessity of action from a certain interest. This might be his own interest or that of another, but in either case the imperative always had to be conditional and could not at all serve as a moral command. This principle I will call the principle of *autonomy* of the will in contrast to all other principles which I accordingly count under heteronomy.

The concept of each rational being as a being that must regard itself as giving universal law through all the maxims of its will, so that it may judge itself and its actions from this standpoint, leads to a very fruitful concept, namely, that of a *realm of ends*.

By "realm" I understand the systematic union of different rational beings through common laws. Because laws determine ends with regard to their universal validity, if we abstract from the personal difference of rational beings and thus from all content of their private ends, we can think of a whole of all ends in systematic connection, a whole of rational beings as ends in themselves as well as of the particular ends which each may set for himself. This is a realm of ends, which is possible on the aforesaid principles. For all rational beings stand under the law that each of them should treat himself and all others never merely as means but in every case also as an end in himself. Thus there arises a systematic union of rational beings through common objective laws. This is a realm which may be called a realm of ends (certainly only an ideal), because what these laws have in view is just the relation of these beings to each other as ends and means.

A rational being belongs to the realm of ends as a member when he gives universal laws in it while also himself subject to these laws. He belongs to it as sovereign when he, as legislating, is subject to the will of no other. The rational being must regard himself always as legislative in a realm of ends possible through the freedom of the will, whether he belongs to it as member or as sovereign. He cannot maintain the latter position merely through the maxims of his will but only when he is a completely independent being without need and with power adequate to his will.

Morality, therefore, consists in the relation of every action to that legislation through which alone a realm of ends is possible. This legislation, however, must be found in every rational being. It must be able to arise from his will, whose principle then is to take no action according to any maxim which would be inconsistent with its being a universal law and thus to act only so that the will through its maxims could regard itself at the same time as universally lawgiving. If now the maxims do not by their nature already necessarily conform to this objective principle of rational beings as universally lawgiving, the necessity of acting according to that principle is called practical constraint, i.e., duty. Duty pertains not to the sovereign in the realm of ends, but rather to each member, and to each in the same degree.

The practical necessity of acting according to this principle, i.e., duty, does not rest at all on feelings, impulses, and inclinations; it rests merely on the relation of rational beings to one another, in which the will of a rational being must always be regarded as legislative, for otherwise it could not be thought of as an end in itself. Reason, therefore, relates every maxim of the will as giving universal laws to every other will and also to every action toward itself; it does so not for the sake of any other practical motive or future advantage but rather from the idea of the dignity of a rational being who obeys no law except that which he himself also gives.

In the realm of ends everything has either a *price* or a *dignity*. Whatever has a price can be replaced by something else as its equivalent; on the other hand, whatever is above all price, and therefore admits of no equivalent, has a dignity.

That which is related to general human inclinations and needs has a *market price*. That which, without presupposing any need, accords with a certain taste, i.e., with pleasure in the mere purposeless play of our faculties, has an *affective price*. But that which constituted the condition under which alone something can be an end in itself does not have mere relative worth, i.e., a price, but an intrinsic worth, i.e., *dignity*.

Now morality is the condition under which alone a rational being can be an end in itself, because only through it is it possible to be a legislative member in the realm of ends. Thus morality and humanity, so far as it is capable of morality, alone have dignity. Skill and diligence in work have a market value; wit, lively imagination, and humor have an affective price; but fidelity in promises and benevolence on principle (not from instinct) have intrinsic worth. Nature and likewise art contain nothing which could replace their lack, for their worth consists not in effects which flow from them, nor in advantage and utility which they procure; it consists only in intentions, i.e., maxims of the will which are ready to reveal themselves in this manner through actions even though success does not favor them. These actions need no recommendation from any subjective disposition or taste in order that they may be looked upon with immediate favor and satisfaction, nor do they have need of any immediate propensity or feeling directed to them. They exhibit the will which performs them as the object of an immediate respect, since nothing but reason is required in order to impose them on the will. The will is not to be cajoled into them, for this, in the case of duties, would be a contradiction. This esteem lets the worth of such a turn of mind be recognized as dignity and puts it infinitely beyond any price, with which it cannot in the least be brought into competition or comparison without, as it were, violating its holiness.

And what is it that justifies the morally good disposition or virtue in making such lofty claims? It is nothing less than the participation it affords the rational being in giving universal laws. He is thus fitted to be a member in a possible realm of ends to which his own nature already destined him. For, as an end in himself, he is destined to be legislative in the realm of ends, free from all laws of nature and obedient only to those which he himself gives. Accordingly, his maxims can belong to a universal legislation to which he is at the same time also subject. A thing has no worth other than that determined for it by the law. The legislation which determines all worth must therefore have a dignity, i.e., unconditional and incomparable worth. For the esteem which a rational being must have for it, only the word "respect" is a suitable expression. Autonomy is thus the basis of the dignity of both human nature and every rational nature. . . .

Reprinted by permission of Simon & Schuster, Inc., from the Macmillan College text *Foundations of the Metaphysics of Morals, 2/E*, translated by Lewis White Beck, Copyright © 1990 by Macmillan College Publishing Company.

The Conscience of Huckleberry Finn

Jonathan Bennett

I

In this paper, I shall present not just the conscience of Huckleberry Finn but two others as well. One of them is the conscience of Heinrich Himmler. He became a Nazi in 1923; he served drably and quietly, but well, and was rewarded with increasing responsibility and power. At the peak of his career he held many offices and commands, of which the most powerful was that of leader of the SS—the principal police force of the Nazi regime. In this capacity, Himmler commanded the whole concentration-camp system, and was responsible for the execution of the so-called "final solution of the Jewish problem." It is important for my purposes that this piece of social engineering should be thought of not abstractly but in concrete terms of Jewish families being marched to what they think are bathhouses, to the accompaniment of loud-speaker renditions of extracts from *The Merry Widow* and *Tales of Hoffmann,* there to be choked to death by poisonous gases. Altogether, Himmler succeeded in murdering about four and a half million of them, as well as several million gentiles, mainly Poles and Russians.

The other conscience to be discussed is that of the Calvinist theologian and philosopher Jonathan Edwards. He lived in the first half of the eighteenth century, and has a good claim to be considered America's first serious and considerable philosophical thinker. He was for many years a widely renowned preacher and Congregationalist minister in New England; in 1748 a dispute with his congregation led him to resign (he couldn't accept their view that unbelievers should be admitted to the Lord's Supper in the hope that it would convert them); for some years after that he worked as a missionary, preaching to Indians through an interpreter; then in 1758 he accepted the presidency of what is now Princeton University, and within two months died from a smallpox inoculation. Along the way he wrote some first-rate philosophy; his book attacking the notion of free will is still sometimes read. Why I should be interested in Edwards's *conscience* will be explained in due course.

I shall use Heinrich Himmler, Jonathan Edwards, and Huckleberry Finn to illustrate different aspects of a single theme, namely the relationship between *sympathy* on the one hand and *bad morality* on the other.

II

All that I can mean by a "bad morality" is a morality whose principles I deeply disapprove of. When I call a morality bad, I cannot prove that mine is better; but when I here call any morality bad, I think you will agree with me that it is bad; and that is all I need.

There could be dispute as to whether the springs of someone's actions constitute a *morality*. I think, though, that we must admit that someone who acts in ways which conflict grossly with our morality may nevertheless have a morality of his own—a set of principles of action which he sincerely assents to, so that for him the problem of acting well or rightly or in obedience to conscience is the problem of conforming to *those* principles. The problem of conscientiousness can arise as acutely for a bad morality as for any other: Rotten principles may be as difficult to keep as decent ones.

As for "sympathy" I use this term to cover every sort of fellow-feeling, as when one feels pity over someone's loneliness, or horrified compassion over his pain, or when one feels a shrinking reluctance to act in a way which will bring misfortune to someone else. These *feelings* must not be confused with *moral judgments*. My sympathy for someone in distress may lead me to help him, or even to think that I ought to help him; but in itself it is not a judgment about what I ought to do but just a *feeling* for him in his plight. We shall get some light on the difference between feelings and moral judgments when we consider Huckleberry Finn.

Obviously, feelings can impel one to action, and so can moral judgments; and in a particular case sympathy and morality may pull in opposite directions. This can happen not just with bad moralities, but also with good ones like yours and mine. For example, a small child, sick and miserable, clings tightly to his mother and screams in terror when she tries to pass him over to the doctor to be examined. If the mother gave way to her sympathy, that is to her feeling for the child's misery and fright, she would hold it close and not let the doctor come near; but don't we agree that it might be wrong for her to act on such a feeling? Quite generally, then, anyone's moral principles may apply to a particular situation in a way which runs contrary to the particular thrusts of fellow-feeling that he has in that situation. My immediate concern is with sympathy in relation to bad morality, but not because such conflicts occur only when the morality is bad.

Now, suppose that someone who accepts a bad morality is struggling to make himself act in accordance with it in a particular situation where his sympathies pull him another way. He sees the struggle as one between doing the right, conscientious thing, and acting wrongly and weakly, like the mother who won't let the doctor come near her sick, frightened baby. Since we don't accept this person's morality, we may see the situation very differently, thoroughly disapproving of the action he regards as the right one, and endorsing the action which from his point of view constitutes weakness and backsliding.

Conflicts between sympathy and bad morality won't always be like this, for we won't disagree with every single dictate of a bad morality. Still, it can happen in the way I have described, with the agent's right action being our wrong one, and vice versa. That is just what happens in a certain episode in Chapter 16 of *The Adventures of Huckleberry Finn,* an episode which brilliantly illustrates how fiction can be instructive about real life.

III

Huck Finn has been helping his slave friend Jim to run away from Miss Watson, who is Jim's owner. In their raft-journey down the Mississippi River, they are near to the place at which Jim will become legally free. Now let Huck take over the story:

> Jim said it made him all over trembly and feverish to be so close to freedom. Well I can tell you it made me all over trembly and feverish, too, to hear him, because I begun to get it through my head that he *was* most free—and who was to blame for it? Why, *me.* I couldn't get that out of my conscience, no how nor no way. . . . It hadn't ever come home to me, before, what this thing was that I was doing. But now it did; and it stayed with me, and scorched me more and more. I tried to make out to myself that *I* warn't to blame, because *I* didn't run Jim off from his rightful owner; but it warn't no use, conscience up and say, every time: "But you knowed he was running for his freedom, and you could a paddled ashore and told somebody." That was so—I couldn't get around that, no way. That was where it pinched. Conscience says to me: "What had poor Miss Watson done to you, that you could see her nigger go off right under your eyes and never say one single word? What did that poor old woman do to you, that you could treat her so mean? . . ." I got to feeling so mean and miserable I most wished I was dead.

Chapter II: Responding to Others

Jim speaks his plan to save up to buy his wife, and then his children, out of slavery; and he adds that if the children cannot be bought he will arrange to steal them. Huck is horrified:

> Thinks I, this is what comes of my not thinking. Here was this nigger which I had as good as helped to run away, coming right out flat-footed and saying he would steal his children—children that belonged to a man I didn't even know; a man that hadn't ever done me no harm.
>
> I was sorry to hear Jim say that, it was such a lowering of him. My conscience got to stirring me up hotter than ever, until at last I says to it: "Let up on me—it ain't too late, yet—I'll paddle ashore at first light, and tell." I felt easy, and happy, and light as a feather, right off. All my troubles was gone.

This is bad morality all right. In his earliest years Huck wasn't taught any principles, and the only one he has encountered since then are those of rural Missouri, in which slave-owning is just one kind of ownership and is not subject to critical pressure. It hasn't occurred to Huck to question those principles. So the action, to us abhorrent, of turning Jim in to the authorities presents itself *clearly* to Huck as the right thing to do.

For us, morality and sympathy would both dictate helping Jim to escape. If we felt any conflict, it would have both these on one side and something else on the other—greed for a reward, or fear of punishment. But Huck's morality conflicts with his sympathy, that is, with his unargued, natural feeling for his friend. The conflict starts when Huck sets off in the canoe towards the shore, pretending that he is going to reconnoiter, but really planning to turn Jim in:

> As I shoved off, [Jim] says: "Pooty soon I'll be a-shout'n for joy, en I'll say, it's all on accounts o' Huck I's a free man . . . Jim won't ever forgit you, Huck; you's de bes' fren' Jim's ever had; en you's de *only* fren' old Jim's got now."
>
> I was paddling off, all in a sweat to tell on him; but when he says this, it seemed to kind of take the tuck all out of me. I went along slow then, and I warn't right down certain whether I was glad I started or whether I warn't. When I was fifty yards off, Jim says:
>
> "Dah you goes, de ole true Huck; de on'y white genlman dat ever kep' his promise to ole Jim." Well, I just felt sick. But I says, I *got* to do it—I can't get *out* of it.

In the upshot, sympathy wins over morality. Huck hasn't the strength of will to do what he sincerely thinks he ought to do. Two men hunting for runaway slaves ask him whether the man on his raft is black or white:

> I didn't answer up prompt. I tried to, but the words wouldn't come. I tried, for a second or two, to brace up and out with it, but I warn't man enough—hadn't the spunk of a rabbit. I see I was weakening; so I just give up trying, and up and says: "He's white."

Quest for Goodness: An Introduction to Ethics

So Huck enables Jim to escape, thus acting weakly and wickedly—he thinks. In this conflict between sympathy and morality, sympathy wins.

One critic has cited this episode in support of the statement that Huck suffers "excruciating moments of wavering between honesty and respectability." That is hopelessly wrong, and I agree with the perceptive comment on it by another critic, who says:

> The conflict waged in Huck is much more serious: He scarcely cares for respectability and never hesitates to relinquish it, but he does care for honesty and gratitude—and both honesty and gratitude require that he should give Jim up. It is not, in Huck, honesty at war with respectability but love and compassion for Jim struggling against his conscience. His decision is for Jim and hell: a right decision made in the mental chains that Huck never breaks. His concern for Jim is and remains *irrational*. Huck finds many reasons for giving Jim up and none for stealing him. To the end Huck sees his compassion for Jim as a weak, ignorant, and wicked felony.[1]

That is precisely correct—and it can have that virtue only because Mark Twain wrote the episode with such unerring precision. The crucial point concerns *reasons*, which all occur on one side of the conflict. On the side of conscience we have principles, arguments, considerations, ways of looking at things:

"It hadn't ever come home to me before what I was doing"
"I tried to make out that I warn't to blame"
"Conscience said 'But you knowed . . .'—I couldn't get around that"
"What had poor Miss Watson done to you?"
"This is what comes of my not thinking"
". . . children that belonged to a man I didn't even know."

On the other side, the side of feeling, we get nothing like that. When Jim rejoices in Huck, as his only friend, Huck doesn't consider the claims of friendship or have the situation "come home" to him in a different light. All that happens is: "When he says this, it seemed to kind of take the tuck all out of me. I went along slow then, and I warn't right down certain whether I was glad I started or whether I warn't." Again, Jim's words about Huck's "promise" to him don't give Huck any *reason* for changing his plan: In his morality promises to slaves probably don't count. Their effect on him is of a different kind: "Well, I just felt sick." And when the moment for final decision comes, Huck doesn't weigh up pros and cons: he simply *fails* to do what he believes to be right—he isn't strong enough, hasn't "the spunk of a rabbit." This passage in the novel is notable not just for its finely wrought irony, with Huck's weakness of will leading him to do the right thing, but also for its masterly handling of the difference between general moral principles and particular unreasoned emotional pulls.

Chapter II: Responding to Others

IV

Consider now another case of bad morality in conflict with human sympathy: the case of the odious Himmler. Here, from a speech he made to some SS generals, is an indication of the content of his morality:

> What happens to a Russian, to a Czech, does not interest me in the slightest. What the nations can offer in the way of good blood of our type, we will take, if necessary by kidnapping their children and raising them here with us. Whether nations live in prosperity or starve to death like cattle interests me only in so far as we need them as slaves to our *Kultur;* otherwise it is of no interest to me. Whether 10,000 Russian females fall town from exhaustion while digging an antitank ditch interests me only in so far as the antitank ditch for Germany is finished.[2]

But has this a moral basis at all? And if it has, was there in Himmler's own mind any conflict between morality and sympathy? Yes there was. Here is more from the same speech:

> I also want to talk to you quite frankly on a very grave matter . . . I mean . . . the extermination of the Jewish race . . . Most of you must know what it means when 100 corpses are lying side by side, or 500, or 1,000. To have stuck it out and at the same time apart from exceptions caused by human weakness—to have remained decent fellows, that is what has made us hard. This is a page of glory in our history which has never been written and is never to be written.

Himmler saw his policies as being hard to implement while still retaining one's human sympathies—while still remaining a "decent fellow." He is saying that only the weak take the easy way out and just squelch their sympathies, and is praising the stronger and more glorious course of retaining one's sympathies while acting in violation of them. In the same spirit, he ordered that when executions were carried out in concentration camps, those responsible "are to be influenced in such a way as to suffer no ill effect in their character and mental attitude." A year later he boasted that the SS had wiped out the Jews

> without our leaders and their men suffering any damage in their minds and souls. The danger was considerable, for there was only a narrow path between the Scylla of their becoming heartless ruffians unable any longer to treasure life, and the Charybdis of their becoming soft and suffering nervous breakdowns.

And there really can't be any doubt that the basis of Himmler's policies was a set of principles which constituted his morality—a sick, bad, wicked *morality*. He described himself as caught in "the old tragic conflict be-

127

tween will and obligation." And when his physician Kersten protested at the intention to destroy the Jews, saying that the suffering involved was "not to be contemplated," Kersten reports that Himmler replied:

> He knew that it would mean much suffering for the Jews. . . . "It is the curse of greatness that it must step over dead bodies to create new life. Yet we must . . . cleanse the soil or it will never bear fruit. It will be a great burden for me to bear."

This, I submit, is the language of morality.

So in this case, tragically, bad morality won out over sympathy. I am sure that many of Himmler's killers did extinguish their sympathies, becoming "heartless ruffians" rather than "decent fellows"; but not Himmler himself. Although his policies ran against the human grain to a horrible degree, he did not sandpaper down his emotional surfaces so that there was no grain there, allowing his actions to slide along smoothly and easily. He did, after all, bear his hideous burden, and even paid a price for it. He suffered a variety of nervous and physical disabilities, including nausea and stomach-convulsions, and Kersten was doubtless right in saying that these were "the expression of a psychic division which extended over his whole life."

This same division must have been present in some of those officials of the Church who ordered heretics to be tortured so as to change their theological opinions. Along with the brutes and the cold careerists, there must have been some who cared, and who suffered from the conflict between their sympathies and their bad morality.

V

In the conflict between sympathy and bad morality, then, the victory may go to sympathy as in the case of Huck Finn, or to morality as in the case of Himmler.

Another possibility is that the conflict may be avoided by giving up, or not ever having, those sympathies which might interfere with one's principles. That seems to have been the case with Jonathan Edwards. I am afraid that I shall be doing an injustice to Edwards's many virtues, and to his great intellectual energy and inventiveness; for my concern is only with the worst thing about him—namely his morality, which was worse than Himmler's.

According to Edwards, God condemns some men to an eternity of unimaginably awful pain, though he arbitrarily spares others—"arbitrarily" because none deserve to be spared:

> Natural men are held in the hand of God over the pit of hell; they have deserved the fiery pit, and are already sentenced to it; and God is

Chapter II: Responding to Others

dreadfully provoked, his anger is as great toward them as to those that are actually suffering the executions of the fierceness of his wrath in hell . . .; the devil is waiting for them, hell is gaping for them, the flames gather and flash about them, and would fain lay hold on them . . .; and . . . there are no means within reach that can be any security to them. . . . All that preserves them is the mere arbitrary will, and unconvenanted unobliged forebearance of an incensed God.[3]

Notice that he says "they have deserved the fiery pit." Edwards insists that men *ought* to be condemned to eternal pain; and his position isn't that this is right because God wants it, but rather that God wants it because it is right. For him, moral standards exist independently of God, and God can be assessed in the light of them (and of course found to be perfect). For example, he says:

> They deserve to be cast into hell; so that . . . justice never stands in the way, it makes no objection against God's using his power at any moment to destroy them. Yea, on the contrary, justice calls aloud for an infinite punishment of their sins.

Elsewhere, he gives elaborate arguments to show that God is acting justly in damning sinners. For example, he argues that a punishment should be exactly as bad as the crime being punished; God is infinitely excellent; so any crime against him is infinitely bad; and so eternal damnation is exactly right as a punishment—it is infinite, but, as Edwards is careful also to say, it is "no more than infinite."

Of course, Edwards himself didn't torment the damned; but the question still arises of whether his sympathies didn't conflict with his *approval* of eternal torment. Didn't he find it painful to contemplate any fellow-human's being tortured for ever? Apparently not:

> The God that holds you over the pit of hell, much as one holds a spider or some loathsome insect over the fire, abhors you, and is dreadfully provoked . . . he is of purer eyes than to bear to have you in his sight; you are ten thousand times so abominable in his eyes as the most hateful venomous serpent is in ours.

When God is presented as being as misanthropic as that, one suspects misanthropy in the theologian. This suspicion is increased when Edwards claims that "the saints in glory will . . . understand how terrible the sufferings of the damned are; yet . . . will not be sorry for [them]."[4] He bases this partly on a view of human nature whose ugliness he seems not to notice:

> The seeing of the calamities of others tends to heighten the sense of our own enjoyments. When the saints in glory, therefore, shall see the doleful state of the damned, how will this heighten their sense of the blessedness of their own state. . . . When they shall see how miserable others of their fellow-creatures are . . . when they shall see the smoke of their torment . . . and hear their dolorous shrieks and cries, and

consider that they in the mean time are in the most blissful state, and shall surely be in it to all eternity; how they will rejoice!

I hope this is less than the whole truth! His other main point about why the saints will rejoice to see the torments of the damned is that it is *right* that they should do so:

> The heavenly inhabitants . . . will have no love nor pity to the damned. . . . [This will not show] a want of spirit of love in them . . . for the heavenly inhabitants will know that it is not fit that they should love [the damned] because they will know then, that God has no love to them, nor pity for them.

The implication that *of course* one can adjust one's feelings of pity so that they conform to the dictates of some authority—doesn't this suggest that ordinary human sympathies played only a small part in Edwards's life?

V

Huck Finn, whose sympathies are wide and deep, could never avoid the conflict in that way; but he is determined to avoid it, and so he opts for the only other alternative he can see—to give up morality altogether. After he has tricked the slave-hunters, he returns to the raft and undergoes a peculiar crisis:

> I got aboard the raft, feeling bad and low, because I knowed very well I had done wrong, and I see it warn't no use for me to try to learn to do right; a body that don't get *started* right when he's little, ain't got no show—when the pinch comes there ain't nothing to back him up and keep him to his work, and so he gets beat. Then I thought a minute, and says to myself, hold on—s'pose you'd a done right and give Jim up; would you feel better than what you do now? No, says I, I'd feel bad— I'd feel just the same way I do now. Well, then, says I, what's the use you learning to do right, when it's troublesome to do right and ain't no trouble to do wrong, and the wages is just the same? I was stuck. I couldn't answer that. So I reckoned I wouldn't bother no more about it, but after this always do whichever come handiest at the time.

Huck clearly cannot conceive of having any morality except the one he has learned—too late, he thinks—from his society. He is not entirely a prisoner of that morality, because he does after all reject it; but for him that is a decision to relinquish morality as such; he cannot envisage revising his morality, altering its content in face of the various pressures to which it is subject, including pressures from his sympathies. For example, he does not begin to approach the thought that slavery should be rejected on moral grounds, or the thought that what he is doing is not theft because a person cannot be owned and therefore cannot be stolen.

Chapter II: Responding to Others

The basic trouble is that he cannot or will not engage in abstract intellectual operations of any sort. In Chapter 33 he finds himself "feeling to blame, somehow" for something he knows he had no hand in; he assumes that this feeling is a deliverance of conscience; and this confirms him in his belief that conscience shouldn't be listened to:

> It don't make no difference whether you do right or wrong, a person's conscience ain't got no sense, and just goes for him *anyway*. If I had a yaller dog that didn't know no more than a person's conscience does, I would poison him. It takes up more than all of a person's insides, and yet ain't no good, nohow.

That brisk, incurious dismissiveness fits well with the comprehensive rejection of morality back on the raft. But this is a digression.

On the raft, Huck decides not to live by principles, but just to do whatever "comes handiest at the time"—always acting according to the mood of the moment. Since the morality he is rejecting is narrow and cruel, and his sympathies are broad and kind, the results will be good. But moral principles are good to have, because they help to protect one from acting badly at moments when one's sympathies happen to be in abeyance. On the highest possible estimate of the role one's sympathies should have, one can still allow for principles as embodiments of one's best feelings, one's broadest and keenest sympathies. On that view, principles can help one across intervals when one's feelings are at less than their best, i.e. through periods of misanthropy or meanness or self-centeredness or depression or anger.

What Huck didn't see is that one can live by principles and yet have ultimate control over their content. And one way such control can be exercised is by checking one's principles in the light of one's sympathies. This is sometimes a pretty straightforward matter. It can happen that a certain moral principle becomes untenable—meaning literally that one cannot hold it any longer—because it conflicts intolerably with the pity or revulsion or whatever that one feels when one sees what the principle leads to. One's experience may play a large part here: Experiences evoke feelings, and feelings force one to modify principles. Something like this happened to the English poet Wilfred Owen, whose experiences in the First World War transformed him from an enthusiastic soldier into a virtual pacifist. I can't document his change of conscience in detail; but I want to present something which he wrote about the way experience can put pressure on morality.

The Latin poet Horace wrote that it is sweet and fitting (or right) to die for one's country—*dulce et decorum est pro patria mori*—and Owen wrote a fine poem about how experience could lead one to relinquish that particular moral principle.[5] He describes a man who is too slow donning his gas mask during a gas attack—"As under a green sea I saw him drowning:" Owen says. The poem ends like this:

131

> In all my dreams before my helpless sight
> He plunges at me, guttering, choking, drowning.
> If in some smothering dreams, you too could pace
> Behind the wagon that we flung him in,
> And watch the white eyes writhing in his face,
> His hanging face, like a devil's sick of sin;
> If you could hear, at every jolt, the blood
> Come gargling from the froth-corrupted lungs,
> Bitter as the cud
> Of vile, incurable sores on innocent tongues,—
> My friend, you would not tell with such high zest
> To children ardent for some desperate glory,
> The old Lie: Dulce et decorum est
> Pro patria mori.

There is a difficulty about drawing from all this a moral for ourselves. I imagine that we agree in our rejection of slavery, eternal damnation, genocide, and uncritical patriotic self-abnegation; so we shall agree that Huck Finn, Jonathan Edwards, Heinrich Himmler, and the poet Horace would all have done well to bring certain of their principles under severe pressure from ordinary human sympathies. But then we can say this because we can say that all those are bad moralities, whereas we cannot look at our own moralities and declare them bad. This is not arrogance: It is obviously incoherent for some one to declare the system of moral principles that he *accepts* to be *bad*, just as one cannot coherently say of anything that one *believes* it but it is *false*.

Still, although I can't point to any of my beliefs and say "That is false," I don't doubt that some of my beliefs *are* false; and so I should try to remain open to correction. Similarly, I accept every single item in my morality—that is inevitable—but I am sure that my morality could be improved, which is to say that it could undergo changes which I should be glad of once I had made them. So I must try to keep my morality open to revision, exposing it to whatever valid pressures there are—including pressures from my sympathies.

I don't give my sympathies a blank check in advance. In a conflict between principle and sympathy, principles ought sometimes to win. For example, I think it was right to take part in the Second World War on the allied side; there were many ghastly individual incidents which might have led someone to doubt the rightness of his participation in that war; and I think it would have been right for such a person to keep his sympathies in a subordinate place on those occasions, not allowing them to modify his principles in such a way as to make a pacifist of him.

Still, one's sympathies should be kept as sharp and sensitive and aware as possible, and not only because they can sometimes affect one's principles or one's conduct or both. Owen, at any rate, says that feelings and sympathies are vital even when they can do nothing but bring pain and distress. In another poem he speaks of the blessings of being numb in one's feelings: "Happy are the men who yet before they are killed/Can let their veins run cold," he says. These are the ones who do not suffer from any compassion which, as Owen puts it, "makes their feet/Sore on the alleys cobbled with their brothers." He contrasts these "happy" ones, who "lose all imagination," with himself and others "who with a thought besmirch/Blood over all our soul." Yet the poem's verdict goes against the "happy" ones. Owen does not say that they will act worse than the others whose souls are besmirched with blood because of their keen awareness of human suffering. He merely says that they are the losers because they have cut themselves off from the human condition:

> By choice they made themselves immune
> To pity and whatever moans in man
> Before the last sea and the hapless stars;
> Whatever mourns when many leave these shores;
> Whatever shares
> The eternal reciprocity of tears.[6]

Endnotes

1. M. J. Sidnell, "Huck Finn and Jim," *The Cambridge Quarterly*, vol. 2, pp. 205–206.
2. Quoted in William L. Shirer, *The Rise and Fall of the Third Reich* (New York, 1960), pp. 937–938. Next quotation: ibid., p. 966. All further quotations relating to Himmler are from Roger Manwell and Heinrich Fraenkel, *Heinrich Himmler* (London, 1965), pp. 132, 197, 184 (twice), 187.
3. Vergilius Ferm (ed.), *Puritan Sage: Collected Writings of Jonathan Edwards* (New York 1953), p. 370. Next three quotations: ibid., p. 366, p. 294 ("no more than infinite"), p. 372.
4. This and the next two quotations are from "The End of the Wicked Contemplated by the Righteous: Or, The Torments of the Wicked in Hell, No Occasion of Grief to the Saints in Heaven," from *The Works of President Edwards* (London, 1817), vol. 4, pp. 507–508, 511–512, and 509 respectively.
5. We are grateful to the Executors of the Estate of Harold Owen, and to Chatto and Windus Ltd. for permission to quote from Wilfred Owen's "Dulce et Decorum Est" and "Insensibility."
6. This paper began life as the Potter Memorial Lecture, given at Washington State University in Pullman, Washington, in 1972.

THE CONSCIENCE OF HUCKLEBERRY FINN From *Philosophy* 49 (1974), pp. 123–134. Reprinted by permission of Cambridge University Press.

Chapter III
Moral Theories and Ethical Perspectives

The word "theory" comes from the Greek *theoria* which means "a way of seeing." A moral theory is a way of seeing, or looking at, the moral dimension of life. A good theory attempts to give a comprehensive and consistent account of morality and provide a basis or ground upon which to justify moral claims. In addition, moral theories include principles which assist individuals in moral decision making.

Historically, two basic types or classifications of moral theories have emerged. Deontological theories (Gk. *deon* = "duty," literally, "that which binds") hold that individuals have basic duties. In other words, as human beings living in a world, there are certain things we must do and certain things we must not do. Right conduct involves knowing and discharging basic duties. On this view, the consequences of an action should not be an issue in moral decision making. Rather, the moral worth of an individual is tied to the performance of particular kinds of actions and to certain motivations.

In contrast, teleological theories (Gk. *telos* = "end" or "purpose") make right and wrong actions a function of an action's consequences or outcomes. Right actions are those whose consequences or intended consequences bring about benefits, either to the society or to the individual while wrong actions are those which do not yield beneficial results.

Three specific deontological theories are presented in this chapter. One type of deontological theory, Divine Command Ethics, grounds morality in God or in God's will. All morality, such theories claim, ultimately derives from and has its source in God. One ought to do what God commands or what God wills and one ought not do those things which God forbids. This approach to ethics is presented in Emil Brunner's, "The Divine Imperative." Brunner argues that the essence of morality is to follow the will of God. But, that God's will can never be defined in terms of absolute principles—this would lead to legalism. Brunner states:

> He [God] claims us for His love, not for an idea of love—and not for a conception of the divine love which can be gained from merely reading the Bible. He claims us for His present, living activity of love, which can only be, and must always remain, His work.

The Bible has been the single most influential source of morality in the Western world. Two of the most widely cited selections from the Bible are included in this chapter. One piece, "The Ten Commandments" is taken from the Old Testament book of Exodus and the other selection, "The Sermon on the Mount" is from the Gospels.

The final selection on Divine Command Ethics comes from the Qur'an, the holy book of Islam. The essence of this religion is embodied in its name. "Islam" means "to submit." For the follower of Islam life is continual submission to the will of God.

A second type of deontological moral theory finds its most powerful expression in the writings of Immanuel Kant. Kant located the groundwork and foundation of morality in human reason and in the logical form of moral imperatives. Reason is a law-giver and it is universal. As such, the moral imperatives handed down by reason will be absolutely binding on all people at all times.

In "Good Will, Duty and the Categorical Imperative," Kant tells us what persons of moral worth do. Such persons act from a good will, one that is "good in itself" and thus act only from the motive of doing what is right. That is, as rational beings we have the capacity to distinguish right from wrong. Kant's categorical imperative states: *Act only on that maxim whereby thou canst at the same time will that it should become a universal law.* As free beings we have a choice. Persons of moral worth choose to do what is right simply because *they* know that it is the right thing to do.

A third type of deontological theory is Intuitionism. The intuitionist holds that all humans have, in the very structure of their being, the intuitive capacity to "know" that certain things ought not to be done, while other things must be done. This type of theory claims that intuitions are the foundation for ethical reasoning.

In his paper, "Intuition: A Foundation for Moral Principles," (published for the first time in this volume), Robert Lorek argues:

> We have good reason to conclude that intuition is a justified foundation for moral principles. If we agree that intuitions are fallible, and defeasible, we can also assume that ethical principles are capable of being revised when conflicting justifications force us to reassess our beliefs. Intuitions are foundational for ethical reasoning, but not in the strict sense foundationalism requires. Intuitions are foundational, if our form of foundationalism allows us to justify our beliefs even though they may be falsified.

Chapter III: Moral Theories and Ethical Perspectives

Because of their power and immediacy, intuitions stand on their own as self-evident, but fallible, principles. As such, they provide an "immediate sense when a *prima facie* justification is right." *Prima facie* means "on the surface" or "at first glance." *Prima facie* duties specify, in a general sense, what human beings must do or must not do before other considerations are taken into account. If one accepts the fallibility of intuitions, Lorek claims that the "appeal to intuitions to establish general moral principles . . . is rational."

The teleological theory of utilitarianism originated with Jeremy Bentham. It was further developed by Bentham's contemporary John Stuart Mill. Bentham explained his "principle of utility" directly:

> By the principle of utility is meant that principle which approves or disapproves of every action whatsoever, according to the tendency which it appears to have to augment or diminish the happiness of the party whose interest is in question: or, what is the same thing in other words, to promote or to oppose that happiness.

To put it simply, an action is right to the extent that it increases happiness and diminishes misery. An action is to be considered wrong in so far as it brings about the opposite effect. "Utility" is the property of producing pleasure or happiness in a conscious being and, by extension, in a community. Bentham devised a "hedonistic calculus" which provided criteria by which one could calculate ratios of pleasures and pains. He proposed that pleasures be evaluated according to their intensity, duration, certainty, propinquity (nearness), fecundity (tendency to lead to other pleasures), purity (tendency *not* to be followed by pain) and extent (the number of persons to whom the pleasure or happiness will benefit).

Suppose that it were possible to do exactly as you pleased! Furthermore, imagine that, in your efforts to seek your own pleasure by employing morally illicit means, you would not have to face up to the consequences of your actions. Why be moral? Plato's "Myth of Gyges" is designed to show that being a just human being is worthwhile for its own sake.

In "Humans Are Not Always Selfish," James Rachels counters the views of "psychological egoism" and "psychological hedonism." These views claim, respectively, that all human beings act, in all cases, for their own selfish ends or in order to derive personal pleasure. He also clears away confusions which blur important distinctions, for example, the differences between the notions of selfishness and self-interest and the difference between an act's object as opposed to the act's motive. He also shows that "egoism," as a doctrine, is internally inconsistent and leads to practical contradictions.

According to Michael C. Brannigan, "the essential aim of Indian philosophy is liberation from suffering." That is, it is to free the individual from

Quest for Goodness: An Introduction to Ethics

the trouble, sorrow and suffering which arises from the world condition of limitation. In order to achieve this end ". . . its various schools [are compelled] to inquire about what constitutes the good life. And two aspects of the good life are significantly compatible: the highest good for the individual, and the highest social good."

"Hindu Perspectives on Ethics" discusses the four goals in life (all of which are legitimate, however, all are not final), the four stages (*asramas*—"rest-stops"), the four main yogas, and the four major castes. The article also explains many key terms, for example: *sannyasa, atman, moksha, karma, dharma, samsara,* etc.

This chapter closes with "Taoist Ethical Perspectives." One of the three major systems of thought in China is Taoism. It's chief source is Lao-tzu's classic *Tao Te Ching (The Book of the Way and Its Power)*. This work provides the key ideas and themes for later Taoist writers, such as Chuang-tzu. It also serves as the philosophical basis for the Taoist religion and figures significantly in traditional Chinese medicine and the martial arts. Excerpts from the *Tao Te Ching* and the *Chuang-tzu* illustrate themes of non-action (wu-wei), the individual life in harmony with the Tao, the superior man [person], and government and the Taoist social ethic.

The *Tao* is "the way." It is the way of ultimate reality. It is the way of nature and, ethically, it is the way an individual ought to live. In other words, the individual ought to gear his or her life to the power of the *Tao*.

The Divine Imperative

Emil Brunner

The Christian conception of the Good differs from every other conception of the Good at this very point: that it cannot be defined in terms of principle at all.

Whatever can be defined in accordance with a principle—whether it be the principle of pleasure or the principle of duty—is legalistic. This means that it is possible—by the use of this principle—to pre-determine "the right" down to the smallest detail of conduct . . . This legalistic spirit corrupts the true conception of the Good from its very roots. The Christian moralist and the extreme individualist are at one in their emphatic rejection of legalistic conduct; they join hands, as it were, in face of the whole host of legalistic moralists; they are convinced that conduct which is regulated by abstract principles can never be good. But equally sternly the Christian moralist rejects the individualistic doctrine of freedom, according to which there is no longer any difference between "right" and "wrong." Rather, in the Christian view, that alone is "good" which is free from all caprice, which takes place in unconditional obedience. There is no Good save obedient behaviour, save the obedient will. But this obedience is rendered not to a law or a principle which can be known beforehand, but only to the free, sovereign will of God. The Good consists in always doing what God wills at any particular moment.

This statement makes it clear that for us the will of God cannot be summed up under any principle, that it is not at our disposal, but that so far as we are concerned the will of God is absolutely free. The Christian is therefore "a free lord over all things," because he stands directly under the personal orders of the free Sovereign God. This is why genuine "Christian conduct"—if we may use this idea as an illustration—is so unaccountable, so unwelcome to the moral rigorist and to the hedonist alike. The moral rigorist regards the Christian as a hedonist, and the hedonist regards him as a rigorist. In reality, the Christian is neither, yet he is also something of both, since he is indeed absolutely *bound* and obedient, but, since he is bound to the *free* loving will of God, he is himself free from all transparent bondage to principles or to legalism. Above all it is important to recognize that even love is not a principle of this kind, neither the love which God Himself *has*, nor the love which He *requires*. Only God Himself defines love in His action. We, for our part, do not know what God is, nor do we know what *love* is, unless we learn to know God in His action, in faith. To be in this His Love, is the commandment. Every attempt to conceive love as a principle leads to this result: it becomes distorted, either in the rigoristic, legalistic sense, or in the hedonistic sense. Man only knows what the love of God is when he sees the way in which God acts, and he only knows how he himself ought to love by allowing himself to be drawn by faith into this activity of God. . . .

But this does not mean that the Christian ethic makes no claim to universal validity. Whatever God demands *can* only be universal, that is, valid for all men, even if those who do not hear this demand do not admit this validity and indeed do not even understand the claim to universal validity. The believer alone clearly perceives that the Good, as it is recognized in faith, is the sole Good, and that all that is otherwise called good cannot lay claim to this title, at least not in the ultimate sense of the word. It is precisely faith and faith alone which knows this: that alone is good which God does; and, indeed, faith really consists in the fact that man knows this—and that he knows it in such a way as it alone can be known, namely, in the recognition of faith. But once man does know this he also knows the unlimited unconditional validity of this conception and of the divine demand. . . .

But what is the function of a system of ethics in regard to the central ethical question: What ought we to do? Can ethics tell us what we are to do? If it could, it would mean that the Christian ethic also is an ethical system based on law and on abstract principles. For where ethics is regarded purely as a science, there general, and to some extent timeless, propositions are stated. If these were to define what we ought to do, then the Good would be defined in legalistic terms. Therefore no such claim can be made either by or for ethics. The service it renders cannot be that of relieving us of the necessity for making moral decisions, but that it prepares the way for such decisions. How this takes place can only be made clear in the explication of the part which is played by law within a morality which is not legalistic. The significance of the law is the same as the significance of ethics, namely: that it prepares the way for a voluntary decision, or for the hearing of the divine command.

. . . *The Good consists simply and solely in the fact* that man receives and deliberately accepts his life as a gift from God, as life dependent on "grace," as the state of "being justified" because it has been granted as a gift, as "justification by faith." Only thus can we know the Will of God, that is, in this revelation of Himself in which He manifests Himself as disinterested, generous Love.

But this Divine giving is not accomplished in any magical way; it simply takes place in the fact that God *"apprehends" man;* God *claims* us for His love, for His generous giving. But this means that He claims our whole existence for Himself, for this love of His; He gives us His love. He gives us His love in such a way that He captures us completely by the power of His love. *To belong* to Him, to this love, and through His love, means that we are the *bondslaves* of this will. To believe means to become a captive, to become His property, or rather, to know that we are His property. The revelation which makes it plain that the will of God is lavish in giving *to* man, makes it equally clear that His will makes a demand *on* man. His will *for* us also means that He wants something *from* us. He claims us for His love. This is His Command. It is the *"new* commandment," because only now can man perceive that it is the command of One who gives before He demands, and who only demands something from us in the act of giving Himself to us. . . .

He claims us for *His* love, not for an *idea* of love—and not for a conception of the divine love which can be gained from merely reading the Bible. He claims us for His present, living activity of love, which can only be, and must always remain, His work. Therefore we can never know beforehand what God will require. God's command can only be perceived at the actual moment of hearing it. It would denote a breaking away from obedience if we were to think of the Divine Command as one which had been enacted once for all, to be interpreted by us in particular instances. To take this line would mean reverting to the legalistic distortion of His love. Love would then have become a "principle." The *free* love of God requires us to remain *free*, that we may be freely at His disposal. *You* cannot say what it means to love here and now; *He* alone can tell you what this means for you at this moment.

The Good is simply what *God* wills that we should do, not that which we should do on the basis of a principle of love. God wills to do something quite definite and particular through us, here and now, something which no other person could do at any time. Just as the commandment of love is absolutely universal so also it is absolutely individual. But just as it is absolutely individual so also it is absolutely devoid of all caprice. "I will guide thee with Mine eye." No one can experience this "moment" save I myself. The Divine Command is made known to us "in the secret place." Therefore it is impossible for us to know it beforehand: to wish to know it beforehand—legalism—is an infringement of the divine honour. The fact that the holiness of God must be remembered when we dwell on His love means that we cannot have His love at our disposal, that it cannot ever be perceived as a universal principle, but only in the act in which He speaks to us Himself; even in His love He remains our *Master* and Lord. But He is our "Lord" in the sense that He tells us Himself what it means to "love," here and now. . . .

It is *His* will that God wills to accomplish in the world: He is not the servant of some purpose outside Himself. God Himself is His own End. In His love, however, He sets up an End outside Himself—without ceasing to be His own End; this "end" is the communion of the creature with Himself, the Creator. This Divine will for "community" is God's Sovereign Will. Therefore salvation, beatitude, the fulfilment of the purpose of life, both for humanity as a whole, and for the individual, is included in God's royal purpose. The tables of prohibition in the Bible may be compared with the notices on power circuits: DO NOT TOUCH! Because God wills to control our life, He commands and He forbids. This is the "eudaemonism" of the Gospel, and at the same time its absolutely serious view of duty. God wills our true happiness; but *He* wills it, and He wills it in such a way that no one else knows what His will is. It remains outside our disposal, and indeed we do not know it. We never know what is right for us, nor what is best for the other person. We go astray when we think that we can deduce this from some principle or another, or from some experience, and we distort the thought of the divine love if we think that we know what He ought to do for us in accordance with His love. But of one thing we may be quite sure: His will is love, even when we do not understand it—when He commands as well as when He gives.

Therefore in His revelation God's will is expressed by His sanctions, by rewards and punishments. God alone gives life; to be with Him is life, to resist Him is ruin. It is impossible to exist apart from God; it is impossible to be neutral towards Him. He who is not for Him is against Him. God's Command means eternal life and God means nothing else than this. He is Love. But His will is utterly serious; it is the will of the Lord of Life and Death. Anyone who—finally—resists Him, will only dash himself to pieces against the rock of His Being. This is the holiness of the love of God. As the divine love cannot be separated from His gift of life, so the Holiness of God cannot be separated from His judicial wrath, the denial and destruction of life. To have a share in the will of God, in the sense of union with His will, means salvation; to resist Him spells utter disaster.

Reprinted from *The Divine Imperative,* by Emil Brunner; translated by Olive Wyon. Copyright © MCMXLVII, by W. L. Jenkins. Used by permission of The Westminster Press, Philadelphia, PA.

The Ten Commandments and the Sermon on the Mount

from The Holy Bible

And God spake all these words, saying,

2 I *am* the LORD thy God, which have brought thee out of the land of Egypt, out of the house of bondage.

3 Thou shalt have no other gods before me.

4 Thou shalt not make unto thee any graven image, or any likeness *of any thing* that *is* in heaven above, or that *is* in the earth beneath, or that *is* in the water under the earth:

5 Thou shalt not bow down thyself to them, nor serve them: for I the LORD thy God *am* a jealous God, visiting the iniquity of the fathers upon the children unto the third and fourth *generation* of them that hate me;

6 And shewing mercy unto thousands of them that love me, and keep my commandments.

7 Thou shalt not take the name of the LORD thy God in vain; for the LORD will not hold him guiltless that taketh his name in vain.

8 Remember the sabbath day, to keep it holy.

9 Six days shalt thou labour, and do all thy work:

10 But the seventh day *is* the sabbath of the LORD thy God: *in it* thou shalt not do any work, thou, nor thy son, nor thy daughter, nor thy manservant, nor thy maidservant, nor thy cattle, nor thy stranger that is within thy gates:

11 For *in* six days the LORD made heaven and earth, the sea, and all that in them *is*, and rested the seventh day: wherefore the LORD blessed the sabbath day, and hallowed it.

12 Honour thy father and thy mother: that thy days may be long upon the land which the LORD thy God giveth thee.

13 Thou shalt not kill.

14 Thou shalt not commit adultery.

15 Thou shalt not steal.

16 Thou shalt not bear false witness against thy neighbour.

17   Thou shalt not covet thy neighbour's house, thou shalt not covet thy neighbour's wife, nor his manservant, nor his maidservant, nor his ox, nor his ass, nor any thing that *is* thy neighbour's.

18   And all the people saw the thunderings, and the lightnings, and the noise of the trumpet, and the mountain smoking: and when the people saw *it*, they removed, and stood afar off. . . .

※ ※ ※

And seeing the multitudes, [Jesus] went up into a mountain: and when he was set, his disciples came unto him:

2   And he opened his mouth, and taught them, saying,

3   Blessed *are* the poor in spirit: for theirs is the kingdom of heaven.

4   Blessed *are* they that mourn: for they shall be comforted.

5   Blessed *are* the meek: for they shall inherit the earth.

6   Blessed *are* they which do hunger and thirst after righteousness: for they shall be filled.

7   Blessed *are* the merciful: for they shall obtain mercy.

8   Blessed *are* the pure in heart: for they shall see God.

9   Blessed *are* the peacemakers: for they shall be called the children of God.

10   Blessed *are* they which are persecuted for righteousness' sake: for theirs is the kingdom of heaven.

11   Blessed are ye, when *men* shall revile you, and persecute *you*, and shall say all manner of evil against you falsely, for my sake.

12   Rejoice, and be exceeding glad: for great *is* your reward in heaven: for so persecuted they the prophets which were before you.

13   Ye are the salt of the earth: but if the salt have lost his savour, wherewith shall it be salted? it is thenceforth good for nothing, but to be cast out, and to be trodden under foot of men.

14   Ye are the light of the world. A city that is set on an hill cannot be hid.

15   Neither do men light a candle, and put it under a bushel, but on a candlestick; and it giveth light unto all that are in the house.

16   Let your light so shine before men, that they may see your good works, and glorify your Father which is in heaven.

17   Think not that I am come to destroy the law, or the prophets: I am not come to destroy, but to fulfil.

18   For verily I say unto you, Till heaven and earth pass, one jot or one tittle shall in no wise pass from the law, till all be fulfilled.

19   Whosoever therefore shall break one of these least commandments, and shall teach men so, he shall be called the least in the kingdom of heaven: but whosoever shall do and teach *them*, the same shall be called great in the kingdom of heaven.

20 For I say unto you, That except your righteousness shall exceed *the righteousness* of the scribes and Pharisees, ye shall in no case enter into the kingdom of heaven.

21 Ye have heard that it was said by them of old time, Thou shalt not kill; and whosoever shall kill shall be in danger of the judgment:

22 But I say unto you, That whosoever is angry with his brother without a cause shall be in danger of the judgment: and whosoever shall say to his brother, Raca, shall be in danger of the council: but whosoever shall say, Thou fool shall be in danger of hell fire.

23 Therefore if thou bring thy gift to the altar, and there rememberest that thy brother hath ought against thee;

24 Leave there thy gift before the altar, and go thy way; first be reconciled to thy brother, and then come and offer thy gift.

25 Agree with thine adversary quickly, whiles thou art in the way with him; lest at any time the adversary deliver thee to the judge, and the judge deliver thee to the officer, and thou be cast into prison.

26 Verily I say unto thee, Thou shalt by no means come out thence, till thou hast paid the uttermost farthing.

27 Ye have heard that it was said by them of old time, Thou shalt not commit adultery:

28 But I say unto you, That whosoever looketh on a woman to lust after her hath committed adultery with her already in his heart.

29 And if thy right eye offend thee, pluck it out, and cast *it* from thee: for it is profitable for thee that one of thy members should perish, and not *that* thy whole body should be cast into hell.

30 And if thy right hand offend thee, cut *it* off, and cast it from thee: for it is profitable for thee that one of thy members should perish, and not *that* thy whole body should be cast into hell.

31 It hath been said, Whosoever shall put away his wife, let him give her a writing of divorcement:

32 But I say unto you, That whosoever shall put away his wife, saving for the cause of fornication, causeth her to commit adultery: and whosoever shall marry her that is divorced committeth adultery.

33 Again, ye have heard that it hath been said by them of old time, Thou shalt not forswear thyself, but shalt perform unto the Lord thine oaths:

34 But I say unto you, Swear not at all; neither by heaven; for it is God's throne:

35 Nor by the earth; for it is his footstool: neither by Jerusalem; for it is the city of the great King.

36 Neither shalt thou swear by thy head, because thou canst not make one hair white or black.

37 But let your communication be, Yea, yea; Nay, nay: for whatsoever is more than these cometh of evil.

38   Ye have heard that it hath been said, An eye for an eye, and a tooth for a tooth:

39   But I say unto you, That ye resist not evil: but whosoever shall smite thee on thy right cheek, turn to him the other also.

40   And if any man will sue thee at the law, and take away thy coat, let him have *thy* cloak also.

41   And whosoever shall compel thee to go a mile, go with him twain.

42   Give to him that asketh thee, and from him that would borrow of thee turn not thou away.

43   Ye have heard that it hath been said, Thou shalt love thy neighbour, and hate thine enemy.

44   But I say unto you, Love your enemies, bless them that curse you, do good to them that hate you, and pray for them which despitefully use you, and persecute you;

45   That ye may be the children of your Father which is in heaven: for he maketh his sun to rise on the evil and on the good, and sendeth rain on the just and on the unjust.

46   For if ye love them which love you, what reward have ye? do not even the publicans the same?

47   And if ye salute your brethren only, what do ye more *than others?* do not even the publicans so?

48   Be ye therefore perfect, even as your Father which is in heaven is perfect.

※ ※ ※

Judge not, that ye be not judged.

2   For with what judgment ye judge, ye shall be judged: and with what measure ye mete, it shall be measured to you again.

3   And why beholdest thou the mote that is in thy brother's eye, but considerest not the beam that *is* in thine own eye?

4   Or how wilt thou say to thy brother, Let me pull out the mote out of thine eye; and, behold, a beam is in thine own eye?

5   Thou hypocrite, first cast out the beam out of thine own eye; and then shalt thou see clearly to cast out the mote out of thy brother's eye.

6   Give not that which is holy unto the dogs, neither cast ye your pearls before swine, lest they trample them under their feet, and turn again and rend you.

7   Ask, and it shall be given you; seek, and ye shall find; knock, and it shall be opened unto you:

8   For every one that asketh receiveth; and he that seeketh findeth; and to him that knocketh it shall be opened.

9   Or what man is there of you, whom if his son ask bread, will he give him a stone?

10   Or if he ask a fish, will he give him a serpent?

11 If ye then, being evil, know how to give good gifts unto your children, how much more shall your Father which is in heaven give good things to them that ask him?

12 Therefore all things whatsoever ye would that men should do to you, do ye even so to them: for this is the law and the prophets.

13 Enter ye in at the strait gate: for wide *is* the gate, and broad *is* the way, that leadeth to destruction, and many there be which go in thereat:

14 Because strait *is* the gate, and narrow *is* the way, which leadeth unto life, and few there be that find it.

15 Beware of false prophets, which come to you in sheep's clothing, but inwardly they are ravening wolves.

16 Ye shall know them by their fruits. Do men gather grapes of thorns, or figs of thistles?

17 Even so every good tree bringeth forth good fruit; but a corrupt tree bringeth forth evil fruit.

18 A good tree cannot bring forth evil fruit, neither *can* a corrupt tree bring forth good fruit.

19 Every tree that bringeth not forth good fruit is hewn down, and cast into the fire.

20 Wherefore by their fruits ye shall know them.

21 Not every one that saith unto me, Lord, Lord, shall enter into the kingdom of heaven; but he that doeth the will of my Father which is in heaven.

22 Many will say to me in that day, Lord, Lord, have we not prophesied in thy name? and in they name have cast out devils? and in thy name done many wonderful works?

23 And then will I profess unto them, I never knew you: depart from me, ye that work iniquity.

24 Therefore whosoever heareth these sayings of mine, and doeth them, I will liken him unto a wise man,which built his house upon a rock:

25 And the rain descended, and the floods came, and the winds blew, and beat upon that house; and it fell not: for it was founded upon a rock.

26 And every one that heareth these sayings of mine, and doeth them not, shall be likened unto a foolish man, which built his house upon the sand:

27 And the rain descended, and the floods came, and the winds blew, and beat upon that house; and it fell: and great was the fall of it.

28 And it came to pass, when Jesus had ended these sayings, the people were astonished at his doctrine:

29 For he taught them as *one* having authority, and not as the scribes.

from The Koran

Muhammad

The Chapter of the Night Journey.[1]

(XVII. Mecca)

In the name of the merciful and compassionate God.

Celebrated be the praises of Him who took His servant a journey by night from the Sacred Mosque[2] to the Remote Mosque,[3] the precinct of which we have blessed, to show him of our signs! verily, He both hears and looks.

And we gave Moses the Book and made it a guidance to the children of Israel: 'Take ye to no guardian but me.'

Seed of those we bore with Noah (in the ark)! verily, he was a thankful servant!

And we decreed to the children of Israel in the Book, 'Ye shall verily do evil in the earth twice,[4] and ye shall rise to a great height (of pride).'

[5] And when the threat for the first (sin) of the two came, we sent over them servants of ours, endued with violence, and they searched inside your houses; and it was an accomplished threat.

Then we rallied you once more against them, and aided you with wealth and sons, and made you a numerous band.

'If ye do well, ye will do well to your own souls; and if ye do ill, it is against them!'

'And when the threat for the last came[5]—to harm your faces and to enter the mosque as they entered it the first time, and to destroy what they had got the upper-hand over with utter destruction.'

It may be that thy Lord will have mercy on you;—but if ye return we will return, and we have made hell a prison for the misbelievers.

Verily, this Qur'ân [Koran] guides to the straightest path, and gives the glad tidings to the believers

[10] who do aright that for them is a great hire; and that for those who believe not in the hereafter, we have prepared a mighty woe.

Man prays for evil as he prays for good; and man was ever hasty.

We made the night and the day two signs; and we blot out the sign of the night and make the sign of the day visible, that ye may seek after plenty from your Lord, and that ye may number the years and the reckoning; and we have detailed everything in detail.

And every man's augury[6] have we fastened on his neck; and we will bring forth for him on the resurrection day a book offered to him wide open.

[15] 'Read thy book thou art accountant enough against thyself to-day!'

He who accepts guidance, accepts it only for his own soul: and he who errs, errs only against it; nor shall one burdened soul bear the burden of another.

Nor would we punish until we had sent an apostle. And when we desired to destroy a city we bade[7] the opulent ones thereof; and they wrought abomination therein; and its due sentence was pronounced; and we destroyed it with utter destruction.

How many generations have we destroyed after Noah! but thy Lord of the sins of his servant is well aware, and sees enough.

Whoso is desirous of this life that hastens away, we will hasten on for him therein what we please,—for whom we please. Then we will make hell for him to broil in—despised and outcast.

[20] But whoso desires the next life, and strives for it and is a believer—these, their striving shall be gratefully received.

To all—these and those—will we extend the gifts of thy Lord; for the gifts of thy Lord are not restricted.

See how we have preferred some of them over others, but in the next life are greater degrees and greater preference.

Put not with God other gods, or thou wilt sit despised and forsaken.

Thy Lord has decreed that ye shall not serve other than Him; and kindness to one's parents, whether one or both of them reach old age with thee; and say not to them, 'Fie!' and do not grumble at them, but speak to them a generous speech.

[25] And lower to them the wing of humility out of compassion, and say, 'O Lord! have compassion on them as they brought me up when I was little!' Your Lord knows best what is in your souls if ye be righteous, and, verily, He is forgiving unto those who come back penitent.

And give thy kinsman his due and the poor and the son of the road; and waste not wastefully, for the wasteful were ever the devil's brothers; and the devil is ever ungrateful to his Lord.

[30] But if thou dost turn away from them to seek after mercy from thy Lord,[8] which thou hopest for, then speak to them an easy speech.

Make not thy hand fettered to thy neck, nor yet spread it out quite open, lest thou shouldst have to sit down blamed and straitened in means.

Verily, thy Lord spreads out provision to whomsoever He will or He doles it out. Verily, He is ever well aware of and sees His servants.

And slay not your children for fear of poverty; we will provide for them; beware! for to slay them is ever a great sin!

And draw not near to fornication; verily, it is ever an abomination, and evil is the way thereof.

[35] And slay not the soul that God has forbidden you, except for just cause; for he who is slain unjustly we have given his next of kin authority; yet let him not exceed in slaying; verily, he is ever helped.

And draw not near to the wealth of the orphan, save to improve it, until he reaches the age of puberty, and fulfil your compacts; verily, a compact is ever enquired of.

And give full measure when ye measure out, and weigh with a right balance; that is better and a fairer determination.

And do not pursue that of which thou hast no knowledge; verily, the hearing, the sight, and the heart, all of these shall be enquired of.

And walk not on the earth proudly; verily, thou canst not cleave the earth, and thou shalt not reach the mountains in height.

Endnotes

1. Also called "The Children of Israel."
2. The Kaabah at Mecca.
3. The Temple at Jerusalem.
4. The two sins committed by the Jews, and for which punishments were threatened and executed, were, first, the murder of Isaiah and the imprisonment of Jeremiah, and second, the murder of John the Baptist.
5. Supply, "we sent foes."
6. That is, "fortune" or "fate," literally, "bird." The Arabs, like the ancient Romans, used to practice divination from the flight of birds.
7. Bade them obey the Apostle.
8. That is, if you are compelled to leave them in order to seek your livelihood; or if your present means are insufficient to enable you to relieve others.

Translated by E. H. Palmer. © 1900 by Oxford University Press.

Good Will, Duty, and the Categorical Imperative

Immanuel Kant

TRANSLATED BY T. K. ABBOTT

Human beings have desires and appetites. They are also rational, capable of knowing what is right, and capable of willing to do it. They can therefore exercise their wills in the rational control of desire for the purpose of right action. This is what persons of moral worth do. According to Kant, to possess moral worth is more important than to possess intelligence, humor, strength, or any other talent of the mind or body. These talents are valuable but moral worth has *absolute* value, commanding not mere admiration but reverence and respect. Human beings who do right merely because it pleases them are not yet intrinsically moral. For had it pleased them they would have done wrong. To act morally is to act from no other motive than the motive of doing what is right. This kind of motive has nothing to do with anything as subjective as pleasure. To do right out of principle is to recognize an objective right that imposes an obligation on any rational being. Moral persons act in such a way that they could will that the principles of their actions should be universal laws for everyone else as well. This is one test of a moral act: Is it the kind of act that everyone should perform? Kant illustrates how this test can be applied to determine whether a given principle is moral and objective or merely subjective. For example, I may wish to break a promise, but that cannot be moral since I cannot will that promise-breaking be a universal practice.

Universal principles impose *categorical* imperatives. An imperative is a demand that I act in a certain fashion. For example, if I want to buy a house, it is imperative that I learn something about houses. But "Learn about houses!" is a *hypothetical* imperative since it is *conditional* on my wanting to buy a house. A *categorical* imperative is unconditional. An example is "Keep your promises." Thus an imperative is not preceded by any condition such as "if you want a good reputation." Hypothetical imperatives are "prudential": "If you want security,

151

buy theft insurance." Categorical imperatives are moral: "Do not lie!" Kant argues that the categorical imperative presupposes the absolute worth of all rational beings as ends in themselves. Thus another formulation of the categorical imperative is, "So act as to treat humanity . . . as an end withal, never as a means only." Kant calls the domain of beings that are to be treated in this way the "kingdom of ends."

Nothing can possibly be conceived in the world, or even out of it, which can be called good, without qualification, except a Good Will. Intelligence, wit, judgment, and the other *talents* of the mind, however they may be named, or courage, resolution, perseverance, as qualities of temperament, are undoubtedly good and desirable in many respects; but these gifts of nature may also become extremely bad and mischievous if the will which is to make use of them, and which, therefore, constitutes what is called *character,* is not good. It is the same with the *gifts of fortune.* Power, riches, honour, even health, and the general well-being and contentment with one's condition which is called *happiness,* inspire pride, and often presumption, if there is not a good will to correct the influence of these on the mind, and with this also to rectify the whole principle of acting, and adapt it to its end. The sight of a being who is not adorned with a single feature of a pure and good will, enjoying unbroken prosperity, can never give pleasure to an impartial rational spectator. Thus a good will appears to constitute the indispensable condition even of being worthy of happiness.

There are even some qualities which are of service to this good will itself, and may facilitate its action, yet which have no intrinsic unconditional value, but always presuppose a good will, and this qualifies the esteem that we justly have for them, and does not permit us to regard them as absolutely good. Moderation in the affections and passions, self-control, and calm deliberation are not only good in many respects, but even seem to constitute part of the intrinsic worth of the person; but they are far from deserving to be called good without qualification, although they have been so unconditionally praised by the ancients. For without the principles of a good will, they may become extremely bad; and the coolness of a villain not only makes him far more dangerous, but also directly makes him more abominable in our eyes than he would have been without it.

A good will is good not because of what it performs or effects, not by its aptness for the attainment of some proposed end, but simply by virtue of the volition, that is, it is good in itself, and considered by itself is to be esteemed much higher than all that can be brought about by it in favour of any inclination, nay, even of the sum-total of all inclinations. Even if it should happen that, owing to special disfavour of fortune, or the niggardly provision of a step-motherly nature, this will should wholly lack power to accomplish its purpose, if with its greatest efforts it should yet achieve nothing, and there should remain only the good will (not, to be sure, a mere wish, but the summoning of all means in our power), then, like a

Chapter III: Moral Theories and Ethical Perspectives

jewel, it would still shine by its own light, as a thing which has its whole value in itself. Its usefulness or fruitlessness can neither add to nor take away anything from this value.

Thus the moral worth of an action does not lie in the effect expected from it, nor in any principle of action which requires to borrow its motive from this expected effect. For all these effects—agreeableness of one's condition, and even the promotion of the happiness of others—could have been also brought about by other causes, so that for this there would have been no need of the will of a rational being; whereas it is in this alone that the supreme and unconditional good can be found. The pre-eminent good which we call moral can therefore consist in nothing else than *the conception of law* in itself, *which certainly is only possible in a rational being,* in so far as this conception, and not the expected effect, determines the will. This is a good which is already present in the person who acts accordingly, and we have not to wait for it to appear first in the result.

But what sort of law can that be, the conception of which must determine the will, even without paying any regard to the effect expected from it, in order that this will may be called good absolutely and without qualification? As I have deprived the will of every impulse which could arise to it from obedience to any law, there remains nothing but the universal conformity of its actions to law in general, which alone is to serve the will as a principle, *i.e.* I am never to act otherwise than *so that I could also will that my maxim should become a universal law.* Here, now, it is the simple conformity to law in general, without assuming any particular law applicable to certain actions, that serves the will as its principle, and must so serve it, if duty is not to be a vain delusion and a chimerical notion. The common reason of men in its practical judgments perfectly coincides with this and always has in view the principle here suggested. Let the question be, for example: May I when in distress make a promise with the intention not to keep it? I readily distinguish here between the two significations which the question may have: Whether it is prudent, or whether it is right, to make a false promise? The former may undoubtedly often be the case. I see clearly indeed that it is not enough to extricate myself from a present difficulty by means of this subterfuge, but it must be well considered whether there may not hereafter spring from this lie much greater inconvenience than that from which I now free myself, and as, with all my supposed *cunning,* the consequences cannot be so easily foreseen but that credit once lost may be much more injurious to me than any mischief which I seek to avoid at present, it should be considered whether it would not be more *prudent* to act herein according to a universal maxim, and to make it a habit to promise nothing except with the intention of keeping it. But it is soon clear to me that such a maxim will still only be based on the fear of consequences. Now it is a wholly different thing to be truthful from duty, and to be so from apprehension of injurious consequences. In the first case, the very notion of the action already implies a law for me; in the second case, I must first look about elsewhere to see what results may be combined with it which would affect myself. For to deviate from the principle of duty is beyond all doubt wicked; but to be unfaithful to my maxim of prudence may often be very advantageous to me, although to abide by it is certainly safer. The shortest way, however, and an unerring one, to discover the answer to this question whether a lying promise is consistent with duty, is to ask myself, Should I be content that my maxim (to extricate myself from difficulty by a false promise) should hold good as a universal law, for myself as well as for others? And should I be able to say to myself, "Everyone may make a deceitful promise when he finds himself in a difficulty from which he cannot otherwise extricate himself"? Then I presently become aware that while I can will the lie, I can by no means will that lying should be a universal law. For with such a law there would be no promises at all, since it would be in vain to allege my intention in regard to my future actions to those who would not believe this allegation, or if they overhastily did so, would pay me back in my own coin. Hence my maxim, as soon as it should be made a universal law, would necessarily destroy itself.

I do not, therefore, need any far-reaching penetration to discern what I have to do in order that my will be morally good. Inexperienced in the course of the world, incapable of being prepared for all its contingencies, I only ask myself: Canst thou also will that thy maxim should be a universal law? If not, then it must be rejected, and that not because of a disadvantage accruing from it to myself or even to others, but because it cannot enter as a principle into a possible universal legislation and reason extorts from me immediate respect for such legislation. I do not indeed as yet *discern* on what this respect is based (this the philosopher may inquire), but at least I understand this, that it is an estimation of the worth which far outweighs all worth of what is recommended by inclination, and that the necessity of acting from *pure* respect for the practical law is what constitutes duty, to which every other motive must give place, because it is the condition of a will being good *in itself*, and the worth of such a will is above everything. . . .

. . . Everything in nature works according to laws. Rational beings alone have the faculty of acting according *to the conception* of laws, that is according to principles, *i.e.* have a *will*. Since the deduction of actions from principles requires *reason*, the will is nothing but practical reason. If reason infallibly determines the will, then the actions of such a being which are recognized as objectively necessary are subjectively necessary also, *i.e.* the will is a faculty to choose *that only* which reason independent on inclination recognizes as practically necessary, *i.e.* as good. But if reason of itself does not sufficiently determine the will, if the latter is subject also to subjective conditions (particular impulses) which do not always coincide with the objective conditions; in a word, if the will does not *in itself* completely accord with reason (which is actually the case with men), then the actions which objectively are recognized as necessary are subjectively contingent, and the determination of such a will according to objective laws is *obligation*, that is to say, the relation of the objective laws to a will that is not thoroughly good is conceived as the determination of the will of a rational being by principles of reason, but which the will from its nature does not of necessity follow.

The conception of an objective principle, in so far as it is obligatory for a will, is called a command (of reason), and the formula of the command is called an Imperative. . . .

Now all *imperatives* command either *hypothetically* or *categorically*. The former represent the practical necessity of a possible action as means to something else that is willed (or at least which one might possibly will). The categorical imperative would be that which represented an action as necessary of itself without reference to another end, *i.e.* as objectively necessary.

Since every practical law represents a possible action as good, and on this account, for a subject who is practically determinable by reason, necessary, all imperatives are formulae determining an action which is necessary according to the principle of a will good in some respects. If now the action is good only as a means to *something else*, then the imperative is *hypothetical;* if it is conceived as good *in itself* and consequently as being necessarily the principle of a will which of itself conforms to reason, then it is *categorical*. . . .

When I conceive a hypothetical imperative, in general I do not know beforehand what it will contain until I am given the condition. But when I conceive a categorical imperative, I know at once what it contains. For as the imperative contains besides the law only the necessity that the maxims shall conform to this law, while the law contains no conditions restricting it, there remains nothing but the general statement that the maxim of the action should conform to a universal law, and it is this conformity alone that the imperative properly represents as necessary.

There is . . . but one categorical imperative, namely, this: *Act only on that maxim whereby thou canst at the same time will that it should become a universal law*.

Now if all imperatives of duty can be deduced from this one imperative as from their principle, then, although it should remain undecided whether what is called duty is not merely a vain notion, yet at least we shall be able to show what we understand by it and what this notion means.

Since the universality of the law according to which effects are produced constitutes what is properly called *nature* in the most general sense (as to form), that is the existence of things so far as it is determined by general laws, the imperative of duty may be expressed thus: *Act as if the maxim of thy action were to become by thy will a universal law of nature*.

We will now enumerate a few duties, adopting the usual division of them into duties to ourselves and to others, and into perfect and imperfect duties.

1. A man reduced to despair by a series of misfortunes feels wearied of life, but is still so far in possession of his reason that he can ask himself whether it would not be contrary to his duty to himself to take his own life. Now he inquires whether the maxim of his action could become a universal law of nature. His maxim is: From self-love I adopt it as a principle to shorten my life when its longer duration is likely to bring more evil than satisfaction. It is asked then simply whether this principle founded on self-love can become a universal law of nature. Now we see at once that a system of nature of which it should be a law to destroy life by means of the very feeling whose special nature it is to impel to the improvement of life would contradict itself, and therefore could not exist as a system of nature; hence that maxim cannot possibly exist as a universal law of nature, and consequently would be wholly inconsistent with the supreme principle of all duty.

2. Another finds himself forced by necessity to borrow money. He knows that he will not be able to repay it, but sees also that nothing will be lent to him, unless he promises stoutly to repay it in a definite time. He desires to make this promise, but he has still so much conscience as to ask himself: Is it not unlawful and inconsistent with duty to get out of a difficulty in this way? Suppose, however, that he resolves to do so, then the maxim of his action would be expressed thus: When I think myself in want of money, I will borrow money and promise to repay it, although I know that I never can do so. Now this principle of self-love or of one's own advantage may perhaps be consistent with my whole future welfare; but the question now is: Is it right? I change then the suggestion of self-love into a universal law, and state the question thus: How would it be if my maxim were a universal law? Then I see at once that it could never hold as a universal law of nature, but would necessarily contradict itself. For supposing it to be a universal law that everyone when he thinks himself in a difficulty should be able to promise whatever he pleases, with the purpose of not keeping his promise, the promise itself would become impossible, as well as the end that one might have in view in it, since no one would consider that anything was promised to him, but would ridicule all such statements as vain pretences.

3. A third finds in himself a talent which with the help of some culture might make him a useful man in many respects. But he finds himself in comfortable circumstances, and prefers to indulge in pleasure rather than to take pains in enlarging and improving his happy natural capacities. He asks, however, whether his maxim of neglect of his natural gifts, besides agreeing with his inclination to indulgence, agrees also with what is called duty. He sees then that a system of nature could indeed subsist with such

a universal law although men (like the South Sea islanders) should let their talents rest, and resolve to devote their lives merely to idleness, amusement, and propagation of their species—in a word, to enjoyment; but he cannot possibly *will* that this should be a universal law of nature, or be implanted in us as such by a natural instinct. For, as a rational being, he necessarily wills that his faculties be developed, since they serve him, and have been given him, for all sorts of possible purposes.

4. A fourth, who is in prosperity, while he sees that others have to contend with great wretchedness and that he could help them, thinks: What concern is it of mine? Let everyone be as happy as Heaven pleases, or as he can make himself; I will take nothing from him nor even envy him, only I do not wish to contribute anything to his welfare or to his assistance in distress! Now no doubt if such a mode of thinking were a universal law, the human race might very well subsist, and doubtless even better than in a state in which everyone talks of sympathy and good-will, or even takes care occasionally to put it into practice, but, on the other side, also cheats when he can, betrays the rights of men, or otherwise violates them. But although it is possible that a universal law of nature might exist in accordance with that maxim, it is impossible to *will* that such a principle should have the universal validity of a law of nature. For a will which resolved this would contradict itself, inasmuch as many cases might occur in which one would have need of the love and sympathy of others, and in which, by such a law of nature, sprung from his own will, he would deprive himself of all hope of the aid he desires. . . .

We have thus established at least this much, that if duty is a conception which is to have any import and real legislative authority for our actions, it can only be expressed in categorical, and not at all in hypothetical imperatives. We have also, which is of great importance, exhibited clearly and definitely for every practical application the content of the categorical imperative, which must contain the principle of all duty if there is such a thing at all. We have not yet, however, advanced so far as to prove *a priori* that there actually is such an imperative, that there is a practical law which commands absolutely of itself, and without any other impulse, and that the following of this law is duty. . . .

Now I say: man and generally any rational being exists as an end in himself, *not merely as a means* to be arbitrarily used by this or that will, but in all his actions, whether they concern himself or other rational beings, must be always regarded at the same time as an end. All objects of the inclinations have only a conditional worth; for if the inclinations and the wants founded on them did not exist, then their object would be without value. But the inclinations themselves being sources of want are so far from having an absolute worth for which they should be desired, that, on the contrary, it must be the universal wish of every rational being to be wholly free from them. Thus the worth of any object which is *to be ac-*

quired by our action is always conditional. Beings whose existence depends not on our will but on nature's, have nevertheless, if they are non-rational beings, only a relative value as means, and are therefore called *things;* rational beings, on the contrary, are called *persons,* because their very nature points them out as ends in themselves, that is as something which must not be used merely as means, and so far therefore restricts freedom of action (and is an object of respect). These, therefore, are not merely subjective ends whose existence has a worth *for us* as an effort of our action, but *objective ends,* that is things whose existence is an end in itself: an end moreover for which no other can be substituted, which they should subserve *merely* as means, for otherwise nothing whatever would possess *absolute worth;* but if all worth were conditioned and therefore contingent, then there would be no supreme practical principle of reason whatever.

If then there is a supreme practical principle or, in respect of the human will, a categorical imperative, it must be one which, being drawn from the conception of that which is necessarily an end for everyone because it is an *an end in itself,* constitutes an *objective* principle of will, and can therefore serve as a universal practical law. The foundation of this principle is: *rational nature exists as an end in itself.* Man necessarily conceives his own existence as being so: so far then this is a *subjective* principle of human actions. But every other rational being regards its existence similarly, just on the same rational principle, that holds for me: so that it is at the same time an objective principle, from which as a supreme practical law all laws of the will must be capable of being deduced. Accordingly the practical imperative will be as follows: *So act as to treat humanity, whether in thine own person or in that of any other, in every case as an end withal, never as means only.* . . .

The conception of every rational being as one which must consider itself as giving all the maxims of its will universal laws, so as to judge itself and its actions from this point of view—this conception leads to another which depends on it and is very fruitful, namely, that of a *kingdom of ends.*

By a *kingdom* I understand the union of different rational beings in a system by common laws. Now since it is by laws that ends are determined as regards their universal validity, hence, if we abstract from the personal differences of rational beings, and likewise from all the content of their private ends, we shall be able to conceive all ends combined in a systematic whole (including both rational beings as ends in themselves, and also the special ends which each may propose of himself), that is to say, we can conceive a kingdom of ends, which on the preceding principles is possible.

For all rational beings come under the *law* that each of them must treat itself and all others *never merely as means,* but in every case *at the same time as ends in themselves.* Hence results a systematic union of rational beings by common objective laws, *i.e.* a kingdom which may be called a kingdom of ends. . . .

GOOD WILL, DUTY, AND THE CATEGORICAL IMPERATIVE *From Fundamental Principles of the Metaphysics of Morals,* by Immanuel Kant. Translated by T. K. Abbott (1898).

Intuition: A Foundation For Moral Principles

Robert Lorek

The appeal to intuitions is a popular, yet controversial avenue in ethical and moral reasoning. It is clearly a recognized method in ethics; but is it rational to give credence to the value of intuitions as a foundation for moral principles? Moral intuitionism claims that it is appropriate and rational to appeal to intuitions in the course of ethical reasoning, even though these intuitions are not based on, or supported by, other beliefs. Certainly, many intuitive claims regarding ethical behavior are the result of biases and incomplete knowledge, and it would be irrational to stand firmly by a principle based solely on bias and incomplete knowledge.

It may be objected that intuitions cannot stand on their own, that they do not have any intrinsic value. Intuitions are valuable not because they are intrinsically valuable, but because they are valued. One can correctly state; intuitions cannot stand on their own, if standing on their own entails that they possess intrinsic value. Just as any belief cannot exist in isolation from other beliefs, intuitions occur within the context of circumstance. They stand on their own in a limited sense. The sense in which intuitions stand on their own stems from their immediacy. Why is immediacy a remark about plausibility, and how does this make intuition foundational in the formation of other justified true beliefs? The immediacy of intuitions entails that they are non-inferential, and pre-theoretical. "In claiming that intuitions are non-inferential, one is claiming that they are not grounded in premises."[1] The sceptical argument against non-inferential justification states: If intuited propositions are not grounded in premises then what we know intuitively, is ultimately unprovable. The sceptic will find the claim that intuitions are not grounded in premises, is not an asset in showing them to be foundational. The sceptical argument must be addressed.

We have an intuitive sense regarding certain moral principles without theorizing about the situation at hand. We have an immediate sense when a prima facie justification is right, as there are also immediate reasons to defeat, override, or outweigh our justification. A common example is my legal and moral obligation to fulfill a promise. When I borrow an item from someone with the implicit intent to return that item when finished, I am obligated to keep my promise. I must return a knife to its owner, due to the prima facie reason that I have an obligation to fulfill my promises. However, the owner of the knife is mentally ill, and has a tendency to become irrationally violent. Intuitively, I defeat my prima facie reason to fulfill a promise and replace it with the better judgement not to return the knife. This judgement to break my promise overrides our previous reason to keep promises, therefore, keeping the knife is the prima facie good. By employing intuitive knowledge relating to fundamental principles of right and wrong, one is able to make a justified moral choice. Our intuition of right and wrong may be fallible; yet our intuition is immediate and it precedes any form of conscious reflection. Referring to intuitive knowledge John Kekes claims: "There is no conscious inference, reflection, or thought in intuiting some situations. The agent spontaneously, instantly, and automatically perceives them that way."[2]

The seeing of facts in and immediate way is a sudden realization or intuition. There exists a point which the facts form a pattern for the agent who came to see those facts as foundational to a justified true belief. What one may intuit, others may realize only after conscious reflection. The limited way in which intuitions stand on their own is their immediate, self evident, yet fallible status. A powerful example of an appeal to our basic moral intuition is the story *The Lottery* by Shirley Jackson; here the author provides a case that appeals to our immediate sense of right and wrong. A rural town holds a traditional yearly lottery, in which the person unfortunate enough to draw a marked piece of paper is stoned to death. All of the townspeople dread the day when they themselves, or their loved ones are chosen in the lottery; yet the practice continues solely because of tradition. The story appeals to our sense of justice. The duty not to harm is a prima facie duty, and the duty to uphold tradition has secondary status to this primary duty. Intuition tells us that the duty not to harm someone overrides an irrational and unjust tradition; therefore we are repulsed and frightened at the prospect of a person being stoned to death for picking the wrong card in a lottery. It is immediately self evident to the reader of *The Lottery*, that there is definitely something wrong with a woman being stoned to death simply because of tradition. The reader of this story does not analyze or form premises, the readers intuit that something is wrong because they are shocked by the townfolk's reasoning.

Is it rational to accept a possibly incorrect intuition to establish a general moral principle? How does one say that some actions are right and certain things are good, when we cannot define 'good'? We may have an intuitive knowledge regarding the universal concept 'good' and we actually rationalize which particular items are good based on that intuitive foundation. Although the intuition may be fallible, we still appeal to that intuition; the fact of the matter being, no other evidence proves that intuition correct, and that intuition is foundational. Nelson Goodman offers a similar view for logic; "we change a general principle which yields particular problems we are not willing to accept, and reject those judgements that violate principles we are not willing to change."[3] In other words, we give the greatest preference to the general principle and judgements resulting from the principle or principles that we are most willing to accept, one that has the greatest intuitive appeal based on our knowledge. Intuitional justification of which actions are right and which things are good, is dependant on circumstances, knowledge, experience, and other factors that may bias their appeal. Intuitions are foundational in forming the universal concepts of right and wrong. Experience, and rational analysis tells us what particular things are good, and which action is right. We observe that intelligent, rational people behave in a certain manner. Our intuitions are often shared by others, thus reinforcing our beliefs, and giving us little reason to doubt them. Most people's intuitions tell them that a lottery in which one person is chosen to die at the hands of her friends, neighbors, and loved ones, is unacceptable. However, we may be biased because we would not want to be the victim; and the story gives us reason to empathize with the victim, not with the townspeople for whom upholding tradition is of the utmost importance.

However biased or fallible it may be to appeal to intuitions to establish general moral principles, it is nonetheless rational to do so. If general moral principles could be established only by that which we could prove with certainty, then moral principles would be difficult, if not impossible, to establish. It is downright irrational to accept only those facts which can be known with certainty. Moral intuitionism does not claim intuitions are dogmatic assertions about the non-evident. Traditional intuitionism may imply such a dogmatic approach. However, intuitions need to be accepted as fallible and defeasible. In maintaining the belief in the strength of an intuition, we generally try to add additional data about which we are fairly certain, and eliminate inconsistencies with other knowledge and beliefs that we find acceptable. When we eliminate inconsistent beliefs arising from our intuitions, we do this by accepting the fallibility of our intuitions, realizing the need to revise our justification or totally discounting the intuition that is leading us into error.

If we claim intuitions are a foundation for ethical reasoning, we are espousing a form of foundationalism. Intuitions will require some sort of positive epistemic status, if they are to yield knowledge.[4] Just as traditional intuitionism has been revised by Ross, Rawls, and others, foundationalism can be revised to allow an intuition to be a foundation and to be justified, even if that intuition may be fallible. Such a form of foundationalism allows for a coherence of values as in reflective equilibrium, and for fallible intuitions to be a foundation for ethical reasoning.[5] Ross's intuitionist theory is plausible if foundationalism allows for the fallibility of intuitions. If Rawls's theory of reflective equilibrium does not provide a necessary condition for the acceptance of ethical principles, but only a sufficient condition, then intuitions still play a major role in ethical reasoning. Intuitions are fallible and are regarded as a foundation for the ethical principles achieved through reflective equilibrium. Some might claim that intuitions, if they are foundational, must stand on their own, because that is what we mean by foundational. Radical foundationalism, such as the foundationalism represented in Descartes' scepticism, requires that foundational beliefs stand on their own and be able to guarantee the certainty of non-foundational beliefs. A modest foundationalism, in which intuitions can be non-inferential foundational beliefs, is the justification for moral principles. Intuitions do stand on their own, however it is only in the limited sense of their immediacy. Intuitional immediacy is definitely primitive, in that there exists no underlying process of reasoning. One infers a conclusion from a premise with immediacy because that premise does not depend on other premises. It is in this sense that intuitions possess their epistemic status as foundational to moral reasoning. Furthermore, beliefs, facts, and all data related to the formation of ethical principles do not stand on their own in the strict sense. Intuitions, beliefs, and facts occur within a context. Intuitions are the insights into facts, not the facts themselves. A strict form of foundationalism does not allow for a coherence of facts, beliefs, and other knowledge claims. Thus it assumes the traditional dogmatic form of intuitionism.

We have good reason to conclude that intuition is a justified foundation for moral principles. If we agree that intuitions are fallible, and defeasible, we can also assume that ethical principles are capable of being revised when conflicting justifications force us to reassess our beliefs. Intuitions are foundational for ethical reasoning, but not in the strict sense that traditional foundationalism requires. Intuitions are foundational, if our form of foundationalism allows us to justify our beliefs even though they may be falsified.

Endnotes

1. Robert Audi."Ethical Reflectionism" Manuscript presented at the University of Nebraska 1993.
2. John Kekes. "Moral Intuition" *American Philosophical Quarterly* Jan 1986 p. 85. Kekes regards intuitions as interpretive rather than merely descriptive. We often misjudge the significance of the facts because of our interpretations.
3. Richard Brandt. *The Theory of the Good and the Right* Clarendon Press Oxford 1979. p.18. Brandt makes reference to Nelson Goodman's *Fact, Fiction, and*

Forecast Bobbs-Merrill Indianapolis Ind. 1965 p. 64. Brandt uses Goodman's view on logic to explain the method in which we appeal to ethical intuitions.
4. Mark Nelson. *Intuitionism and Subjectivism* "Metaphilosophy" Jan/Apr 1991 p. 116. Nelson refers to Richard' Hare's objection to intuitionism.
5. Robert Audi. "The Foundationalism-Coherentism Controversy" Manuscript presented in Seminar on Rationality. University of Nebraska. 1993 From *The Structure of Justification* Cambridge Press 1993. Robert Audi refers to a moderate form of foundationalism or "Fallibilistic Foundationalism."

The Principle of Utility

Jeremy Bentham

Of the Principle of Utility

Nature has placed mankind under the governance of two sovereign masters, *pain* and *pleasure*. It is for them alone to point out what we ought to do, as well as to determine what we shall do. On the one hand the standard of right and wrong, on the other the chain of causes and effects, are fastened to their throne. They govern us in all we do, in all we say, in all we think: every effort we can make to throw off our subjection, will serve but to demonstrate and confirm it. In words a man may pretend to abjure their empire: but in reality he will remain subject to it all the while. The *principle of utility* recognizes this subjection, and assumes it for the foundation of that system, the object of which is to rear the fabric of felicity by the hands of reason and of law. Systems which attempt to question it, deal in sounds instead of sense, in caprice instead of reason, in darkness instead of light.

But enough of metaphor and declamation: it is not by such means that moral science is to be improved.

The principle of utility is the foundation of the present work; it will be proper therefore at the outset to give an explicit and determinate account of what is meant by it. By the principle of utility is meant that principle which approves or disapproves of every action whatsoever, according to the tendency which it appears to have to augment or diminish the happiness of the party whose interest is in question: or, what is the same thing in other words, to promote or to oppose that happiness. I say of every action whatsoever; and therefore not only of every action of a private individual, but of every measure of government.

By utility is meant that property in any object, whereby it tends to produce benefit, advantage, pleasure, good, or happiness, (all this in the present case comes to the same thing) or (what comes again to the same thing) to prevent the happening of mischief, pain, evil, or unhappiness to the party whose interest is considered: if that party be the community in general, then the happiness of the community: if a particular individual, then the happiness of that individual.

The interest of the community is one of the most general expressions that can occur in the phraseology of morals: no wonder that the meaning of it is often lost. When it has a meaning, it is this. The community is a fictitious *body*, composed of the individual persons who are considered as constituting as it were its *members*. The interest of the community then is, what?—the sum of the interests of the several members who compose it.

It is in vain to talk of the interests of the community, without understanding what is the interest of the individual. A thing is said to promote the interest, or to be *for* the interest, of an individual, when it tends to add to the sum total of his pleasures: or, what comes to the same thing, to diminish the sum total of his pains.

An action then may be said to be conformable to the principle of utility, or, for shortness sake, to utility (meaning with respect to the community at large), when the tendency it has to augment the happiness of the community is greater than any it has to diminish it.

A measure of government (which is but a particular kind of action, performed by a particular person or persons) may be said to be conformable to or dictated by the principle of utility when in like manner the tendency which it has to augment the happiness of the community is greater than any which it has to diminish it.

When an action, or in particular a measure of government, is supposed by a man to be conformable to the principle of utility, it may be convenient, for the purposes of discourse, to imagine a kind of law or dictate, called a law or dictate of utility: and to speak of the action in question, as being conformable to such law or dictate.

A man may be said to be a partisan of the principle of utility, when the approbation or disapprobation he annexes to any action, or to any measure, is determined by and proportioned to the tendency which he conceives it to have to augment or to diminish the happiness of the community: or in other words, to its conformity or unconformity to the laws or dictates of utility.

Of an action that is conformable to the principle of utility one may always say either that it is one that ought to be done, or at least that it is not one that ought not to be done. One may say also, that it is right it should be done; at least that it is not wrong it should be done: that it is a right action; at least that it is not a wrong action. When thus interpreted, the words *ought*, and *right* and *wrong*, and others of that stamp, have a meaning: when otherwise, they have none.

Has the rectitude of this principle been ever formally contested? It should seem that it had, by those who have not known what they have been meaning. Is it susceptible of any direct proof? It should seem not: for that which is used to prove every thing else, cannot itself be proved: a chain of proofs must have their commencement somewhere. To give such proof is as impossible as it is needless.

Not that there is or ever has been that human creature breathing, however stupid or perverse, who has not on many, perhaps on most occasions of his life, deferred to it. By the natural constitution of the human frame, on most occasions of their lives men in general embrace this principle, without thinking of it: if not for the ordering of their own actions, yet for the trying of their own actions, as well as of those of other men. There have been, at the same time, not many, perhaps, even of the most intelligent, who have been disposed to embrace it purely and without reserve. There are even few who have not taken some occasion or other to quarrel with it, either on account of their not understanding always how to apply it, or on account of some prejudice or other which they were afraid to examine into, or could not bear to part with. For such is the stuff that man is made of: in principle and in practice, in a right track and in a wrong one, the rarest of all human qualities is consistency.

When a man attempts to combat the principle of utility, it is with reasons drawn, without his being aware of it, from that very principle itself. His arguments, if they prove any thing, prove not that the principle is *wrong*, but that, according to the applications he supposes to be made of it, it is *misapplied*. Is it possible for a man to move the earth? Yes; but he must first find out another earth to stand upon.

To disprove the propriety of it by arguments is impossible; but, from the causes that have been mentioned, or from some confused or partial view of it, a man may happen to be disposed not to relish it. Where this is the case, if he thinks the settling of his opinions on such a subject worth the trouble, let him take the following steps, and at length, perhaps, he may come to reconcile himself to it.

Let him settle with himself, whether he would wish to discard this principle altogether; if so, let him consider what it is that all his reasonings (in matters of politics especially) can amount to?

If he would, let him settle with himself whether he would judge and act without any principle, or whether there is any other he would judge and act by?

If there be, let him examine and satisfy himself whether the principle he thinks he has found is really any separate intelligible principle; or whether it be not a mere principle in words, a kind of phrase, which at bottom expresses neither more nor less than the mere averment of his own unfounded sentiments; that is, what in another person he might be apt to call caprice?

If he is inclined to think that his own approbation or disapprobation, annexed to the idea of an act, without any regard to its consequences, is a sufficient foundation for him to judge and act upon, let him ask himself whether his sentiment is to be a standard of right and wrong, with respect to every other man, or whether every man's sentiment has the same privilege of being a standard to itself?

In the first case, let him ask himself whether his principle is not despotical, and hostile to all the rest of human race?

In the second case, whether it is not anarchical, and whether at this rate there are not as many different standards of right and wrong as there are men? and whether even to the same man, the same thing, which is right to-day, may not (without the least change in its nature) be wrong to-morrow? and whether the same thing is not right and wrong in the same place at the same time? and in either case, whether all argument is not at an end? and whether, when two men have said, "I like this;" and "I don't like it;" they can (upon such a principle) have any thing more to say?

If he should have said to himself, No: for that the sentiment which he proposes as a standard must be grounded on reflection, let him say on what particulars the reflection is to turn? if on particulars having relation to the utility of the act, then let him say whether this is not deserting his own principle and borrowing assistance from that very one in opposition to which he sets it up: or if not on those particulars, on what other particulars?

If he should be for compounding the matter, and adopting his own principle in part, and the principle of utility in part, let him say how far he will adopt it?

When he has settled with himself where he will stop; then let him ask himself how he justifies to himself the adopting it so far? and why he will not adopt it any farther?

Admitting any other principle than the principle of utility to be a right principle, a principle that it is right for a man to pursue; admitting (what is not true) that the word *right* can have a meaning without reference to utility, let him say whether there is any such thing as a *motive* that a man can have to pursue the dictates of it: if there is, let him say what that motive is, and how it is to be distinguished from those which enforce the dictates of utility: if not, then lastly let him say what it is this other principle can be good for?

▨ ▨ ▨

Pleasures then, and the avoidance of pains, are the *ends* which the legislator has in view: it behooves him therefore to understand their *value*. Pleasures and pains are the *instruments* he has to work with: it behooves him therefore to understand their force, which is again, in other words, their value.

To a person considered *by himself*, the value of a pleasure or pain considered *by itself*, will be greater or less, according to the four following circumstances:

1. Its *intensity*.
2. Its *duration*.
3. Its *certainty* or *uncertainty*.
4. Its *propinquity* or *remoteness*.

These are the circumstances which are to be considered in estimating a pleasure or a pain considered each of them by itself. But when the value of any pleasure or pain is considered for the purpose of estimating the tendency of any *act* by which it is produced, there are two other circumstances to be taken into the account; these are,

5. Its *fecundity* or the chance it has of being followed by sensations of the same, kind: that is, pleasures, if it be a pleasure: pains, if it be a pain.
6. Its *purity* or the chance it has of not being followed by sensations of the opposite kind: that is, pains, if it be a pleasure: pleasures, if it be a pain.

These two last, however, are in strictness scarcely to be deemed properties of the pleasure or the pain itself; they are not, therefore, in strictness to be taken into the account of the value of that pleasure or that pain. They are in strictness to be deemed properties only of the act, or other event, by which such pleasure or pain has been produced; and accordingly are only to be taken into the account of the tendency of such act or such event.

To a *number* of persons, with reference to each of whom the value of a pleasure or a pain is considered, it will be greater or less, according to seven circumstances: to wit, the six preceding ones; *viz.*

1. Its *intensity*.
2. Its *duration*.
3. Its *certainty* or *uncertainty*.
4. Its *propinquity* or *remoteness*.
5. Its *fecundity*.
6. Its *purity*.

And one other; to wit:

7. Its *extent*; that is, the number of persons to whom it *extends*; or (in other words) who are affected by it.

To take an exact account then of the general tendency of any act, by which the interests of a community are affected, proceed as follows. Begin with any one person of those whose interest seem most immediately to be affected by it: and take an account,

1. Of the value of each distinguishable *pleasure* which appears to be produced by it in the *first* instance.
2. Of the value of each *pain* which appears to be produced by it in the *first* instance.

3. Of the value of each pleasure which appears to be produced by it *after* the first. This constitutes the *fecundity* of the first *pleasure* and the *impurity* of the first pain.
4. Of the value of each *pain* which appears to be produced by it after the first. This constitutes the *fecundity* of the first *pain*, and the *impurity* of the first pleasure.
5. Sum up all the values of all the *pleasures* on the one side, and those of all the pains on the other. The balance, if it be on the side of pleasure, will give the *good* tendency of the act upon the whole, with respect to the interests of that *individual* person; if on the side of pain, the *bad* tendency of it upon the whole.
6. Take an account of the *number* of persons whose interests appear to be concerned; and repeat the above process with respect to each. *Sum* up the numbers expressive of the degrees of *good* tendency, which the act has, with respect to each individual, in regard to whom the tendency of it is *good* upon the whole: do this again with respect to each individual, in regard to whom the tendency of it is *bad* upon the whole. Take the *balance*; which, if on the side of *pleasure*, will give the general *good tendency* of the act, with respect to the total number or community of individuals concerned; if on the side of pain, the general *evil tendency*, with respect to the same community.

It is not to be expected that this process should be strictly pursued previously to every moral judgment, or to every legislative or judicial operation. It may, however, be always kept in view: and as near as the process actually pursued on these occasions approaches to it, so near will such process approach to the character of an exact one.

The same process is alike applicable to pleasure and pain, in whatever shape they appear: and by whatever denomination they are distinguished: to pleasure, whether it be called *good* (which is properly the cause or instrument of pleasure) or *profit* (which is distant pleasure, or the cause or instrument of distant pleasure), or *convenience*, or *advantage*, *benefit*, *emolument*, *happiness*, and so forth; to pain, whether it be called *evil* (which corresponds to good), or *mischief*, or *inconvenience*, or *disadvantage*, or *loss*, or *unhappiness*, and so forth.

Nor is this a novel and unwarranted, any more than it is a useless theory. In all this there is nothing but what the practice of mankind, whatsoever they have a clear view of their own interest, is perfectly conformable to. An article of property, an estate in land, for instance, is valuable, on what account? On account of the pleasures of all kinds which it enables a man to produce, and what comes to the same thing the pains of all kinds which it enables him to avert. But the value of such an article of property is universally understood to rise or fall according to the length or shortness of the time which a man has in it: the certainty or uncertainty of its coming into possession: and the nearness or remoteness of the time at which, if at all, it is to come into possession. As to the *intensity* of the pleasures which a man may derive from it, this is never thought of, because it depends upon the use which each particular person may come to make of it; which cannot be estimated till the particular pleasures he may come to derive from it, or the particular pains he may come to exclude by means of it, are brought to view. For the same reason, neither does he think of the *fecundity* or *purity* of those pleasures.

THE PRINCIPLE OF UTILITY Excerpted from Jeremy Bentham, *The Principles of Morals and Legislation* (1789).

Humans Are Always Selfish
(The Ring of Gyges)

Plato

. . . First, I will state what is commonly held about the nature of justice and its origin; secondly, I shall maintain that it is always practiced with reluctance, not as good in itself, but as a thing one cannot do without; and thirdly, that this reluctance is reasonable, because the life of injustice is much the better life of the two—so people say. . . . Accordingly, I shall set an example by glorifying the life of injustice with all the energy that I hope you will show later in denouncing it and exalting justice in its stead. Will that plan suit you?

Nothing could be better, I replied. Of all subjects this is one on which a sensible man must always be glad to exchange ideas.

Good, said Glaucon. Listen then, and I will begin with my first point: the nature and origin of justice.

What people say is that to do wrong is, in itself, a desirable thing; on the other hand, it is not at all desirable to suffer wrong, and the harm to the sufferer outweighs the advantage to the doer. Consequently, when men have had a taste of both, those who have not the power to seize the advantage and escape the harm decide that they would be better off if they made a compact neither to do wrong nor to suffer it. Hence they began to make laws and covenants with one another; and whatever the law prescribed they called lawful and right. That is what right or justice is and how it came into existence; it stands half-way between the best thing of all—to do wrong with impunity—and the worst, which is to suffer wrong without the power to retaliate. So justice is accepted as a compromise, and valued, not as good in itself, but for lack of power to do wrong; no man worthy of the name, who had that power, would ever enter into such a compact with anyone; he would be mad if he did. That, Socrates, is the nature of justice according to this account, and such the circumstances in which it arose.

Chapter III: Moral Theories and Ethical Perspectives

The next point is that men practice it against the grain, for lack of power to do wrong. How true that is, we shall best see if we imagine two men, one just, the other unjust, given full license to do whatever they like, and then follow them to observe where each will be led by his desires. We shall catch the just man taking the same road as the unjust; he will be moved by self-interest, the end which it is natural to every creature to pursue as good, until forcibly turned aside by law and custom to respect the principle of equality.

Now, the easiest way to give them that complete liberty of action would be to imagine them possessed of the talisman found by Gyges, the ancestor of the famous Lydian. The story tells how he was a shepherd in the King's service. One day there was a great storm, and the ground where his flock was feeding was rent by an earthquake. Astonished at the sight, he went down into the chasm and saw, among other wonders of which the story tells, a brazen horse, hollow, with windows in its sides. Peering in, he saw a dead body, which seemed to be of more than human size. It was naked save for a gold ring, which he took from the finger and made his way out. When the shepherds met, as they did every month, to send an account to the King of the state of his flocks, Gyges came wearing the ring. As he was sitting with the others, he happened to turn the bezel of the ring inside his hand. At once he became invisible, and his companions, to his surprise, began to speak of him as if he had left them. Then, as he was fingering the ring, he turned the bezel outwards and became visible again. With that, he set about testing the ring to see if it really had this power, and always with the same result: according as he turned the bezel inside or out he vanished and reappeared. After this discovery he contrived to be one of the messengers sent to the court. There he seduced the Queen, and with her help murdered the King and seized the throne.

Now suppose there were two such magic rings, and one were given to the just man, the other to the unjust. No one, it is commonly believed, would have such iron strength of mind as to stand fast in doing right or keep his hands off other men's goods, when he could go to the marketplace and fearlessly help himself to anything he wanted, enter houses and sleep with any woman he chose, set prisoners free and kill men at his pleasure, and in a word go about among men with the powers of a god. He would behave no better than the other; both would take the same course. Surely this would be strong proof that men do right only under compulsion; no individual thinks of it as good for him personally, since he does wrong whenever he finds he has the power. Every man believes that wrongdoing pays him personally much better, and, according to this theory, that is the truth. Granted full license to do as he liked, people would think him a miserable fool if they found him refusing to wrong his neighbors or to touch their belongings, though in public they would keep up a pretence of praising his conduct, for fear of being wronged themselves. So much for that. . . .

Abridged and reprinted from *The Republic of Plato*. Translated by F. M. Cornford (1941). By permission of Oxford University Press.

Humans Are Not Always Selfish

James Rachels

1. Our ordinary thinking about morality is full of assumptions that we almost never question. We assume, for example, that we have an obligation to consider the welfare of other people when we decide what actions to perform or what rules to obey; we think that we must refrain from acting in ways harmful to others, and that we must respect their rights and interests as well as our own. We also assume that people are in fact capable of being motivated by such considerations, that is, that people are not wholly selfish and that they do sometimes act in the interests of others.

Both of these assumptions have come under attack by moral sceptics, as long ago as by Glaucon in Book II of Plato's *Republic.* Glaucon recalls the legend of Gyges, a shepherd who was said to have found a magic ring in a fissure opened by an earthquake. The ring would make its wearer invisible and thus would enable him to go anywhere and do anything undetected. Gyges used the power of the ring to gain entry to the Royal Palace where he seduced the Queen, murdered the King, and subsequently seized the throne. Now Glaucon asks us to determine that there are two such rings, one given to a man of virtue and one given to a rogue. The rogue, of course, will use his ring unscrupulously and do anything necessary to increase his own wealth and power. He will recognize no moral constraints on his conduct, and, since the cloak of invisibility will protect him from discovery, he can do anything he pleases without fear of reprisal. So, there will be no end to the mischief he will do. But how will the so-called virtuous man behave? Glaucon suggests that he will behave no better than the rogue; "No one, it is commonly believed, would have such iron strength of mind as to stand fast in doing right or keep his hands off other men's goods, when he could go to the market-place and fearlessly help himself to anything he wanted, enter houses and sleep with any woman he chose, set prisoners free and kill men at his pleasure, and in a word go about among men with the powers of a god. He would behave no better than the other; both would take the same course."[1] Moreover, why shouldn't he? Once he is freed from the fear of reprisal, why shouldn't a man simply do what he pleases, or what he thinks is best for himself? What reason is there for him to continue being "moral" when it is clearly not to his own advantage to do so?

These sceptical views suggested by Glaucon have come to be known as *psychological egoism* and *ethical egoism* respectively. Psychological egoism is the view that all men are selfish in everything that they do, that is, that the only motive from which anyone ever acts is self-interest. On this view, even when men are acting in ways apparently calculated to benefit others, they are actually motivated by the belief that acting in this way is to their own advantage, and if they did not believe this, they would not be doing that action. Ethical egoism is, by contrast, a normative view about how men *ought* to act. It is the view that, regardless of how men do in fact behave, they have no obligation to do anything except what is in their own interests. According to the ethical egoist, a person is always justified in doing whatever is in his own interests, regardless of the effect on others.

Clearly, if either of these views is correct, then "the moral institution of life" (to use Butler's well-turned phrase) is very different than what we normally think. The majority of mankind is grossly deceived about what is, or ought to be, the case, where morals are concerned.

2. Psychological egoism seems to fly in the face of the facts. We are tempted to say: "Of course people act unselfishly all the time. For example, Smith gives up a trip to the country, which he would have enjoyed very much, in order to stay behind and help a friend with his studies, which is a miserable way to pass the time. This is a perfectly clear case of unselfish behavior, and if the psychological egoist thinks that such cases do not occur, then he is just mistaken." Given such obvious instances of "unselfish behavior," what reply can the egoist make? There are two general arguments by which he might try to show that all actions, including those such as the one just outlined, are in fact motivated by self-interest. Let us examine these in turn:

a. The First argument goes as follows. If we describe one person's action as selfish, and another person's action as unselfish, we are overlooking the crucial fact that in both cases, assuming that the action is done voluntarily, *the agent is merely doing what he most wants to do*. If Smith stays behind to help his friend, that only shows that he wanted to help his friend more than he wanted to go to the country. And why should he be praised for his "unselfishness" when he is only doing what he most wants to do? So, since Smith is only doing what he wants to do, he cannot be said to be acting unselfishly.

This argument is so bad that it would not deserve to be taken seriously except for the fact that so many otherwise intelligent people have been taken in by it. First, the argument rests on the premise that people never voluntarily do anything except what they want to do. But this is patently false; there are at least two classes of actions that are exceptions to this generalization. One is the set of actions which we may not want to do, but which we do anyway as a means to an end which we want to achieve; for example, going to the dentist in order to stop a toothache, or going to work every day in order to be able to draw our pay at the end of the month. These cases may be regarded as consistent with the spirit of the egoist argument, however, since the ends mentioned are wanted by the agent. But the other set of actions are those which we do, not because we want to, nor even because there is an end which we want to achieve, but because we feel ourselves *under an obligation* to do them. For example, someone may do something because he has promised to do it, and thus feels obligated, even though he does not want to do it. It is sometimes suggested that in such cases we do the action because, after all, we want to keep our promises; so, even here, we are doing what we want. However, this dodge will not work: if I have promised to do something, and if I do not want to do it then it is simply false to say that I want to keep my promise. In such cases we feel a conflict precisely because we do *not* want to do what we feel obligated to do. It is reasonable to think that Smith's action falls roughly into this second category: he might stay behind, not because he wants to, but because he feels that his friend needs help.

But suppose we were to concede, for the sake of the argument, that all voluntary action is motivated by the agent's wants, or at least that Smith is so motivated. Even if this were granted, it would not follow that Smith is acting selfishly or from self-interest. For if Smith wants to do something that will help his friend, even when it means forgoing his own enjoyments, that is precisely what makes him *un*selfish. What else could unselfishness be, if not wanting to help others? Another way to put the same point is to say that it is the *object* of a want that determines whether it is selfish or not. The mere fact that I am acting on *my* wants does not mean that I am acting selfishly; that depends on *what it is* that I want. If I want only my own good, and care nothing for others, then I am selfish; but if I also want other people to be well-off and happy, and if I act on *that* desire, then my action is not selfish. So much for this argument.

b. The second argument for psychological egoism is this. Since so-called unselfish actions always produce a sense of self-satisfaction in the agent,[2] and since this sense of satisfaction is a pleasant state of consciousness, it follows that the point of the action is really to achieve a pleasant state of consciousness, rather than to bring about any good for others. Therefore, the action is "unselfish" only at a superficial level of analysis. Smith will feel much better with himself for having stayed to help his friend—if he had gone to the country, he would have felt terrible about it—and that is the real point of the action. According to a well-known story, this argument was once expressed by Abraham Lincoln:

Mr. Lincoln once remarked to a fellow-passenger on an old-time mudcoach that all men were prompted by selfishness in doing good. His fellow-passenger was antagonizing this position when they were passing over a corduroy bridge that spanned a slough. As they crossed this bridge they espied an old razor-backed sow on the bank making a terrible noise because her pigs had got into the slough and were in danger of drowning. As the old coach began to climb the hill, Mr. Lincoln called out, "Driver, can't you stop just a moment?" Then Mr. Lincoln jumped out, ran back, and lifted the little pigs out of the mud and water and placed them on the bank. When he returned, his companion remarked: "Now, Abe, where does selfishness come in on this little episode?" "Why, bless your soul, Ed, that was the very essence of selfishness. I should have had no peace of mind all day had I gone on and left that suffering old sow worrying over those pigs. I did it to get peace of mind, don't you see?"[3]

This argument suffers from defects similar to the previous one. Why should we think that merely because someone derives satisfaction from helping others this makes him selfish? Isn't the unselfish man precisely the one who *does* derive satisfaction from helping others, while the selfish man does not? If Lincoln "got peace of mind" from rescuing the piglets, does this show him to be selfish, or, on the contrary, doesn't it show him to be compassionate and good-hearted? (If a man were truly selfish, why should it bother his conscience that *others* suffer—much less pigs?) Similarly, it is nothing more than shabby sophistry to say, because Smith takes satisfaction in helping his friend, that he is behaving selfishly. If we say this rapidly, while thinking about something else, perhaps it will sound all right; but if we speak slowly, and pay attention to what we are saying, it sounds plain silly.

Moreover, suppose we ask *why* Smith derives satisfaction from helping his friend. The answer will be, it is because Smith cares for him and wants him to succeed. If Smith did not have these concerns, then he would take no pleasure in assisting him; and these concerns, as we have already seen, are the marks of unselfishness, not selfishness. To put the point more generally: if we have a positive attitude toward the attainment of some goal, then we may derive satisfaction from attaining that goal. But the *object* of our attitude is the *attainment of that goal*; and we must want to attain the goal *before* we can find any satisfaction in it. We do not, in other words, desire some sort of "pleasurable consciousness" and then try to figure out how to achieve it; rather, we desire all sorts of different things—money, a new fishing boat, to be a better chess player, to get a promotion in our work, etc.—and because we desire these things, we derive satisfaction from attaining them. And so, if someone desires the welfare and happiness of another person, he will derive satisfaction from that; but this does not mean that this satisfaction is the object of his desire, or that he is in any way selfish on account of it.

Chapter III: Moral Theories and Ethical Perspectives

It is a measure of the weakness of psychological egoism that these insupportable arguments are the ones most often advanced in its favor. Why, then, should anyone ever have thought it a true view? Perhaps because of a desire for theoretical simplicity: In thinking about human conduct, it would be nice if there were some simple formula that would unite the diverse phenomena of human behavior under a single explanatory principle, just as simple formulae in physics bring together a great many apparently different phenomena. And since it is obvious that self-regard is an overwhelmingly important factor in motivation, it is only natural to wonder whether all motivation might not be explained in these terms. But the answer is clearly No; while a great many human actions are motivated entirely or in part by self-interest, only by a deliberate distortion of the facts can we say that all conduct is so motivated. This will be clear, I think, if we correct three confusions which are commonplace. The exposure of these confusions will remove the last traces of plausibility from the psychological egoist thesis.

The first is the confusion of selfishness with self-interest. The two are clearly not the same. If I see a physician when I am feeling poorly, I am acting in my own interest but no one would think of calling me "selfish" on account of it. Similarly, brushing my teeth, working hard at my job, and obeying the law are all in my self-interest but none of these are examples of selfish conduct. This is because selfish behavior is behavior that ignores the interests of others, in circumstances in which their interests ought not to be ignored. This concept has a definite evaluative flavor; to call someone "selfish" is not just to describe his action but to condemn it. Thus, you would not call me selfish for eating a normal meal in normal circumstances (although it may surely be in my self-interest); but you would call me selfish for hoarding food while others about are starving.

The second confusion is the assumption that every action is done *either* from self-interest or from other-regarding motives. Thus, the egoist concludes that if there is no such thing as genuine altruism then all actions must be done from self-interest. But this is certainly a false dichotomy. The man who continues to smoke cigarettes, even after learning about the connection between smoking and cancer, is surely not acting from self-interest, not even by his own standard—self-interest would dictate that he quit smoking at once—and he is not acting altruistically either. He *is*, no doubt, smoking for the pleasure of it, but all that this shows is that undisciplined pleasure-seeking and acting from self-interest are very different, This is what led Butler to remark that "The thing to be lamented is, not that men have so great regard to their own good or interest in the present world, for they have not enough."[4]

The last two paragraphs show *(a)* that it is false that all actions are selfish, and *(b)* that it is false that all actions are done out of self-interest. And it should be noted that these two points can be made, and were, without any appeal to putative examples of altruism.

The third confusion is the common but false assumption that a concern for one's own welfare is incompatible with any genuine concern for the welfare of others. Thus, since it is obvious that everyone (or very nearly everyone) does desire his own well-being, it might be thought that no one can really be concerned with others. But again, this is false. There is no inconsistency in desiring that everyone, including oneself *and* others, be well-off and happy. To be sure, it may happen on occasion that our own interests conflict with the interests of others, and in these cases we will have to make hard choices. But even in these cases we might sometimes opt for the interests of others, especially when the others involved are our family or friends. But more importantly, not all cases are like this: sometimes we are able to promote the welfare of others when our own interests are not involved at all. In these cases not even the strongest self-regard need prevent us from acting considerately toward others.

Once these confusions are cleared away, it seems to me obvious enough that there is no reason whatever to accept psychological egoism. On the contrary, if we simply observe people's behavior with an open mind, we may find that a great deal of it is motivated by self-regard, but by no means all of it; and that there is no reason to deny that "the moral institution of life" can include a place for the virtue of beneficence.[5]

3. The ethical egoist would say at this point, "Of course it is possible for people to act altruistically, and perhaps many people do act that way—but there is no reason why they *should* do so. A person is under no obligation to do anything except what is in his own interests."[6] This is really quite a radical doctrine. Suppose I have an urge to set fire to some public building (say, a department store) just for the fascination of watching the spectacular blaze: according to this view, the fact that several people might be burned to death provides no reason whatever why I should not do it. After all, this only concerns *their* welfare, not my own, and according to the ethical egoist the only person I need think of is myself.

Some might deny that ethical egoism has any such monstrous consequences. They would point out that it is really to my own advantage not to set fire—for if I do that I may be caught and put into prison (unlike Gyges, I have no magic ring for protection). Moreover, even if I could avoid being caught it is still to my advantage to respect the rights and interests of others, for it is to my advantage to live in a society in which people's rights and interests are respected. Only in such a society can I live a happy and secure life; so, in acting kindly toward others, I would merely be doing my part to create and maintain the sort of society which it is to my advantage to have.[7] Therefore, it is said, the egoist would not be such a bad man; he would be as kindly and considerate as anyone else, because he would see that it is to his own advantage to be kindly and considerate.

This is a seductive line of thought, but it seems to be mistaken. Certainly it is to everyone's advantage (including the egoist's) to preserve a stable society where people's interests are generally protected. But there is no reason for the egoist to think that merely because *he* will not honor the rules of the social game, decent society will collapse. For the vast majority of people are not egoists, and there is no reason to think that they will be converted by his example—especially if he is discreet and does not unduly flaunt his style of life. What this line of reasoning shows is not that the egoist himself must act benevolently, but that he must encourage *others* to do so. He must take care to conceal from public view his own self-centered method of decision-making, and urge others to act on precepts very different from those on which he is willing to act.

The rational egoist, then, cannot advocate that egoism be universally adopted by everyone. For he wants a world in which his own interests are maximized; and if other people adopted the egoistic policy of pursuing their own interests to the exclusion of his interests, as he pursues his interests to the exclusion of theirs, then such a world would be impossible. So he himself will be an egoist, but he will want others to be altruists.

This brings us to what is perhaps the most popular "refutation" of ethical egoism current among philosophical writers—the argument that ethical egoism is at bottom inconsistent because it cannot be universalized.[8] The argument goes like this:

To say that any action or policy of action is *right* (or that it *ought* to be adopted) entails that it is right for *anyone* in the same sort of circumstances. I cannot, for example, say that it is right for me to lie to you, and yet object when you lie to me (provided, of course, that the circumstances are the same). I cannot hold that it is all right for me to drink your beer and then complain when you drink mine. This is just the requirement that we be consistent in our evaluations; it is a requirement of logic. Now it is said that ethical egoism cannot meet this requirement because, as we have already seen, the egoist would not want others to act in the same way that he acts. Moreover, suppose he *did* advocate the universal adoption of egoistic policies: he would be saying to Peter, "You ought to pursue your own interests even if it means destroying Paul"; and he would be saying to Paul, "You ought to pursue your own interest even if it means destroying Peter," The attitudes expressed in these two recommendations seem clearly inconsistent—he is urging the advancement of Peter's interest at one moment, and countenancing their defeat at the next. Therefore, the argument goes, there is no way to maintain the doctrine of ethical egoism as a consistent view about how we ought to act. We will fall into inconsistency whenever we try.

What are we to make of this argument? Are we to conclude that ethical egoism has been refuted? Such a conclusion, I think, would be unwarranted; for I think that we can show, contrary to this argument, how ethical egoism can be maintained consistently. We need only to interpret the egoist's position in a sympathetic way: we should say that he has in mind a certain kind of world which he would prefer over all others; it would be a world in which his own interests were maximized, regardless of the effects on other people. The egoist's primary policy of action, then, would be to act in such a way as to bring about, as nearly as possible, this sort of world. Regardless of however morally reprehensible we might find it, there is nothing *inconsistent* in someone's adopting this as his ideal and acting in a way calculated to bring it about. And if someone did adopt this as his ideal, then he would not advocate universal egoism; as we have already seen, he would want other people to be altruists. So, if he advocates any principles of conduct for the general public, they will be altruistic principles. This would not be inconsistent; on the contrary, it would be perfectly consistent with his goal of creating a world in which his own interests are maximized. To be sure, he would have to be deceitful; in order to secure the good will of others, and a favorable hearing for his exhortations to altruism, he would have to pretend that he was himself prepared to accept altruistic principles. But again, that would be all right; from the egoist's point of view, this would merely be a matter of adopting the necessary means to the achievement of his goal—and while we might not approve of this, there is nothing inconsistent about it. Again, it might be said: "He advocates one thing, but does another. Surely *that's* inconsistent." But it is not; for what he advocates and what he does are both calculated as means to an end (the *same* end, we might note); and as such, he is doing what is rationally required in each case. Therefore, contrary to the previous argument, there is nothing inconsistent in the ethical egoist's view. He cannot be refuted by the claim that he contradicts himself.

Is there, then, no way to refute the ethical egoist? If by "refute" we mean show that he has made some *logical* error, the answer is that there is not. However, there is something more that can be said. The egoist challenge to our ordinary moral convictions amounts to a demand for an explanation of why we should adopt certain policies of action, namely policies in which the good of others is given importance. We can give an answer to this demand, albeit an indirect one. The reason one ought not to do action that would hurt other people is: other people would be hurt. The reason one ought to do actions that would benefit other people is: other people would be benefited. This may at first seem like a piece of philosophical sleight-of-hand, but it is not. The point is that the welfare of human beings is something that most of us value for *its own sake*, and not merely for the sake of something else. Therefore, when *further* reasons are demanded for valuing the welfare of human beings, we cannot point to anything further to satisfy this demand. It is not that we have no reason for pursuing these policies, but that our reason is that these policies are for the good of human beings.

So: if we are asked "Why shouldn't I set fire to this department store?" one answer would be "Because if you do, people may be burned to death." This is a complete, sufficient reason which does not require qualification or supplementation of any sort. If someone seriously wants to know why this action shouldn't be done, that's the reason. If we are pressed further and asked the sceptical question "But why shouldn't I do actions that will harm others?" we may not know what to say—but this is because the questioner has included in his question the very answer we would like to give: "Why shouldn't you do actions that will harm others? Because, doing those actions would harm others."

The egoist, no doubt, will not be happy with this. He will protest that *we* may accept this as a reason, but *he* does not. And here the argument stops: there are limits to what can be accomplished by argument, and if the egoist really doesn't care about other people—if he honestly doesn't care whether they are helped or hurt by his actions—then we have reached those limits. If we want to persuade him to act decently toward his fellow humans, we will have to make our appeal to such other attitudes as he does possess, by threats, bribes, or other cajolery. That is all that we can do.

Though some may find this situation distressing (we would like to be able to show that the egoist is just *wrong*), it holds no embarrassment for common morality. What we have come up against is simply a fundamental requirement of rational action, namely, that the existence of reasons for action always depends on the prior existence of certain attitudes in the agent. For example, the fact that a certain course of action would make the agent a lot of money is a reason for doing it only if the agent wants to make money; the fact that practicing at chess makes one a better player is a reason for practicing only if one wants to be a better player; and so on. Similarly, the fact that a certain action would help the agent is a reason for doing the action only if the agent cares about his own welfare, and the fact that an action would help others is a reason for doing it only if the agent cares about others. In this respect ethical egoism and what we might call ethical altruism are in exactly the same fix: both require that the agent *care* about himself, or about other people, before they can get started.

So a nonegoist will accept "It would harm another person" as a reason not to do an action simply because he cares about what happens to that other person. When the egoist says that he does *not* accept that as a reason, he is saying something quite extraordinary. He is saying that he has no affection for friends or family, that he never feels pity or compassion, that he is the sort of person who can look on scenes of human misery with complete indifference, so long as he is not the one suffering. Genuine egoists, people who really don't care at all about anyone other than themselves, are rare. It is important to keep this in mind when thinking about ethical egoism; it is easy to forget just how fundamental to human psychological makeup the feeling of sympathy is. Indeed, a man without any sympathy at all would scarcely be recognizable as a man; and that is what makes ethical egoism such a disturbing doctrine in the first place.

4. There are, of course, many different ways in which the sceptic might challenge the assumptions underlying our moral practice. In this essay I

have discussed only two of them, the two put forward by Glaucon in the passage that I cited from Plato's *Republic*. It is important that the assumptions underlying our moral practice should not be confused with particular judgments made within that practice. To defend one is not to defend the other. We may assume—quite properly, if my analysis has been correct—that the virtue of beneficence does, and indeed should, occupy an important place in "the moral institution of life"; and yet we may make constant and miserable errors when it comes to judging when and in what ways this virtue is to be exercised. Even worse, we may often be able to make accurate moral judgments, and know what we ought to do, but not do it. For these ills, philosophy, alone is not the cure.

Endnotes

1. *The Republic of Plato*, translated by F. M. Cornford (Oxford, 1941), p. 45.
2. Or, as it is sometimes said, "It gives him a clear conscience," or "He couldn't sleep at night if he had done otherwise," or "He would have been ashamed of himself for not doing it," and so on.
3. Frank C. Sharp, *Ethics* (New York, 1928), pp. 74–75. Quoted from the Springfield (Ill.) *Monitor* in the *Outlook*, vol. 56, p. 1059.
4. *The Works of Joseph Butler*, edited by W. E. Gladstone (Oxford, 1896), vol. II, p. 26. It should be noted that most of the points I am making against psychological egoism were first made by Butler. Butler made all the important points; all that is left for us is to remember them.
5. The capacity for altruistic behavior is not unique to human beings. Some interesting experiments with rhesus monkeys have shown that these animals will refrain from operating a device for securing food if this causes other animals to suffer pain. See Masserman, Wechkin, and Terris, "'Altruistic' Behavior in Rhesus Monkeys," *The American Journal of Psychiatry*, vol. 121 (1964), 584–585.
6. I take this to be the view of Ayn Rand, in so far as I understand her confusing doctrine.
7. Cf. Thomas Hobbes, *Leviathan* (London, 1651), chap. 17.
8. See, for example, Brian Medlin, "Ultimate Principles and Ethical Egoism," *Australian Journal of Philosophy*, vol. 35 (1957), 111–118; and D. H. Monro, *Empiricism and Ethics* (Cambridge, 1967), chap 16.

From James Rachels, "Egoism and Moral Scepticism." Copyright 1972 by James Rachels. Reprinted by permission of the author.

Hindu Perspectives on Ethics

Michael C. Brannigan

The essential aim of Indian philosophy is liberation from suffering. This compels its various schools to inquire about what constitutes the good life. And two aspects of the good life are significantly compatible: the highest good for the individual, and the highest social good.

Let us review some fundamental themes in the Indian quest for this good life.

Basic Themes in Hindu Ethics

Life's Four Goals In Indian thought, there are four basic aims in life:

- To acquire some degree of material well-being
- To experience pleasure
- To live virtuously
- To attain spiritual awakening

These goals are not equally important. The highest goal is spiritual awakening. By itself, material well-being will not bring about immortality or liberation from suffering. Nevertheless, Hindus acknowledge the human need for some material security. What is crucial is our attitude toward this need. As for pleasure, there is an important distinction between that which is good and that which is pleasing. We all seek pleasure and to avoid pain. Yet pleasure in itself is not a good, but rather an instrumental good that enables other goods to come about, the highest being the spiritual pleasure attained through self-realization.

Life's Four Stages Orthodox Indians believe that there are four stages in life. These stages—called *asramas*, meaning "rest-stops"—are student, householder, forest dweller, and hermit (*sannyasa*). The four stages are viewed as successive steps to spiritual awakening and perfection. This perfection is possible because our very nature is itself divine, or *atman*. Though not legally required, they are held up as ideals to strive for.

The *student* stage is a period of disciplined learning that is totally committed to proper study, especially of the teachings of the Vedas. There is a special relationship between the instructor and the student, for the teacher is viewed as a spiritual mentor.

The *householder* stage commences with marriage and the establishment of a family. A stable family life is essential to the cohesiveness of a society. During this time, the attainment of material security (*artha*) is important for the well-being of the family. Moreover, devotion to family life is a means of transcending one's own self interests.

The third stage is that of the *forest dweller*. At this point, individuals, having fulfilled familial responsibilities, are now ready for retreat from the family in order to nourish their spiritual nature and genuine selves. Again, this is a means to that spiritual realization that is the ultimate aim in orthodox Indian thought.

Finally, the *hermit*, in the stage of *sannyasa*, is the person who has disconnected himself from the world. This person is known as the *sannyasin*, whose highest goal is to achieve *moksha*, or spiritual awakening. The *sannyasin* embarks upon a solitary venture, no longer connected to family and society.

Dharma *Dharma*, an important idea in Indian ethics, comes from the root *dhr*, meaning "to nourish." Its meaning is traced back to the Rig Veda's use of *rita*, or order of the universe. The principle of *rita* is not confined to the physical realm, but is applied even more crucially to the moral level. This means that the universal moral order necessitates the priority of virtue.

Generally, *dharma* means that which is morally correct. *Dharma* also demands fulfillment of one's duties in accordance with one's role. Here is the advice given by a teacher to his student in the *Taittiriya Upanishad*:

> "Speak the truth. Do your duty [dharma]. Study the Wedas [Vedas]. Give what is fitting to the teacher; marry, continue the family. Neither neglect your spiritual nor your worldly welfare. Always learn and teach. Forget neither God nor ancestor. Your mother your goddess, your father your God, your guest your God, your teacher your God; copy our good deeds along, so escape blame.
> "Look for men greater than us, welcome them, give them hospitality."

Dharma therefore means right action, and it includes viewing others as we view ourselves. In this way, we would be less inclined to harm another, just as we do not want to be harmed. *Dharma* must be an essential quality within us, for realizing our nature entails realizing our moral character as well.

Chapter III: Moral Theories and Ethical Perspectives

Moksha *Moksha*, the supreme goal in orthodox Indian thought, refers to genuine spiritual awakening. (For Buddhists, the highest state is called *nirvana*.) Yet, *moksha* has acquired a variety of meanings. For instance, in the Samkhya and Nyaya-Vaisheshika schools, *moksha* is negatively defined as liberation from suffering and misery. The Vedanta schools describe *moksha* positively as the highest bliss. In any case, *moksha* means liberation from *samsara*, the wheel of birth, death, and rebirth.

The many ways to achieve this highest goal of spiritual awakening can be reduced to three major paths, referred to as yogas: karma yoga, bhakti yoga, and jnana yoga. Yoga means "yoke" in the sense of joining together. It can mean the joining together of body and mind, or the joining together of oneself with Reality, *atman* and *Brahman*, realized as one in essence.

Karma yoga is a popular path to enlightenment. This is the way of action, or the way of work, and the path by which our labor and occupation bring us closer to personal realization. The Hindus stress the importance of fulfilling our duties in line with our class.

What is necessary, however, is that we fulfill our duties without being attached to them. In other words, we should work without concern for the consequences of our work. This means that we should not perform our responsibilities *in order* to be recognized or praised. As we will see, a highly important teaching in the *Bhagavad Gita* is to not be attached to the fruits of one's efforts. As long as we are attached to what we do, we work from a self-interested reference point, still enmeshed by desires. The ultimate goal is *moksha*, and not recognition, praise, fame, or reward. The way of action is particularly emphasized, for example, in the Mimamsa school.

Bhakti yoga, which appeals to our more interiorized needs, is the path of devotion and of prayer. This is the path of love of *Brahman* or God. This path satisfies our emotional needs to express devotion through prayer and sacrifice. The notion of *Brahman* as *nirguna* (without qualities or attributes) does not satisfy our need for some positive, more concrete image with which we can more readily identify. Even the attributes of *sat-cit-ananda* (being-consciousness-bliss) can be less satisfying.

Bhakti yoga can lead to union with the divine in the most intimate way. Bhakti yoga is expressed in the religious sects of Saivism and Vaisnavism. (Saivism is a sect that emphasizes devotion to God as Shiva; Vaisnavism is a branch that emphasizes devotion to Vishnu.) The philosophical schools that especially underscore the way of devotion are the Vedanta teachings of Ramanuja and Madhva:

> Lead me from the unreal to the real!
> Lead me from darkness to light!
> Lead me from death to immortality!

Jnana yoga addresses another need in us—the need to know. It is the way to *moksha* through knowledge. Proper knowledge is necessary if we are to root out our natural ignorance of our real nature. Our most fundamental error lies in mistaking our ego for our true self. Awakening to the truth of *tat tvam asi* can occur through cultivation of knowledge.

This knowledge is not purely cerebral, but instead a knowledge that involves the total person from the depths of his or her being. It is a knowing that is immediate and total. Yet, in order to gain this intuitive insight, both the cultivation of intellect and the proper state of mind are important. Jnana yoga is quite involved, entailing personal, moral cultivation and intensive study and meditation. The way of knowledge is the focus in Advaita Vedanta, in Jainism, and in Buddhism.

Karma Any discussion of ethics in Indian philosophy must take into account the belief that our particular quality of existence is to some extent the result of our ethical conduct in former lives. In past existences we have accumulated karma that determines our next rebirth. This will be examined more closely in Chapter 6. However, a review of the meaning of karma is crucial to an understanding of Indian ethics.

Literally, karma refers to an "act" or deed. It is a law pertaining to the moral sphere; it is the principle of moral causality. This means that each deed and thought brings about its specific effect, if not in this life, then in another. This effect is at least twofold: (1) An act or thought produces its particular negative or positive effect, and (2) It contributes to the formation of that person's moral character. A habit of good deeds results in good character, whereas a habit of bad deeds produces bad character. Each action and thought either enhances or detracts from our moral personality.

What is especially important in karma is that we are the sole determiners of what we become. Indians generally believe that we are the ultimate managers of our destiny. Therefore, even though, due to past karma, we are born into a particular class, we still possess the freedom to affect our destinies. Although we are often constrained by our circumstances and conditions, as humans we still possess the free will to determine how we respond to those conditions. The law of karma is not a rigid determinism that rules out freedom; rather, it places a premium on individual responsibility for one's actions. It remains one of the most profound and far-reaching teachings in Indian thought.

Our human existence has a special status with respect to karma: We are chained to the wheel of *samsara*, of birth, death, and rebirth. Yet, this does not guarantee constant rebirth in a human form. Rebirths usually occur in other realms (as animals or insects, for example) and on different planes. Let us be clearer.

As we live, we accumulate karma. Just think of the remarkable amount of karma we accrue in one day, let alone in one lifetime. When we die, we have karma that has not been actualized or effected. We can call this our karmic residue. In other words, not all karma exhausts itself right away, and instead it becomes a latent force in later rebirths. Much of this residue

Chapter III: Moral Theories and Ethical Perspectives

is spent in our rebirths in other forms; only occasionally are we reborn in human form.

However, only humans can bring about karma. In other words, our rebirths in other psycho-physical forms are the result of the products of our karma, even though as humans we can also experience the product of our karma. But we can produce karma only as humans because only as humans do we possess the reason and free will that constitutes moral and immoral behavior.

Therefore, only humans can experience *moksha*, the spiritual awakening that liberates us from the cycle of *samsara*. Remember that the goal in Indian thought is not longevity, but breaking out of *samsara* and realizing total freedom.

Hindus believe that being born into a particular social caste is the result of one's karma. Therefore, this caste system reinforced the teaching of karma. The complex caste system in India had many divisions comprising four main classes that constituted the society: *brahmanas*, or priest-teachers; *kshatriyas*, or warriors; *vaisyas*, or traders and merchants; and *shudras*, or laborers. Those outside society were considered outcasts, referred to as "untouchables."

Brahmanas were the spiritual guides of the community. They were the educators and teachers of the Vedas and were sought out for spiritual advice. *Ksatriyas* were the protectors of the community. Many were soldiers and enforcers of the laws, responsible for protecting society from invasion. *Vaisyas* were the merchants and professionals responsible for maintaining the economic state of the community, including farmers, cattle raisers, and traders. *Shudras* were the laborers. It is important to realize that the status of the laborer was not at first viewed as inferior to that of other classes, for the laborer played a valuable part in the functioning of society.

Within this division of labor, Indian society was able to maintain harmony and complementarity among the different classes. The purpose behind this allotment of responsibilities was the collective well-being.

The Sanskrit word for class is *varna*, which literally means "color." Throughout its history, India managed to assimilate a variety of racial groups, including the indigenous Dravidians, the conquering Aryans, Persians, Greeks, and Huns. Although *varna* may have originally referred to the pigmentation of the skin, color later referred to one's character.

In connection with this, recall the Samkhya theory of the three *gunas*: clarity, activity, and passivity. Each individual possesses these *gunas* in varying degrees. Personal growth consisted of progressing through the predominant *gunas* from passivity to activity to clarity. (These same three *gunas* were also represented by black, red, and white, respectively.) Furthermore, it was believed that just as individuals had certain predominant *gunas*, the same could be said for certain classes. For example, the *brahmanas* possessed more clarity, or *sattva*, which is why they were the accepted teachers and spiritual leaders. The warriors possessed more activity, or *rajas*; the traders and merchants possessed more passivity, or *tamas*. The laborers had little development of any of these *gunas*. So we see that class membership was originally intended to be determined by character, not by birth.

The social rules among the classes were not always hard-and-fast duties, for occasionally they were amenable to varying circumstances. There are abundant examples of individuals infringing upon social rules and justifying their actions through an appeal to personal conscience. In other words, the class system did not obliterate the importance of personal conscience. However, it is crucial that one be able to properly discriminate between personal conscience and personal desires. Within this class system, the freedom of the individual to pursue his or her own moral path is not absolutely prohibited. There are examples of *brahmanas* who became warriors in the *kshatriya* class. Switching castes, however, was generally discouraged as a social practice, and it was important that members of various castes adhere to the prescribed rules of their cast. Such rules were set up as ideal, social, ethical codes.

Bhagavad Gita: The Meaning of Dharma

The *Bhagavad Gita* is one of the most influential works in Indian thought. The action takes place just before the Pandavas battle their cousins, the Kauravas. Arjuna becomes despondent and experiences a moral conflict: He is reluctant to fight against his cousins, for it is clear that the outcome of the battle will mean death for many of them and for his own family and friends as well. In a heartrending scene, just as Arjuna is about to cast his weapons down, Krishna consoles him and engages him in a discussion about the nature of action and duty, or *dharma*. Consequently, Krishna reveals his true, divine nature to Arjuna, and Arjuna achieves an understanding that transcends the ordinary human level of knowledge. The work is a powerful account of the meaning of action and *dharma* in the context of this moral conflict.

It is clear that Arjuna comes to this battle with designs for victory. After all, he and his Pandava brothers are the rightful inheritors of the kingdom, which was unjustly taken from them by the Kaurava clan. Even on the eve of battle, Arjuna reassures his elder brother that their cause is just.

Arjuna's feelings change, however, when he actually confronts the enemy. Faced with imminent bloodshed, pangs of distress wrack him. He does not suddenly transform into a pacifist opposed to all forms of violence; such a view is inconsistent with his lifestyle as a warrior. Arjuna realizes that war will not only destroy family and friends, but will lead to

Chapter III: Moral Theories and Ethical Perspectives

the decline of social order, with its emphasis on clan authority. Many elders will be killed, further eroding the social order.

Despondent, Arjuna presents all sorts of reasons for throwing down his weapons to Krishna, who listens patiently. In many respects Arjuna is not simply surrendering to waves of emotion, for he presents some moral grounds for not fighting. His reasoning is essentially utilitarian, perceiving the long-range devastating results of war for all the parties involved. And these considerations come into sharp conflict with what he intellectually knows to be his duty.

Krishna's response to Arjuna's personal quandary can be interpreted on a number of levels. On the same basic, human level, Krishna provides Arjuna reasons why he should fight. He chastises Arjuna's emotional attachment to the body, arguing that death does not truly occur because the soul is immortal. Krishna speaks of the immortal self:

> Never is he born nor dies;
> Never did he come to be, nor will he ever come to be again:
> Unborn, eternal, everlasting he—primeval:
> He is not slain when the body is slain.
>
> If a man knows him as indestructible,
> Eternal, unborn, never to pass away,
> How and whom can he cause to be slain
> Or slay?

Furthermore, Krishna points out to Arjuna some undesirable consequences that would result if Arjuna refuses to fight:

> But if thou wilt not wage this war
> Prescribed by thy (caste-) duty,
> Then, by casting off both honour and (caste-) duty,
> Thou wilt bring evil on thyself
>
> Yes, this thy dishonour will become a byword
> In the mouths of men in ages yet to come;
> And dishonour in a man well-trained to honour
> [Is an ill] surpassing death.

Now Krishna raises the most crucial argument: A moral act can only be such if there is no personal attachment to the results (gains or otherwise) of the act. Motives of personal benefit and profit have no part in ethical action:

> Work alone is thy proper business,
> Never the fruits [it may produce];
> Let not your motive be the fruit of work,
> Nor your attachment to [mere] worklessness (*akarma*).

Krishna's rebuttals are presented on the human plane that Arjuna well understands. However, Krishna is a god in disguise, and his most overpowering attempt to move Arjuna from his lethargy comes when he shares with Arjuna a perspective that goes beyond the limited human plane. Arjuna is thus compelled to view his dilemma in a different light, and from Krishna's cosmic and divine view the dilemma disappears.

This vision is transformative. From his limited human perspective, Arjuna was attached to his actions; from his new perspective, he is freed from such attachment. In this all-embracing cosmic vision, all of his former concerns are essentially irrelevant. Arjuna is now spiritually enlightened, and in his enlightened state the ethical conflict disappears. From this perspective, he realizes he must do what he had intellectually known all along—his duty.

Dharma, or action without attachment to its results, does not mean purposeless action, for action is only meaningful if there is some purpose behind it. Nor is *dharma* that which is without desire. Desireless action is again meaningless action. *Dharma*, or right action, derives from the essential attitude one takes toward purpose and desire.

As long as action occurs within a self-referential context, it is wrong action and not *dharma*. One cannot escape action, for living is acting. Yet the goal is to act properly; the aim is right action or *dharma*. Therefore, the primary yoga emphasized in the *Bhagavad Gita* is that of action, or karma yoga.

Mimamsa School: Metaphysical Status of Dharma

The primary teaching in this school concerns the meaning and significance of *dharma*, or "right action." Basically, right action is that which follows the Vedic prescriptions. Sometimes the term *dharma* is translated as "duty" (as it often is in the *Bhagavad Gita*). Jaimini, the founder of the Mimamsa school, refers to *dharma* as a command to action. And the prescribed actions in the Veda concern rituals, prayers, sacrifices, and other social duties.

An important idea in this school is that the effects of these acts will take place—if not in this life, then in another. Therefore, an act's effect lies in a state of latent actualization. The renowned philosopher in the school, Kumarila, assigned the term *apurva* to this latent state.

What we have in the Mimamsa school is a metaphysical status bestowed upon *dharma*. *Dharma* is the foundational force behind all things and is that which keeps all things together. Due to its unseen energy, results often occur much later than the performance of the actual cause. In other words, in this dynamic idea of activity, causation itself is dynamic. The action we perform continues beyond the activity itself to eventually bring about an effect.

Taoist Ethical Perspectives

Lao-tzu and Chuang-tzu

Individual Life in Harmony with the Tao[1]

Non-Action[2]

Nonaction makes its exemplifier the lord of all fame; nonaction serves him as the treasury of all plans; nonaction fits him for the burden of all offices; nonaction makes him the lord of all wisdom. The range of his action is inexhaustible, but there is nowhere any trace of his presence. He fulfills all that he has received from Heaven, but he does not see that he was the recipient of anything. A pure vacancy of all purpose is what characterizes him. When the perfect man employs his mind, it is a mirror. It conducts nothing and anticipates nothing; it responds to what is before it, but does not retain it. Thus he is able to deal successfully with all things, and injures none.

> [16] Vacancy should be brought to the utmost degree,
> And that of stillness guarded with unwearying vigor.
> All things go through their processes of activity,
> And then we see them return to their original state.
> When things (in the vegetable world) have displayed their
>   luxuriant growth,
> We see each of them return to its root.
> This returning to their root is what we call the state of
>   stillness;
> And that stillness may be called a reporting that they have
>   fulfilled their appointed end.
> The report of that fulfillment is the regular, unchanging rule.

To know that unchanging rule is to be intelligent;
Not to know it leads to wild movements and evil results.

The knowledge of that unchanging rule produces a grand
   capacity and forbearance,
And that capacity and forbearance lead to a community of
   feeling with all things.
From this community of feeling comes a kingliness of
   character;
And he who is king-like goes on to be heavenlike.
In that likeness to heaven he possesses the Tao.
Possessed of the Tao, he endures long;
And to the end of his bodily life, is exempt from all danger of
   decay.

[22] The partial becomes complete;
The crooked, straight;
The empty, full;
The worn out, new.
He whose desires are few gets them;
He whose desires are many goes astray.

Therefore the sage holds in his embrace the one thing
   (humility),
And manifests it to all the world.
He is free from self-display, and therefore he shines;
From self-assertion, and therefore he is distinguished;
From self-boasting, and therefore his merit is acknowledged;
From self-complacency, and therefore he acquires superiority.

It is because he is thus free from striving that therefore no one
   in the world is able to strive with him.
The saying of the ancients that "the partial becomes complete"
   was not vainly spoken—
All real completion is comprehended under it.

[29) If any one should wish to get the kingdom for himself
   and to get this by what he does,
I see that he will not succeed.
The kingdom is a spirit-like thing,
And cannot be gotten by active doing.
He who would so win it destroys it;
He who would hold it in his grasp loses it.
The course and nature of things is such that
   What was in front is now behind;

What warmed soon we freezing find.
Strength is of weakness oft the spoil;
The store in ruins mocks our toil.
Hence the sage puts away excessive effort, extravagance, and indulgence.

[33] He who knows other men is discerning;
He who knows himself is intelligent.
He who overcomes others is strong;
He who overcomes himself is mighty.
He who is satisfied with his lot is rich;
He who goes on acting with energy has a firm will.
He who does not fail in the requirements of his position continues long;
He who dies and yet does not perish, has longevity.

[44] Fame or life—
Which do you hold more dear?
Life or wealth—
To which would you adhere?
Keep life and lose those other things;
Keep them and lose your life—
Which brings sorrow and pain more near?

Thus we may see:
Who cleaves to fame
Rejects what is more great;
Who loves large stores
Gives up the richer state.

Who is content
Needs fear no shame.
Who knows to stop
Incurs no blame.
From danger free
Live long shall he.[3]

The Superior Man[4]

The Master said, "The Tao overspreads and sustains all things. How great it is in its overflowing influence! The superior man ought by all means to remove from his mind all that is contrary to it. Acting without action is what is called Heavenlike. Speech coming forth of itself is what is called a mark of the true Virtue. Loving men and benefiting things is what is called Benevolence. Seeing wherein things that are different yet agree is what is called being Great. Conduct free from the ambition of being distinguished above others is what is called being Generous. The possession in himself of a myriad points of difference is what is called being Rich. Therefore to hold fast the natural attributes is what is called the Guiding Line of government; the perfecting of those attributes is what is called its Establishment; accordance with the Tao is what is called being Complete; and not allowing anything external to affect the will is what is called being Perfect.

When the Superior man understands these ten things, he keeps all matters as it were sheathed in himself, showing the greatness of his mind; and through the outflow of his doings all things move and come to him. Being such, he lets the gold lie hid in the hill, and the pearls in the deep; he considers not property or money to be any gain; he keeps aloof from riches and honors; he rejoices not in long life, and grieves not for early death; he does not account prosperity a glory, nor is ashamed of indigence; he would not grasp at the gain of the whole world to be held as his own private portion; he would not desire to rule over the whole world as his own private distinction. His distinction is in understanding that all things belong to the one treasury, and that death and life should be viewed in the same way."

The Master said, "How still and deep is the place where the Tao resides! How limpid is its purity! Metal and stone without It would give forth no sound. They have indeed the power of sound in them, but if they be not struck, they do not emit it. Who can determine the qualities that are in all things?

"The man of kingly qualities holds on his way unoccupied, and is ashamed to busy himself with the conduct of affairs. He establishes himself in what is the root and source of his capacity, and his wisdom grows to be spiritlike. In this way his attributes become more and more great, and when his mind goes forth, whatever things come in his way, it lays hold of them and deals with them. Thus, if there were not the Tao, the bodily form would not have life, and its life, without the attributes of the Tao, would not be manifested. Is not he who preserves the body and gives the fullest development to the life, who establishes the attributes of the Tao and clearly displays It, possessed of kingly qualities? How majestic is he in his sudden issuings forth, and in his unexpected movements, when all things follow him!—This we call the man whose qualities fit him to rule.

"He sees where there is the deepest obscurity; he hears where there is no sound. In the midst of the deepest obscurity, he alone sees and can distinguish various objects; in the midst of a soundless abyss, he alone can hear a harmony of notes. Therefore where one deep is succeeded by a greater, he can people all with things; where one mysterious range is followed by another that is more so, he can lay hold of the subtlest character of each. In this way in his dealings with all things, while he is farthest from having anything, he can yet give to them what they seek; while he is always hurrying forth, he yet returns to his resting place; now large, now small; now long, now short; now distant, now near."

Government[5]

[3] Not to value and employ men of superior ability is the way to keep the people from rivalry among themselves;
Not to prize articles which are difficult to procure is the way to keep them from becoming thieves;
Not to show them what is likely to excite their desires is the way to keep their minds from disorder.

Therefore the sage, in the exercise of his government:
Empties their minds, fills their bellies;
Weakens their wills, and strengthens their bones.
He constantly keeps them without knowledge and without desire,
And where there are those who have knowledge, he keeps them from presuming to act on it.
When there is this abstinence from action, good order is universal.

[10] When the intelligent and animal souls are held together in one embrace, they can be kept from separating.
When one gives undivided attention to the vital breath, and brings it to the utmost degree of pliancy, he can become as a baby.
When he has cleansed away the most mysterious sights (of his imagination), he can become without a flaw.

In loving the people and ruling the state, cannot he proceed without any purpose of action?
In the opening and shutting of his gates of heaven, cannot he do so as a female bird?[6]
While his intelligence reaches in every direction, cannot he appear to be without knowledge?
The Tao produces all things and nourishes them;
It produces them and does not claim them as its own;
It does all, and yet does not boast of it;
It presides over all, and yet does not control them.
This is what is called its "mysterious quality."

[18] When the Great Tao ceased to be observed, benevolence and righteousness came into vogue.

Then appeared wisdom and shrewdness, and there ensued
   great hypocrisy.
When harmony no longer prevailed throughout the six
   kinships, filial sons found their manifestation;
When the states and clans fell into disorder, loyal ministers
   appeared.

[57] A state may be ruled by correction;
Weapons of war may be used with crafty dexterity;
But the kingdom is made one's own only by freedom from
   action and purpose.
How do I know that it is so? By these facts:
In the kingdom the multiplication of prohibitions increases the
   poverty of the people;
The more implements people have to add to their profit, the
   greater disorder is there in the state and clan;
The more acts of crafty dexterity that men possess, the more
   do strange contrivances appear;
The more display there is of legislation, the more thieves and
   robbers there are.

Therefore a sage has said, "I will do nothing, and the people
   will be transformed by themselves;
I will be fond of keeping still, and the people will by
   themselves become correct.
I will take no trouble about it, and the people will by
   themselves become rich;
I will manifest no ambition, and the people will by themselves
   attain to genuine simplicity."

[64] That which is at rest is easily held;
Before a thing has indicated its presence, it is easy to take
   measures against it.
That which is brittle is easily broken;
That which is very small is easily dispersed.
Action should be taken before a thing has made its
   appearance;
Other should be secured before disorder has begun.
The tree which fills the arms grew from the tiniest sprout;
The tower of nine stories rose from a heap of earth;
The journey of a thousand li[7] began with a single step.
He who acts does harm;
He who takes hold of a thing loses his hold.
The sage does not act, and therefore does no harm;
He does not lay hold, and therefore does not lose his hold.
But people in their conduct of affairs are constantly ruining

them when they are on the eve of success.
If they were as careful at the end as they are at the beginning, they would not ruin them.

Therefore the sage desires what other men do not desire, and does not prize things difficult to get;
He learns what others do not learn, and turns back to what the multitude has passed by.
Thus he helps the natural development of all things, and does not dare to act.

[31] Weapons, however beautiful, are instruments of evil omen,
Hateful, it may be said, to all creatures.
Therefore they who have the Tao do not like to employ them.
The superior man ordinarily considers the left hand the most honorable place, but in time of war the right hand.
Those sharp weapons are instruments of evil omen.

They are not the instruments of the superior man;
He uses them only on the compulsion of necessity.
Calm and repose are what he prizes; victory by force of arms is to him undesirable.
To consider this desirable would be to delight in the slaughter of men;
And he who delights in the slaughter of men cannot get his will in the kingdom.

On occasions of festivity to be on the left hand is the prized position; on occasions of mourning, the right hand.
The second in command of the army has his place on the left; the general has his on the right;
This place is assigned to him [the general] just as in the rites of mourning.
He who has killed multitudes of men should weep for them with the bitterest grief;
The victor in battle has his place just as in those rites of mourning.

Endnotes

1. *Tao Te Ching* 16, 22, 29, 33, 44
2. *Live long shall he*: lines like that in the Tao Te Ching encouraged later Taoist esoteric practices about gaining long life and even immortality through religious practices.
3. *Chang-tzu*, book 7
4. *Chang-tzu*, book 12
5. *Tao Te Ching* 3, 10, 18, 57, 64, 31
6. *as a female bird*: with the yin of nonaction.
7. *li*: about one-third of a mile.

Chapter IV
Relativism

Relativism, in one form or another, has existed as a topic for philosophical discussion for at least twenty-five hundred years. Centuries before Christ, the Greek philosopher Protagoras declared, "Man is the measure of all things." But, it was not until the twilight of the nineteenth century, when Nietzsche boldly declared, "God is dead," that relativism became a serious challenge to traditionally accepted moral beliefs. Nietzsche's announcement, for many, sounded the death knoll for all "absolutes" and wrenched the center out from western civilization.

Relativism is the view that there are many standards of morality—not just one. Furthermore, this view implies that no single standard is more correct than any other but, only, different. Morality, it is claimed, is culturally conditioned and varies from place to place, from society to society, from historical time to historical time, and, perhaps, from individual to individual.

In "The Age of Relativism," Luther Binkley cites key works in the development of relativism in its various forms. He treats the topic from the anthropological, sociological, philosophical, psychological, literary and dramatic perspectives which emerged in the late nineteenth and early twentieth centuries. He includes the views of Walter Lippman, Westermarck, Durkheim, Sumner, Mannheim, Ruth Benedict, John Barth, Samuel Beckett, Eugene Ionesco, Jean Genet, Albert Camus and B. F. Skinner. Brinkley calls attention to the fact that relativism has initiated diverse cultural reactions: dogmatic rejection, despair and absurdity, boredom, an awakening from "dogmatic slumber," a re-examination and refinement of traditional beliefs which had been uncritically accepted, and manipulation of fellow human beings for profit and power. Because the findings of many social scientists (i.e. descriptive ethics) show that "different cultures professed radically different values" it followed that ". . . there was no justification for our traditional belief that our values were the only ones which sane men could adopt."

Quest for Goodness: An Introduction to Ethics

The phrase, "When in Rome, do as the Romans" has often been invoked to illustrate the point of view of moral relativism. Frank Burton's article, "When In Rome . . ." clarifies the important distinction between subjectivism and relativism. He shows that while subjectivism may be legitimately located within the realm of relativism, it is a perspective which is limited to the views of individuals. *Subjectivism* is the view that "all ethical evaluations merely reflect the preferences of the person, . . . they merely express the feelings of the individual." *Relativism,* on the other hand, holds that all moral evaluations are arbitrary preferences which are dependent on ". . .the individual, the situation, the culture and the times." According to this way of looking at morality, "conflicting ethical positions could be equally valid."

Burton also traces the historical development of relativism from Greek philosophy to modern philosophy. His essay includes Herskovit's insightful essay, *Cultural Relativism and Cultural Values.* This article provides many examples of ethical practices and values from a variety of cultures. In addition, it discusses enculturation and ethnocentrism.

Nietzsche claims that, historically, there have been only two types of morality: the *master morality* and the *slave morality.* The highest type of human being is the self assertive individual. Fulfillment in life and nobility originate from "an impulse generated by the super-abundance of power." The "noble man" is a determiner of values. "The noble man," Nietzsche says, "honors in himself the powerful one, him also who has power over himself, who knows how to speak and how to keep silence. . . ." It is the noble and powerful individual that confers honor on things; it is this one who is a creator of values. In this type of self-assertion lies the highest and best expression of human freedom.

David Hume's, "Morality As Based on Sentiment," is perhaps the most influential expression of the position of ethical subjectivism. This essay could also have been included in the preceding chapter on "Moral Theories and Ethical Perspectives." It is included here because subjectivism, as an ethical perspective, properly lies within the realm of relativism. Ethical Subjectivism is a theory about the nature of morality. "It maintains," says Hume, "that morality is determined by sentiment." In this essay Hume insists that morality belongs not to the *speculative* area of philosophy, but to the *practical.* He also insists that one cannot derive "ought" from "is" and that morality must be grounded in matters of fact. Hume also believed conduct should be guided by a general sentiment of beneficence toward all humankind.

William Sumner was an American sociologist and anthropologist. In the well known article that follows Sumner makes a case for cultural relativism. He believed there can be no universal right or wrong. His essay explains how societies satisfy certain human needs through habitual and accepted behavior. *Folkways,* Sumner states, "extend over the whole of life." They are prescriptive in nature and provide a framework within

Chapter IV: Relativism

which members of a given society form judgments about others. Over time, folkways are raised to a higher institutionalized societal plane and are termed *mores*. Mores are the directive moral force in a given society. The directive moral force of a society is objectified by laws and moral codes. The later are mechanical and practical and vary from society to society.

"According to the absolutists," writes W. T. Stace, "there is but one eternally true and valid moral code. The moral code applies with rigid impartiality to all men. What is a duty for me must likewise be a duty for you." An ethical absolutist does not dispute the fact that "moral customs and moral ideas differ from country to country and from age to age." From these facts, however, it does not necessarily follow that ethics are relative. Stace points out that merely to "think something is right does not make it right, even for them." Furthermore, he claims, "Nor does the fact that we think the same things wrong make them wrong. They are *in themselves* either right or wrong." His article attempts to clarify and justify this view.

Carl Wellman wrote, in "The Implications of Cultural Relativity," that, "it is often thought that the discoveries of anthropology have revolutionary implications for ethics." In fact, it is commonly, though uncritically, thought that the scientific study of cultures has undermined all belief in ethical absolutes. Wellman did not question the findings of the anthropologists nor their particular contributions to descriptive ethics, but he asked what these empirical findings imply. Furthermore, he asked what, if anything, about these discoveries might force human beings to revise their ethics. Wellman's work is filled with examples of ethical practices from various cultures and reports about the various things which cultural anthropologists find to be relative. In each case he asked: "What does this imply for ethics?"

Mary Midgley looks carefully and critically at a way of thinking about morality which is becoming increasingly prevalent. Midgley calls this position "moral isolationism." She says, "It consists in simply denying that we can ever understand any culture except our own well enough to make judgments about it." She continues that those who endorse this view "feel that the respect and tolerance due from one system to another forbids us ever to take up a critical position to any other culture."

Midgley sees no merit in the position of moral isolationism. She uses the remote example of the Japanese Samurai practice of "trying out one's new sword on a chance wayfarer" in order to help the reader understand what is involved in making accurate moral judgments about another culture. She concludes: "Morally as well as physically, there is only one world, and we all have to live in it."

As a backdrop to Midgley's article, "Japanese Ethical Perspectives" seemed to be an appropriate selection. This article could have also been placed in the previous chapter, "Moral Theories and Ethical Perspectives" "It is often said," writes Michael Brannigan, "that the spirit of Japanese ethics is typified in the code of Bushido, or the Way of the Warrior." This spirit is embodied in the Samurai and it is threefold. First, one must die moment by moment. The fact of death frees one to live. Second, one must engage in service to Lord, Shogun or family. This is *giri*. *Giri* is the duty to service and a manifestation of loyalty. Third, the Samurai must always act from a pure heart—i.e., one that is free from worldly attachments and self-interest. By way of exacting physical and mental discipline the Samurai forges a union of mind and body. From this oneness the Samurai is able to act immediately, intuitively and fearlessly for he has no sense of self.

C. S. Lewis was both a popular and prolific writer who dealt primarily with Christian themes. "The Law of Human Nature" was reprinted from his widely read book, *Mere Christianity*. Lewis held that within the context of moral discourse, standards are explicitly stated or tacitly assumed. When a person makes a moral claim, he or she is appealing to a standard that one expects the other to know about. According to Lewis:

> Quarreling means trying to show that the other man is wrong. And there would be no sense in trying to do that unless you and he had some sort of agreement as to what Right and Wrong are; just as there would be no sense in saying that a footballer had committed a foul unless there was some agreement about the rules of football.

There is, Lewis claimed, what was once called a universal Law of Nature. This law works with the exactness of scientific laws, like the law of gravity. However, unlike gravity, human beings are free to obey or disobey the Law of Nature but will reap the benefits or consequences of their acts. The Law of Nature dictates how human beings ought to behave; it is the idea of decency, or morality. It is the Rule of Right and Wrong. Lewis believed that God was the force behind this law and that is why it is universal and absolute.

The Age of Relativism

Luther Binkley

Our age has often been called an age of relativism. During the so-called Jazz Age of the Twenties Walter Lippmann observed that "the acids of modernity" had dissolved the religious certainties of the past. The influence of the scientific method and the growth of industrial and urban society were largely responsible, he believed, for the loss of faith in absolutes. Even in the realm of morals the codes we had inherited from the Hebrews of the Old Testament were beginning to dissolve in the spirit of a new age.[1] Lippman's insights were confirmed by the findings of many social scientists who found in their studies that different cultures professed radically different values, thus suggesting that there was no justification for our traditional belief that our values were the only ones which sane men could adopt.

The most sustained treatment of relativism in ethics was by Edward Westermarck, whose studies show a blend of anthropological, sociological and philosophical interests. In the *Origin and Development of Moral Ideas* (1906) and *Ethical Relativity* (1932) he shows the great diversity among the moral judgments of different societies and individuals. Some of these differences in moral standards may be accounted for by differences in environment, in religion, and in beliefs, but many of them represented what he considered to be unresolvable moral differences. In providing examples of the latter type of moral differences, he referred to the various concepts held by different societies and by individuals as to how widely within or beyond the group the principles of morality apply, and what should be done when one's interests clash with those of others. These differences in moral judgment led Westermarck to conclude that ethics is based on emotional reactions in which there is a basic impulse to repay the good or evil that has been done to oneself. Westermarck held an individualistic theory of ethics to the extent that he maintained that what one calls good is that which arouses in him the emotion of approval, while that is considered bad which arouses the emotion of disapproval. He did point out, however, that no one can develop arbitrarily his own emotions of approval or disapproval. They are really conditioned to a great extent by the moral emotions held in the particular age and locality in which the person is living. Thus, moral standards were found to vary from age to age as well as from culture to culture.[2] Because Westermarck supported his conclusions with a wealth of historical data, his theory of moral relativism seemed to many minds convincing.

In addition to the monumental study of morals in various societies by Westermarck, several other scholars tended to support his findings. Emile Durkheim, who was primarily interested in sociology, in studying primitive societies suggested that the facts of human behavior were more important than ethical theories. One had first to understand how men did in fact act, before one could say anything meaningful about how they ought to act. Herein, he asserted, was one of the great mistakes made by most philosophers. They had pronounced their ideal ethical codes with little reference to the actual nature of man and his behavior. Durkheim stressed more than Westermarck did the role of society in forming one's moral standards. The feelings of approval or disapproval which characterize good and bad conduct, he suggested, are determined by the opinions of society as a unit rather than by the individuals of the society. For Durkheim the supreme authority concerning moral values is the particular society in which one happens to live. The peculiar urgency which attaches to moral commands is due to the fact that they originate in the society and not simply in individuals. But these commands are relativistic, on the basis of this kind of analysis, for they have no validity beyond the particular societies in which they appear.[3]

William Graham Sumner, the first significant American sociologist, also contributed to the belief that moral values are relative in maintaining that moral judgments were accurately described as non-rational manifestations of social forces. Moral values, according to him, are part of the folkways of a given society. Folkways are the customary ways by which man seeks to satisfy his basic needs. When folkways have a certain coerciveness about them, and when the implication is drawn that obeying them is good for the society which developed them, then they have become *mores*. That which we call good is, according to this view, only that to which we refer when we are expressing in forceful language the prevailing customs of our present society. But he also found that these customs varied from society to society, and that they tended to change within any given society from time to time. Philosophy and ethics then become nothing more than attempts to give some rational order to the prevailing folkways, and the reason for each age having its own distinctive philosophy is simply that each age attempts anew to rationalize its favorite customs, folkways and mores. No man can lift himself outside of the mores of his group, and Sumner insisted that the religious prophet or the social reformer was no exception to this rule. For Sumner morals are simply social customs which are more rigidly fixed and enforced than are such customs as styles in dress.[4]

Karl Mannheim has gone even further and has maintained that modes of thought are always conditioned by their social origins. All our ways of thinking are ideologies, according to Mannheim, even though we usually reserve the word to refer disparagingly to views with which we are in disagreement. As he puts it, the ethical system of any country at any time is simply an ideological expression by the prevailing group in power regarding the conduct it values as socially useful. All moral values and norms are then relative; an absolute standard is unobtainable. In fact, Mannheim maintained that even the very concepts of good and of right are purely ideological. It is true that he admitted that for a particular culture one ideology may be practicably more useful than another, but he found no way to stand apart from all ideologies so as to find a universal value.[5]

We might cite many more writers who have contributed to the prevailing relativistic climate in this century, but we have probably already made clear the converging lines of evidence from the social sciences which seem to suggest that "all values are relative."[6] We take for granted today that there are different patterns of culture; not all societies have adopted the same basic values as traditional Western civilization. What remains to be done, however, is to point out that there are conflicting judgments as to what relativism in morals implies.

One popular interpretation of the belief that all values are relative holds then that all values become equally arbitrary and irrational. According to this view, there is no rational justification for any act that an individual does; to save a human life is as irrational as to commit murder. One author has summarized this position as follows:

> It all depends on where you are,
> It all depends on when you are,
> It all depends on what you feel,
> It all depends on how you feel.
> It all depends on how you're raised,
> It all depends on what is praised,
> What's right today is wrong tomorrow,
> Joy in France, in England sorrow.
> It all depends on point of view,
> Australia or Timbuctoo,
> In Rome do as the Romans do.
> If tastes just happen to agree,
> Then you have morality.
> But where they are conflicting trends,
> It all depends, it all depends. . . .[7]

Sometimes, this interpretation of relativism is used to justify one's own conduct, even if it harms other people. If all values are relative, and I "get my kicks" in a different way than you, then it is claimed that you have no right to object to my behavior. Thus, "All values are relative" is often used as an emotive justification of any conduct whatsoever. As the hero of John Barth's novel *The Floating Opera* puts it: "The reasons for which people assign value to things are always ultimately (though not necessarily immediately) arbitrary, irrational."[8]

The logical conclusion of this kind of an interpretation of relativism is found in the contemporary Theatre of the Absurd. The plays of Samuel Beckett, Eugène Ionesco, and Jean Genet reflect the breakdown of the belief in rationality and in the traditional Hebraic-Christian values which marked the recent past. The drama of the absurd not only deals with the futility and uselessness of the ordinary activities of men, but also with the emptiness in men's hearts resulting from the loss of the traditional values of Western civilization. In Beckett's *Waiting for Godot* the main characters, Estragon and Vladimir, carry on meaningless conversations in order to pass the time. Day after day they wait for Godot, who never arrives, and yet they continue to wait, despite the absurdity of their behavior. One day is like any other day, and there is no sense of purpose or meaning to their lives. They discuss separating from each other, hanging themselves, moving to some other spot, but reject all these possibilities. To do anything at all is absurd, and so they might just as well continue in their senseless and eternal waiting. Their constant chatter and antics seem to have only one justification:

VLADIMIR: That passed the time.
ESTRAGON: It would have passed in any case.
VLADIMIR: Yes, but not so rapidly.
 Pause
ESTRAGON: What do we do now?
VLADIMIR: I don't know.
ESTRAGON: Let's go.
VLADIMIR: We can't.
ESTRAGON: Why not?
VLADIMIR: We're waiting for Godot.
ESTRAGON: *(despairingly)* Ah![9]

Another aspect often present in the drama of the absurd stresses the overwhelming horror individuals face in having to cope with a vast world in the face of the impossibility of really having authentic communication with anyone else. In Ionesco's *The Chairs* an old married couple in their nineties await the arrival of a distinguished crowd of people who have been invited to hear the message which the old man will deliver at the end of his life. But since the old man is no orator, he has hired a professional orator to deliver his message. The guests arrive but are never seen or heard; instead the two old people fill the stage with chairs to seat them and carry on endless polite conversation with the empty chairs. The absurdity of attempting to communicate one's wisdom with other human beings is nicely satirized by the spectacle of the empty chairs on the stage. But the ending of the play portrays an even greater absurdity. The old man, convinced that the orator will deliver his message, jumps into the sea, followed by his wife. The professional orator faces the crowd of empty chairs, and prepares to speak. However, he is deaf and dumb and hence makes only an inarticulate gurgling noise. He then attempts to write something on a blackboard, but this is nothing more than a jumble of meaningless letters. Obviously, both in form and content, this play shows the ultimate meaninglessness and absurdity of man's existences[10]

Jean Genet's plays attack the traditional values of Western civilization head on. All of us are portrayed as actors playing roles, and each role is shown to be empty, absurd, and meaningless. In *The Balcony* the scene is set in a fetishistic house of ill-repute, where people go in order to enact the roles which they really would prefer to play in the society in which they live. Despite a violent revolution being waged outside in the "real world" the clients, including the chief of police, continue to come to this establishment where they can act out whatever roles they desire. Ironically, the leader of the revolutionary band comes to the brothel to enact the role of chief of police. The mirrors in the house reflect the false images which men assume in their roles of fantasy, but Genet suggests that these images are not any more unreal than the roles most men actually perform in the outside world. Irma, proprietress of the house of illusions, makes this point in her speech to the audience at the end of the play: "You must now go home, where everything—you can be quite sure—will be even falser than here."[11]

The connection between the absurd and man's loss of belief in the traditional values of the past was clearly expressed by Albert Camus in *The Myth of Sisyphus:*

> A world that can be explained even with bad reasons is a familiar world. But, on the other hand, in a universe suddenly divested of illusions and lights, man feels an alien, a stranger. His exile is without remedy since he is deprived of the memory of a lost home or the hope of a promised land. This divorce between man and his life, the actor and his setting, is properly the feeling of absurdity.[12]

The theatre of the absurd is an attempt to portray the nature of human life when one comes to accept the belief that there are no values which are better than any others, that all life is therefore senseless and meaningless. It is an attempt to force man to confront his life with full awareness of the reality of arbitrary and irrational choices. If one is outraged and shocked by the themes and devices of the theatre of the absurd, one should recall that these dramatists believe that only by a new kind of play can we be awakened from our present conformism and moral insensibility. As Ionesco put it: "To tear ourselves away from the everyday, from habit, from mental laziness which hides from us the strangeness of reality, we must receive something like a real bludgeon blow."[13] The theatre of the absurd has sought to accomplish this mission; to reveal to the audience the absurdity of all value commitments if one believes that all values are equally irrational and arbitrary.

There is, however, a more justifiable interpretation of relativism than the one which we have discussed. This view maintains that moral judgments are relative to something or to some persons; they are not merely irrational and arbitrary whims. This kind of interpretation does not deny the findings of the social scientists for it recognizes that moral standards have in fact varied from culture to culture, from era to era, and even among the individuals in a particular society. In our own society, for example, it is clear that not all people hold the same moral judgments concerning euthanasia or birth control. But to maintain that moral evaluations are relative to our time in history and to the culture of which we are a part is not, according to this interpretation, to disparage morals but rather to help us to formulate more coherent and consistent basic principles for acting in our modern world. Just as science is relative to the age in which it is formulated, so quite naturally are our moral standards and judgments. Everyone knows that the physical sciences have changed radically in their basic principles since the time of their founding several centuries ago, and many scientists expect that similar changes are quite likely to occur in the future. What is not so often recognized is that no one argues that since science has changed so radically in several hundred years, any one is justified in holding arbitrary and irrational beliefs about scientific issues since all such beliefs are relative to the time in which they are formulated. Our understanding of human behavior and of the nature of man has also changed radically in the past several centuries, but this is no reason to maintain that therefore all values are equally absurd, arbitrary and irrational.

It is important that we do not mislead the reader to believe that this second interpretation of the significance of relativism rests on the assumption that moral values are exactly like scientific theories. Far from it, for while this kind of interpretation of relativism does call attention to the fact that scientific theories change and are in that sense relative to the age in which they are proclaimed, it also recognizes that there are crucial differences between believing in a scientific theory and committing oneself to a value judgment. The crucial tests for subscribing to a scientific theory depend upon the ability to explain observable events in terms of the theory, and to permit predictions of how similar events will occur in the future. A scientific theory concerning human behavior would attempt to explain man's actions in terms of a general theory, and then the theory would be accepted or rejected according to its success in predicting future behavior. We have no over-arching general scientific theory of human behavior as yet, although many social scientists claim that we know enough about man for some general explanations and predictions to be made. B. F. Skinner, the Harvard psychologist, has made some extremely penetrating generalizations about human behavior as a result of his experimentation with positive reinforcement as a factor in human conditioning.[14] But while this may tell us how man in fact behaves, and what techniques we can use to condition him to behave in other ways, this scientific study does not tell us how man *ought* to behave. Whenever we ask such questions as "What ought I to do?" we have gone beyond the facts and scientific theories and are asking for a value judgment.

To clarify the distinction we are drawing between facts and values let us consider an example from our own day. The mass media, such as television, have profited from the social scientists' study of human behavior. It is not by accident that television commercials seek to associate their products with the things which most men enjoy or desire. If we can be made to associate a particular brand of cigarettes with the virility of the cowboys of the old West, then we may be conditioned into not only smoking but also into purchasing that particular brand. Even more effective, however, will be to have the cowboy offer one of his cigarettes to a beautiful woman. The appeal will then be made to both the desire of males to be virile, strong he-men, and to the females to be feminine and beautiful. Advertising tries to find out what most people like, and then it seeks for ways by means of which it can associate the products of its clients with these human desires. The degree of success of these conditioning procedures can be determined by any one of you. Do you buy any cola beverage, any brand of aspirin? Or do you ask for a particular brand? If you ask for a particular brand, did you ever try to find out why? Does that brand of cola really taste better? Is that particular brand of aspirin any better than any other brand? Or have you been conditioned by the mass media to associate cola and aspirin with particular brands?

The reader will probably grant that the mass media do indeed condition us to behave in certain way, but he might ask "Is it right for them to do so?" In the light of the evidence which suggests that there is a connection between the smoking of cigarettes and cancer, should not cigarette manufacturers discontinue their advertising campaigns? Is it right for them to continue to associate cigarette smoking with relaxation and pleasure, with really being a mature man? When questions such as these are raised we have entered the area of value judgments. Notice, however, that not every one would say that cigarette manufacturers should discontinue their advertising. An appeal could well be made for the right of the individual to make his own choice as to whether or not he wished to smoke. One might even argue that the states need the tax dollars which they get from the sale of cigarettes, or that the stockholders in the cigarette companies have a right to expect these companies to do everything they can to show a profit. Indeed, would not preventing cigarette companies from engaging in advertising campaigns be a violation of their rights in a free enterprise economy? This issue raises some very basic questions about values. Are economic values to be considered as more important than those of the health of the general populace? Is pleasure of the moment to be valued higher than a long life? Does a state have the right to prohibit its citizens from obtaining pleasure in the ways they choose, if some of their chosen behavior may be injurious to their health or welfare? Who is ultimately to make these decisions? The individual himself? The state, acting for the individual through the representatives he has elected to Congress?

It is possible to reply that a rational man who understands the techniques employed in advertising can resist the pressures brought to bear upon him to use certain products. Furthermore, there are many conflicting voices raised, and we have the opportunity to choose from among them the ones which we believe to be correct. And, of course, each one of us likes to think of himself as one of those rational individuals who makes his own decisions. Suppose, however, that we had been reared in a society like that described by Skinner in *Walden Two*. Frazier, the head of Walden Two, uses his knowledge of human conditioning to train all the inhabitants of this utopian community to cooperate with each other. Competition is unheard of. All the frustrations and conflicts which we experience in our present world are eliminated. The conditioning process has been so thorough that none of the inhabitants raise any questions about the goals of this "ideal" community. Frazier invites some scholars from the outside world to his Walden Two so that they can observe how well he has succeeded. In a discussion with the philosopher in the group of visitors, Frazier proclaims:

> "This *is* the Good Life. We know it. It's a fact, not a theory. It has an experimental justification, not a rational one. As for your conflict of principles, that's an experimental question, too. We don't puzzle our little minds over the outcome of Love versus Duty. We simply arrange a world in which serious conflicts occur as seldom as possible or, with a little luck, not at all."[15]

But the philosopher's main reservation about Walden Two was not grasped by Frazier. Clearly it was a fact that he had conditioned the people in this community to respond in far more cooperative and peaceful ways than they do in our contemporary world. The philosopher, however, asked in effect, "Is this really the Good Life? Ought man to be conditioned into behaving docilely? Is the absence of all competition and conflict a good thing? How would it ever be possible for a genius or an exceptionally creative man to develop in Walden Two? Is not a genius, who rejects the values of his day, of more worth than thousands of conforming robot-like men? Why should Frazier determine the values to which the entire community would be conditioned to conform? What right did any man have to so completely determine the lives of others?" These were questions concerning values, not concerning facts and scientific theories.

The reader should now understand that to make a value judgment is to express a preference; it is to make an estimation of worth. We all make

Chapter IV: Relativism

value judgments every day of our lives. In such a simple act as choosing to spend ten dollars to see a play, rather than to buy a book, one is expressing the belief that at that particular time seeing that particular play will be more worthwhile than buying that particular book. Furthermore, in such an act, we also can see what this second kind of interpretation of relativism maintains. One is not maintaining that it is always better to see a play than to buy a book; to do so would be to subscribe to an absolute value judgment. Rather, one's judgment is based upon the comparison of a particular play with a particular book at a particular time. If one had not recently bought a great many books, one might have chosen to buy a particular novel instead of going to the play. If one has been reading a great deal lately, and desires some form of relaxing entertainment, he might very well choose to see a particular musical comedy. Clearly, one would not maintain that everyone ought to make exactly the same choice as he made, but notice also that one's decision is not completely arbitrary, for reasons can be given for making the value judgment.

Our concern here, however, will be with more basic and general value commitments, rather than with particular decisions. What do I most want out of Life? Is my personal integrity of greater value to me than success? Should I always be oriented so as to seek my own welfare, even if it is at the expense of others? Should my values not happen to agree with those generally held by my society, ought I to follow my own convictions anyway? These and many other questions like them raise general questions concerning one's basic values in terms of which many of one's everyday choices are made. This second interpretation of relativism, which we have been considering, reminds us that even these more basic commitments are related to specific persons who are living in a particular period of history. We must, therefore, not become the slaves of the principles of the past, but rather seek honestly for the most rationally defensible values which will assist in making our world a more humane one in which to live. Moral values then are not arbitrary; they are relative to man.

Relativism in moral theory need not, therefore, lead one into despair and absurdity; rather it may be seen as a liberating force requiring that each man make a serious effort to choose those values which he finds to be most meaningful for himself and society. John Barth has the hero of *The Floating Opera* reject the view he held earlier concerning the absurdity of values. After many years of thought and life he realizes:

> If there are no absolutes, then a value is no less authentic, no less genuine, no less compelling, no less "real," for its being relative! It is one thing to say "Values are *only* relative"; quite another, and more thrilling, to remove the pejorative adverb and assert "There *are* relative values!" These, at least, we have, and if they are all we have, then in *no way whatsoever* are they inferior.[16]

213

Quest for Goodness: An Introduction to Ethics

We shall examine in later chapters the positions adopted concerning moral relativism by the proponents of different value orientations for our century. We shall find that some of these writers, such as Marx, Nietzsche and Freud, fully accept moral relativism as an inevitable fact in the modern world; while others, such as Kierkegaard and Fromm, attempt to defend a commitment to absolute or objective values. That we live in an age of pluralism will become quite apparent when we examine the views of contemporary theologians, some of whom frankly call for a new morality based on relativism. But we must not get ahead of our story. In addition to our century being called an age of relativism, we are often told that it is an age dominated by pragmatism. Let us see what this suggests about our contemporary moral climate.

Endnotes

1. Walter Lippman, *A Preface to Morals* (New York: Macmillan, 1929), *passim*.
2. Edward Westermarck, *Ethical Relativity* (Paterson, N.J.: Littlefield, Adams & Co., 1960), *passim*.
3. Emile Durkheim, *The Elementary Form's of the Religious Life,* trans. by Joseph Ward Swain (New York: Collier Books, 1961), *passim*.
4. William Graham Sumner, *Folkways: A Study of the Sociological Importance of Usages, Manners, Customs, Mores, and Morals* (New York: The New American Library of World Literature, Inc., 1960).
5. Karl Mannheim, *Ideology and Utopia: An Introduction to the Sociology of Knowledge,* trans. by Louis Wirth and Edward Shils (New York: A Harvest Book, Harcourt, Brace & World, Inc., 1936).
6. Among works which have appeared recently, the reader might be interested in referring to Ruth Benedict, *Patterns of Culture* (Boston: Houghton Mifflin Co., 1934), and the numerous anthropological writings of Margaret Mead.
7. Quoted in Abraham Edel, *Ethical Judgment: The Use of Science in Ethics* (New York: The Free Press, A Division of The Macmillan Co., 1955), p. 16. Edel himself does not subscribe to this kind of an interpretation of ethical relativity; in fact his book is an excellent attempt to find a common human basis for morality.
8. John Barth, *The Floating Opera* (New York: An Avon Library Book, 1956), p. 216.
9. Samuel Beckett, *Waiting for Godot: A Tragicomedy in Two Acts* (New York: Grove Press, Inc., 1954), pp. 31–32.
10. Eugene Ionesco, *Four Plays: The Bald Soprano, The Lesson, Jack or the Submission, The Chairs, trans.* by Donald M. Allen (New York: Grove Press, Inc., 1958).
11. Jean Genet, *The Balcony,* trans. by Bernard Frechtman (New York: Grove Press, Inc., 1958), p.115.
12. Albert Camus, *The Myth of Sisyphus and Other Essays,* trans. by Justin O'Brien (New York: Vintage Books, Inc., Random House, 1959), p. 5.

13. Eugene Ionesco, "Discovering the Theatre," in *Theatre in the Twentieth Century,* ed. by Robert W. Corrigan (New York: Grove Press, Inc., 1965), p. 86.
14. B. F. Skinner, *Science and Human Behavior* (New York: The Free Press, A Division of Macmillan Publishing Co., 1965), *passim.*
15. B. F. Skinner, *Walden Two* (New York: Macmillan, 1962), p. 161.
16. Barth, *The Floating Opera,* p. 271.

Source: Luther J. Binkley, *Conflict of Ideals* (New York, 1969), pp. 2–11. Copyright © 1969 by Litton Educational Publishing, Inc. Reprinted by permission of D. Van Nostrand Company.

When in Rome . . .

Burton F. Porter

When the general relativist position is applied solely to the field of ethics it takes the form of claiming that all value judgments are a reflection of personal and societal attitudes. From a relativist standpoint someone who judges stealing to be wrong is only expressing a personal distaste for stealing or reporting the fact that his society disapproves of it. He is not telling us anything about the nature of stealing or recognizing any inherent wrongdoing in taking someone else's property. The same is said to be true of a person who praises courage, loyalty, justice, patriotism, or compassion. Some of these values are more widespread than others but none is universal and each varies according to the society's perspective. To the relativist all moral evaluations are considered to be arbitrary preferences, depending entirely upon the individual, the situation, the culture, and the times. Conflicting ethical positions could be equally valid.

Within this ethical realm, a distinction may be made between relativism and subjectivism. When this is done, *subjectivism* refers to the theory that all ethical evaluations merely reflect the preferences of the person. They do not necessarily describe social attitudes and they certainly do not identify any qualities intrinsic to an act; they merely express the feelings of the individual. If those feelings were different, then the values would also be different. For example, to state that keeping promises is important means nothing more than that the person likes promise-keeping and perhaps that he wishes everyone else did also. It may give him a sense of security, the positive self-image that says he is someone to be trusted, and the confident feeling that he can depend upon other people when they give their word. Whatever the motivation may be, the moral judgment is nothing more than an autobiographical statement; it tells us something about the psychology of the speaker but nothing about the nature of the act.

Subjectivism differs from relativism then by emphasizing the personal nature of ethical evaluations. In other words, the subjectivist interprets a value judgment to mean "X suits my taste, it appeals to me," whereas the relativist views it as a report that "our society approves of X."

Chapter IV: Relativism

In contrast to both theories ethical *objectivism* maintains that certain actions really are right and others are wrong, that some goals in living are inherently worth seeking and others are worthless. That is, the objectivist maintains that ethical standards do exist and that judgments can legitimately be made about human conduct. These standards are thought to be transcultural, objective, and unchanging and for that reason authoritative in settling disagreements about right and wrong, good and bad.

For example, the judgment Women should not be treated as inferior to men could be assumed to be an objectively true proposition. Or Slavery is unjust could be taken as an accurate evaluation of the institution of slavery. In neither case, according to the objectivist, are we simply describing our society's attitudes or evincing our personal dislikes; we are making judgments about the offensiveness of these practices. An objectivist might also assert the intrinsic worth of generosity, pity, or trust and the intrinsic wrongness of deceit, theft, or torture. Such evaluations could also be considered insights into the nature of these actions.

The objectivist does not maintain that he has certain knowledge of the objective standards but only that there are such standards to be known. He will admit that a perfect understanding of moral principles is impossible but he takes this as his ideal and measures his progress by the degree to which he gains moral awareness. He argues against the relativist and subjectivist: Because no one can know everything about right and wrong conduct, it does not follow that no knowledge is possible or that one person's opinion is as good as another's.

In the same way that we can differentiate between ethical relativism and objectivism, a distinction can be made between ethical objectivism and a logical extension of that position called *universalism*. The theory of universalism maintains that actions that are intrinsically right are forever right. That is, an act that can be judged right in itself therefore is right for all people, at all times, and in all places. For example, if we value respect for another person's bodily integrity and this belief is a truly valid principle, then it holds true everywhere and for everyone. Consequently, the violent act of rape, which denies the factor of consent and violates a person's body, is wrong whenever it occurs.

The universalist is actually carrying objectivism one step further, asserting universality to intrinsically correct values. In linguistic terms it is the claim that "right" implies "ought": Whatever is right should always be done. It would be very odd, the universalist thinks, to claim that an act is valuable but to deny that everyone ought to do it. It would be equally peculiar to claim that an act is wrong in one place yet right in another (e.g., rape), or that something formerly wrong has become right. The moral nature of actions does not change even if our perception of them does. The difficult part lies in recognizing their essential nature and making value judgments that are correct in terms of that reality. But at least we have to assume that conduct correctly judged as right or wrong would be so absolutely and universally.

The lines of disagreement are thereby drawn, with the relativist and subjectivist on one side and the objectivist and universalist on the other. But which position is correct? Are there values that transcend time and place, are things right in themselves, or are all values arbitrary and dependent upon one's society or personal temperament? Can one make something trivial important by taking it seriously? Is an action right if people think it so or could people be mistaken in their moral judgments? Could an ideal be valuable whether or not anyone realizes it? Does conduct become right because of society's beliefs or could a society be wrong in what it believes, holding various acts to be commendable when in fact they are abominable?

Relativism in Greek Philosophy

In intellectual history the debate over this question goes back at least as far as Plato (c. 427–347 B.C.). We will discuss Plato's broader views later, but during that period of history there were a group of Greek thinkers who were known as Sophists—itinerant philosophers who taught the skills of practical success. They often were accused of being persuasive rather than logical in their reasoning and more concerned with their fees than with the integrity of teaching. (Sophistry, in fact, has become a name for fallacious arguments that have the appearance of being correct.) The important point for our purposes is that they shared a common belief in relativism and were the first philosophers to hold such a position.

In Plato's most famous dialogue, *The Republic,* a celebrated discussion takes place between Socrates and a Sophist named Thrasymachus over the issue of justice, and as the dialogue proceeds it comes to include the larger issue of ethical relativism. Socrates, who is either a spokesman for Plato's ideas or the person whose words Plato recorded, asks for a sound definition of justice. Thrasymachus replies that "justice is nothing else than the interest of the stronger." He then elaborates upon his position in political terms by saying

> "have you never heard that forms of government differ; there are tyrannies, and there are democracies, and there are aristocracies?"
> "Yes, I know." Socrates replies.
> "And the government is the ruling power in each state?"
> "Certainly."
> "And the different forms of government make laws democratical, aristocratical, tyrannical, with a view to their several interests; and these laws, which are made by them for their own interests, are the justice which they deliver to their subjects, and him who transgresses

them they punish as a breaker of the law, and unjust. And that is what I mean when I say that in all states there is the same principle of justice, which is the interest of the government; and as the government must be supposed to have power, the only reasonable conclusion is, that everywhere there is one principle of justice, which is the interest of the stronger."

In this passage Thrasymachus claims that might makes right; whatever laws a government has the power to enforce thereby become just because of that power. Justice changes then according to the various forms of governments that are established and is wholly relative to the rulers' interests.

The Sophist Gorgias is another early representative of relativism and he expressed his views in three propositions for which he is renowned. The first proposition consists of the bald pronouncement that right and wrong have no objective validity. If an action were right then we would be morally bound to perform it whenever the occasion arose. But because ethical values are merely the product of tradition and custom, right and wrong have no claim upon us. There are only actions that further our purposes and those that obstruct our self-interest.

The second proposition is that even if there were universal standards of right and wrong we could never have knowledge of them. We can only accept the moral ideas that we have experienced in our own nation and are never able to transcend the limitations of that cultural experience. Different peoples hold different values because of the beliefs that prevail in their particular social environments and to escape into a realm of objective understanding is utterly impossible.

Gorgias addresses a final eventuality in his third proposition, that even if objective standards existed and they could be grasped by exceptional individuals such truths could never be communicated. For no one would be receptive to new insights that were at variance with the accepted customs and beliefs. The discoverers of such ideas would be shunned or persecuted as dangerous radicals, and their ideas would be condemned as heresy.

These three propositions—that values do not exist, that if they did exist they would be unknowable, and that if they were knowable they would be incommunicable—clearly place Gorgias in the relativist camp. In an overall sense he is convinced that right and wrong are terms that merely reflect our personal advantage; to think otherwise, he believes, is hypocrisy.

Besides Thrasymachus and Gorgias, another Sophist named Protagoras appears to have been the father of the group as well as the most eminent and powerful spokesman for the relativist position. He is referred to as the Great Sophist and one of Plato's dialogues, named the *Protagoras*, offers a very sympathetic rendering of his views.

It was Protagoras who said, "Man is the measure of all things, of the existence of the things that are and the nonexistence of the things that are not." This *Homo Mensura* or Man-Measure theory was derived from Protagoras' views about perception. In the dialogue the *Theaetetus* Plato attributes to him the paradigm of the wind, which can be expressed as follows: When a wind blows it will be felt by a person with fever as chilly but to another person it will be perceived as refreshing. Now if the same wind can appear both chilly and refreshing, then the wind itself does not possess qualities but is what it appears to be to each person. The same is true of the perception of tastes, textures, colors, aromas, and sounds. (This point sometimes is expressed by saying that to an ant silk is rough and a pin drop loud.)

Protagoras applies the same principle to moral values. Whether a child speaks Greek or Persian, he says, depends on the nation in which he is born, and by the same token, whether one believes in abandoning unwanted babies to die is a cultural accident. So long as a person holds certain beliefs they are true to him, for right and wrong are whatever we say they are.

Relativism in Modern Philosophy

The relativist position did not die with the ancient thinkers. It has been argued by numerous philosophers throughout history and continues to be affirmed to the present day. Some of the most notable figures in the relativist camp were Thomas Hobbes (1588–1679), Benedict Spinoza (1632–1677), David Hume (1711–1776), and more contemporaneously the Pragmatists William James (1842–1910) and John Dewey (1859–1952), A. J. Ayer (1910–) the chief spokesman for Logical Positivism, and Jean-Paul Sartre (1905–1980) the dean of French Existentialism. Even the British philosopher Bertrand Russell at one time expressed a relativist position when he said, "there can be no such thing as 'sin' in any absolute sense; what one man calls 'sin' another may call 'virtue,' and though they may dislike each other on account of this difference, neither can convict the other of intellectual error." It would be useful therefore to examine some of the arguments they offer, taking Hume as a representative of what is termed *modern* philosophy and A. J. Ayer as an example of contemporary philosophic thinking.

David Hume held a position of ethical relativism in the eighteenth century but from a very different standpoint than that of Thrasymachus. In the following celebrated passage from his book *An Enquiry Concerning Human Understanding* Hume first divides genuine knowledge into two categories:

> All the objects of human reason or inquiry may naturally be divided into two kinds, to wit, *Relations of Ideas,* and *Matters of Fact*. Of the

Chapter IV: Relativism

first kind are the sciences of Geometry, Algebra, and Arithmetic; and in short, every affirmation which is either intuitively or demonstratively certain. *That the square of the hypothenuse is equal to the square of the two sides,* is a proposition which expresses a relation between these figures. *That three times five is equal to the half of thirty,* expresses a relation between these numbers. Propositions of this kind are discoverable by the mere operation of thought, without dependence on what is anywhere existent in the universe. Though there never were a circle or a triangle in nature, the truths demonstrated by Euclid would forever retain their certainty and evidence.

Matters of fact, which are the second objects of human reason, are not ascertained in the same manner; nor is our evidence of their truth, however great, of a like nature with the foregoing. The contrary of every matter of fact is still possible; because it can never imply a contradiction, and is conceived by the mind with the same facility and distinctness, as if ever so conformable to reality. *That the sun will not rise tomorrow* is no less intelligible a proposition, and implies no more contradiction than the affirmation, *that it will rise.* . . .

To paraphrase and update Hume's distinction, relations of ideas are judged according to the meaning of the terms involved. The sentence All circles are round is a true statement because part of the meaning of the term *circle* is that it is a round figure; the predicate of the sentence is contained in the subject. Because of the logic of the two concepts and their relation, we can assert that the proposition is true. The same can be said of All bachelors are unmarried males; All murals are on walls; and All mammals breathe air. These statements may be obvious and trivial but they also are necessarily true; the conceptual relationship makes them undeniable.

Matters of fact, on the other hand, are not established by examining the logic but by determining whether the proposition accurately describes the external world. For example, the truth of the statement All fish have dorsal fins cannot be determined by analyzing the concept of fish to see whether having dorsal fins is implied. Rather, we would have to check the facts. We might consult an ichthyologist, refer to a text on marine biology, or conduct a study ourselves of every species of fish. Whatever steps we took to find out, we would be comparing the statement to what is actually the case in the world.

Hume, incidentally, maintains that matters of fact are verified by showing a cause-effect connection between the statement and some fact that proves it. For instance, if we were to find a watch on a deserted island we would have to conclude that people had once been there, for the effect, that is the watch, could only have been caused by people having created it. The same type of proof applies to all factual assertions, Hume declares, therefore we should treat the study of cause-effect connections as crucial in testing the truth of matters of fact. Hume himself went on to develop one of the most radical concepts of causality ever devised.

The application of Hume's distinction to ethics is that moral judgments are neither relations of ideas nor matters of fact. The truth of a principle such as Love thine enemy cannot be proven either by the meaning of the terms involved or by reference to external facts. Moral judgments therefore occupy a state of limbo; their truth lies beyond all verification. Hume writes:

> In every system of morality which I have hitherto met with, I have always remarked, that the author proceeds for some time in the ordinary way of reasoning, and establishes the being of a god, or makes observations concerning human affairs; when of a sudden I am surpriz'd to find, that instead of the usual copulations of propositions, *is* and *is not*, I meet with no proposition that is not connected with an *ought*, or an *ought not*. This change is imperceptible; but it is, however, of the last consequence. For as this ought or ought not, expresses some new relation or affirmation, 'tis necessary that it should be observed and explained . . . and [I] am persuaded that this small attention would subvert all the vulgar systems of morality, and let us see, that the distinction of vice and virtue is not founded merely on the relations of objects, nor is perceived by reason.

Hume is implying here that ethical assertions (the *ought* and *ought not*) do not fall into either of the two categories of genuine knowledge. According to his view then, we can have no knowledge of any actual right or wrong.

In the history of philosophy, Hume's position has been echoed by numerous voices all of which reached the same skeptical conclusion regarding values. A theory known as *Positivism,* founded by the French philosopher Auguste Comte (1798–1857), was especially militant in maintaining that only scientific claims can be true. And Hume's position emerged again (but in "linguistic" form) in the twentieth century movement called *Logical Positivism.* A. J. Ayer was one of its leading spokesmen and in his influential book *Language, Truth and Logic* he presents a basic standard for determining when a sentence is meaningful and when it is meaningless. Ayer calls this the Verification Principle and describes it as follows:

> The criterion which we use to test the genuineness of apparent statements of fact is the criterion of verifiability. We say that a sentence is factually significant to any given person, if, and only if, he knows how to verify the proposition which it purports to express—that is, if he knows what observations would lead him, under certain conditions, to accept the proposition as being true, or reject it as being false. If, on the other hand, the putative proposition is of such a character that the assumption of its truth, or falsehood, is consistent with any assumption whatsoever concerning the nature of his future experience, then, as far as he is concerned, it is, if not a tautology, a mere pseudo-proposition. The sentence expressing it may be emotionally significant to him; but

it is not literally significant.

The implication of the Verification Principle is that various types of sentences previously regarded as perfectly meaningful were now to be regarded as meaningless. Sentences about religion, art, emotions, history—all were judged as nonsense because they could not be verified by any empirical (i.e., sense) observations. Most important for our purposes, value judgments were also declared meaningless on the same grounds: No empirical tests could confirm or deny them.

The Logical Positivists were arguing that a sentence such as The cat is on the mat is clearly meaningful, because we know how to go about verifying its truth. If we experience a certain shape and size, a mewing sound, a particular odor, and can feel soft fur then these sense particulars constitute proof that the proposition is true. But how can anyone test an alleged proposition such as Honesty is praiseworthy or To forgive is divine. Sentences of this kind are beyond all possible verification; therefore they are not false but, worse still, they are utterly senseless.

All ethical assertions fall into this category. They are meaningless and therefore incapable of being judged either true or false. It is as though we were saying, "'Twas brillig, and the slithy toves/ Did gyre and gimble in the wabe," that is, expressing a parody of meaningful language. Ayer writes:

> If I say to someone, "You acted wrongly in stealing that money," I am not stating anything more than if I had simply said, "You stole that money." In adding that this action is wrong I am not making any further statement about it. I am simply evincing my moral disapproval of it. It is as if I had said "You stole that money," in a peculiar tone of horror. . . .
>
> It is clear that there is nothing said here which can be true or false. Another man may disagree with me about the wrongness of stealing, in the sense that he may not have the same feelings about stealing as I have, and he may quarrel with me on account of my moral sentiments. But he cannot, strictly speaking, contradict me. For in saying that a certain type of action is right or wrong, I am not making any factual statement, not even a statement about my own state of mind. I am merely expressing certain moral sentiments.

Cultural Relativism and Cultural Values

Melville Herskovits

Cultural relativism, in all cases, must be sharply distinguished from concepts of the relativity of individual behavior, which would negate all social controls over conduct. . . . The very core of cultural relativism is the social discipline that comes of respect for differences—mutual respect. Emphasis on the worth of many ways of life, not one, is an affirmation of the values in each culture. Such emphasis seeks to understand and to harmonize goals, not to judge and destroy those that do not dovetail with our own.

All peoples form judgments about ways of life different from their own. When systematic study is undertaken, comparison gives rise to classification, and scholars have devised many schemes for classifying ways of life. Moral judgments have been drawn regarding the ethical principles that guide the behavior and mold the value systems of different peoples. Their economic and political structures and their religious beliefs have been ranked in order of complexity, efficiency, desirability. Their art, music, and literary forms have been weighed.

It has become increasingly evident, however, that evaluations of this kind stand or fall with the acceptance of the premises from which they derive. In addition, many of the criteria on which judgment is based are in conflict, so that conclusions drawn from one definition of what is desirable will not agree with those based on another formulation.

A simple example will illustrate this. There are not many ways in which the primary family can be constituted. One man may live with one woman, one woman may have a number of husbands, one man may have a number of wives. But if we evaluate these forms according to their function of perpetuating the group, it is clear that they perform their essential tasks. Otherwise, the societies wherein they exist would not survive.

Such an answer will, however, not satisfy all those who have undertaken to study cultural evaluation. What of the moral questions inherent in the practice of monogamy as against polygamy, the adjustment of children raised in households where, for example, the mothers must compete on behalf of their offspring for the favors of a common husband? If monogamy is held to be the desired form of marriage, the responses to these questions are predetermined. But when we consider these questions from the point of view of those who live in polygamous societies, alternative answers, based on different conceptions of what is desirable, may be given.

Let us consider, for example, the life of a plural family in the West African culture of Dahomey. . . . Here, within a compound, live a man and his wives. The man has his own house, as has each of the women and her children, after the basic African principle that two wives cannot successfully inhabit the same quarters. Each wife in turn spends a native week of four days with the common husband, cooking his food, washing his cloths, sleeping in his house, and then making way for the next. Her children, however, remain in their mother's hut. With pregnancy, she drops out of this routine, and ideally, in the interest of her child's health and her own, does not again visit her husband until the child has been born and weaned. This means a period of from three to four years, since infants are nursed two years and longer.

The compound, made up of these households, is a cooperative unit. The women who sell goods in the market, or make pottery, or have their gardens, contribute to its support. This aspect, though of great economic importance, is secondary to the prestige that attaches to the larger unit. This is why one often finds a wife not only urging her husband to acquire a second spouse but even aiding him by loans or gifts to make this possible.

Tensions do arise between the women who inhabit a large compound. Thirteen different ways of getting married have been recorded in this society, and in a large household those wives who are married in the same category tend to unite against all others. Competition for the regard of the husband is also a factor, when several wives try to influence the choice of an heir in favor of their own sons. Yet all the children of the compound play together, and the strength of the emotional ties between the children of the same mother more than compensates for whatever stresses may arise between brothers and sisters who share the same father but are of different mothers. Cooperation, moreover, is by no means a mere formality among the wives. Many common tasks are performed in friendly unison, and there is solidarity in the interest of women's prerogatives, or where the status of the common husband is threatened.

We may now return to the criteria to be applied in drawing judgments concerning polygamous as against monogamous families. The family structure of Dahomey is obviously a complex institution. If we but consider the possible lines of personal relations among the many individuals concerned, we see clearly how numerous are the ramifications of reciprocal right and obligation of the Dahomean family. The effectiveness of the Dahomean family is, however, patent. It has, for untold generations, performed its function of rearing the young; more than this, the very size of the group gives it economic resources and a resulting stability that might well be envied by those who live under different systems of family organization. Moral values are always difficult to establish, but at least in this society marriage is clearly distinguished from casual sex relations and from prostitution, in its supernatural sanctions and in the prestige it confers, to say nothing of the economic obligation toward spouse and prospective offspring explicitly accepted by one who enters into a marriage.

Numerous problems of adjustment do present themselves in an aggregate of this sort. It does not call for much speculation to understand the plaint of the head of one large compound when he said: "One must be something of a diplomat if one has many wives." Yet the sly digs in proverb and song, and the open quarreling, involve no greater stress than is found in any small rural community where people are also thrown closely together for long periods of time. Quarrels between co-wives are not greatly different from disputes over the back fence between neighbors. And Dahomeans who know European culture, when they argue for their system, stress the fact that it permits the individual wife to space her children in a way that is in accord with the best precepts of modern gynecology.

Thus polygamy, when looked at from the point of view of those who practice it, is seen to hold values that are not apparent from the outside. A similar case can be made for monogamy, however, when it is attacked by those who are enculturated to a different kind of family structure. And what is true of a particular phase of culture such as this, is also true of others. Evaluations are *relative* to the cultural background out of which they arise.

Cultural relativism is in essence an approach to the question of the nature and role of values in culture. It represents a scientific, inductive attack on an age-old philosophical problem, using fresh, cross-cultural data, hitherto not available to scholars, gained from the study of the underlying value-systems of societies having the most diverse customs. The principle of cultural relativism, briefly stated, is as follows: *Judgments are based on experience, and experience is interpreted by each individual in terms of his own enculturation.* Those who hold for the existence of fixed values will find materials in other societies that necessitate a reinvestigation of their assumptions. Are there absolute moral standards, or are moral standards effective only as far as they agree with the orientations of a given people at a given period of their history? We even approach the problem of the ultimate nature of reality itself. Cassirer . . . holds that reality can only be experienced through the symbolism of language. Is reality, then, not defined and redefined by the ever-varied symbolisms of the innumerable languages of mankind? Answers to questions such as these represent one of the most profound contributions of anthropology to the analysis of man's place in the world. When we reflect that such intangibles as right and wrong, normal and abnormal, beautiful and plain are absorbed as a person learns the ways of the group into which he is born, we see that we are dealing here with a process of first importance. Even the facts of the physical world are discerned through the enculturative screen, so that the perception of time, distance, weight, size, and other "realities" is mediated by the conventions of any given group.

No culture, however, is a closed system of rigid molds to which the behavior of all members of a society must conform. The psychological reality of culture tells us that a culture, as such, can *do* nothing. It is but the summation of the behavior and habitual modes of thought of the persons who make up a particular society. Though by learning and habit these individuals conform to the ways of the group into which they have been born, they nonetheless vary in their reactions to the situations of living they commonly meet. They vary, too, in the degree to which they desire change, as whole cultures vary. This is but another way in which we see that culture is flexible and holds many possibilities of choice within its framework, and that to recognize the values held by a given people in no wise implies that these values are a constant factor in the lives of succeeding generations of the same group.

How the ideas of a people mediate their approach even to the physical world can be made plain by a few examples. Indians living in the southwestern part of the United States think in terms of *six* cardinal points rather than four. In addition to north, south, east and west, they include the directions "up" and "down." From the point of view that the universe is three dimensional, these Indians are entirely realistic. Among ourselves, even in airplane navigation, where three dimensions must be coped with as they need not by those who keep to the surface of the earth, we separate direction from height in instruments and in our thinking about position. We operate, conceptually, on two distinct planes. One is horizontal— "We are traveling ENE." One is vertical —"We are now cruising at 8000 feet:"

Or take a problem in the patterning of sound. We accept the concept of the wave length, tune pianos in accordance with a mechanically determined scale, and are thus conditioned to what we call true pitch. Some persons, we say, have absolute pitch; that is, a note struck or sung at random will immediately be given its place in the scale–"That's B flat." A composition learned in a given key, when transposed, will deeply trouble such a person, though those who are musically trained but do not have true pitch will enjoy such a transposed work, if the *relation* of each note to every other has not been disturbed. Let us assume that it is proposed to study whether this ability to identify a note is an inborn trait, found among varying but small percentages of individuals in various societies. The difficulty of probing such a question appears immediately once we discover that but few peoples have fixed scales, and none other than ourselves has the concept of true pitch! Those living in cultures without mechanically tuned and true instruments are free to enjoy notes that are as much as a quarter-tone "off," as we would say. As for the patterned progressions in which the typical scales and modal orientations of any musical convention are set, the number of such systems, each of which is consistent within its own limits, is infinite . . .

The very definition of what is normal or abnormal is relative to the phenomenon of possession as found among African and New World Negroes. The supreme expression of their religious experience, possession, is a psychological state wherein a displacement of personality occurs when the god "comes to the head" of the worshipper. The individual thereupon is held to be the deity himself. This phenomenon has been described in pathological terms by many students whose approach is non-anthropological, because of its surface resemblance to cases in the records of medical practitioners, psychological clinicians, psychiatrists, and others. The hysteria-like trances, where persons, their eyes tightly closed, move about excitedly and presumably without purpose or design, or roll on the ground, muttering meaningless syllables, or go into a state where their bodies achieve complete rigidity, are not difficult to equate with the neurotic and even psychotic manifestations of abnormality found in Euroamerican society.

Yet when we look beneath behavior to meaning, and place such apparently random acts in their cultural frame of reference, such conclusions become untenable. For *relative to the setting in which these possession experiences occur, they are not to be regarded as abnormal at all,* much less psychopathological. They are *culturally* patterned, and often induced by learning and discipline. The dancing or other acts of the possessed persons are so stylized that one who knows this religion can identify the god possessing a devotee by the behavior of the individual possessed. Furthermore, the possession experience does not seem to be confined to emotionally unstable persons. Those who "get the god" run the gamut of personality types found in the group. Observation of persons who frequent the cults, yet who, in the idiom of worship "have nothing in the head" and thus never experience possession, seems to show that they are far less adjusted than those who do get possessed. Finally, the nature of the possession experience in these cultures is so disciplined that it may only come to a given devotee under particular circumstances. In West Africa and Brazil the gods come only to those who have been designated in advance by the priest of their group, who lays his hands on their heads. In Haiti, for an initiate not a member of the family group giving a rite to become possessed at a ceremony is considered extremely "bad form" socially and a sign of spiritual weakness, evidence that the god is not under the control of his worshipper.

The terminology of psychopathology, employed solely for descriptive purposes, may be of some utility. But the connotation it carries of psychic

Chapter IV: Relativism

instability, emotional imbalance, and departure from normality recommends the use of other words that do not invite such a distortion of cultural reality. For in these Negro societies, the meaning this experience holds for the people falls entirely in the realm of understandable, predictable, normal behavior. This behavior is known and recognized by all members as an experience that may come to any one of them, and is to be welcomed not only for the psychological security it affords, but also for the status, economic gain, aesthetic expression, and emotional release it vouchsafes the devotee.

※ ※ ※

The primary mechanism that directs the evaluation of culture is *ethnocentrism*. Ethnocentrism is the point of view that one's own way of life is to be preferred to all others. Flowing logically from the process of early enculturation, it characterizes the way most individuals feel about their own culture, whether or not they verbalize their feeling. Outside the stream of Euroamerican culture, particularly among nonliterate peoples, this is taken for granted and is to be viewed as a factor making for individual adjustment and social integration. For the strengthening of the ego, identification with one's own group, whose ways are implicitly accepted as best, is all-important. It is when, as in Euroamerican culture, ethnocentrism is rationalized and made the basis of programs of action detrimental to the well-being of other peoples that it gives rise to serious problems.

The ethnocentrism of nonliterate peoples is best illustrated in their myths, folk tales, proverbs, and linguistic habits. It is manifest in many tribal names whose meaning in their respective languages signifies "human beings." The inference that those to whom the name does not apply are outside this category is, however, rarely, if ever, explicitly made. When the Suriname Bush Negro, shown a flashlight, admires it and then quotes the proverb: "White man's magic isn't black man's magic," he is merely reaffirming his faith in his own culture. He is pointing out that the stranger, for all his mechanical devices, would be lost in the Guiana jungle without the aid of his Bush Negro friends.

A myth of the origin of human races, told by the Cherokee Indians of the Great Smoky Mountains, gives another instance of this kind of ethnocentrism. The Creator fashioned man by first making and firing an oven and then, from dough he had prepared, shaping three figures in human form. He placed the figures in the oven and waited for them to get done. But his impatience to see the result of this, his crowning experiment in the work of creation, was so great that he removed the first figure too soon. It was sadly underdone—pale, an unlovely color, and from it descended the white people. His second figure had fared well. The timing was accurate, the form, richly browned, that was to be the ancestor of the Indians, pleased him in every way. He so admired it, indeed, that he neglected to take out of the oven the third form, until he smelled it burning. He threw open the door, only to find this last one charred and black. It was regrettable, but there was nothing to be done; and this was the first Negro.[1]

This is the more usual form that ethnocentrism takes among many peoples—a gentle insistence on the good qualities of one's own group, without any drive to extend this attitude into the field of action. With such a point of view, the objectives, sanctioned modes of behavior, and value systems of peoples with whom one's own group comes into contact can be considered in terms of their desirability, then accepted or rejected without any reference to absolute standards. That differences in the manner of achieving commonly sought objectives may be permitted to exist without a judgment being entered on them involves a reorientation in thought for those in the Euroamerican tradition, because in this tradition, a difference in belief or behavior too often implies something is worse, or less desirable, and must be changed.

The assumption that the cultures of nonliterate peoples are of inferior quality is the end product of a long series of developments in our intellectual history. It is not often recalled that the concept of progress, that strikes so deep into our thinking, is relatively recent. It is, in fact, a unique product of our culture. It is a part of the same historic stream that developed the scientific tradition and that developed the machine, thus giving Europe and America the final word in debates about cultural superiority. "He who makes the gun-powder wields the power," runs a Dahomean proverb. There is no rebuttal to an argument, backed by cannon, advanced to a people who can defend their position with no more than spears, or bows and arrows, or at best a flint-lock gun.

With the possible exception of technological aspects of life, however, the proposition that one way of thought or action is better than another is exceedingly difficult to establish on the grounds of any universally acceptable criteria. Let us take food as an instance. Cultures are equipped differently for the production of food, so that some peoples eat more than others. However, even on the subsistence level, there is no people who do not hold certain potential foodstuffs to be unfit for human consumption. Milk, which figures importantly in our diet, is rejected as food by the peoples of southeastern Asia. Beef, a valued element of the Euroamerican cuisine, is regarded with disgust by Hindus. Nor need compulsions be this strong. The thousands of cattle that range the East African highlands are primarily wealth to be preserved, and not a source of food. Only the cow that dies is eaten—a practice that, though abhorrent to us, has apparently done no harm to those who have been following it for generations.

Totemic and religious taboos set up further restrictions on available foodstuffs, while the refusal to consume many other edible and nourishing substances is simply based on the enculturative conditioning. So strong is this conditioning that prohibited food consumed unwittingly may induce such a physiological reaction as vomiting. All young animals provide succulent meat, but the religious abhorrence of the young pig by the Mohammedan is no stronger than the secular rejection of puppy steaks or colt chops by ourselves. Ant larvae, insect grubs, locusts—all of which have caloric values and vitamin content—when roasted or otherwise cooked, or even when raw, are regarded by many peoples as delicacies. We never eat them, however, though they are equally available to us. On the other hand, some of the same peoples who feed on these with gusto regard substances that come out of tin cans as unfit for human consumption. . . .

※ ※ ※

Before we terminate our discussion of cultural relativism, it is important that we consider questions that are raised when the cultural-relativistic position is advanced. "It may be true," it is argued, "that human beings live in accordance with the ways they have learned. These ways may be regarded by them as best. A people may be so devoted to these ways that they are ready to fight and die for them. In terms of survival value, their effectiveness may be admitted, since the group that lives in accordance with them continues to exist. But does this mean that all systems of moral values, all concepts of right and wrong, are founded on such shifting sands that there is no need for morality, for proper behavior, for ethical codes? Does not a relativistic philosophy, indeed, imply a negation of these?"

To hold that values do not exist because they are relative to time and place is to fall prey to a fallacy that results from a failure to take into account the positive contribution of the relativistic position. For cultural relativism is a philosophy that recognizes the values set up by every society to guide its own life and that understands their worth to those who live by them, though they may differ from one's own. Instead of underscoring differences from absolute norms that, however objectively arrived at, are nonetheless the product of a given time or place, the relativistic point of view brings into relief the validity of every set of norms for the people who have them, and the values these represent.

It is essential, in considering cultural relativism, that we differentiate absolutes from universals. *Absolutes* are fixed, and, as far as convention is concerned, are not admitted to have variation, to differ from culture to culture, from epoch to epoch. *Universals*, on the other hand, are those least common denominators to be extracted from the range of variation that all phenomena of the natural or cultural world manifest. If we apply the distinction between these two concepts in drawing an answer to the points raised in our question, these criticisms are found to lose their force. To say that there is no absolute criterion of values or morals, or even, psychologically, of time or space, does not mean that such criteria, in differing *forms*, do not comprise universals in human culture. Morality is a universal, and so is enjoyment of beauty, and some standard for truth. The many forms these concepts take are but products of the particular historical experience of the societies that manifest them. In each, criteria are subject to continuous questioning, continuous change. But the basic conceptions remain, to channel thought and direct conduct, to give purpose to living.

In considering cultural relativism, also, we must recognize that it has three quite different aspects, which in most discussions of it tend to be disregarded. One of these is methodological, one philosophical, and one practical. As it has been put:

> As method, relativism encompasses the principle of our science that, in studying a culture, one seeks to attain as great a degree of objectivity as possible; that one does not judge the modes of behavior one is describing, or seek to change them. Rather, one seeks to understand the sanctions of behavior in terms of the established relationships within the culture itself, and refrains from making interpretations that arise from a preconceived frame of reference. Relativism as philosophy concerns the nature of cultural values, and, beyond this, the implications of an epistemology that derives from a recognition of the force of enculturative conditioning in shaping thought and behavior. Its practical aspects involve are the application—the practice—of the philosophical principles derived from this method, to the wider, cross-cultural scene.

We may follow this reasoning somewhat further.

> In these terms, the three aspects of cultural relativism can be regarded as representing a logical sequence which, in a broad sense, the historical development of the idea has also followed. That is, the methodological aspect, whereby the data from which the epistemological propositions flow are gathered, ordered and assessed, came first. For it is difficult to conceive of a systematic theory of cultural relativism—as against a generalized idea of live-and-let-live—without the pre-existence of the massive ethnographic documentation gathered by anthropologists concerning the similarities and differences between cultures the world over. Out of these data came the philosophical position, and with the philosophical position came speculation as to its implications for conduct.[2]

Cultural relativism, in all cases, must be sharply distinguished from concepts of the relativity of individual behavior, which would negate all social controls over conduct. Conformity to the code of the group is a requirement for any regularity in life. Yet to say that we have a right to expect conformity to the code of our day for ourselves does not imply that we need expect, much less impose, conformity to our code on persons who live by other codes. The very code of cultural relativism is the social discipline that comes of respect for differences—of mutual respect. Emphasis on the worth of many ways of life, not one, is an affirmation of the values in each culture. Such emphasis seeks to understand and to harmonize goals, not to judge and destroy those that do not dovetail with our own. Cultural history teaches that, important as it is to discern and study the parallelisms in human civilizations, it is no less important to discern and study the different ways man has devised to fulfill his needs.

That it has been necessary to consider questions such as have been raised reflects an enculturative experience wherein the prevalent system of morals is not only consciously inculcated, but its exclusive claim to excellence emphasized. There are not many cultures, for example, where a rigid dichotomy between good and evil, such as we have set up, is insisted upon. Rather it is recognized that good and evil are but the extremes of a continuously varied scale between these poles that produces only different degrees of greyness. We thus return to the principle enunciated earlier, that "judgments are based on experience, and experience is interpreted by each individual in terms of his enculturation." In a culture where absolute values are stressed, the relativism of a world that encompasses many ways of living will be difficult to comprehend. Rather, it will offer a field day for value judgments based on the degree to which a given body of customs resembled or differs from those of Euroamerican culture.[3]

Once comprehended, however, and employing the field methods of the scientific student of man, together with an awareness of the satisfactions the most varied bodies of custom yield, this position gives us a leverage to lift us out of the ethnocentric morass in which our thinking about ultimate values has for so long bogged down. With a means of probing deeply into all manner of differing cultural orientations, of reaching into the significance of the ways of living of different peoples, we can turn again to our own culture with fresh perspective, and an objectivity that can be achieved in no other manner.

Evaluation

Relativism appears to be a solid scientific theory with extensive philosophic support and a spirit congenial to the awareness of the twentieth century. It is certainly beneficial in promoting receptivity toward foreign codes of behavior and in reminding us of the diversity of moral viewpoints. We become much more flexible and much less self-righteous if we realize that our way of living is not the only way in which human life can be organized. And we are reluctant to force our values on others through missionaries or the military if we take all values as equally valid. A liberal, live-and-let-live attitude prevails in which we respect each individual's way of life—what the Germans call *leben und leben lassen*.

Nevertheless, although certain social gains follow from the relativist assumptions, the question of its truth must be addressed. An idea can be beneficial but not true, and ideas certainly aren't true because they are beneficial. Wishing does not make it so, any more than denying reality can make the truth disappear, which is the ostrich mentality. For good or ill, we must ask ourselves whether the relativist is correct in what he claims.

1. First of all with regard to the philosophic claims of David Hume and A. J. Ayer, both seem guilty of excluding the possibility of objective morality by peremptorily defining what is to count as a genuine or meaningful assertion. They both seem to say that the only claims worth considering (apart from logical relations of ideas) are those that can be tested by the senses, that is, empirically verifiable propositions. But that criterion is highly arbitrary and would eliminate an entire range of discourse. Statements such as The sunset is beautiful, The meal is delicious, and even I am in love with you would be considered worthless. This is hardly in keeping with our ordinary assumptions, and neither philosopher gives us any good reasons as to why the empirically verifiable alone is worth saying.

It has also been pointed out that neither Hume's classification of two types of genuine knowledge nor Ayer's Verification Principle is provable according to its author's own criterion. Neither one is based on empirical evidence (or logical relations) and, thus by the relativist's own standards, must be considered specious or meaningless.

2. Aside from the problems inherent in particular philosophic claims, relativism in its broadest sense can be charged with contradicting itself. For when the relativist argues that everything is relative and that this proposition is absolutely true, he becomes involved in affirming and denying his own claim. If everything is relative then nothing is absolutely true including that principle itself. Or differently put, in saying that everything is relative, the statement is not thought to be relative but absolute; therefore not everything is relative. In the same way, it is logically inconsistent for the subjectivist to claim that his position is objectively true, if everything is a subjective matter.

If the relativist tries to make his position more consistent by saying that the statement everything is relative is also a relative statement, then no one need take it seriously. For the statement then becomes a trivial one, relative to the speaker's society or disposition.

The relativist then can be consistent but say very little or maintain that he is really right and contradict himself. Neither choice is a very happy one and neither one does much to make the relativist position rationally convincing.

The same logical problem, incidentally, confronts any skeptical position regarding knowledge. If the skeptic declares that there is no knowledge, then this statement is not knowledge either or he contradicts himself. And the situation is not improved by changing the claim to There is no truth.

3. Another problem arises if relativism is taken in the subjectivist sense of claiming that whatever an individual believes to be true is true to him. For this would produce the logically impossible situation in which two contradictory statements would both have to be judged as true if each was maintained by someone. We would have to say, for example, that a square has four sides and that a square does not have four sides if two people took opposing views about it. Both positions would have to be considered correct if it is assumed that each individual is right to himself, and this is patently absurd.

The lesson to be learned here is that thinking does not make it so. We can be mistaken in what we believe, and whether we have judged matters correctly or incorrectly is determined by the reality we are attempting to describe. This is apparent in the previous example when one realizes that two contradictory propositions cannot both be true; this Principle of Noncontradiction, as it is called, is one of the most basic laws of thought. No statement can be both true and false; at least one position would have to be mistaken. And the decision as to which position is incorrect would be made in terms of the actual state of affairs.

It should be added that even if everyone were in accord about an idea that would not establish it as so, because truth is not dependent on what people think is the case but on what the case happens to be. As one philosopher phrases it,

> A fundamental distinction must be drawn between the way the world is and what we say about it, even if we all happen to agree. We could all be wrong. Some of the most important commitments we make in our life could be based on error. What is true and what we think is true need not coincide. This simple statement seems self-evident, since it merely draws attention to human fallibility in general, and our own in particular.

Socrates offers a similar criticism of the subjectivist view when he objects to the definition of justice offered by Thrasymachus. In the passage quoted earlier from *The Republic,* Thrasymachus had argued that justice is nothing other than the interests of the stronger. Socrates then proceeds to question this definition in the following way. He asks Thrasymachus,

> "Do you admit that it is just for subjects to obey their rulers?"
> "I do."
> "But are the rulers of states absolutely infallible, or are they sometimes liable to error?"
> "To be sure. . . . they are liable to err."
> "Then in making their laws they may sometimes make them rightly, and sometimes not?"
> "True."
> "When they make them rightly, they make them agreeably to their interest; when they are mistaken, contrary to their interest; you admit that?"

"Yes."

"And the laws which they make must be obeyed by their subjects—and that is what you call justice?"

"Doubtless."

"Then justice, according to your argument, is not only obedience to the interest of the stronger but the reverse?"

"What is that you are saying?. . ."

"I am only repeating what you are saying, I believe. But let us consider: Have we not admitted that the rulers may be mistaken about their own interest in what they command, and also that to obey them is justice? Has not that been admitted?"

"Yes."

"Then you must also have acknowledged justice not to be the interest of the stronger, when the rulers unintentionally command things to be done which are to their own injury. For if, as you say, justice is the obedience which the subject renders to their commands, in that case, O wisest of men, is there any escape from the conclusion that the weaker are commanded to do, not what is for the interest, but what is for the injury of the stronger?"

In other words, doing what the stronger commands could mean doing what is good for them or doing what is bad for them, depending on whether they had understood where their best interests lie. Justice then could work out to be that which harms the stronger, which is just the opposite of what Thrasymachus intended.

For our purposes the important point is that no moral values are determined by what an individual asserts. Even if we hold the cynical view of values as mere self-interest (as Thrasymachus does with regard to justice), the individual would be correct or incorrect in his decision according to what his best interests actually were. And just as people can be mistaken about what is good for them, they can be mistaken about what is truly fair, equitable, or honest. In no case does believing something make it right; values are independent of the individual or the ruling political form. This is Plato's point and it applies equally well to the relativism of Protagoras and Gorgias.

4. Another criticism of ethical relativism has to do with the assumption that differing moral values among cultures show that no objective standards exist. Is that conclusion really justified?

To begin with, the diversity in values worldwide may be more apparent than actual. For example, it seems as though a society that condones a husband killing his wife's lover and a society that condemns such action are in fundamental disagreement. To the one the husband has behaved honorably, to the other he is a base criminal. However, these may be superficial differences masking common principles. Both societies will probably have laws prohibiting murder and have strong beliefs in the protection of human life. They will differ only in their definitions as to what constitutes murder, that is, taking life unjustifiably. In the same way, a tribe that practices hospitality toward neighboring tribes and one that acts with enmity toward its neighbors may appear to be exhibiting diverse values. However, both may share a common belief in the value of hospitality. To the first that would include adjacent tribes, whereas to the second it would only apply to other families within the tribe. The difference may be over what constitutes a neighbor and a stranger and who therefore is entitled to the gift of hospitality.

In other words the underlying values may be the same and the disagreement may not stem from moral differences at all. As some anthropologists have pointed out, there certainly seems to be widespread agreement over the worth of values such as group loyalty, courage, and parental affection for the young. Likewise, deceit, ingratitude, and stealing are broadly condemned. The evidence therefore points to a certain unanimity on fundamental moral principles, and what is taken as cultural diversity in values may only be differences in the application or meaning of those principles.

As a prime example it has been claimed that the Golden Rule is one of the oldest principles of a distinctly universal character. Witness the following comparative list, drawn mainly from chief religions of the world:

Confucianism
   What you don't want done to yourself, don't do to others.
   —Sixth Century B.C.

Buddhism
   Hurt not others with that which pains thyself.
   —Fifth Century B.C.

Jainism
   In happiness and suffering, in joy and grief, we should regard all creatures as we regard our own self, and should therefore refrain from inflicting upon others such injury as would appear undesirable to us if inflicted upon ourselves.
   —Fifth Century B.C.

Zoroastrianiasm
   Do not do unto others all that which is not well for oneself.
   —Fifth Century B.C.

Classical Philosophy
   May I do to others as I would that they should do unto me.
   Plato—Fourth Century B.C.

Hinduism
   Do naught to others which if done to thee would cause thee pain.
   Mahabharata—Third Century B.C.

Judaism
   What is hateful to yourself, don't do to your fellow man.
   Rabbi Hillel—First Century B.C.

Christianity
Whatsoever ye would that men should do to you, do ye even so to them.
Jesus of Nazareth—First Century A.D.

Sikhism
Treat others as thou wouldst be treated thyself.
—Sixteenth Century A.D.

However, even if moral disagreement does exist, disagreement that cannot be explained away in terms of a substratum of shared values, that still would not demonstrate the relativity of values. For the fact that societies disagree about values does not prove that each is right; it only shows that each society believes itself to be right. It still makes good sense to ask which has come closest to the truth and which is farthest away from the mark.

To take an analogy from science, the fact that disease used to be attributed to evil spirits or the influences of the four humors and that cures were thought of in terms of exorcism or bloodletting does not imply that disease has no real cause. The multiplicity of beliefs about these matters does not warrant the conclusion that everything is relative to the time and place and one person's opinion is as good as another's. Rather, the medical researcher assumes that diseases have actual causes and that cures can be effected by properly identifying those causes. He attributes the variety of past beliefs about disease to the greater clarity or dimness with which people have perceived the truth. At various times people may have been very ignorant and superstitious or remarkably perceptive (as with herbal remedies). But as a scientist he takes it for granted that there is a truth to be known and that assumption provides the motivation for his research.

In the same way the objectivist sees the multiplicity of moral beliefs not as evidence of relativism but as a manifestation of greater or lesser understanding of genuine values—values that he also tries to grasp in his systematic and rigorous way. Notice that he does not doubt the facts of cultural diversity but only the interpretation of those facts—that moral relativity follows from them.

5. But couldn't it be argued that the reverse might be true? Couldn't the diversity of moral views at different times and places indicate the relativity of morals and not any universal standard variously perceived? After all two interpretations are possible, so why choose the objectivist one?

This consideration introduces the concept of burden of proof which is usually taken as an argument against the relativist view. According to this concept, the burden of proof in a dispute is always on the side that takes the unusual position. For example, in an argument over what factors were responsible for World War II the person who says it was due to the astrological influence of the stars would have to prove that contention, otherwise it would be appropriate to assume that the economic conditions in Germany, the humiliation of the Treaty of Versailles, the charismatic leadership of Hitler, and so forth were responsible for the war. In other words, the person who adopts a theory that is out of the ordinary must prove his case, while the person who maintains a customary or commonsensical view is justified in holding that view until it is disproven.

In the dispute over the relativity or objectivity of values the burden of proof falls on the relativist, and the question is whether he has in fact established his position. For people ordinarily believe that certain values are truly important, that indiscriminate killing, for example, is terribly wrong and the preservation of life is a moral obligation. If assumptions of this kind are mistaken then that has to be proven, and it does not seem that the relativist has succeeded in demonstrating it. He has only shown the wide range of values among cultures and in different historical periods, and that does not prove all values are relative. Therefore, the objectivist position, which is in accord with common human experience, can be maintained with some confidence.

In summation then we can see that relativism is basically self-contradictory or inconsistent in numerous ways and that cultural diversity does not warrant the conclusion that values have no objective basis.

Oddly enough, relativism cannot even claim the social benefit of fostering tolerance, as several philosophers have shown. For by advocating the value of tolerance the relativist is presupposing that this value has objective worth and denying his own position. He is extolling tolerance from the standpoint of a moral system that he believes everyone should accept. In other words, by claiming the virtue of tolerance for his position the relativist gives the game away, for tolerance at least is assumed to be objectively valuable.

Perhaps Socrates had the last laugh regarding relativism when he argued against Protagoras in the *Theaetetus* by saying "and the best of the joke is that he acknowledges the truth of their opinions who believe his own opinions to be false for he admits that the opinions of all men are true." That is, if man is the measure of all things and whatever a person believes is true because he believes it, then the person who believes relativism is false would be correct in his belief. Relativism therefore collapses of its own weight.

Endnotes

1. This unpublished myth was told F. M. Olbrechts of Brussels, Belgium, in the course of field work among the Cherokee. His having made it available is gratefully acknowledged. A similar tale has been recorded from the Albany Cree, at Moose Factory, according to information received from F. Voget.

Quest for Goodness: An Introduction to Ethics

2. M. J. Herskovits, 1951, p. 24.
3. Instances of the rejection of relativism on philosophical grounds, by writers who attempt to reconcile the principle of absolute values with the diversity of known systems, are to be found in E. Vivas, 1950, pp. 27–42, and D. Bidney, 1953a, pp. 689–95, 1953b, pp. 423–29. Both of these discussions, also, afford examples of the confusion that results when a distinction is not drawn between the methodological, philosophical, and practical aspects of relativism. For a critical consideration of relativism that, by implication, recognizes these differences, see R. Redfield, 1953, pp. 144 ff.

Reprinted by permission from Melville Herskovits, *Cultural Relativism* (New York: Random House, 1972), 11–34, some footnotes have been deleted.

Self-Assertion

Friedrich Nietzsche

From "The Birth of Tragedy"[1]

It is an eternal phenomenon: the insatiate will can always, by means of an illusion spread over things, detain its creatures in life and compel them to live on. One is chained by the Socratic love of knowledge and the delusion of being able thereby to heal the eternal wound of existence; another is ensnared by art's seductive veil of beauty fluttering before his eyes; still another by the metaphysical comfort that beneath the flux of phenomena eternal life flows on indestructibly: to say nothing of the more ordinary and almost more powerful illusions which the will has always at hand. These three planes of illusion are on the whole designed only for the more nobly formed natures, who in general feel profoundly the weight and burden of existence, and must be deluded by exquisite stimulants into forgetfulness of their sorrow. All that we call culture is made up of these stimulants; and, according to the proportion of the ingredients, we have either a dominantly *Socratic* or *artistic* or *tragic* culture: or if historical exemplifications are wanted, there is either an Alexandrian or a Hellenic or a Buddhistic culture.

Our whole modern world is entangled in the net of Alexandrian culture. It proposes as its ideal the theoretical man equipped with the greatest forces of knowledge, and laboring in the service of science, whose archetype and progenitor is Socrates. All our educational methods have originally this ideal in view: every other form of existence must struggle on wearisome beside it, as something tolerated, but not intended. In an almost alarming manner, the cultured man was for a long time found only in the form of the scholar: even our poetical arts have been forced to evolve from learned imitations, and in the main effect, that of rhyme, we still recognize the origin of our poetic form from artistic experiments with a non-indigenous, thoroughly learned language. How unintelligible must *Faust*, the modern cultured man, who is in himself intelligible, have appeared to a true Greek—Faust, storming unsatisfied through all the faculties, devoted to magic and the devil from a desire for knowledge; Faust, whom we have but to place beside Socrates for the purpose of comparison, in order to see that modern man is beginning to divine the limits of this Socratic love of perception and yearns for a coast in the wide waste of the ocean of knowledge. When Goethe on one occasion said to Eckermann with reference to Napoleon: "Yes, my good friend, there is also a productiveness of deeds," he reminded us in a charmingly naive manner that the non-theorist is something incredible and astounding to modern man; so that we again have need of the wisdom of Goethe to discover that such a surprising form of existence is not only comprehensible, but even pardonable.

Now, we must not hide from ourselves what is concealed at the heart of this Socratic culture: Optimism, with its delusion of limitless power! Well, we must not be alarmed if the fruits of this optimism ripen—if society, leavened to the very lowest strata by this kind of culture, gradually begins to tremble with wanton agitations and desires, if the belief in the earthly happiness of all, if the belief in the possibility of such a general intellectual culture is gradually transformed into the threatening demand for such an Alexandrian earthly happiness, into the conjuring up of a Euripidian *deus ex machina*. Let us mark this well: the Alexandrian culture, to be able to exist permanently, requires a slave class, but, with its optimistic view of life, it denies the necessity of such a class, and consequently, when the effect of its beautiful seductive and tranquilizing utterance about the "dignity of man" and the "dignity of labor" is over, it gradually drifts toward a dreadful destruction. There is nothing more terrible than a barbaric slave class, who have learned to regard their existence as an injustice, and now prepare to avenge, not only themselves, but all future generations. In the face of such threatening storms, who dares to appeal with any confidence to our pale and exhausted religions, whose very foundations have degenerated into "learned" religions?—so that myth, the necessary prerequisite of every religion, is already paralyzed everywhere, and even in this domain the optimistic spirit—which we have just designated as the destroying germ of society—has attained the mastery.

While the evil slumbering in the heart of theoretical culture gradually begins to disquiet modern man, while he anxiously ransacks the stores of his experience for means to avert the danger, though he has no great faith in these means; while he, therefore, begins to divine the consequences of his position: great, universally gifted natures have contrived, with an incredible amount of thought, to make use of the paraphernalia of science itself, in order to point out the limits and the relativity of knowledge generally, and thus definitely to deny the claim of science to universal validity and universal aims: with which demonstration the illusory notion was for

Chapter IV: Relativism

the first time recognized as such, which pretends, with the aid of causality, to be able to fathom the innermost essence of things. The extraordinary courage and wisdom of *Kant* and *Schopenhauer* have succeeded in gaining the most difficult victory, the victory over the optimism hidden in the essence of logic, which optimism in turn is the basis of our culture. While this optimism, resting on apparently unobjectionable *aeternae veritates*, had believed in the intelligibility and solvability of all the riddles of the universe, and had treated space, time, and causality as totally unconditioned laws of the most universal validity, Kant, on the other hand, showed that in reality these served only to elevate the mere phenomenon, the work of Maya, to the position of the sole and highest reality, putting it in place of the innermost and true essence of things, and thus making impossible any knowledge of this essence or, in Schopenhauer's words, lulling the dreamer still more soundly asleep. With this knowledge a culture is inaugurated which I venture to call a tragic culture; the most important characteristic of which is that wisdom takes the place of science as the highest end, wisdom, which uninfluenced by the seductive distractions of the sciences, turns with unmoved eye to a comprehensive view of the world, and seeks to conceive therein, with sympathetic feelings of love, the eternal suffering as its own. Let us imagine a rising generation with this bold vision, this heroic desire for the magnificent, let us imagine the valiant step of these dragon-slayers, the proud daring with which they turn their backs on all the effeminate doctrines of optimism that they may "live resolutely," wholly, and fully: Would it not be necessary for the tragic man of this culture, with his self-discipline of seriousness and terror, to desire a new art, the art of metaphysical comfort—namely, tragedy—to claim it as, Helen, and exclaim with Faust:

> Und sollt ich nicht, sehnsuechtigster Gewald,
> Ins Leben ziehn die einzigste Gestalt?
> [And must I not satisfy my longing,
> By bringing this incomparable beauty to life?]

But now that the Socratic culture can only hold the scepter of its infallibility with trembling hands; now that it has been shaken from two directions—once by the fear of its own conclusions which it at length begins to surmise, and again, because it no longer has its former naive confidence in the eternal validity of its foundations—it is a sad spectacle to see how the dance of its thought rushes longingly on ever-new forms, to embrace them, and then, shuddering, lets them go suddenly as Mephistopheles does the seductive Lamaiae. It is certainly the sign of the "breach" which all are wont to speak of as the fundamental tragedy of modern culture that the theoretical man, alarmed and dissatisfied at his own conclusions, no longer dares entrust himself to the terrible ice-stream of existence: he runs timidly up and down the bank. So thoroughly has he been spoiled by his optimistic views, that he no longer wants to have anything whole, with all of nature's cruelty attaching to it. Besides, he feels that a culture based on the principles of science must be destroyed when it begins to grow *illogical*, that is, to retreat before its own conclusions. Our art reveals this universal trouble: in vain does one depend imitatively on all great productive periods and natures; in vain does one accumulate the entire "World-Literature" around modern man for his comfort; in vain does one place one's self in the midst of the art-styles and artists of all ages, so that one may give names to them as Adam did to the beasts: one still continues eternally hungry, the "critic" without joy and energy, the Alexandrian man, who is at bottom a librarian and corrector of proofs, and who, pitiable wretch, goes blind from the dusty books and printers' errors.

From "Beyond Good and Evil"[2]

In a tour through the many finer and coarser moralities which have hitherto prevailed or still prevail on the earth, I found certain traits recurring regularly together, and connected with one another, until finally two primary types revealed themselves to me, and a radical distinction was brought to light. There is *master-morality* and *slave-morality*. I would at once add, however, that in all higher and mixed civilizations, there are also attempts at the reconciliation of the two moralities; but one finds still oftener the confusion and mutual misunderstanding of them, indeed, sometimes their close juxtaposition—even in the same man, within one soul. The distinctions of moral values have either originated in a ruling caste, pleasantly conscious of being different from the ruled—or among the ruled class, the slaves and dependents of all sorts. In the first case, when it is the rulers who determine the conception "good," it is the exalted, proud disposition which is regarded as the distinguishing feature, and that which determines the order of rank. The noble type of man separates from himself the beings in whom the opposite of this exalted, proud disposition displays itself: he despises them. Let it at once be noted that in this first kind of morality the antithesis "good" and "bad" means practically the same as "noble" and "despicable"; the antithesis "good" and "*evil*" is of a different origin. The cowardly, the timid, the insignificant, and those thinking merely of narrow utility are despised; moreover, also, the distrustful, with their constrained glances, the self-abasing, the dog-like kind of men who let themselves be abused, the mendicant flatterers, and above all the liars:—it is a fundamental belief of all aristocrats that the common people are untruthful. "We truthful ones"—the nobility in ancient Greece called themselves. It is obvious that everywhere the designations of moral value were at first applied to *men*, and were only derivatively and at a later period applied to *actions*; it is a gross mistake, therefore, when historians of morals start questions like, "Why have sympathetic actions been praised?" The noble type of man regards *himself* as a determiner of values: he does not require to be approved of, he passes the judgment: "What is injurious in itself"; he knows that it is he himself only who confers honor on things; he is a *creator of values*. He honors whatever he recognizes in himself: such morality is self-glorification. In the foreground there is the feeling of plenitude, of power which seeks to overflow, the happiness of high tension, the consciousness of a wealth which would fain give and bestow: the noble man also helps the unfortunate, but not—or scarcely— out of pity, but rather from an impulse generated by the super-abundance of power. The noble man honors in himself the powerful one, him also who has power over himself, who knows how to speak and how to keep silence, who takes pleasure in subjecting himself to severity and hardness, and has reverence for all that is severe and hard. "Wotan placed a hard heart in my breast," says an old Scandinavian Saga: it is thus rightly expressed from the soul of a proud Viking. Such a type of man is even proud of *not* being made for sympathy; the hero of the Saga therefore adds warningly: "He who has not a hard heart when young, will never have one." The noble and brave who think thus are the furthest removed from the morality which sees precisely in sympathy, or in acting for the good of others, or in *désinteressement,* the characteristic of the moral; faith in oneself, pride in oneself, a radical enmity and irony towards "selflessness," belong as definitely to noble morality, as do a careless scorn and precaution in presence of sympathy and the "warm heart"—it is the powerful who *know* how to honor, it is their art, their domain for invention. The profound reverence for age and for tradition—all law rests on this double reverence, the belief and prejudice in favor of ancestors and unfavorable to newcomers, is typical in the morality of the powerful; and if, reversely, men of "modern ideas' believe almost instinctively in "progress" and the "future," and are more and more lacking in respect for old age, the ignoble origin of these "ideas" has complacently betrayed itself thereby. A morality of the ruling class, however, is more especially foreign and irritating to present-day taste in the sternness of its principle that one has duties only to one's equals; that one may act towards beings of a lower rank, towards all that is foreign, just as seems good to one, or "as the heart desires," and in any case "beyond good and evil": it is here that sympathy and similar sentiments can have a place. The ability and obligation to exercise prolonged gratitude and prolonged revenge—both only within the circle of equals, artfulness in retaliation, *raffinement* of the idea in friendship, a certain necessity to have enemies (as outlets for the emotions of envy, quarrelsomeness, arrogance—in fact in order to be a good *friend*): all these are typical characteristics of the noble morality, which, as has been pointed out, is not the morality of "modern ideas," and is therefore at present difficult to realize, and also to unearth and disclose. It is otherwise with the second type of morality, *slave-morality*. Supposing that the abused, the oppressed, the suffering, the unemancipated, the weary, and those uncertain of themselves, should moralize, what will be the common element in their moral estimates? Probably a pessimistic suspicion with regard to the entire situation of man will find expression, perhaps a condemnation of man, together with this situation. The slave has an unfavorable eye for the virtues of the powerful; he has a skepticism and distrust, a *refinement* of distrust of everything "good" that is there honored—he would fain persuade himself that the very happiness there is not genuine. On the other hand, *those* qualities which serve to alleviate the existence of sufferers are brought into prominence and flooded with light; it is here that sympathy, the kind, helping hand, the warm heart, patience, diligence, humility, and friendliness attain to honor; for here these are the most useful qualities, and almost the only means of supporting the burden of existence. Slave-morality is essentially the morality of utility. Here is the seat of the origin of the famous antithesis "good" and "evil": power and dangerousness are assumed to reside in the evil, a certain dreadfulness, subtlety, and strength, which do not admit of being despised. According to slave-morality, therefore, the "evil" man arouses fear; according to master-morality it is precisely the "good" man who arouses fear and seeks to arouse it, while the bad man is regarded as the despicable being. The contrast attains its maximum when, in accordance with the logical consequences of slave-morality, a shade of depreciation—it may be slight and well-intentioned—at last attaches itself to the "good" man of his morality; because, according to the servile mode of thought, the good man must in any case be the *safe* man: he is good-natured, easily deceived, perhaps a little stupid, *un bonhomme*. Everywhere that slave-morality gains the ascendancy, language shows a tendency to approximate the significations of the words "good" and "stupid." A last fundamental difference: the desire for *freedom*, the instinct for happiness, and the refinements of the feeling of liberty belong as necessarily to slave-morals and morality, as artifice and enthusiasm in reverence and devotion are the regular symptoms of an aristocratic mode of thinking and estimating. Hence we can understand without further detail why love *as a passion*—it is our European speciality—must absolutely be of noble origin; as is well known, its invention is due to the Provençal poet-cavaliers, those brilliant ingenious men of the *"gai-saber,"* to whom Europe owes so much and almost owes itself.

From "The Genealogy of Morals"[2]

The revolt of the slaves in morals begins in the very principle of *resentment* becoming creative and giving birth to values—a resentment experienced by creatures who, deprived as they are of the proper outlet of action, are forced to find their compensation in an imaginary revenge. While every aristocratic morality springs from a triumphant affirmation of its own demands, the slave morality says "no" from the very outset to what is "outside itself," and "not itself": and this "no" is its creative deed. This volte-face of the valuing standpoint—this *inevitable* gravitation to the objective instead of back to the subjective—is typical of "resentment": the slave-morality requires as the condition of its existence an external and objective world; to employ physiological terminology, it requires objective stimuli to be capable of action at all—its action is fundamentally a reaction. The contrary is the case when we come to the aristocrat's system of values: it acts and grows spontaneously, it merely seeks its antithesis in order to pronounce a more grateful and exultant "yes" to its own self; its negative conception, "low," "vulgar," "bad," is merely a pale lateborn foil in comparison with its positive and fundamental conception (saturated as it is with life and passion), of "we aristocrats, we good ones, we beautiful ones, we happy ones."

When the aristocratic morality goes astray and commits sacrilege on reality, this is limited to that particular sphere, with which it is *not* sufficiently acquainted—a sphere, in fact, from the real knowledge of which it disdainfully defends itself. It misjudges, in some cases, the sphere which it despises, the sphere of the common vulgar man and the low people: on the other hand, due weight should be given to the consideration that in any case the mood of contempt, of disdain, of superciliousness, even on the supposition that it *falsely* portrays the object of its contempt, will always be far removed from that degree of falsity which will always characterize the attacks—in effigy, of course—of the vindictive hatred and revengefulness of the weak in onslaughts on their enemies. In point of fact, there is in contempt too strong an admixture of nonchalance, of casualness, of boredom, of impatience, even of personal exultation, for it to be capable of distorting its victim into a real caricature or a real monstrosity. Attention again should be paid to the almost benevolent *nuances* which, for instance, the Greek nobility imparts into all the words by which it distinguishes the common people from itself, note how continuously a kind of pity, care, and consideration imparts its honeyed *flavor*, until at last almost all the words which are applied to the vulgar man survive finally, as expressions for "unhappy," "worthy of pity"—and how, conversely, "bad," "low," "unhappy" have never ceased to ring in the Greek ear with a tone in which "unhappy" is the predominant note: this is a heritage of the old noble aristocratic morality, which remains true to itself even in contempt. The "well-born" simply *felt* themselves the "happy"; they did not have to manufacture their happiness artificially through looking at their enemies, or in cases to talk and lie themselves into happiness (as is the custom with all resentful men); and similarly, complete men as they were, exuberant with strength, and consequently *necessarily* energetic, they were too wise to dissociate happiness from action—activity becomes in their minds necessarily counted as happiness—all in sharp contrast to the "happiness" of the weak and the oppressed, with their festering venom and malignity, among whom happiness appears essentially as a narcotic, a deadening, a quietude, a peace, a "Sabbath," an enervation of the mind and relaxation of the limbs, in short, a purely *passive* phenomenon. While the aristocratic man lived in confidence and openness with himself, the resentful man, on the other hand, is neither sincere nor naive, nor honest and candid with himself. His soul *squints*; his mind loves hidden crannies, tortuous paths and backdoors, everything secret appeals to him as *his* word, *his* safety, *his* balm; he is past master in silence, in not forgetting, in waiting, in provisional self-depreciation and self-abasement. A race of such *resentful* men will of necessity eventually prove more *prudent* than any aristocratic race, it will honor prudence on quite a distinct scale, as, in fact, a paramount condition of existence, while prudence among aristocratic men is apt to be tinged with a delicate flavor of luxury and refinement; so among them it plays nothing like so integral a part as that complete certainty of function of the governing *unconscious* instincts, or as indeed a certain lack of prudence, such as a vehement and valiant charge, whether against danger or the enemy, or as those ecstatic bursts of rage, love, reverence, gratitude, by which at all times noble souls have recognized each other. When the resentment of the aristocratic man manifests itself, it fulfills and exhausts itself in an immediate reaction, and consequently instills no *venom*: on the other hand, it never manifests itself at all in countless instances, when in the case of the feeble and weak it would be inevitable. An inability to take seriously for any length of time their enemies, their disasters, their *misdeeds*—that is the sign of the full strong natures who possess a superfluity of molding plastic force, that heals completely and produces forgetfulness: a good example of this in the modern world is Mirabeau, who had no memory for any insults and meannesses which were practised on him, and who was only incapable of forgiving because he forgot. Such a man indeed shakes off with a shrug many a worm which would have buried itself in another; it is only in characters like these that we see the possibility (supposing, of course, that there is such a possibility in the world) of the real "*love* of one's enemies." What respect for his enemies is found, forsooth, in an aristocratic man—and such a reverence is already a bridge to love! He insists on having his enemy to himself as his distinction. He tolerates no other enemy but a man in whose character there is nothing to despise and much to honor! On the other hand, imagine the "enemy" as the resentful man conceives him—and it is here exactly that we see his work, his creativeness; he has conceived "the evil enemy," "the evil one," and indeed that is the root idea from which he now evolves as a contrasting and corresponding figure, a "good one," himself—his very self!

The method of this man is quite contrary to that of the aristocratic man, who conceives the root idea "good" spontaneously and straight away, that

Chapter IV: Relativism

is to say, out of himself, and from that material then creates for himself a concept of "bad"! This "bad" of aristocratic origin and that "evil" out of the cauldron of unsatisfied hatred—the former an imitation, and "extra," an additional nuance; the latter, on the other hand, the original, the beginning, the essential act in the conception of a slave-morality—these two words "bad" and "evil," how great a difference do they mark, in spite of the fact that they have an identical contrary in the idea good. But the idea "good" is *not* the same: much rather let the question be asked, "Who is really evil according to the meaning of the morality of resentment?" In all sternness let it be answered thus: *just* the good man of the other morality, just the aristocrat, the powerful one, the one who rules, but who is distorted by the venomous eye of resentfulness, into a new color, a new signification, a new appearance. This particular point we would be the last to deny: the man who learned to know those "good" ones only as enemies, learned at the same time not to know them only as *"evil enemies,"* and the same men who *inter pares* were kept so rigorously in bounds through convention, respect, custom, and gratitude, though much more through mutual vigilance and jealousy *inter pares,* these men who in their relations with each other find so many new ways of manifesting consideration, self-control, delicacy, loyalty, pride and friendship, these men are in reference to what is outside their circle (where the foreign element, a *foreign* country, begins) not much better than beasts of prey, which have been let loose. They enjoy their freedom from all social control, they feel that in the wilderness they can give vent with impunity to that tension which is produced by enclosure and imprisonment in the peace of society, they *revert* to the innocence of the beast-of-prey conscience, like jubilant monsters, who perhaps come from a ghostly bout of murder, arson, rape, and torture, with bravado and a moral equanimity, as though merely some wild student's prank had been played, perfectly convinced that the poets have now an ample theme to sing and celebrate. It is impossible not to recognize at the core of all these aristocratic races a beast of prey; the magnificent *blond brute*, avidly rampant for spoil and victory; this hidden core needed an outlet from time to time, the beast must get loose again, must return into the wilderness—the Roman, Arabic, German, and Japanese nobility, the Homeric heroes, the Scandinavian Vikings, are all alike in this need. It is the aristocratic races who have left the idea "Barbarian" on all the tracks in which they have marched; nay, a consciousness of this very barbarianism, and even a pride in it, manifests itself even in their highest civilization (for example, when Pericles says to his Athenians in that celebrated, funeral oration, "Our audacity has forced a way over every land and sea, rearing everywhere imperishable memorials of itself for *good* and for *evil*").

. . . Granted the truth of the theory now believed to be true, that the very *essence of all civilizations is* to *train* out of man the beast of prey, a tame and civilized animal, it follows indubitably that we must regard as the real tools of civilization all those instincts of reaction and resentment, by the help of which the aristocratic races, together with their ideas, were finally degraded and over-powered; though that has not yet come to be synonymous with saying that the bearers of those tools also *represented* the civilization. It is rather the contrary that is not only probable—nay, it is *palpable* today; these bearers of vindictive instincts that have to be bottled up, these descendants of all European and non-European slavery, especially of the pre-Aryan population—these people, I say, represent the *decline* of humanity! These "tools of civilization" are a disgrace to humanity, and constitute in reality more of an argument against civilization, more of a reason why civilization should be suspected. One may be perfectly justified in being always afraid of the blond beast that lies at the core of all aristocratic races, and in being on one's guard: but who would not a hundred times prefer to be afraid, when one at the same times admires, than to be immune from fear, at the cost of being perpetually obsessed with the loathsome spectacle of the distorted, the dwarfed, the stunted, the envenomed? And is that not our fate? What produces today our repulsion towards "man"? for we *suffer* from "man," there is no doubt about it. It is not fear; it is rather that we have nothing more to fear from men; it is that the worm "man" is in the foreground and pullulates; it is that the "tame-man," the wretched mediocre and unedifying creature, has learned to consider himself a goal and a pinnacle, an inner meaning, an historic principle, a "higher man"; yes, it is that he has a certain right so to consider himself, in so far as he feels that in contrast to that excess of deformity, disease, exhaustion, and effeteness whose order is beginning to pollute present-day Europe, he at any rate has achieved a relative success, he at any rate still says "yes" to life. . . .

But let us come back to it; the problem of *another* origin of the good—of the good, as the resentful man has thought it out—demands its solution. It is not surprising that the lambs should bear a grudge against the great birds of prey for taking the little lambs. And when the lambs say among themselves, "Those birds of prey are evil, and he who is far removed from being a bird of prey, who is rather its opposite, a lamb—is he not good?" then there is nothing to cavil at in the setting up of this ideal, though it may also be that the birds of prey will regard it a little sneeringly, and perchance say to themselves, "*We* bear no grudge against them, these good lambs, we even like them: nothing is tastier than a tender lamb." To require of strength that it should *not* express itself as strength, that it should not be a wish to overpower, a wish to overthrow, a wish to become master, a thirst for enemies and antagonisms and triumphs, is just as absurd as to require of weakness that it should express itself as strength. A quantum of force is just such a quantum of movement, will, action; rather it is nothing else than just those very phenomena of moving, willing, acting, and can only appear otherwise in the misleading errors of language (and the fundamental fallacies of reason which have become petrified therein), which understands, and understands wrongly, all working as conditioned by a worker, by a "subject." And just exactly as the people separate the lightning from its flash, and interpret the latter as a thing done, as the working of a subject which is called lightning, so also does the popular morality separate strength from the expression of strength, as though behind the strong man there existed some indifferent neutral *substratum*, which enjoyed a *caprice* and *option* as to whether or not it should express strength. But there is no such *substratum*, there is no "being" behind doing, working, becoming; "the doer" is a mere appanage to the action. The action is everything. In point of fact, the people duplicate the doing, when they make the lightning lighten, that is a "doing-doing"; they make the same phenomenon first a cause, and then, secondly, the effect of that cause. The scientists fail to improve matters when they say, "Forces move, force causes," and so on. Our whole science is still, in spite of all its coldness, of all its freedom from passion, a dupe of the tricks of language, and has never succeeded in getting rid of that superstitious changeling "the subject" (the atom, to give another instance, is such a changeling just as the Kantian "Thing-in-itself"). What wonder if the suppressed and stealthily simmering passions of revenge and hatred exploit for their own advantage their belief, and indeed hold no belief with a more steadfast enthusiasm than this—"that the strong has the *option* of being weak, and the bird of prey of being a lamb." Thereby do they win for themselves the right of attributing to the birds of prey the *responsibility* for being birds of prey: when the oppressed, downtrodden, and overpowered say to themselves with the vindictive guile of weakness, "Let us be otherwise than the evil, namely, good! and good is everyone who does not oppress, who hurts no one, who does not attack, who does not pay back, who hands over revenge to God, who holds himself, as we do, in hiding; who goes out of the way of evil, and demands, in short, little from life; like ourselves the patient, the meek, the just"—yet all this, in its cold and unprejudiced interpretation, means nothing more than "once for all, the weak are weak; it is good to do *nothing for which we are not strong enough*"; but this dismal state of affairs, this prudence of the lowest order, which even insects possess (which in a great danger are fain to sham death so as to avoid doing "too much") has, thanks to the counterfeiting and self-deception of weakness, come to masquerade in the pomp of an ascetic, mute, and expectant virtue, just as though the *very* weakness of the weak—that is, forsooth, its *being*, its working, its whole unique inevitable inseparable reality—were a strong result, something wished, chosen, a deed, an act of *merit*. This kind of man finds the belief in a neutral, free-choosing "subject" *necessary* from an instinct of self-preservation, of self-assertion, in which every lie is fain to sanctify itself. The subject (or to use popular language, the *soul*) has perhaps proved itself the best dogma in the world simply because it rendered possible to the horde of mortal, weak, and oppressed individuals of every kind, that most sublime specimen of self-deception, the interpretation of weakness as freedom, of being this, or being that, *as merit*.

Endnotes

1. From *The Philosophy of Nietzsche*. Reprinted by permission of Random House. Copyright 1927 and renewed 1955 by The Modern Library, Inc. It is a violation of the law to reproduce this selection by any means whatsoever without the written permission of the copyright holder.
2. Reprinted by permission of George Allen & Unwin Ltd., London.

Morality as Based on Sentiment

David Hume

Those who affirm that virtue is nothing but a conformity to reason; that there are eternal fitnesses and unfitnesses of things, which are the same to every rational being that considers them; that the immutable measures of right and wrong impose an obligation, not only on human creatures, but also on the Deity himself: All these systems concur in the opinion, that morality, like truth, is discern'd merely by ideas, and by their juxtaposition and comparison. In order, therefore, to judge of these systems, we need only consider, whether it be possible, from reason alone, to distinguish betwixt moral good and evil, or whether there must concur some other principles to enable us to make that distinction.

If morality had naturally no influence on human passions and actions, 'twere in vain to take such pains to inculcate it; and nothing wou'd be more fruitless than that multitude of rules and precepts, with which all moralists abound. Philosophy is commonly divided into *speculative* and *practical*, and as morality is always comprehended under the latter division, 'tis supposed to influence our passions and actions, and to go beyond the calm and indolent judgments of the understanding. And this is confirm'd by common experience, which informs us, that men are often govern'd by their duties, and are deter'd from some actions by the opinion of injustice, and impend to others by that of obligation.

Since morals, therefore, have an influence on the actions and affections, it follows, that they cannot be deriv'd from reason; and that because reason alone, as we have already prov'd, can never have any such influence. Morals excite passions, and produce or prevent actions. Reason of itself is utterly impotent in this particular. The rules of morality, therefore, are not conclusions of our reason.

. . . Take any action allow'd to be vicious: Wilful murder, or instance. Examine it in all lights, and see if you can find that matter of fact, or real existence, which you call *vice*. In whichever way you take it, you find only certain passions, motives, volitions and thoughts. There is no other matter of fact in the case. The vice entirely escapes you, as long as you consider the object. You never can find it, till you turn your reflexion into your own breast, and find a sentiment of disapprobation, which arises in you, towards this action. Here is a matter of fact; but 'tis the object of feeling, not of reason. It lies in yourself, not in the object. So that when you pronounce any action or character to be vicious, you mean nothing, but that from the constitution of your nature you have a feeling or sentiment of blame from the contemplation of it.

. . . I cannot forbear adding to these reasonings an observation, which may, perhaps, be found of some importance. In every system of morality, which I have hitherto met with, I have always remark'd, that the author proceeds for some time in the ordinary way of reasoning, and establishes the being of a God, or makes observations concerning human affairs; when of a sudden I am surpriz'd to find, that instead of the usual copulations of propositions, *is*, and *is not*, I meet with no proposition that is not connected with an *ought*, or an *ought not*. This change is imperceptible; but is, however, of the last consequence. For as this *ought*, or *ought not*, expresses some new relation or affirmation, 'tis necessary that it shou'd be observ'd and explain'd; and at the same time that a reason should be given, for what seems altogether inconceivable, how this new relation can be a deduction from others, which are entirely different from it. But as authors do not commonly use this precaution, I shall presume to recommend it to the readers; and am persuaded, that this small attention wou'd subvert all the vulgar systems of morality, and let us see, that the distinction of vice and virtue is not founded merely on the relations of objects, nor is perceiv'd by reason.

※ ※ ※

Examine the crime of *ingratitude*, for instance, which has place wherever we observe good-will expressed and known, together with good-offices performed, on the one side, and a return of ill-will or indifference with ill-offices or neglect on the other: anatomize all these circumstances and examine, by your reason alone, in what consists the demerit or blame. You never will come to any issue or conclusion.

Reason judges either of *matter of fact* or of *relations*. Enquire then, *first*, where is that matter of fact which we here call *crime*; point it out, determine the time of its existence, describe its essence or nature, explain the sense or faculty to which it discovers itself. It resides in the mind of the person who is ungrateful. He must, therefore, feel it and be conscious of it. But nothing is there, except the passion of ill-will or absolute indifference. You cannot say, that these, of themselves, always and in all circumstances are crimes. No, they are only crimes when directed towards persons who have before expressed and displayed good-will towards us. Consequently, we may infer that the crime of ingratitude is not any particular individual *fact*, but arises from a complication of circumstances which, being presented to the spectator, excites the *sentiment* of blame by the particular structure and fabric of his mind.

This representation, you say, is false. Crime, indeed, consists not in a particular *fact*, of whose reality we are assured by *reason*, but it consists in certain *moral relations*, discovered by reason, in the same manner as we discover by reason the truths of geometry or algebra. But what are the relations, I ask, of which you here talk? In the case stated above, I see first good-will and good-offices in one person, then ill-will and ill-offices, in the other. Between these, there is a relation of *contrariety*. Does the crime consist in that relation? But suppose a person bore me ill-will or did me ill-offices, and I, in return, were indifferent towards him, or did him good offices. Here is the same relation of *contrariety*, and yet my conduct is often highly laudable. Twist and turn this matter as much as you will, you can never rest the morality on relation, but must have recourse to the decisions of sentiment.

When it is affirmed that two and three are equal to the half of ten, this relation of equality I understand perfectly. I conceive that, if ten be divided into two parts, of which one has as many units as the other, and if any of these parts be compared to two added to three, it will contain as many units as that compound number. But when you draw thence a comparison to moral relations, I own that I am altogether at a loss to understand you. A moral action, a crime, such as ingratitude, is a complicated object. Does the morality consist in the relation of its parts to each other? How? After what manner? Specify the relation: be more particular and explicit in your propositions, and you will easily see their falsehood.

No, say you, the morality consists in the relation of actions to the rule of right; and they are denominated good or ill, according as they agree or disagree with it. What then is this rule of right? In what does it consist? How is it determined? By reason, you say, which examines the moral relations of actions. So that moral relations are determined by the comparison of action to a rule. And that rule is determined by considering the moral relations of objects. Is not this fine reasoning?

All this is metaphysics, you cry. That is enough; there needs nothing more to give a strong presumption of falsehood. Yes, reply I, here are metaphysics surely; but they are all on your side, who advance an abstruse hypothesis which can never be made intelligible, nor quadrate with any particular instance or illustration. The hypothesis which we embrace is plain. It maintains that morality is determined by sentiment. It defines virtue to be *whatever mental action or quality gives to a spectator the pleasing sentiment of approbation*; and vice the contrary. We then proceed to examine a plain matter of fact, to wit, what actions have this influence. We consider all the circumstances in which these actions agree, and thence endeavour to extract some general observations with regard to these sentiments. If you call this metaphysics and find anything abstruse here, you need only conclude that your turn of mind is not suited to the moral sciences.

From David Hume, *A Treatise of Human Nature* (1740), Book III, Part I, Section 1; and *An Inquiry Concerning the Principles of Morals* (1751), Appendix I.

Ethics Are Relative

William Sumner

1. *Definition and mode of origin of the folkways.* If we put together all that we have learned from anthropology and ethnography about primitive men and primitive society, we perceive that the first task of life is to live. Men begin with acts, not with thoughts. Every moment brings necessities which must be satisfied at once. Need was the first experience, and it was followed at once by a blundering effort to satisfy it. It is generally taken for granted that men inherited some guiding instincts from their beast ancestry, and it may be true, although it has never been proved. If there were such inheritances, they controlled and aided the first efforts to satisfy needs. Analogy makes it easy to assume that the ways of beasts had produced channels of habit and predisposition along which dexterities and other psychophysical activities would run easily. Experiments with newborn animals show that in the absence of any experience of the relation of means to ends, efforts to satisfy needs are clumsy and blundering. The method is that of trial and failure, which produces repeated pain, loss, and disappointments. Nevertheless, it is a method of rude experiment and selection. The earliest efforts of men were of this kind. Need was the impelling force. Pleasure and pain, on the one side and the other, were the rude constraints which defined the line on which efforts must proceed. The ability to distinguish between pleasure and pain is the only psychical power which is to be assumed. Thus ways of doing things were selected which were expedient. They answered the purpose better than other ways, or with less toil and pain. Along the course on which efforts were compelled to go, habit, routine, and skill were developed. The struggle to maintain existence was carried on, not individually, but in groups. Each profited by the other's experience; hence there was concurrence towards that which proved to be most expedient. All at last adopted the same way for the same purpose; hence the ways turned into customs and became, mass phenomena. Instincts were developed in connection with them. In this way folkways arise. The young learn them by tradition, imitation, and authority. The folkways, at a time, provide for all the needs of life then and

there. They are uniform, universal in the group, imperative, and invariable. As time goes on, the folkways become more and more arbitrary, positive, and imperative. If asked why they act in a certain way in certain cases, primitive people always answer that it is because they and their ancestors always have done so. A sanction also arises from ghost fear. The ghosts of ancestors would be angry if the living should change the ancient folkways.

3. *Folkways are made unconsciously.* It is of the first importance to notice that, from the first acts by which men try to satisfy needs, each act stands by itself, and looks no further than the immediate satisfaction. From recurrent needs arise habits for the individual and customs for the group, but these results are consequences which were never conscious, and never foreseen or intended. They are not noticed until they have long existed, and it is still longer before they are appreciated. Another long time must pass, and a higher stage of mental development must be reached, before they can be used as a basis from which to deduce rules for meeting, in the future, problems whose pressure can be foreseen. The folkways, therefore, are not creations of human purpose and wit. They are like products of natural forces which men unconsciously set in operation, or they are like the instinctive ways of animals, which are developed out of experience, which reach a final form of maximum adaptation to an interest, which are handed down by tradition and admit of no exception or variation, yet change to meet new conditions, still within the same limited methods, and without rational reflection or purpose. From this it results that all the life of human beings, in all ages and stages of culture, is primarily controlled by a vast mass of folkways handed down from the earliest existence of the race, having the nature of the ways of other animals, only the topmost layers of which are subject to change and control, and have been somewhat modified by human philosophy, ethics, and religion, or by other acts of intelligent reflection. . . .

28. *Folkways due to false inference.* Furthermore, folkways have been formed by accident, that is, by irrational and incongruous action, based on pseudo-knowledge. In Molembo a pestilence broke out soon after a Portuguese had died there. After that the natives took all possible measures not to allow any white man to die in their country. On the Nicobar islands some natives who had just begun to make pottery died. The art was given up and never again attempted. White men gave to one Bushman in a kraal a stick ornamented with buttons as a symbol of authority. The recipient died leaving the stick to his son. The son soon died. Then the Bushmen brought back the stick lest all should die. Until recently no building of incombustible materials could be built in any big town of the central province of Madagascar, on account of some ancient prejudice. . . . Soon after the Yakuts saw a camel for the first time smallpox broke out amongst them.

Chapter IV: Relativism

They thought the camel to be the agent of the disease. A woman amongst the same people contracted an endogamous marriage. She soon afterwards became blind. This was thought to be on account of the violation of ancient customs. A very great number of such cases could be collected. In fact they represent the current mode of reasoning of nature people. It is their custom to reason that, if one thing follows another, it is due to it. A great number of customs are traceable to the notion of the evil eye, many more to ritual notions of uncleanness. No scientific investigation could discover the origin of the folkways mentioned if the origin had not chanced to become known to civilized men. We must believe that the known cases illustrate the irrational and incongruous origin of many folkways. In civilized history also we know that customs have owed their origin to "historical accident"—the vanity of a princess, the deformity of a king, the whim of a democracy, the love intrigue of a statesman or prelate. By the institutions of another age it may be provided that no one of these things can affect decisions, acts, or interests, but then the power to decide the ways may have passed to clubs, trades unions, trust, commercial rivals, wire-pullers, politicians, and political fanatics. In these cases also the causes and origins may escape investigation.

29. Harmful folkways. There are folkways which are positively harmful. Very often these are just the ones for which a definite reason can be given. The destruction of a man's goods at his death is a direct deduction from other-worldliness; the dead man is supposed to want in the other world just what he wanted here. The destruction of a man's goods at his death was a great waste of capital, and it must have had a disastrous effect on the interests of the living, and must have very seriously hindered the development of civilization. With this custom we must class all the expenditure of labor and capital on graves, temples, pyramids, rites, sacrifices, and support of priests, so far as these were supposed to benefit the dead. The faith in goblinism produced other-worldly interests which over-ruled ordinary worldly interests. Foods have often been forbidden which were plentiful, the prohibition of which injuriously lessened the food supply. There is a tribe of Bushmen who will eat no goat's flesh, although goats are the most numerous domestic animals in the district. Where totemism exists it is regularly accompanied by a taboo on eating the totem animal. Whatever may be the real principle in totemism, it overrules the interest in an abundant food supply. "The origin of the sacred regard paid to the cow must be sought in the primitive nomadic life of the Indo-European race," because it is common to Iranians and Indians of Hindostan. The Libyans ate oxen but not cows. The same was true of the Phoenicians and Egyptians. In some cases the sense of a food taboo is not to be learned. It may have been entirely capricious. Mohammed would not eat lizards because he thought them the offspring of a metamorphosed clan of Israelites. On the other hand, the protective taboo which forbade killing crocodiles, pythons, cobras, and other animals enemies of man was harmful to his interests, whatever the motive. "It seems to be a fixed article of belief throughout southern India that all who have willfully or accidentally killed a snake, especially a cobra, will certainly be punished, either in this life or the next, in one of three ways: either by childlessness, or by leprosy, or by ophthalmia." Where this faith exists man has a greater interest to spare a cobra than to kill it. India furnishes a great number of cases of harmful mores. "In India every tendency of humanity seems intensified and exaggerated. No country in the world is so conservative in its traditions, yet no country has undergone so many religious changes and vicissitudes." "Every year thousand perish of disease that might recover if they would take proper nourishment, and drink the medicine that science prescribes, but which they imagine that their religion forbids them to touch." . . .

30. How "true" and "right" are found. If a savage puts his hand too near the fire, he suffers pain and draws it back. He knows nothing of the laws of the radiation of heat, but his instinctive action conforms to that law as if he did know it. If he wants to catch an animal for food, he must study its habits and prepare a device adjusted to those habits. If it fails, he must try again, until his observation is "true" and his device is "right." All the practical and direct element in the folkways seems to be due to common sense, natural reason, intuition, or some other original mental endowment. It seems rational (or rationalistic) and utilitarian. Often in the mythologies this ultimate rational element was ascribed to the teaching of a god or a culture hero. In modern mythology it is accounted for as "natural."

Although the ways adopted must always be really "true" and "right" in relation to facts, for otherwise they could not answer their purpose, such is not the primitive notion of true and right.

31. The folkways are "right." Rights. Morals. The folkways are the "right" ways to satisfy all interests because they are traditional, and exist in fact. They extend over the whole of life. There is a right way to catch game, to win a wife, to make one's self appear, to cure disease, to honor ghosts, to treat comrades or strangers, to behave when a child is born, on the warpath, in council, and so oil in all cases which can arise. The ways are defined on the negative side, that is, by taboos. The "right" way is the way which the ancestors used and which has been handed down. The tradition is its own warrant. It is not held subject to verification by experience. The notion of right is in the folkways. It is not outside of them, of independent origin, and brought to them to test them. In the folkways, whatever is, is right. This is because they are traditional, and therefore contain in themselves the authority of the ancestral ghosts. When we come to the folkways we are at the end of our analysis. The notion of right and ought is the same in regard to all the folkways, but the degree of it varies with the importance of the interest at stake. The obligation of conformable and cooperative action is far greater under fear and war than in other matters, and the social sanctions are severer, because group interests are supposed to be at stake. Some usages contain only a slight element of right and ought. It may well be believed that notions of right and duty, and of social welfare, were first developed in connection with ghost fear and other-worldliness, and therefore that, in that field also, folkways were first raised to mores. "Rights" are the rules of mutual give and take in the competition of life which are imposed on comrades in the in-group, in order that the peace may prevail there which is essential to the group strength. Therefore rights can never be "natural" or "God-given," or absolute in any sense. The morality of a group at a time is the sum of the taboos and prescriptions in the folkways by which right conduct is defined. Therefore morals can never be intuitive. They are historical, institutional, and empirical.

World philosophy, life policy, right, rights, and morality are all products of the folkways. They are reflections on, and generalizations from, the experience of pleasure and pain which is won in efforts to carry on the struggle for existence under actual life conditions. The generalizations are very crude and vague in their germinal forms. They are all embodied in folklore, and all our philosophy and science have been developed out of them.

15. Ethnocentrism is the technical name for this view of things in which one's own group is the center of everything, and all others are scaled and rated with reference to it. Folkways correspond to it to cover both the inner and the outer relation. Each group nourishes its own pride and vanity, boasts itself superior, exalts its own divinities, and looks with contempt on outsiders. Each group thinks its own folkways the only right ones, and if it observes that other groups have other folkways, these excite its scorn. Opprobrious epithets are derived from these differences. "Pig-eater," "cow-eater," "uncircumcised," "jabberers," are epithets of contempt and abomination. The Tupis called the Portuguese by a derisive epithet descriptive of birds which have feathers around their feet, on account of trousers. For our present purpose the most important fact is that ethnocentrism leads a people to exaggerate and intensify everything in their own folkways which is peculiar and which differentiates them from others. It therefore strengthens the folkways.

34. Definition of the mores. When the elements of truth and right are developed into doctrines of welfare, the folkways are raised to another plane. They then become capable of producing inferences, developing into new forms, and extending their constructive influence over men and society. Then we call them the mores. The mores are the folkways, including the philosophical and ethical generalizations as to societal welfare which are suggested by them, and inherent in them, as they grow.

42. Purpose of the present work. "Ethology" would be a convenient term for the study of manners, customs, usages, and mores, including the study of the way in which they are formed, how they grow or decay, and how they affect the interests which it is their purpose to serve. The Greeks applied the term "ethos" to the sum of the characteristic usages, ideas, standards, and codes by which a group was differentiated and individualized in character from other groups. "Ethics" were things which pertained to the ethos and therefore the things which were the standard of right. The Romans used "mores" for customs in the broadest and richest sense of the word, including the notion that customs served welfare, and had traditional and mystic sanction, so that they were properly authoritative and sacred. It is a very surprising fact that modern nations should have lost these words and the significant suggestions which inhere in them. The English language has no derivative noun from "mores," and no equivalent for it. The French *moeurs* is trivial compared with "mores." The German *sitte* renders "mores" but very imperfectly. The modern peoples have made morals and morality a separate domain, by the side of religion, philosophy, and politics. In that sense, morals is an impossible and unreal category. It has no existence, and can have none. The word "moral" means what belongs or appertains to the mores. Therefore the category of morals can never be defined without reference to something outside of itself. Ethics, having lost connection with the ethos of a people, is an attempt to systematize the current notions of right and wrong upon some basic principle, generally with the purpose of establishing morals on an absolute doctrine, so that it shall be universal, absolute, and everlasting. In a general way also, whenever a thing can be called moral or connected with some ethical generality, it is thought to be "raised," and disputants whose method is to employ ethical generalities assume especial authority for themselves and their views. These methods of discussion are most employed in treating of social topics, and they are disastrous to sound study of facts, They help to hold the social sciences under the dominion of metaphysics. The abuse has been most developed in connection with political economy, which has been almost robbed of the character of a serious discipline by converting its discussions into ethical disquisitions.

43. Why use the word mores? "Ethica," in the Greek sense, or "ethology," as above defined, would be good names for our present work. We aim to study the ethos of groups, in order to see how it arises, its power and influence, the modes of its operation on members of the group, and the various attributes of it (ethica). "Ethology" is a very unfamiliar word. It has been used for the mode of setting forth manners, customs, and mores in satirical comedy. The Latin word "mores" seems to be, on the whole, more practically convenient and available than any other for our purpose, as a name for the folkways with the connotations of right and truth in respect to welfare embodied in them. The analysis and definition above given show that in the mores we must recognize a dominating force in history, constituting a condition as to what can be done, and as to the methods which can be employed.

44. Mores are a directive force. Of course the view which has been stated is antagonistic to the view that philosophy and ethics furnish creative and determining forces in society, and history. That view comes down to us from the Greek philosophy and it has now prevailed so long that all current discussion conforms to it. Philosophy and ethics are pursued as independent disciplines, and the results are brought to the science of society and to statesmanship and legislation as authoritative dicta . . . . It can be seen also that philosophy and ethics are products of the folkways. They are taken out of the mores, but are never original and creative; they are secondary and derived. They often interfere in the second stage of the sequence—act, thought, act. Then they produce harm, but some ground is furnished for the claim that they are creative or at least regulative. In fact, the real process in great bodies of men is not one of deduction from any great principle of philosophy or ethics. It is one of minute efforts to live well under existing conditions, which efforts are repeated indefinitely by great numbers, getting strength from habit and from the fellowship of united action. The resultant folkways become coercive. All are forced to conform, and the folkways dominate the societal life. Then they seem true and right, and arise into mores as the norm of welfare. Thence are produced faiths, ideas, doctrines, religions, and philosophies, according to the stage of civilization and the fashions of reflection and generalization.

61. The mores and institutions. Institutions and laws are produced out of mores. An institution consists of a concept (idea, notion, doctrine, interest) and a structure. The structure is a framework, or apparatus, or perhaps only a number of functionaries set to cooperate in prescribed ways at a certain conjuncture. The structure holds the concept and furnishes instrumentalities for bringing it into the world of facts and action in a way to serve the interests of men in society. Institutions are either crescive or enacted. They are crescive when they take shape in the mores, growing by the instinctive efforts by which the mores are produced. Then the efforts, through long use, become definite and specific. Property, marriage, and religion are the most primary institutions. They began in folkways. They became customs. They developed into mores by the addition of some philosophy of welfare, however crude. Then they were made more definite and specific as regards the rules, the prescribed acts, and the apparatus to be employed. This produced a structure and the institution was complete. Enacted institutions are products of rational invention and intention. They belong to high civilization. Banks are institutions of credit founded on usages which can be traced back to barbarism. There came a time when, guided by rational reflection on experience, men systematized and regulated the usages which had become current, and thus created positive institutions of credit, defined by law and sanctioned by the force of the state. Pure enacted institutions which are strong and prosperous are hard to find. It is too difficult to invent and create an institution for a purpose, out of nothing. The electoral college in the Constitution of the United States is an example. In that case the democratic mores of the people have seized upon the device and made of it something quite different from what the inventors planned. All institutions have come out of mores, although the rational element in them is sometimes so large that their origin in the mores is not to be ascertained except by an historical investigation (legislatures, courts, juries, joint stock companies, the stock exchange). Property, marriage, and religion are still almost entirely in the mores. Amongst nature men any man might capture and hold a woman at any time, if he could. He did it by superior force which was its own supreme justification. But his act brought his group and her group into war, and produced harm to his comrades. They forbade capture, or set conditions for it. Beyond the limits, the individual might still use force, but his comrades were no longer responsible. The glory to him, if he succeeded, might be all the greater. His control over his captive was absolute. Within the prescribed conditions, "capture" became technical and institutional, and rights grew out of it. The woman had a status which was defined by custom, and was very different from the status of a real captive. Marriage was the institutional relation, in the society and under its sanction, of a woman to a man, where the woman had been obtained in a prescribed way. She was then a "wife." What her rights and duties were was defined by the mores, as they are to-day in all civilized society.

62. Laws. Acts of legislation come out of the mores. In low civilization all societal regulations are customs and taboos, the origin of which is unknown. Positive laws are impossible until the stage of verification, reflection, and criticism is reached. Until that point is reached there is only customary law, or common law. The customary law may be codified and systematized with respect to some philosophical principles, and yet remain customary. The codes of Manu and Justinian are examples. Enactment is not possible until reverence for ancestors has been so much weakened that it is no longer thought wrong to interfere with traditional customs by positive enactment. Even then there is reluctance to make enactments, and there is a stage of transition during which traditional customs are extended by interpretation to cover new cases and to prevent evils. Legislation, however, has to seek standing ground on the existing mores, and it soon becomes apparent that legislation, to be strong, must be consistent with the mores. Things which have been in the mores are put under police regulation and later under positive law. It is sometimes said that "public opinion" must ratify and approve police regulations, but this statement rests on an imperfect analysis. The regulations must conform to the mores, so that the public will not think them too lax or too strict. The mores of our urban and rural populations are not the same; consequently legislation about intoxicants which is made by one of these sections of the population does not succeed when applied to the other. The regulation of drinking places, gambling places, and disorderly houses has passed through the abovementioned stages. It is always a question of expediency whether to leave a subject under the mores, or to make a police regulation for it, or to put it into criminal law. Betting, horse racing, dangerous sports, electric cars, and vehicles are cases now of things which seem to be passing under positive enactment and out of the unformulated control of the mores. When an enactment is made there is a sacrifice of the elasticity and automatic self-adaptation of custom, but an enactment is specific and is provided with sanctions. Enactments come into use when conscious purposes are formed, and it is believed that specific devices can be framed by which to realize such purposes in the society. Then also prohibitions take the place of taboos, and punishments are planned to be deterrent rather than revengeful. The mores of different societies, or of different ages, are characterized by greater or less readiness and confidence in regard to the use of positive enactments for the realization of societal purposes.

63. How laws and institutions differ from mores. When folkways have become institutions or laws they have changed their character and are to be distinguished from the mores. The element of sentiment and faith inheres in the mores. Laws and institutions have a rational and practical character, and are more mechanical and utilitarian. The great difference is that institutions and laws have a positive character, while mores are unformulated and undefined. There is a philosophy implicit in the folkways; when it is made explicit it becomes technical philosophy. Objectively regarded, the mores are the customs which actually conduce to welfare under existing life conditions. Acts under the laws and institutions are conscious and voluntary; under the folkways they are always unconscious and involuntary, so that they have the character of natural necessity. Educated reflection and skepticism can disturb this spontaneous relation. The laws, being positive prescriptions, supersede the mores so far as they are adopted. It follows that the mores come into operation where laws and tribunals fail. The mores cover the great field of common life where there are no laws or police regulations. They cover an immense and undefined domain, and they break the way in new domains, not yet controlled at all. The mores, therefore, build up new laws and police regulations in time.

83. Inertia and rigidity of the mores. We see that we must conceive of the mores as a vast system of usages, covering the whole of life, and serving all its interests; also containing in themselves their own justification by tradition and use and wont, and approved by mystic sanctions until, by rational reflection, they develop their own philosophical and ethical generalizations, which are elevated into "principles" of truth and right. They coerce and restrict the newborn generation. They do not stimulate to thought, but the contrary. The thinking is already done and is embodied in the mores. They never contain any provision for their own amendment. They are not questions, but answers, to the problem of life. They present themselves as final and unchangeable, because they present answers which are offered as "the truth." No world philosophy, until the modern scientific world philosophy, and that only within a generation or two, has ever presented itself as perhaps transitory, certainly incomplete, and liable to be set aside tomorrow by more knowledge. No popular world philosophy or life policy ever can present itself in that light. It would cost too great a mental strain. All the groups whose mores we consider far inferior to our own are quite as well satisfied with theirs as we are with ours. The goodness or badness of mores consists entirely in their adjustment to the life conditions and the interests of the time and place . . . . Therefore it is a sign of ease and welfare when no thought is given to the mores, but all cooperate in them instinctively. The nations of southeastern Asia show us the persistency of the mores, when the element of stability and rigidity in them becomes predominant. Ghost fear and ancestor worship tend to establish the persistency of the mores by dogmatic authority, strict taboo, and weighty sanctions. The mores then lose their naturalness and vitality. They are stereotyped. They lose all relation to expediency. They become an end in themselves. They are imposed by imperative authority without regard to interests or conditions (caste, child marriage, widows). When any society falls under the dominion of this disease in the mores it must disintegrate before it can live again. In that diseased state of the mores all learning consists in committing to memory the words of the sages of the past who established the formulae of the mores. Such words are "sacred writings," a sentence of which is a rule of conduct to be obeyed quite independently of present interests, or of any rational considerations.

232. Mores and morals; social code. For every one the mores give the notion of what ought to be. This includes the notion of what ought to be done, for all should cooperate to bring to pass, in the order of life, what ought to be. All notions of propriety, decency, chastity, politeness, order, duty, right, rights, discipline, respect, reverence, cooperation, and fellowship, especially all things in regard to which good and ill depend entirely on the point at which the line is drawn, are in the mores. The mores can make things seem right and good to one group or one age which to another seem antagonistic to every instinct of human nature. The thirteenth century bred in every heart such a sentiment in regard to heretics that inquisitors had no more misgivings in their proceedings than men would have now if they should attempt to exterminate rattlesnakes. The sixteenth century gave to all such notions about witches that witch persecutors thought they were waging war on enemies of God and man. Of course the inquisitors and witch persecutors constantly developed the notions of heretics and witches. They exaggerated the notions and then gave them back again to the mores, in their expanded form, to inflame the hearts of men with terror and hate and to become, in the next stage, so much more fantastic and ferocious motives. Such is the reaction between the mores and the acts of the living generation. The world philosophy of the age is never anything but the reflection on the mental horizon, which is formed out of the mores of the ruling ideas which are in the mores themselves. It is, from a failure to recognize the to and fro in this reaction that the current notion arises that mores are produced by doctrines. The "morals" of an age are never anything but the consonance between what is done and what the mores of the age require. The whole revolves on itself, in the relation of the specific to the general, within the horizon formed by the mores. Every attempt to win an outside standpoint from which to reduce the whole to an absolute philosophy of truth and right based on an unalterable principle, is a delusion. New elements are brought in only by new conquests of nature through science and art. The new conquests change the conditions of life and the interests of the members of the society. Then the mores change by adaptation to new conditions and interests. The philosophy and ethics then follow to account for and justify the changes in the mores; often, also, to claim that they have caused the changes. They never do anything but draw new lines of bearing between the parts of the mores and the horizon of thought within which they are inclosed, and which is a deduction from the mores. The horizon is widened by more knowledge, but for one age it is just as much a generation from the mores as for another. It is always unreal. It is only a product of thought. The ethical philosophers select points on this horizon from which to take their bearings, and they think that they have won some authority for their systems when they travel back again from the generalization to the specific custom out of which it was deduced. The cases of the inquisitors and witch persecutors who toiled arduously and continually for their chosen ends, for little or no reward, show us the relation between mores on the one side and philosophy, ethics, and religion on the other.

494. Honor, seemliness, common sense, conscience. Honor, common sense, seemliness, and conscience seem to belong to the individual domain. They are reactions produced in the individual by the societal environment. Honor is the sentiment of what one owes to one's self. It is an individual prerogative and an ultimate individual standard. Seemliness is conduct which befits one's character and standards. Common sense, in the current view, is a natural gift and universal outfit. As to honor and seemliness, the popular view seems to be that each one has a fountain of inspiration in himself to furnish him with guidance. Conscience might be added as another natural or supernatural "voice," intuition, and part of the original outfit of all human beings as such. If these notions could be verified, and if they proved true, no discussion of them would be in place here, but as to honor it is a well known and undisputed fact that societies have set codes of honor and standards of it which were arbitrary, irrational, and both individually and socially inexpedient, as ample experiment has proved. These codes have been and are imperative, and they have been accepted and obeyed by great groups of men who, in their own judgment, did not believe them sound. These codes came out of the folkways of the time and place. Then comes the question whether it is not always so. Is honor, in any case, anything but the code of one's duty to himself which he has accepted from the group in which he was educated? Family, class, religious sect, school, occupation, enter into the social environment. In every environment there is a standard of honor. When a man thinks that he is acting most independently, on his personal prerogative, he is at best only balancing against each other the different codes in which he has been educated, e.g., that of the trades union against that of the Sunday school, or of the school against that of the family. What we think "natural" and universal, and to which we attribute an objective reality, is the sum of traits whose origin is so remote, and which we share with so many, that we do not know when or how we took them up, and we can remember no rational selection by which we adopted them. The same is true of common sense. It is the stock of ways of looking at things which we acquired unconsciously by suggestion from the environment in which we grew up. Some have more common sense than others, because they are more docile to suggestion, or have been taught to make judgments by people who were strong and wise. Conscience also seems best explained as a sum of principles of action which have in one's character the most original, remote, undisputed, and authoritative position, and to which questions of doubt are habitually referred. If these views are accepted, we have in honor, common sense, and conscience other phenomena of the folkways, and the notions of eternal truths of philosophy or ethics, derived from somewhere outside of men and their struggles to live well under the conditions of earth, must be abandoned as myths.

438. Specification of the subject. The ethnographers write of a tribe that the "morality" in it, especially of the women, is low or high, etc. This is the technical use of morality—as a thing pertaining to the sex relation only or especially, and the ethnographers make their propositions by applying our standards of sex behavior, and our form of the sex taboo, to judge the folkways of all people. All that they can properly say is that they find a great range and variety of usages, ideas, standards, and ideals, which differ greatly from ours. Some of them are far stricter than ours. Those we do not consider nobler than ours. We do not feel that we ought to adopt any ways because they are more strict than our traditional ones. We consider many to be excessive, silly, and harmful. A Roman senator was censured for impropriety because he kissed his wife in the presence of his daughter.

439. Meaning of "immoral." When, therefore, the ethnographers apply condemnatory or depreciatory adjectives to the people whom they study, they beg the most important question which we want to investigate; that is, What are standards, codes, and ideas of chastity, decency, propriety, modesty, etc., and whence do they arise? The ethnographical facts contain the answer to this question . . . . "Immoral" never means an thing but contrary to the mores of the time and place. Therefore the mores and the morality may move together, and there is no permanent or universal standard by which right and truth in regard to these matters can be established and different folkways compared and criticized.

From W. G. Sumner, *Folkways* (Boston: Ginn, 1907), chaps. 1, 2, 5, and 11. Copyright 1907 by W. G. Sumner.

Ethics Are Not Relative

W. T. Stace

There is an opinion widely current nowadays in philosophical circles which passes under the name of "ethical relativity." Exactly what this phrase means or implies is certainly far from clear. But unquestionably it stands as a label for the opinions of a group of ethical philosophers whose position is roughly on the extreme left wing among the moral theorizers of the day. And perhaps one may best understand it by placing it in contrast with the opposite kind of extreme view against which, undoubtedly, it has arisen as a protest. For among moral philosophers one may clearly distinguish a left and a right wing. Those of the left wing are the ethical relativists. They are the revolutionaries, the clever young men, the up to date. Those of the right wing we may call the ethical absolutists. They are the conservatives and the old-fashioned.

Ethical Absolutism

According to the absolutists there is but one eternally true and valid moral code. This moral code applies with rigid impartiality to all men. What is a duty for me must likewise be a duty for you. And this will be true whether you are an Englishman, a Chinaman, or a Hottentot. If cannibalism is an abomination in England or America, it is an abomination in central Africa, notwithstanding that the African may think otherwise. The fact that he sees nothing wrong in his cannibal practices does not make them for him morally right. They are as much contrary to morality for him as they are for us. The only difference is that he is an ignorant savage who does not know this. There is not one law for one man or race of men, another for another. There is not one moral standard for Europeans, another for Indians, another for Chinese. There is but one law, one standard, one morality, for all men. And this standard, this law, is absolute and unvarying.

Moreover, as the one moral law extends its dominion over all the comers of the earth, so too it is not limited in its application by any considerations of time or period. That which is right now was right in the centuries of Greece and Rome, nay, in the very ages of the, cave man. That which is evil now was evil then. If slavery is morally wicked today, it was morally wicked among the ancient Athenians, notwithstanding that their greatest men accepted it as a necessary condition of human society. Their opinion did not make slavery a moral good for them. It only showed that they were, in spite of their otherwise noble conceptions, ignorant of what is truly right and good in this matter.

The ethical absolutist recognizes as a fact that moral customs and moral ideas differ from country to country and from age to age. This indeed seems manifest and not to be disputed. We think slavery morally wrong, the Greeks thought it morally unobjectionable. The inhabitants of New Guinea certainly have very different moral ideas from ours. But the fact that the Greeks or the inhabitants of New Guinea think something right does not make it right, even for them. Nor does the fact that we think the same things wrong make them wrong. They are *in themselves* either right or wrong. What we have to do is to discover which they are. What anyone thinks makes no difference. It is here just as it is in matters of physical science. We believe the earth to be a globe. Our ancestors may have thought it flat. This does not show that it *was* flat, and is *now* a globe. What it shows is that men having in other ages been ignorant about the shape of the earth have now learned the truth. So if the Greeks thought slavery morally legitimate, this does not indicate that it was for them and in that age morally legitimate, but rather that they were ignorant of the truth of the matter.

The ethical absolutist is not indeed committed to the opinion that his own, or our own, moral code is the true one. Theoretically at least he might hold that slavery is ethically justifiable, that the Greeks knew better than we do about this, that ignorance of the true morality lies with us and not with them. All that he is actually committed to is the opinion that, whatever the true moral code may be, it is always the same for all men in all ages. His view is not at all inconsistent with the belief that humanity has still much to learn in moral matters. If anyone were to assert that in five hundred years the moral conceptions of the present day will appear as barbarous to the people of that age as the moral conceptions of the middle ages appear to us now, he need not deny it. If anyone were to assert that the ethics of Christianity are by no means final, and will be superseded in future ages by vastly nobler moral ideals, he need not deny this either. For it is of the essence of his creed to believe that morality is in some sense objective, not man-made, not produced by human opinion; that its principles are real truths about which men have to learn—just as they have to learn about the shape of the world—about which they may have been ignorant in the past, and about which therefore they may well be ignorant now.

Thus although absolutism is conservative in the sense that it is regarded by the more daring spirits as an out of date opinion, it is not necessarily conservative in the sense of being committed to the blind support of existing moral ideas and institutions. If ethical absolutists are sometimes conservative in this sense too, that is their personal affair. Such conservatism is accidental, not essential to the absolutist's creed. There is no logical reason, in the nature of the case, why an absolutist should not be a communist, an anarchist, a surrealist, or an upholder of free love. The fact that he is usually none of these things may be accounted for in various ways. But it has nothing to do with the sheer logic of his ethical position. The sole opinion to which he is committed is that whatever is morally right (or wrong)—be it free love or monogamy or slavery or cannibalism or vegetarianism—is morally right (or wrong) for all men at all times.

Usually the absolutist goes further than this. He often maintains, not merely that the moral law is the same for all the men on this planet—which is, after all, a tiny speck in space—but that in some way or in some sense it has application everywhere in the universe. He may express himself by saying that it applies to all "rational beings"—which would apparently include angels and the men on Mars (if they are rational). He is apt to think that the moral law is a part of the fundamental structure of the universe. But with this aspect of absolutism we need not, at the moment, concern ourselves. At present we may think of it as being simply the opinion that there is a single moral standard for all human beings.

※ ※ ※

Historical Causes for the Acceptance of Absolutism. This brief and rough sketch of ethical absolutism is intended merely to form a background against which we may the more clearly indicate, by way of contrast, the theory of ethical relativity. Up to the present, therefore, I have not given any of the reasons which the absolutist can urge in favour of his case. It is sufficient for my purpose at the moment to state *what* he believes, without going into the question of *why* he believes it. But before proceeding to our next step—the explanation of ethical relativity—I think it will be helpful to indicate some of the historical causes (as distinguished from logical reasons) which have helped in the past to render absolutism a plausible interpretation of morality as understood by European peoples.

Our civilization is a Christian civilization. It has grown up, during nearly two thousand years, upon the soil of Christian monotheism. In this soil our whole outlook upon life, and consequently all our moral ideas, have their roots. They have been moulded by this influence. The wave of religious scepticism which, during the last half century, has swept over us, has altered this fact scarcely at all. The moral ideas even of those who most violently reject the dogmas of Christianity with their intellects are still Christian ideas. This will probably remain true for many centuries even if Christian theology, as a set of intellectual beliefs, comes to be wholly rejected by every educated person. It will probably remain true so long as our civilization lasts. A child cannot, by changing in later life his intellectual creed, strip himself of the early formative moral influences of his childhood, though he can no doubt modify their results in various minor ways. With the outlook on life which was instilled into him in his early days he, in large measure, lives and dies. So it is with a civilization. And our civilization, whatever religious or irreligious views it may come to hold or reject, can hardly escape within its lifetime the moulding influences of its Christian origin. Now ethical absolutism was, in its central ideas, the product of Christian theology.

The connection is not difficult to detect. For morality has been conceived, during the Christian dispensation, as issuing from the will of God. That indeed was its single and all-sufficient source. There would be no point, for the naive believer in the faith, in the philosopher's questions regarding the foundations of morality and the basis of moral obligation. Even to ask such questions is a mark of incipient religious scepticism. For the true believer the author of the moral law is God. What pleases God, what God commands—that is the definition of right. What displeases God, what he forbids, that is the definition of wrong. Now there is, for the Christian Monotheist, only one God ruling over the entire universe. And this God is rational, self-consistent. He does not act upon whims. Consequently his will and his commands must be the same everywhere. They will be unvarying for all peoples and in all ages. If the heathen have other moral ideas than ours—inferior ideas—that can only be because they live in ignorance of the true God. If they knew God and his commands, their ethical precepts would be the same as ours.

Polytheistic creeds may well tolerate a number of diverse moral codes. For the God of the western hemisphere might have different views from those entertained by the God of the eastern hemisphere. And the God of the north might issue to his worshippers commands at variance with the commands issued to other peoples by the God of the south. But a monotheistic religion implies a single universal and absolute morality.

This explains why ethical absolutism, until very recently, was not only believed by philosophers but *taken for granted without any argument.* . . .

Ethical Relativism

We can now turn to the consideration of ethical relativity . . . . The revolt of the relativists against absolutism is, I believe, part and parcel of the general revolutionary tendency of our times. In particular it is a result of the decay of belief in the dogmas of orthodox religion. Belief in absolutism was supported, as we have seen, by belief in Christian monotheism. And now that, in an age of widespread religious scepticism, that support is withdrawn, absolutism tends to collapse. Revolutionary movements are as a rule, at any rate in their first onset, purely negative. They attack and destroy. And ethical relativity is, in its essence, a purely negative creed. It is simply a denial of ethical absolutism. That is why the best way of explaining it is to begin by explaining ethical absolutism. If we understand that what the latter asserts the former denies, then we understand ethical relativity.

Any ethical position which denies that there is a single moral standard which is equally applicable to all men at all times may fairly be called a species of ethical relativity. There is not, the relativist asserts, merely one moral law, one code, one standard. There are many moral laws, codes, standards. What morality ordains in one place or age may be quite different from what morality ordains in another place or age. The moral code of Chinamen is quite different from that of Europeans, that of African savages quite different from both. Any morality, therefore, is relative to the age, the place, and the circumstances in which it is found. It is in no sense absolute.

This does not mean merely—as one might at first sight be inclined to suppose—that the very same kind of action which is *thought* right in one country and period may be *thought* wrong in another. This would be a mere platitude, the truth of which everyone would have to admit. Even the absolutist would admit this—would even wish to emphasize it—since he is well aware that different peoples have different sets of moral ideas, and his whole point is that some of these sets of ideas are false. What the relativist means to assert is, not this platitude, but that the very same kind of action which *is* right in one country and period may *be* wrong in another. And this, far from being a platitude, is a very startling assertion.

It is very important to grasp thoroughly the difference between the two ideas. For there is reason to think that many minds tend to find ethical relativity attractive because they fail to keep them clearly apart. It is so very obvious that moral ideas differ from country to country and from age to age. And it is so very easy, if you are mentally lazy, to suppose that to say this means the same as to say that no universal moral standard exists—or in other words that it implies ethical relativity. We fail to see that the word "standard" is used in two different senses. It is perfectly true that, in one sense, there are many variable moral standards. We speak of judging a man by the standard of his time. And this implies that different times have different standards. And this, of course, is quite true. But when the word "standard" is used in this sense it means simply the set of moral ideas current during the period in question. It means what people *think* right, whether as a matter of fact it *is* right or not. On the other hand when the absolutist asserts that there exists a single universal moral "standard," he is not using the word in this sense at all. He means by "standard" what is right as distinct from what people merely think right. His point is that although what people think right varies in different countries and periods, yet what actually is right is everywhere and always the same. And it follows that when the ethical relativist disputes the position of the absolutist and denies that any universal moral standard exists he too means by "standard" what actually is right. But it is exceedingly easy, if we are not careful, to slip loosely from using the word in the first sense to using it in the second sense; and to suppose that the variability of moral beliefs is the same thing as the variability of what really is moral. And unless we keep the two senses of the word "standard" distinct, we are likely to think the creed of ethical relativity much more plausible than it actually is.

The genuine relativist, then, does not merely mean that Chinamen may think right what Frenchmen think wrong. He means that what is wrong for the Frenchman may *be* right for the Chinaman. And if one enquires how, in those circumstances, one is to know what actually is right in China or in France, the answer comes quite glibly. What is right in China is the same as what people think right in China; and what is right in France is the same as what people think right in France. So that, if you want to know what is moral in any particular country or age all you have to do is to ascertain what are the moral ideas current in that age or country. Those ideas are, *for that age or country*, right. Thus what is morally right is identified with what is thought to be morally right, and the distinction which we made above between these two is simply denied. To put the same thing in another way, it is denied that there can be or ought to be any distinction between the two senses of the word "standard." There is only one kind of standard of right and wrong, namely, the moral ideas current in any particular age or country.

Moral right *means* what people think morally right. It has no other meaning. What Frenchmen think right is, therefore, right *for Frenchmen*. And evidently one must conclude—though I am not aware that relativists are anxious to draw one's attention to such unsavoury but yet absolutely necessary conclusions from their creed—that cannibalism is right for people who believe in it, that human sacrifice is right for those races which practice it, and that burning widows alive was right for Hindus until the British stepped in and compelled the Hindus to behave immorally by allowing their widows to remain alive.

When it is said that, according to the ethical relativist, what is thought right in any social group is right for that group, one must be careful not to misinterpret this. The relativist does not, of course, mean that there actually is an objective moral standard in France and a different objective standard in England, and that French and British opinions respectively give us correct information about these different standards. His point is rather that there are no objectively true moral standards at all. There is no single universal objective standard. Nor are there a variety of local objective standards. All standards are subjective. People's subjective feelings about morality are the only standards which exist.

To sum up. The ethical relativist consistently denies, it would seem, whatever the ethical absolutist asserts. For the absolutist there is a single universal moral standard. For the relativist there is no such standard. There are only local, ephemeral, and variable standards. For the absolutist there are two senses of the word "standard." Standards in the sense of sets of current moral ideas are relative and changeable. But the standard in the sense of what is actually morally right is absolute and unchanging. For the relativist no such distinction can be made. There is only one meaning of the word standard, namely, that which refers to local and variable sets of moral ideas. Or if it is insisted that the word must be allowed two meanings, then the relativist will say that there is at any rate no actual example of a standard in the absolute sense, and that the word as thus used is an empty name to which nothing in reality corresponds so that the distinction between the two meanings becomes empty and useless. Finally—though this is merely saying the same thing in another way—the absolutist makes a distinction between what actually is right and what is thought right. The relativist rejects this distinction and identifies what is moral with what is thought moral by certain human beings or groups of human beings. . . .

Arguments in Favor of Ethical Relativity. . . . The first [argument] is that which relies upon the actual varieties of moral "standards" found in the world. It was easy enough to believe in a single absolute morality in older times when there was no anthropology, when all humanity was divided clearly into two groups, Christian peoples and the "heathen." Christian peoples knew and possessed the one true morality. The rest were savages whose moral ideas could be ignored. But all this is changed. Greater knowledge has brought greater tolerance. We can no longer exalt our own morality as alone true, while dismissing all other moralities as false or inferior. The investigations of anthropologists have shown that there exist side by side in the world a bewildering variety of moral codes. On this topic endless volumes have been written, masses of evidence piled up. Anthropologists have ransacked the Melanesian Islands, the jungles of New Guinea, the steppes of Siberia, the deserts of Australia, the forests of central Africa, and have brought back with them countless examples of weird, extravagant, and fantastic "moral" customs with which to confound us. We learn that all kinds of horrible practices are, in this, that, or the other place, regarded as essential to virtue. We find that there is nothing, or next to nothing, which has always and everywhere been regarded as morally good by all men. Where then is our universal morality? Can we, in face of all this evidence, deny that it is nothing but an empty dream?

This argument, taken by itself, is a very weak one. It relies upon a single set of facts—the variable moral customs of the world. But this variability of moral ideas is admitted by both parties to the dispute, and is capable of ready explanation upon the hypothesis of either party. The relativist says that the facts are to be explained by the non-existence of any absolute moral standard. The absolutist says that they are to be explained by human ignorance of what the absolute moral standard is. And he can truly point out that men have differed widely in their opinions about all manner of topics including the subject-matters of the physical sciences—just as much as they differ about morals. And if the various different opinions which men have held about the shape of the earth do not prove that it has no one real shape, neither do the various opinions which they have held about morality prove that there is no one true morality.

Thus the facts can be explained equally plausibly on either hypothesis. There is nothing in the facts themselves which compels us to prefer the relativistic hypothesis to that of the absolutist. And therefore the argument fails to prove the relativist conclusion. If that conclusion is to be established, it must be by means of other considerations.

This is the essential point. But I will add some supplementary remarks. The work of the anthropologists, upon which ethical relativists seem to rely so heavily, has as a matter of fact added absolutely nothing *in principle* to what has always been known about the variability of moral ideas. Educated people have known all along that the Greeks tolerated sodomy, which in modern times has been regarded in some countries as an abominable crime; that the Hindus thought it a sacred duty to burn their widows; that trickery, now thought despicable, was once believed to be a virtue; that terrible torture was thought by our own ancestors only a few centuries ago to be a justifiable weapon of justice; that it was only yesterday that western peoples came to believe that slavery is immoral. Even the ancients knew very well that moral customs and ideas vary—witness the writings of Herodotus. Thus the principle of the variability of moral ideas was well understood long before modern anthropology was ever heard of. Anthropology has added nothing to the knowledge of this principle except a mass of new and extreme examples of it drawn from very remote sources. But to multiply examples of a principle already well known and universally admitted adds nothing to the argument which is built upon that principle. The discoveries of the anthropologists have no doubt been of the highest importance in their own sphere. But in my considered opinion they have thrown no new light upon the special problems of the moral philosopher.

Although the multiplication of examples has no logical bearing on the argument, it does have an immense *psychological* effect upon people's minds. These masses of anthropological learning are impressive. They are propounded in the sacred name of "science." If they are quoted in support of ethical relativity—as they often are—people *think* that they must prove something important. They bewilder and over-awe the simple-minded, batter down their resistance, make them ready to receive humbly the doctrine of ethical relativity from those who have acquired a reputation by their immense learning and their claims to be "scientific." Perhaps this is why so much ado is made by ethical relativists regarding the anthropological evidence. But we must refuse to be impressed. We must discount all this mass of evidence about the extraordinary moral customs of remote peoples. Once we have admitted—as everyone who is instructed must have admitted these last two thousand years without any anthropology at all—the principle that moral ideas vary, all this new evidence adds nothing to the argument. And the argument itself proves nothing for the reasons already given. . . .

[Another] argument in favour of ethical relativity. . . . consists in alleging that no one has ever been able to discover upon what foundation an absolute morality could rest, or from what source a universally binding moral code could derive its authority.

If, for example, it is an absolute and unalterable moral rule that all men ought to be unselfish, from whence does this *command* issue? For a command it certainly is, phrase it how you please. There is no difference in meaning between the sentence "You ought to be unselfish" and the sentence "Be unselfish." Now a command implies a commander. An obligation implies some authority which obliges. Who is this commander, what this authority? Thus the vastly difficult question is raised of *the basis of moral obligation.* Now the argument of the relativist would be that it is impossible to find any basis for a universally binding moral law; but that it is quite easy to discover a basis for morality if moral codes are admitted to be variable, ephemeral, and relative to time, place, and circumstance.

. . . I am assuming that it is no longer possible to solve this difficulty by saying naively that the universal moral law is based upon the uniform commands of God to all men. There will be many, no doubt, who will dispute this. But I am not writing for them. I am writing for those who feel the necessity of finding for morality a basis independent of particular religious dogmas. And I shall therefore make no attempt to argue the matter.

The problem which the absolutist has to face, then, is this. The religious basis of the one absolute morality having disappeared, can there be found for it any other, any secular, basis? If not, then it would seem that we cannot any longer believe in absolutism. We shall have to fall back upon belief in a variety of perhaps mutually inconsistent moral codes operating over restricted areas and limited periods. No one of these will be better, or more true, than any other. Each will be good and true for those living in those areas and periods. We shall have to fall back, in a word, on ethical relativity. . . .

Arguments Against Ethical Relativity. . . . Ethical relativity, in asserting that the moral standards of particular social groups are the only standards which exist, renders meaningless all propositions which attempt to compare these standards with one another in respect of their moral worth. And this is a very serious matter indeed. We are accustomed to think that the moral ideas of one nation or social group may be "higher" or "lower" than those of another. We believe, for example, that Christian ethical ideals are nobler than those of the savage races of central Africa. Probably most of us would think that the Chinese moral standards are higher than those of the

Chapter IV: Relativism

inhabitants of New Guinea. In short we habitually compare one civilization with another and judge the sets of ethical ideas to be found in them to be some better, some worse. The fact that such judgments are very difficult to make with any justice, and that they are frequently made on very superficial and prejudiced grounds, has no bearing on the question now at issue. The question is whether such judgments have any *meaning*. We habitually assume that they have.

But on the basis of ethical relativity they can have none whatever. For the relativist must hold that there is no *common* standard which can be applied to the various civilizations judged. Any such comparison of moral standards implies the existence of some standard which is applicable to both. And the existence of any standard is precisely what the relativist denies. According to him the Christian standard is applicable only to Christians, the Chinese standard only to Chinese, the New Guinea standard only to the inhabitants of New Guinea.

What is true of comparisons between the moral standards of different races will also be true of comparisons between those of different ages. It is not unusual to ask such questions as whether the standard of our own day is superior to that which existed among our ancestors five hundred years ago. And when we remember that our ancestors employed slaves, practiced barbaric physical tortures, and burnt people alive, we may be inclined to think that it is. At any rate we assume that the question is one which has meaning and is capable of rational discussion. But if the ethical relativist is right, whatever we assert on this subject must be totally meaningless. For here again there is no common standard which could form the basis of any such judgments.

This in its turn implies that the whole notion of moral *progress* is a sheer delusion. Progress means an advance from lower to higher, from worse to better. But on the basis of ethical relativity it has no meaning to say that the standards of this age are better (or worse) than those of a previous age. For there is no common standard by which both can be measured. . . .

If these arguments are valid, the ethical relativist cannot really maintain that there is anywhere to be found a moral standard binding upon anybody against his will. And he cannot maintain that, even within the social group, there is a common standard as between individuals. And if that is so, then even judgments to the effect that one man is morally better than another become meaningless. All moral valuation thus vanishes. There is nothing to prevent each man from being a rule unto himself. The result will be moral chaos and the collapse of all effective standards. . . .

But even if we assume that the difficulty about defining moral groups has been surmounted, a further difficulty presents itself. Suppose that we have not definitely decided what are the exact boundaries of the social group within which a moral standard is to be operative. And we will assume—as is invariably done by relativists themselves—that this group is to be some actually existing social community such as a tribe or nation. How are we to know, even then, what actually *is* the moral standard within that group? How is anyone to know? How is even a member of the group to know? For there are certain to be within the group—at least this will be true among advanced peoples—wide differences of opinion as to what is right, what wrong. Whose opinion, then, is to be taken as representing *the* moral standard of the group? Either we must take the opinion of the majority within the group, or the opinion of some minority. If we rely upon the ideas of the majority, the results will be disastrous. Wherever there is found among a people a small band of select spirits, or perhaps one man, working for the establishment of higher and nobler ideals than those commonly accepted by the group, we shall be compelled to hold that, for that people at that time, the majority are right, and that the reformers are wrong and are preaching what is immoral. We shall have to maintain, for example, that Jesus was preaching immoral doctrines to the Jews. Moral goodness will have to be equated always with the mediocre and sometimes with the definitely base and ignoble. If on the other hand we say that the moral standard of the group is to be identified with the moral opinions of some minority, then what minority is this to be? We cannot answer that it is to be the minority composed of the best and most enlightened individuals of the group. This would involve us in a palpably vicious circle. For by what standard are these individuals to be judged the best and the most enlightened? There is no principle by which we could select the right minority. And therefore we should have to consider every minority as good as every other. And this means that we should have no logical right whatever to resist the claim of the gangsters of Chicago—if such a claim were made that their practices represent the highest standards of American morality. It means in the end that every individual is to be bound by no standard save his own.

The ethical relativists are great empiricists. What is the actual moral standard of any group can only be discovered, they tell us, by an examination on the ground of the moral opinions and customs of that group. But will they tell us how they propose to decide, when they get to the ground, which of the many moral opinions they are sure to find there is *the* right one in that group? To some extent they will be able to do this for the Melanesian Islanders—from whom apparently all lessons in the nature of morality are in future to be taken. But it is certain that they cannot do it for advanced peoples whose members have learnt to think for themselves and to entertain among themselves a wide variety of opinions. They cannot do it unless they accept the calamitous view that the ethical option of the majority is always right. We are left therefore once more with the conclusion that, even within a particular social group, anybody's moral opinion is as good as anybody else's, and that every man is entitled to be judged by his own standards.

Finally, not only is ethical relativity disastrous in its consequences for moral theory. It cannot be doubted that it must tend to be equally disastrous in its impact upon practical conduct. If men come really to believe that one moral standard is as good as another, they will conclude that their own moral standard has nothing special to recommend it. They might as well then slip down to some lower and easier standard. It is true that, for a time, it may be possible to hold one view in theory and to act practically upon another. But ideas, even philosophical ideas, are not so ineffectual that they can remain for ever idle in the upper chambers of the intellect. In the end they seep down to the level of practice. They get themselves acted on. . . .

These, then, are the main arguments which the anti-relativist will urge against ethical relativity. And perhaps finally he will attempt a diagnosis of the social, intellectual, and psychological conditions of our time to which the emergence of ethical relativism is to be attributed. His diagnosis will be somewhat as follows.

We have abandoned, perhaps with good reason, the oracles of the past. Every age, of course, does this. But in our case it seems that none of us knows any more whither to turn. We do not know what to put in the place of that which has gone. What ought we, supposedly civilized peoples, to aim at? What are to be our ideals? What is right? What is wrong? What is beautiful? What is ugly? No man knows. We drift helplessly in this direction and that. We know not where we stand nor whither we are going.

There are, of course, thousands of voices frantically shouting directions. But they shout one another down, they contradict one another, and the upshot is mere uproar. And because of this confusion there creeps upon us an insidious scepticism and despair. Since no one knows what the truth is, we will deny that there is any truth. Since no one knows what right is, we will deny that there is any right. Since no one knows what the beautiful is, we will deny that there is any beauty. Or at least we will say—what comes to the same thing—that what people (the people of any particular age, region, society)—think to be true is true *for them*; that what people think morally right is morally right *for them*; that what people think beautiful is beautiful *for them*. There is no common and objective standard in any of these matters. Since all the voices contradict one another, they must be all equally right (or equally wrong, for it makes no difference which we say). It is from the practical confusion of our time that these doctrines issue. When all the despair and defeatism of our distracted age are expressed in abstract concepts, are erected into a philosophy, it is then called relativism—ethical relativism, aesthetic relativism, relativity of truth. Ethical relativity is simply defeatism in morals.

And the diagnosis will proceed. Perhaps, it will say, the current pessimism as to our future is unjustified. But there is undoubtedly a wide spread feeling that our civilization is rushing downwards to the abyss. If this should be true, and if nothing should check the headlong descent, then perhaps some historian of the future will seek to disentangle the causes. The causes will, of course, be found to be multitudinous and enormously complicated. And one must not exaggerate the relative importance of any of them. But it can hardly be doubted that our future historian will include somewhere in his list the failure of the men of our generation to hold steadfastly before themselves the notion of an (even comparatively) unchanging moral idea. He will cite that feebleness of intellectual and moral grasp which has led them weakly to harbour the belief that no one moral aim is really any better than any other, that each is good and true for those who entertain it. This meant, he will surely say, that men had given up in despair the struggle to attain moral truth. Civilization lives in and through its upward struggle. Whoever despairs and gives up the struggle, whether it be an individual or a whole civilization, is already inwardly dead.

From W. T. Stace, *The Concept of Morals*. Copyright 1937 by The Macmillan Company, renewed 1965 by The Macmillan Company. Reprinted by permission of the publisher.

The Ethical Implications of Cultural Relativity

Carl Wellman

It is often thought that the discoveries of anthropology have revolutionary implications for ethics. Readers of Sumner, Benedict, and Herskovits are apt to come away with the impression that the only moral obligation is to conform to one's society, that polygamy is as good as monogamy, or that no ethical judgment can be rationally justified. While these anthropologists might complain that they are being misinterpreted, they would not deny that their real intent is to challenge the traditional view of morals. Even the anthropologist whose scientific training has made him skeptical of sweeping generalities and wary of philosophical entanglements is inclined to believe that the scientific study of cultures has undermined the belief in ethical absolutes of any kind.

Just what has been discovered that forces us to revise our ethics? Science has shown that certain things that were once thought to be absolute are actually relative to culture. Something is relative to culture when it varies with and is causally determined by culture. Clearly, nothing can be both relative to culture and absolute, for to be absolute is to be fixed and invariable, independent of man and the same for all men.

Exactly which things are relative and in what degree is a question still being debated by cultural anthropologists. Important as this question is, I do not propose to discuss it. It is the empirical scientists who must tell us which things vary from culture to culture and to what extent each is causally determined by its culture. It is not for me to question the findings of the anthropologists in this area. Instead, let me turn to the philosophical problem of the implications of cultural relativity. Assuming for the moment that cultural relativity is a fact, what follows for ethics?

What follows depends in part upon just what turns out to be relative. Anthropologists are apt to use the word "values" to refer indiscriminately to the things which have value, the characteristics which give these things their value, the attitudes of the persons who value these things, and the judgments of those people that these things have value. Similarly, one finds it hard to be sure whether "morals" refers to the mores of a people, the set of principles an observer might formulate after observing their conduct, the practical beliefs the people themselves entertain, or the way they feel about certain kinds of conduct. Until such ambiguities are cleared up, one hardly knows what is being asserted when it is claimed that "values" or "morals" are relative.

It seems to me there are at least ten quite different things of interest to the ethicist that the anthropologist might discover to be relative to culture: mores, social institutions, human nature, acts, goals, value experiences, moral emotions, moral concepts moral judgments, and moral reasoning. Since I can hardly discuss all the ethical conclusions that various writers have tried to draw from these different facts of cultural relativity, what I propose to do is to examine critically the reasoning by which one ethical conclusion might be derived from each of them.

I

It has long been recognized that mores are relative to culture. Mores are those customs which are enforced by social pressure. They are established patterns of action to which the individual is expected to conform and from which he deviates only at the risk of disapproval and punishment. It seems clear that mores vary from society to society and that the mores of any given society depend upon its culture. What does this imply for ethics?

The conclusion most frequently drawn is that what is right in one society may be wrong in another. For example, although it would be wrong for one of us to kill his aged parents, this very act is right for an Eskimo. This is because our mores are different from those of Eskimo society, and it is the mores that make an act right or wrong.

Let us grant, for the sake of discussion, that different societies do have different mores. Why should we grant that the mores make an act right or wrong? It has been claimed that this is true by definition. "Right" simply means according to the mores, and "wrong" means in violation of the mores. There is something to be said for this analysis of our concepts of right and wrong. It seems to explain both the imperativeness and the impersonality of obligation.

The "ought" seems to tell one what to do and yet to be more than the command of any individual; perhaps its bindingness lies in the demands of society. Attractive as this interpretation appears at first glance, I cannot accept it. It can be shown that no naturalistic analysis of the meaning of ethical words is adequate. In addition, this particular analysis is objectionable in that it makes it self-contradictory to say that any customary way of acting is wrong. No doubt, social reformers are often confused, but they are not always inconsistent.

If the view that the mores make an act right or wrong is not true by definition, it amounts to the moral principle that one ought always to conform to the mores of his society. None of the ways in which this principle is usually supported is adequate. (a) Any society unconsciously develops those mores which are conducive to survival and well-being under its special circumstances. Each individual ought to obey the mores of his society because this is the best way to promote the good life for the members of that society. I admit that there is a tendency for any society to develop those mores which fit its special circumstances, but I doubt that this is more than a tendency. There is room for reform in most societies. and this is particularly true when conditions are changing for one reason or another. (b) One ought to obey the mores of his society because disobedience would tend to destroy those mores. Without mores any society would lapse into a state of anarchy that would be intolerable for its members. It seems to me that this argument deserves to be taken seriously, but it does not prove that one ought always to obey the mores of his society. What it does show is that one ought generally to obey the mores of his society and that whenever he considers disobedience, he should give due weight to the effects of his example upon social stability. (c) One ought to obey the mores of his society because disobedience tends to undermine their existence. It is important to preserve the mores, not simply to avoid anarchy, but because it is their mores which give shape and meaning to the life of any people. I grant that the individual does tend to think of his life in terms of the mores of his group and that anything which disrupts those mores tends to rob his life of significance. But once again, all this shows is that one should conform to the mores of his society on the whole. Although there is some obligation to conformity, this is not the only nor the most important obligation on the member of any society.

Therefore, it does not seem to me that one can properly say that the mores make an act right or wrong. One cannot define the meaning of these ethical words in terms of the mores, nor can one maintain the ethical principle that one ought always to obey the mores of his society. If the mores do not make acts right or wrong, the fact that different societies have different mores does not imply that the same kind of act can be right in one society and wrong in another.

II

Cultural relativity seems to apply to institutions as well as to mores. A social institution is a type of organization; it involves a pattern of activity in which two or more people play recognized roles. The family, the church, the government, the liberal arts college, the bridge club are all social institutions. Institutions can be classified more or less specifically. Thus monogamy, polygamy, and polyandry are specific institutions which fall under the generic institution of the family. Since the specific form an institution takes seems to vary from society to society depending upon the culture of that society, let us grant that social institutions are relative to culture. What does this imply for ethics?

A conclusion that is sometimes drawn is that we should never try to adopt an institution from another society or seek to impose one of our institutions upon another people. The main argument for this view is that each institution is an expression of the total culture of which it is a part. To try to take an institution out of its cultural environment is sure to maim or even kill it; to try to bring an institution into an alien culture is likely to disorganize and even destroy that cultural pattern. Thus the attempt to transport an institution from one society to another will fail to achieve its intended result and will produce many unintended and socially undesirable effects.

No doubt the attempt to import or export a social institution is often a dismal failure. The transported institution becomes a mere caricature of its former self, and the society into which it is introduced becomes demoralized or even destroyed. Extreme caution is certainly necessary. But is it not incautious to conclude that the attempt will always fail? The most glaring examples of cultural demoralization and destruction, such as the intervention of the white man in Africa, have involved much more than the imposition of one or two institutions. Moreover, some institutions may be less alien to a given culture than others. If so, there might be some institutions that the society could adopt with only minor modifications. In fact, societies seem to have been borrowing from one another for centuries. While the effects of this borrowing have often been bad, they have not always been totally destructive or even grossly demoralizing. Occasionally they may have been beneficial. It seems unnecessary to conclude that we should never import or export an institution from the fact that social institutions are culturally relative.

III

Another thing which may be relative to culture is human nature. As soon as one ponders the differences between the Chinese aristocrat and the Australian bushman, the American tycoon and the Indian yogi, one finds it hard to believe that there is anything basic to human nature which is shared by all men. And reflection upon the profound effects of enculturation easily leads one to the conclusion that what a man is depends upon the society in which he has been brought up. Therefore, let us assume that human nature is culturally relative and see what this implies.

This seems to imply that no kind of action, moral character, or social institution is made inevitable by human nature. This conclusion is important because it cuts the ground out from under one popular type of justification in ethics. For example, capitalism is sometimes defended as an ideal on the grounds that this is the only economic system that is possible in the light of man's greedy and competitive nature. Or it might be claimed that adultery is permissible because the ideal of marital fidelity runs counter to man's innate drives or instincts. If there is no fixed human nature, such arguments are left without any basis.

One may wonder, however, whether the only alternatives are an entirely fixed and an entirely plastic human nature. It might be that enculturation could mold a human being but only within certain limits. These limits might exist either because certain parts of human nature are not at all plastic or because all parts are only moderately plastic. For example, it might turn out that the need for food and the tendency to grow in a certain way cannot be modified at all by enculturation, or it might turn out that every element in human nature can be modified in some ways but not in others. In either case, what a man becomes would depend partly upon enculturation and partly upon the nature of the organism being enculturated.

Thus cultural relativity may be a matter of degree. Before we can decide just what follows from the fact that human nature is relative to culture, we must know how far and in what ways it is relative. If there are certain limits to the plasticity of human nature, these do rule out some kinds of action, character, or institution. But anthropology indicates that within any such limits a great many alternatives remain. Human nature may make eating inevitable, but what we eat and when we eat and how we eat is up to us. At least we can say that to the degree that human nature is relative to culture no kind of action, moral character, or social institution is made possible by human nature.

IV

It has been claimed that acts are also relative to culture. This is to say that the same general type of action may take on specific differences when performed in different societies because those societies have different cultures. For example, it is one thing for one of us to kill his aged parent; it is quite a different thing for an Eskimo to do such an act. One difference lies in the consequences of these two acts. In our society, disposing of old and useless parents merely allows one to live in greater luxury; to an Eskimo this act may mean the difference between barely adequate subsistence and malnutrition for himself and his family. What are we to make of this fact that the nature of an act is culturally relative?

One possible conclusion is that the same kind of act may be right in one society and wrong in another. This presupposes that the rightness of an act depends upon its consequences and that it consequences may vary from society to society. Since I accept these presuppositions, I agree that the rightness or wrongness of an act is relative to its social context.

It is important, however, to distinguish this conclusion from two others with which it is often confused. To say that the rightness of an act is relative to the society in which it is performed is not to say that exactly the same sort of act can be both right and wrong. It is because the social context makes the acts different in kind that one can be right while the other is wrong. Compare an act of infanticide in our society with an act of infanticide in some South Seas society. Are these two acts, the same or different? They are of the same kind inasmuch as both are acts of killing an infant. On the other hand, they are different in that such an act may be necessary to preserve the balance between family size and food resources in the South Seas while this is not the case in our society. These two acts are generically similar but specifically different; that is, they belong to different species of the same genus. Therefore, the conclusion that the same kind of act may be right in one society and wrong in another does not amount to saying that two acts which are precisely the same in every respect may differ in rightness or wrongness.

Neither is this conclusion to be confused with the view that acts are made right or wrong by the mores of society. No doubt our society disapproves of infanticide and some South Seas societies approve of it, but it is not this which makes infanticide wrong for us and right for them. If infanticide is wrong for us and right for them, it is because acts of infanticide have very different consequences in our society and in theirs, not because the practice is discouraged here and customary there.

V

The goals that individuals or groups aim for also seem relative to culture. What objects people select as goals varies from society to society depending upon the cultures of those societies. One group may strive for social prestige and the accumulation of great wealth, another may aim at easy comfort and the avoidance of any danger, a third may seek military glory and the conquest of other peoples. What follows from this fact of cultural relativity?

This fact is often taken as a basis for arguing that it is impossible to compare the value of acts, institutions, or total ways of life belonging to different societies. The argument rests on the assumptions that acts, institutions, and ways of life are means directed at certain ends, that means can be evaluated only in terms of their ends, and that ends are incommensurable with respect to value.

Granted these assumptions, the argument seems a good one, but I doubt that ends are really incommensurable. It seems to me that we can recognize that certain ends are more worth while than others, for example that pleasure is intrinsically better than pain. I may be mistaken, but until this has been shown, the conclusion that it is impossible to compare the value of acts, institutions, or ways of life belonging to different societies has not been established.

VI

People from different societies apparently experience the same object or situation in quite different ways depending upon the cultural differences between their societies. The satisfying experience that a cultured Chinese might derive from eating bird's nest soup would be diametrically opposed to the experience I would undergo if I forced myself to gulp down my helping of that exotic dish out of politeness. Again, an experience which I would greatly value, sitting in the bleachers watching the Red Sox clinch the pennant, would be nothing but a boring observation of meaningless motions accompanied by the sensations of scorching sun, trickling sweat, and unyielding benches to a Hottentot visitor. In large measure the nature of any experience is determined by the process of enculturation that the experiencer has undergone. Thus, value experiences are also relative to culture.

It might seem to follow that the same experience could be good to one person and bad to another, but this is just what does *not* follow. The difference in value stems from the fact that, although confronted with similar objects or situations, the two people have very different experiences. The nature of a person's experience depends upon the kind of person he has become through the process of enculturation as much as upon the external stimulus. It would be a mistake to conclude that qualitatively identical experiences are good to me and bad to the Hottentot. Although he and I are in the same ballpark watching the same game, we are having very different experiences.

What one should conclude is that the same kind of object or situation can have different values to people from different societies. This follows from the fact that the nature of a person's experience depends in large measure upon the way in which he has been enculturated, together with the assumption that the value of any object or situation depends upon its effects on experience. Since my ethical view is that the value of objects and situations is derived from their impact upon experience, I accept the conclusion that the same kind of object or situation can have very different values to people who come from different cultures.

VII

It appears that moral emotions are also relative to culture. What a person desires, approves, or feels guilty about seems to vary from society to society depending upon the cultural differences between those societies. What does the fact that moral emotions are culturally relative imply for ethics?

One possible conclusion would be that the same kind of act or person can be morally good in one society and morally bad in another. This is supposed to follow from the fact that the same kind of act or person can be approved in one society and disapproved in another together with the view that to be morally good or bad is simply to be approved or disapproved.

That infanticide is approved in certain South Seas societies and disapproved in ours need not be doubted. That infanticide constitutes exactly the same kind of act in the two societies is, as we have seen, more dubious. But even if it did, I would not accept the conclusion in question; for I would not admit that the moral value of any act or person depends upon whether it is approved or disapproved. That the grounds for moral evaluation lie outside the moral emotions can be seen by the fact that it always makes sense to ask someone *why* he approves or disapproves of something. If approving or disapproving made its object morally good or bad, there would be no need of such justification. Thus, the fact that moral emotions are culturally relative does not prove that identical acts or persons can be morally good in one society and morally bad in another.

VIII

Both linguistic and psychological studies have suggested that people living in different societies conceptualize their experience in different ways. Probably, moral concepts vary from society to society depending upon the cultural backgrounds from which they arise. The ancient Greek thought of virtue quite differently from the modern American; the Christian conception of obligation is probably absent from the mind of the African who has escaped the influence of any missionary. What are we to conclude from the fact that moral concepts are relative to culture?

The obvious implication appears to be that people of different cultural backgrounds are almost sure to disagree on any ethical questions. Obvious as it may seem, this is not implied at all. In fact, people using different concepts could never disagree, for disagreement presupposes that both parties are thinking in the same terms. For one thing, on what question are they supposed to be disagreeing? If each person is using his own set of concepts, each person formulates his own question in his own terms. And if the two persons do not have any common set of ethical concepts there is no way for formulating a single question that will be intelligible to both of them. Again, in what sense do their respective answers disagree? When an American says that Poland is undemocratic and a Russian insists that it is a fine example of democracy, it appears that they are disagreeing. No doubt they do disagree in many ways, but not in their utterances. Their statements are quite compatible, for they are using the word "democracy" in different senses. Similarly, people of different cultures would only seem to disagree if they attached different concepts to their ethical words.

The proper conclusion to draw is that any comparison between the ethical views of the members of different cultures can be only partial. As long as each view is stated only in its own terms, there can be no comparison between them; comparison becomes possible only when they are stated in the same set of concepts. But if the sets of concepts are not identical, any translation of one view into the language of the other or of both into some neutral language will be approximate at best. Even where something approaching adequate translation is possible, some of the meaning will be lost or something will be added that was not in the original concept. For this reason, any claim that the ethical views of people in different societies are either identical or contradictory is likely to tell only part of the story. To some extent, at least, the ethics of different cultures are incommensurate.

IX

The aspect of cultural relativity most often emphasized is that pertaining to moral judgments. Objects that the members of one society think to be good are considered bad by another group; acts considered wrong in one society are thought of as right in another. Moreover, these differences in judgments of value and obligation seem to reflect cultural differences between the respective societies. There is a great deal of evidence to suggest that ethical judgments are relative to culture.

To many anthropologists and philosophers it is a corollary of this fact that one of a set of contrary ethical judgments is no more valid than another, or, put positively, that all ethical judgments are equally valid. Unfortunately, there is a crucial ambiguity lurking in this epistemological thicket. Ethical judgments might have equal validity either because all are valid or because none are: similarly, one ethical judgment might be no more valid than another either because both are equally valid or because both are equally lacking in validity. Since these two interpretations are quite different, let us consider them separately.

On the first interpretation, the conclusion to be drawn from the fact that ethical judgments are relative to culture is that every moral judgment is valid for the society in which it is made. Instead of denying the objective validity of ethical judgments, this view affirms it, but in a qualified form which will allow for the variations in ethical belief.

There seem to be three main ways of defending this position. (a) Ethical judgments have objective validity because it is possible to justify them rationally. However, this validity is limited to a given society because the premises used in such justification are those which are agreed upon in that society. Since there are no universally accepted premises, no universal validity is possible. I would wish to deny that justification is real if it is limited in this way. If all our reasoning really does rest on certain premises which can be rejected by others without error, then we must give up the claim to objective validity. When I claim validity for ethical judgments, I intend to claim more than that it is possible to support them with logical arguments; I also claim that it is incorrect to deny the premises of such arguments. (b) Any ethical judgment is an expression of a total pattern of culture. Hence it is possible to justify any single judgment in terms of its coherence with the total cultural configuration of the judger. But one cannot justify the culture as a whole, for it is not part of a more inclusive pattern. Therefore, ethical judgments have objective validity, but only in terms of a given cultural pattern. I would make the same objection to this view as to the preceding one. Since it allows justification to rest upon an arbitrary foundation, it is inadequate to support any significant claim to objective validity. (c) Any ethical judgment has objective validity because it is an expression of a moral code. The validity of a moral code rests on the fact that without conformity to a common code social cohesion breaks down, leading to disastrous results. Since any given moral code provides cohesion for one and only one society, each ethical judgment has validity for a single society. There are at least two difficulties with this defense of objectivity. Surely one could deny some ethical judgments without destroying the entire moral code they reflect; not every judgment could be shown to be essential to social stability. Moreover, the argument seems to rest on the ethical judgment that one ought not to contribute to the breakdown of social stability. How is this judgment to be shown to be valid? One must either appeal to some other basis of validity or argue in a circle. None of these arguments to show that every moral judgment is valid for the society in which it is made is adequate.

On the second interpretation, the conclusion to be drawn from the fact that moral judgments are relative to culture is that moral judgments have no objective validity. This amounts to saying that the distinction between true and false, correct and incorrect, does not apply to such judgments. This conclusion obviously does not follow simply from the fact that people disagree about ethical questions. We do not deny the objective validity of scientific judgments either on the grounds that different scientists propose alternative theories or on the grounds that the members of some societies hold fast to many unscientific beliefs.

Why, then, does the fact that moral judgments are relative to culture imply that they have no objective validity? (a) Individuals make different ethical judgments because they judge in terms of different frames of references and they adopt these frames of reference uncritically from their cultures. Since ethical judgments are the product of enculturation rather than reasoning, they cannot claim rational justification. I do not find this argument convincing, for it seems to confuse the origin of a judgment with its justification. The causes of a judgment are one thing; the reasons for or against it are another. It remains to be shown that any information about what causes us to judge as we do has any bearing on the question of whether or not our judgments are correct. (b) It is impossible to settle ethical questions by using the scientific method. Therefore, there is no objective way to show that one ethical judgment is any more correct than another, and, in the absence of any method of establishing the claim to objective validity, it makes no sense to continue to make the claim. I will concede that, if there is no rational method of establishing ethical judgments, then we might as well give up the claim to objective validity. And if the scientific method is restricted to the testing of hypotheses by checking the predictions they imply against the results of observation and experiment, it does seem to be inapplicable to ethical questions. What I will not concede is the tacit assumption that the scientific method is the only method of establishing the truth. Observation and experimentation do not figure prominently in the method used by mathematicians. I even wonder whether the person who concludes that ethical judgments have no objective validity can establish *this* conclusion by using the scientific method. The fact that ethical judgments cannot be established scientifically does not by itself prove that they cannot be established by any method of reasoning. (c) There might be some method of settling ethical disputes, but it could not be a method of reasoning. Any possible reasoning would have to rest upon certain premises. Since the members of different societies start from different premises, there is no basis for argument that does not beg the question. I suspect, however, that we have been looking for our premises in the wrong place. The model of deduction tempts us to search for very general premises from which all our more specific judgments can be deduced. Unfortunately, it is just in this area of universal moral principles that disagreement seems most frequent and irremedial. But suppose that these ethical generalizations are themselves inductions based upon particular moral judgments. Then we could argue for or against them in terms of relatively specific ethical judgments and the factual judgments that are in turn relevant to these. Until this possibility is explored further, we need not admit that there is no adequate basis for ethical reasoning. Thus it appears that none of these refutations of the objective validity of ethical judgments is really conclusive.

The fact that ethical judgments are relative to culture is often taken to prove that no ethical judgment can claim to be any more valid than any of its contraries. I have tried to show that on neither of the two possible interpretations of this conclusion does the conclusion necessarily follow from the fact of cultural relativity.

X

Finally, moral reasoning might turn out to be relative to culture. When some ethical statement is denied or even questioned, the person who made the statement is apt to leap to its defense. He attempts to justify his statement by producing reasons to support it. But speakers from different societies tend to justify their statements in different ways. The difference in their reasoning may be of two kinds. Either their reasoning may rest on different assumptions or they may draw inferences in a different manner. That is, the arguments they advance may either start from different premises or obey different logics. We can ignore the former case here; for it boils down to a difference in their judgments, and we have discussed that at length in the receding section. Instead let us assume that people who belong to different societies tend to draw their moral conclusions according to different logics depending upon their respective cultures. What difference would it make if moral reasoning were thus culturally relative?

The most interesting conclusion that might be drawn from the fact that moral reasoning is relative to culture is that it has no objective validity: The claim, to objective validity is empty where it cannot be substantiated. But how could one justify the claim that any given kind of moral reasoning is valid? To appeal to the same kind of reasoning would be circular. To appeal to some other kind of reasoning would not be sufficient to justify this kind; for each kind of reasoning involves principles of inference which go beyond, and therefore cannot be justified by appealing to, any other kind.

I find this line of argument inconclusive for several reasons. First, it is not clear that a given kind of reasoning cannot be justified by appealing to a different kind of reasoning. In fact, this seems to be a fairly common practice in logic. Various forms of syllogistic arguments can be shown to be valid by reducing them to arguments of the form Barbara. Again, a logician will sometimes justify certain rules for natural deduction by an involved logical argument which does not itself use these same rules. Second, in what sense is it impossible to show another person that my moral arguments are valid? I can show him that the various moral arguments I advance conform to the principles of my logic. If he does not accept these principles, he will remain unconvinced. This may show that I cannot persuade him that my arguments are valid, but does it show that I have not proved that they are? It is not obvious that persuading a person and proving a point are identical. Third, is the claim to objective validity always empty in the absence of any justification for it? Perhaps some reasoning is ultimate in that it requires no further justification. To assume the opposite seems to lead to an infinite regress. If every valid justification stands in need of further justification, no amount of justification would ever be sufficient.

I do not claim to have established the objective validity of moral reasoning. I am not even sure how that validity might be established or even whether it needs to be established. All I have been trying to do is to suggest that such validity is not ruled out by the fact, if it is a fact, that moral reasoning is relative to culture.

No doubt the reader will wish to challenge my acceptance or rejection of this or that particular conclusion. Quite apart from such specific ethical questions, however, there are certain over-all logical conclusions which seem to me inevitable. (1) What conclusions one can legitimately draw from the facts of cultural relativity will depend upon *which* facts one starts from. It is worth distinguishing between the relativity of mores, social institutions, human nature, acts, goals, value experiences, moral emotions, moral concepts, moral judgments, and moral reasoning; for each of these has different implications for ethics. (2) By themselves the facts of cultural relativity do not imply anything for ethics. Any argument that is both interesting and valid requires additional premises. Thus it is only in conjunction with certain statements that go beyond anthropology that the findings of anthropology have any bearing at all on ethics. (3) What conclusions one should draw will obviously depend upon which of these additional premises one accepts. Therefore, one's ethical and epistemological theory will determine the significance one will attach to cultural relativity. (4) Before we can criticize or even understand the arguments by which ethical conclusions are derived from the facts of such relativity, we must make these additional premises explicit and see what can be said for or against them. My main purpose in this paper has been to make a start in this complicated yet crucial task.

Source: Carl Wellman, "The Ethical Implications of Cultural Relativity," *Journal of Philosophy,* Vol. LX, No. 7 (March 1963), pp. 169–184. Reprinted by permission of the Journal and the author.

Trying Out One's New Sword

Mary Midgley

All of us are, more or less, in trouble today about trying to understand cultures strange to us. We hear constantly of alien customs. We see changes in our lifetime which would have astonished our parents. I want to discuss here one very short way of dealing with this difficulty, a drastic way which many people now theoretically favour. It consists in simply denying that we can ever understand any culture except our own well enough to make judgments about it. Those who recommend this hold that the world is sharply divided into separate societies, sealed units, each with its own system of thought. They feel that the respect and tolerance due from one system to another forbids us ever to take up a critical position to any other culture. Moral judgment, they suggest, is a kind of coinage valid only in its country of origin.

I shall call this position 'moral isolationism'. I shall suggest that it is certainly not forced upon us, and indeed that it makes no sense at all. People usually take it up because they think it is a respectful attitude to other cultures. In fact, however, it is not respectful. Nobody can respect what is entirely unintelligible to them. To respect someone, we have to know enough about him to make a *favorable* judgment, however general and tentative. And we do understand people in other cultures to this extent. Otherwise a great mass of our most valuable thinking would be paralysed.

To show this, I shall take a remote example, because we shall probably find it easier to think calmly about it than we should with a contemporary one, such as female circumcision in Africa or the Chinese Cultural Revolution. The principles involved will still be the same. My example is this. There is, it seems, a verb in classical Japanese which means 'to try out one's new sword on a chance wayfarer'. (The word is *tsujigiri*, literally 'crossroads-cut'.) A samurai sword had to be tried out because, if it was to work properly, it had to slice through someone at a single blow, from the shoulder to the opposite flank. Otherwise, the warrior bungled his stroke. This could injure his honour, offend his ancestors, and even let down his emperor. So tests were needed, and wayfarers had to be expended. Any wayfarer would do—provided, of course, that he was not another Samurai. Scientists will recognize a familiar problem about the rights of experimental subjects.

Now when we hear of a custom like this, we may well reflect that we simply do not understand it; and therefore are not qualified to criticize it at all, because we are not members of that culture. But we are not members of any other culture either, except our own. So we extend the principle to cover all extraneous cultures, and we seem therefore to be moral isolationists. But this is, as we shall see, an impossible position. Let us ask what it would involve.

We must ask first: Does the isolating barrier work both ways? Are people in other cultures equally unable to criticize *us?* This question struck me sharply when I read a remark in *The Guardian* by an anthropologist about a South American Indian who had been taken into a Brazilian town for an operation, which saved his life. When he came back to his village, he made several highly critical remarks about the white Brazilians' way of life. They may very well have been justified. But the interesting point was that the anthropologist called these remarks 'a damning indictment of Western civilization'. Now the Indian had been in that town about two weeks. Was he in a position to deliver a damning indictment? Would we ourselves be qualified to deliver such an indictment on the Samurai, provided we could spend two weeks in ancient Japan? What do we really think about this?

My own impression is that we believe that outsiders can, in principle, deliver perfectly good indictments—only, it usually takes more than two weeks to make them damning. Understanding has degrees. It is not a slapdash yes-or-no matter. Intelligent outsiders can progress in it, and in some ways will be at an advantage over the locals. But if this is so, it must clearly apply to ourselves as much as anybody else.

Our next question is this: Does the isolating barrier between cultures block praise as well as blame? If I want to say that the Samurai culture has many virtues, or to praise the south American Indians, am I prevented from doing *that* by my outside status? Now, we certainly do need to praise other societies in this way. But it is hardly possible that we could praise them effectively if we could not, in principle, criticize them. Our praise would be worthless if it rested on definite grounds, if it did not flow from some understanding. Certainly we may need to praise things which we do not *fully* understand. We say 'there's something very good here, but I can't quite make out what it is yet'. This happens when we want to learn from strangers. And we can learn from strangers. But to do this we have to distinguish between those strangers who are worth learning from and those who are not. Can we then judge which is which?

This brings us to our third question: What is involved in judging? Now plainly there is no question here of sitting on a bench in a red robe and sentencing people. Judging simply means forming an opinion, and expressing it if it is called for. Is there anything wrong about this? Naturally, we ought to avoid forming—and expressing—*crude* opinions, like that of a simple-minded missionary, who might dismiss the whole Samurai culture as entirely bad, because it is non-Christian. But this is a different objection. The trouble with crude opinions is that they are crude, whoever forms them, not that they are formed by the wrong people. Anthropologists, after all, are outsiders quite as much as missionaries. Moral isolationism forbids us to form *any* opinions on these matters. Its ground for doing so is that we don't understand them. But there is much that we don't understand in our own culture too. This brings us to our last question: If we can't judge other cultures, can we really judge our own? Our efforts to do so will be much damaged if we are really deprived of our opinions about other societies, because these provide the range of comparison, the spectrum of alternatives against which we set what we want to understand. We would have to stop using the mirror which anthropology so helpfully holds up to us.

In short, moral isolationism would lay down a general ban on moral reasoning. Essentially, this is the programme of immoralism, and it carries a distressing logical difficulty. Immoralists like Nietzsche are actually just a rather specialized sect of moralists. They can no more afford to put moralizing out of business than smugglers can afford to abolish customs regulations. The power of moral judgment is, in fact, not a luxury, not a perverse indulgence of the self-righteous. It is a necessity. When we judge something to be bad or good, better or worse than something else, we are taking it as an example to aim at or avoid. Without opinions of this sort, we would have no framework of comparison for our own policy, no chance of profiting by other people's insights or mistakes. In this vacuum, we could form no judgments on our own actions.

Now it would be odd if Homo sapiens had really got himself into a position as bad as this—a position where his main evolutionary asset, his brain, was so little use to him. None of us is going to accept this sceptical diagnosis. We cannot do so, because our involvement in moral isolationism does not flow from apathy, but from a rather acute concern about human hypocrisy and other forms of wickedness. But we polarize that concern around a few selected moral truths. We are rightly angry with those who despise, oppress or steamroll other cultures. We think that doing these things is actually *wrong*. But this is itself a moral judgment. We could not condemn oppression and insolence if we thought that all our condemnations were just a trivial local quirk of our own culture. We could still less do it if we tried to stop judging altogether.

Real moral scepticism, in fact, could lead only to inaction, to our losing all interest in moral questions, most of all in those which concern other societies. When we discuss these things, it becomes instantly clear how far we are from doing this. Suppose, for instance, that I criticize the bisecting Samurai, that I say his behaviour is brutal. What will usually happen next is

Chapter IV: Relativism

that someone will protest, will say that I have no right to make criticisms like that of another culture. But it is most unlikely that he will use this move to end the discussion of the subject. Instead, he will justify the Samurai. He will try to fill in the background, to make me understand the custom, by explaining the exalted ideals of discipline and devotion which produced it. He will probably talk of the lower value which the ancient Japanese placed on individual life generally. He may well suggest that this is a healthier attitude than our own obsession with security. He may add, too, that the wayfarers did not seriously mind being bisected, that in principle they accepted the whole arrangement.

Now an objector who talks like this is implying that it *is* possible to understand alien customs. That is just what he is trying to make me do. And he implies, too, that if I do succeed in understanding them, I shall do something better than giving up judging them. He expects me to change my present judgment to a truer one—namely, one that is favourable. And the standards I must use to do this cannot just be Samurai standards. They have to be ones current in my own culture. Ideals like discipline and devotion will not move anybody unless he himself accepts them. As it happens, neither discipline nor devotion is very popular in the West at present. Anyone who appeals to them may well have to do some more arguing to make *them* acceptable before he can use them to explain the Samurai. But if he does succeed here, he will have persuaded us, not just that there was something to be said for them in ancient Japan, but that there would be here as well.

Isolating barriers simply cannot arise here. If we accept something as a serious moral truth about one culture, we can't refuse to apply it—in however different an outward form—to other cultures as well, wherever circumstance admit it. If we refuse to do this, we just are not taking the other culture seriously. This becomes clear if we look at the last argument used by my objector—that of justification by consent of the victim. It is suggested that sudden bisection is quite in order, *provided* that it takes place between consenting adults. I cannot now discuss how conclusive this justification is. What I am pointing out is simply that it can only work if we believe that *consent* can make such a transaction respectable—and this is a thoroughly modern and Western idea. It would probably never occur to a Samurai; if it did, it would surprise him very much. It is *our* standard. In applying it, too, we are likely to make another typically Western demand. We shall ask for good factual evidence that the wayfarers actually do have this rather surprising taste—that they are really willing to be bisected. In applying Western standards in this way, we are not being confused or irrelevant. We are asking the questions which arise *from where we stand,* questions which we can see the sense of. We do this because asking questions which you can't see the sense of is humbug. Certainly we can extend our questioning by imaginative effort. We can come to understand other societies better. By doing so, we may make their questions our own, or we may see that they are really forms of the questions which we are asking already. This is not impossible. It is just very hard work. The obstacles which often prevent it are simply those of ordinary ignorance, laziness and prejudice.

If there were really an isolating barrier, of course, our own culture could never have been formed. It is no sealed box, but a fertile jungle of different influences—Greek, Jewish, Roman, Norse, Celtic and so forth, into which further influences are still pouring—American, Indian, Japanese, Jamaican, you name it. The moral isolationist's picture of separate, unmixable cultures is quite unreal. People who talk about British history usually stress the value of this fertilizing mix, no doubt rightly. But this is not just an odd fact about Britain. Except for the very smallest and most remote, all cultures are formed out of many streams. All have the problem of digesting and assimilating things which, at the start, they do not understand. All have the choice of learning something from this challenge, or alternatively, of refusing to learn, and fighting it mindlessly instead.

This universal predicament has been obscured by the fact that anthropologists used to concentrate largely on very small and remote cultures, which did not seem to have this problem. These tiny societies, which had often forgotten their own history, made neat, self-contained subjects for study. No doubt it was valuable to emphasize their remoteness, their extreme strangeness, their independence of our cultural tradition This emphasis was, I think, the root of moral isolationism. But, as the tribal studies themselves showed, even there the anthropologists were able to interpret what they saw and make judgments—often favourable—about the tribesmen. And the tribesmen, too, were quite equal to making judgments about the anthropologists—and about the tourists and Coca-Cola salesmen who followed them. Both sets of judgments, no doubt, were somewhat hasty, both have been refined in the light of further experience. A similar transaction between us and the Samurai might take even longer. But that is no reason for deeming it impossible. Morally as well as physically, there is only one world, and we all have to live in it.

Japanese Ethical Perspectives

Michael C. Brannigan

Bushido

It is often said that the spirit of Japanese ethics is typified in the code of Bushido, or the Way of the Warrior. One exponent is Yamago Soko, a scholar of the Kogakuha school who constructed a rather stern Bushido code in which the welfare of the group supersedes individual concerns. Bushido exacts self-discipline and loyalty to one's lord, which are to be instilled through diligent training, both physical and mental. Let us look at some features of Bushido.

Preparing to Die: Two Kinds of Death

A classic manifesto of this code is the *Hagakure*, attributed to Yamamoto Tsunetomo (c. 1716), in which we find the famous expression:

"Bushido consists in dying—that is my conclusion."

What does this mean? "Dying" means a number of things for the samurai. First, it refers to that physical death for which the samurai must always be prepared. The true samurai is ready to die at any moment, which allows the freedom to be fully present to the moment.

In order to be successful in a life-and-death encounter, the samurai must be absolutely present in both mind and body. He cannot be distracted by thoughts that pull him away from the moment. The art of swordsmanship demands complete awareness and a molding together of mind and body:

> When one eternally repeats his vow to die at any moment at the call of his duty every morning and every evening, one can act freely in Bushido at a moment's notice, thus fulfilling his duties as a feudal vassal without a flaw, even to the last moment of his life.

In this terse statement we see the meaning of Bushido. The ever-present thought of death actually frees one from clinging to life.

Fear of dying comes from clinging to this life and from the desire to live. It is this clinging to life that the samurai must die to. This is the second meaning of "dying." Dying is a letting-go or detachment from one's desires. This is why the samurai trains himself to die by constantly absorbing himself with the thought of death. The samurai must overcome any denial of death. By training himself to be ready to die, ironically enough, the warrior allows himself the freedom to be fully present in confrontation.

Giri

> The alpha and omega of a samurai's life is service, service, service—nothing but service.

One of the most important virtues in Bushido is loyalty, which is done out of duty, called *giri* whether to one's liege lord, or shogun, or family. This is foremost in the mind of the samurai, so much so that he is willing to die for his lord.

We must be careful not to confuse this loyalty with blind loyalty. A samurai may question the actions or motives of his lord, even though this could mean the risk of death. A true samurai is not a passive follower, but one who thinks independently while remaining loyal to his lord. For example, in a recent film by Akira Kurosawa, *Ran*, there is an incident in which a retainer refuses to honor the request of his lord's wife to go out and bring back the head of the lord's sister. Instead, he returns with the head of a stone fox, insinuating that the cunning wife was herself a fox.

It is not purely out of duty that a samurai is loyal, but rather from a commitment to service. Service was often considered the proper response to the protection and care the lord has provided for his retainers, and it is to be performed in the spirit of gratitude. A relatively recent example of this was the service performed by young fighter pilots who volunteered to die for their country during the kamikaze attacks toward the end of World War II. Just before their mission, many of them wrote letters of gratitude for both their country and their families.

Pure Heart

In addition to these two requirements of preparedness for death and service, the Bushido code also requires an immediate response that is "pure." The samurai must be pure in heart, for then he can respond immediately to a situation.

Self-interested motives, whether conscious or unconscious, can obstruct a pure heart. Furthermore, a warrior may deliberate on factors such as the consequences of his actions. In order to be pure in heart, one must act immediately without attachment to any thought of the possible rewards of one's actions. (As we saw in the *Bhagavad Gita,* this is one of the core teachings of Krishna.) In this way, the samurai trains himself to act without self-reference.

So, we see a strong Stoic emphasis in Bushido, a strict control over one's emotions and desires. At the same time, there is the strict cultivation of such other-directed virtues as compassion and fortitude. The four "vows" mentioned in the *Hagakure* are:

> Never to be outdone in the Way of the Samurai.
> To be of good use to the master.
> To be filial to my parents.
> To manifest great compassion, and to act for the sake of Man.

In view of these features—dying at each moment, unending service, and purity of heart—the spirit of Bushido reflects basic values expressed throughout Japan's history. In other words, what the notions of dying, service, and sincerity have in common is the absence of self-interest. As we have seen, this is an important and constant element in Japanese ethics. Bushido ultimately means the dying of the self. It means not having private interests at the center of one's morality.

Nishida Kitaro and the Unifying Power of Consciousness

Nishida's approach to ethics cannot be separated from his analysis of reality. The two go together, so that the "good" that is to be sought after is the reality that transcends our ordinary subject-object duality. The good can be attained in true Buddhist fashion only by a letting go, or by forgetting of self.

In his *An Inquiry into the Good,* Nishida criticized a number of philosophical positions that focus on only a part of the human psyche. For

Nishida, the good can be attained only when all faculties are balanced in a healthy synthesis. He called this the "unifying power of consciousness."

This "unifying power of consciousness" is the true "personality" existing deep within each of us. Realizing this personality is realizing the good. Yet even though we tend to break consciousness down into disparate elements, such as intellect, will, and feeling,

> [t]he true unity of consciousness is a pure and simple activity that comes forth of itself, unhindered by oneself; it is the original state of independent, self-sufficient consciousness, with no distinction among knowledge, feeling, and volition, and no separation of subject and object.

Nishida admitted that properly knowing what is good and what is not good is a fundamental problem. Let us briefly review his critique of some traditional ethical theories.

First, the class of theories he called "intuitive" were found to be unsatisfactory. *Intuition* is a term that lacks clarity. Further, he chastised the "authority theory," which posits morality in absolute terms of what is and is not good. The authority rests upon some external figure or text. Nishida ruled out any morality based on fear and power.

Next, Nishida examined the rationalist theories (what he called "dianoetic ethics") in which knowledge and reason play major roles. These theories assume a link between what is good and what is true. Proponents therefore appeal to our rational natures as human beings. The problem with this approach is that while it extols reason, it also downplays other aspects of our human psyche such as will and desire:

> Even Confucius' maxim, "Do not do unto others what you would not have others do unto you," is nearly meaningless without the motivation of sympathy. If abstract logic were the motivation of the will, then those who are most adept at reasoning would be the best people. No one can deny, however, that ignorant people are sometimes actually better than those who have knowledge.

Grounding morality solely on reason does not satisfactorily value the complexity of the personality, with its feelings and volition.

Nishida then went on to criticize hedonist theories that state that the good is personal pleasure. Hedonism is built on the edifice of self.

Nishida viewed utilitarianism as hedonism on a wider scale. In utilitarianism, pleasure is broadened to mean collective well-being in terms of what is publicly pleasing. He found fault with this because, first of all, not all pleasures are the same, and second, the self-interested viewpoint is not the only perspective. Nishida claimed that "Humans have an innate instinct of altruism." Furthermore, it would be wrong to presume that pleasures are the only goals that humans seek.

Nishida then proceeded to claim that the good is attained when one discovers the self, and that is reality. "Thus, to seek the good and to return to it is to know the true reality of the self." At the same time, in true Zen fashion, the good can be reached only by emptying the self.

Watsuji Tetsuro and Aidagara

Whereas Nishida is known primarily for his attempt to inscribe a metaphysical system as well as a new logic, Watsuji is prominent in the area of ethics. He was both a historian of Japanese ethics, and a formulator of a unique ethical position.

An intriguing work is his *Fudo (Climate and Culture),* written in 1928–29. As we saw earlier, Watsuji was so impressed with Heidegger's *Being and Time* that he wrote *Fudo* to complement Heidegger's emphasis on time modality. *Fudo* addresses the familiar (though taken-for-granted) realm of spatiality. Watsuji sought to account for the role of space and geography in the formation of cultural attitudes. In other words, just as Heidegger argued that we are by nature future-oriented beings, Watsuji contended that we are by nature outward-bound.

The final selection at the end of this chapter is taken from *Fudo,* which literally means "wind and earth" and generally means "climate"; it indicates the geography and environment that act to effect a culture's outlook and character. The term *fudo* suggests a reciprocity between climate and cultural disposition. For Watsuji, "climate" is a broad notion, and it encompasses not only the environmental, but also interpersonal features—our social geography.

Watsuji studied three kinds of climate—monsoon, desert, and pastoral—and contended that each endows inhabitants with a unique temperament. The monsoon climate, to which both Japan and India belong, is a strong factor in producing a culture that emphasizes compliance, cooperation, and (sometimes) submission. Desert climates, such as we find in African and Arab countries, tend to evoke a more aggressive, almost warlike temperament. Greece and most of Europe typify a pastoral, grassy climate, which tends to produce a more rational disposition.

Watsuji claimed that the more compliant temperament in Japan has a bearing on its moral demeanor. For instance, its monsoon climate naturally manifests itself sporadically and in extremes. Such is the case with the Japanese, who sometimes react in extreme and unpredictable ways.

For Watsuji, *aidagara,* "in-betweenness," remains an underlying element in ethics. Ethics must be grounded on the relationality of our existence. In other words, I am defined by my relationship within my various relevant groupings: marriage, family, community, society, culture, world, and universe. *Aidagara* gives a more Japanese stamp to morality.

To illustrate, the Japanese term for ethics is *rinri*, consisting of two characters. The first, *rin*, points to the communal bond or relationship with others. The second, *ri*, means reason, or the principle of relationality of self and other. In addition, as we stated earlier, the character for "man" represents a "being-involved-in-the-world."

The Law of Human Nature

C. S. Lewis

Every one has heard people quarrelling. Sometimes it sounds funny and sometimes it sounds merely unpleasant; but however it sounds, I believe we can learn something very important from listening to the kinds of things they say. They say things like this: "How'd you like it if anyone did the same to you?"—"That's my seat, I was there first"—"Leave him alone, he isn't doing you any harm"—"Why should you shove in first?"—"Give me a bit of your orange, I gave you a bit of mine"—"Come on, you promised." People say things like that every day, educated people as well as uneducated, and children as well as grown-ups.

Now what interests me about all these remarks is that the man who makes them is not merely saying that the other man's behaviour does not happen to please him. He is appealing to some kind of standard of behaviour which he expects the other man to know about. And the other man very seldom replies: "To hell with your standard." Nearly always he tries to make out that what he has been doing does not really go against the standard, or that if it does there is some special excuse. He pretends there is some special reason in this particular case why the person who took the seat first should not keep it, or that things were quite different when he was given the bit of orange, or that something has turned up which lets him off keeping his promise. It looks, in fact, very much as if both parties had in mind some kind of Law or Rule of fair play or decent behaviour or morality or whatever you like to call it, about which they really agreed. And they have. If they had not, they might, of course, fight like animals, but they could not *quarrel* in the human sense of the word. Quarrelling means trying to show that the other man is in the wrong. And there would be no sense in trying to do that unless you and he had some sort of agreement as to what Right and Wrong are; just as there would be no sense in saying that a footballer had committed a foul unless there was some agreement about the rules of football.

Now this Law or Rule about Right and Wrong used to be called the Law of Nature. Nowadays, when we talk of the "laws of nature" we usually mean things like gravitation, or heredity, or the laws of chemistry. But when the older thinkers called the Law of Right and Wrong "the Law of Nature," they really meant the Law of *Human* Nature. The idea was that, just as all bodies are governed by the law of gravitation and organisms by biological laws, so the creature called man also had *his* law—with this great difference, that a body could not choose whether it obeyed the law of gravitation or not, but a man could choose either to obey the Law of Human Nature or to disobey it.

We may put this in another way. Each man is at every moment subjected to several sets of law but there is only one of these which he is free to disobey. As a body, he is subjected to gravitation and cannot disobey it; if you leave him unsupported in mid-air, he has no more choice about falling than a stone has. As an organism, he is subjected to various biological laws which he cannot disobey any more than an animal can. That is, he cannot disobey those laws which he shares with other things; but the law which is peculiar to his human nature, the Law he does not share with animals or vegetables or inorganic things, is the one he can disobey if he chooses.

This law was called the Law of Nature because people thought that every one knew it by nature and did not need to be taught it. They did not mean, of course, that you might not find an odd individual here and there who did not know it, just as you find a few people who are colour-blind or have no ear for a tune. But taking the race as a whole, they thought that the human idea of decent behaviour was obvious to every one. And I believe they were right. If they were not, then all the things we said about the war were nonsense. What was the sense in saying the enemy were in the wrong unless Right is a real thing which the Nazis at bottom knew as well as we did and ought to have practiced? If they had no notion of what we mean by right, then, though we might still have had to fight them, we could no more have blamed them for that than for the colour of their hair.

I know that some people say the idea of a Law of Nature or decent behaviour known to all men is unsound, because different civilisations and different ages have had quite different moralities.

But this is not true. There have been differences between their moralities, but these have never amounted to anything like a total difference. If anyone will take the trouble to compare the moral teaching of, say, the ancient Egyptians, Babylonians, Hindus, Chinese, Greeks and Romans, what will really strike him will be how very like they are to each other and to our own. Some of the evidence for this I have put together in the appendix of another book called *The Abolition of Man;* but for our present purpose I need only ask the reader to think what a totally different morality would mean. Think of a country where people were admired for running away in battle, or where a man felt proud of doublecrossing all the people who had been kindest to him. You might just as well try to imagine a country where two and two made five. Men have differed as regards what

Chapter IV: Relativism

people you ought to be unselfish to—whether it was only your own family, or your fellow countrymen, or everyone. But they have always agreed that you ought not to put yourself first. Selfishness has never been admired. Men have differed as to whether you should have one wife or four. But they have always agreed that you must not simply have any woman you liked.

But the most remarkable thing is this. Whenever you find a man who says he does not believe in a real Right and Wrong, you will find the same man going back on this a moment later. He may break his promise to you, but if you try breaking one to him he will be complaining "It's not fair" before you can say Jack Robinson. A nation may say treaties do not matter; but then, next minute, they spoil their case by saying that the particular treaty they want to break was an unfair one. But if treaties do not matter, and if there is no such thing as Right and Wrong—in other words, if there is no Law of Nature what is the difference between a fair treaty and an unfair one? Have they not let the cat out of the bag and shown that, whatever they say, they really know the Law of Nature just like anyone else?

It seems, then, we are forced to believe in a real Right and Wrong. People may be sometimes mistaken about them, just as people sometimes get their sums wrong; but they are not a matter of mere taste and opinion any more than the multiplication table. Now if we are agreed about that, I go on to my next point, which is this. None of us are really keeping the Law of Nature. If there are any exceptions among you, I apologize to them. They had much better read some other work, for nothing I am going to say concerns them. And now, turning to the ordinary human beings who are left:

I hope you will not misunderstand what I am going to say. I am not preaching, and Heaven knows I do not pretend to be better than anyone else. I am only trying to call attention to a fact; the fact that this year, or this month, or, more likely, this very day, we have failed to practice ourselves the kind of behaviour we expect from other people. There may be all sorts of excuses for us. That time you were so unfair to the children was when you were very tired. That slightly shady business about the money—the one you have almost forgotten came when you were very hard up. And what you promised to do for old So-and-so and have never done—well, you never would have promised if you had known how frightfully busy you were going to be. And as for your behaviour to your wife (or husband) or sister (or brother) if I knew how irritating they could be, I would not wonder at it—and who the dickens am I, anyway? I am just the same. That is to say, I do not succeed in keeping the Law of Nature very well, and the moment anyone tells me I am not keeping it, there starts up in my mind a string of excuses as long as your arm. The question at the moment is not whether they are good excuses. The point is that they are one more proof of how deeply, whether we like it or not, we believe in the Law of Nature. If we do not believe in decent behaviour, why should we be so anxious to make excuses for not having behaved decently? The truth is, we believe in decency so much—we feel the Rule of Law pressing on us so—that we cannot bear to face the fact that we are breaking it, and consequently we try to shift the responsibility. For you notice that it is only for our bad behaviour that we find all these explanations. It is only our bad temper that we put down to being tired or worried or hungry; we put our good temper down to ourselves.

These, then, are the two points I wanted to make. First, that human beings, all over the earth, have this curious idea that they ought to behave in a certain way, and cannot really get rid of it. Secondly, that they do not in fact behave in that way. They know The Law of Nature; they break it. These two facts are the foundation of all clear thinking about ourselves and the universe we live in.

Chapter V
Vice and Virtue

What kind of person am I? What kind of person can and will I become? The ethics of vice and virtue judges the moral worth of individuals on the basis of character and not on the performance of external actions. The later can deceive. The key question, according to James Rachels, is "What traits of character make one a good person?"

Vices, such as cowardice, jealousy, envy, greed, gluttony, and spite, are examples of morally undesirable character traits. These traits become imbedded in the life of a man or woman through the indulgence of degrading appetites, lack of self-discipline and education, and habitual practice of degrading or immoral conduct. Vices render the possessor base and ignoble. The base person is not controlled by reason but by impulse. The ignoble person is discontent and anxiety ridden. His or her lifestyle is plagued by inner tension and chaos. This stormy inner life manifests itself in outer deeds which are corrupt, ignoble, and immoral.

In contrast, virtues are "human excellences." That is, they are character traits, such as honesty, loyalty, courage, wisdom, and temperance, which render the life of the possessor morally, intellectually, and practically superior. Even though the virtuous person, like the vicious individual, lives in a world of trouble, the life of the virtuous person is characterized by inner strength, contentment, happiness, and purpose.

Plutarch was an ancient Greek moralist. His *Lives* is a classic. The selection on "Vice" is as relevant today as it was nearly two thousand years ago. Plutarch observes that there exists a condition in human affairs which "deceives most people, who think that, if they surround themselves with vast houses, and get together a mass of slaves and money, they shall live pleasantly." How many people today believe that their happiness is dependent on the possession of material things? How many people invest their lives in the pursuit of things in order to become happy?

In contrast to this view, Plutarch maintains that "a pleasant and happy life comes not from external things, but, on the contrary, man draws on his own character as a source from which to add the element of pleasure and joy to the things which surround him."

The vicious individual cannot escape him or herself. Vice, says Plutarch, "is a settled tenet of his very vitals always." He continues:

> ... in travelling vice is a troublesome companion because of arrogance, at dinner an expensive companion owing to gluttony, and a distressing bedfellow, since by anxieties, cares and jealousies it drives out and destroys sleep.

Because of the effects produced by the outworking of vice, "the soul is overwhelmed and confounded." The vicious person is petty and incapable of enjoying the external things which they covet and, sometimes, acquire. In contrast, the person of virtue, "... will be luxurious in poverty, and live like a king." Furthermore, "If you become a philosopher," Plutarch claims, "you will not live unpleasantly, but you will learn to submit pleasantly anywhere and with any resources."

St. Augustine recalls the time when he and his friends stole some pears and threw the fruit to the pigs. On reflection he ponders the motivation for this act. "I willed to commit the theft," he says, and "I stole a thing of which I had plenty of my own and of much better quality." This act, Augustine reasoned, was an expression of corrupted human nature and rebellion against God. He concludes, "We did this to do what pleased us for the reason that it was forbidden."

In "The Depths of Vice," St. Augustine looks at the anatomy of evil. In his discussion he lists a number of vices and describes the various manifestations of these vices:

> pride imitates loftiness of mind . . .
> what does ambition seek, except honor and glory . . .
> the cruelty of the mighty desires to be feared . . .
> the caresses of the wanton call for love . . .
> curiosity pretends to be a desire for knowledge . . .
> ignorance itself and folly are cloaked over the names of simplicity and innocence . . .
> sloth . . . seeks rest . . .
> luxury of life desires to be called plenty and abundance . . .
> prodigality casts but the shadow of liberality
> avarice desires to possess many things
> envy contends for excellence . . .
> anger seeks vengeance . . .
> fear shrinks back at sudden and unusual things threatening what it loves . . .
> sadness wastes away over things now lost in which desire once took delight. . .
> (and), the soul commits fornication when it is turned away from you (God).

Chapter V: Vice and Virtue

"Jealousy, Envy and Spite" is taken from Kant's lectures on ethics. He observes that "there are two methods by which men arrive at an opinion of their worth: by comparing themselves with the idea of perfection and by comparing themselves with others." Only the first method is a proper standard.

But, people often compare themselves to others. When this improper standard is used it opens the door to jealousy, grudging and emulation. Other vices such as envy, spite, ingratitude and malice follow. Three vices, ingratitude, envy, and malice, are "devilish," according to Kant, because they imply a direct inclination to evil.

Peter Abelard, one of the great philosophers of the Middle Ages, views vice as a certain "defect of the mind" which disposes individuals to bad actions. That is, he is concerned to show how it is that the morally defective individual gives in to sin. Failure to exercise self control is "to be beaten by one's lower self." He claims that when we allow ourselves to act on evil impulses, "we fall below ourselves."

Having base desires is not sin. Sin occurs when a man or woman consents to those base desires and permits the "overlordship" of moral defects. This consent to base impulse is sin and this is nothing less than contempt for God.

Tu-Wei Ming conducts a new inquiry into *jen* as a living metaphor. In part, this inquiry frees the term from the limitations of traditional interpretation and the fixity of uncritical and unreflective acceptance of the scholarly tradition.

In Chinese thought, *jen* is typically regarded as the highest and central virtue. The term is variously translated as "goodness" "human-heartedness," "love" "benevolent love" "virtue," and "humanity." It is more. *Jen* is "a holistic manifestation of humanity in its commonest and highest state of perfection."

Because the individual in Chinese culture is not viewed independently of relationships, "the pursuit of *jen* is never a lonely struggle." Tu-Wei Ming writes:

> From the *jen* perspective, "a man of humanity," wishing to establish his own character, also establishes the character of others, and wishing to fully manifest himself, also helps others to fully manifest themselves. . . . The task of *jen,* far from being an internal, subjective search for one's own individuality, depends as much on meaningful communal inquiry as on self-scrutiny.

Alasdair MacIntyre calls attention to the fact that the ancient Greek word *arete* is translated as both "virtue" and "excellence." In heroic societies, the notion of excellence is closely tied into the virtue of courage and the related notion of strength. *Kudos,* glory, is then attributed to that one who excels as a mark of recognition by the family or the community. The virtue of courage is also tied intimately to the other virtues and to the concepts of friendship, fate and death. "The critical point," says MacIntyre, is that "morality and social structure are in fact one and the same in heroic societies."

All choices and meanings arise within a certain narrative context and framework of rules and precepts. However, the framework itself is never chosen. Within this concrete context the individual is accountable to fulfill a particular role.

> Identity in heroic society involves particularity and accountability. I am answerable for doing or failing to do what anyone who occupies my role owes to others and this accountability terminates only with death. I have until my death to do what I have to do. It is to, for and with specific individuals that I must do what I ought, and it is to these same and other individuals, members of the same local community, that I am accountable.

MacIntrye concludes that the type of social structure necessary for heroic virtues is "irrevocably lost," but, nevertheless, there are important lessons that can be learned from heroic societies.

Aristotle's "Habit and Virtue" is, in part, a guideline for moral education. It attempts to answer the question, "How does one become virtuous?" Aristotle's answer would be, roughly, education and training.

According to Aristotle, one is born with the capacity to become virtuous but individuals are not virtuous by nature. Virtuocity results from habit and right habits are cultivated by education and training. Furthermore, Aristotle tells us that it is the responsibility of the state to ensure that this is accomplished. He says:

> For the legislator makes the citizens good by habituating them, and this is the wish of every legislator; if he fails to do it well he misses his goal. [The right] habituation is what makes the difference between a good political system and a bad one.

"A state [of character]," Aristotle teaches, "arises from [the repetition of] similar activities." The right sort of habituation avoids excess, on the one hand, and deficiency, on the other. This habituation must also be concerned with pleasure and pain.

Jean-Louis Servan-Schreiber discussed the need for the virtue of courage. Why do we need courage? Servan-Schreiber answers that "courage allows us to live better, not only our last minute better, but even more important, every minute and day that went before." Furthermore, he tells us that "there are only two important kinds of courage: the courage to die and the courage to get up in the morning." Having courage "is a matter of leading my life in the best possible way, even when there is no witness but myself"

Benjamin Franklin is undoubtedly America's "universal man." Franklin was self-taught and yet achieved international stature. He was an accomplished businessman, printer, writer, politician, statesman, diplomat, ambassador, civil servant, scientist, philosopher and inventor. "Thirteen Virtues" is taken from his *Autobiography*.

Franklin realized that moral understanding is not sufficient if one wishes to become a good person. Inclination and habit are often stronger than the understanding. From his own readings on the moral virtues, Franklin developed a list of virtues with practical affirmations and action-guiding maxims: "My intention," Franklin declared, "being to acquire the *habitude* of all these virtues." Franklin's method was to work on one virtue at a time until he achieved mastery. Upon mastering all thirteen, Franklin reasoned that he would have realized a high degree of self-mastery.

James Rachels' article, "The Ethics of Virtue," draws together much of the thinking discussed thus far on vice and virtue and moral theories (Chapter III). Rachels looks at both the ethics of virtue and the ethics of right action. They lead us in different directions, Rachels reasons, because they start by asking fundamentally different questions. These questions also embody and make manifest certain assumptions about morality. The former asks: "What traits of character make one a good person?" and the later asks: "What is the right thing to do?"

Rachels develops the background of these two fundamental approaches to ethics and reopens the question, "Should we return to the ethics of virtue?" His conclusion is that a theory of virtue ethics will be incomplete, however the virtues may be revived and developed as a valuable supplement to modern theories of obligation.

Vice

Plutarch

1. Clothes are supposed to make a man warm, not of course by warming him themselves in the sense of adding their warmth to him, because each garment by itself is cold, and for this reason very often persons who feel hot and feverish keep changing from one set of clothes to another; but the warmth which a man gives off from his own person the clothing, closely applied to the body, confines and enwraps, and does not allow it, when thus imprisoned in the body, to be dissipated again. Now the same condition existing in human affairs deceives most people, who think that, if they surround themselves with vast houses, and get together a mass of slaves and money, they shall live pleasantly. But a pleasant and happy life comes not from external things, but, on the contrary, man draws on his own character as a source from which to add the element of pleasure and joy to the things which surround him.

> Bright with a blazing fire a house looks far more cheerful,

and wealth is pleasanter, and repute and power more resplendent, if with them goes the gladness which springs from the heart; and so too men bear poverty, exile, and old age lightly and gently in proportion to the serenity and mildness of their character.

2. As perfumes make coarse and ragged garments fragrant, but the body of Anchises gave off a noisome exudation,

> Damping the linen robe adown his back,

so every occupation and manner of life, if attended by virtue, is untroubled and delightful, while, on the other hand, any admixture of vice renders those things which to others seem splendid, precious, and imposing, only troublesome, sickening, and unwelcome to their possessors.

> This man is happy deemed 'mid public throng,
> But when he opes his door he's thrice a wretch;
> His wife controls, commands, and always fights.

Chapter V: Vice and Virtue

Yet it is not difficult for any man to get rid of a bad wife if he be a real man and not a slave; but against his own vice it is not possible to draw up a writing of divorcement and forthwith to be rid of troubles and to be at peace, having arranged to be by himself. No, his vice, a settled tenant of his very vitals always, both at night and by day,

> Burns, but without e'er a brand, and consigns to an eld all untimely.

For in travelling vice is a troublesome companion because of arrogance, at dinner an expensive companion owing to gluttony, and a distressing bed-fellow, since by anxieties, cares and jealousies it drives out and destroys sleep. For what slumber there may be is a sleep and repose for the body only, but for the soul terrors, dreams, and agitations, because of superstition.

> When grief o'ertakes me as I close my eyes,
> I'm murdered by my dreams.

says one man. In such a state do envy, fear, temper, and licentiousness put a man. For by day vice, looking outside of itself and conforming its attitude to others, is abashed and veils its emotions, and does not give itself up completely to its impulses, but often-times resists them and struggles against them; but in the hours of slumber, when it has escaped from opinion and law, and got away as far as possible from feeling fear or shame, it sets every desire stirring, and awakens its depravity and licentiousness. It "attempts incest," as Plato says, partakes of forbidden meats, abstains from nothing which it wishes to do, but revels in lawlessness so far as it can, with images and visions which end in no pleasure or accomplishment of desire, but have only the power to stir to fierce activity the emotional and morbid propensities.

3. Where, then, is the pleasure in vice, if in no part of it is to be found freedom from care and grief, or contentment or tranquillity or calm? For a well-balanced and healthy condition of the body gives room for engendering the pleasures of the flesh; but in the soul lasting joy and gladness cannot possibly be engendered, unless it provide itself first with cheerfulness, fearlessness, and courageousness as a basis to rest upon, or as a calm tranquillity that no billows disturb; otherwise, even though some hope or delectation lure us with a smile, anxiety suddenly breaks forth, like a hidden rock appearing in fair weather, and the soul is overwhelmed and confounded.

4. Heap up gold, amass silver, build stately promenades, fill your hourse with slaves and the city with your debtors; unless you lay level the emotions of your soul, put a stop to your insatiate desires, and quit yourself of fears and anxieties, you are but decanting wine for a man in a fever, offering honey to a bilious man, and preparing tid-bits and dainties for sufferers from colic or dysentery, who cannot retain them or be strength-

ened by them, but are only brought nearer to death thereby. Does not your observation of sick persons teach you that they dislike and reject and decline the finest and costliest viands which their attendants offer and try to force upon them; and then later, when their whole condition has changed, and good breathing, wholesome blood, and normal temperature have returned to their bodies, they get up and have joy and satisfaction in eating plain bread with cheese and cress? It is such a condition that reason creates in the soul. You will be contented with your lot if you learn what the honourable and good is. You will be luxurious in poverty, and live like a king, and you will find no less satisfaction in the care-free life of a private citizen than in the life connected with high military or civic office. If you become a philosopher, you will live not unpleasantly, but you will learn to subsist pleasantly anywhere and with any resources. Wealth will give your gladness for the good you will do to many, poverty for your freedom from many cares, repute for the honours you will enjoy, and obscurity for the certainty that you shall not be envied.

VICE Reprinted by permission of the publishers and the Loeb Classical Library from Plutarch's *Moralia*, trans. by Frank Cole Babbit, Cambridge, Mass.: Harvard University Press, 1928, 1956, 1962.

The Depths of Vice

Saint Augustine

I wish to bring back to mind my past foulness and the carnal corruptions of my soul. This is not because I love them, but that I may love you, my God. Out of love for your love I do this. In the bitterness of my remembrance, I tread again my most evil ways, so that you may grow sweet to me, O sweetness that never fails, O sweetness happy and enduring, whichs gathers me together again from that disordered state in which I lay in shattered pieces, wherein, turned away from you, the one, I spent myself upon the many. For in my youth, I burned to get my fill of hellish things. I dared to run wild in different darksome ways of love. My comeliness wasted away. I stank in your eyes, but I was pleasing to myself and I desired to be pleasing to the eyes of men. . . .

The Stolen Fruit

Surely, Lord, your law punishes theft, as does that law written on the hearts of men, which not even iniquity itself blots out. What thief puts up with another thief with a calm mind? Not even a rich thief will pardon one who steals from him because of want. But I willed to commit theft, and I did so, not because I was driven to it by any need, unless it were by poverty of justice, and dislike of it, and by a glut of evildoing. For I stole a thing of which I had plenty of my own and of much better quality. Nor did I wish to enjoy that thing which I desired to gain by theft, but rather to enjoy the actual theft and the sin of theft.

In a garden nearby to our vineyard there was a pear tree, loaded with fruit that was desirable neither in appearance nor in taste. Late one night—to which hour, according to our pestilential custom, we had kept our street games—a group of very bad youngsters set out to shake down and rob this tree. We took great loads of fruit from it, not for our own eating, but rather to throw it to the pigs; even if we did eat a little of it, we did this to do what pleased us for the reason that it was forbidden. . . .

When there is discussion concerning a crime and why it was committed, it is usually held that there appeared possibility that the appetites would obtain some of these goods, which we have termed lower, or there was fear of losing them. These things are beautiful and fitting, but in comparison with the higher goods, which bring happiness, they are mean and base. A man commits murder: why did he do so? He coveted his victim's wife or his property; or he wanted to rob him to get money to live on; or he feared to be deprived of some such thing by the other; or he had been injured, and burned for revenge. Would anyone commit murder without reason and out of delight in murder itself? Who can believe such a thing? Of a certain senseless and utterly cruel man it was said that he was evil and cruel without reason. Nevertheless, a reason has been given, for he himself said, "I don't want to let my hand or will get out of practice through disuse." Why did he want that? Why so? It was to the end that after he had seized the city by the practice of crime, he would attain to honors, power, and wealth, and be free from fear of the law and from trouble due to lack of wealth or from a guilty conscience. Therefore, not even Catiline himself loved his crimes, but something else, for sake of which he committed them.

The Anatomy of Evil

What was it that I, a wretch, loved in you, my act of theft, my deed of crime done by night, done in the sixteenth year of my age? You were not beautiful, for you were but an act of thievery. In truth, are you anything at all, that I may speak to you? The fruit we stole was beautiful, for it was your creation, O most beautiful of all beings, creator of all things, God the good, God the supreme good and my true good. Beautiful was the fruit, but it was not what my unhappy soul desired. I had an abundance of better pears, but those pears I gathered solely that I might steal. The fruit I gathered I threw away, devouring in it only iniquity, and that I rejoiced to enjoy. For if I put any of that fruit into my mouth, my sin was its seasoning. But now, O Lord my God, I seek out what was in that theft to give me delight, and lo, there is no loveliness in it. I do not say such loveliness as there is in justice and prudence, or in man's mind, and memory, and senses, and vigorous life, nor that with which the stars are beautiful and glorious in their courses, or the land and the sea filled with their living kinds, which by new births replace those that die, nor even that flawed and shadowy beauty found in the vices that deceive us.

For pride imitates loftiness of mind, while you are the one God, highest above all things. What does ambition seek, except honor and glory,

Chapter V: Vice and Virtue

while you alone are to be honored above all else and are glorious forever? The cruelty of the mighty desires to be feared: but who is to be feared except the one God, and from his power what can be seized and stolen away, and when, or where, or how, or by whom? The caresses of the wanton call for love; but there is naught more caressing than your charity, nor is anything to be loved more wholesomely than your truth, which is beautiful and bright above all things. Curiosity pretends to be a desire for knowledge, while you know all things in the highest degree. Ignorance itself and folly are cloaked over the names of simplicity and innocence, because nothing more simple than you can be found. What is more innocent than you, whereas to evil men their own works are hostile? Sloth seeks rest as it were, but what sure rest is there apart from the Lord? Luxury of life desires to be called plenty and abundance; you are the fullness and the unfailing plenty of incorruptible pleasure. Prodigality casts but the shadow of liberality, while you are the most affluent giver of all good things. Avarice desires to possess many things, and you possess all things. Envy contends for excellence: what is more excellent than you? Anger seeks vengeance: who takes vengeance with more justice than you? Fear shrinks back at sudden and unusual things threatening what it loves, and is on watch for its own safety. But for you what is unusual or what is sudden? Or who can separate you from what you love? Where, except with you, is there firm security? Sadness wastes away over things now lost in which desire once took delight. It did not want this to happen, whereas from you nothing can be taken away.

Thus the soul commits fornication when it is turned away from you and, apart from you, seeks such pure, clean things as it does not find except when it returns to you. In a perverse way, all men imitate you who put themselves far from you, and rise up in rebellion against you. Even by such imitation of you they prove that you are the creator of all nature, and that therefore there is no place where they can depart entirely from you.

What, therefore did I love in that theft of mine, in what manner did I perversely or viciously imitate my Lord? Did it please me to go against your law, at least by trickery, for I could not do so with might? Did it please me that as a captive I should imitate a deformed liberty, by doing with impunity things illicit bearing a shadowy likeness of your omnipotence? Behold, your servant flees from his Lord and follows after a shadow! O rottenness! O monstrous life and deepest death! Could a thing give pleasure which could not be done lawfully, and which was done for no other reason but because it was unlawful? . . .

Evil Communications

What was my state of mind? Truly and clearly, it was most base, and woe was it to me who had it. Yet, what was it? Who understands his sins? It was like a thing of laughter, which reached down as it were into our hearts, that we were tricking those who did not know what we were doing and would most strenuously resent it. Why, then, did even the fact that I did not do it alone give me pleasure? Is it because no one can laugh readily when he is alone? No one indeed does laugh readily when alone. However, individual men, when alone and when no one else is about, are sometimes overcome by laughter if something very funny affects their senses or strikes their mind. But that deed I would not have done alone, alone I would never have done it.

Behold, the living record of my soul lies before you, my God. By myself I would not have committed that theft in which what pleased me was not what I stole but the fact that I stole. This would have pleased me not at all if I had done it alone; nor by-myself would I have done it at all. O friendship too unfriendly! Unfathomable seducer of the mind, greed to do harm for fun and sport, desire for another's injury, arising not from desire for my own gain or for vengeance, but merely when someone says, "Let's go! Let's do it!" and it is shameful not to be shameless!

A Soul in Waste

Who can untie this most twisted and intricate mass of knots? It is a filthy thing: I do not wish to think about it; I do not wish to look upon it. I desire you, O justice and innocence, beautiful and comely to all virtuous eyes, and I desire this unto a satiety that can never be satiated. With you there is true rest and life untroubled. He who enters into you enters into the joy of his Lord, and he shall have no fear, and he shall possess his soul most happily in him who is the supreme good. I fell away from you, my God, and I went astray, too far astray from you, the support of my youth, and I became to myself a land of want.

THE DEPTHS OF VICE From *The Confessions of St. Augustine.* Translated by John K. Ryan. Copyright © 1960 by Doubleday and Company, Inc. Reprinted by permission of the publisher.

Desire and Sin

Peter Abelard

Prologue

In the study of morals we deal with the defects or qualities of the mind which dispose us to bad or good actions. Defects and qualities are not only mental, but also physical. There is bodily weakness; there is also the endurance which we call strength. There is sluggishness or speed; blindness or sight. When we now speak of defects, therefore, we pre-suppose defects of the mind, so as to distinguish them from the physical ones. The defects of the mind are opposed to the qualities; injustice to justice; cowardice to constancy; intemperance to temperance.

Chapter I. The Defect of Mind Bearing upon Conduct

Certain defects or merits of mind have no connection with morals. They do not make human life a matter of praise or blame. Such are dull wits or quick insight; a good or a bad memory; ignorance or knowledge. Each of these features is found in good and bad alike. They have nothing to do with the system of morals, nor with making life base or honourable. To exclude these we safeguarded above the phrase 'defects of mind' by adding 'which dispose to bad actions,' that is, those defects which incline the will to what least of all either should be done or should be left undone.

Chapter II. How Does Sin Differ from a Disposition to Evil?

Defect of this mental kind is not the same thing as sin. Sin, too, is not the same as a bad action. For example, to be irascible, that is, prone or easily roused to the agitation of anger is a defect and moves the mind to unpleasantly impetuous and irrational action. This defect, however, is in the mind so that the mind is liable to wrath, even when it is not actually roused to it. Similarly, lameness, by reason of which a man is said to be lame, is in the man himself even when he does not walk and reveal his lameness. For the defect is there though action be lacking. So, also, nature or constitution renders many liable to luxury. Yet they do not sin because they are like this, but from this very fact they have the material of a struggle whereby they may, in the virtue of temperance, triumph over themselves and win the crown. As Solomon says: 'Better a patient than a strong man; and the Lord of his soul than he that taketh a city.' (Prov. xvi, 32.) For religion does not think it degrading to be beaten by man; but it is degrading to be beaten by one's lower self. The former defeat has been the fate of good men. But, in the latter, we fall below ourselves. The Apostle commends victory of this sort; 'No one shall be crowned who has not truly striven.' (2 Tim. ii, 5.) This striving, I repeat, means standing less against men than against myself, so that defects may not lure me into base consent. Though men cease to oppose us, our defects do not cease. The fight with them is the more dangerous because of its repetition. And as it is the more difficult, so victory is the more glorious. Men, however much they prevail over us, do not force baseness upon us, unless by their practice of vice they turn us also to it and overcome us through our own wretched consent. They may dominate our body; but while our mind is free, there is no danger to true freedom. We run no risk of base servitude. Subservience to vice, not to man, is degradation. It is the overlordship of defects and not physical serfdom which debases the soul.

Chapter III. Definition of 'Defect' and of Sin

Defect, then, is that whereby we are disposed to sin. We are, that is, inclined to consent to what we ought not to do, or to leave undone what we ought to do. Consent of this kind we rightly call sin. Here is the reproach of the soul meriting damnation or being declared guilty by God. What is that consent but to despise God and to violate His laws? God cannot be set at enmity by injury, but by contempt. He is the highest power, and is not diminished by any injury, but He avenges contempt of Himself. Our sin, therefore, is contempt of the Creator. To sin is to despise the Creator; that is, not to do for Him what we believe we should do for Him, or, not to renounce what we think should be renounced on His behalf. We have defined sin negatively by saying that it means not doing or not renouncing what we ought to do or renounce. Clearly, then, we have shown that sin has no reality. It exists rather in *not being* than in *being*. Similarly we could define shadows by saying: The absence of light where light usually is.

Perhaps you object that sin is the desire or will to do an evil deed, and that this will or desire condemns us before God in the same way as the will to do a good deed justifies us. There is as much quality, you suggest, in the good will as there is sin in the evil will; and it is no less 'in being' in the latter than in the former. By willing to do what we believe to be pleasing to God we please Him. Equally, by willing to do what we believe to be displeasing to God, we displease Him and seem either to violate or despise His nature.

But diligent attention will show that we must think far otherwise of this point. We frequently err, and from no evil will at all. Indeed, the evil will itself, when restrained, though it may not be quenched, procures the palm-wreath for those who resist it. It provides, not merely the materials for combat, but also the crown of glory. It should be spoken of rather as a certain inevitable weakness than as sin. Take, for example, the case of an innocent servant whose harsh master is moved with fury against him. He pursues the servant, drawing his sword with intent to kill him. For a while the servant flies and avoids death as best he can. At last, forced all unwillingly to it, he kills his master so as not to be killed by him. Let anyone say what sort of evil will there was in this deed. His will was only to flee from death and preserve his own life. Was this an evil will? You reply: 'I do not think this was an evil will. But the will that he had to kill the master who was pursuing him was evil.' Your answer would be admirable and acute if you could show that the servant really willed what you say that he did. But, as I insisted, he was unwillingly forced to his deed. He protracted his master's life as long as he could, knowing that danger also threatened his own life from such a crime. How, then was a deed done voluntarily by which he incurred danger to his own life? . . .

Sin, therefore, is sometimes committed without an evil will. Thus sin cannot be defined as 'will.' True, you will say, when we sin under constraint, but not when we sin willingly, for instance, when we will to do something which we know ought not to be done by us. There the evil will and sin seem to be the same thing. For example a man sees a woman; his concupiscence is aroused; his mind is enticed by fleshly lust and stirred to base desire. This wish, this lascivious longing, what else can it be, you say, than sin?

I reply: What if that wish may be bridled by the power of temperance? What if its nature is never to be entirely extinguished but to persist in struggle and not fully fail even in defeat? For where is the battle if the antagonist is away? Whence the great reward without grave endurance? When the fight is over nothing remains but to reap the reward. Here we strive in contest in order elsewhere to obtain as victors a crown. Now, for a contest, an opponent is needed who will resist, not one who simply submits. This opponent is our evil will over which we triumph when we subjugate it to the divine will. But we do not entirely destroy it. For we needs must ever expect to encounter our enemy. What achievement before God is it if we undergo nothing contrary to our own will, but merely practice what we please? Who will be grateful to us if in what we say we do for him we merely satisfy our own fancy?

You will say, what merit have we with God in acting willingly or unwillingly? Certainly none: I reply. He weighs the intention rather than the deed in his recompense. Nor does the deed, whether it proceed from a good or an evil will, add anything to the merit, as we shall show shortly. But when we set His will before our own so as to follow His and not ours, our merit with God is magnified, in accordance with that perfect word of Truth: 'I came not to do mine own will, but the will of Him that sent me.' (John vi, 38.) To this end He exhorts us: 'If anyone comes to me, and does not hate father, and mother . . . yea his own soul also, he is not worthy of me.' (Luke xiv, 26.) That is to say, 'unless a man renounces his parents' influence and his own will and submits himself to my teaching, he is not worthy of me.' Thus we are bidden to hate our father, not to destroy him. Similarly with our own will. We must not be led by it; at the same time, we are not asked to root it out altogether.

When the Scripture says: 'Go not after your own desires' (Eccles. xviii, 30) . . . I think that it is plain that no natural physical delight can be set down as sin, nor can it be called guilt for men to delight in what, when it is done, must involve the feeling of delight.

For example, if anyone obliged a monk, bound in chains, to lie among women, and the monk by the softness of the couch and by contact with his fair flatterers is allured into delight, though not into consent, who shall presume to designate guilt the delight which is naturally awakened?

You may urge, with some thinkers, that the carnal pleasure, even in lawful intercourse, involves sin. Thus David says: 'Behold in sin was I conceived.' (Ps. 1, 7.) And the Apostle, when he had said: 'Ye return to it again' (I Cor. vii, 5), adds nevertheless, 'This I say by way of concession, not of command.' (ibid., v, 6.) Yet authority rather than reason, seems to dictate the view that we should allow simple physical delight to be sin. For, assuredly, David was conceived not in fornication, but in matrimony: and concession, that is forgiveness, does not, as this standpoint avers, condone when there is no guilt to forgive. As for what David meant when he says that he had been conceived 'in iniquity' or 'in sin' and does not say 'whose' sin, he referred to the general curse of original sin, wherein from the guilt of our first parents each is subject to damnation, as it is elsewhere stated: 'None are pure of stain, not the infant a day old, if he has life on this earth.' As the blessed Jerome reminds us and as manifest reason teaches, the soul of a young child is without sin. If, then, it is pure of sin, how is it also impure by sinful corruption? We must understand the infant's purity from sin in reference to its personal guilt. But its contact with sinful corruption, its 'stain,' is in reference to penalty owed by mankind because of Adam's sin. He who has not yet perceived by reason what he ought to do cannot be guilty of contempt of God. Yet he is not free from the contamination of the sin of his first parents, from which he contracts the penalty, though not the guilt, and bears in penalty what they committed in guilt. When, therefore, David says that he was conceived in iniquity or sin, he sees himself subject to the general sentence of damnation from the guilt of his racial parents, and he assigns the sins, not to his father and mother but to his first parents. . . .

We come, then, to this conclusion, that no one who sets out to assert that all fleshly desire is sin may say that the sin itself is increased by the doing of it. For this would mean extending the consent of the soul into the exercise of the action. In short, one would be stained not only by consent to baseness, but also by the mire of the deed, as if what happens externally in the body could possibly soil the soul. Sin is not, therefore, increased by the doing of an action: and nothing mars the soul except what is of its own nature, namely consent. This we affirmed was alone sin, preceding action in will, or subsequent to the performance of action. Although we wish for, or do, what is unseemly, we do not therefore sin. For such deeds not uncommonly occur without there being any sin. On the other hand, there may be consent without the external effects, as we have indicated. There was wish without consent in the case of the man who was attracted by a woman whom he caught sight of, or who was tempted by his neighbour's fruit, but who was not enticed into consent. There was evil consent without evil desire in the servant who unwillingly killed his master.

Certain acts which ought not to be done often are done, and without any sin, when, for instance, they are committed under force or ignorance. No one, I think, ignores this fact. A woman under constraint of violence, lies with another's husband. A man, taken by some trick, sleeps with one whom he supposed to be his wife, or kills a man, in the belief that he himself has the right to be both judge and executioner. Thus to desire the wife of another or actually to lie with her is not sin. But to consent to that desire or to that action is sin. This consent to covetousness the law calls covetousness in saying: 'Thou shalt not covet.' (Deut. v, 21.) Yet that which we cannot avoid ought not to be forbidden, nor that wherein, as we said, we do not sin. But we should be cautioned about the consent to covetousness. So, too, the saying of the Lord must be understood: 'Whosoever shall look upon a woman to desire her.' (Matt. v, 28.) That is, whosoever shall so look upon her as a slip into consent to covetousness, 'has already committed adultery with her in his heart' (Matt. v, 28), even though he may not have committed adultery in deed. He is guilty of sin, though there be no sequel to his intention. . . .

Blessed Augustine, in his careful view of this question, reduces every sin or command to terms of charity and covetousness, and not to works. 'The law,' he says, 'inculcates nothing but charity, and forbids nothing but covetousness.' The Apostle, also, asserts: 'All the law is contained in one word: thou shalt love thy neighbour as thyself,' (Rom. xiii, 8, 10), and again, 'Love is the fulfilling of the law.' (ibid.)

Whether you actually give alms to a needy person, or charity makes you ready to give, makes no difference to the merit of the deed. The will may be there when the opportunity is not. Nor does it rest entirely with you to deal with every case of need which you encounter. Actions which are right and actions which are far from right are done by good and bad men alike. The intention alone separates the two classes of men . . .

Briefly to summarize the above argument: Four things were postulated which must be carefully distinguished from one another.

1. Imperfection of soul, making us liable to sin.
2. Sin itself, which we decided is consent to evil or contempt of God.
3. The will or desire of evil.
4. The evil deed.

To wish is not the same thing as to fulfil a wish. Equally, to sin is not the same as to carry out a sin. In the first case, we sin by consent of the soul: the second is a matter of the external effect of an action, namely, when we fulfil in deed that whereunto we have previously consented. When, therefore, temptation is said to proceed through three stages, suggestion, delight, consent, it must be understood that, like our first parents, we are frequently led along these three paths to the commission of sin. The devil's persuasion comes *first* promising from the taste of the forbidden fruit immortality. Delight follows. When the woman sees the beautiful tree, and perceives that the fruit is good, her appetite is whetted by the anticipated pleasure of tasting. This desire she ought to have repressed, so as to obey God's command. But in consenting to it, she was drawn *secondly* into sin. By penitence she should have put right this fault, and obtained pardon. Instead, she *thirdly* consummated the sin by the deed. Eve thus passed through the three stages to the commission of sin.

By the same avenues we also arrive not at sin, but at the action of sin, namely, the doing of an unseemly deed through the suggestion or prompting of something within us. If we already know that such a deed will be pleasant, our imagination is held by anticipatory delight and we are tempted thereby in thought. So long as we give consent to such delight, we sin. Lastly, we pass to the third stage, and actually commit the sin.

It is agreed by some thinkers that carnal suggestion, even though the person causing the suggestion be not present, should be included under sinful suggestion. For example, a man having seen a woman falls into a sensual desire of her. But it seems that this kind of suggestion should simply be called delight. This delight, and other delights of the like kind, arise naturally and, as we said above, they are not sinful. The Apostle calls them 'human temptations.' No temptation has taken you yet which was not common to men. God is faithful, and will not suffer you to be tempted above what you are able; but will, with the temptation make a way of escape, that you may be able to bear it.' By temptation is meant, in general, any movement of the soul to do something unseemly, whether in wish or consent. We speak of human temptation without which it is hardly or never possible for human weakness to exist. Such are sexual desire, or the pleasures of the table. From these the Psalmist asks to be delivered when he says: 'Deliver me from my wants, O Lord' (Ps. xxiv, 17); that is, from the temptations of natural and necessary appetites that they may not influence him into sinful consent. Or, he may mean: 'When this life is over, grant me to be without those temptations of which life has been full.'

When the Apostle says: 'No temptation has taken you but what is human,' his statement amounts to this: Even if the soul be stirred by that delight which is, as we said, human temptation, yet God would not lead the soul into that consent wherein sin consists. Someone may object: But by what power of our own are we able to resist those desires? We may reply: 'God is faithful, who will not allow you to resist those desires? We may reply: 'God is faithful, who will not allow you to be tempted,' as the Scripture says. In other words: We should rather trust him than rely upon ourselves. He promises help, and is true to his promises. He is faithful, so that we should have complete faith in him. Out of pity God diminishes the degree of human temptation, does not suffer us to be tempted above what we are able, in order that it may not drive us to sin at a pace we cannot endure, when, that is, we strive to resist it. Then, too, God turns the temptation to our advantage: for He trains us thereby so that the recurrence of temptation causes us less care, and we fear less the onset of a foe over whom we have already triumphed, and whom we know how to meet. . . .

DESIRE AND SIN From *Abelard's Ethics*. Translated by R. McCallum. Reprinted by permission of the publisher, Basil Blackwell Publisher Limited.

Jealousy, Envy, and Spite

Immanuel Kant

There are two methods by which men arrive at an opinion of their worth: by comparing themselves with the idea of perfection and by comparing themselves with others. The first of these methods is sound; the second is not, and it frequently even leads to a result diametrically opposed to the first. The idea of perfection is a proper standard, and if we measure our worth by it, we find that we fall short of it and feel that we must exert ourselves to come nearer to it; but if we compare ourselves with others, much depends upon who those others are and how they are constituted, and we can easily believe ourselves to be of great worth if those with whom we set up comparison are rogues. Men love to compare themselves with others, for by that method they can always arrive at a result favourable to themselves. They choose as a rule the worst and not the best of the class with which they set up comparison; in this way their own excellence shines out. If they choose those of greater worth the result of the comparison is, of course, unfavourable to them.

When I compare myself with another who is better than I, there are but two ways by which I can bridge the gap between us. I can either do my best to attain to his perfections, or else I can seek to depreciate his good qualities. I either increase my own worth, or else I diminish his so that I can always regard myself as superior to him. It is easier to depreciate another than to emulate him, and men prefer the easier course. They adopt it, and this is the origin of jealousy. When a man compares himself with another and finds that the other has many more good points, he becomes jealous of each and every good point he discovers in the other, and tries to depreciate it so that his own good points may stand out. This kind of jealousy may be called grudging. The other species of the genus jealousy, which makes us try to add to our good points so as to compare well with another, may be called emulating jealousy. The jealousy of emulation is, as we have stated, more difficult than the jealousy of grudge and so is much the less frequent of the two.

Chapter V: Vice and Virtue

Parents ought not, therefore, when teaching their children to be good, to urge them to model themselves on other children and try to emulate them, for by so doing they simply make them jealous. If I tell my son, "Look, how good and industrious John is," the result will be that my son will bear John a grudge. He will think to himself that, but for John, he himself would be the best, because there would be no comparison. By setting up John as a pattern for imitation I anger my son, make him feel a grudge against this so-called paragon, and I instil jealousy in him. My son might, of course, try to emulate John, but not finding it easy, he will bear John ill-will. Besides, just as I can say to my son, "Look, how good John is," so can he reply: "Yes, he is better than I, but are there not many who are far worse? Why do you compare me with those who are better? Why not with those who are worse than I?" Goodness must, therefore, be commended to children in and for itself. Whether other children are better or worse has no bearing on the point. If the comparison were in the child's favour, he would lose all ground of impulse to improve his own conduct. To ask our children to model themselves on others is to adopt a faulty method of upbringing, and as time goes on the fault will strike its roots deep. It is jealousy that parents are training and presupposing in their children when they set other children before them as patterns. Otherwise, the children would be quite indifferent to the qualities of others. They will find it easier to belittle the good qualities of their patterns than to emulate them, so they will choose the easier path and learn to show a grudging disposition. It is true that jealousy is natural, but that is no excuse for cultivating it. It is only a motive, a reserve in case of need. While the maxims of reason are still undeveloped in us, the proper course is to use reason to keep it within bounds. For jealousy is only one of the many motives, such as ambition, which are implanted in us because we are designed for a life of activity. But so soon as reason is enthroned, we must cease to seek perfection in emulation of others and must covet it in and for itself. Motives must abdicate and let reason bear rule in their place.

Persons of the same station and occupation in life are particularly prone to be jealous of each other. Many business-men are jealous of each other; so are many scholars, particularly in the same line of scholarship; and women are liable to be jealous of each other regarding men.

Grudge is the displeasure we feel when another has an advantage; his advantage makes us feel unduly small and we grudge it him. But to grudge a man his share of happiness is envy. To be envious is to desire the failure and unhappiness of another not for the purpose of advancing our own success and happiness but because we might then ourselves be perfect and happy as we are. An envious man is not happy unless all around him are unhappy; his aim is to stand alone in the enjoyment of his happiness. Such is envy, and we shall learn below that it is satanic. Grudge, although it too should not be countenanced, is natural. Even a good-natured person may at times be grudging. Such a one may, for instance, begrudge those around him their jollity when he himself happens to be sorrowful; for it is hard to bear one's sorrow when all around are joyful. When I see everybody enjoying a good meal and I alone must content myself with inferior fare, it upsets me and I feel a grudge; but if we are all in the same boat I am content. We find the thought of death bearable, because we know that all must die; but if everybody were immortal and I alone had to die, I should feel aggrieved. It is not things themselves that affect us, but things in their relation to ourselves. We are grudging because others are happier than we. But when a good-natured man feels happy and cheerful, he wishes that every one else in the world were as happy as he and shared his joy; he begrudges no one his happiness.

When a man would not grant to another even that for which he himself has no need, he is spiteful. Spite is a maliciousness of spirit which is not the same thing as envy. I may not feel inclined to give to another something which belongs to me, even though I myself have no use for it, but it does not follow that I grudge him his own possessions, that I want to be the only one who has anything and wish him to have nothing at all. There is a deal of grudge in human nature which could develop into envy but which is not itself envy. We feel pleasure in gossiping about the minor misadventures of other people; we are not averse, although we may express no pleasure thereat, to hearing of the fall of some rich man; we may enjoy in stormy weather, when comfortably seated in our warm, cosy parlour, speaking of those at sea, for it heightens our own feeling of comfort and happiness; there is grudge in all this, but it is not envy.

The three vices which are the essence of vileness and wickedness are ingratitude, envy, and malice. When these reach their full degree they are devilish.

Men are shamed by favours. If I receive a favour, I am placed under an obligation to the giver; he has a call upon me because I am indebted to him. We all blush to be obliged. Noble-minded men accordingly refuse to accept favours in order not to put themselves under an obligation. But this attitude predisposes the mind to ingratitude. If the man who adopts it is noble-minded, well and good; but if he be proud and selfish and has perchance received a favour, the feeling that he is beholden to his benefactor hurts his pride and, being selfish, he cannot accommodate himself to the idea that he owes his benefactor anything. He becomes defiant and ungrateful. His ingratitude might even conceivably assume such dimensions that he cannot bear his benefactor and becomes his enemy. Such ingratitude is of the devil; it is out of all keeping with human nature. It is inhuman to hate and persecute one from whom we have reaped a benefit, and if such conduct were the rule it would cause untold harm. Men would then be afraid to do good to anyone lest they should receive evil in return for their good. They would become misanthropic.

Chapter V: Vice and Virtue

The second devilish vice is envy. Envy is in the highest degree detestable. The envious man does not merely want to be happy; he wants to be the only happy person in the world; he is really contented only when he sees nothing but misery around him. Such an intolerable creature would gladly destroy every source of joy and happiness in the world.

Malice is the third kind of viciousness which is of the devil. It consists in taking a direct pleasure in the misfortunes of others. Men prone to this vice will seek, for instance, to make mischief between husband and wife, or between friends, and then enjoy the misery they have produced. In these matters we should make it a rule never to repeat to a person anything that we may have heard to his disadvantage from another, unless our silence would injure him. Otherwise we start an enmity and disturb his peace of mind, which our silence would have avoided, and in addition we break faith with our informant. The defence against such mischief-makers is upright conduct. Not by words but by our lives we should confute them. As Socrates said: We ought so to conduct ourselves that people will not credit anything spoken in disparagement of us.

These three vices—ingratitude *(ingratitudo qualificata)*, envy, and malice—are devilish because they imply a direct inclination to evil. There are in man certain indirect tendencies to wickedness which are human and not unnatural. The miser wants everything for himself, but it is no satisfaction to him to see that his neighbour is destitute. The evilness of a vice may thus be either direct or indirect. In these three vices it is direct.

We may ask whether there is in the human mind an immediate inclination to wickedness, an inclination to the devilish vices. Heaven stands for the acme of happiness, hell for all that is bad, and the earth stands midway between these two extremes; and just as goodness which transcends anything which might be expected of a human being is spoken of as being angelic, so also do we speak of devilish wickedness when the wickedness oversteps the limits of human nature and becomes inhuman. We may take it for granted that the human mind has no immediate inclination to wickedness, but is only indirectly wicked. Man cannot be so ungrateful that he simply must hate his neighbour; he may be too proud to show his gratitude and so avoid him, but he wishes him well. Again, our pleasure in the misfortune of another is not direct. We may rejoice, for example, in a man's misfortunes, because he was haughty, rich and selfish; for man loves to preserve equality. We have thus no direct inclination towards evil as evil, but only an indirect one. But how are we to explain the fact that even young children have the spirit of mischief strongly developed? For a joke, a boy will stick a pin in an unsuspecting playmate, but it is only for fun. He has no thought of the pain the other must feel on all such occasions. In the same spirit he will torture animals; twisting the cat's tail or the dog's. Such tendencies must be nipped in the bud, for it is easy to see where they will lead. They are, in fact, something animal, something of the beast of prey which is in us all, which we cannot overcome, and the source of which we cannot explain. There certainly are in human nature characteristics for which we can assign no reason. There are animals too who steal anything that comes their way, though it is quite useless to them; and it seems as if man has retained this animal tendency in his nature.

Ingratitude calls for some further observations here. To help a man in distress is charity; to help him in less urgent needs is benevolence; to help him in the amenities of life is courtesy. We may be the recipients of a charity which has not cost the giver much and our gratitude is commensurate with the degree of good-will which moved him to the action. We are grateful not only for what we have received but also for the good intention which prompted it, and the greater the effort it has cost our benefactor, the greater our gratitude.

Gratitude may be either from duty or from inclination. If an act of kindness does not greatly move us, but if we nevertheless feel that it is right and proper that we should show gratitude, our gratitude is merely prompted by a sense of duty. Our heart is not grateful, but we have principles of gratitude. If however, our heart goes out to our benefactor, we are grateful from inclination. There is a weakness of the understanding which we often have cause to recognize. It consists in taking the conditions of our understanding as conditions of the thing understood. We can estimate force only in terms of the obstacles it overcomes. Similarly, we can only estimate the degree of good will in terms of the obstacles it has to surmount. In consequence we cannot comprehend the love and goodwill of a being for whom there are no obstacles. If God has been good to me, I am liable to think that after all it has cost God no trouble, and that gratitude to God would be mere fawning on my part. Such thoughts are not at all unnatural. It is easy to fear God, but not nearly so easy to love God from inclination because of our consciousness that God is a being whose goodness is unbounded but to whom it is no trouble to shower kindness upon us. This is not to say that such should be our mental attitude; merely that when we examine our hearts, we find that this is how we actually think. It also explains why to many races God appeared to be a jealous God, seeing that it cost Him nothing to be more bountiful with His goodness; it explains why many nations thought that their gods were sparing of their benefits and that they required propitiating with prayers and sacrifices. This is the attitude of man's heart; but when we call reason to our aid we see that God's goodness must be of a high order if He is to be good to a being so unworthy of His goodness. This solves our difficulty. The gratitude we owe to God is not gratitude from inclination, but from duty, for God is not a creature like ourselves, and can be no object of our inclinations.

We ought not to accept favours unless we are either forced to do so by dire necessity or have implicit confidence in our benefactor (for he ceases to be our friend and becomes our benefactor) that he will not regard it as

Chapter V: Vice and Virtue

placing us under an obligation to him. To accept favours indiscriminately and to be constantly seeking them is ignoble and the sign of a mean soul which does not mind placing itself under obligations. Unless we are driven by such dire necessity that it compels us to sacrifice our own worth, or unless we are convinced that our benefactor will not account it to us as a debt, we ought rather to suffer deprivation than accept favours, for a favour is a debt which can never be extinguished. For even if I repay my benefactor tenfold, I am still not even with him, because he has done me a kindness which he did not owe. He was the first in the field, and even if I return his gift tenfold I do so only as repayment. He will always be the one who was the first to show kindness and I can never be beforehand with him.

The man who bestows favours can do so either in order to make the recipient indebted to him or as an expression of his duty. If he makes the recipient feel a sense of indebtedness, he wounds his pride and diminishes his sense of gratitude. If he wishes to avoid this he must regard the favours he bestows as the discharge of a duty he owes to mankind, and he must not give the recipient the impression that it is a debt to be repaid. On the other hand, the recipient of the favour must still consider himself under an obligation to his benefactor and must be grateful to him. Under these conditions there can be benefactors and beneficiaries. A right-thinking man will not accept kindnesses, let alone favours. A grateful disposition is a touching thing and brings tears to our eyes on the stage, but a generous disposition is lovelier still. Ingratitude we detest to a surprising degree; even though we are not ourselves the victims of it, it angers us to such an extent that we feel inclined to intervene. But this is due to the fact that ingratitude decreases generosity.

Envy does not consist in wishing to be more happy than others—that is grudge—but in wishing to be the only one to be happy. It is this feeling which makes envy so evil. Why should not others be happy along with me? Envy shows itself also in relation to things which are scarce. Thus the Dutch, who as a nation are rather envious, once valued tulips at several hundreds of florins apiece. A rich merchant, who had one of the finest and rarest specimens, heard that another had a similar specimen. He thereupon bought it from him for 2,000 florins and trampled it underfoot, saying that he had no use for it, as he already possessed a specimen, and that he only wished that no one else should share that distinction with him. So it is also in the matter of happiness.

Malice is different. A malicious man is pleased when others suffer, he can laugh when others weep. An act which willfully brings unhappiness is cruel; when it produces physical pain it is bloodthirsty. Inhumanity is all these together, just as humanity consists in sympathy and pity, since these differentiate man from the beasts. It is difficult to explain what gives rise to a cruel disposition. It may arise when a man considers another so evilly disposed that he hates him. A man who believes himself hated by another, hates him in return, although the former may have good reason to hate him. For if a man is hated because he is selfish and has other vices, and he knows that he is hated for these reasons, he hates those who hate him although these latter do him no injustice. Thus kings who know that they are hated by their subjects become even more cruel. Equally, when a man has done a good deed to another, he knows that the other loves him, and so he loves him in return, knowing that he himself is loved. Just as love is reciprocated, so also is hate. We must for our own sakes guard against being hated by others lest we be affected by that hatred and reciprocate it. The hater is more disturbed by his hatred than is the hated.

JEALOUSY, ENVY, AND SPITE From "Jealousy, Envy, and Grudge" from *Lectures on Ethics* by Immanuel Kant, Translated by Louis Enfield (Harper & Row, 1963). Reprinted by permission of Methuen and Company Ltd.

Jen *as a Living Metaphor in the Confucian* Analects

Tu-Wei Ming

In an article surveying Chinese and Western interpretations of *jen* (humanity), Wing-tsit Chan maintains that Confucius in the *Analects* was the first to conceive of *jen* as the general virtue "which is basic, universal and the source of all specific virtues." "Although Confucius' concept of *jen* as the general virtue is unmistakable," Chan further observes, "he never defined it."[1] Chan's position that in the hierarchy of values in Confucian symbolism *jen* occupies the central position around which other cardinal virtues are ordered, although *jen* in itself is never specified, seems self-evidently true in light of traditional Chinese and Japanese exegeses.

To my knowledge, the only serious challenge to this interpretive consensus is Herbert Fingarette's focused investigation on *li* as the "holy rite" in the human community. In *Confucius—The Secular as Sacred*, Fingarette argues that the metaphor of an inner psychic life is not even a "rejected possibility" in the *Analects* and that the way of Confucius' *jen* should be understood as "where reciprocal good faith and respect are expressed through the specific forms defined in *li*."[2] The purpose of the present article is to conduct a new inquiry into *jen* as a living metaphor, while bearing in mind Fingarette's highly provocative reflections.

I. *The Rhetorical Situation.* To the modern inquirer who has been steeped in the art of argumentation, Confucius may appear to be "a prosaic and parochial moralizer," his collected sayings "an archaic irrelevance."[3] This initial response is likely to become an unreflective fixity, if the inquirer is mainly concerned with philological issues as matters of fact.[4] Needless to say, a study geared only to explicating the stylistic nuances of the original text leaves many questions unasked. And since "unasked questions are unlikely to be answered,"[5] the impression that Confucius was an outmoded ethical teacher, the study of whom is only *historically significant*,[6]

337

will remain persistent. In what sense can Confucius be understood and appreciated as, for example, in Fingarette's words, "a thinker with profound insight and with an imaginative vision of man equal in its grandeur to any I know"?[7]

To begin, I would suggest that the mode of articulation in the *Analects* is a form of what Wayne C. Booth has forcefully argued for as "the rhetoric of assent."[8] In such a rhetorical situation, the internal lines of communication are predicated on a view of human nature significantly different from that of the pseudo-scientific assertion that ideally man is a rational atomic mechanism in a universe that is value-free. Rather, the basic assumptions are as follows: human beings come into existence through symbolic interchange. We are "created in the process of sharing intentions, values, meanings; in fact more like each other than different, more valuable in our commonality than in our idiosyncrasies: not, in fact, anything at all when considered separately from our relations."[9] Viewed from this perspective, the whole world defined in terms of the polarities "individual" and "society" shifts: "even usage of words like *I, my, mine, self,* must be reconsidered, because the borderlines between the self and the other have either disappeared or shifted sharply."[10]

It is in this connection that Fingarette's perceptive observation becomes singularly pertinent:

> The images of the inner man and of his inner conflict are not essential to a concept of man as a being whose dignity is the consummation of a life of subtlety and sophistication, a life in which human conduct can be intelligible in natural terms and yet be attuned to the sacred, a life in which the practical, the intellectual and the spiritual are equally revered and are harmonized in the one act—the act of *li.*[11]

Indeed, intent on underscoring the commonality, communicability, and community of the human situation, the rhetoric of assent affirms not only the malleability of human nature but also the perfectibility of undivided selves through group sharing and mutual exhortation. Yet this is neither a license for unbridled romantic assertion nor a belief in dogmatic scientific manipulation, but an attempt to establish "a commonsensical defense of the way we naturally, inescapably, work upon each other,"[12] without resorting to the "clean linearity" of an argumentative procedure. Elsewhere, I have used the notion of "fiduciary community" as opposed to an "adversary system" in describing this kind of psychic as well as social ethos.[13]

The philosophical anthropology predicated on this rhetorical insight maintains that "man is essentially a self-making-and-remaking, symbol-manipulating [worker], an exchanger of information, a communicator, a persuader and manipulator, an inquirer."[14] The symbolic exchange wherein self-identification and group awareness in both cognitive and affective senses take place thus becomes the primary human milieu. Against this background, the dialogical encounters couched in analogical reasoning are by no means "an unsound form of the inductive argument."[15] For their persuasive power lies not in the straightness of a logical sequence devoid of emotion but in its appeal to common sense, good reasons, and a willingness to participate in the creation of sharable values.

Of course, as Wayne Booth observes, "we have no reason to assume that the world is rational in the sense of harmonizing all our 'local' values; in fact we know that at every moment it presents . . . sharp clashes among good reasons."[16] Actually, there is no assumption in the *Analects* like the one found in the objectivists' claim that "all truly reasonable men will always finally agree."[17] On the contrary, it is taken for granted that reasonable men of diverse personalities will have differing visions of the Way. As I have pointed out in my reflection on the Confucian perception of adulthood, "[s]ince the Way is not shown as a norm that establishes a fixed pattern of behavior, a person cannot measure the success or failure of his conduct in terms of the degree of approximation to an external ideal."[18] Consequently, "[e]ven among Confucius' closest disciples, the paths of self-realization are varied. Between Yen Hui's premature death and Tseng Tzu's longevity, there are numerous manifestations of adulthood."[19]

However, the multiplicity of paths in realizing the Way is not at all in conflict with the view that the pursuit of the Way necessitates a continuous process of symbolic exchange through the sharing of communally cherished values with other selves. The self as a center of relationships rather than as an isolable individual is such a fundamental premise in the *Analects* that man as "an ultimately autonomous being" is unthinkable, and the manifestation of the authentic self is impossible "except in matrices of human converse."[20]

The conversations in the *Analects* so conceived are not merely instructive sayings of the Master but intersubjectively validated ideas, communal values exemplified by life experiences of the speakers in the act of *li*. Since the act of *li* entails the participation of others, the rhetorical situation in the *Analects* is, in an existential sense, characterized not by the formula of the teacher speaking to the student but by the ethos in which the teacher answers in response to the student's concrete questioning. And the exchange as a whole echoes a deep-rooted concern, a tacit communal quest, for self-realization as a collaborative effort. Understandably, in the Confucian tradition, teaching *(chiao)* and learning *(hsüeh)* for both the teacher and the student are inseparable, indeed interchangeable.

※ ※ ※

II. *The Semiotic Structure: Jen as a Sign.* It is commonly accepted that etymologically *jen* consists of two parts, one a simple ideogram of a human figure, meaning the self, and the other with two horizontal strokes, suggesting human relations.[21] Peter Boodberg, obviously following this interpretive tradition in "Semasiology of Some Primary Confucian Concepts," proposes that *jen* be rendered as "co-humanity." And, based upon a phonological analysis of related words in ancient Chinese pronunciation, he further proposes that a root meaning of *jen* should be softness, weakness, and, I presume by implication, pliability.[22]

Boodberg's claims, far from being a novel reading of the classics, can be substantiated by the vast lore of Chinese and Japanese scholarship on the subject. In a recent study on the evolution of *jen* in pre-Confucian times, the author summarizes her findings by identifying the original meanings of *jen* in terms of two semiotic foci: (1) as the tender aspect of human feelings; namely, love and (2) as an altruistic concern for others, and, thus a mature manifestation of humanity.[23] But in either case, *jen* functions as a particular virtue, often contrasted with other equally important virtues, such as *li* (propriety), *hsin* (faithfulness), *i* (righteousness), *chih* (intelligence), and *yung* (bravery). Therefore, it is quite conceivable that 'a man of *jen* could be neither brave nor intelligent, for his tenderness may become a sign of weakness and his altruistic concern for others, an obstacle in achieving a realistic appraisal of the objective conditions.

The author then concludes that the concept of *jen* in the *Analects* seems to have been a crystallization of these two trends in the early Spring and Autumn period. In her words, the creative synthesis of Confucius skillfully integrates *jen* as *"ai-jen"* (love and care for others) and *jen* as *"ch'eng-jen"* (fully human or adult in the ethical sense).[24] Thus, in the *Analects*, *jen* is elevated to a general virtue, more embracing than any of the other core Confucian virtues. Surely, "love" remains a defining characteristic of *jen*, but as the scope of *jen* becomes qualitatively broadened, it is no longer possible to conceive of *jen* merely as a localized value. Indeed, a man of *jen* is necessarily brave and intelligent, although it is not at all impossible that a brave man or an intelligent man falls short of being a *jen* man. In a deeper sense, through the general virtue of *jen*, such values as bravery and intelligence are being transvalued. Bravery and intelligence as contributing elements in the symbolic structure of *jen* must now be understood as courage and wisdom.

Genetic reasons aside, this quantum leap of intellectual sophistication is perhaps the main reason *jen*, in the *Analects*, appears to be discouragingly complex. Methodologically, it seems that one problem is particularly germane to the complexity of the semiotic structure of *jen*: let us call it the problem of linkage. Before undertaking a brief analysis of this problem, however, it should be noted from the outset that the lack of a definitional statement about what *jen* is in itself in the *Analects* must not be construed as the Master's deliberate heuristic device to hide an esoteric truth from his students. "My friends, I know you think that there is something I am keeping from you. There is nothing at all that I keep from you. There is nothing which I do that is not shown to you, my friends" (7:23). On the contrary, Confucius seems absolutely serious in his endeavor to transmit the true

Chapter V: Vice and Virtue

sense of *jen*, as he understood and experienced it, to his students. After all, as numerous scholars have already stated, it is *jen* rather than *chih, yung,* or *li* that really features prominently and uniquely in the *Analects.*

Although Confucius "rarely spoke of profit, fate, or *jen*," (9:1) his recorded remarks on *jen* by far surpass his comments on any other virtues in the *Analects.* Of course, each recorded articulation on the subject is but a clue to the all-inclusive virtue, or in Waley's words, the "mystic entity."[25] Among the hundred and five references to *jen* in 58 out of 498 chapters of the *Analects*,[26] there are, to be sure, statements that appear to be conflicting or paradoxical assertions. A mechanistic cataloguing of these statements is not likely to develop a coherent interpretation of *jen*. A more elaborate strategy is certainly required.

First, we must not pass lightly over what seem to be only cliché virtues ascribed to those who are thought to manifest *jen*: "courteous," "diligent," "faithful," "respectful," "broad," and "kind" (13:19, 14:5, 17:6). For these traditional virtues provide the map of common sense and good reasons on which *jen* is located.[27] However, the tenderness of *jen* is also closely linked with such virtues as "brave," "steadfast," and "resolute." Accordingly only those of *jen* know how to love men and how to hate them (4:3), for the feelings of love and hate can be impartially expressed as fitting responses to concrete situations only by those who have reached the highest level of morality.[28] This is predicated on the moral principle that those who sincerely strive to become *jen* abstain from evil will (or, if you wish, hatred); as a result, they can respond to a value-laden and emotion-charged situation in a disinterested but compassionate manner. The paradox, rather than obscurity, is quite understandable in terms of Confucius' characterization of the accommodating and compromising hyperhonest villager as the spoiler of virtue (17:13). A man of *jen* refuses to tolerate evil because he has no evil will toward others; his ability to hate is thus a true indication that he has no penned up hatred in his heart.[29]

The problem of linkage is particularly pronounced when *jen* is connected with two other important concepts, *chih* and *li.* Our initial puzzlement over the precise relationship of *jen* to *chih* or *li* can be overcome, if *jen* is conceived of as a complex of attitude and disposition in which the other two important concepts are integral parts or contributing factors. In other words, *jen* is like a source in which symbolic exchange comes into existence. By implication, it is in *jen's* "field of influence"[30] that the meanings of *chih* and *li* are shaped. They in turn enrich *jen's* resourcefulness. Without stretching the point, I would suggest that the relationship of *jen* to *chih* or to *li* is analogous to the statement that "a man of *jen* certainly also possesses courage, but a brave man is not necessarily *jen*" (14:5). To be sure, in the courts of communal exchange, as exemplified in the rhetorical situation of the *Analects*, the presence of *jen* without *li* and *chih* is illegitimate. Furthermore, the examples of *li* as ritualism and *chih* as cleverness clearly indicate that *li* or *chih* without *jen*, easily degenerates into formalism or insensitivity. Thus, a man who is not *jen* can have nothing to do with *li* (3:3), because the true spirit of *li* is always grounded in *jen*.

Whether or not *jen* and *chih* are like "two wings, one supporting the other,"[31] in the Confucian ethical system, the two frequently appear as a pair (4:2, 6:21, 9:28, 12:22, 15:32, 14:30). The contrast between mountain, tranquillity, and longevity symbolizing the man of *jen* on the one hand, and water, movement, and happiness symbolizing the man of *chih*, on the other (6:21), gives one the impression that *jen* and *chih* seem to represent two equally significant styles of life. Confucius' preference, however, becomes clear when he asserts that without *jen*, a man cannot for long endure either adversity or prosperity and that those who are *jen* rest content in *jen*; those who are *chih* pursue *jen* with facility (4:2). The necessity for *jen* to sustain *chih* and the desirability for *chih* to reach *jen* is shown in a crucial passage which states that "even if a man's *chih* is sufficient for him to attain it without *jen* to hold it, he will lose it again" (15:32).

Chih in the *Analects* may occasionally be put in a negative light to mean fragmented or nonessential knowledge (15:33); sometimes the absence of *chih* can convey a sense of receptivity and flexibility (9:7), and even its opposite, *yü* (stupidity or folly), may in extraordinary situations be applauded as a demonstration of inner strength (5:20). *Jen*, by contrast, is always understood as "Goodness" (Arthur Waley), "Human-heartedness" (E. R. Hughes), "Love" (Derk Bodde), "Benevolent Love" (H. H. Dubs), "Virtue" (H. G. Creel), and "Humanity" (W. T. Chan). The practice of qualifying *jen* with such adjectives as "false" *(chia)* and "womanish," *(fu-jen chih jen)* which appear in later writings in ancient China, is completely absent in the *Analects*. In the light of the preceding discussion, it seems that, while *jen* and *chih* appear as mutually complementary virtues in Confucian symbolism, *jen* is unquestionably a more essential characterization of the Confucian Way.

Therefore, it may not be far-fetched to suggest that *jen* is in a subtle way linked up with virtually all other basic Confucian concepts. Yet its relation to any of them is neither obscure nor mystical. I believe that a systematic inquiry into each occurrence of the linkage problem should eventually yield the fruit of a coherent semiotic structure of *jen*. The matter involved is no less complex than what the scholarly tradition of *ko-i* has demonstrated. But through "matching concepts" or, more dramatically, through a series of wrestlings with the meanings of each pair of ideas in terms of comparative analysis, *jen's* true face should not be concealed for long.

At the present juncture, we may tentatively conclude: Confucius refused to grant *jen* to Tzu-lu despite his talents in political leadership and to Jan Ch'iu despite his virtuosity in state rituals (5:7); he also resisted the temptation to characterize the loyalty *(chung)* of Tzu-wen and the purity *(ch'ing)* of Ch'en Wen Tzu as *jen* (5:18), not because *jen* implies "an inner mysterious realm" but because *jen* symbolizes a holistic manifestation of humanity in its commonest and highest state of perfection.

※ ※ ※

III. *The Semantic Locus: Jen as a Symbol.* When we shift our attention from the linkage problem to focus on *jen* as a problem in itself, we are easily struck by the assurance that *jen* is immediately present if desired: "Is *jen* far away? As soon as I want it, there it is right by me" (7:29). Also, we are told that although it is difficult to find one who really loves *jen*, each person has sufficient strength to pursue its course without relying upon external help (4:6). This sense of immediacy and infallibility assumes a new shade of meaning when, in Tseng Tzu's imagery, *jen* becomes a heavy burden to be shouldered throughout one's life (8:7). Indeed, *jen* can be realized only after one has done what is difficult (6:20).

The paradoxical situation in which jen presents itself both as a given reality and as an inaccessible ideal is further complicated by a group of passages in the *Analects*, orienting our thoughts to the absolute seriousness with which *jen* is articulated. Thus, the *chün-tzu* (profound person) is instructed never to abandon *jen* "even for the lapse of a single meal;" instead, "he is never so harried but that he cleaves to this; never so tottering but that he cleaves to this" (4:5). *Jen* must come before any other consideration (4:6); it is a supreme value. more precious than one's own life and therefore an idea worth dying for (15:8).

Yet the pursuit of *jen* is never a lonely struggle. It is not a quest for inner truth or spiritual purity isolable from an "outer" or public realm; From the *jen* perspective, "a man of humanity, wishing to establish his own character, also establishes the character of others, and wishing to fully manifest himself, also helps others to fully manifest themselves. The ability to take what is near at hand as an example may be called the method of realizing *jen*" (6:28). The task of *jen*, far from being an internal, subjectivistic search for one's own individuality, depends as much on meaningful communal inquiry as on self-scrutiny.

Tseng Tzu's daily self-examination is a case in point. The effort of personal cultivation certainly suggests a spiritual-moral dimension not reducible to social considerations, but the three areas of concern—loyalty to others, faithfulness to friends and commitment to learning (1:4), are so much an integral part of the "symbolic interchange" mentioned earlier that Master Tseng's message is clearly in the realm of human relations. The self so conceived is a kind of value-creating field in which the fiduciary community exists and is realized by a tradition of selves in continuous interaction with selves. It is in this connection, I believe, that Confucius insisted that true learning be specified as learning for the sake of the self (14:25).

However, an essential characterization of *jen* impels us to go beyond the behavioristic approach, no matter how comprehensive it purports to be. In fact, the reason *jen* seems to be "surrounded with paradox and mystery in the *Analects*"[32] is also relevant here. The four-word phrase, *"ke-chi fu-li,"* wrongly rendered by Arthur Waley as "he who can himself submit to ritual,"[33] clearly shows that the attainment of *jen* involves both self-mastery and returning to ritual. The interpretation that "the man who can submit himself to *li* is *jen*" misses the point in a fundamental way.[34] And, by implication, the portrayal of *jen* as a disposition "after one has mastered the skills of action required by *li"* is probably an inadequate view of the linkage problem.[35] *Jen* is not simply "a matter of the person's deciding to submit to *li* (once he has the objective skill to do so);"[36] rather, it is a matter of inner strength and self-knowledge, symbolizing an inexhaustible source for creative communal expression.

The primacy of *jen* over *li* and the inseparability of *li* from *jen,* a thesis I tried to develop in my study *"Li* as Process of Humanization,"[37] can be substantiated by Confucius' response to Lin Fang who asked about "the foundation of *li."* After having noted the importance of the question, the Master recommended that "in ceremonies, be thrifty rather than extravagant, and in funerals, be deeply sorrowful rather than shallow in sentiment" (3:4). Obviously the emphasis is not on role performance but on "the raw stuff of humanity." Therefore, it is not at all surprising that the Master was very pleased with Tzu-hsia when he understood that "just as the painting comes from the plain groundwork, ritual comes afterwards" (3:8).

The centrality of self-mastery to the practice of *jen* can be shown in Confucius' remark that "a man who is strong, resolute, simple, and slow to speak is near to *jen*" (13:27). In fact, notwithstanding the danger of psychologizing the *Analects,* it is important to note that the text contains many ideas specifying that the mature personal stance is determined not merely by social approval but more importantly by personal integrity, as in freeing oneself from arbitrariness of opinion, dogmatism, obstinacy, and egoism (9:4). Accordingly, dispositional qualities resulting from spiritual-moral cultivation, such as cordiality, frankness, courteousness, temperance, and deference, are thought to be bases upon which proper human intercourse should be conducted (1:10). This particular concern for self improvement clearly underlies Confucius' suggestion that looking out for faults is a way of recognizing *jen* (4:7). The vigilant way of overcoming one's moral and spiritual "sickness" is nothing other than constantly "looking within" (12:4).

It is in this sense, I think, that the controversial notion of *yu* (sorrow, worry, trouble, anxiousness) in the *Analects* does signify a "subjective state" not provable or demonstratable by ordinary hard tests.[38] In fact it is a reflection of personal knowledge or inner awareness, comparable to what Michael Polanyi calls a kind of in-dwelling.[39] Surely, *yu* is related to "the notion of objective uncertainty and unsettledness with possible ominous import,"[40] but it is much more than a matter of objective comportment. The characterization that the man of *jen* is not *yu* (9:28, 14:30) suggests, at least on the surface, that *yu* is the opposite of *jen.*[41] However,

Confucius makes it clear that virtue without proper cultivation, ignorance of the task of learning, inability to change according to the words of the righteous, and failure in rectifying faults are examples of *yu* (7:3).

The context in which "the man of *jen* is not *yu*" occurs should put the issue in proper perspective. Two passages conveying essentially the same idea have a parallel syntactical structure: The wise are not perplexed; the brave are not fearful; the *jen* are not *yu*. To be sure, the brave are not fearful, but Confucius instructed the fearless Tzu-lu that his "associate must be able to approach difficulties with a sense of fear and eventually manage to succeed by strategy" (7:10). Similarly, since the person who is aware of his ignorance really knows (2:17), the wise is he who can put aside the points of which he is in doubt (2:18). Along the same line of thinking, Confucius can speak of himself as so joyful and eager in learning and teaching that he forgets *yu* and ignores the onset of old age (7:18), precisely because he is *yu* with regard to the Tao and not to his private lot (15:31).[42]

The absence of the language and imagery, of a purely psychological nature, or for that matter of a purely sociological nature, should not trouble us in the least. After all, recent developments in psychology and sociology as well as in philosophy in the West have already rendered the sharp contrast between "individual" and "society" not only undesirable but empirically unsound.

※ ※ ※

IV. *The Interpretive Task.* It should become obvious by now that "the deepest meaning of the thought of Confucius and, paradoxically, its application to our time" is yet to be discerned by a systematic and open-minded inquiry into the *Analects*. Fingarette is certainly right in concluding that "[t]he noble man who most perfectly [has] given up self, ego, obstinacy and personal pride (9:4) follows not profit but the Way."[43] Nevertheless, I cannot help wondering whether such a man, having come to fruition as a person, is really a "Holy Vessel."[44] I would rather contend that it is precisely in the recognition that "the profound person is not a vessel" (2:12) that the interpretive task of true humanity in the *Analects* begins.

Endnotes

1. Wing-tsit Chan, "Chinese and Western Interpretations of *Jen* (Humanity)," Journal of Chinese Philosophy 2 (1975); 109.
2. Herbert Fingarette, *Confucius—The Secular as Sacred* (New York: Harper & Row, 1972), p. 42.
3. Ibid., vii. Of course, Fingarette makes it clear that this initial response of his to the *Analects* was short-lived.

4. The word "philological" is used here simply to designate the methods of linguistic analysis in the Ch'ien-Chia tradition of Ch'ing scholarship. I am aware that "philology" in terms of the principles of Böckh's Philologie, signifying "the recognition of that which was once cognized," can be philosophically meaningful. I am indebted to Masao Maruyama for this insight. See his *Studies in the Intellectual History of Tokugawa Japan,* trans. Mikiso Hane (Princeton: Princeton University Press, 1974), xx.
5. Fingarette, *Confucius,* ix.
6. It is important to note that "historically significant" in the Levensonian sense is comparable to the idea of "traditionalistic," which means that the "heritage" in question has little modern relevance, because it is no longer a living tradition.
7. Fingarette, Confucius, vii.
8. Wayne C. Booth, *Modern Dogma and the Rhetoric of Assent* (Chicago: The University of Chicago Press, 1974). I am indebted to my colleague, Leonard Nathan, for calling my attention to this seminal work.
9. Ibid., p. 134.
10. Ibid. Also, cf. Fingarette, pp. 72–73.
11. Fingarette, Confucius, p. 36.
12. Booth, *Modern Dogma,* p. 141.
13. Tu Wei-ming, *Centrality and Commonality: An Essay on Chung-yung* (Honolulu: The University Press of Hawaii, 1976), pp. 52–99.
14. Booth, *Modern Dogma,* p. 136.
15. Based on Monroe C. Beardsley's *Thinking Straight: Principles of Reasoning for Readers and Writers* (Englewood Cliffs, NJ.: Prentice-Hall, 1966), pp. 130–36; 284, quoted in Booth, *Modern Dogma,* p. 141.
16. Booth, *Modern Dogma,* p. 110.
17. Ibid., p. 111.
18. Tu Wei-ming, "The Confucian Perception of Adulthood," *Daedalus* 105, no. 2 (Spring, 1976), 110.
19. Ibid., 121.
20. Booth, *Modern Dogma,* p. 132. Also, see Fingarette, *Confucius,* p. 34.
21. I am aware that this etymological reading of the sign, traceable to the Han lexicographer Hsü Shen, may itself have been influenced by the Confucian tradition. See Wing-tsit Chan, "Chinese and Western Interpretations," 108–109.
22. Peter Boodberg, "The Semasiology of Some Primary Confucian Concepts," *Philosophy East and West* 2, no. 4 (October, 1953), 317–332. For Chan's critical remarks on Boodberg's phonological analysis of *jen,* see Wing-tsit Chan, "Chinese and Western Interpretations," 125.
23. Fang Ying-hsien, "Yüan-jen lun—tzu Shih Shu chih K'ung Tzu shih-tai kuan-nien chih yen-pien," (On the origins of *jen*_the transformation of the idea from the time of the *Poetry* and the *History* to the time of Confucius) *Ta-lu tsa-chib* 52, no. 3 (March, 1976), 22–34.
24. Ibid., 33.
25. Arthur Waley, *The Analects of Confucius* (London: Allen & Unwin, 1938), p. 28.
26. Based upon Wing-tsit Chan, "Chinese and Western Interpretations," 107.
27. Cf. Fingarette, *Confucius,* p. 41.
28. Ibid., p. 40.

29. Thus, I cannot go along with Fingarette's observation that "it becomes all too evident that the concept *jen* is obscure." See ibid.
30. Booth, *Modern Dogma,* p. 126n.
31. Wing-tsit Chan, *A Source Book in Chinese Philosophy* (Princeton: Princeton University Press, 1973), p. 30.
32. Fingarette, *Confucius*, p. 37.
33. Waley, p. 162. See my critique of Waley's interpretive account, "The Creative Tension between Jen and Li," *Philosophy East and West* 18, no. 2 (April, 1968), 30–31.
34. Fingarette, *Confucius.*, p. 42.
35. Ibid., p. 51.
36. Ibid.
37. "Li as Process of Humanization," *Philosophy East and West* 22, no. 2 (April, 1972): 188.
38. Booth. *Modern Dogma,* p. 116.
39. Michael Polanyi, *Personal Knowledge: Towards a Post-Critical Philosophy* (New York: Harper & Row, 1964), pp. 173, 344, 378.
40. Fingarette, *Confucius*, p. 46.
41. Ibid., p. 43.
42. It is in this sense that I must take issue with Figarette's interpretive position, see ibid., pp. 45–47.
43. Ibid., p. 79.
44. Ibid.

The Virtues of the Superior Man[1]

Confucius

[1.1] The Master said, "Is it not pleasant to learn with a constant perseverance and application? Is it not delightful to have friends coming from distant quarters? Is he not a man of complete virtue, who feels no discomposure though men may take no note of him?"

The philosopher Yu said, "Few are those who, being filial and fraternal, are fond of offending their superiors. There have been none, who, not liking to offend their superiors, have been fond of stirring up confusion. The superior man bends his attention to the foundation. That being established, all practical courses naturally grow up. Filial piety and fraternal submission—are they not the root of all benevolent actions?"

The Master said, "Fine words and an insinuating appearance are seldom associated with true virtue."

The philosopher Tsang said, "I daily examine myself on three points: whether, in transacting business for others, I have been faithful; whether, in dealings with friends, I have been sincere; whether I have mastered and practiced the instructions of my teacher.". . .

[6] The Master said, "A youth, when at home, should be filial, and away from home he should be respectful to his elders. He should be earnest and truthful. He should overflow in love to all, and cultivate the friendship of good people. When he has time and opportunity, after the performance of these things, he should employ them in the arts."

Tsze-hsia said, "If a man withdraws his mind from the love of beauty, and applies it as sincerely to the love of the virtuous; if, in serving his parents, he can exert his utmost strength; if, in serving his prince, he can devote his life; if, in his dealings with his friends, his words are sincere although men say that he has not learned, I will certainly say that he has."

The Master said, "If the scholar is not serious, he will not call forth any veneration, and his learning will not be solid. Hold faithfulness and sincerity as first principles. Have no friends not equal to yourself. When you have faults, do not fear to abandon them."

The philosopher Tsang said, "Let there be a careful attention to perform the funeral rites to parents, and let them be followed when long gone with the ceremonies of sacrifice. Then the virtue of the people will resume its proper excellence.". . .

[14] The Master said, "He who aims to be a man of complete virtue in his food does not seek to gratify his appetite, nor in his dwelling place does he seek the appliances of ease. He is earnest in what he does, and careful in his speech. He frequents the company of men of principle that he may be rectified. Such a person may be said indeed to love to learn."

[15.17] The Master said, "The superior man considers righteousness to be essential in every thing. He performs it according to the rules of propriety. He brings it forth in humility. He completes it with sincerity. This is indeed a superior man."

The Master said, "The superior man is distressed by his lack of ability. He is not distressed by his lack of fame."

The Master said, "The superior man dislikes the thought of his name not being mentioned after his death."

[20] The Master said, "What the superior man seeks is in himself. What the inferior man seeks is in others."

The Master said, "The superior man is dignified, but does not wrangle. He is sociable, but not a partisan."

The Master said, "The superior man does not promote a man simply on account of his words, nor does he put aside good words because of the man."

Tsze-kung asked, saying, "Is there one word which may serve as a rule of practice for all one's life?" The Master said, "Is not Reciprocity[9] such a word? What you do not want done to yourself, do not do to others."

Benevolence[2]

The Master said, "Virtuous manners constitute the excellence of a neighborhood. If a man in selecting a residence does not fix on one where such manners prevail, how can he be wise?"

The Master said, "Those who are without virtue cannot abide long either in a condition of poverty and hardship, or in a condition of enjoyment. The virtuous rest in virtue; the wise desire virtue."

The Master said, "It is only the [truly] virtuous man who can love, or who can hate, others."

The Master said, "If the will is set on virtue, there will be no practice of wickedness."

[5] The Master said, "Riches and honors are what men desire. If it cannot be obtained in the proper way, they should not be held. Poverty and a low condition are what men dislike. If it cannot be obtained in the proper way, they should not be avoided. If a superior man abandons virtue, how can he fulfill the requirements of that name? The superior man does not, even for the space of a single meal, act contrary to virtue. In moments of haste, he clings to it. In seasons of danger, he clings to it."

The Master said, "I have not seen a person who loved virtue, or one who hated what was not virtuous. He who loved virtue would esteem nothing above it. He who hated what is not virtuous would practice virtue in such a way that he would not allow anything that is not virtuous to approach his person. Is any one able for one day to apply his strength to virtue? I have not seen the case in which his strength would be sufficient. Should there possibly be any such case, I have not seen it."

The Actions of Filial Piety[3]

The sovereign king orders the chief minister to send down his lessons of virtue to the millions of the people . . .

[4] [After getting properly] dressed [in the morning], [sons] should go to their parents and parents-in-law."[11] On getting to where they are, with bated breath and gentle voice they should ask if their clothes are too warm or too cold, whether they are ill or pained, or uncomfortable in any part. If they are, they should proceed reverently to stroke and scratch the place. They should in the same way, going before or following after, help and support their parents in leaving or entering the apartment. In bringing in the basin for them to wash, the younger will carry the stand and the elder the water. They will beg to be allowed to pour out the water, and when the washing is concluded, they will hand them the towel. They will ask whether they want anything, and then respectfully bring it. All this they will do with an appearance of pleasure to make their parents feel at ease. They should bring gruel, thick or thin, spirits or juice, soup with vegetables, beans, wheat, spinach, rice, millet, maize, and glutinous millet— whatever they wish, in fact. They should bring dates, chestnuts, sugar and honey to sweeten their dishes; the ordinary or the large-leaved violets, leaves of elm-trees, fresh or dry, and the most soothing rice-water to lubricate them; and fat and oil to enrich them. The parents will be sure to taste them, and when they have done so, the young people should withdraw . . .

From the time that sons receive an official appointment,[12] they and their father occupy different parts of their residence. But at dawn, the son will pay his respects, and express his affection by the offer of pleasant delicacies. At sunrise he will retire, and he and his father will attend to their

Chapter V: Vice and Virtue

different duties. At sundown, the son will pay his evening visit in the same way....

[10] While the parents are both alive, at their regular meals, morning and evening, the eldest son and his wife will encourage them to eat everything, and what is left after all, they themselves will eat. When the father is dead, and the mother still alive, the eldest son should wait upon her at her meals. The wives of the other sons will do with what is left as in the former case. The children should have the sweet, soft and oily things that are left.

When sons and their wives are ordered to do anything by their parents, they should immediately respond and reverently proceed to do it. In going forward or backward, or turning round, they should be careful and serious. While going out or coming in, while bowing or walking, they should not presume to belch, sneeze, or cough, to yawn or stretch themselves, to stand on one foot, or to lean against anything, or to look askance. They should not dare to spit or snivel, nor if it is cold to put on more clothes, nor if they itch anywhere, to scratch themselves. Unless for reverent attention to something, they should not presume to bare their [parents'] shoulders or chest. Unless it be in wading, they should not hold up their clothes. Of their private dress and coverlet, they should not display the inside. They should not allow the spittle or snivel of their parents to be seen. They should ask leave to rinse away any dirt on their caps or girdles, and to wash their clothes that are dirty with lye that has been prepared for the purpose; and to stitch together, with needle and thread, any tear....

Sons and sons' wives, who are filial and reverential, when they receive an order from their parents should not refuse or delay executing it. When their parents give them anything to eat or drink, which they do not like, they will nevertheless taste it and wait for their further orders. When they give them clothes which are not to their liking, they will put them on, and wait in the same way. If their parents give them anything to do, and then employ another to take their place, although they do not like the arrangement, they will in the meantime give it into his hands and let him do it, doing it again if it is not done well....

When sons and their wives have not been filial and reverential, the parents should not be angry and resentful with them, but endeavor to instruct them. If they will not receive instruction, they should then be angry with them. If that anger does no good, they can then drive out the son, and send the wife away, yet not publicly showing why they have treated them so.

[15] If a parent has a fault, the son should with bated breath, and bland aspect, and gentle voice, admonish him. If the admonition does not take effect, he will be more reverential and more filial; and when the father seems pleased, he will repeat the admonition. If he should be displeased with this, rather than allow him to commit an offense against anyone in the

neighborhood or countryside, the son should strongly protest. If the parent is angry and more displeased, and beat him till the blood flows, he should not presume to be angry and resentful, but be still more reverential and more filial.

The Attitude of Filial Piety[4]

[2.5] Mang asked what filial piety was. The Master said, "It is 'not being disobedient.'" Soon after, as Fan Ch'ih was driving him, the Mister told him, saying, "Mang-sun asked me what filial piety was, and I answered him—'not being disobedient." Fan Ch'ih said, "What did you mean?" The Master replied, "That parents, when alive, should be served according to propriety; that, when dead, they should be buried according to propriety; and that they should be sacrificed to according to propriety."

Mang Wu asked what filial piety was. The Master said, "Do not make your parents anxious about anything else than your being sick."

Tsze-yu asked what filial piety was. The Master said, "Filial piety nowadays means the support of one's parents. But dogs and horses likewise are able to do something in the way of support. Without reverence, what is there to distinguish the one support given from the other?"

Tsze-hsia asked what filial piety was. The Master said, "The difficulty is with the countenance. When their elders have any troublesome affairs and the young do their work, and when the young have plenty of wine and food to set before their elders, how can this be considered filial piety?"

[4.18] The Master said, "In serving his parents, a son may protest to them, but gently; when he sees that they do not incline to follow his advice, he shows an increased degree of reverence, but does not abandon his purpose; and should they punish him, he does not allow himself to murmur."

The Master said, "While his parents are alive, the son may not leave his home area to a far distance. If he does go away, he must have a fixed place to which he goes."[13]

[20] The Master said, "If the son for three years[14] does not alter from the way of his father, he may be called filial."

The Master said, "The age of one's parents should always be kept in the memory, as an reason for joy and for fear."

[13.18] The duke of Sheh informed Confucius, saying, "Among us here are those who may be styled upright in their conduct. If their father stole a sheep, they will bear witness to the fact." Confucius said, "Among us, in our part of the country, those who are upright are different from this. The father conceals the misconduct of the son, and the son conceals the misconduct of the father. Uprightness is to be found in this."

Propriety[5]

The Master said, "If a man lacks the virtues proper to humanity, what has he to do with the rites of propriety? If a man is without the virtues proper to humanity, what has he to do with music?"

Lin Fang asked what was the first thing to be attended to in ceremonies. The Master said, "A great question indeed! In festive ceremonies, it is better to be sparing than extravagant. In the ceremonies of mourning, it is better that there be deep sorrow than a minute attention to observances.". . .

[8] Tsze-hsia asked, "What is the meaning of the passage, 'The pretty dimples of her artful smile! The well-defined black and white of her eye! The plain ground for the colors'?"[15] The Master said, "The business of laying on the colors follows [the preparation of] the plain ground." "Ceremonies then are a subsequent thing?" The Master said, "It is you, Shang, who can bring out my meaning. Now I can begin to talk about the Odes with you."

The Master said, "I could describe the ceremonies of the Hsia dynasty, but Chi cannot sufficiently attest my words. I could describe the ceremonies of the Yin dynasty, but Sung cannot sufficiently attest my words. [They can not do so] because of the insufficiency of their records and wise men. If those were sufficient, I could adduce them in support of my words.". . .

[12] He sacrificed to the dead as if they were present.[16] He sacrificed to the spirits as if the spirits were present. The Master said, "I consider my not being present at the sacrifice as if I did not sacrifice."

Wang-sun Chia asked, "What is the meaning of the saying, 'It is better to pay court to the furnace than to the southwest corner'?"[17] The Master said, "Not so. He who offends against Heaven has none to whom he can pray."

The Master said, "Chou had the advantage of viewing the two past dynasties. How complete and elegant are its regulations! I follow Chou."

[15] The Master, when he entered the Grand Temple,[18] asked about everything. Someone said, "Who says that the son of the man of Tsau knows the rules of propriety! He has entered the grand temple and asks about everything." The Master heard the remark, and said, "This [behavior of mine] is indeed a rule of propriety.". . .

[17] Tzu-kung wished to do away with the offering of a sheep connected with the inauguration of the first day of each month. The Master said, "Tzu, you love the sheep; I love the ceremony."[19]

The Master said, "The full observance of the rules of propriety in serving one's prince is accounted by people to be flattery."

The duke Ting asked how a prince should employ his ministers, and how ministers should serve their prince. Confucius replied, "A prince should employ his minister according to the rules of propriety; ministers should serve their prince with faithfulness."

The Way[6]

Confucius said, "When good government prevails in the empire, ceremonies, music, and punitive military expeditions proceed from the son of Heaven. When bad government prevails in the empire, ceremonies, music, and punitive military expeditions proceed from the princes. When these things proceed from the princes, as a rule, the cases will be few in which they do not lose their power in ten generations. When they proceed from the great officers of the princes, as a rule, the cases will be few in which they do not lose their power in five generations. When the subsidiary ministers of the great officers hold in their grasp the orders of the state, as a rule, the cases will be few in which they do not lose their power in three generations. When right principles prevail in the kingdom, government will not be in the hands of the great officers. When right principles prevail in the kingdom, there will be no discussions among the common people."

The Love of Learning[7]

The Master said, "Yu, have you heard the six words to which are attached six faults?" Yu replied, "I have not." "Sit down, and I will tell them to you. There is the love of being benevolent without the love of learning; the fault here leads to a foolish simplicity. There is the love of knowing without the love of learning; the fault here leads to dissipation of mind. There is the love of being sincere without the love of learning; the fault here leads to an injurious disregard of consequences. There is the love of straightforwardness without the love of learning; the fault here leads to rudeness. There is the love of boldness without the love the learning; the fault here leads to insubordination. There is the love of firmness without the love of learning; the fault here leads to extravagant conduct."

The Master said, "My children, why do you not study the *Book of Poetry?* The Odes serve to stimulate the mind. They may be used for purposes of self-contemplation. They teach the art of sociability. They show how to regulate feelings of resentment. From them you learn the more immediate duty of serving one's father, and the remoter duty of serving one's prince. From them we become largely acquainted with the names of birds, beasts, and plants.". . .

[12] The Master said, "He who puts on an appearance of stern firmness, while inwardly he is weak, is like one of the small, common people. Yes, is he not like the thief who breaks through, or climbs over, a wall?"

Endnotes

1. Analects I.I–4, 69, 14; 15.17–23
2. Analects 4.1–6
3. Analects 3.3–4, 8–9, 12–15, 17–19
4. Classic of Rites 10.1, 4, 7, 10–11, 13–15
5. Analects 2.5–9; 4.18–21; 13.18
6. Analects 16.2
7. Analects 17.8–9, 12
9. *Reciprocity*: the virtue *shu*.
10. Taken with editing, from James Legge, trans., *The Sacred Books of China: The Texts of Confucianism,* part 3, *Sacred Books of the East,* vol. 27 (Oxford, Oxford University Press, 1885), pp. 449–457.
11. The passage presupposes that one's parents have an apartment or room in one's house, typically the case in traditional China.
12. *official appointment*: in a government position.
13. *a fixed place:* so his parents know where he is.
14. *for three years:* after the death of the father.
15. A poem from the *Odes.*
16. A traditional saying.
17. A traditional saying, meaning that it is better to serve the gods of food than the ancestral spirits of the shrine (at the southwest corner of the Chinese house).
18. *the Grand Temple:* in the state of Lu.
19. Also translated, "Tzu, you love the sheep, but I love the sacrifice."

The Virtues in Heroic Societies

Alasdair MacIntyre

The word *aretê*, which later comes to be translated as 'virtue,' is in the Homeric poems used for excellence of any kind; a fast runner displays the *aretê* of his feet (*Iliad* 20.411) and a son excels in his father in every kind of *aretê*—as athlete, as soldier and in mind (*Iliad* 15.642). This concept of virtue or excellence is more alien to us than we are apt at first to recognise. It is not difficult for us to recognise the central place that strength will have in such a conception of human excellence or the way in which courage will be one of the central virtues, perhaps the central virtue. What is alien to our conception of virtue is the intimate connection in heroic society between the concept of courage and its allied virtues on the other hand and the concepts of friendship, fate and death on the other.

Courage is important, not simply as a quality of individuals, but as the quality necessary to sustain a household and a community. *Kudos*, glory, belongs to the individual who excels in battle or in contest as a mark of recognition by his household and his community. Other qualities linked to courage also merit public recognition because of the part they play in sustaining the public order. In the Homeric poems cunning is such a quality because cunning may have its achievements where courage is lacking or courage fails. In the Icelandic sagas a wry sense of humour is closely bound up with courage. In the saga account of the battle of Clontarf in 1014, where Brian Boru defeated a Viking army, one of the norsemen, Thorstein, did not flee when the rest of his army broke and ran, but remained where he was, tying his shoestring. An Irish leader, Kerthialfad, asked him why he was not running. 'I couldn't get home tonight,' said Thorstein. 'I live in Iceland.' Because of the joke, Kerthialfad spared his life.

To be courageous is to be someone on whom reliance can be placed. Hence courage is an important ingredient in friendship. The bonds of friendship in heroic societies are modelled on those of kinship. Sometimes friendship is formally vowed, so that by the vow the duties of brothers are mutually incurred. Who my friends are and who my enemies, is as clearly defined as who my kinsmen are. The other ingredient of friendship is

Chapter V: Vice and Virtue

fidelity. My friend's courage assures me of his power to aid me and my household; my friend's fidelity assures me of his will. My household's fidelity is the basic guarantee of its unity. So in women, who constitute the crucial relationships within the household, fidelity is the key virtue. Andromache and Hector, Penelope and Odysseus are friends *(philos)* as much as are Achilles and Patroclus.

What I hope this account makes clear already is the way in which any adequate account of the virtues in heroic society would be impossible which divorced them from their context in its social structure, just as no adequate account of the social structure of heroic society would be possible which did not include an account of the heroic virtues. But to put it this way is to understate the crucial point: morality and social structure are in fact one and the same in heroic society. There is only one set of social bonds. Morality as something distinct does not yet exist. Evaluative questions *are* questions of social fact. It is for this reason that Homer speaks always of *knowledge* of what to do and how to judge. Nor are such questions difficult to answer, except in exceptional cases. For the given rules which assign men their place in the social order and with it their identity also prescribe what they owe and what is owed to them and how they are to be treated and regarded if they fail and how they are to treat and regard others if those others fail.

Without such a place in the social order, a man would not only be incapable of receiving recognition and response from others; not only would others not know, but he would not himself know who he was. It is precisely because of this that heroic societies commonly have a well-defined status to which any stranger who arrives in the society from outside can be assigned. In Greek the word for 'alien' and the word for 'guest' are the same word. A stranger has to be received with hospitality, limited but well-defined. When Odysseus encounters the Cyclopes the question as to whether they possess *themis* (the Homeric concept of *themis* is the concept of customary law shared by all civilised peoples) is to be answered by discovering how they treat strangers. In fact they eat them—that is, for them strangers have no recognised human identity.

We might thus expect to find in heroic societies an emphasis upon the contrast between the expectations of the man who not only possesses courage and its allied virtues, but who also has kinsmen and friends on the one hand and the man lacking all these on the other. Yet one central theme of heroic societies is also that death waits for both alike. Life is fragile, men are vulnerable and it is of the essence of the human situation that they are such. For in heroic societies life is the standard of value. If someone kills you, my friend or brother, I owe you their death and when I have paid my debt to you their friend or brother owes them my death. The more extended my system of kinsmen and friends, the more liabilities I shall incur of a kind that may end in my death.

357

Moreover there are powers in the world which no one can control. Human life is invaded by passions which appear sometimes as impersonal forces, sometimes as gods. Achilles' wrath disrupts Achilles as well as his relationship to the other Greeks. These forces and the rules of kinship and friendship together constitute patterns of an ineluctable kind. Neither willing nor cunning will enable anyone to evade them. Fate is a social reality and the descrying of fate an important social role. It is no accident that the prophet or the seer flourishes equally in Homeric Greece, in saga Iceland and in pagan Ireland.

The man therefore who does what he ought moves steadily towards his fate and his death. It is defeat and not victory that lies at the end. To understand this is itself a virtue; indeed it is a necessary part of courage to understand this. But what is involved in such understanding? What would have been understood if the connections between courage, friendship, fidelity, the household, fate and death had been grasped? Surely that human life has a determinate form, the form of a certain kind of story. It is not just that poems and sagas narrate what happens to men and women, but that in their narrative form poems and sagas capture a form that was already present in the lives which they relate.

'What is character but the determination of incident?' wrote Henry James. 'What is incident but the illustration of character?' But in heroic society character of the relevant kind can only be exhibited in a succession of incidents and the succession itself must exemplify certain patterns. Where heroic society agrees with James is that character and incident cannot be characterised independently of each other. So to understand courage as a virtue is not just to understand how it may be exhibited in character, but also what place it can have in a certain kind of enacted story. For courage in heroic society is a capacity not just to face particular harms and dangers but to face a particular kind of pattern of harms and dangers, a pattern in which individual lives find their place and which such lives in turn exemplify.

What epic and saga then portray is a society which already embodies the form of epic or saga. Its poetry articulates its form of individual and social life. To say this is still to leave open the question of whether there ever were such societies; but it does suggest that if there were such societies they could only be adequately understood through their poetry. Yet epic and saga are certainly not simple mirror images of the society they profess to portray. For it is quite clear that the poet or the saga writer claims for himself a kind of understanding which is denied to the characters about whom he writes. The poet does not suffer from the limitations which define the essential condition of his characters. Consider especially the *Iliad*.

As I said earlier of heroic society in general, the heroes in the *Iliad* do not find it difficult to know what they owe one another, they feel *aidôs*—

Chapter V: Vice and Virtue

a proper sense of shame—when confronted with the possibility of wrongdoing, and if that is not sufficient, other people are always at hand to drive home the accepted view. Honour is conferred by one's peers and without honour a man is without worth. There is indeed in the vocabulary available to Homer's characters no way for them to view their own culture and society as if from the outside. The evaluative expressions which they employ are mutually interdefined and each has to be explained in terms of the others.

Let me use a dangerous, but illuminating analogy. The rules which govern both action and evaluative judgment in the *Iliad* resemble the rules and the precepts of a game such as chess. It is a question of fact whether a man is a good chess player, whether he is good at devising end-game strategies, whether a move is the right move to make in a particular situation. The game of chess presupposes, indeed is partially constituted by, agreement on how to play chess. Within the vocabulary of chess it makes no sense to say 'That was the one and only move which would achieve checkmate, but was it the right move to make?' And therefore someone who said this and understood what he was saying would have to be employing some notion of 'right' which receives its definition from outside chess, as someone might ask this whose purpose in playing chess was to amuse a small child rather than to win.

One reason why the analogy is dangerous is that we do play games such as chess for a variety of purposes. But there is nothing to be made of the question: for what purpose do the characters in the *Iliad* observe the rules that they observe and honour the precepts which they honour? It is rather the case that it is only within their framework of rules and precepts that they are able to frame purposes at all; and just because of this the analogy breaks down in another way, too. All questions of choice arise within the framework; the framework itself therefore cannot be chosen.

There is thus the sharpest of contrasts between the emotivist self of modernity and the self of the heroic age. The self of the heroic age lacks precisely that characteristic which we have already seen that some modern moral philosophers take to be an essential characteristic of human selfhood: the capacity to detach oneself from any particular standpoint or point of view, to step backwards, as it were, and view and judge that standpoint or point of view from the outside. In heroic society there is no 'outside' except that of the stranger. A man who tried to withdraw himself from his given position in heroic society would be engaged in the enterprise of trying to make himself disappear.

Identity in heroic society involves particularity and accountability. I am answerable for doing or failing to do what anyone who occupies my role owes to others and this accountability terminates only with death. I have until my death to do what I have to do. Moreover this accountability is particular. It is to, for and with specific individuals that I must do what I ought, and it is to these same and other individuals, members of the same local community, that I am accountable. The heroic self does not itself aspire to universality even although in retrospect we may recognise universal worth in the achievements of that self.

The exercise of the heroic virtues thus requires both a particular kind of human being and a particular kind of social structure. Just because this is so, an inspection of the heroic virtues may at first sight appear irrelevant to any general enquiry into moral theory and practice. If the heroic virtues require for their exercise the presence of a kind of social structure which is now irrevocably lost—as they do—what relevance can they possess for us? Nobody now can be a Hector or a Gisli. The answer is that perhaps what we have to learn from heroic societies is twofold: first that all morality is always to some degree tied to the socially local and particular and that the aspirations of the morality of modernity to a universality freed from all particularity is an illusion; and secondly that there is no way to possess the virtues except as part of a tradition in which we inherit them and our understanding of them from a series of predecessors in which series heroic societies hold first place. . . .

From *After Virtue: A Study in Moral Philosophy* by Alasdair MacIntyre. Copyright © 1981, by University of Notre Dame Press, Notre Dame, Indiana 46556. Reprinted by permission.

Habit and Virtue

Aristotle

Virtues of Character in General

How a Virtue of Character is Acquired

Virtue, then, is of two sorts, virtue of thought and virtue of character. Virtue of thought arises and grows mostly from teaching, and hence needs experience and time. Virtue of character [i.e. of *ethos*] results from habit [*ethos*]; hence its name "ethical," slightly varied from "*ethos*."

Virtue comes about, not by a process of nature, but by habituation

Hence it is also clear that none of the virtues of character arises in us naturally.

(1) What is natural cannot be changed by habituation

For if something is by nature [in one condition], habituation cannot bring it into another condition. A stone, e.g., by nature moves downwards, and habituation could not make it move upwards, not even if you threw it up ten thousand times to habituate it; nor could habituation make fire move downwards, or bring anything that is by nature in one condition into another condition.

Thus the virtues arise in us neither by nature nor against nature, but we are by nature able to acquire them, and reach our complete perfection through habit.

(2) Natural capacities are not acquired by habituation

Further, if something arises in us by nature, we first have the capacity for it, and later display the activity. This is clear in the case of the senses; for we did not acquire them by frequent seeing or hearing, but already had them when we exercised them, and did not get them by exercising them.

Virtues, by contrast, we acquire, just as we acquire crafts, by having previously activated them. For we learn a craft by producing the same product that we must produce when we have learned it, becoming builders, e.g., by building and harpists by playing the harp; so also, then, we become just by doing just actions, temperate by doing temperate actions, brave by doing brave actions.

(3) Legislators concentrate on habituation

What goes on in cities is evidence for this also. For the legislator makes the citizens good by habituating them, and this is the wish of every legislator; if he fails to do it well he misses his goal. [The right] habituation is what makes the difference between a good political system and a bad one.

(4) Virtue and vice are formed by good and bad actions

Further, just as in the case of a craft, the sources and means that develop each virtue also ruin it. For playing the harp makes both good and bad harpists, and it is analogous in the case of builders and all the rest; for building well makes good builders, building badly, bad ones. If it were not so, no teacher would be needed, but everyone would be born a good or a bad craftsman.

It is the same, then, with the virtues. For actions in dealings with [other] human beings make some people just, some unjust; actions in terrifying situations and the acquired habit of fear or confidence make some brave and others cowardly. The same is true of situations involving appetites and anger; for one or another sort of conduct in these situations makes some people temperate and gentle, others intemperate and irascible.

Conclusion: The importance of habituation

To sum up, then, in a single account: A state [of character] arises from [the repetition of] similar activities. Hence we must display the right activities, since differences in these imply corresponding differences in the states. It is not unimportant, then, to acquire one sort of habit or another, right from our youth; rather, it is very important, indeed all-important.

Chapter V: Vice and Virtue

What is the right sort of habituation?

This is an appropriate question, for the aim of ethical theory is practical

Our present inquiry does not aim, as our others do, at study; for the purpose of our examination is not to know what virtue is, but to become good, since otherwise the inquiry would be of no benefit to us. Hence we must examine the right way to act, since, as we have said, the actions also control the character of the states we acquire.

First, then, actions should express correct reason. That is a common [belief], and let us assume it; later we will say what correct reason is and how it is related to the other virtues.

But let us take it as agreed in advance that every account of the actions we must do has to be stated in outline, not exactly. As we also said at the start, the type of accounts we demand should reflect the subject-matter; and questions about actions and expediency, like questions about health, have no fixed [and invariable answers].

And when our general account is so inexact, the account of particular cases is all the more inexact. For these fall under no craft or profession, and the agents themselves must consider in each case what the opportune action is, as doctors and navigators do.

The account we offer, then, in our present inquiry is of this inexact sort; still, we must try to offer help.

The right sort of habituation must avoid excess and deficiency

First, then, we should observe that these sorts of states naturally tend to be ruined by excess and deficiency. We see this happen with strength and health, which we mention because we must use what is evident as a witness to what is not. For both excessive and deficient exercises ruin strength; and likewise, too much or too little eating or drinking ruins health, while the proportionate amount produces, increases and preserves it.

The same is true, then, of temperance, bravery and the other virtues. For if, e.g., someone avoids and is afraid of everything, standing firm against nothing, he becomes cowardly, but if he is afraid of nothing at all and goes to face everything, he becomes rash. Similarly, if he gratifies himself with every pleasure and refrains from none, he becomes intemperate, but if he avoids them all, as boors do, he becomes some sort of insensible person. Temperance and bravery, then, are ruined by excess and deficiency but preserved by the mean.

The same actions, then, are the sources and causes both of the emergence and growth of virtues and of their ruin; but further, the activities of the virtues will be found in these same actions. For this is also true of more evident cases, e.g. strength, which arises from eating a lot and from withstanding much hard labour, and it is the strong person who is most able to do these very things. It is the same with the virtues. Refraining from pleasures makes us become temperate, and when we have become temperate we are most able to refrain from pleasures. And it is similar with bravery; habituation in disdaining what is fearful and in standing firm against it makes us become brave, and when we have become brave we shall be most able to stand firm.

Pleasure and pain are important in habituation

But [actions are not enough]; we must take as a sign of someone's state his pleasure or pain in consequence of his action. For if someone who abstains from bodily pleasures enjoys the abstinence itself, then he is temperate, but if he is grieved by it, he is intemperate. Again, if he stands firm against terrifying situations and enjoys it, or at least does not find it painful, then he is brave, and if he finds it painful, he is cowardly.

[Pleasures and pains are appropriately taken as signs] because virtue of character is concerned with pleasures and pains.

Virtue is concerned with pleasure and pain

(1) For it is pleasure that causes us to do base actions, and pain that causes us to abstain from fine ones. Hence we need to have had the appropriate upbringing—right from early youth, as Plato says—to make us find enjoyment or pain in the right things; for this is the correct education.

(2) Further, virtues are concerned with actions and feelings; but every feeling and every action implies pleasure or pain; hence, for this reason too, virtue is concerned with pleasures and pains.

(3) Corrective treatment [for vicious actions] also indicates [the relevance of pleasure and pain], since it uses pleasures and pains; it uses them because such correction is a form of medical treatment and medical treatment naturally operates through contraries.

(4) Further, as we said earlier, every state of soul is naturally related to and concerned with whatever naturally makes it better or worse; and pleasures and pains make people worse, from pursuing and avoiding the wrong ones, at the wrong time, in the wrong ways, or whatever other distinctions of that sort are needed in an account.

These [bad effects of pleasure and pain] are the reason why people actually define the virtues as ways of being unaffected and undisturbed [by pleasures and pains]. They are wrong, however, because they speak [of being unaffected] unconditionally, not of being unaffected in the right or wrong way, at the right or wrong time, and the added specifications.

We assume, then, that virtue is the sort of state [with the appropriate specifications] that does the best actions concerned with pleasures and

Chapter V: Vice and Virtue

pains, and that vice is the contrary. The following points will also make it evident that virtue and vice are concerned with the same things.

(5) There are three objects of choice—fine, expedient and pleasant—and three objects of avoidance—their contraries, shameful, harmful and painful. About all these, then, the good person is correct and the bad person is in error, and especially about pleasure. For pleasure is shared with animals, and implied by every object of choice, since what is fine and what is expedient appear pleasant as well.

(6) Further, since pleasure grows up with all of us from infancy on, it is hard to rub out this feeling that is dyed into our lives; and we estimate actions as well [as feelings], some of us more, some less, by pleasure and pain. Hence, our whole inquiry must be about these, since good or bad enjoyment or pain is very important for our actions.

(7) Moreover, it is harder to fight pleasure than to fight emotion, [though that is hard enough], as Heracleitus says. Now both craft and virtue are concerned in every case with what is harder, since a good result is even better when it is harder. Hence, for this reason also, the whole inquiry, for virtue and political science alike, must consider pleasures and pains; for if we use these well, we shall be good, and if badly, bad.

In short, virtue is concerned with pleasures and pains; the actions that are its sources also increase it or, if they are done differently, ruin it; and its activity is concerned with the same actions that are its sources.

But our claims about habituation raise a puzzle: How can we become good without being good already?

However, someone might raise this puzzle: "What do you mean by saying that to become just we must first do just actions and to become temperate we must first do temperate actions? For if we do what is grammatical or musical, we must already be grammarians or musicians. In the same way, then, if we do what is just or temperate, we must already be just or temperate."

First reply: Conformity versus understanding

But surely this is not so even with the crafts, for it is possible to produce something grammatical by chance or by following someone else's instructions. To be a grammarian, then, we must both produce something grammatical and produce it in the way in which the grammarian produces it, i.e. expressing grammatical knowledge that is in us.

Second reply: Crafts versus virtues

Moreover, in any case what is true of crafts is not true of virtues. For the products of a craft determine by their own character whether they have been produced well; and so it suffices that they are in the right state when they have been produced. But for actions expressing virtue to be done temperately or justly [and hence well] it does not suffice that they are themselves in the right state. Rather, the agent must also be in the right state when he does them. First, he must know [that he is doing virtuous actions]; second, he must decide on them, and decide on them for themselves; and, third, he must also do them from a firm and unchanging state.

As conditions for having a craft these three do not count, except for the knowing itself. As a condition for having a virtue, however, the knowing counts for nothing, or [rather] for only a little, whereas the other two conditions are very important, indeed all-important. And these other two conditions are achieved by the frequent doing of just and temperate actions.

Hence actions are called just or temperate when they are the sort that a just or temperate person would do. But the just and temperate person is not the one who [merely] does these actions, but the one who also does them in the way in which just or temperate people do them.

It is right, then, to say that a person comes to be just from doing just actions and temperate from doing temperate actions; for no one has even a prospect of becoming good from failing to do them.

Virtue requires habituation, and therefore requires practice, not just theory

The many, however, do not do these actions but take refuge in arguments, thinking that they are doing philosophy, and that this is the way to become excellent people. In this they are like a sick person who listens attentively to the doctor, but acts on none of his instructions. Such a course of treatment will not improve the state of his body; any more than will the many's way of doing philosophy improve the state of their souls.

ID VIRTUE From *Nicomachean Ethics* by Aristotle. Translated by Terence Irwin (Indianapolis, IN: Hackett, 1985), pp. 33–40. Reprinted by permission of the publisher.

Courage

Jean-Louis Servan-Schreiber

There are only two important kinds of courage: the courage to die and the courage to get up in the morning. All other courage stems from these or is inspired by them. But, with or without courage, we cannot avoid facing either death or a new day. They are moments from which there is no escape. So why do we need courage? What difference does it make, since these two events are in fact unavoidable?

Death awaits the condemned, both he who is dragged, trembling and sobbing, to the scaffold, and he who patriotically proclaims, "Give me Liberty, or give me Death!" It was not in dying that Nathan Hale displayed great courage, it was in choosing to face up to it, to exist fully to the very end. The difference may seem slight, but it is crucial. Nathan Hale lived the last minute of his life *better*.

Courage allows us to live better, not only our last minute better, but even more important, every minute and day that went before. Courage plays a part in everything we do, even when we aren't aware of it.

There are cases where the absence of courage makes all the difference. Raoul Dautry, a member of the Cabinet of the Third French Republic, told how, one day in 1938, when he was in Germany for the dedication of a new dam, he found himself standing behind Adolf Hitler on the edge of a hundred-and-fifty-foot-high concrete wall. "Shall I push him over?" he asked himself. But he didn't have the nerve. Of course, he would have been shot down by storm troopers, but his death would probably have forestalled millions of others. Who, though, can reproach him for failing to act? None of us can swear that, in his place, we would have had the immediate courage to shove the Führer into the void.

A more commonplace incident: I am riding a train when I see a woman who attracts me. I want to talk with her, but my nerve fails me. A few moments later, she gets out and the chance is gone. No courage, nothing happens.

We could say that courage has two different aspects. When we are faced with the inevitable, such as when we confront death, it determines our attitude; when we confront daily uncertainty, it conditions the outcome. But are these two aspects of courage so different? We can only speak of courage when in situations where we can make a choice. But, like Nathan Hale, even facing death we still have a choice, our way of facing it.

All that follows in this book will confirm that we cannot take action without courage. And since we are constantly moving from one action to another without any awareness that we are especially endowed with courage, then, plainly, courage can be there without our being aware of it.

When I get up in the morning after only three hours sleep, it demands a bit—however small—of courage. But if it is in order to start on an exciting trip, I get myself into the bathroom without much trouble. It took some small piece of courage to overcome being tired, but my high motivation, much more powerful, made me unaware of it.

Traditionally, courage has been seen as a moral or spiritual virtue, often with military connotations. This was the courage celebrated by the ancient Greeks, typified by Achilles. Later our civilization had the Captains Courageous, facing a storm at sea; Joan of Arc climbing the ramparts of Orléans; John Wayne in *The Alamo* falling, outnumbered, while firing his last round. All folklore of the past, which has played a part in relegating courage to the shelf of spare parts, no longer in demand . . .

But the courage of which we have daily need has little to do with the courage of Joan of Arc. Without either special merit or vainglory, *it's a matter of leading my life in the best possible way, even when there is no witness but myself.* So it is not a moralizing kind of courage I need, it is a psychological wellspring, necessary to my existence.

Just lately, after her son had committed suicide, one of my friends found the note he had left behind. "Mother, you didn't tell me that it takes courage to live." All of our generation have cherished the hope that progress, prosperity, technology, a more just and better organized world, would make courage—which we instinctively couple with trials, tribulations, and fatality—a virtue of times gone by.

And not unreasonably. The great wars were far behind us. The last battles of Victorian ethics had been dynamited by protesting students in the 1960s. Education floundered in a psychoanalytical soup, presenting the individual as the end-product of his instincts and his unconscious. If anyone was at fault it was our parents, or society.

In trying to forget centuries of poverty and constraints, we thought we had no more need of old-fashioned virtues such as will, effort, discipline, and courage.

Psychologists, therapists, and teachers hardly dared to pronounce any of these words unless they be taken for old-fashioned fools. And not illogically. The hope that a revolution would better everything at once was a constant of our times. The spread of the gospel according to Freud, antibiotics, and supermarkets led us to hope for uncomplicated happiness. The

Chapter V: Vice and Virtue

"Death of History," and its painful reminders of our past, was even spoken of, as if we could do without a past.

But times, and our mood, changed again. The economic recessions of the 1970s don't explain it all. In fact, the ninety percent of the population not unemployed suffered only a slight decline in its personal income. But it was enough to signal that progress had come to an end.

Only five years elapsed between the naive slogan "Anything Goes" and the shock of the oil crisis. There were brutal disappointments. The system didn't work. Economists were running out of answers. The bureaucracy of government did not respond to change, and our future seemed uncertain. The dogma of our century, that social remedies ensure us protection from uncertainty and bad luck, began to waver. On the heels of our new idealism came an old saying, "Heaven helps those who help themselves." Our economic woes have led to another and deeper, although implicit, conclusion. *Progress hasn't altered Man's fate, the human condition.*

Modern life puts us up against some of the same problems as those Shakespeare faced. And so we now seek out and dust off the lifejacket we had so hastily thrown away; once more we take an interest in will, effort, and courage.

Many of the ideas voiced here may seem as old as the world, which indeed they are. But although humanity's problems are not new, each one of us has to face them for the first time in our own lives. Every generation in its turn passes through the labyrinth.

From *The Song of Roland* to *For Whom the Bell Tolls* we have referred to the same kind of courage. The last man of the rear guard holds the pass and gives up his life for his comrades, whether blowing Roland's horn or wielding a machine gun. Those heroes, though, are dead. The courage that interests us here is not a springboard to posthumous glory; it is a force that keeps us in one piece, that prevents us from breaking up amid the vicissitudes of daily life.

The modern warrior—you and me—is a strategist throughout the course of his life; a tactician throughout his days. He defends, above all, his inner cohesion and logic. Gone are the mad charges, the clash of battlelines, so murderous, yet so simple to play out. The new hand-to-hand combat, whose battleground is within the individual, is all the fiercer in that it is complex and without retreat.

If courage has once more become indispensable, it is because no one else can win this battle for me, no one can fight in my place.

Faced with a solitude by no means new, but which more and more shows itself, I have only everyday courage, often subtle, only occasionally more demanding. It is not along the line of "In case of accident, break glass," but, rather, like "Apply several times daily, as needed." It is courage as a style, as an ecological principle, to help me feel more free, more whole, even if I am all alone. Sometimes a single capsule, sometimes the entire box.

The course of life is long and challenging. If we examine it closely we see everywhere examples of courage. Finding ways in which to cope, to remain unscathed, occupy us all. But I have a dawning suspicion that protection is to be found in courage rather than in life insurance. The reasons, however, may not be obvious to everyone, and that is why the matter deserves sharper examination.

Thirteen Virtues

Benjamin Franklin

It was about this time I conceiv'd the bold and arduous project of arriving at moral perfection. I wish'd to live without committing any fault at any time; I would conquer all that either natural inclination, custom, or company might lead me into. As I knew, or thought I knew, what was right and wrong, I did not see why I might not always do the one and avoid the other. But I soon found I had undertaken a task of more difficulty than I had imagined. While my care was employ'd in guarding against one fault, I was often surprised by another; habit took the advantage of inttention: inclination was sometimes too strong for reason. I concluded, at length, that the mere speculative conviction that it was our interest to be completely virtuous, was not sufficient to prevent our slipping; and that the contrary habits must be broken, and good ones acquired and established, before we can have any dependence on a steady, uniform rectitude of conduct. For this purpose I therefore contrived the following method.

In the various enumerations of the moral virtues I had met with in my reading, I found the catalogue more or less numerous, as different writers included more or fewer ideas under the same name. Temperance, for example, was by some confined to eating and drinking, while by others it was extended to mean the moderating every other pleasure, appetite, inclination or passion, bodily or mental, even to our avarice and ambition. I propos'd to myself, for the sake of clearness, to use rather more names, with fewer ideas annex'd to each, than a few names with more ideas; and I included under thirteen names of virtues all that at that time occurr'd to me as necessary or desirable, and annexed to each a short precept, which fully express'd the extent I gave to its meaning.

These names of virtues, with their precepts were:

1. TEMPERANCE.
    Eat not to dullness; drink not to elevation.

2. SILENCE.
   Speak not but what may benefit others or yourself; avoid trifling conversation.
3. ORDER.
   Let all your things have their places; let each part of your business have its time.
4. RESOLUTION.
   Resolve to perform what you ought; perform without fail what you resolve.
5. FRUGALITY.
   Make no expense but to do good to others or yourself; *i. e.,* waste nothing.
6. INDUSTRY.
   Lose no time; be always employ'd in something useful; cut off all unnecessary actions.
7. SINCERITY.
   Use no hurtful deceit; think innocently and justly and, if you speak, speak accordingly.
8. JUSTICE.
   Wrong none by doing injuries, or omitting the benefits that are your duty.
9. MODERATION.
   Avoid extreams; forbear resenting injuries so much as you think they deserve.
10. CLEANLINESS.
    Tolerate no uncleanliness in body, cloaths, or habitation.
11. TRANQUILLITY.
    Be no disturbed at trifles, or at accidents common or unavoidable.
12. CHASTITY.
    Rarely use venery but for health or offspring, never to dulness, weakness, or the injury of your own or another's peace or reputation.
13. HUMILITY.
    Imitate Jesus and Socrates.

My intention being to acquire the *habitude* of all these virtues, I judg'd it would be well not to distract my attention by attempting the whole at once, but to fix it on one of them at a time; and, when I should be master of that, then to proceed to another, and so on, till I should have gone thro' the thirteen; and, as the previous acquisition of some might facilitate the acquisition of certain others, I arrang'd them with that view, as they stand above.

The Ethics of Virtue

James Rachels

> The concepts of obligation, and duty—*moral* obligation and *moral* duty, that is to say—and of what is *morally* right and wrong, and of the *moral* sense of "ought," ought to be jettisoned.... It would be a great improvement if, instead of "morally wrong," one always named a genus such as "untruthful," "unchaste," "unjust."
> G. E. M. Anscombe, *Modern Moral Philosophy* (1958)

1. The Ethics of Virtue and the Ethics of Right Action

In thinking about any subject it makes a great deal of difference what questions we begin with. In Aristotle's *Nicomachean Ethics* (ca. 325 B.C.), the central questions are about *character*. Aristotle begins by asking "What is the good of man?" and his answer is that "The good of man is an activity of the soul in conformity with virtue." To understand ethics, therefore, we must understand what makes someone a virtuous person, and Aristotle, with a keen eye for the details, devotes much space to discussing such particular virtues as courage, self-control, generosity, and truthfulness. The good man is the man of virtuous character, he says, and so the virtues are taken to be the subject matter of ethics.

Although this way of thinking is closely identified with Aristotle, it was not unique to him—it was also the approach taken by Socrates, Plato, and a host of other ancient thinkers. They all approached the subject by asking: *What traits of character make one a good person?* and as a result "the virtues" occupied center stage in all of their discussions.

As time passed, however, this way of thinking about ethics came to be neglected. With the coming of Christianity a new set of ideas was introduced. The Christians, like the Jews, were monotheists who viewed God as a lawgiver, and for them righteous living meant obedience to the divine commandments. The Greeks had viewed reason as the source of practical wisdom—the virtuous life was, for them, inseparable from the life of reason. But St. Augustine, the fourth-century Christian thinker who was to be enormously influential, distrusted reason and taught that moral goodness depends on subordinating oneself to the will of God. Therefore, when the medieval philosophers discussed the virtues, it was in the context of Divine Law. The "theological virtues"—faith, hope, charity, and, of course, *obedience*—came to have a central place.

After the Renaissance, moral philosophy began to be secularized once again, but philosophers did not return to the Greek way of thinking. Instead, the Divine Law was replaced by its secular equivalent, something called the *Moral Law*. The Moral Law, which was said to spring from human reason rather than divine fiat, was conceived to be a system of rules specifying which actions are right. Our duty as moral agents, it was said, is to follow its directives. Thus modern moral philosophers approached their subject by asking a fundamentally different question than the one that had been asked by the ancients. Instead of asking: *What traits of character make one a good person?* they began by asking: *What is the right thing to do?* This led them in a different direction. They went on to develop theories, not of virtue, but of rightness, and obligation:

- Each person ought to do whatever will best promote his or her own interests. (Ethical Egoism)
- We ought to do whatever will promote the greatest happiness for the greatest number. (Utilitarianism)
- Our duty is to follow rules that we could consistently will to be universal laws—that is, rules that we would be willing to have followed by all people in all circumstances. (Kant's theory)
- The right thing to do is to follow the rules that rational, self-interested people can agree to establish for their mutual benefit. (The Social Contract Theory)

And these are the familiar theories that have dominated modern moral philosophy from the seventeenth century on.

2. *Should We Return to the Ethics of Virtue?*

Recently a number of philosophers have advanced a radical idea: they have suggested that modern moral philosophy is bankrupt and that, in order to salvage the subject, we should return to Aristotle's way of thinking.

This idea was first put forth in 1958 when the distinguished British philosopher G. E. M. Anscombe published an article called "Modern Moral

Philosophy" in the academic journal *Philosophy*. In that article she suggested that modern moral philosophy is misguided because it rests on the incoherent notion of a "law" without a lawgiver. The very concepts of obligation, duty, and rightness, on which modern moral philosophers have concentrated their attention, are inextricably linked to this nonsensical idea. Therefore, she concluded, we should stop thinking about obligation, duty, and rightness. We should abandon the whole project that modern philosophers have pursued and return instead to Aristotle's approach. This means that the concept of virtue should once again take center stage.

In the wake of Anscombe's article a flood of books and essays appeared discussing the virtues, and "virtue theory" soon became a major option in contemporary moral philosophy. There is, however, no settled body of doctrine on which all these philosophers agree. Compared to such theories as Utilitarianism, virtue theory is still in a relatively undeveloped state. Yet the virtue theorists are united in believing that modern moral philosophy has been on the wrong track and that a radical reorientation of the subject is needed.

In what follows we shall first take a look at what the theory of virtue is like. Then we shall consider some of the reasons that have been given for thinking that the ethics of virtue is superior to other, more modern ways of approaching the subject. And at the end we will consider whether a "return to the ethics of virtue" is really a viable option.

3. The Virtues

A theory of virtue should have, several components. First, there should be an explanation of what a virtue is. Second, there should be a list specifying which character traits are virtues. Third, there should be an explanation of what these virtues consist in. Fourth, there should be an explanation of why these qualities are good ones for a person to have. Finally, the theory should tell us whether the virtues are the same for all people or whether they differ from person to person or from culture to culture.

What Is Virtue? The first question that must be asked is: *What is a virtue?* Aristotle suggested one possible answer. He said that a virtue is a trait of character that is manifested in habitual actions. The virtue of honesty is not possessed by someone who tells the truth only occasionally or whenever it is to his own advantage. The honest person is truthful as a matter of principle; his actions "spring from a firm and unchangeable character."

This is a start, but it is not enough. It does not distinguish virtues from vices, for vices are also traits of character manifested in habitual action. Edmund L. Pincoffs, a philosopher at the University of Texas, has made a suggestion that takes care of this problem. Pincoffs suggests that virtues and vices are qualities that we refer to in deciding whether someone is to be sought or avoided. "Some sorts of persons we prefer; others we avoid," he says. "The properties on our list [of virtues and vices] can serve as reasons for preference or avoidance."

We seek out people for different purposes, and this makes a difference to the virtues that are relevant. In looking for an auto mechanic, we want someone who is skillful, honest, and conscientious; in looking for a teacher, we want someone who is knowledgeable, articulate, and patient. Thus the virtues associated with auto repair are different from the virtues associated with teaching. But we also assess people *as people*, in a more general way: and so we have the concept, not just of a good mechanic or a good teacher, but of a good person. The moral virtues are the virtues of persons as such.

Taking our cue from Pincoffs, then, we may define a virtue as *a trait of character, manifested in habitual action, that it is good for a person to have.*

What Are the Virtues? What, then, *are* the virtues? Which traits of character should be fostered in human beings? There is no short answer, but the following is a partial list:

benevolence	fairness	reasonableness
civility	friendliness	self-confidence
compassion	generosity	self-control
conscientiousness	honesty	self-discipline
cooperativeness	industriousness	self-reliance
courage	justice	tactfulness
courteousness	loyalty	thoughtfulness
dependability	moderation	tolerance

The list could be expanded, of course, with other traits added. But this is a reasonable start.

What Do These Virtues Consist In? It is one thing to say, in a general way, that we should be conscientious and compassionate; it is another thing to try to say exactly what these character traits consist in. Each of the virtues has its own distinctive features and raises its own distinctive problems. There isn't enough space here to consider all the items on our list, but we may examine four of them briefly.

1. *Courage.* According to Aristotle, virtues are means poised between extremes; a virtue is "the mean by reference to two vices: the one of excess and the other of deficiency." Courage is a mean between the extremes of cowardice and foolhardiness—it is cowardly to run away from all danger; yet it is foolhardy to risk too much.

Courage is sometimes said to be a military virtue because it is so obviously needed to accomplish the soldier's task. Soldiers do battle; battles are fraught with danger; and so without courage the battle will be lost. But soldiers are not the only ones who need courage. Courage is needed by anyone who faces danger—and at different times this includes all of us. A scholar who spends his timid and safe life studying medieval literature might seem the very opposite of a soldier. Yet even he might become ill and need courage to face a dangerous operation. As Peter Geach (a contemporary British philosopher) puts it:

> Courage is what we all need in the end, and it is constantly needed in the ordinary course of life: by women who are with child, by all of us because our bodies are vulnerable, by coalminers and fishermen and steel-workers and lorry-drivers.

So long as we consider only "the ordinary course of life," the nature of courage seems unproblematic. But unusual circumstances present more troublesome types of cases. Consider a Nazi soldier, for example, who fights valiantly—he faces great risk without flinching—but he does so in an evil cause. Is he courageous? Geach holds that, contrary to appearances, the Nazi soldier does not really possess the virtue of courage at all. "Courage in an unworthy cause," he says, "is no virtue; still less is courage in an evil cause. Indeed I prefer not to call this non-virtuous facing of danger 'courage.'"

It is easy to see Geach's point. Calling the Nazi soldier "courageous" seems to praise his performance, and we should not want to praise it. Instead we would rather he behaved differently. Yet neither does it seem quite right to say that he is *not* courageous—after all, look at how he behaves in the face of danger. To get around this problem perhaps we should just say that he displays *two* qualities of character, one that is admirable (steadfastness in facing danger) and one that is not (a willingness to defend a despicable regime). He is courageous all right, and courage is an admirable thing; but because his courage is deployed in an evil cause, his behavior is *on the whole* wicked.

2. *Generosity*. Generosity is the willingness to expend one's resources to help others. Aristotle says that, like courage, it is also a mean between extremes: it stands somewhere between stinginess and extravagance. The stingy person gives too little, the extravagant person gives too much. But how much is enough?

The answer will depend to some extent on what general ethical view we accept. Jesus, another important ancient teacher, said that we must give all we have to help the poor. The possession of riches, while the poor starve, was in his view unacceptable. This was regarded by those who heard him as a hard teaching and it was generally rejected. It is still rejected by most people today, even by those who consider themselves to be his followers.

The modern utilitarians are, in this regard at least, Jesus' moral descendants. They hold that in every circumstance it is one's duty to do whatever will have the best overall consequences for everyone concerned. This means that we should be generous with our money until the point has been reached at which further giving would be more harmful to us than it would be helpful to others.

Why do people resist this idea? Partly it may be a matter of selfishness; we do not want to make ourselves poor by giving away what we have. But there is also the problem that adopting such a policy would prevent us from living normal lives. Not only money but time is involved. Our lives consist in projects and relationships that require a considerable investment of both. An ideal of "generosity" that demands spending our money and time as Jesus and the utilitarians recommend would require that we abandon our everyday lives and live very differently.

A reasonable interpretation of the demands of generosity might, therefore, be something like this: we should be as generous with our resources as is consistent with conducting our ordinary lives in a minimally satisfying way. Even this, though, will leave us with some awkward questions. Some people's ordinary lives are quite extravagant—think of a rich person whose everyday life includes luxuries without which he would feel deprived. The virtue of generosity, it would seem, cannot exist in the context of a life that is too sumptuous, especially when there are others about whose basic needs are unmet. To make this a "reasonable" interpretation of the demands of generosity, we need a conception of ordinary life that is itself not too extravagant.

3. *Honesty.* The honest person is, first of all, someone who does not lie. But is that enough? There are other ways of misleading people than by lying. Geach tells the story of St. Athanasius, who "was rowing on a river when the persecutors came rowing in the opposite direction: 'Where is the traitor Athanasius?' 'Not far away,' the Saint gaily replied, and rowed past them unsuspected."

Geach approves of Athanasius's deception even though he thinks it would have been wrong to tell an outright lie. Lying, Geach thinks, is always forbidden: a person possessing the virtue of honesty will not even consider it. Indeed, on his view that is what the virtues are: they are dispositions of character that simply *rule out* actions that are incompatible with them. Honest people will not lie, and so they will have to find other ways to deal with difficult situations. Athanasius was clever enough to do so. He told the truth, even if it was a deceptive truth.

Of course, it is hard to see why Athanasius's deception was not also dishonest. What nonarbitrary principle would approve of misleading people by one means but not by another? But whatever we think about this, the larger question is whether virtue requires adherence to absolute rules. Concerning honesty, we may distinguish two views of the matter:

1. That an honest person will never lie and
2. That an honest person will never lie except in rare circumstances when there are compelling reasons why it must be done.

Chapter V: Vice and Virtue

There is no obvious reason why the first view must be accepted. On the contrary, there is reason to favor the second. To see why, we need only to consider why lying is a bad thing in the first place. The explanation might go like this:

Our ability to live together in communities depends on our capacities of communication. We talk to one another, read one another's writing, exchange information and opinions, express our desires to one another, make promises, ask and answer questions, and much more. Without these sorts of interchanges, social living would be impossible. But in order for these interchanges to be successful, we must be able to assume that there are certain rules in force: we must be able to rely on one another to speak honestly.

Moreover, when we accept someone's word we make ourselves vulnerable to harm in a special way. By accepting what they say and modifying our beliefs accordingly, we place our welfare in their hands. If they speak truthfully, all is well. But if they lie, we end up with false beliefs; and if we act on those beliefs, we end up doing foolish things. It is *their fault*: we trusted them, and they let us down. This explains why being given the lie is distinctively offensive. It is at bottom a violation of trust. (It also explains, incidentally, why lies and "deceptive truths" may seem morally indistinguishable. Both may violate trust in the same fashion.)

None of this, however, implies that honesty is the *only* important value or that we have an obligation to deal honestly with *everyone* who comes along, regardless of who they are and what they are up to. Self-preservation is also an important matter, especially protecting ourselves from those who would harm us unjustly. When this comes into conflict with the rule against lying it is not unreasonable to think it takes priority. Suppose St. Athanasius had told the persecutors "I don't know him," and as a result they went off on a wild goose chase. Later, could they sensibly complain that he had violated their trust? Wouldn't they have forfeited any right they might have had to the truth from him when they set out unjustly to persecute him?

4. *Loyalty to Family and Friends*. At the beginning of Plato's dialogue *Euthyphro*, Socrates learns that Euthyphro, whom he has encountered near the entrance to the court, has come there to prosecute his father for murder. Socrates expresses surprise at this and wonders whether it is proper for a son to bring charges against his father. Euthyphro sees no impropriety, however: for him, a murder is a murder. Unfortunately, the question is left unresolved as their discussion moves on to other matters.

The idea that there is something morally special about family and friends is, of course, familiar. We do not treat our family and friends as we would treat strangers. We are bound to them by love and affection and we do things for them that we would not do for just anybody. But this is not merely a matter of our being nicer to people we like. The nature of our relationships with family and friends is different from our relationships with other people, and part of the difference is that our *duties and responsibilities* are different. This seems to be an integral part of what friendship is. How could I be your friend and yet have no duty to treat you with special consideration?

If we needed proof that humans are essentially social creatures, the existence of friendship would supply all we could want. As Aristotle said, "No one would choose to live without friends, even if he had all other goods":

> How could prosperity be safeguarded and preserved without friends? The greater it is the greater are the risks it brings with it. Also, in poverty and all other kinds of misfortune men believe that their only refuge consists in their friends. Friends help young men amid error; to older people they give the care and help needed to supplement the failing powers of action which infirmity brings.

Friends give help, to be sure, but the benefits of friendship go far beyond material assistance. Psychologically, we would be lost without friends. Our triumphs seem hollow unless we have friends to share them with, and our failures are made bearable by their understanding. Even our self-esteem depends in large measure on the assurances of friends: by returning our affection, they confirm our worthiness as human beings.

If we need friends, we need no less the qualities of character that enable us to *be* a friend. Near the top of the list is loyalty. Friends can be counted on. They stick by one another even when the going is hard, and even when, objectively speaking, the friend might deserve to be abandoned. They make allowances for one another; they forgive offenses and they refrain from harsh judgments. There are limits, of course: sometimes a friend will be the only one who can tell us hard truths about ourselves. But criticism is acceptable from friends because we know that, even if they scold us privately, they will not embarrass us in front of others.

None of this is to say that we do not have duties to other people, even to strangers. But they are different duties, associated with different virtues. Generalized beneficence is a virtue, and it may demand a great deal, but it does not require for strangers the same level of concern that we have for friends. Justice is another such virtue; it requires impartial treatment for all. But because friends are loyal, the demands of justice apply less certainly between them.

That is why Socrates is surprised to learn that Euthyphro is prosecuting his father. The relationship that we have with members of our family may be even closer than that of friendship; and so, as much as we might admire his passion for justice, we still may be startled that Euthyphro could take the same attitude toward his father that he would take toward someone else who had committed the same crime. It seems inconsistent with the proper regard of a son. The point is still recognized by the law today. In the United States, as well as in some other countries, a wife cannot be compelled to testify in court against her husband, and vice versa.

Why Are the Virtues Important? We said that virtues are traits of character that are good for people to have. This only raises the further question of *why* the virtues are desirable. Why is it a good thing for a person to be courageous, generous, honest, or loyal? The answer, of course, may vary depending on the particular virtue in question. Thus:

- Courage is a good thing because life is full of dangers and without courage we would be unable to cope with them.
- Generosity is desirable because some people will inevitably be worse off than others and they will need help.
- Honesty is needed because without it relations between people would go wrong in myriad ways.
- Loyalty is essential to friendship—friends stick by one another, even when they are tempted to turn away.

Looking at this list suggests that each virtue is valuable for a different reason. However, Aristotle believed it is possible to give a more general answer to our question: he thought that the virtuous person will fare better in life. The point is not that the virtuous will be richer—that is obviously not so, or at least it is not always so. The point is that the virtues are needed to conduct our lives well.

To see what Aristotle is getting at, consider the kinds of creatures we are and the kinds of lives we lead. On the most general level, we are rational and social beings who both want and need the company of other people. So we live in communities among friends, family, and fellow citizens. In this setting, such qualities as loyalty, fairness, and honesty are needed for interacting with all those other people successfully. (Imagine the difficulties that would be experienced by someone who habitually manifested the opposite qualities in his or her social life.) On a more individual level, our separate lives might include working at a particular kind of job and having particular sorts of interests. Other virtues may be necessary for successfully doing that job or pursuing those interests—perseverance and industriousness might be important. Again, it is part of our common human condition that we must sometimes face danger or temptation; and so courage and self-control are needed. The upshot is that, despite their differences, the virtues all have the same general sort of value: they are all qualities needed for successful human living.

Are the Virtues the Same for Everyone? Finally, we may ask whether there is *one* set of traits that is desirable for all people. Should we even speak of *the* good person, as though all good people come from a single mold? This assumption has often been challenged. Friedrich Nietzsche, for example, did not think that there is only one kind of human goodness. In his flamboyant way, Nietzsche observes:

> How naive it is altogether to say: "Man *ought* to be such-and-such!" Reality shows us an enchanting wealth of types, the abundance of a lavish play and change of forms—and some wretched loafer of a moralist comments: "No! Man ought to be different." He even knows what man should he like, this wretched bigot and prig: he paints himself on the wall and exclaims, "*Ecce homo!*"

There is obviously something to this. The scholar who devotes his life to understanding medieval literature and the professional soldier are very different kinds of people. A Victorian woman who would never expose a knee in public and a modern woman on a bathing-beach have very different standards of modesty. And yet all may be admirable in their own ways.

There is, then, an obvious sense in which the virtues may be thought of as differing from person to person. Because people lead different kinds of lives, have different sorts of personalities, and occupy different social roles, the qualities of character that they manifest may differ.

It is tempting to go even further and say simply that the virtues differ in different societies. After all, the kind of life that is possible for an individual will depend on the society in which he or she lives. A scholar's life is possible only in a society that has institutions, such as universities, that define and make possible the life of a scholar. The same could be said of a football player, a priest, or an interior decorator. Societies provide systems of values, institutions, and ways of life within which individual lives are fashioned. The traits of character that are needed to occupy these roles will differ, and so the traits needed to live successfully will differ. Thus the virtues will be different. In light of all this, why shouldn't we just say that which qualities are virtues will depend on the ways of life that are created and sustained by particular societies?

To this it may be countered that *there are some virtues that will be needed by all people in all times.* This was Aristotle's view, and he was probably right. Aristotle believed that we all have a great deal in common, despite our differences. "One may observe," he said, "in one's travels to distant countries the feelings of recognition and affiliation that link every human being to every other human being." Even in the most disparate societies, people face the same basic problems and have the same basic needs. Thus:

- Everyone needs courage, because no one (not even the scholar) is so safe that danger may not sometimes arise.
- In every society there will be property to be managed, and decisions to be made about who gets what, and in every society there will be some people who are worse off than others; so generosity is always to be prized.
- Honesty in speech is always a virtue because no society can exist without communication among its members.

- Everyone needs friends, and to have friends one must be a friend; so everyone needs loyalty.

This sort of list could—and in Aristotle's hands it does—go on and on.

To summarize, then, it may be true that in different societies the virtues are given somewhat different interpretations, and different sorts of actions are counted as satisfying them; and it may be true that some people, because they lead particular sorts of lives in particular sorts of circumstances, will have occasion to need some virtues more than others. But it cannot be right to say simply that whether any particular character trait is a virtue is never anything more than a matter of social convention. The major virtues are mandated not by social convention but by basic facts about our common human condition.

4. Some Advantages of Virtue Ethics

As we noted above, some philosophers believe that an emphasis on the virtues is superior to other ways of thinking about ethics. Why? A number of reasons have been suggested. Here are three of them.

1. *Moral motivation.* First, virtue ethics is appealing because it provides a natural and attractive account of moral motivation. The other theories seem deficient on this score. Consider the following example.

You are in the hospital recovering from a long illness. You are bored and restless, and so you are delighted when Smith arrives to visit. You have a good time chatting with him; his visit is just the tonic you needed. After a while you tell Smith how much you appreciate his coming: he really is a fine fellow and a good friend to take the trouble to come all the way across town to see you. But Smith demurs; he protests that he is merely doing his duty. At first you think Smith is only being modest, but the more you talk, the clearer it becomes that he is speaking the literal truth. He is not visiting you because he wants to, or because he likes you, but only because he thinks it is his duty to "do the right thing," and on this occasion he has decided it is his duty to visit you—perhaps because he knows of no one else who is more in need of cheering up or no one easier to get to.

This example was suggested by Michael Stocker in an influential article that appeared in the *Journal of Philosophy* in 1976. Stocker comments that surely you would be very disappointed to learn Smith's motive; now his visit seems cold and calculating and it loses all value to you. You thought he was your friend, but now you learn otherwise. Stocker says about Smith's behavior: "Surely there is something lacking here—and lacking in moral merit or value."

Of course, there is nothing wrong with what Smith *did*. The problem is his *motive*. We value friendship, love, and respect; and we want our relationships with people to be based on mutual regard. Acting from an abstract sense of duty, or from a desire to "do the right thing," is not the same. We would not want to live in a community of people who acted only from such motives, nor would we want to *be* such a person. Therefore, the argument goes, theories of ethics that emphasize only right action will never provide a completely satisfactory account of the moral life. For that, we need a theory that emphasizes personal qualities such as friendship, love, and loyalty—in other words, a theory of the virtues.

2. *Doubts about the "ideal" of impartiality.* A dominant theme of modern moral philosophy has been impartiality—the idea that all persons are morally equal, and that in deciding what to do we should treat everyone's interests as equally important. (Of the four theories of "right action" listed above, only Ethical Egoism, a theory with few adherents, denies this.) John Stuart Mill put the point well when he wrote that "Utilitarianism requires [the moral agent] to be as strictly impartial as a benevolent and disinterested spectator.". . .

It may be doubted, though, whether impartiality is really such an important feature of the moral life. Consider one's relationships with family and friends. Are we really impartial where their interests are concerned? And should we be? A mother loves her children and cares for them in a way that she does not care for other children. She is partial to them through and through. But is there anything wrong with that? Isn't it exactly the way a mother *should* be? Again, we love our friends and we are willing to do things for them that we would not do for just anyone. Is there anything wrong with *that*? On the contrary, it seems that the love of family and friends is an inescapable feature of the morally good life. Any theory that emphasizes impartiality will have a difficult time accounting for this.

A moral theory that emphasizes the virtues, however, can account for all this very comfortably. Some virtues are partial and some are not. Love and friendship involve partiality toward loved ones and friends; beneficence toward people in general is also a virtue, but it is a virtue of a different kind. What is needed, on this view, is not some general requirement of impartiality, but an understanding of the nature of these different virtues and how they relate to one another.

3. *Virtue ethics and feminism.* Finally, we may notice a connection between the ethics of virtue and some concerns voiced by feminist thinkers. Feminists have argued that modern moral philosophy incorporates a subtle male bias. It isn't just that the most renowned philosophers have all been men, or that many of them have been guilty of sexist prejudice in what they have said about women. The bias is more systematic, deeper, and more interesting than that.

To see the bias, we need first to notice that social life has traditionally been divided into public and private realms, with men in charge of public affairs and women assigned responsibility for life's more personal and private dimensions. Men have dominated political and economic life, while women have been consigned to home and hearth. *Why* there has been this division would, in a different context, be a matter of some interest. Perhaps it is due to some inherent difference between men and women that suits them for the different roles. Or it may be merely a matter of social custom. But for present purposes, the cause of this arrangement need not concern us. It is enough to note that it has existed for a long time.

The public and private realms each have their own distinctive concerns. In politics and business, one's relations with other people are frequently impersonal and contractual. Often the relationship is adversarial—they have interests that conflict with our own. So we negotiate; we bargain and make deals. Moreover, in public life our decisions may affect large numbers of people whom we do not even know. So we may try to calculate, in an impersonal way, which decisions will have the best overall outcome for the most people.

In the world of home and hearth, however, things are different. It is a smaller-scale environment. In it, we are dealing mainly with family and friends, with whom our relationships are more personal and intimate. Bargaining and calculating play a much smaller role. Relations of love and caring are paramount.

Now with this in mind, think again about the theories of "right action that have dominated modern moral philosophy—theories produced by male philosophers whose sensibilities were shaped by their own distinctive sorts of experience. The influence of that experience is plain. Their theories emphasize impersonal duty, contracts, the harmonization of competing interests, and the calculation of costs and benefits. The concerns that accompany private life—the realm in which women traditionally dominate—are almost wholly absent. The theory of virtue may be seen as a corrective to this imbalance. It can make a place for the virtues of private life as well as the rather different virtues that are required by public life. It is no accident that feminist philosophers are among those who are now most actively promoting the idea of a return to the ethics of virtue.

5. *The Incompleteness of Virtue Ethics*

The preceding arguments make an impressive case for two general points: first, that an adequate philosophical theory of ethics must provide an understanding of moral character; and second, that modern moral philosophers have failed to do this. Not only have they neglected the topic; what is more, their neglect has led them sometimes to embrace doctrines that *distort* the nature of moral character. Suppose we accept these conclusions. Where do we go from here?

One way of proceeding would be to develop a theory that combines the best features of the right action approach with insights drawn from the virtues approach—we might try to improve utilitarianism, Kantianism, and the like by adding to them a better account of moral character. Our total theory would then include an account of the virtues, but that account would be offered only as a supplement to a theory of right action. This sounds sensible, and if such a project could be carried out successfully, there would obviously be much to be said in its favor.

Some virtue theorists, however, have suggested that we should proceed differently. They have argued that the ethics of virtue should be considered as an *alternative* to the other sorts of theories—as an independent theory of ethics that is complete in itself. We might call this "radical virtue ethics." Is this a viable view?

Virtue and Conduct. As we have seen, theories that emphasize right action seem incomplete because they neglect the question of character. Virtue theory remedies this problem by making the question of character its central concern. But as a result, virtue theory runs the risk of being incomplete in the opposite way. Moral problems are frequently problems about what we should *do*. It is not obvious how, according to virtue theory, how should we go about deciding what to do. What can this approach tell us about the assessment, not of character, but of action?

The answer will depend on the spirit in which virtue theory is offered. If a theory of the virtues is offered only as a supplement to a theory of right action, then when the assessment of action is at issue the resources of the total theory will be brought into play and some version of utilitarian or Kantian policies (for example) will be recommended. On the other hand, if the theory of virtue is offered as an independent theory intended to be complete in itself, more drastic steps must be taken. Either the theory will have to jettison the notion of "right action" altogether or it will have to give some account of the notion derived from the conception of virtuous character.

Although it sounds at first like a crazy idea, some philosophers have in fact argued that we should simply get rid of such concepts as "morally right action." Anscombe says that "it would be a great improvement" if we stopped using such notions altogether. We could still assess conduct as better or worse, she says, but we would do so in other terms. Instead of saying that an action was "morally wrong" we would simply say that it was "untruthful" or "unjust"—terms derived from the vocabulary of virtue. On her view, we need not say anything more than this to explain why an action is to be rejected.

But it is not really necessary for radical virtue theorists to jettison such notions as "morally right." Such notions can be retained but given a new interpretation within the virtue framework. This might be done as follows. First, it could be said that actions are to be assessed as right or wrong in the familiar way, by reference to the reasons that can be given for or against them: we ought to do those actions that have the best reasons in their favor. However, *the reasons cited will all be reasons that are connected with the virtues*—the reasons in favor of doing an act will be that it is honest, or generous, or fair, and the like; while the reasons against doing it will be that it is dishonest, or stingy, or unfair, and the like. This analysis could be summed up by saying that our duty is to act virtuously—the "right thing to do," in other words, is whatever a virtuous person would do.

The Problem of Incompleteness. We have now sketched the radical virtue theorist's way of understanding what we ought to do. Is that understanding sufficient? The principal problem for the theory is the problem of incompleteness.

First, consider what it would mean in the case of a typical virtue—the virtue of honesty. Suppose a person is tempted to lie, perhaps because lying offers some advantage in a particular situation. The reason he or she should not lie, according to the radical virtue ethics approach, is simply because doing so would be dishonest. This sounds reasonable enough. But what does it mean to be honest? Isn't an honest person simply one who follows such rules as "Do not lie"? It is hard to see what honesty consists in if it is not the disposition to follow such rules.

But we cannot avoid asking *why* such rules are important. Why shouldn't a person lie, especially when there is some advantage to be gained from it? Plainly we need an answer that goes beyond the simple observation that doing so would be incompatible with having a particular character trait; we need an explanation of why it is better to have this trait than its opposite. Possible answers might be that a policy of truth-telling is on the whole to one's own advantage; or that it promotes the general welfare; or that it is needed by people who must live together relying on one another. The first explanation looks suspiciously like Ethical Egoism; the second is utilitarian; and the third recalls contractarian ways of thinking. In any case, giving any explanation at all seems to take us beyond the limits of unsupplemented virtue theory.

Second, it is difficult to see how unsupplemented virtue theory could handle cases of moral *conflict*. Suppose you must choose between A and B, when it would be dishonest but kind to do A, and honest but unkind to do B. (An example might be telling the truth in circumstances that would be hurtful to someone.) Honesty and kindness are both virtues, and so there are reasons both for and against each alternative. But you must do one or the other—you must either tell the truth, and be unkind, or not tell the truth, and be dishonest. So which should you do? The admonition to act virtuously does not, by itself, offer much help. It only leaves you wondering which virtue takes precedence. It seems that we need some more general guidance, beyond that which radical virtue theory can offer, to resolve such conflicts.

Is There a Virtue That Matches Every Morally Good Reason for Doing Something? The problem of incompleteness points toward a more general theoretical difficulty for the radical virtue ethics approach. As we have seen, according to this approach the reasons for or against doing an action must always be associated with one or more virtues. Thus radical virtue ethics is committed to the idea that *for any good reason that may be given in favor of doing an action, there is a corresponding virtue that consists in the disposition to accept and act on that reason.* But this does not appear to be true.

Suppose, for example, that you are a legislator and you must decide how to allocate funds for medical research—there isn't enough money for everything, and you must decide whether to invest resources in AIDS research or in some other worthy project. And suppose you decide it is best in these circumstances to do what will benefit the most people. Is there a virtue that matches the disposition to do this? If there is, perhaps it should be called "acting like a utilitarian." Or, to return to our example of moral conflicts—is there a virtue connected with every principle that can be invoked to resolve conflicts between the other virtues? If there is, perhaps it is the "virtue" of wisdom—which is to say, the ability to figure out and do what is on the whole best. But this gives away the game. If we posit such "virtues," only to make all moral decision making fit into the preferred framework, we will have saved radical virtue ethics, but at the cost of abandoning its central idea.

Conclusion. For these reasons, it seems best to regard the theory of virtue as part of an overall theory of ethics rather than as a complete theory in itself. The total theory would include an account of all the considerations that figure in practical decision making, together with their underlying rationale. The question, then, will be whether such a total view can accommodate *both* an adequate conception of right action *and* a related conception of virtuous character in a way that does justice to both.

I can see no reason why this is not possible. Our overall theory might begin by taking human welfare—or the welfare of all sentient creatures, for that matter—as the surpassingly important value. We might say that, from a moral point of view, we should want a society in which all people can lead happy and satisfying lives. We could then go on to consider both the question of what sorts of actions and social policies would contribute to this goal *and* the question of what qualities of character are needed to create and sustain individual lives. An inquiry into the nature of virtue could profitably be conducted from within the perspective that such a larger view would provide. Each could illuminate the other; and if each part of the overall theory has to be adjusted a bit here and there to accommodate the other, so much the better for truth.

Chapter VI
Lying and Veracity

Is it ever morally acceptable to lie? Are some lies harmless? Why do people lie? How do individuals feel when they discover they have been lied to? What is the relationship of lies to truth? What is truth? Is the whole truth attainable? What is the basis of trust? This chapter will look in-depth at the above questions.

Mark Twain is a noted American humorist and novelist. In his unique style, which is both insightful and delightful, Twain helps us to think more deeply about lying as well as truth-telling. "Lying," he says, "is universal—we all do it; we all must do it." However, he bemoans the fact that people lie so poorly and so thoughtlessly. He is pained to see lying, once a noble art, prostituted and vulgarized. But, Mark Twain is also concerned with, what he perceives as, the growing prevalence of the "brutal truth." He claims that, "An injurious truth has no merit over an injurious lie."

His essay concludes with a challenge to the reader to examine his or her own conversation, objectives, and motives. He asks that one become more thoughtful and judicious in speech. Since one must lie, then

> . . . the wise thing is for us diligently to train ourselves to lie thoughtfully, judiciously; to lie with a good object, and not an evil one; to lie for others' advantage, and not our own; to lie healingly, charitably, humanely, not cruelly, hurtfully, maliciously; to lie gracefully and graciously, not awkwardly and clumsily; to lie firmly, frankly, squarely, with head erect, not haltingly, fortuitously, with pusillanimous mien, as being ashamed of our high calling.

Charles Fried opens up the structure of lies and of truth in relation to the structure of persons. He begins by noting that, "the evil of lying is as hard to pin down as it is strongly felt." What, specifically, is wrong with lying? Why must individuals not lie? "Lying is wrong," he states:

... because when I lie I set up a relationship which is essentially exploitive. It violates the principle of respect, for I must affirm that the mind of another is available to me in a way in which I cannot agree my mind would be available to him ... when I do intentional physical harm, I say that your body, your person, is available for my purposes. When I lie, I lay claim to your mind.

The article, "On the Supposed Right to Tell Lies from Benevolent Motives," is an extension of Kant's moral philosophy. Earlier chapters of this book have considered Kant's view on respect for persons, his discussions of a good will and the moral law, and, of course, the categorical imperative. Many people uncritically assume that well-intentioned lies and lies told from benevolent motives are morally justified. Kant explicitly denies this. In contrast he maintains: "To be truthful (honest) in all declarations is therefore a sacred, unconditional command of reason, and not to be limited to any expediency."

Henry Sidgwick examines the duty of veracity. This duty has often been assumed to be an absolute moral duty. Many moralists claim that individuals must follow the positive maxim "to speak the truth" and, further, that this maxim admits of no exceptions. Sidgwick holds that , on examination, it is not obvious that individuals have such an unconditional duty. At least, "patient reflection will show that this view is not really confirmed by the Common Sense of mankind."

Sidgwick examines several ethical positions from Intuitionism to the ethics of Kant and shows the many Common Sense exceptions to the duty of veracity. He concludes by stating that there is a strong, but not formally conclusive, utilitarian ground for speaking the truth.

Concerning the concept of truth, Sissela Bok states:

> ... no concept intimidates and yet draws thinkers so powerfully. From the beginnings of human speculation about the world, the questions of what truth is and whether we can attain it have loomed large. Every philosopher has had to grapple with them. Every religion seeks to answer them.

Bok briefly discusses the ancient Greek concept of truth as *aletheia* as bringing material to life. She calls the reader's attention to the important distinction between epistemological "truth" and ethical "truthfulness" or "truth-telling." This accomplishes two main points: First, it clarifies the notion of truth and, secondly, it removes the skeptic from the ethical or moral domain. In closing, Bok defines intentional deception and lying as follows;

> When we undertake to deceive others intentionally, we communicate messages meant to mislead them, meant to make them believe what we ourselves do not believe. We can do this through gesture, through disguise, by means of action or inaction, even through silence. Which of these innumerable deceptive messages are also lies? I shall define a lie as any intentionally deceptive message which is *stated*.

Chapter VI: Lying and Veracity

In "Truthfulness, Deceit, and Trust," Bok shows the importance of truthfulness, the subtle dimensions of deceit, and the dynamics which play out in the relationships which embody the above terms.

She begins by showing that there is common ground which deceit shares with violence. Boks states: "Deceit and violence—these are the two forms of deliberate assault on human beings. Both can coerce people into acting against their will." Yet, this very fact attests to the underlying centrality of truthfulness, some level of which "has always been seen as essential to human society." Furthermore, she continues, "a society . . . whose members were unable to distinguish truthful messages from deceptive ones, would collapse."

Next, Bok considers discrepant perspectives toward lying. Here one sees clearly the differences in the outlook of the deceiver and the one deceived, as well as the divergent viewpoints of the liar and the dupe. She concludes this essay with a discussion of the notions of trust and veracity:

> . . . trust in some degree of veracity functions as a *foundation* of relations among human beings; when this trust shatters or wears away, institutions collapse.

Advertising is responsible for selling a great deal more than products. Advertising sells us self-concepts, notions of beauty and success, and images of love, friendship and the good life. Today, advertising is an inescapable fact of life. How does advertising work? Wherein is its power? In what subtle ways does advertising control and manipulate people? In "Sex, Lies, and Advertising," feminist Gloria Steinem, cofounder of Ms. Magazine, writes from personal experience about the uses, abuses, and goals of advertising.

On the Decay of the Art of Lying

Mark Twain

Observe, I do not mean to suggest that the *custom* of lying has suffered any decay or interruption—no, for the Lie, as a Virtue, a Principle, is eternal; the Lie, as a recreation, a solace, a refuge in time of need, the fourth Grace, the tenth Muse, man's best and surest friend, is immortal, and cannot perish from the earth while this Club remains. My complaint simply concerns the decay of the *art* of lying. No high-minded man, no man of right feeling, can contemplate the lumbering and slovenly lying of the present day without grieving to see a noble art so prostituted. In this veteran presence I naturally enter upon this scheme with diffidence; it is like an old maid trying to teach nursery matters to the mothers in Israel. It would not become me to criticize you, gentlemen, who are nearly all my elders—and my superiors, in this thing—and so, if I should here and there *seem* to do it, I trust it will in most cases be more in a spirit of admiration than of faultfinding; indeed, if this finest of the fine arts had everywhere received the attention, encouragement, and conscientious practice and development which this Club has devoted to it, I should not need to utter this lament, or shed a single tear. I do not say this to flatter: I say it in a spirit of just and appreciative recognition.

[It had been my intention, at this point, to mention names and give illustrative specimens, but indications observable about me admonished me to beware of particulars and confine myself to generalities.]

No fact is more firmly established than that lying is a necessity of our circumstances—the deduction that it is then a Virtue goes without saying. No virtue can reach its highest usefulness without careful and diligent cultivation—therefore, it goes without saying, that this one ought to be taught in the public schools—at the fireside—even in the newspapers. What chance has the ignorant, uncultivated liar against the educated expert? What chance have I against Mr. Per—against a lawyer? *Judicious* lying is what the world needs. I sometimes think it were even better and safer not

Chapter VI: Lying and Veracity

to lie at all than to lie injudiciously. An awkward, unscientific lie is often as ineffectual as the truth.

Now let us see what the philosophers say. Note that venerable proverb: Children and fools *always* speak the truth. The deduction is plain—adults and wise persons *never* speak it. Parkman, the historian, says, "The principle of truth may itself be carried into an absurdity." In another place in the same chapter he says, "The saying is old that truth should not be spoken at all times; and those whom a sick conscience worries into habitual violation of the maxim are imbeciles and nuisances." It is strong language, but true. None of us could *live* with an habitual truth-teller; but, thank goodness, none of us has to. An habitual truth-teller is simply an impossible creature; he does not exist; he never has existed. Of course there are people who *think* they never lie, but it is not so—and this ignorance is one of the very things that shame our so-called civilization. Everybody lies—every day; every hour; awake; asleep; in his dreams; in his joy; in his mourning; if he keeps his tongue still, his hands, his feet, his eyes, his attitude, will convey deception—and purposely. Even in sermons—but that is a platitude.

In a far country where I once lived the ladies used to go around paying calls, under the humane and kindly pretense of wanting to see each other; and when they returned home, they would cry out with a glad voice, saying, "We made sixteen calls and found fourteen of them out"—not meaning that they found out anything against the fourteen—no, that was only a colloquial phrase to signify that they were not at home—and their manner of saying it expressed their lively satisfaction in that fact. Now their pretense of wanting to see the fourteen—and the other two whom they had been less lucky with—was that commonest and mildest form of lying which is sufficiently described as a deflection from the truth. Is it justifiable? Most certainly. It is beautiful, it is noble; for its object is, *not* to reap profit, but to convey a pleasure to the sixteen. The iron-souled truth-monger would plainly manifest, or even utter the fact that he didn't want to see those people—and he would be an ass, and inflict a totally unnecessary pain. And next, those ladies in that far country—but never mind, they had a thousand pleasant ways of lying, that grew out of gentle impulses, and were a credit to their intelligence and an honor to their hearts. Let the particulars go.

The men in that far country were liars, every one. Their mere howdy-do was a lie, because *they* didn't care how you did, except they were undertakers. To the ordinary inquirer you lied in return; for you made no conscientious diagnosis of your case, but answered at random, and usually missed it considerably. You lied to the undertaker, and said your health was failing—a wholly commendable lie, since it cost you nothing and pleased the other man. If a stranger called and interrupted you, you said with your hearty tongue, "I'm glad to see you," and said with your heartier soul, "I wish you were with the cannibals and it was dinner-time." When he went, you said regretfully, "*Must* you go?" and followed it with a "Call again;" but you did no harm, for you did not deceive anybody nor inflict any hurt, whereas the truth would have made you both unhappy.

I think that all this courteous lying is a sweet and loving art, and should be cultivated. The highest perfection of politeness is only a beautiful edifice, built, from the base to the dome, of graceful and gilded forms of charitable and unselfish lying.

What I bemoan is the growing prevalence of the brutal truth. Let us do what we can to eradicate it. An injurious truth has no merit over an injurious lie. Neither should ever be uttered. The man who speaks an injurious truth, lest his soul be not saved if he do otherwise, should reflect that that sort of a soul is not strictly worth saving. The man who tells a lie to help a poor devil out of trouble, is one of whom the angels doubtless say, "In, here is an heroic soul who casts his own welfare into jeopardy to succor his neighbor's; let us exalt this magnanimous liar."

An injurious lie is an uncommendable thing; and so, also, and in the same degree, is an injurious truth—a fact which is recognized by the law of libel.

Among other common lies, we have the *silent* lie—the deception which one conveys by simply keeping still and concealing the truth. Many obstinate truth-mongers indulge in this dissipation, imagining that if they *speak* no lie, they lie not at all. In that far country where I once lived, there was a lively spirit, a lady whose impulses were always high and pure, and whose character answered to them. One day I was there at dinner, and remarked in a general way, that we are all liars. She was amazed, and said, "Not *all?*" It was before "Pinafore's" time, so I did not make the response which would naturally follow in our day, but frankly said, "Yes, *all*—we are all liars; there are no exceptions." She looked almost offended, and said, "Why, do you include *me?*" "Certainly," I said, "I think you even rank as an expert. She said, "'Sh-sh! the children!" So the subject was changed in deference to the children's presence, and we went on talking about other things. But as soon as the young people were out of the way, the lady came warmly back to the matter and said, "I have made it the rule of my life to never tell a lie; and I have never departed from it in a single instance." I said, "I don't mean the least harm or disrespect, but really you have been lying like smoke ever since I've been sitting here. It has caused me a good deal of pain, because I am not used to it." She required of me an instance—just a single instance. So I said:

"Well, here is the unfilled duplicate of the blank which the Oakland hospital people sent to you by the hand of the sick-nurse when she came here to nurse your little nephew through his dangerous illness. This blank asks all manner of questions as to the conduct of that sick-nurse: 'Did she ever sleep on her watch? Did she ever forget to give the medicine?' and so forth and so on. You are warned to be very careful and explicit in your answers, for the welfare of the service requires that the nurses be promptly fined or otherwise punished for derelictions. You told me you were perfectly delighted with that nurse—that she had a thousand perfections and only one fault: you found you never could depend on her wrapping Johnny up half sufficiently while he waited in a chilly chair for her to rearrange the warm bed. You filled up the duplicate of this paper, and sent it back to the hospital by the hand of the nurse. How did you answer this question—'Was the nurse at any time guilty of a negligence which was likely to result in the patient's taking cold?' Come—everything is decided by a bet here in California: ten dollars to ten cents you lied when you answered that question." She said, "I didn't; I *left it blank!*" "Just so—you have told a *silent* lie; you have left it to be inferred that you had no fault to find in that matter." She said, "Oh, was that a lie? And how *could* I mention her one single fault, and she so good?—it would have been cruel." I said, "One ought always to lie, when one can do good by it; your impulse was right, but your judgment was crude; this comes of unintelligent practice. Now observe the result of this inexpert deflection of yours. You know Mr. Jones's Willie is lying very low with scarlet fever; well, your recommendation was so enthusiastic that that girl is there nursing him, and the worn-out family have all been trustingly sound asleep for the last fourteen hours, leaving their darling with full confidence in those fatal hands, because you, like young George Washington, have a reputa—However, if you are not going to have anything to do, I will come around to-morrow and we'll attend the funeral together, for, of course, you'll naturally feel a peculiar interest in Willie's case—as personal a one, in fact, as the undertaker."

But that was all lost. Before I was halfway through she was in a carriage and making thirty miles an hour toward the Jones mansion to save what was left of Willie and tell all she knew about the deadly nurse. All of which was unnecessary, as Willie wasn't sick; I had been lying myself. But that same day, all the same, she sent a line to the hospital which filled up the neglected blank, and stated the *facts*, too, in the squarest possible manner,

Now, you see, this lady's fault was *not* in lying, but only in lying injudiciously. She should have told the truth, *there*, and made it up to the nurse with a fraudulent compliment further along in the paper. She could have said, "In one respect the sick-nurse is perfection—when she is on watch, she never snores." Almost any little pleasant lie would have taken the sting out of that troublesome but necessary expression of the truth.

Lying is universal—we *all* do it; we all *must* do it. Therefore, the wise thing is for us diligently to train ourselves to lie thoughtfully, judiciously; to lie with a good object, and not an evil one; to lie for others' advantage, and not our own; to lie healingly, charitably, humanely, not cruelly, hurtfully, maliciously; to lie gracefully and graciously, not awkwardly and clumsily; to lie firmly, frankly, squarely, with head erect, not haltingly, tortuously, with pusillanimous mien, as being ashamed of our high calling. Then shall we be rid of the rank and pestilent truth that is rotting the land; then shall we be great and good and beautiful, and worthy dwellers in a world where even benign Nature habitually lies, except when she promises execrable weather. Then—But I am but a new and feeble student in this gracious art; I cannot instruct *this* Club.

Joking aside, I think there is much need of wise examination into what sorts of lies are best and wholesomest to be indulged, seeing we *must* all lie and *do* all lie, and what sorts it may be best to avoid—and this is a thing which I feel I can confidently put into the hands of this experienced Club—a ripe body, who may be termed, in this regard, and without undue flattery, Old Masters.

The Evil of Lying

Charles Fried

The evil of lying is, has hard to pin down as it is strongly felt. Is lying wrong or is it merely something bad? If it is bad, why is it bad—is it bad in itself or because of some tendency associated with it? Compare lying to physical harm. Harm is a state of the world and so it can only be classified as bad; the wrong I argued for was the *intentional doing* of harm. Lying, on the other hand, can be wrong, since it is an action. But the fact that lying is an action does not mean that it *must* be wrong rather than bad. It might be that the action of lying should be judged as just another state of the world—a time-extended state, to be sure, but there is no problem about that—and as such it would count as a negative element in any set of circumstances in which it occurred. Furthermore, if lying is judged to be bad it can be bad in itself, like something ugly or painful, or it can be bad only because of its tendency to produce results that are bad in themselves,

If lying were bad, not wrong, this would mean only that, other things being equal, we should avoid lies. And if lying were bad not in itself but merely because of its tendencies, we would have to avoid lies only when those tendencies were in fact likely to be realized. In either case lying would be permissible to produce a net benefit, including the prevention of more or worse lies. By contrast the categorical norm "Do not lie" does not evaluate states of affairs but is addressed to moral agents, forbidding lies. Now if lying is wrong it is also bad in itself, for the category of the intrinsically bad is weaker and more inclusive than the category of the wrong. And accordingly, many states of the world are intrinsically bad (such as destruction of valuable property) but intentional acts bringing them about are not necessarily wrong.

Bentham plainly believed that lying is neither wrong nor even intrinsically bad: "Falsehood, take it by itself, consider it as not being accompanied by any other material circumstances, nor therefore productive of any material effects, can never, upon the principle of utility, constitute any offense at all." By contrast, Kant and Augustine argued at length that lying is wrong. Indeed, they held that lying is not only wrong *unless* excused or justified in defined ways (which is my view) but that lying is always wrong. Augustine sees lying as a kind of defilement, the liar being tainted by the lie, quite apart from any consequences of the lie. Kant's views are more complex. He argues at one point that lying undermines confidence and trust among men generally: "Although by making a false statement I do no wrong to him who unjustly compels me to speak, yet I do wrong to men in general. . . . I cause that declarations in general find no credit, and hence all rights founded on contract should lose their force; and this is a wrong to mankind." This would seem to be a consequentialist argument, according to which lying is bad only insofar as it produces these bad results. But elsewhere he makes plain that he believes these bad consequences to be necessarily, perhaps even conceptually linked to lying. In this more rigoristic vein, he asserts that lying is a perversion of one's uniquely human capacities irrespective of any consequences of the lie, and thus lying is not only intrinsically bad but wrong.

Finally, a number of writers have taken what looks like an intermediate position: the evil of lying is indeed identified with its consequences, but the connection between lying and those consequences, while not a necessary connection, is close and persistent, and the consequences themselves are pervasive and profound, Consider this passage from a recent work by G. F. Warnock:

> I do not necessarily do you any harm at all by deed or word if I induce you to believe what is not in fact the case; I may even do you good, possibly by way, for example, of consolation or flattery. Nevertheless, though deception is not thus necessarily directly damaging it is easy to see how crucially important it is that the natural inclination to have recourse to it should be counteracted. It is, one might say, not the implanting of false beliefs that is damaging, but rather the generation of the suspicion that they may be being implanted. For this undermines trust; and, to the extent that trust is undermined, all cooperative undertakings, in which what one person can do or has reason to do is dependent on what others have done, are doing, or are going to do, must tend to break down. . . . There is no sense in my asking you for your opinion on some point, if I do not suppose that your answer will actually express your opinion (verbal communication is doubtless the most important of all our cooperative undertakings).

Warnock does not quite say that truth-telling is good in itself or that lying is wrong, yet the moral quality of truth-telling and lying is not so simply instrumental as it is, for instance, for Bentham. Rather, truth-telling seems to bear a fundamental, pervasive relation to the human enterprise, just by lying appears to be fundamentally subversive of that enterprise. What exactly is the nature of this relation? How does truth-telling bear to human goods a relation which is more than instrumental but less than necessary?

Chapter VI: Lying and Veracity

The very definition of lying makes plain that consequences are crucial, for lying is intentional and the intent is an intent to produce a consequence: false belief. But how can I then resist the consequentialist analysis of lying? Lying is an attempt to produce a certain effect on another, and if that effect (consequence) is not bad, how can lying be wrong? I shall have to argue, therefore, that to lie is to intend to produce an effect which always has something bad about it, an effect moreover of the special sort that it is wrong to produce it intentionally. To lay that groundwork for my argument about lying, I must consider first the moral value of truth.

Truth and Rationality

A statement is true when the world is the way the statement says it is. Utilitarians insist (as in the quotation from Bentham above) that truth, like everything else, has value just exactly as it produces value—pleasure, pain, the satisfaction or frustration of desire. And of course it is easy to show that truth (like keeping faith, not harming the innocent, respecting rights) does not always lead to the net satisfactions of desire, to the production of utility. It may *tend* to do so, but that tendency explains only why we should discriminate between occasions when truth does and when it does not have value—an old story. It is an old story, for truth—like justice, respect, and self-respect—has a value which consequentialist analyses (utilitarian or any other) do not capture. Truth, like respect, is a foundational value.

The morality of right and wrong does not count the satisfaction of desire as the overriding value. Rather, the integrity of persons, as agents and as the objects of the intentional agency of others, has priority over the attainment of the goals which agents choose to attain. I have sought to show how respect for physical integrity is related to respect for the person. The person, I argued, is not just a locus of potential pleasure and pain but an entity with determinate characteristics. The person is, among other things, necessarily an incorporated, a physical, not an abstract entity. In relation to truth we touch another necessary aspect of moral personality: the capacity for judgment, and thus for choice. It is that aspect which Kant used to ground his moral theory, arguing that freedom and rationality are the basis for moral personality. John Bawls makes the same point, arguing that "moral personality and not the capacity for pleasure and pain . . . [is] the fundamental aspect of the self. . . . The essential unity of the self is . . . . provided by the concept of right." The concept of the self is prior to the goods which the self chooses, and these goods gather their moral significance from the fact that they have been chosen by moral beings—beings capable of understanding and acting on moral principles.

In this view freedom and rationality are complementary capacities, or aspects of the same capacity, which is moral capacity. A man is free insofar as he is able to act on a judgment because he perceives it to be correct; he is free insofar as he may be moved to action by the judgments his reason offers to him. This is the very opposite of the Humean conception of reason as the slave of the passions. There is no slavery here. The man who follows the steps of a mathematical argument to its conclusion because he judges them to be correct is free indeed. To the extent that we choose our ends we are free; and as to objectively valuable ends which we choose because we see their value, we are still free.

Now, rational judgment is true judgment, and so the moral capacity for rational choice implies the capacity to recognize the matter on which choice is to act and to recognize the kind of result our choices will produce. This applies to judgments about other selves and to judgments in which one locates himself as a person among persons, a self among selves. These judgments are not just arbitrary suppositions: *they are judged to be true of the world.* For consider what the self would be like if these judgments were not supposed to be true. Maybe one might be content to be happy in the manner of the fool of Athens who believed all the ships in the harbor to be his. But what of our perceptions of other people? Would we be content to have those whom we love and trust the mere figments of our imaginations? The foundational values of freedom and rationality imply the foundational value of truth, for the rational man is the one who judges aright, that is, truly. Truth is not the same as judgment, as rationality; it is rather the proper subject of judgment. If we did not seek to judge truly, and if we did not believe we could judge truly, the act of judgment would not be what we know it to be at all.

Judgment and thus truth are *part* of a structure which as a whole makes up the concept of self. A person's relation to his body and the fact of being an incorporated self are another part of that structure. These two parts are related. The bodily senses provide matter for judgments of truth, and the body includes the physical organs of judgment.

The Wrong of Lying

So our capacity for judgment is foundational and truth is the proper object of that capacity, but how do we get to the badness of lying, much less its categorical wrongness? The crucial step to be supplied has to do not with the value of truth but with the evil of lying. We must show that to lie to someone is to injure him in a way that particularly touches his moral personality. From that, the passage is indeed easy to the conclusion that to inflict such injury intentionally (remember that all lying is by hypothesis

Chapter VI: Lying and Veracity

intentional) is not only bad but wrong. It is this first, crucial step which is difficult. After all, a person's capacity for true judgment is not necessarily impaired by inducing in him a particular false belief. Nor would it seem that a person suffers a greater injury in respect to that capacity when he is induced to believe a falsity than when we intentionally prevent him from discovering the truth, yet only in the first case do we lie. Do we really do injury to a person's moral personality when we persuade him falsely that it rained yesterday in Bangkok—a fact in which he has no interest? And do we do him more injury than when we fail to answer his request for yesterday's football scores, in which he is mildly interested? Must we not calculate the injury by the *other* harm it does; disappointed expectations, lost property, missed opportunities, physical harm? In this view, lying would be a way of injuring a person in his various substantive interests—a way of stealing from him, hurting his feelings, perhaps poisoning him—but then the evil of lying would be purely instrumental, not wrong at all.

All truth, however irrelevant or trivial, has value, even though we may cheerfully ignore most truths, forget them, erase them as encumbrances from our memories. The value of every truth is shown just in the judgment that the only thing we must not do is falsify truth. Truths are like other people's property, which we can care nothing about but may not use for our own purposes. It is as if the truth were not ours (even truth we have discovered and which is known only to us), and so we may not exercise an unlimited dominion over it. Our relations to other people have a similar structure: we may perhaps have no duty to them, we may be free to put them out of our minds to make room for others whom we care about more, but we may not harm them. And so we may not falsify truth. But enough of metaphors—what does it mean to say that the truth is not ours?

The capacity for true judgment is the capacity to arrive at judgments which are in fact true of the world as it exists apart from our desires, our choices, our values. It is the world presented to us by true judgments—including true judgments about ourselves—which we then make the subject of our choices, our valuation. Now, if we treat the truth as our own, it must be according to desire or valuation. But for rational beings these activities are supposed to depend on truth; we are supposed to desire and choose according to the world as it is. To choose that something not be the case when it is in fact the case is very nearly self-contradictory—for choice is not *of* truth but *on the basis of* truth. To deliberate about whether to believe a truth (not whether it is indeed true—another story altogether) is like deciding whether to cheat at solitaire. All this is obvious. In fact I suppose one cannot even coherently talk about choosing to believe something one believes to be false. And this holds equally for all truths—big and little, useful, useless, and downright inconvenient. But we do and must calculate *about* (and not just *with*) truths all the time as we decide what truths to acquire, what to forget. We decide all the time not to pursue some inquiry because it is not worth it. Such calculations surely must go forward on the basis of what truths are useful, given one's plans and desires. Even when we pursue truth for its own sake, we distinguish between interesting and boring truths.

Considering what truth to acquire or retain differs, however, from deliberately acquiring false beliefs. All truths are acquired as propositions correctly (truly) corresponding to the world, and in this respect, all truths are equal. A lie, however, has the form and occupies the role of truth in that it too purports to be a proposition about the world; only the world does not correspond to it. So the choice of a lie is not like a choice among truths, for the choice of a lie is a choice to affirm as the basis for judgment a proposition which does not correspond to the world. So, when I say that truth is foundational, that truth precedes choice, what I mean is *not* that this or that truth is foundational but that judging according to the facts is foundational to judging at all. A scientist may deliberate about which subject to study and, having chosen his subject, about the data worth acquiring, but he cannot even deliberate as a scientist about whether to acquire false data. Clearly, then, there is something funny (wrong?) about lying to oneself, but how do we go from there to the proposition that it is wrong to lie to someone else? After all, much of the peculiarity about lying to oneself consists in the fact that it seems not so much bad as downright self-contradictory, logically impossible, but that does not support the judgment that it is wrong to lie to another. I cannot marry myself, but that hardly makes it wrong to marry someone else.

Let us imagine a case in which you come as close as you can to lying to yourself: You arrange some operation, some fiddling with your brain that has no effect other than to cause you to believe a proposition you know to be false and also to forget entirely the prior history of how you came to believe that proposition. It seems to me that you do indeed harm yourself in such an operation. This is because a free and rational person wishes to have a certain relation to reality: as nearly perfect as possible. He wishes to build his conception of himself and the world and his conception of the good on the basis of truth. Now if he affirms that the truth is available for fiddling in order to accommodate either his picture of the world or his conception of the good, then this affirms that reality is dependent on what one wants, rather than what one wants being fundamentally constrained by what there is. Rationality is the respect for this fundamental constraint of truth. This is just another way of saying that the truth is prior to our plans and prospects and must be respected whatever our plans might be. What if the truth we "destroy" by this operation is a very trivial and irrelevant truth—the state of the weather in Bangkok on some particular day? There is still an injury to self, because the fiddler must have some purpose in his fiddling. If it is a substantive purpose, then the truth is in fact relevant to that purpose, and my argument holds. If it is just to show it can be done, then he is only trying to show he can do violence to his rationality—a kind of moral blasphemy. Well, what if it is a very *little* truth? Why, then, it is a very little injury he does himself—but that does not undermine my point.

Now, when I lie to you, I do to you what you cannot actually do to yourself—brain-fiddling being only an approximation. The nature of the injury I would do to myself, if I could, explains why lying to you is to do you harm, indeed why it is wrong. The lie is an injury because it produces an effect (or seeks to) which a person as a moral agent should not wish to have produced in him, and thus it is as much an injury as any other effect which a moral agent would not wish to have produced upon his person. To be sure, some people may want to be lied to. That is a special problem; they are like people who want to suffer (not just are willing to risk) physical injury. In general, then, I do not want you to lie to me in the same way that as a rational man I would not lie to myself if I could. But why does this make lying wrong and not merely bad?

Lying is wrong because when I lie I set up a relation which is essentially exploitative. It violates the principle of respect, for I must affirm that the mind of another person is available to me in a way in which I cannot agree my mind would be available to him—for if I do so agree, then I would not expect my lie to be believed. When I lie, I am like a counterfeiter: I do not want the market flooded with counterfeit currency; I do not want to get back my own counterfeit bill. Moreover, in lying to you, I affirm such an unfairly unilateral principle in respect to an interest and capacity which is crucial, as crucial as physical integrity: your freedom and your rationality. When I do intentional physical harm, I say that your body, your person, is available for my purposes. When I lie, I lay claim to your mind.

Lying violates respect and is wrong, as is any breach of trust. Every lie is a broken promise, and the only reason this seems strained is that in lying the promise is made and broken at the same moment. Every lie necessarily implies—as does every assertion—an assurance, a warranty of its truth. The fact that the breach accompanies the making should, however, only strengthen the conclusion that this is wrong. If promise-breaking is wrong, then a lie must be wrong, since there cannot be the supervening factor of changed circumstances which may excuse breaches of promises to perform in the future.

The final one of the convergent strands that make up the wrong of lying is the shared, communal nature of language. This is what I think Kant had in mind when he argued that a lie does wrong "to men in general." If whether people stood behind their statements depended wholly on the particular circumstances of the utterance, then the whole point of communication would be undermined. For every utterance would simply be the occasion for an analysis of the total circumstances (speaker's and hearer's) in order to determine what, if anything, to make of the utterance. And though we do often wonder and calculate whether a person is telling the truth, we do so from a baseline, a presumption that people do stand behind their statements. After all, the speaker surely depends on such a baseline. He wants us to think that he is telling the truth. Speech is a paradigm of communication, and all human relations are based on some form of communication. Our very ability to think, to conceptualize, is related to speech. Speech allows the social to penetrate the intimately personal. Perhaps that is why Kant's dicta seem to vacillate between two positions: lying as a social offense, and lying as an offense against oneself; the requirement of an intent to deceive another, and the insistence that the essence of the wrong is not injury to another but to humanity. Every lie violates the basic commitment to truth which stands behind the social fact of language.

I have already argued that bodily integrity bears a necessary relation to moral integrity, so that an attack upon bodily integrity is wrong, not just bad. The intimate *and* social nature of truth make the argument about lying stronger. For not only is the target aspect of the victim crucial to him as a moral agent but, by lying, we attack that target by a means which itself offends his moral nature; the means of attack are social means which can be said to belong as much to the victim as to his assailant. There is not only the attack at his moral vitals, but an attack with a weapon which belongs to him. Lying is, thus, a kind of treachery. (*Kind of* treachery? Why not treachery pure and simple?) It is as if we not only robbed a man of his treasure but in doing so used his own servants or family as our agents. That speech is our *common* property, that it belongs to the liar, his victim and all of us makes the matter if anything far worse.

So this is why lying is not only bad (a hurt), but wrong, why lying is wrong apart from or in addition to any other injury it does, and why lying seems at once an offense against the victim and against mankind in general, an offense against the liar himself, and against the abstract entity, truth. Whom do you injure when you pass a counterfeit bill?

What about little pointless lies? Do I really mean they are wrong? Well, yes, even a little lie is wrong, *if* it is a true piece of communication, an assertion of its own truth and not just a conventional way of asserting nothing at all or something else (as in the case of polite or diplomatic formulas). A little lie is a little wrong, but it is still something you must not do.

On a Supposed Right to Tell Lies from Benevolent Motives

Immanuel Kant

In the work called *France*, for the year 1797, Part VI., No. 1, on Political Reactions, by *Benjamin Constant*, the following passage occurs, p. 123:—

"The moral principle that it is one's duty to speak the truth, if it were taken singly and unconditionally, would make all society impossible. We have the proof of this in the very direct consequences which have been drawn from this principle by a German philosopher, who goes so far as to affirm that to tell a falsehood to a murderer who asked us whether our friend, of whom he was in pursuit, had not taken refuge in our house, would be a crime."

The French philosopher opposes this principle in the following manner, p. 124:—"It is a duty to tell the truth. The notion of duty is inseparable from the notion of right. A duty is what in one being corresponds to the right of another. Where there are no rights there are no duties. To tell the truth then is a duty, but only towards him who has a right to the truth. But no man has a right to a truth that injures others." The πρωτον ψενδος [false beginning] here lies in the statement that *"To tell the truth is a duty, but only towards him who has a right to the truth."*

It is to be remarked, first, that the expression "to have a right to the truth" is unmeaning. We should rather say, a man has a right to his own *truthfulness* (*veracitas*), that is, to subjective truth in his own person. For to have a right objectively to truth would mean that, as in *meum* and *tuum* generally, it depends on his *will* whether a given statement shall be true or false, which would produce a singular logic.

Now, the *first* question is whether a man—in cases where he cannot avoid answering Yes or No—has the *right* to be untruthful. The *second* question is whether, in order to prevent a misdeed that threatens him or some one else, he is not actually bound to be untruthful in a certain statement to which an unjust compulsion forces him.

Truth in utterances that cannot be avoided is the formal duty of a man to everyone, however great the disadvantage that may arise from it to him or any other; and although by making a false statement I do no wrong to him who unjustly compels me to speak, yet I do wrong to men in general in the most essential point of duty, so that it may be called a lie (though not in the jurist's sense), that is, so far as in me lies I cause that declarations in general find no credit, and hence that all rights founded on contract should lose their force; and this is a wrong which is done to mankind.

If, then, we define a lie merely as an intentionally false declaration towards another man, we need not add that it must injure another; as the jurists think proper to put in their definition (*mendacium est falsiloquium in praejudicium alterius*). For it always injures another; if not another individual, yet mankind generally, since it vitiates the source of justice. This benevolent lie *may*, however, by *accident* (*casus*) become punishable even by civil laws; and that which escapes liability to punishment only by accident may be condemned as a wrong even by external laws. For instance, if you have *by a lie* hindered a man who is even now planning a murder, you are legally responsible for all the consequences. But if you have strictly adhered to the truth, public justice can find no fault with you, be the unforeseen consequence what it may. It is possible that whilst you have honestly answered Yes to the murderer's question, whether his intended victim is in the house, the latter may have gone out unobserved, and so not have come in the way of the murderer, and the deed therefore have not been done; whereas, if you lied and said he was not in the house, and he had really gone out (though unknown to you), so that the murderer met him as he went, and executed his purpose on him, then you might with justice be accused as the cause of his death. For, if you had spoken the truth as well as you knew it, perhaps the murderer while seeking for his enemy in the house might have been caught by neighbours coming up and the deed been prevented. Whoever then *tells a lie*, however good his intentions may be, must answer for the consequences of it, even before the civil tribunal, and must pay the penalty for them, however unforeseen they may have been; because truthfulness is a duty that must be regarded as the basis of all duties founded on contract, the laws of which would be rendered uncertain and useless if even the least exception to them were admitted.

To be *truthful* (honest) in all declarations is therefore a sacred unconditional command of reason, and not to be limited to any expediency.

M. Constant makes a thoughtful and sound remark on the decrying of such strict principles, which it is alleged lose themselves in impracticable ideas, and are therefore to be rejected (p. 123):—"In every case in which a principle proved to be true seems to be inapplicable, it is because we do not know the *middle principle* which contains the medium of its application." He adduces (p. 121) the doctrine of *equality* as the first link forming

Chapter VI: Lying and Veracity

the social chain (p. 121): "namely, that no man can be bound by any laws except those to the formation of which he has contributed. In a very contracted society this principle may be directly applied and become the ordinary rule without requiring any middle principle. But in a very numerous society we must add a new principle to that which we here state. This middle principle is, that the individuals may contribute to the formation of the laws either in their own person or by *representatives*. Whoever would try to apply the first principle to a numerous society without taking in the middle principle would infallibly bring about its destruction. But this circumstance, which would only show the ignorance or incompetence of the lawgiver, would prove nothing against the principle itself." He concludes (p. 125) thus: "A principle recognized as truth must, therefore, never be abandoned, however obviously danger may seem to be involved in it." (And yet the good man himself abandoned the unconditional principle of veracity on account of the danger to society, because he could not discover any middle principle which would serve to prevent this danger; and, in fact, no such principle is to be interpolated here.)

Retaining the names of the persons as they have been here brought forward, "the French philosopher" confounds the action by which one does harm (*nocet*) to another by telling the truth, the admission of which he cannot avoid, with the action by which he does him *wrong* (*lædit*). It was merely an *accident* (*casus*) that the truth of the statement did harm to the inhabitant of the house; it was not a free *deed* (in the juridical sense). For to admit his right to require another to tell a lie for his benefit would be to admit a claim opposed to all law. Every man has not only a right, but the strictest duty to truthfulness in statements which he cannot avoid, whether they do harm to himself or others. He himself, properly speaking, does not do harm to him who suffers thereby; but this harm is caused by accident. For the man is not free to choose, since (if he must speak at all) veracity is an unconditional duty. The "German philosopher" will therefore not adopt as his principle the proposition (p. 124): "It is a duty to speak the truth, but only to him who has *a right to the truth*," first on account of the obscurity of the expression, for truth is not a possession the right to which can be granted to one, and refused to another; and next and chiefly, because the duty of veracity (of which alone we are speaking here) makes no distinction between persons towards whom we have this duty, and towards whom we may be free from it; but is an *unconditional duty* which holds in all circumstances.

Now, in order to proceed from a *metaphysic* of Right (which abstracts from all conditions of experience) to a principle of *politics* (which applies these notions to cases of experience), and by means of this to the solution of a problem of the latter in accordance with the general principle of right, the philosopher will enunciate:—1. An *Axiom*, that is, an apodictically certain proposition, which follows directly from the definition of external right (harmony of the *freedom* of each with the freedom of all by a universal law). 2. A *Postulate* of external public *law* as the united will of all on the principle of *equality*, without which there could not exist the freedom of all. 3. A *Problem*; how it is to be arranged that harmony may be maintained in a society, however large, on principles of freedom and equality (namely, by means of a representative system); and this will then become a principle of the *political system*, the establishment and arrangement of which will contain enactments which, drawn from practical knowledge of men, have in view only the mechanism of administration of justice, and how this is to be suitably carried out. Justice must never be accommodated to the political system, but always the political system to justice.

"A principle recognized as true (I add, recognized *à priori*, and therefore apodictic) must never be abandoned, however obviously danger may seep to be involved in it," says the author. Only here we must not understand the danger of *doing harm* (accidentally), but of *doing wrong*; and this would happen if the duty of veracity, which is quite unconditional, and constitutes the supreme condition of justice in utterances, were made conditional and subordinate to other considerations; and although by a certain lie I in fact do no wrong to any person, yet I infringe the principle of justice in regard to all indispensably necessary statements *generally* (I do wrong formally, though not materially); and this is much worse than to commit an injustice to any individual, because such a deed does not presuppose any principle leading to it in the subject. The man who, when asked whether in the statement he is about to make he intends to speak truth or not, does not receive the question with indignation at the suspicion thus expressed towards him that he might be a liar, but who asks permission first to consider possible exceptions, is already a liar (*in potentia*), since he shows that he does not recognize veracity as a duty in itself, but reserves exceptions from a rule which in its nature does not admit of exceptions, since to do so would be self-contradictory.

All practical principles of justice must contain strict truths, and the principles here called middle principles can only contain the closer definition of their application to actual cases (according to the rules of politics), and never exceptions from them, since exceptions destroy the universality, on account of which alone they bear the name of principles.

The Duty of Veracity

Henry Sidgwick

1. It may easily seem that when we have discussed Benevolence, Justice, and the observance of Law and Contract, we have included in our view the whole sphere of social duty, and that whatever other maxims we find accepted by Common Sense must be subordinate to the principles which we have been trying to define.

For whatever we owe definitely to our fellow-men, besides the observance of special contracts, and of positive laws, seems—at least by a slight extension of common usage—to be naturally included under Justice: while the more indefinite obligations which we recognize seem to correspond to the goodwill which we think ought to exist among all members of the human family, together with the stronger affections appropriate to special relations and circumstances. And hence it may be thought that the best way of treating the subject would have been to divide Duty generally into Social and Self-regarding, and again to subdivide the former branch into heads which I have discussed one by one; afterwards adding such minor details of duty as have obtained special names and distinct recognition. And this is perhaps the proper place to explain why I did not adopt this course. The division of duties into Social and Self-regarding, though obvious, and acceptable enough as a rough *prima facie* classification, does not on closer examination seem exactly appropriate to the Intuitional Method. For these titles naturally suggest that the happiness or well-being, of the agent or of others, is always the end and final determinant of right action: whereas the Intuitional doctrine is, that at least certain kinds of conduct are prescribed absolutely, without reference to their ulterior consequences. And if a more general meaning be given to the terms, and by Social duties we understand those which consist in the production of certain effects upon others, while in the Self-regarding we aim at producing certain effects upon ourselves, the division is still an unsuitable one. For these consequences are not clearly recognized in the enunciation of common rules of morality: and in many cases we produce marked effects both on ourselves and on others, and it is not easy to say which (in the view of Common Sense) are most important: and again, this principle of division would sometimes make it necessary to cut in two the class of duties prescribed under some common notion; as the same rule may govern both our social and our solitary conduct. Take, for example, the acts morally prescribed under the head of Courage. It seems clear that the prominence given to this Virtue in historic systems of morality has been due to the great social importance that must always attach to it, so long as communities of men are continually called upon to fight for their existence and well-being: but still the quality of bravery is the same essentially, whether it be exhibited for selfish or social ends.

It is no doubt true that when we examine with a view to definition the kinds of conduct commended or prescribed in any list of Virtues commonly recognized, we find, to a great extent, that the maxims we obtain are clearly not absolute and independent; that the quality denoted by our term is admittedly only praiseworthy in so far as it promotes individual or general welfare, and becomes blameworthy—though remaining in other respects the same—when it operates adversely to these ends. We have already noticed this result in one or two instances, and it will be illustrated at length in the following chapters. But though this is the case to a great extent, it is, for our present purpose, of special importance to note the— real or apparent—exceptions to the rule; because they are specially characteristic of the method that we call Intuitionism.

One of the most important of these exceptions is Veracity: and the affinity in certain respects of this duty—in spite of fundamental differences—to the duty of Good Faith or Fidelity to Promises renders it convenient to examine the two in immediate succession. Under either head a certain correspondence between words and facts is prescribed: and hence the questions that arise when we try to make the maxims precise are somewhat similar in both cases. For example, just as the duty of Good Faith did not lie in conforming our acts to the *admissible* meaning of certain words, but to the meaning which we knew to be put on them by the promisee; so the duty of Truthspeaking is not to utter words which *might*, according to common usage, produce in other minds beliefs corresponding to our own, but words which we believe will have this effect on the persons whom we address. And this is usually a very simple matter, as the natural effect of language is to convey our beliefs to other men, and we commonly know quite well whether we are doing this or not. A certain difficulty arises, as in the case of promises, from the use of set forms imposed either by law or by custom. . . . In the case of formulæ imposed by law—such (*e.g.*) as declarations of religious belief—it is doubtful whether we may understand the terms in any sense which they commonly bear, or are to take them in the sense intended by the Legislature that imposed them; and again, a difficulty is created by the gradual degradation or perversion of their meaning, which results from the strong inducements offered for their general acceptance; for thus they are continually strained and stretched until a new

Chapter VI: Lying and Veracity

general understanding seems gradually to grow up as to the meaning of certain phrases; and it is continually disputed whether we may veraciously use the phrases in this new signification. A similar process continually alters the meaning of conventional expressions current in polite society. When a man declares that he 'has great pleasure in accepting' a vexatious invitation, or is 'the obedient servant' of one whom he regards as an inferior, he uses phrases which were probably once deceptive. If they are so no longer, Common Sense condemns as over-scrupulous the refusal to use them where it is customary to do so. But Common Sense seems doubtful and perplexed where the process of degradation is incomplete, and there are still persons who may be deceived: as in the use of the reply that one is 'not at home' to an inconvenient visitor from the country.

However, apart from the use of conventional phrases, the rule 'to speak the truth' is not generally difficult of application in conduct. And many moralists have regarded this, from its simplicity and definiteness, as a quite unexceptional instance of an ethical axiom. I think, however, that patient reflection will show that this view is not really confirmed by the Common Sense of mankind.

※ ※ ※

2. In the first place, it does not seem clearly agreed whether Veracity is an absolute and independent duty, or a special application of some higher principle. We find (*e.g.*) that Kant regards it as a duty owed to oneself to speak the truth, because 'a lie is an abandonment or, as it were, annihilation of the dignity of man.' And this seems to be the view in which lying is prohibited by the code of honour, except that it is not thought (by men of honour as such) that the dignity of man is impaired by *any* lying: but only that lying for selfish ends, especially under the influence of fear, is mean and base. In fact there seems to be circumstances under which the code of honour prescribes lying. Here, however, it may be said to be plainly divergent from the morality of Common Sense. Still, the latter does not seem to decide clearly whether truthspeaking is absolutely a duty, needing no further justification: or whether it is merely a general right of each man to have truth spoken to him by his fellows, which right however may be forfeited or suspended under certain circumstances. Just as each man is thought to have a natural right to personal security generally, but not if he is himself attempting to injure others in life and property: so if we may even kill in defence of ourselves and others, it seems strange if we may not lie, if lying will defend us better against a palpable invasion of our rights: and Common Sense does not seem to prohibit this decisively. And again, just as the orderly and systematic slaughter which we call war is thought perfectly right under certain circumstances, though painful and revolting: so in the word-contests of the law-courts, the lawyer is commonly held to be justified in untruthfulness within strict rules and limits: for an advocate is thought to be over-scrupulous who refuses to say what he knows to be

411

false, if he is instructed to say it. Again, where deception is designed to benefit the person deceived, Common Sense seems to concede that it may sometimes be right: for example, most persons would not hesitate to speak falsely to an invalid, if this seemed the only way of concealing facts that might produce a dangerous shock: nor do I perceive that any one shrinks from telling fictions to children, on matters upon which it is thought well that they should not know the truth. But if the lawfulness of benevolent deception in any case be admitted, I do not see how we can decide when and how far it is admissible, except by considerations of expediency; that is, by weighing the gain of any particular deception against the imperilment of mutual confidence involved in all violation of truth.

The much argued question of religious deception ('pious fraud') naturally suggests itself here. It seems clear, however, that Common Sense now pronounces against the broad rule, that falsehoods may rightly be told in the interests of religion. But there is a subtler form in which the same principle is still maintained by moral persons. It is sometimes said that the most important truths of religion cannot be conveyed into the minds of ordinary men, except by being enclosed, as it were, in a shell of fiction; so that by relating such fictions as if they were facts, we are really performing an act of substantial veracity. Reflecting upon this argument, we see that it is not after all so clear wherein Veracity consists. For from the beliefs immediately communicated by any set of affirmations inferences are naturally drawn, and we may clearly foresee that they will be drawn. And though commonly we intend that both the beliefs immediately communicated and the inferences drawn from them should be true, and a person who always aims at this is praised as candid and sincere: still we find relaxation of the rule prescribing this intention claimed in two different ways by at least respectable sections of opinion. For first, as was just now observed, it is sometimes held that if a conclusion is true and important, and cannot be satisfactorily communicated otherwise, we may lead the mind of the hearer to it by means of fictitious premises. But the exact reverse of this is perhaps a commoner view: viz. that it is only an absolute duty to make our actual affirmations true; for it is said that though the ideal condition of human converse involves perfect sincerity and candour, and we ought to rejoice in exhibiting these virtues where we can, still in our actual world concealment is frequently necessary to the well-being of society, and may be legitimately effected by any means short of actual falsehood. Thus it is not uncommonly said that in defence of a secret we may not indeed *lie*, *i.e.* produce directly beliefs contrary to fact; but we may "turn a question aside," *i.e.* produce indirectly, by natural inference from our answer, a negatively false belief; or "throw the inquirer on a wrong scent," *i.e.* produce similarly a positively false belief. These two methods of concealment are known respectively as *suppressio veri* and *suggestio falsi*, and many think them legitimate under certain circumstances: while others say that if deception is to be practiced at all, it is mere formalism to object to any one mode of effecting it more than another.

On the whole, then, reflection seems to show, that the rule of Veracity, as commonly accepted, cannot be elevated into a definite moral axiom: for there is no real agreement as to how far we are bound to impart true beliefs to others: and while it is contrary to Common Sense to exact absolute candour under all circumstances, we yet find no self-evident secondary principle, clearly defining when it is not to be exacted.

※ ※ ※

3. There is, however, one method of exhibiting *a priori* the absolute duty of Truth, which we must not overlook; as, if it be valid, it would seem that the exceptions and qualifications above mentioned have been only admitted by Common Sense from inadvertence and shallowness of thought.

It is said that if it were once generally understood that lies were justifiable under certain circumstances, it would immediately become quite useless to tell the lies, because no one would believe them; and that the moralist cannot lay down a rule which, if generally accepted, would be suicidal. To this there seem to be three answers. In the first place it is not necessarily an evil that men's confidence in each other's assertions should, *under certain peculiar circumstances*, be impaired or destroyed: it may even be the very result which we should most desire to produce: *e.g.* it is obviously a most effective protection for legitimate secrets that it should be universally understood and expected that those who ask questions which they have no right to ask will have lies told them: nor, again, should we be restrained from pronouncing it lawful to meet deceit with deceit, merely by the fear of impairing the security which rogues now derive from the veracity of honest men. No doubt the ultimate result of general unveracity under the circumstances would be a state of things in which such falsehoods would no longer be told: but unless this ultimate result is undesirable, the prospect of it does not constitute a reason why the falsehoods should not be told so long as they are useful. But, secondly, since the beliefs of men in general are not formed purely on rational grounds, experience shows that unveracity may long remain partially effective under circumstances where it is generally understood to be legitimate. We see this in the case of the law-courts. For though jurymen are perfectly aware that it is considered the duty of an advocate to state as plausibly as possible whatever he has been instructed to say on behalf of any criminal he may defend, still a skilful pleader may often produce an impression that he sincerely believes his client to be innocent: and it remains a question of casuistry how far this kind of hypocrisy is justifiable. But, finally, it cannot be assumed as certain that it is never right to act upon a maxim of which the universal application would be an undoubted evil. This assumption may seem to be involved in what was previously admitted as an ethical axiom, that what is right for me must be right for 'all persons under similar conditions.' But reflection will show that there is a special case within the range of the axiom in which its application is necessarily self-limiting, and excludes the practical universality which the axiom appears to suggest: *i.e.* where the agent's conditions include (1) the knowledge that his maxim is not universally accepted, and (2) a reasoned conviction that his act will not tend to make it so, to any important extent. For in this case the axiom will practically only mean that it will be right for all persons to do as the agent does, if they are sincerely convinced that the act will not be widely imitated; and this conviction must vanish if it *is* widely imitated. It can hardly be said that these conditions are impossible: and if they are possible, the axiom that we are discussing can only serve, in its present application, to direct our attention to an important danger of unveracity, which constitutes a strong—but not formally conclusive—utilitarian ground for speaking the truth.

Is the "Whole Truth" Attainable?

Sissela Bok

"I was born for this, I came into the world for this: to bear witness to the truth; and all who are on the side of truth listen to my voice."
"Truth?" said Pilate, "what is that?" —John 18.37

If, like truth, the lie had but one face, we would be on better terms. For we would accept as certain the opposite of what the liar would say. But the reverse of truth has a hundred thousand faces and an infinite field. —Montaigne, *Essays*

Like freedom, truth is a bare minimum or an illusory ideal (the truth, the whole truth, and nothing but the truth about, say, the battle of Waterloo or the *Primavera*).
—J. L. Austin, "Truth," *Philosophical Papers*

The "Whole Truth"

Is it not naïve to set forth on a general exploration of lying and truth-telling? Some will argue that the task is impossible. Life is too complex, they will say, and societies too diverse. How can one compare the bargaining in an Eastern bazaar, the white lies of everyday life, the lie for national defense, and that to spare a dying child? Is it not arrogant and myopic to conceive of doing so?

And even if these variations could somehow be encompassed, the argument continues, how can we ever attain the truth about any complex matter—the battle of Waterloo, in Austin's example—or even a single circumstance? How can one, in fact, do full justice to the words used in court: "The truth, the whole truth, and nothing but the truth"?

These words mock our clumsy efforts to remember and convey our experiences. The "whole truth" has seemed so obviously unattainable to some as to cause them to despair of human communication in general. They see so many barriers to prevent us from obtaining truthful knowledge, let alone communicating it; so many pitfalls in conveying what we mean.

How can a physician, for example, tell the "whole truth" to a patient about a set of symptoms and their causes and likely effects? He certainly does not know all there is to know himself. Even all he does know that might have a bearing—incomplete, erroneous, and tentative though it be—could not be conveyed in less than weeks or even months. Add to these difficulties the awareness that everything in life and experience connects, that all is a "seamless web" so that nothing can be said without qualifications and elaborations in infinite regress, and a sense of lassitude begins to steal over even the most intrepid.

This book is intended as a reply to such arguments. The whole truth *is* out of reach. But this fact has very little to do with our choices about whether to lie or to speak honestly, about what to say and what to hold back. These choices can be set forth, compared, evaluated. And when they are, even rudimentary distinctions can give guidance.

If arrogance there be, it lies rather in the immobilizing impatience with all that falls short of the "whole truth." This impatience helps explain why the contemporary debate about deception is so barren. Paradoxically, the reluctance to come to grips with *deception* can stem from an exalted and all-absorbing preoccupation with *truth*.

"Truth"—no concept intimidates and yet draws thinkers so powerfully. From the beginnings of human speculation about the world, the questions of what truth is and whether we can attain it have loomed large. Every Philosopher has had to grapple with them.[1] Every religion seeks to answer them.

One pre-Socratic Greek tradition saw truth—*aletheia*—as encompassing all that we remember: singled out through memory from everything that is destined for Lethe, "the river of forgetfulness." The oral tradition required that information be memorized and repeated, often in song, so as not to be forgotten, Everything thus memorized—stories about the creation of the world, genealogies of gods and heroes, advice about health—all partook of truth, even if in another sense completely fabricated or erroneous. In this early tradition, repeating the songs meant keeping the material alive and thus "true," just as creating works of art could be thought of as making an object true, bringing it to life.

Only gradually did the opposition between truth and error come to be thought central to philosophy, and the nature of verification itself spotlighted. The immense preoccupation with epistemology took hold with

Plato and has never diminished since. In logic, in epistemology, in theology, and in metaphysics, the topic of "truth" has continued to absorb almost limitless energies. And since the strands from these diverse disciplines are not always disentangled, a great many references to "truth" remain of unsurpassed vagueness.

Truth and Truthfulness

In all such speculation, there is great risk of a conceptual muddle, of not seeing the crucial differences between two domains: the *moral* domain of intended truthfulness and deception, and the much vaster domain of truth and falsity in general. The moral question of whether you are lying or not is not *settled* by establishing the truth or falsity of what you say. In order to settle this question, we must know whether you *intend your statement to mislead*.

The two domains often overlap, and up to a point each is indispensable to the other. But truth and truthfulness are not identical, any more than falsity and falsehood. Until the differences are seen, and the areas of overlap and confusion spotlighted, little progress can be made in coping with the moral quandaries of lying.

The two domains are sometimes taken to be identical. This can happen whenever some believe that they have access to a truth so complete that all else must pale by comparison. Many religious documents or revelations claim to convey what is true. Those who do not accept such a belief are thought to live in error, in ignorance, even in blindness. At times, the refusal of nonbelievers to accept the dogma or truth revealed to the faithful is called, not merely an error, but a lie. The battle is seen as one between upholders of the faith and the forces of deception and guile.[2] Thus Bonhoeffer writes that:

> Jesus calls Satan "the father of the lie." (John 8.44) The lie is primarily the denial of God as He has evidenced Himself to the world. "Who is a liar but he that denieth that Jesus is the Christ?" (I John 2.22)

Convinced that they know the truth—whether in religion or in politics—enthusiasts may regard lies for the sake of this truth as justifiable. They may perpetrate so-called pious frauds to convert the unbelieving or strengthen the conviction of the faithful. They see nothing wrong in telling untruths for what they regard as a much "higher" truth.

In the history of human thought, we find again and again such a confusion of the two domains. It is not unrelated to the traditions which claim that truth exists, that it can be revealed, that one can hope to come face to face with it. Even Nietzsche, at war with such traditions, perpetuates the confusion:

> There is only *one* world, and that world is false, cruel, contradictory, misleading, senseless. [. . .] We need lies to vanquish this reality, this "truth," we need lies in order to live. [. . .] That lying is a necessity of life is itself a part of the terrifying and problematic character of existence.

The several meanings of the word "false" only add to the ease of confusing the two domains. For whereas "false" normally has the larger sense which includes all that is wrong or incorrect, it takes on the narrower, moral sense when applied to persons. A false person is not one merely wrong or mistaken or incorrect; it is one who is intentionally deceitful or treacherous or disloyal. Compare, to see the difference, a "false note" and a "false friend"; a "false economy" and a "false witness."[3]

Any number of appearances and words can mislead us; but only a fraction of them are *intended* to do so. A mirage may deceive us, through no one's fault. Our eyes deceive us all the time. We are beset by self-delusion and bias of every kind. Yet we often know when we mean to be honest or dishonest. Whatever the essence of truth and falsity, and whatever the sources of error in our lives, *one* such source is surely the human agent, receiving and giving out information, intentionally deflecting, withholding, even distorting it at times.[4] Human beings, after all, provide for each other the most ingenious obstacles to what partial knowledge and minimal rationality they can hope to command.

We must single out, therefore, from the countless ways in which we blunder misinformed through life, that which is done with the *intention to mislead*; and from the countless partial stabs at truth, those which are intended to be truthful. Only if this distinction is clear will it be possible to ask the moral question with rigor. And it is to this question alone—the intentional manipulation of information—that the court addresses itself in its request for "the truth, the whole truth, and nothing but the truth."

But one obstacle remains. Even after the two domains of the ethical and the epistemological are set apart, some argue that the latter should have priority. It is useless to be overly concerned with truthfulness, they claim, so long as one cannot know whether human beings are capable of knowing and conveying the truth in the first place. Such a claim, if taken seriously, would obviously make the study of truth-telling and deception seem pointless and flat. Once again, the exalted and all-absorbing preoccupation with "truth" then comes to nourish the reluctance to confront falsehood.

Skeptics have questioned the easy certitudes of their fellows from the earliest times. The most extreme among them have held that nothing can be known at all; sometimes they have gone very far in living out such a belief. Cratylus, a contemporary of Socrates, is said to have refused discussion of any kind. He held that the speakers and the words in any conversation would be changing and uncertain. He therefore merely wiggled his finger in response to any words to show that he had heard them but that a reply would be pointless. And Pyrrho, in the third century b.c., denied that anything could be known and concluded that nothing could therefore be said to be honorable or dishonorable, just or unjust.

For these radical skeptics, just as for those who believe that complete and absolute truth can be theirs, ethical matters of truth-telling and deception melt into insignificance by comparison with the illumination of truth and the dark void of its absence. As a result, both groups largely ignore the distinctions between truthfulness and falsehood in their intense quest for certainty regarding truth.

But the example of Cratylus shows how difficult it is to live up to thoroughgoing skepticism. Most thinkers who confuse intentional deception and falsity nevertheless manage to distinguish between the two in their ordinary lives. And those who consider the study of "truth" to be prior to any use of information put such concerns aside in their daily routines. They make informed choices of books in libraries; of subway connections and tools and food; they take some messages to be more truthful than others, and some persons as more worthy of their trust than others.

Ordinary decisions can no doubt be made in spite of theoretical beliefs which confuse truth and truth-telling, or which set epistemological certainty ahead of ethical analysis. But the fact remains that moral choice is often harmed thereby; for to the extent that one has radical doubts about the reliability of all knowledge, to that extent the moral aspects of how human beings treat one another, how they act, and what they say to each other, may lose importance. Worst of all, this loss is especially likely to afflict one's own moral choices. For whereas it is only prudent to support morality in others, we are more hospitable to doubts about the possibility of moral choice when it comes to our own decisions.

The most important reason why philosophers have done so little to analyze the problems of deception goes beyond particular views about truth, and truthfulness, and is more general. In most fields, theory is more congenial, less frustrating, than application. Ethics is no different. Many hesitate to grapple with concrete ethical problems, intertwined as they are with psychological and political strands rendering choice so difficult. Why tackle such choice when there are so many abstract questions of meaning and definition, of classification and structure, which remain to challenge the imagination?

As philosophy has become an increasingly academic and specialized enterprise, this hesitation has grown. But it was always there. Thus Epictetus, in the first century a.d., refers to it as follows, using the "principle not to speak falsely" as his example:

> The primary and most necessary part of philosophy is the application of principles, as for instance the principle not to speak falsely.
> The second part is that of the arguments, as in "Wherefore ought one not to speak falsely?"

> The third confirms these, and distinguishes between them, as in "Wherefore is that an argument?" For what is an argument, what a consequence, what a contradiction [conflict], what truth, what falsehood?
>
> Therefore, the third part is necessary because of the second, and the second because of the first; while the first is the most necessary, and is where we ought to remain. But we do the reverse; we squander our time in the third part, and to it goes all our zeal, while we utterly neglect the first. And thus we do lie, but are ready with the arguments which prove that one ought not to lie.

Applied ethics, then, has seemed uncongenial and lacking in theoretical challenge to many moral philosophers even apart from any belief in epistemological priority and from muddles about the meaning of "truth." As a result, practical moral choice comes to be given short shrift; and never more so than in the case of lies. To be sure, many do make some mention of lying. It is often used as an example, or ruled out in some summary manner. But such analysis cannot help but seem inadequate to those confronting difficult problems in their lives—wondering, perhaps, whether to lie to protect a client's confidences, or to keep shattering news from a sick man.

For all these reasons, deception commands little notice. This absence of real analysis is reflected also in teaching and in codes of professional ethics. As a result, those who confront difficult moral choices between truthfulness and deception often make up their own rules. They think up their own excuses and evaluate their own arguments. I shall take these up in the chapters to come. But one deserves mention here, for it results from a misuse of skepticism by those who wish to justify their lies, giving rise to a clearly fallacious argument. It holds that since we can never know the truth or falsity of anything anyway, it does not matter whether or not we lie when we have a good reason for doing so. Some have used this argument to explain why they and their entire profession must regretfully forego the virtue of veracity in dealing with clients. Such a view is stated, for example, by an eminent physician in an article frequently referred to in medical literature:

> Above all, remember that it is meaningless to speak of telling the truth, the whole truth, and nothing but the truth to a patient. It is meaningless because it is impossible—a sheer impossibility. [. . .] Since telling the truth is impossible, there can be no sharp distinction between what is true and what is false.
>
> [. . .] Far older than the precept, "the truth, the whole truth, and nothing but the truth," is another that originates within our profession, that has always been the guide of the best physicians, and, if I may venture a prophecy, will always remain so: So far as possible, do no

harm. You can do harm by the process that is quaintly called telling the truth. You can do harm by lying. [. . .] But try to do as little harm as possible.

The same argument is often used by biomedical investigators who claim that asking subjects for their informed consent to be used in research is meaningless because it is impossible to obtain a *genuinely* informed consent. It is used by government officials who decide not to inform citizens of a planned war or emergency measure. And very often, it is then supplemented by a second argument: Since there is an infinite gradation between what is truthful and what is deceitful, no lines can be drawn and one must do what one considers best on other grounds.

Such arguments draw on our concerns with the adequacy of information to reach a completely unwarranted conclusion: one that gives *carte blanche* to what those who lie take to be well-meant lies. The difference in perspectives is striking. These arguments are made by the liar but never by those lied to. One has only to imagine how the professionals who argue in this way would respond if their dentists, their lawyers, or their insurance agents used similar arguments for deceiving *them*. As dupes we know what as liars we tend to blur—that information can be more or less adequate; that even where no clear lines are drawn, rules and distinctions may, in fact, be made; and that truthfulness can be required even where full "truth" is out of reach.

The fact that the "whole truth" can never be reached in its entirety should not, therefore, be a stumbling block in the much more limited inquiry into questions of truth-telling and falsehood. It *is* possible to go beyond the notion that epistemology is somehow prior to ethics. The two nourish one another, but neither can claim priority. It is equally possible to avoid the fallacies which arise from the confusion of "truth" and "truthfulness," and to draw distinctions with respect to the adequacy and relevance of the information reaching us. It is therefore legitimate to go on to define deception and to analyze the moral dilemmas it raises.

Defining Intentional Deception and Lying

When we undertake to deceive others intentionally, we communicate messages meant to mislead them, meant to make them believe what we ourselves do not believe. We can do so through gesture, through disguise, by means of action or inaction, even through silence. Which of these innumerable deceptive messages are also lies? I shall define as a lie any intentionally deceptive message which is *stated*. Such statements are most often made verbally or in writing, but can of course also be conveyed via smoke signals, Morse code, sign language, and the like. Deception, then, is the larger category, and lying forms part of it.[5]

This definition resembles some of those given by philosophers and theologians, but not all. For it turns out that the very choice of definition has often presented a moral dilemma all its own. Certain religious and moral traditions were rigorously opposed to all lying. Yet many adherents wanted to recognize at least a few circumstances when intentionally misleading statements could be allowed. The only way out for them was, then, to define lies in such a way that some falsehoods did not count as lies. Thus Grotius, followed by a long line of primarily Protestant thinkers, argued that speaking falsely to those—like thieves—to whom truthfulness is not owed cannot be called lying. Sometimes the rigorous tradition was felt to be so confining that a large opening to allowable misstatements was needed. In this way, casuist thinkers developed the notion of the "mental reservation," which, in some extreme formulations, can allow you to make a completely misleading statement, so long as you add something in your own mind to make it true. Thus, if you are asked whether you broke somebody's vase, you could answer "No," adding in your own mind the mental reservation "not last year" to make the statement a true one.

Such definitions serve the special purpose of allowing persons to subscribe to a strict tradition yet have the leeway in actual practice which they desire. When the strict traditions were at their strongest, as with certain forms of Catholicism and Calvinism, such "definitional" ways out often flourished. Whenever a law or rule is so strict that most people cannot live by it, efforts to find loopholes will usually ensue; the rules about lying are no exception.

I see nothing wrong with either a narrow or a wider definition of lying, so long as one retains the prerogative of morally evaluating the intentionally misleading statements, no matter whether they fall within the category of lying or outside it.[6] But a narrower definition often smuggles in a moral term which in itself needs evaluation. To say, for instance, that it is *not* lying to speak falsely to those with no right to your information glides over the vast question of what it means to have such a right to information. In order to avoid this difficulty, I shall use instead a more neutral, and therefore wider, definition of a lie: an intentionally deceptive message in the form of a *statement*.

All deceptive messages, whether or not they are lies, can also be more or less affected by self-deception, by error, and by variations in the actual intention to deceive. These three factors can be looked at as filters of irregular thickness, distortion, and color that alter the ways in which a message is experienced by both deceived and deceivers. To complicate matters further, someone who intends to deceive can work *with* these filters and manipulate them; he can play on the biases of some persons, the imagination of others, and on errors and confusion throughout the system.

Chapter VI: Lying and Veracity

The interaction of these filters through which communication passes and is perceived is immensely complex. Each year we learn more about the complexity of communication, and about the role of the brain in sending and receiving messages. We see the intricate capacities of each person for denial, deflection, distortion, and loss of memory; but also for accuracy, regeneration, and invention. Add the fact that communication takes place over a period of time, sometimes long, and often between more than two persons. The many experiments on rumors show how information can be distorted, added to, partially lost, when passed from one person to another, until it is almost unrecognizable even though no one may have intended to deceive.

Merely trying to encompass these factors in our minds can lead to discouragement about the ethics of deception. It is for this reason that I propose that we remove the filters in the chapters that follow, so as to look primarily at clear-cut lies—lies where the intention to mislead is obvious, where the liar knows that what he is communicating is not what he believes, and where he has not deluded himself into believing his own deceits. We must, of course, always keep the filters in mind and never forget the underlying complexity. But with clear-cut lies we can make much sharper distinctions than if we look first at all the subtler variations. And it is important to try to resolve some of the problems these lies pose. After all, many of the most searing moral choices involve deciding whether or not to tell an outright lie.

If we could gain greater clarity for these choices and thereby narrow the margin of remaining doubt, we might then return to all the borderline difficulties with firmer ground under our feet. In the pages to come, therefore, clear-cut lies will often be singled out and considered separately. What do such lies do to our perception and our choices? And when might they be justified?

Endnotes

1. A glance at the Index of the recently published *Encyclopedia of Philosophy* reveals the contrast. As mentioned in the Introduction, it has no reference to "lying" or "deception." "Truth," on the other hand, receives over 100 references.
2. The confusion between "error" and "lie" underlying such a belief occasionally gives rise to the conclusion that those who are in possession of the truth—and thus not liars—are both infallible and incapable of lying. In order to sort out just what is meant by any one such claim, it is necessary to ask: Is the person believed infallible incapable of lying? of other forms of deceit? of being wrong? of being deceived? and with respect to what forms of knowledge? *Cf.* a Sufi

saying: "The pious would not deceive and the intelligent man can not be deceived." *A Sufi Rule for Novices*, ed. Menahem Wilson (Cambridge, Mass.: Harvard University Press, 1975), p. 41.

3. To further complicate matters, there are, of course, many uses of "false" to mean "deceitful" or "treacherous" which do not apply directly to persons, but rather to what persons have intended to be misleading. A "false trail," a "false ceiling," or a "false clue" carry different overtones of deceptiveness.
4. Messages between human beings can suffer from a number of unintended distortions or interferences, originating either at the source, en route, or at the reception. The speaker, for example, may be mistaken, inarticulate, or using a language unknown to the listener. En route, the message may be deflected by outside noise, by atmospheric conditions, by interruption. At the receiving end, deafness, fatigue, language problems, or mental retardation may affect the reception of the message.
5. It is perfectly possible to define "lie" so that it is identical with "deception." This is how expressions like "living a lie" can be interpreted. For the purposes of this book, however, it is best to stay with the primary distinction between deceptive *statements*—lies—and all the other forms of deception.
6. Consider the analogy with defining "hitting people." Say that you have religious texts which proscribe all "hitting" of people absolutely. Then, if you still want to be allowed to hit another, perhaps in self-defense or in play, you will find it useful to define "hitting" so as not to include the kinds you wish to allow. You may say, then, that "hitting" people is to be defined as striking them when you have no right to do so.

Truthfulness, Deceit, and Trust

Sissela Bok

> Suppose men imagined there was no obligation to veracity, and acted accordingly; speaking as often against their own opinion as according to it; would not all pleasure of conversation be destroyed, and all confidence in narration? Men would only speak in bargaining, and in this too would soon lose all mutual confidence.
> —Francis Hutcheson, *A System of Moral Philosophy*

> A great man—what is he? . . . He rather lies than tells the truth; it requires more spirit and *will*. There is a solitude within him that is inaccessible to praise or blame, his own justice that is beyond appeal.
> —Friedrich Nietzsche, *The Will to Power*

> Lying, after all, is suggestive of game theory. It involves at least two people, a liar and someone who is lied to; it transmits information, the credibility and veracity of which are important; it influences some choice another is to make that the liar anticipates; the choice to lie or not to lie is part of the liar's choice of strategy; and the possibility of a lie presumably occurs to the second party, and may be judged against some *a priori* expectations; and the payoff configurations are rich in their possibilities . . .
> —Thomas Schelling, "Game Theory and the Study of Ethical Systems"

Lying and Choice

Deceit and violence—these are the two forms of deliberate assault on human beings. Both can coerce people into acting against their will. Most harm that can befall victims through violence can come to them also through deceit. But deceit controls more subtly, for it works on belief as well as action. Even Othello, whom few would have dared to try to subdue by force, could be brought to destroy himself and Desdemona through falsehood.

The knowledge of this coercive element in deception, and of our vulnerability to it, underlies our sense of the *centrality* of truthfulness. Of course, deception—again like violence—can be used also in self-defense, even for sheer survival. Its use can also be quite trivial, as in white lies. Yet its potential for coercion and for destruction is such that society could scarcely function without some degree of truthfulness in speech and action.[1]

Imagine a society, no matter how ideal in other respects, where word and gesture could never be counted upon. Questions asked, answers given, information exchanged—all would be worthless. Were all statements randomly truthful or deceptive, action and choice would be undermined from the outset. There must be a minimal degree of trust in communication for language and action to be more than stabs in the dark. This is why some level of truthfulness has always been seen as essential to human society, no matter how deficient the observance of other moral principles. Even the devils themselves, as Samuel Johnson said, do not lie to one another, since the society of Hell could not subsist without truth any more than others.

A society, then, whose members were unable to distinguish truthful messages from deceptive ones, would collapse. But even before such a general collapse, individual choice and survival would be imperiled. The search for food and shelter could depend on no expectations from others. A warning that a well was poisoned or a plea for help in an accident would come to be ignored unless independent confirmation could be found.

All our choices depend on our estimates of what is the case; these estimates must in turn often rely on information from others. Lies distort this information and therefore our situation as we perceive it, as well as our choices. A lie, in Hartmann's words, "injures the deceived person in his life; it leads him astray."

To the extent that knowledge gives power, to that extent do lies affect the distribution of power, they add to that of the liar, and diminish that of the deceived, altering his choices at different levels. A lie, first, may misinform, so as to obscure some objective, something the deceived person wanted to do or obtain. It may make the *objective* seem unattainable or no longer desirable. It may even create a new one, as when Iago deceived Othello into wanting to kill Desdemona.

Lies may also eliminate or obscure relevant *alternatives*, as when a traveler is falsely told a bridge has collapsed. At times, lies foster the belief that there are more alternatives than is really the case; at other times, a lie may lead to the unnecessary loss of confidence in the best alternative. Similarly, the estimates of *costs and benefits* of any action can be endlessly varied through successful deception. The immense toll of life and human welfare from the United States' intervention in Vietnam came at least in part from the deception (mingled with self-deception) by those who channeled overly optimistic information to the decision-makers.

Finally, the degree of *uncertainty* in how we look at our choices can be manipulated through deception. Deception can make a situation falsely uncertain as well as falsely certain. It can affect the objectives seen, the alternatives believed possible, the estimates made of risks and benefits. Such a manipulation of the dimension of certainty is one of the main ways to gain power over the choices of those deceived. And just as deception can initiate actions a person would otherwise never have chosen, so it can prevent action by obscuring the necessity for choice. This is the essence of camouflage and of the cover-up—the creation of apparent normality to avert suspicion.

Everyone depends on deception to get out of a scrape, to save face, to avoid hurting the feelings of others. Some use it much more consciously to manipulate and gain ascendancy. Yet all are intimately aware of the threat lies can pose, the suffering they can bring. This two-sided experience which we all share makes the singleness with which either side is advocated in action all the more puzzling. Why are such radically different evaluations given to the effects of deception, depending on whether the point of view is that of the liar or the one lied to?

The Perspective of the Deceived

Those whose learn that they have been lied to in an important matter—say, the identity of their parents, the affection of their spouse, or the integrity of their government—are resentful, disappointed, and suspicious. They feel wronged; they are wary of new overtures. And they look back on their past beliefs and actions in the new light of the discovered lies. They see that they were manipulated, that the deceit made them unable to make choices for themselves according to the most adequate information available, unable to act as they would have wanted to act had they known all along.

It is true, of course, that personal, informed choice is not the only kind available to them. They may *decide* to abandon choosing for themselves and let others decide for them—as guardians, financial advisors, or political representatives. They may even decide to abandon choice based upon information of a conventional nature altogether and trust instead to the stars or to throws of the dice or to soothsayers.

But such alternatives ought to be personally chosen and not surreptitiously imposed by lies or other forms of manipulation. Most of us would resist loss of control over which choices we want to delegate to others and which ones we want to make ourselves, aided by the best information we can obtain. We resist because experience has taught us the consequences when others choose to deceive us, even "for our own good." Of course, we know that many lies are trivial. But since we, when lied to, have no way to judge which lies are the trivial ones, and since we have no confidence that liars will restrict themselves to just such trivial lies, the perspective of the deceived leads us to be wary of all deception.

Nor is this perspective restricted to those who are actually deceived in any given situation. Though only a single person may be deceived, many others may be harmed as a result. If a mayor is deceived about the need for new taxes, the entire city will bear the consequences. Accordingly, the perspective of the deceived is shared by all those who feel the consequences of a lie, whether or not they are themselves lied to. When, for instance the American public and world opinion were falsely led to believe that bombing in Cambodia had not begun, the Cambodians themselves bore the heaviest consequences, though they can hardly be said to have been deceived about the bombing itself.

An interesting parallel between skepticism and determinism exists here. Just as skepticism denies the possibility of *knowledge*, so determinism denies the possibility of *freedom*. Yet both knowledge, and freedom to act on it are required for reasonable choice. Such choice would be denied to someone genuinely convinced—to the very core of his being—of both skepticism and determinism. He would be cast about like a dry leaf in the wind. Few go so far. But more may adopt such views selectively, as when they need convenient excuses for lying. Lies, they may then claim, do not add to or subtract from the general misinformation or "unfreedom" of those lied to. Yet were they to adopt the perspective of the deceived, such excuses for lying to them would seem hollow indeed. Both skepticism and determinism have to be bracketed—set aside—if, moral choice is to retain the significance for liars that we, as deceived, know it has in our lives.

Deception, then, can be coercive. When it succeeds, it can give power to the deceiver—power that all who suffer the consequences of lies would not wish to abdicate. From this perspective, it is clearly unreasonable to assert that people should be able to lie with impunity whenever they want to do so. It would be unreasonable, as well, to assert such a right even in the more restricted circumstances where the liars claim a good reason for lying. This is especially true because lying so often accompanies every *other* form of wrongdoing, from murder and bribery to tax fraud and theft. In refusing to condone such a right to decide when to lie and when not to, we are therefore trying to protect ourselves against lies which help to execute or cover up all other wrongful acts.

For this reason, the perspective of the deceived supports the statement by Aristotle:

> Falsehood is in itself mean and culpable, and truth noble and full of praise.

There is an initial imbalance in the evaluation of truth-telling and lying. Lying requires a *reason*, while truth-telling does not. It must be excused; reasons must be produced, in any one case, to show why a particular lie is not "mean and culpable."

The Perspective of the Liar

Those who adopt the perspective of would-be-liars, on the other hand, have different concerns. For them, the choice is often a difficult one. They may believe, with Machiavelli, that "great things" have been done by those who have "little regard for good faith." They may trust that they can make wise use of the power that lies bring. And they may have confidence in their own ability to distinguish the times when good reasons support their decision to lie.

Liars share with those they deceive the desire not to *be* deceived. As a result, their choice to lie is one which they would like to reserve for themselves while insisting that others be honest. They would prefer, in other words, a "free-rider" status, giving them the benefits of lying without the risks of being lied to. Some think of this free-rider status as for them alone. Others extend it to their friends, social group, or profession. This category of persons can be narrow or broad; but it does require as a necessary backdrop the ordinary assumptions about the honesty of most persons. The free rider trades upon being an exception, and could not exist in a world where everybody chose to exercise the same prerogatives.

At times, liars operate as if they believed that such a free-rider status is theirs and that it excuses them. At other times, on the contrary, it is the very fact that others *do* lie that excuses their deceptive stance in their own eyes. It is crucial to see the distinction between the freeloading liar and the liar whose deception is a strategy for survival in a corrupt society.[2]

All want to avoid being deceived by *others* as much as possible. But many would like to be able to weigh the advantages and disadvantages in a more nuanced way whenever they are themselves in the position of choosing whether or not to deceive. They may invoke special reasons to lie—such as the need to protect confidentiality or to spare someone's feelings. They are then much more willing, in particular, to exonerate a well-intentioned lie on their own part; dupes tend to be less sanguine about the good intentions of those who deceive them.

But in this benevolent self-evaluation by the liar of the lies he might tell, certain kinds of disadvantage and harm are almost always overlooked. Liars usually weigh only the immediate harm to others from the lie against the benefits they want to achieve. The flaw in such an outlook is that it ignores or underestimates two additional kinds of harm—the harm that lying does to the liars themselves and the harm done to the general level of trust and social cooperation. Both are cumulative; both are hard to reverse.

How is the liar affected by his own lies? The very fact that he *knows* he has lied, first of all, affects him. He may regard the lie as an inroad on his integrity; he certainly looks at those he has lied to with a new caution. And if they find out that he has lied, he knows that his credibility and the respect for his word have been damaged. When Adlai Stevenson had to go before the United Nations in 1961 to tell falsehoods about the United States' role in the Bay of Pigs invasion, he changed the course of his life. He may not have known beforehand that the message he was asked to convey was untrue; but merely to carry the burden of being the means of such deceit must have been difficult. To lose the confidence of his peers in such a public way was harder still.

Granted that a public lie on an important matter, once revealed, hurts the speaker, must we therefore conclude that *every* lie has this effect? What of those who tell a few white lies once in a while? Does lying hurt them in the same way? It is hard to defend such a notion. No one trivial lie undermines the liar's integrity. But the problem for liars is that they tend to see *most* of their lies in this benevolent light and thus vastly underestimate the risks they run. While no one lie always carries harm for the liar, then, there is *risk* of such harm in most.

These risks are increased by the fact that so few lies are solitary ones. It is easy, a wit observed, to tell a lie, but hard to tell only one. The first lie "must be thatched with another or it will rain through." More and more lies may come to be needed; the liar always has more mending to do. And the strains on him become greater each time—many have noted that it takes an excellent memory to keep one's untruths in good repair and disentangled. The sheer energy the liar has to devote to shoring them up is energy the honest man can dispose of freely.

After the first lies, moreover, others can come more easily. Psychological barriers wear down; lies seem more necessary, less reprehensible; the ability to make moral distinctions can coarsen; the liar's perception of his chances of being caught may warp. These changes can affect his behavior in subtle ways; even if he is not found out he will then be less trusted than those of unquestioned honesty. And it is inevitable that more frequent lies *do* increase the chance that some will be discovered. At that time, even if the liar has no personal sense of loss of integrity[3] from his deceitful practices, he will surely regret the damage to his credibility which their discovery brings about. Paradoxically, once his word is no longer trusted, he will be left with greatly *decreased* power—even though a lie often does bring at least a short-term gain in power over those deceived.

Even, if the liar cares little about the risks to others from his deception, therefore, all these risks to himself argue in favor of at least weighing any decision to lie quite seriously. Yet such risks rarely enter his calculations.

Chapter VI: Lying and Veracity

Bias skews all judgment, but never more so than in the search for good reasons to deceive. Not only does it combine with ignorance and uncertainty so that liars are apt to overestimate their own good will, high motives, and chances to escape detection; it leads also to overconfidence in their own imperviousness to the personal entanglements, worries, and loss of integrity which might so easily beset them.

The liar's self-bestowed free-rider status, then, can be as corrupting as all other unchecked exercises of power. There are, in fact, very few "free rides" to be had through lying. I hope to examine, in this book, those exceptional circumstances where harm to self and others from lying is less likely, and procedures which can isolate and contain them. But the chance of harm to liars can rarely be ruled out altogether.

Bias causes liars often to ignore the second type of harm as well. For even if they make the effort to estimate the consequences to *individuals*—themselves and others—of their lies, they often fail to consider the many ways in which deception can spread and give rise to practices very damaging to human communities. These practices clearly do not affect only isolated individuals. The veneer of social trust is often thin. As lies spread—by imitation, or in retaliation, or to forestall suspected deception—trust is damaged. Yet trust is a social good to be protected just as much as the air we breathe or the water we drink. When it is damaged, the community as a whole suffers; and when it is destroyed, societies falter and collapse.

We live at a time when the harm done to trust can be seen first-hand. Confidence in public officials and in professionals has been seriously eroded. This, in turn, is a most natural response to the uncovering of practices of deceit for high-sounding aims such as "national security" or the "adversary system of justice." It will take time to rebuild confidence in government pronouncements that the CIA did not participate in a Latin American coup, or that new figures show an economic upturn around the corner. The practices engendering such distrust were entered upon, not just by the officials now so familiar to us, but by countless others, high and low, in the government and outside it, each time for a reason that seemed overriding.

Take the example of a government official hoping to see Congress enact a crucial piece of antipoverty legislation. Should he lie to a Congressman he believes unable to understand the importance and urgency of the legislation, yet powerful enough to block its passage? Should he tell him that, unless the proposed bill is enacted, the government will push for a much more extensive measure?

In answering, shift the focus from this case taken in isolation to the vast practices of which it forms a part. What is the effect on colleagues and subordinates who witness the deception, so often resulting from such a choice? What is the effect on the members of Congress as they inevitably learn of a proportion of these lies? And what is the effect on the electorate as it learns of these and similar practices? Then shift back to the narrower world of the official troubled about the legislation he believes in, and hoping by a small deception to change a crucial vote.

It is the fear of the harm lies bring that explains statements such as the following from Revelations (22.15), which might otherwise seem strangely out of proportion:

> These others must stay outside [the Heavenly City]: dogs, medicine-men, and fornicators, and murderers, and idolaters, and everyone of false life and false speech.

It is the deep-seated concern of the multitude which speaks here; there could be few contrasts greater than that between this statement and the self-confident, individualistic view by Machiavelli:

> Men are so simple and so ready to obey present necessities, that one who deceives will always find those who allow themselves to be deceived.

Discrepant Perspectives

The discrepancy of perspectives explains the ambiguity toward lying which most of us experience. While we know the risks of lying, and would prefer a world where others abstained from it, we know also that there are times when it would be helpful, perhaps even necessary, if we ourselves could deceive with impunity. By itself, each perspective is incomplete. Each can bias moral judgments and render them shallow. Even the perspective of the deceived can lead to unfounded, discriminatory suspicions about persons thought to be untrustworthy.

We need to learn to shift back and forth between the two perspectives, and even to focus on both at once, as in straining to see both aspects of an optical illusion. In ethics, such a double focus leads to applying the Golden Rule: to strain to experience one's acts not only as subject and agent but as recipient, sometimes victim. And while it is not always easy to put oneself in the place of someone affected by a fate one will never share, there is no such difficulty with lying. We all know what it is to lie, to be told lies, to be correctly or falsely suspected of having lied. In principle, we can all readily share both perspectives. What is important is to make that effort as we consider the lies we would like to be able to tell. It is at such times of choice and judgment that the Golden Rule is hardest to follow. The Muslim mystic Al-Ghazali recommended the shift in perspectives in the following words:

> If you want to know the foulness of lying for yourself, consider the lying of someone else and how you shun it and despise the man who lies and regard his communication as foul. Do the same with regard to all your own vices, for you do not realize the foulness of your vices from your own case, but from someone else's.

The parallel between deception and violence as seen from these two perspectives is, once again, striking. For both violence and deception are means not only to unjust coercion, but also to self-defense and survival. They have been feared and circumscribed by law and custom, when seen from the perspective of those affected by lies and by assaults. In religion and in ethics alike, they have been proscribed, and advice has been given on how to cope with the oppression in their wake.

But they have also been celebrated through the ages when seen from the perspective of the agent, the liar, the forceful man. The hero uses deceit to survive and to conquer. When looked at from this point of view, both violence and deceit are portrayed with bravado and exultation. Nietzsche and Machiavelli are their advocates, epic poetry their home. See, for example, how Athena, smiling, addresses Odysseus in the *Odyssey*:

> Whoever gets around you must be sharp
> and guileful as a snake; even a god
> might bow to you in ways of dissimulation.
> You! You chameleon!
> Bottomless bag of tricks! Here in your own country
> would you not give your stratagems a rest
> or stop spellbinding for an instant?
>
> You play a part as if it were your own tough skin.
> No more of this, though. Two of a kind, we are,
> contrivers, both. Of all men now alive
> you are the best in plots and story telling.
> My own fame is for wisdom among the gods—
> deceptions, too.

The Principle of Veracity

The perspective of the deceived, then, reveals several reasons why lies are undesirable. Those who share it have cause to fear the effects of undiscovered lies on the choices of liars and dupes. They are all too aware of the impact of discovered and suspected lies on trust and social cooperation. And they consider not only the individual lie but the practice of which it forms a part, and the long-term results which it can have.

For these reasons, I believe that we must at the, very least accept as an initial premise Aristotle's view that lying is "mean and culpable" and that truthful statements are preferable to lies in the absence of special considerations. This premise gives an initial negative weight to lies. It holds that they are not neutral from the point of view of our choices; that lying requires explanation, whereas truth ordinarily does not. It provides a counterbalance to the crude evaluation by liars of their own motives and of the consequences of their lies. And it places the burden of proof, squarely on those who assume the liar's perspective.

This presumption against lying can also be stated so as to stress the positive worth of truthfulness or veracity. I would like, in the chapters to come, to refer to the "principle of veracity" as an expression of this initial imbalance in our weighing of truthfulness and lying.

It is not necessarily a principle that overrides all others, nor even the one most frequently appealed to. Nor is it, obviously, sufficient by itself—witness the brutal but honest regime or the tormentor who prides himself on his frankness. Rather, trust in some degree of veracity functions as a *foundation* of relations among human beings; when this trust shatters or wears away, institutions collapse.[4]

Such a principle need not indicate that all lies should be ruled out by the initial negative weight given to them, nor does it even suggest what kinds of lies should be prohibited. But it does make at least one immediate limitation on lying: in any situation where a lie is a possible choice, one must first seek truthful alternatives. If lies and truthful statements appear to achieve the same result or appear to be as desirable to the person contemplating lying the lies should be ruled out. And only where a lie is the *last resort* can one even begin to consider whether or not it is morally justified. Mild as this initial stipulation sounds, it would, if taken seriously, eliminate a great many lies told out of carelessness or habit or unexamined good intentions.

When we try to move beyond this agreement on such an initial premise, the first fork in the road is presented by those who believe that *all* lies should be categorically ruled out. Such a position not only assigns a negative weight to lies; it sees this weight as so overwhelming that no circumstances can outweigh it. If we choose to follow that path, the quest for circumstances when lying is justified is obviously over.

Endnotes

1. But truthful statements, though they are not meant to deceive, can, of course, themselves be coercive and destructive; they can be used as weapons, to wound and do violence.
2. While different, the two are closely linked. If enough persons adopt the free-rider strategy for lying, the time will come when all will feel pressed to lie to survive.

Chapter VI: Lying and Veracity

3. The word "integrity" comes from the same roots which have formed "intact" and "untouched." It is used especially often in relation to truthfulness and fair dealing and reflects, I believe, the view that by lying one hurts oneself. The notion of the self-destructive aspects of doing wrong is part of many traditions. See, for example, the *Book of Mencius*: "Every man has within himself these four beginnings [of humanity, righteousness, decorum, wisdom]. The man who considers himself incapable of exercising them is destroying himself." See Merle Severy, ed., *Great Religions of the World* (Washington, D.C.: National Geographic Society, 1971), p. 167; and W.A.C.H. Dobson trans., *Mencius* (Toronto: University of Toronto Press, 1963), p. 132.
4. The function of the principle of veracity as a foundation is evident when we think of trust. I can have different kinds of trust: that you will treat me fairly, that you will have my interests at heart, that you will do me no harm. But if I do not trust your word, can I have genuine trust in the first three? If there is no confidence in the truthfulness of others, is there any way to assess their fairness, their intentions to help or to harm? How, then, can they be trusted? *Whatever* matters to human beings, trust is the atmosphere in which it thrives.

Sex, Lies, and Advertising

Gloria Steinem

About three years ago, as *glasnost* was beginning and *Ms.* seemed to be ending, I was invited to a press lunch for a Soviet official. He entertained us with anecdotes about new problems of democracy in his country. Local Communist leaders were being criticized in their media for the first time, he explained, and they were angry.

"So I'll have to ask my American friends," he finished pointedly. "how more *subtly* to control the press." In the silence that followed, I said, "Advertising."

The reporters laughed, but later, one of them took me aside: How *dare* I suggest that freedom of the press was limited? How dare I imply that his newsweekly could be influenced by ads?

I explained that I was thinking of advertising's media-wide influence on most of what we read. Even newsmagazines use "soft" cover stories to sell ads, confuse readers with "advertorials,"[1] and occasionally self-censor on subjects known to be a problem with big advertisers.

But, I also explained, I was thinking especially of women's magazines. There, it isn't just a little content that's devoted to attracting ads, it's almost all of it. That's why advertisers—not readers—have always been the problem for *Ms.* As the only women's magazine that didn't supply what the ad world euphemistically describes as "supportive editorial atmosphere" or "complementary copy" (for instance, articles that praise food/fashion/beauty subjects to "support" and "complement" food/fashion/beauty ads), *Ms.* could never attract enough advertising to break even.

"Oh, *women's* 's magazines," the journalist said with contempt. "Everybody knows they're catalogs—but who cares? They have nothing to do with journalism."

I can't tell you how many times I've had this argument in 25 years of working for many kinds of publications. Except as moneymaking machines—"cash cows" as they are so elegantly called in the trade—women's

Chapter VI: Lying and Veracity

magazines are rarely taken seriously. Though changes being made by women have been called more far-reaching than the industrial revolution—and though many editors try hard to reflect some of them in the few pages left to them after all the ad-related subjects have been covered—the magazines serving the female half of this country are still far below the journalistic and ethical standards of news and general interest publications. Most depressing of all, this doesn't even rate an exposé.

If *Time* and *Newsweek* had to lavish praise on cars in general and credit General Motors in particular to get GM ads, there would be a scandal—maybe a criminal investigation. When women's magazines from *Seventeen* to *Lear's* praise beauty products in general and credit Revlon in particular to get ads, it's just business as usual.

1

When *Ms.* began, we didn't consider *not* taking ads. The most important reason was keeping the price of a feminist magazine low enough for most women to afford. But the second and almost equal reason was providing a forum where women and advertisers could talk to each other and improve advertising itself. After all, it was (and still is) as potent a source of information in this country as news or TV and movie dramas.

We decided to proceed in two stages. First, we would convince makers of "people products" used by both men and women but advertised mostly to men—cars, credit cards, insurance, sound equipment, financial services, and the like—that their ads should be placed in a women's magazine. Since they were accustomed to the division between editorial[2] and advertising in news and general interest magazines, this would allow our editorial content to be free and diverse. Second, we would add the best ads for whatever traditional "women's products" (clothes, shampoo, fragrance, food, and so on) that surveys showed *Ms.* readers used. But we would ask them to come in *without* the usual quid pro quo of "complementary copy."

We knew the second step might be harder. Food advertisers have always demanded that women's magazines publish recipes and articles on entertaining (preferably ones that name their products) in return for their ads; clothing advertisers expect to be surrounded by fashion spreads (especially ones that credit their designers); and shampoo, fragrance, and beauty products in general usually insist on positive editorial coverage of beauty subjects, plus photo credits besides. That's why women's magazines look the way they do. But if we could break this link between ads and editorial content, then we wanted good ads for "women's products," too.

By playing their part in this unprecedented mix of *all* the things our readers need and use, advertisers also would be rewarded: Ads for products like cars and mutual funds would find a new growth market; the best ads for women's products would no longer be lost in oceans of ads for the same category; and both would have access to a laboratory of smart and caring readers whose response would help create effective ads for other media as well.

I thought then that our main problem would be the imagery in ads themselves. Car-makers were still draping blondes in evening gowns over the hoods like ornaments. Authority figures were almost always male, even in ads for products that only women used. Sadistic, he-man campaigns even won industry praise. (For instance, *Advertising Age* had hailed the infamous Silva Thin cigarette theme, "How to Get a Woman's Attention: Ignore Her," as "brilliant.") Even in medical journals, tranquilizer ads showed depressed housewives standing beside piles of dirty dishes and promised to get them back to work.

Obviously, *Ms.* would have to avoid such ads and seek out the best ones—but this didn't seem impossible. *The New Yorker* had been selecting ads for aesthetic reasons for years, a practice that only seemed to make advertisers more eager to be in its pages. *Ebony* and *Essence* were asking for ads with positive black images, and though their struggle was hard, they weren't being called unreasonable.

Clearly, what *Ms.* needed was a very special publisher and ad sales staff. I could think of only one woman with experience on the business side of magazines—Patricia Carbine, who recently had become a vice president of *McCall's* as well as its editor in chief—and the reason I knew her name was a good omen. She had been managing editor at *Look* (really *the* editor, but its owner refused to put a female name at the top of his masthead) when I was writing a column there. After I did an early interview with Cesar Chavez, then just emerging as a leader of migrant labor, and the publisher turned it down because he was worried about ads from Sunkist, Pat was the one who intervened. As I learned later, she had told the publisher she would resign if the interview wasn't published. Mainly because *Look* couldn't afford to lose Pat, it *was* published (and the ads from Sunkist never arrived).

Though I barely knew this woman, she had done two things I always remembered: put her job on the line in a way that editors often talk about but rarely do, and been so loyal to her colleagues that she never told me or anyone outside *Look* that she had done so.

Fortunately, Pat did agree to leave *McCall's* and take a huge cut in salary to become publisher of *Ms.* She became responsible for training and inspiring generations of young women who joined the *Ms.* ad sales force, many of whom went on to become "firsts" at the top of publishing. When *Ms.* first started, however, there were so few women with experience selling space that Pat and I made the rounds of ad agencies ourselves. Later, the fact that *Ms.* was asking companies to do business in a different way meant our saleswomen had to make many times the usual number of calls—first to convince agencies and then client companies besides—and

Chapter VI: Lying and Veracity

to present endless amounts of research. I was often asked to do a final ad presentation, or see some higher decision-maker, or speak to women employees so executives could see the interest of women they worked with. That's why I spent more time persuading advertisers than editing or writing for *Ms.* and why I ended up with an unsentimental education in the seamy underside of publishing that few writers see (and even fewer magazines can publish).

Let me take you with us through some experiences, just as they happened:

• Cheered on by early support from Volkswagen and one or two other car companies, we scrape together time and money to put on a major reception in Detroit. We know U.S. car-makers firmly believe that women choose the upholstery, not the car, but we are armed with statistics and reader mail to prove the contrary: A car is an important purchase for women, one that symbolizes mobility and freedom.

But almost nobody comes. We are left with many pounds of shrimp on the table, and quite a lot of egg on our face. We blame ourselves for not guessing that there would be a baseball pennant play-off on the same day, but executives go out of their way to explain they wouldn't have come anyway. Thus begins ten years of knocking on hostile doors, presenting endless documentation, and hiring a full-time saleswoman in Detroit: all necessary before *Ms.* gets any real results.

This long saga has a semihappy ending: foreign and, later, domestic car-makers eventually provided *Ms.* with enough advertising to make cars one of our top sources of ad revenue. Slowly, Detroit began to take the women's market seriously enough to put car ads in other women's magazines, too, thus freeing a few pages from the hothouse of fashion-beauty-food ads.

But long after figures showed a third, even a half, of many car models being bought by women, U.S. makers continued to be uncomfortable addressing women. Unlike foreign car-makers, Detroit never quite learned the secret of creating intelligent ads that exclude no one, and then placing them in women's magazines to overcome past exclusion. (*Ms.* readers were so grateful for a routine Honda ad featuring rack and pinion steering, for instance, that they sent fan mail.) Even now, Detroit continues to ask, "Should we make special ads for women?" Perhaps that's why some foreign cars still have a disproportionate share of the U.S. women's market.

• In the *Ms.* Gazette, we do a brief report on a congressional hearing into chemicals used in hair dyes that are absorbed through the skin and may be carcinogenic. Newspapers report this too, but Clairol, a Bristol-Myers subsidiary that makes dozens of products—a few of which have just begun to advertise in *Ms.*—is outraged. Not at newspapers or news magazines, just at us. It's bad enough that *Ms.* is the only women's magazine refusing to provide the usual "complementary" articles and beauty photos, but to criticize one of their categories—*that* is going too far.

439

We offer to publish a letter from Clairol telling its side of the story. In an excess of solicitousness, we even put this letter in the Gazette, not in Letters to the Editors where it belongs. Nonetheless—and in spite of surveys that show *Ms.* readers are active women who use more of almost everything Clairol makes than do the readers of any other women's magazine—*Ms.* gets almost none of these ads for the rest of its natural life.

Meanwhile, Clairol changes its hair-coloring formula, apparently in response to the hearings we reported.

- Our saleswomen set out early to attract ads for consumer electronics: sound equipment, calculators, computers, VCRs, and the like. We know that our readers are determined to be included in the technological revolution. We know from reader surveys that *Ms.* readers are buying this stuff in numbers as high as those of magazines like *Playboy*, or "men 18 to 34," the prime targets of the consumer electronics industry. Moreover, unlike traditional women's products that our readers buy but don't need to read articles about, these are subjects they want covered in our pages. There actually *is* a supportive editorial atmosphere.

"But women don't understand technology," say executives at the end of ad presentations. "Maybe not," we respond, "but neither do men—and we all buy it."

"If women *do* buy it," say the decision-makers, "they're asking their husbands and boyfriends what to buy first." We produce letters from *Ms.* readers saying how turned off they are when salesmen say things like "Let me know when your husband can come in."

After several years of this, we get a few ads for compact sound systems. Some of them come from JVC, whose vice president, Harry Elias, is trying to convince his Japanese bosses that there is something called a women's market. At his invitation, I find myself speaking at huge trade shows in Chicago and Las Vegas, trying to persuade JVC dealers that showrooms don't have to be locker rooms where women are made to feel unwelcome. But as it turns out, the shows themselves are part of the problem. In Las Vegas, the only women around the technology displays are seminude models serving champagne. In Chicago, the big attraction is Marilyn Chambers, who followed Linda Lovelace of *Deep Throat* fame as Chuck Traynor's captive and/or employee. VCRs are being demonstrated with her porn videos.

In the end, we get ads for a car stereo now and then, but no VCRs; some IBM personal computers, but no Apple or Japanese ones. We notice that office magazines like *Working Woman* and *Savvy* don't benefit as much as they should from office equipment ads either. In the electronics world, women and technology seem mutually exclusive. It remains a decade behind even Detroit.

- Because we get letters from little girls who love toy trains, and who ask our help in changing ads and box-top photos that feature little boys only, we try to get toy-train ads from Lionel. It turns out that Lionel executives

Chapter VI: Lying and Veracity

have been concerned about little girls. They made a pink train, and were surprised when it didn't sell.

Lionel bows to consumer pressure with a photograph of a boy and a girl—but only on some of their boxes. They fear that, if trains are associated with girls, they will be devalued in the minds of boys. Needless to say, *Ms.* gets no train ads, and little girls remain a mostly unexplored market. By 1986, Lionel is put up for sale.

But for different reasons, we haven't had much luck with other kinds of toys either. In spite of many articles on child-rearing; an annual listing of nonsexist, multiracial toys by Letty Cottin Pogrebin; Stories for Free Children, a regular feature also edited by Letty; and other prizewinning features for or about children, we get virtually no toy ads. Generations of *Ms.* saleswomen explain to toy manufacturers that a larger proportion of *Ms.* readers have preschool children than do the readers of other women's magazines, but this industry can't believe feminists have or care about children.

• When *Ms.* begins, the staff decides not to accept ads for feminine hygiene sprays or cigarettes: they are damaging and carry no appropriate health warnings. Though we don't think we should tell our readers what to do, we do think we should provide facts so they can decide for themselves. Since the anti-smoking lobby has been pressing for health warnings on cigarette ads, we decide to take them only as they comply.

Philip Morris is among the first to do so. One of its brands, Virginia Slims, is also sponsoring women's tennis and the first national polls of women's opinions. On the other hand, the Virginia Slims theme, "You've come a long way, baby," has more than a "baby" problem. It makes smoking a symbol of progress for women.

We explain to Philip Morris that this slogan won't do well in our pages, but they are convinced its success with some women means it will work with *all* women. Finally, we agree to publish an ad for a Virginia Slims calendar as a test. The letters from readers are critical—and smart. For instance: Would you show a black man picking cotton, the same man in a Cardin suit, and symbolize the antislavery and civil rights movements by smoking? Of course not. But instead of honoring the test results, the Philip Morris people seem angry to be proven wrong. They take away ads for *all* their many brands.

This costs *Ms.* about $250,000 the first year. After five years, we can no longer keep track. Occasionally, a new set of executives listens to *Ms.* saleswomen, but because we won't take Virginia Slims, not one Philip Morris product returns to our pages for the next 16 years.

Gradually, we also realize our naiveté in thinking we could decide against taking cigarette ads. They became a disproportionate support of magazines the moment they were banned on television, and few magazines could compete and survive without them; certainly not *Ms.*, which lacks so many other categories. By the time statistics in the 1980s showed that women's rate of lung cancer was approaching men's, the necessity of taking cigarette ads has become a kind of prison.

- General Mills, Pillsbury, Carnation, Del Monte, Dole, Kraft, Stouffer, Hormel, Nabisco: You name the food giant, we try it. But no matter how desirable the *Ms.* readership, our lack of recipes is lethal.

We explain to them that placing food ads *only* next to recipes associates food with work. For many women, it is a negative that works *against* the ads. Why not place food ads in diverse media without recipes (thus reaching more men, who are now a third of the shoppers in supermarkets anyway), and leave the recipes to specialty magazines like *Gourmet* (a third of whose readers are also men)?

These arguments elicit interest, but except for an occasional ad for a convenience food, instant coffee, diet drinks, yogurt, or such extras as avocados and almonds, this mainstay of the publishing industry stays closed to us. Period.

- Traditionally, wines and liquors didn't advertise to women: Men were thought to make the brand decisions, even if women did the buying. But after endless presentations, we begin to make a dent in this category. Thanks to the unconventional Michel Roux of Carillon Importers (distributors of Grand Marnier, Absolut Vodka, and others), who assumes that food and drink have no gender, some ads are leaving their men's club.

Beermakers are still selling masculinity. It takes *Ms.* fully eight years to get its first beer ad (Michelob). In general, however, liquor ads are less stereotyped in their imagery—and far less controlling of the editorial content around them—than are women's products. But given the underrepresentation of other categories, these very facts tend to create a disproportionate number of alcohol ads in the pages of *Ms.* This in turn dismays readers worried about women and alcoholism.

- We hear in 1980 that women in the Soviet Union have been producing feminist *samizdat* (underground, self-published books) and circulating them throughout the country. As punishment, four of the leaders have been exiled. Though we are operating on our usual shoestring, we solicit individual contributions to send Robin Morgan to interview these women in Vienna.

The result is an exclusive cover story that includes the first news of a populist peace movement against the Afghanistan occupation, a prediction of *glasnost* to come, and a grassroots, intimate view of Soviet women's lives. From the popular press to women's studies courses, the response is great. The story wins a Front Page award.

Nonetheless, this journalistic coup undoes years of efforts to get an ad schedule from Revlon. Why? Because the Soviet women on our cover *are not wearing makeup.*

- Four years of research and presentations go into convincing airlines that women now make travel choices and business trips. United, the first airline to advertise in *Ms.*, is so impressed with the response from our

Chapter VI: Lying and Veracity

readers that one of its executives appears in a film for our ad presentations. As usual, good ads get great results.

But we have problems unrelated to such results. For instance: Because American Airlines flight attendants include among their labor demands the stipulation that they could choose to have their last names preceded by "*Ms.*" on their name tags—in a long-delayed revolt against the standard, "I am your pilot. Captain Rothgart, and this is your flight attendant, Cindy Sue"—American officials seem to hold the magazine responsible. We get no ads.

There is still a different problem at Eastern. A vice president cancels subscriptions for thousands of copies on Eastern flights. Why? Because he is offended by ads for lesbian poetry journals in the *Ms.* Classified. A "family airline," as he explains to me coldly on the phone, has to "draw the line somewhere."

It's obvious that *Ms.* can't exclude lesbians and serve women. We've been trying to make that point ever since our first issue included an article by and about lesbians, and both Suzanne Levine, our managing editor, and I were lectured by such heavy hitters as Ed Kosner, then editor of *Newsweek* (and now of *New York Magazine*), who insisted that *Ms.* should "position" itself *against* lesbians. But our advertisers have paid to reach a guaranteed number of readers, and soliciting new subscriptions to compensate for Eastern would cost $150,000 plus rebating money in the meantime.

Like almost everything ad-related, this presents an elaborate organizing problem. After days of searching for sympathetic members of the Eastern board, Frank Thomas, president of the Ford Foundation, kindly offers to call Roswell Gilpatrick, a director of Eastern. I talk with Mr. Gilpatrick, who calls Frank Borman, then the president of Eastern. Frank Borman calls me to say that his airline is not in the business of censoring magazines: *Ms.* will be returned to Eastern flights.

• Women's access to insurance and credit is vital, but with the exception of Equitable and a few other ad pioneers, such financial services address men. For almost a decade after the Equal Credit Opportunity Act passes in 1974, we try to convince American Express that women are a growth market—but nothing works.

Finally, a former professor of Russian named Jerry Welsh becomes head of marketing. He assumes that women should be cardholders, and persuades his colleagues to feature women in a campaign. Thanks to this 1980s series, the growth rate for female cardholders surpasses that for men.

For this article, I asked Jerry Welsh if he would explain why American Express waited so long. "Sure," he said, "they were afraid of having a 'pink' card."

• Women of color read *Ms.* in disproportionate numbers. This is a source of pride to *Ms.* staffers, who are also more racially representative than the editors of other women's magazines. But this reality is obscured by ads filled with enough white women to make a reader snowblind.

Quest for Goodness: An Introduction to Ethics

Pat Carbine remembers mostly "astonishment" when she requested African American, Hispanic, Asian, and other diverse images. Marcia Ann Gillespie, a *Ms.* editor who was previously the editor in chief of *Essence*, witnesses ad bias a second time: Having tried for *Essence* to get white advertisers to use black images (Revlon did so eventually, but L'Oréal, Lauder, Chanel, and other companies never did), she sees similar problems getting integrated ads for an integrated magazine. Indeed, the ad world often creates black and Hispanic ads only for black and Hispanic media. In an exact parallel of the fear that marketing a product to women will endanger its appeal to men, the response is usually, "But your [white] readers won't identify."

In fact, those we are able to get—for instance, a Max Factor ad made for *Essence* that Linda Wachner gives us after she becomes president—are praised by white readers, too. But there are pathetically few such images.

• By the end of 1986, production and mailing costs have risen astronomically, ad income is flat, and competition for ads is stiffer than ever. The 60/40 preponderance of edit over ads that we promised to readers becomes 50/50; children's stories, most poetry, and some fiction are casualties of less space; in order to get variety into limited pages, the length (and sometimes the depth) of articles suffers; and, though we do refuse most of the ads that would look like a parody in our pages, we get so worn down that some slip through. Still, readers perform miracles. Though we haven't been able to afford a subscription mailing in two years, they maintain our guaranteed circulation of 450,000.

Nonetheless, media reports on *Ms.* often insist that our unprofitability must be due to reader disinterest. The myth that advertisers simply follow readers is very strong. Not one reporter notes that other comparable magazines our size (say, *Vanity Fair* or *The Atlantic*) have been losing more money in one year than *Ms.* has lost in 16 years. No matter how much never-to-be-recovered cash is poured into starting a magazine or keeping one going, appearances seem to be all that matter. (Which is why we haven't been able to explain our fragile state in public. Nothing causes ad flight like the smell of nonsuccess.)

My healthy response is anger. My not-so-healthy response is constant worry. Also an obsession with finding one more rescue. There is hardly a night when I don't wake up with sweaty palms and pounding heart, scared that we won't be able to pay the printer or the post office; scared most of all that closing our doors will hurt the women's movement.

Out of chutzpa and desperation, I arrange a lunch with Leonard Lauder, president of Estée Lauder. With the exception of Clinique (the brainchild of Carol Phillips), none of Lauder's hundreds of products has been advertised in *Ms.* A year's schedule of ads for just three or four of them could save us. Indeed, as the scion of a family-owned company whose ad practices are followed by the beauty industry, he is one of the few men who could liberate many pages in all women's magazines just by changing his mind about "complementary copy."

Over a lunch that costs more than we can pay for some articles, I explain the need for his leadership. I also lay out the record of *Ms.*: more literary and journalistic prizes won, more new issues introduced into the mainstream, new writers discovered, and impact on society than any other magazine; more articles that became books, stories that became movies, ideas that became television series, and newly advertised products that became profitable; and, most important for him, a place for his ads to reach women who aren't reachable through any other women's magazine. Indeed, if there is one constant characteristic of the ever changing *Ms.* readership, it is their impact as leaders. Whether it's waiting until later to have first babies, or pioneering PABA as sun protection in cosmetics, *whatever* they are doing today, a third to a half of American women will be doing three to five years from now. It's never failed.

But, he says, *Ms.* readers are not *our* women. They're not interested in things like fragrance and blush-on. If they were, *Ms.* would write articles about them.

On the contrary, I explain, surveys show they are more likely to buy such things than the readers of, say, *Cosmopolitan* or *Vogue*. They're good customers because they're out in the world enough to need several sets of everything: home, work, purse, travel, gym, and so on. They just don't need to read articles about these things. Would he ask a men's magazine to publish monthly columns on how to shave before he advertised Aramis products (his line for men)?

He concedes that beauty features are often concocted more for advertisers than readers. But *Ms.* isn't appropriate for his ads anyway, he explains. Why? Because Estée Lauder is selling "a kept-woman mentality."

I can't quite believe this. Sixty percent of the users of his products are salaried, and generally resemble *Ms.* readers. Besides, his company has the appeal of having been started by a creative and hardworking woman, his mother, Estée Lauder.

That doesn't matter, he says. He knows his customers, and they would *like* to be kept women. That's why he will never advertise in *Ms.*

※ ※ ※

In November 1987, by vote of the Ms. Foundation for Education and Communication (*Ms.*'s owner and publisher, the media subsidiary of the Ms. Foundation for Women), *Ms.* was sold to a company whose officers, Australian feminists Sandra Yates and Anne Summers, raised the investment money in their country that *Ms.* couldn't find in its own. They also started *Sassy* for teenage women.

In their two-year tenure, circulation was raised to 550,000 by investment in circulation mailings, and, to the dismay of some readers, editorial features on clothes and new products made a more traditional bid for ads.

Nonetheless, ad pages fell below previous levels. In addition, *Sassy*, whose fresh voice and sexual frankness were an unprecedented success with young readers, was targeted by two mothers from Indiana who began, as one of them put it, "calling every Christian organization I could think of." In response to this controversy, several crucial advertisers pulled out.

Such links between ads and editorial content was a problem in Australia, too, but to a lesser degree. "Our readers pay two times more for their magazines," Anne explained, "so advertisers have less power to threaten a magazine's viability."

"I was shocked," said Sandra Yates with characteristic directness. "In Australia, we think you have freedom of the press—but you don't."

Since Anne and Sandra had not met their budget's projections for ad revenue, their investors forced a sale. In October 1989, *Ms.* and *Sassy* were bought by Dale Lang, owner of *Working Mother, Working Woman*, and one of the few independent publishing companies left among the conglomerates. In response to a request from the original *Ms.* staff—as well as to reader letters urging that *Ms.* continue, plus his own belief that *Ms.* would benefit his other magazines by blazing a trail—he agreed to try the ad-free, reader-supported *Ms.* . . . and to give us complete editorial control.

2

In response to the workplace revolution of the 1970s, traditional women's magazines—that is, "trade books" for women working at home—were joined by *Savvy, Working Woman*, and other trade books for women working in offices. But by keeping the fashion/beauty/entertainment articles necessary to get traditional ads and then adding career articles besides, they inadvertently produced the anti-feminist stereotype of Super Woman. The male-imitative, dress-for-success woman carrying a briefcase became the media image of a woman worker, even though a blue-collar woman's salary was often higher than her glorified secretarial sister's, and though women at a real briefcase level are statistically rare. Needless to say, these dress-for-success women were also thin, white, and beautiful.

In recent years, advertisers' control over the editorial content of women's magazines has become so institutionalized that it is written into insertion orders or dictated to ad salespeople as official policy. The following are recent typical orders to women's magazines:
• Dow's Cleaning Products stipulates that ads for its Vivid and Spray 'n Wash products should be adjacent to "children or fashion editorial"; ads for Bathroom Cleaner should be next to "home furnishing/family" features; and so on for other brands. "If a magazine fails for half the brands or more," the Dow order warns, "it will be omitted from further consideration."

- Bristol-Myers, the parent of Clairol, Windex, Drano, Bufferin, and much more, stipulates that ads be placed next to "a full page of compatible editorial."
- S.C. Johnson & Son, makers of Johnson Wax, lawn and laundry products, insect sprays, hair sprays, and so on, orders that its ads *"should not be opposite extremely controversial features or material antithetical to the nature/copy of the advertised product."* (Italics theirs.)
- Maidenform, manufacturer of bras and other apparel, leaves a blank for the particular product and states: "The creative concept of the ——— campaign, and the very nature of the product itself appeal to the positive emotions of the reader/consumer. Therefore, it is imperative that all editorial adjacencies reflect that same positive tone. The editorial must not be negative in content or lend itself contrary to the ——— product imagery/message (e.g., *editorial relating to illness, disillusionment, large size fashion, etc.*)." (Italics mine.)
- The De Beers diamond company, a big seller of engagement rings, prohibits magazines from placing its ads with "adjacencies to hard news or anti/love-romance themed editorial."
- Procter & Gamble, one of this country's most powerful and diversified advertisers, stands out in the memory of Anne Summers and Sandra Yates (no mean feat in this context): Its products were not to be placed in *any* issue that included *any* material on gun control, abortion, the occult, cults, or the disparagement of religion. Caution was also demanded in any issue covering sex or drugs, even for educational purposes.

Those are the most obvious chains around women's magazines. There are also rules so clear they needn't be written down: for instance, an overall "look" compatible with beauty and fashion ads. Even "real" nonmodel women photographed for a woman's magazine are usually made up, dressed in credited clothes, and retouched out of all reality. When editors do include articles on less-than-cheerful subjects (for instance, domestic violence), they tend to keep them short and unillustrated. The point is to be "upbeat." Just as women in the street are asked, "Why don't you smile, honey?" women's magazines acquire an institutional smile.

Within the text itself, praise for advertisers' products has become so ritualized that fields like "beauty writing" have been invented. One of its frequent practitioners explained seriously that "It's a difficult art. How many new adjectives can you find? How much greater can you make a lipstick sound? The FDA restricts what companies can say on labels, but we create illusion. And ad agencies are on the phone all the time pushing you to get their product in. A lot of them keep the business based on how many editorial clippings they produce every month. The worst are products," like Lauder's as the writer confirmed, "with their own name involved. It's all ego."

Often, editorial becomes one giant ad. Last November, for instance. *Lear's* featured an elegant woman executive on the cover. On the contents page, we learned she was wearing Guerlain makeup and Samsara, a new fragrance by Guerlain. Inside were full-page ads for Samsara and Guerlain anti-wrinkle cream. In the cover profile, we learned that this executive was responsible for launching Samsara and is Guerlain's director of public relations. When the *Columbia Journalism Review* did one of the few articles to include women's magazines in coverage of the influence of ads, editor Frances Lear was quoted as defending her magazine because "this kind of thing is done all the time."

Often, advertisers also plunge odd-shaped ads into the text, no matter what the cost to the readers. At *Woman's Day*, a magazine originally founded by a supermarket chain, editor in chief Ellen Levine said, "The day the copy had to rag around a chicken leg was not a happy one."

Advertisers are also adamant about where in a magazine their ads appear. When Revlon was not placed as the first beauty ad in one Hearst magazine, for instance, Revlon pulled its ads from *all* Hearst magazines. Ruth Whitney, editor in chief of *Glamour*, attributes some of these demands to "ad agencies wanting to prove to a client that they've squeezed the last drop of blood out of a magazine." She also is, she says, "sick and tired of hearing that women's magazines are controlled by cigarette ads." Relatively speaking, she's right. To be as censoring as are many advertisers for women's products, tobacco companies would have to demand articles in praise of smoking and expect glamorous photos of beautiful women smoking their brands.

I don't mean to imply that the editors I quote here share my objections to ads: Most assume that women's magazines have to be the way they are. But it's also true that only former editors can be completely honest. "Most of the pressure came in the form of direct product mentions," explains Sey Chassler, who was editor in chief of *Redbook* from the sixties to the eighties. "We got threats from the big guys, the Revlons, blackmail threats. They wouldn't run ads unless we credited them."

"But it's not fair to single out the beauty advertisers because these pressures came from everybody. Advertisers want to know two things: What are you going to charge me? What *else* are you going to do for me? It's a holdup. For instance, management felt that fiction took up too much space. They couldn't put any advertising in that. For the last ten years, the number of fiction entries into the National Magazine Awards has declined.

"And pressures are getting worse. More magazines are more bottomline oriented because they have been taken over by companies with no interest in publishing.

"I also think advertisers do this to women's magazines especially," he concluded, "because of the general disrespect they have for women."

※ ※ ※

Even media experts who don't give a damn about women's magazines are alarmed by the spread of this ad-edit linkage. In a climate *The Wall*

Street Journal describes as an unacknowledged Depression for media, women's products are increasingly able to take their low standards wherever they go. For instance: Newsweeklies publish uncritical stories on fashion and fitness. *The New York Times Magazine* recently ran an article on "firming creams," complete with mentions of advertisers. *Vanity Fair* published a profile of one major advertiser, Ralph Lauren, illustrated by the same photographer who does his ads, and turned the lifestyle of another, Calvin Klein, into a cover story. Even the outrageous *Spy* has toned down since it began to go after fashion ads.

And just to make us really worry, films and books, the last media that go directly to the public without having to attract ads first, are in danger, too. Producers are beginning to depend on payments for displaying products in movies, and books are now being commissioned by companies like Federal Express.

But the truth is that women's products—like women's magazines—have never been the subjects of much serious reporting anyway. News and general interest publications, including the "style" or "living" sections of newspapers, write about food and clothing as cooking and fashion, and almost never evaluate such products by brand name. Though chemical additives, pesticides, and animal fats are major health risks in the United States, and clothes, shoddy or not, absorb more consumer dollars than cars, this lack of information is serious. So is ignoring the contents of beauty products that are absorbed into our bodies through our skins, and that have profit margins so big they would make a loan shark blush.

3

What could women's magazines be like if they were as free as books? as realistic as newspapers? as creative as films? as diverse as women's lives? We don't know.

But we'll only find out if we take women's magazines seriously. If readers were to act in a concerted way to change traditional practices of *all* women's magazines and the marketing of *all* women's products, we could do it. After all, they are operating on our consumer dollars; money that we now control. You and I could:

- write to editors and publishers (with copies to advertisers) that we're willing to pay more for magazines with editorial independence, but will not continue to pay for those that are just editorial extensions of ads;
- write to advertisers (with copies to editors and publishers) that we want fiction, political reporting, consumer reporting—whatever is, or is not, supported by their ads;

- put as much energy into breaking advertising's control over content as into changing the images in ads, or protesting ads for harmful products like cigarettes;
- support only those women's magazines and products that take *us* seriously as readers and consumers.
- Those of us in the magazine world can also use the carrot-and-stick technique. For instance: Pointing out that, if magazines were a regulated medium like television, the demands of advertisers would be against FCC rules. Payola and extortion could be punished. As it is, there are probably illegalities. A magazine's postal rates are determined by the ratio of ad to edit pages, and the former costs more than the latter. So much for the stick.

The carrot means appealing to enlightened self-interest. For instance: There are many studies showing that the greatest factor in determining an ad's effectiveness is the credibility of its surroundings. The "higher the rating of editorial believability," concluded a 1987 survey by the *Journal of Advertising Research*, the higher the rating of the advertising." Thus, an impenetrable wall between edit and ads would also be in the best interest of advertisers.

Unfortunately, few agencies or clients hear such arguments. Editors often maintain the false purity of refusing to talk to them at all. Instead, they see ad salespeople who know little about editorial, are trained in business as usual, and are usually paid by commission. Editors might also band together to take on controversy. That happened once when all the major women's magazines did articles in the same month on the Equal Rights Amendment. It could happen again.

It's almost three years away from life between the grindstones of advertising pressures and readers' needs. I'm just beginning to realize how edges got smoothed down—in spite of all our resistance.

I remember feeling put upon when I changed "Porsche" to "car" in a piece about Nazi imagery in German pornography by Andrea Dworkin—feeling sure Andrea would understand that Volkswagen, the distributor of Porsche and one of our few supportive advertisers, asked only to be far away from Nazi subjects. It's taken me all this time to realize that Andrea was the one with a right to feel put upon.

Even as I write this, I get a call from a writer for *Elle*, who is doing a whole article on where women part their hair. Why, she wants to know, do I part mine in the middle?

It's all so familiar. A writer trying to make something of a nothing assignment; an editor laboring to think of new ways to attract ads; readers assuming that other women must want this ridiculous stuff; more women suffering for lack of information, insight, creativity, and laughter that could be on these same pages.

I ask you: Can't we do better than this?

Endnotes

1. **advertorial** Advertisement designed to mimic the appearance of a feature article.—Eds.
2. **editorial** In the magazine industry, all non-advertising content in a magazine, including regular columns and feature articles.—Eds.

Chapter VII
Self-Deception and Integrity

Self-knowledge is the key to avoiding self-deception and it is the key element to living with integrity. But, how well do we really know ourselves? To what degree and extent are men and women strangers to themselves? How can human beings avoid the traps of self-deception and the folly of life? On the other hand, what precisely is the relationship of self-knowledge to integrity? What is integrity? How does this differ from mere honesty? What does it mean to live a life with integrity?

Bishop Butler concludes that self-deception "undermines the whole principle of good." It is, he contends, a "deep and calm source of delusion" which is worse than even that wickedness which issues forth from common vicious passions.

Human beings, for the most part, lack a high degree of self-knowledge and routinely overestimate their own goodness and moral worth. This is due, Butler asserts, from either a lack of critical self-reflection or self-love. As a result of wrong views of self, the judgments people make concerning their own lives are often skewed and erroneous. Self-deceit lies close to the heart of vice in general which, Butler says, "consists in having an unreasonable and too great regard for ourselves, in comparison of others."

At one extreme Butler claims the general ignorance of self is manifest in wrong judgments in all areas concerning self. In many other instances, a particular passion or object of self-interest may lie at the center of wrong self-judgments. Self-deception and self-partiality are especially prevalent in those areas of human life which are not governed by fixed determinate rules.

Does self-deceit, in fact, imply self-knowledge? Do individuals engaged in self-deception routinely avoid the company of those who would reprove or condemn them? Butler uses the extreme example of King David to help the reader see how patterns of self-deception may arise in his or her own life.

Do people intentionally mislead themselves? Sissela Bok asks, "How, if not through such intentional misleading of self, can someone fail to notice that his work leads nowhere, that he lives beyond his means, that his marriage is a farce?" She claims that secrecy lies at the center of self-deception: "We keep secret from ourselves the truth we cannot face."

Bok then shows how the issues of self-deception invite moral concern. She reminds the reader that Petrarch warned against self-deception and called it, "the most deadly thing in life." Plato, of course, argued that if one could know and discern what is right and true, one would surely choose it. Hence, all error, wickedness, and evil acts flow from ignorance or, as others more pessimistically claim, self-deception. Yet, how is it then that we have self-deceit or a "split self," "bad faith," a "false consciousness," and "defense mechanisms?" Regardless of the metaphor one uses are not these pleas for ignorance nothing more than psychological attempts on the part of individuals to acquit themselves of responsibility? If, as Kant claimed, "ought implies can" then it follows that a certain knowledge must accompany moral obligation and, if a person can, by way of self-deceit, claim ignorance, then it follows they cannot be morally responsible. Bok then goes on to discuss the subtle ways in which secrecy is related to self-deception.

Roger Ames traces the Chinese concept *hsin*, "living up to one's word," in the Confucian *Analects*. "Living up to one's word" is, for Confucius, a necessary condition for achieving personhood. Confucius states: "I am not aware that one can become a person without living up to his word *(hsin).*"

> It *(hsin)* is integrally related to the notions of "being sparing in one's words" *(chin)* and "doing one's best as oneself" *(chung)*. Because living up to one's word is more than simply a willingness or even a promise to accord with what one says, it is perhaps close to the archaic notion of "plighting one's troth": the claim that one has the acquired ability, acumen and resources to enact and make real what one says."

"Living up to one's word" is actualizing genuine personhood. Integrity deals with extending this authentic personhood to all in the process of existence. It is, for example, not only a basis for friendship but an essential factor in establishing interpersonal credibility. It should be stressed that one must in addition live up to the "right" word. According to Ames:

> *Hsin* requires the articulation, disclosure, and realization of personal significance. If a person is true to his word, he has made himself a source of meaning in the world, meaning that can be realized and transmitted by others. Thus, the *Analects* records (1/13): "Living up to one's word *(hsin)* comes close to significating *(yi)* in that these words (as articulations of significance) can then be repeated. . . ." Of course, where one's words are *not* grounded in, and informed by significance *(yi)* and, as a consequence, are not lived up to, they hardly bear repeating.

Chapter VII: Self-Deception and Integrity

In "Integrity: Wholeness of Standards and Actions," Charles Watson looks at the nature and meaning of integrity, discusses the benefits of living with integrity, and shows examples of integrity within the business community. "Integrity" comes from the Latin, *integritas,* meaning whole or complete. He tells us that "the person with integrity is undivided. His standards and actions are sound, and they are one. This person is consistent in what he says and does."

Watson also tells us that the person who lives with integrity is not exempt from life's difficulties and troubles. However, the person of integrity is not overcome by difficulties:

> Often admired and always respected, the person with integrity faces many of the same difficulties and opportunities others do, but somehow negotiates his way through life's bends and snags on a higher plane and above the confusion that engulfs those of less solid character. Where others stumble or fall because of character flaws, this person is able to stride forward freely.

In 399 B.C., the philosopher Socrates was brought before an Athenian court and put on trial for his life. He was found guilty by a jury composed of 501 citizen-jurors and was sentenced to death. After an extended period of time in prison, Socrates was executed. Plato's "Apology" tells us of the life and trial of Socrates.

The word "apology" means "defense." However, the precise meaning of the term may only be gleaned by considering its etymology. The Greek, *apologia,* means to defend one's life, by speech, before a tribunal or judgment seat. This method of defense required that the accused be able to give an answer of "truth" in the face of accusation and to "set the record straight" by making a self-disclosure. To give an *apologia,* one must be in a position to account for one's own life—to articulate personal values and commitments and to justify them. It is a matter of stating with clarity where one stands in life and thus to say, precisely, what it is that one lives for.

Socrates had conducted his life according to the maxim: "The unexamined life is not worth living." In doing so, he had acquired a high degree of self-knowledge and personal integrity. He refused to compromise his integrity, his deepest values and convictions, even when faced with death. After his conviction and sentencing, Socrates exhorted his judges, condemners, and accusers to "be of good cheer about death, and know of a certainty, that no evil can happen to a good man, either in life or after death."

Lynne McFall highlights three features which are essential to the person who desires to live with integrity. The key features are coherence, importance and attitude. Integrity is a state of being undivided and therefore requires coherence and consistency within one's set of principles or commitments. Furthermore, these commitments must be of great importance. Finally, the individual of integrity must assume, at least implicitly, a certain attitude. McFall states:

An attitude essential to the notion of integrity is that there are some things that one is not prepared to do, or some things one must do. . . . This principle requires that some of one's commitments be unconditional.

In other words, a person of integrity understands that he or she is claimed by the moral dimension of human existence.

Upon Self-Deceit

Bishop Butler

And Nathan said to David, Thou art the man. 2 *Samuel* 12.7

These words are the application of Nathan's parable to David, upon occasion of his adultery with Bathsheba, and the murder of Uriah her husband. The parable, which is related in the most beautiful simplicity, is this: *There were two men in one city; the one rich, and the other poor: The rich man had exceeding many flocks and herds: but the poor man had nothing, save one little ewe lamb, which he had bought and nourished up: and it grew up together with him, and with his children: it did eat of his own meat, and drank of his own cup, and lay in his bosom, and was unto him as a daughter. And there came a traveller unto the rich man, and he spared to take of his own flock and of his own herd, to dress for the wayfaring man that was come unto him; but took the poor man's lamb, and dressed it for the man that was come to him. And David's anger was greatly kindled against the man; and he said to Nathan, As the Lord liveth, the man that hath done this thing shall surely die: and he shall restore the lamb fourfold, because he did this thing, and because he had not pity.* David passes sentence, not only that there should be a fourfold restitution made; but the proceeds to the rigour of justice, *the man that hath done this thing shall die:* and this judgment is pronounced with the utmost indignation against such an act of inhumanity; *As the Lord liveth, he shall surely die: and his anger was greatly kindled against the man.* And the Prophet answered, *Thou art the man.* He had been guilty of much greater inhumanity, with the utmost deliberation, thought, and contrivance. Near a year must have passed, between the time of the commission of his crimes, and the time of the Prophet's coming to him; and it does not appear from the story, that he had in all this while the least remorse or contrition.

Nothing is more strange than our self-partiality.

There is not any thing, relating to men and characters, more surprising and unaccountable, than this partiality to themselves, which is observable in many; as there is nothing of more melancholy reflection, respecting morality, virtue, and religion. Hence it is that many men seem perfect strangers to their own characters. They think, and reason, and judge quite differently upon any matter relating to themselves, from what they do in cases of others where they are not interested. Hence it is one hears people exposing follies, which they themselves are eminent for; and talking with great, severity against particular vices, which, if all the world be not mistaken, they themselves are notoriously guilty of. This self-ignorance and self-partiality may be in all different degrees. It is a lower degree of it which David himself refers to in these words, *Who can tell how oft he offendeth? O cleanse thou me from my secret faults*. This is the ground of that advice of Elihu to Job: *Surely it is meet to be said unto God,—That which I see not, teach thou me; if I have done iniquity, I will do no more*. And Solomon saw this thing in a very strong light, when he said, *He that trusteth his own heart is a fool*.

Hence the 'Know thyself' of the ancients.

This likewise was the reason why that precept, *Know thyself*, was so frequently inculcated by the philosophers of old. For if it were not for that partial and fond regard to ourselves, it would certainly be no great difficulty to know our own character, what passes within, the bent and bias of our mind; much less would there be any difficulty in judging rightly of our own actions. But from this partiality it frequently comes to pass, that the observation of many men's being themselves last of all acquainted with what falls out in their own families, may be applied to a nearer home, to what passes within their own breasts.

Usual temper: (a) absence of mistrust: (b) assumption that all is right: (c) disregard of precept, when against ourselves.

There is plainly, in the generality of mankind, an absence of doubt or distrust, in a very great measure, as to their moral character and behaviour;

and likewise a disposition to take for granted, that all is right and well with them in these respects. The former is owing to their not reflecting, not exercising their judgment upon themselves; the latter; to self-love. I am not speaking of that extravagance, which is sometimes to be met with; instances of persons declaring in words at length, that they never were in the wrong, nor had ever any diffidence to the justness of their conduct, in their whole lives. No, these people are too far gone to have anything said to them. The thing before us is indeed of this kind, but in a lower degree, and confined to the moral character; somewhat of which we almost all of us have, without reflecting upon it. Now consider how long, and how grossly, a person of the best understanding might be imposed upon by one of whom he had not any suspicion, and in whom he placed an entire confidence; especially if there were friendship and real kindness in the case: surely this holds even stronger with respect to that self we are all so fond of. Hence arises in men a disregard of reproof and instruction, rules of conduct and moral discipline, which occasionally come in their way: a disregard, I say, of these; not in every respect, but in this single one, namely, as what may be of service to them in particular towards mending their own hearts and tempers, and making them better men. It never in earnest comes into their thoughts, whether such admonitions may not relate, and be of service to themselves; and this quite distinct from a positive persuasion to the contrary, a persuasion from reflection that they are innocent and blameless in those respects. Thus we may invert the observation which is somewhere made upon Brutus, that he never read, but in order to make himself a better man. It scarce comes into the thoughts of the generality of mankind, that this use is to be made of moral reflections which they meet with; that this use, I say, is to be made of them by themselves, for every body observes and wonders that it is not done by others.

Also exclusive self-interest.

Further, there are instances of persons having so fixed and steady an eye upon their own interest, whatever they place it in, and the interest of those whom they consider as themselves, as in a manner to regard nothing else; their views are almost confined to this alone. Now we cannot be acquainted with, or in any propriety of speech be said to know any thing, but what we attend to. If therefore they attend only to one side, they really will not, cannot see or know what is to be alleged on the other. Though a man hath the best eyes in the world, he cannot see any way but that which he turns them. Thus these persons, without passing over the least, the most minute thing, which can possibly be urged in favour of themselves, shall overlook entirely the plainest and most obvious things on the other side.

They inquire only to justify.

And whilst they are under the power of this temper, thought and consideration upon the matter before them has scarce any tendency to set them right: because they are engaged; and their deliberation concerning an action to be done, or reflection upon it afterwards, is not to see whether it be right, but to find out reasons to justify or palliate it; palliate it, not to others, but to themselves.

With self-ignorance, perhaps, only in the favourite propensity.

In some there is to be observed a general ignorance of themselves, and wrong way of thinking and judging in every thing relating to themselves; their fortune, reputation, every thing in which self can come in: and this perhaps attended with the rightest judgment in all other matters. In others this partiality is not so general, has not taken hold of the whole man, but is confined to some particular favourite passion, interest, or pursuit; suppose ambition, covetousness, or any other. And these persons may probably judge and determine what is perfectly just and proper, even in things in which they themselves are concerned, if these things have no relation to their particular favourite passion or pursuit. Hence arises that amazing incongruity, and seeming inconsistency of character, from whence slight observers take it for granted, that the whole is hypocritical and false; not being able otherwise to reconcile the several parts: whereas in truth there is real honesty, so far as it goes. There is such a thing as men's being honest to such a degree, and in such respects, but no further. And this, as it is true, so it is absolutely necessary to be taken notice of, and allowed them; such general and undistinguishing censure of their whole character, as designing and false, being one main thing which confirms them in their self-deceit. They know that the whole censure is not true; and so take for granted that no part of it is.

The judgment is perverted through the passions.

But to go on with the explanation of the thing itself: Vice in general consists in having an unreasonable and too great regard to ourselves, in comparison of others. Robbery and murder is never from the love of injustice or cruelty,

Chapter VII: Self-Deception and Integrity

but to gratify some other passion, to gain some supposed advantage: and it is false selfishness alone, whether cool or passionate, which makes a man resolutely pursue that end, be it ever so much to the injury of another. But whereas, in common and ordinary wickedness, this unreasonableness, this partiality and selfishness, relates only, or chiefly, to the temper and passions in the characters we are now considering, it reaches to the understanding, and influences the very judgment. And, besides that general want of distrust and diffidence concerning our own character, there are, you see, two things, which may thus prejudice and darken the understanding itself: that overfondness for ourselves, which we are all so liable to; and also being under the power of any particular passion or appetite, or engaged in any particular pursuit. And these, especially the last of the two, may be in so great a degree, as to influence our judgment, even of other persons and their behaviour. Thus a man, whose temper is former to ambition or covetousness, shall even approve of them sometimes in others. . . .

Frequent difficulty of defining: enhanced by vice.

It is to be observed then, that as there are express determinate acts of wickedness, such as murder, adultery, theft: so, on the other hand, there are numberless cases in which the vice and wickedness cannot be exactly defined; but consists in a certain general temper and course of action, or in the neglect of some duty, suppose charity or any other; whose bounds and degrees are not fixed. This is the very province of self-deceit and self-partiality: here it governs without check or control. For what commandment is there broken? Is there a transgression where there is no law? A vice which cannot be defined?

Whoever will consider the whole commerce of human life, will see that a great part, perhaps the greatest part, of the intercourse amongst mankind, cannot be reduced to fixed determinate rules. Yet in these cases there is a right and a wrong: a merciful, a liberal, a kind and compassionate behaviour, which surely is our duty; and in an unmerciful contracted spirit, an hard and oppressive course of behaviour, which is most certainly immoral and vicious. But who can define precisely, wherein that contracted spirit and hard usage of others consist, as murder and theft may be defined? There is not a word in our language, which expresses more detestable wickedness than *oppression*: yet the nature of this vice cannot be so exactly stated, nor the bounds of it so determinately marked, as that we shall be able to say in all instances, where rigid right and justice ends, and oppression begins. In these cases there is great latitude left, for every one to determine for, and consequently to deceive himself. It is chiefly in these cases that self-deceit comes in; as every one must see that there is much larger scope for it here, than in express, single, determinate acts of wickedness. . . .

It is safer to be wicked in the ordinary way, than from this corruption lying at the root.

Upon the whole it is manifest, that there is such a thing as this self-partiality and self-deceit: that in some persons it is to a degree which would be thought incredible, were not the instances before our eyes; of which the behaviour of David is perhaps the highest possible one, in a single particular case; for there is not the least appearance, that it reached his general character: that we are almost all of us influenced by it in some degree, and in some respects: that therefore every one ought to have an eye to and beware of it. And all that I have further to add upon this subject is, that either there is a difference between right and wrong, or there is not: religion is true, or it is not. If it be not, there is no reason for any concern about it: but if it be true, it requires real fairness of mind and honesty of heart. And, if people will be wicked, they had better of the two be so from the common vicious passions without such refinements, than from this deep and calm source of delusion; which undermines the whole principle of good; darkens that light, that *candle of the Lord within*, which is to direct our steps; and corrupts conscience, which is the guide of life.

UPON SELF-DECEIT from *Fifteen Sermons upon Human Nature* by Joseph Butler (1726).

Secrecy and Self-Deception
Sissela Bok

Misleading Oneself

Petrarch kept by his bedside a book he called his *Secret, or The Soul's Conflict with Passion*, which he intended for his personal use alone. It reveals a remarkable self-analysis. With the Lady Truth listening in silence, Petrarch conducts three dialogues with Saint Augustine, the thinker whom he admired above all others. Early in the first dialogue, Saint Augustine warns Petrarch against self-deception, "the most deadly thing in life." When Petrarch asks to know more, Augustine answers:

> O race of mortal men, this it is above all makes me astonished and fearful for you, when I behold you, of your own free will, clinging to your miseries; pretending that you do not know the peril hanging over your heads, and if one brings it under your very eyes, you try to thrust it from your sight and put it far off.

What was it about which human beings were so insistent on deluding themselves? What was the peril they refused to see, though it was hanging over their heads?

Sin and death, and above all the likelihood of suffering eternally after death: these were the perils of which Petrarch's Saint Augustine warned. In the face of this danger, nothing would suffice but to give up all other interests, all passions for the life of this world—for love and for studies and politics, in Petrarch's own case—and to devote all thought to the care of one's soul by contemplating one's sinfulness and the nearness of death.

Before and after Petrarch, a great many thinkers have similarly warned of the corrosive and perversely self-destructive nature of such avoidance of the truth, of the lies we tell ourselves, and of the secrets we keep from ourselves. But they have seen far different truths—equally obvious in their

463

own minds—as the ones we so obstinately reject through self-deception. In our time, Marx and Freud have signaled, as false consciousness and defense mechanisms, the clinging to illusion that stands in the way of becoming free. Only through unmasking, demystification, above all interpretation, can we break through the web of illusion and become aware of our role in perpetuating it.

Some have claimed that we would not only become more free through the dispelling of self-deceit, but also more capable of acting morally and of leading nobler lives. Echoing Plato, they have argued that if only we could discern what is right and what is true, we would surely choose it. Others have held, more pessimistically, that self-deception may be our only shield against knowledge that would otherwise cripple us—that without what Ibsen called our "life-lies", we could not survive.

Whatever the role they assign to self-deception, most have taken its presence for granted. To see the self as deceiving itself has seemed the only way to explain what might otherwise be incomprehensible: a person's failure to acknowledge what is too obvious to miss. How, if not through such intentional misleading of self, can someone fail to notice that his work leads nowhere, that he lives beyond his means, that his marriage is a farce? How else can so many patients listen to a doctor's explanation of their life-threatening disease, respond as if they understood, yet know nothing about it a few hours later?

Postulating such self-inflicted ignorance helps point to the biases and weaknesses besetting perception and testifies to the perennial effort to understand human failures that would otherwise seem inexplicable. And it is secrecy that lies at the center of such self-deception: the secrecy that is part of all deception. In deceiving ourselves, according to such a view, we keep secret from ourselves the truth we cannot face.[1]

As helpful as such a view may be, it is also a troubling one. For exactly how can one be both insider and outsider thus, keeping secrets from oneself, even lying to oneself? How can one simultaneously know and ignore the same thing, hide it, and remain in the dark about it?[2] The paradoxical nature of such a view also seems to undercut reasoned choice *about* secrecy. If there is a deceiving and a deceived part in any one individual, then should one part only (and if so, which?) be considered responsible for choices made in such a state of self-deception? Which part is it that can exercise discretion or any other form of moral judgment? And how can we know that it is not deceiving itself in so doing? If we cannot, finally, then how can we even begin to sort out the moral problems of choice and responsibility?

On all counts, the view of the self keeping secrets from itself seems paradoxical. In this, it is not merely problematic, as are so many concepts concerning relations *between* people when used instead with respect to the self: duties to oneself, for example, or promises to oneself. These do not have the element of paradox inherent in the notion of keeping secrets

Chapter VII: Self-Deception and Integrity

from oneself. For while we can envision so construing duties and promises that they apply, in somewhat different form, to oneself as well as to others, it is much harder to envision just how one goes about keeping a secret from oneself—being at once included and shut out.

The most sustained effort to overcome this seeming paradox has been that of psychoanalysis. Its view of human defense mechanisms is surely much more complex than the standard versions of self-deception. Freud's therapy was based on the assumption that people repress much of what they seem not to know, or to have forgotten, and that this material is capable of being retrieved. Heinz Hartmann argued that "a great part of psychoanalysis can be described as a theory of self-deceptions and of misjudgments of the external world." And a number of psychiatrists have described all unconscious material as secrets kept from the self by the self. They have categorized as secret all that they could infer a person to have forgotten or repressed, relying on Freud's partitioning of the psyche, and on his imagery of strata, resistances, censors, and conflicting forces ranging back and forth across regions of differing accessibility.

The very profusion of metaphors that Freud brought in to convey such a picture of internal, self-imposed secrecy or deceit has not escaped criticism. Sartre, among others, has derided the idea of the unconscious keeping secrets from the conscious; he has argued that Freud needed to postulate a process complete with "censor, conceived of as a line of demarcation, with customs, passport division, currency control, etc.," in order to re-establish within the self the duality of deceiver and deceived. Freud, he argued, has merely interposed these barriers in order to overcome the paradox, and must then in turn overcome the duality itself through recourse to a "magic unity."

Having criticized Freud's attempt to overcome the contradiction inherent in attributing self-deception and concealment from self, Sartre proceeded to set forth an even more improbable theory of self-deception as "bad faith." It is the denial that consciousness directs toward itself, and results from the fear of facing the abyss of one's own freedom. Sartre did nothing to overcome the paradox inherent in such bad faith; instead he underlined it by claiming, "I must know, as deceiver, the truth that is masked from me as deceived. . . . Better still, I have to know this truth very precisely in order to hide it from myself the more carefully."

"Bad faith," for Sartre, carried a stronger overtone of blame than "self-deception." Because it is something one intends and is aware of, one is morally responsible for being in such a state, and for what one does or avoids as a result. But the concept also reflects Sartre's ambivalence toward moral reasoning. He intended throughout his life to set forth a complete moral theory, announcing such a project repeatedly, only to postpone it and finally to abandon it altogether. His extraordinarily subtle understanding of human motives may have flourished best in the absence of such a theory, and indeed might well have undermined it. Yet he also had a judgmental, often moralizing attitude toward those persons and groups he opposed. The concept of bad faith combined fluidity and blame in such a way as to allow him to assign moral responsibility without indicating just how he had arrived at his conclusions.

Not only did Sartre not offer criteria for determining when bad faith is and is not present; he never explained how he could retain the paradox of lying to oneself without contradiction. Rather than weakening the paradox, as Freud had, and introducing some distance between deceiver and deceived by means of the unconscious and of the processes of censorship, Sartre merely blurred it. He attributed to bad faith a mysterious quality of "evanescence" and described it as oscillating in perpetuity between good faith and cynicism. Many, he argued, live in a continuous state of bad faith with intermittent and sudden awakenings in either direction.

Freud, on the other hand, remained profoundly concerned throughout his career to overcome the paradox. He was still struggling to do so in the last article he wrote, which he had to leave unfinished. In this article, Freud postulated that the ego of a person in analysis must, when young, "have behaved in a remarkable manner" under the influence of "a powerful trauma." The child must have been tormented both by the desire to satisfy a strong instinct and by fear of the dangers that might ensue through doing so. The response is a split whereby the child both satisfies the instinct symbolically and rejects any knowledge concerning the matter:

> The two contrary reactions to the conflict persist as the centre-point of a split in the ego. The whole process seems so strange to us because we take for granted the synthetic nature of the workings of the ego. But we are clearly at fault in this. The synthetic function of the ego, though it is of such extraordinary importance, is subject to particular conditions and is liable to a whole series of disturbances.

By means of the split ego, Freud thought to do away with the paradox while allowing that the process did seem strange. Others have argued, in a similar vein, that a split self or even several selves are at work in self-deception to guard against anxiety-producing knowledge.

Yet on closer inspection the contradiction remains. The view of the split ego or self is but another metaphor—and an even more personalized one—for the mind in conflict. No more than the image of the self keeping secrets from itself or the unconscious from the conscious can it explain the complex defense mechanisms to which human beings resort, nor avert the paradox of both knowing and not knowing the same thing at the same time, both keeping a secret and ignoring it.

Neither such mutually secretive parts of the ego or the self, nor even the deception by a split ego or self, can be shown to be either present or absent in any one person. As a result, someone presumed to be lying to himself—about incestuous fantasies, for example, or hatred too painful to confront—has no convincing way to deny the fact. Every effort at refuting the notion can arguably be seen as further proof of resistance, and of the force with which one part of the self is suppressing the secret truth. Anyone can then impute such "secrets" to anyone else, and point to a disavowal as further proof of their existence. A glance at the psychiatric literature will yield innumerable examples of such reasoning. A person's secrets, in such an extended view, may then turn out to encompass not only all that he knowingly conceals but also what he has forgotten or never noticed, and even all that he is imagined to be keeping from consciousness or from part of his ego.

The concept of "self-deception," and those of "split self," "bad faith," "false consciousness," and "defense mechanisms" are nevertheless compelling metaphors. They point to internal conflicts and self-imposed defeats that we all recognize as debilitating. These metaphors are surely not empty ones: they remind us of all that stands in the way of perceiving and thinking. We cannot easily do without these metaphors; the danger comes when we begin to take them for *explanations*. As metaphors, they help us to see the paradoxes of human failure to perceive and react; as explanations of how the paradoxes are overcome, they short-circuit understanding and become misleading in their own right—one more way in which we avoid trying to understand the complexity that underlies our experience of paradox. They function then as what I. A. Richards called "premature ultimates," bringing inquiry to an end too suddenly.

At such times, these concepts blur the distinction between intentional concealment and ignorance; between lies and all the other ways in which one can influence perception and action; and between deceiving and being deceived. As a result, they permit some people to impute clear-cut intention, directness, and simplicity to the intricate processes of coping with information, while at the same time allowing others to dismiss the questions of responsibility and intention altogether. Each of the two responses obstructs the effort to sort out just what part individuals do play in what we take for self-deception. Before considering how to try to avoid these oversimplified responses, it is worthwhile to look at the difficulties each can give rise to in practice.

Attributing Self-Deception

Because self-deception and secrecy from self point to self-inflicted and often harmful ignorance, they invite moral concern: judgments about responsibility, efforts to weigh the degree of harm imposed by such ignorance, and questions of how to help reverse it. If the false belief is judged harmless and even pleasurable, as may be the case with the benevolent light in which most of us see our minor foibles, few would consider interfering. But clearly there are times when people are dangerously wrong about themselves. The anorexic girl close to starving to death who thinks that she looks fat in the mirror, and the alcoholic who denies having a drinking problem, are both in need of help; yet the help cannot consist merely in interference, but must somehow bring about a recognition on their part of their need and the role they play in not perceiving it accurately.

Judgments about when and how to try to help people one takes to be in self-inflicted danger depend on the nature and the seriousness of the danger, as well as on how rational one thinks they are. To attribute self-deception to people is to regard them as less than rational concerning the danger one takes them to be in, and makes intervention, by contrast, seem more legitimate. But this is itself dangerous because of the difficulties of establishing that there is self-deception in the first place. Some feel as certain that anyone who does not believe in their deity, their version of the inevitable march of history, or their views of the human psyche deceives himself as they might feel about the self-deception of the anorexic and the alcoholic. Frequently, the more improbable their own views, the stronger is their need to see the world as divided up into those who perceive the self-evident and those who persist in deluding themselves.

Aiding the victims of such imputed self-deception can be hard to resist for true believers and enthusiasts of every persuasion. If they come to believe that all who do not share their own views are not only wrong but actually know they are wrong in one part of their selves that keeps the other in the dark, they can assume that it is an act of altruism to help the victimized, deceived part see through the secrecy and the self-deception. What could be more legitimate than helping to bring about a change, that one takes the self-deceived person's more rational self to desire?

Zealots can draw on their imputing self-deception to nonbelievers in yet another way, to nourish any tendency they might have to a conspiracy theory. If they see the self—their own and that of others—as a battleground for a conspiracy, they may then argue that anyone who disagrees with them thereby offers proof that his mind has been taken over by the forces they are striving to combat. It is not long before they come to see the most disparate events not only as connected but as *intended* to connect. There are no accidents, they persuade themselves; nothing is too trivial or improbable to count as evidence of such intent.

Indeed, calling something trivial or far-fetched counts, for holders of such theories, as further evidence of its significance. And denying what they see as self-evident is still more conclusive proof. How well we recognize the tone in which the eminent sixteenth-century philosopher and jurist Jean Bodin denounced those who scoffed at the belief in the existence of witches. Their protestations of disbelief, he declared, showed that they were most likely witches themselves. He wrote of the pact that "confessed" witches—among them several judges and a doctor of theology—said they had signed with Satan. It obliged them to ridicule all talk of witchcraft as superstitious invention and contrary to reason. They persuaded many naïve persons, Bodin insisted, whose arrogance and self-deception was such that they would dismiss as impossible even the actions of witches that were right before their eyes.

By itself, the scope for abuse is of course no argument against a theory that postulates self-deception. But the frequent lack of criteria for attributing self-deception or its absence represents a problem for any such theory and increases the likelihood that it will be misapplied.

Another way to misapply such a theory is to invoke it to explain away guilt. In this way, the populations in Nazi Germany and elsewhere who claim to have been ignorant of concentration camps in their vicinity deny what was too obvious to be in any sense a secret. Ignorance, even though self-imposed, is put forward as an excuse. Admitting the knowledge, on the other hand, would call for a response of approval and collaboration, or toleration, or outright rejection. In the last case, a choice of stance would be required: whether or not to voice one's rejection, or act to put it into effect, and at what personal risk.

The Plea of Self-Imposed Ignorance

If we agree with Kant that "ought implies can" and that no one should therefore be held morally responsible for failing to do what he cannot do, then we must hold, further, that no one can be blamed for failing to do what he did not know needed doing. A paraplegic cannot be blamed for not trying to rescue a drowning child, nor can a swimmer asleep on the beach. Both capacity to act and knowledge that acting is required must be present for there to be moral obligation, and responsibility for its breach.

At times, even pleas of ignorance do not suffice to acquit one of responsibility. If one has the obligation to remain alert to signs of danger—say, as a lifeguard on the beach—then the fact that one failed to do so gives no excuse. And even without having it as one's job to be aware of danger to others, there are many times when one would feel at fault for not perceiving it. Between full responsibility to know and none at all the gradations are numerous; and it is with respect to making such determinations that the issues of self-deception enter in. How does self-ignorance resemble or differ from other forms of ignorance? Does its self-inflicted aspect add or remove responsibility? in what ways are the strategies of avoidance by those who claim ignorance of avoidable cruelty and suffering like being asleep while children drown?

Albert Speer has explored his responsibility for the Nazi atrocities and its relation to ignorance and delusion in his book *Inside the Third Reich*. As a member of Hitler's government and of his innermost circle of advisers, Speer had much more direct responsibility for the government's actions than he would have had purely as a citizen. He details the elaborate forms of avoidance and of rationalization whereby he maintained his self-respect at the time.

Speer not only knew about the persecution of Jews and the slave-labor practices and the concentration camps; first as Hitler's principal architect and later as minister of armament, he took an active part in the design of the munitions factories, fully aware of the inhumane treatment of the prisoners who worked there. Yet he talked himself into believing that his work was strictly that of an architect and administrator, and that it was not his role to agonize over "political" matters.

In this way Speer refused to confront the atrocities in an other than abstract way. The day after the Kristallnacht in November 1938, driving by the smoking remnants of Berlin's synagogue, he remembers being disturbed, not by the destruction and all it stood for, but by the disorder and messiness that disturbed his architect's sense of design. And later in his career, his friend Karl Hanke warned him not to visit Auschwitz. Rather than ask why, he purposely did not follow up this line of inquiry with anyone.

> I did not query him, I did not query Himmler. I did not query Hitler. I did not speak with personal friends. I did not investigate—for I did not want to know what was happening there. . . . from fear of discovering something which might have made me turn away from my course, I had closed my eyes. This deliberate blindness outweighs whatever good I may have done or tried to do in the last period of the war. Those activities shrink to nothing in the face of it. Because I failed at that time, I still feel, to this day, responsible for Auschwitz in a wholly personal way."

As Speer rightly recognized, he was not in a position to deny responsibility. His failure to seek out the information about Auschwitz and to respond to all the evidence right before his eyes was inexcusable. Considering all that he already knew, any residual ignorance on his part of such matters, whether incurred through self-deception or not, was beside the point.

It would certainly be excessive, on the other hand, to stretch the notion of moral responsibility so far as to cover all that individuals ignore or fail to notice, or all the situations in which we perceive some rationalization or other strategy of avoidance. We are obviously not responsible for much that we do not know, or do not know that we should look into; the less so if we have no duty in the first place to respond to the situation of which we are ignorant—because we have no power to change it, or because it lies outside our reach. At other times, we do acknowledge responsibility, but only partially, as when we should have noticed, but didn't, that a friend was becoming severely depressed, or that a family member brought home far more money than he was being paid at work.

Chapter VII: Self-Deception and Integrity

In many such cases when ignorance and avoidance of knowledge blend, the lines are hard to draw. We are especially likely to deceive ourselves, as Bishop Butler pointed out, precisely where the lines of responsibility are blurred.

> Whoever will consider the whole commerce of human life, will see that a great part, perhaps the greatest part, of the intercourse amongst mankind, cannot be reduced to fixed determinate rules. Yet in these cases there is a right and a wrong: a merciful, a liberal, a kind and compassionate behavior, which surely is our duty; and an unmerciful contracted spirit, an hard and oppressive course of behavior, which is most certainly immoral and vicious. But who can define precisely, wherein that contracted spirit and hard usage of others consist, as murder and theft may be defined? There is not a word in our language which expresses more detestable wickedness than *oppression*: yet the nature of this vice cannot be so exactly stated, nor the bounds of it so determinately marked, as that we shall be able to say in all instances, when rigid right and justice ends, and oppression begins. In these cases there is great latitude left, for everyone to determine for, and consequently to deceive himself.

Ignorance, Error, Bias, and Avoidance.

> *If the doors of perception were cleansed, everything*
> *would appear to man se it is, infinite.*
> *For man has closed himself up, till he sees all things*
> *thro' the narrow chinks of his cavern.*
>   WILLIAM BLAKE, *The Marriage of Heaven and Hell*

How might we disentangle the factors that are lumped together in the notion of keeping secrets from oneself, or deceiving oneself? And how sort out the destructive forms these factors take from much-needed self-protection?

Consider all the possible knowledge that an individual might acquire: with all the openness and acuity in the world, he could acquire only a minute portion of this knowledge, even in principle. Every direction chosen forecloses innumerable others. And even out of the limited amount of knowledge available to him in theory, he could respond, as a practical matter, only to a fraction. Thousands of sensory impressions reach the average individual per second, according to some estimates: the vast majority of these are dealt with—adapted to or rejected—at the simplest organic levels. Had we no such protection from all the information that bombards us, we would be exposed to far more than we could cope with:

471

it would be like having no skin. At such an organic level, it makes no sense to speak of secrecy and deception toward the self.

A related form of rejecting knowledge is what is known as "psychic numbing." It comes much closer to what is often called self-deception, yet it can be a reflex response to overwhelming pain or fear. Recall an intensely painful experience, and notice that it is impossible to recapture the sheer physical sense of that pain. In the same way, the initial impact of suffering may wear off with repeated exposure, leaving us incapable of responding to what at first aroused sharp reactions. This numbing can be dangerous when it lowers resistance to avoidable injuries; but without the capacity for some such self-protection we might be condemned to relive endlessly our most unbearable memories or fears.

Of the remaining messages that reach the individual, each may be more or less accurate, complete, diffused, hard to decipher, intertwined with or in conflict with other messages, and deflected or impaired en route. Add, now, his own characteristics as a recipient: his deafness, or fatigue, his difficulties of memory and of understanding; his habits, biases, hopes, and fears. He starts out, in sum, with information already severely winnowed out, incomplete, erroneous, twisted, confused, and conflicting. To label as secrecy from self all the resulting ignorance and error is to try to lend purposiveness to much that is haphazard and accidental in human responses. By attributing to individuals powers to keep such knowledge at bay, one internalizes the ancient belief in all-knowing powers that keep secret from human beings all that they do not know.

Other processes come closer to achieving self-imposed ignorance. Compartmentalization allows us to avoid responding to situations that would otherwise require us to make a choice. Beliefs or messages may be kept separate, never confronted with one another, and thus never seen to be contradictory. We may postpone following through with a troublesome lead, or succeed in not spelling out exactly what it will mean to take a certain action. And rationalization helps us to incorporate and to disarm threatening information.

Of all the responses that seem clearly self-deceptive to many, denial is most striking. Doctors find, for example, that among seriously ill patients who learn that death is near, at least 20 percent have no memory after a few days of having received such news. Faced with intolerable anxiety, they have blocked out the information. In such responses, there are aspects of secrecy, but not the concealment that is the core of secrecy, nor the deception of self that many imagine. Rather, the responses of denial are linked with the element of separation, of setting aside and sifting apart that is present in all secrecy, and also with that of the unspoken and the unspeakable.

Sometimes the setting aside is quite conscious and in no way secret to the self, as in much procrastination. The same is true of conscious refusals

Chapter VII: Self-Deception and Integrity

to spend much time worrying about possible but unlikely dangers about which one can do nothing, such as the chance of being struck by lightning. Such dismissals of concern are often eminently reasonable as are similar means by which people compensate for misfortune and handicaps. One psychiatrist, Arnold Beisser, has written of the way physicians may misinterpret as denial of illness what he regards, rather, as affirming attitudes that contribute to health. He has used his own experience of severe physical handicap to show how the focus can shift between degrees of awareness of one's condition:

> I am actively engaged in my profession and, when doing so, am absorbed with the tasks at band. I am frequently asked such questions as, "How do you bear spending your life in a wheelchair?" On such occasions I am aware that my attention is redirected from what I am doing in an affirmative way to what I am unable to do in accordance with the standards implied by the question. Thus when what I cannot do becomes foreground, I am aware that I am disabled; while I am working or carrying out my social or family activities, my disability becomes background and my competence and health are foreground.

Most of us shift focus in similar ways, without thinking of the changes as evidence of denial. We should be no hastier in attributing denial to others at those times when we realize that they do not, any more than ourselves, maintain a constant and acute awareness of the full extent and variety of their problems.

There are nevertheless times when we might all agree that denial is present: times when someone seems to block information completely, about the death of a family member, for example, or the diagnosis of cancer. For some, such blockage is a temporary reflex only, allowing them time to regroup their forces and to begin to take it all in. For others, it is permanent.

It is when the combined forms of avoidance no longer merely filter but block needed information, when they are no longer temporary but permanent, and when they prevent people from doing something about a danger which could be averted or alleviated, that they do the greatest disservice. Far from protecting individuals, avoidance then leaves them defenseless against threats they could otherwise have tried to combat. To block out knowledge of the symptoms of a disease that is curable in its early stages is a common form of such avoidance. On a collective scale, the inability to think about the growing likelihood of a nuclear devastation exhibits it at its most irrational. For whereas all the forms of avoidance can be protective of self when they avert attention from an unlikely danger, or one about which nothing can be done, they have the opposite effect whenever there is something one could do if one responded in time.

Without a doubt, the various forms of avoidance and rejection I have mentioned do point to striking responses to threatening or unusable information. However supportive they may be on occasion, their cumulative burden is great. True, we could not survive if bombarded ceaselessly by information of a useless, threatening, or unduly burdening nature. But we struggle along with such thick layers of bias and rationalization, compartmentalization and denial, that our choices suffer immeasurably.

In answer to the question raised earlier, whether the concept of secrecy from oneself might not undercut all efforts to pursue the ethics of secrecy or indeed any questions of moral choice and responsibility, I would therefore argue that such a concept can, but need not, undercut these efforts. It can blur moral inquiry and permit moral reflection to run in comfortable, well-worn circles. But when the processes of avoidance that it points to are studied more closely, we find that they undercut some, but far from all, questions of responsibility; and that even as they reveal the extent of our present ignorance about the interactions of organic and other obstacles to perception, they underline the need for moral inquiry, not its impossibility. Given the role of these processes, the ways in which they skew or shut out knowledge, and the resulting ignorance, error, and uncertainty, what is the role of moral deliberation?

While such deliberation can counteract these forces, it can undoubtedly never dissolve them; and so one of its most important tasks must be to remain mindful of them and to devise means of reducing their sway, but also to watch how they are imputed: to whom, on what grounds, and with what power to bring about changes. Consider once again, from this point of view, Petrarch's *Secret*, containing the dialogues between Saint Augustine and himself in response to Saint Augustine's exhortations that he recognize his self-delusion and set aside his passionate interest in the world and in his studies so as to contemplate sin, death, and the life to come, Petrarch agonized and demurred. To the very end, he refused to obey his mentor fully.

> Indeed I owe you a great debt of gratitude . . . for you have cleansed my darkened sight and scattered the thick clouds of error in which I was involved. And how shall I express my thankfulness to Her also, the Spirit of Truth? And now, as She and you have your dwelling-place in heaven, and I must still abide on earth, and, as you see, am greatly perplexed and troubled, not knowing for how long this must be, I implore you, do not forsake me. . . . I will be true to myself, so far as in me lies. . . . I am not ignorant that, as you said a few minutes before, it would be much safer to attend only to the care of my soul. . . . But I have not the strength to resist that old bent for study altogether.

We who are the beneficiaries of Petrarch's "old bent for study" cannot but cheer his independent spirit. Many others have faltered when pressed to acknowledge self-deception of a particular kind and to accept the world-view urged upon them. Consider in this light the generations of women who have been told that their drive toward self-expression and

Chapter VII: Self-Deception and Integrity

independence stemmed from a lack of feminine modesty or of piety, or more recently, from sexual envy of men. At such times, imputations of self-deception have reinforced the pressure on women to conform to whatever stereotype of femininity prevailed. Whatever the current dogma, countless men and women have been similarly persuaded that their efforts to think for themselves revealed the sin of pride, the error of ideological deviation, or some grievous failure of psychological insight.

Efforts, to understand the nature of self-deception and its links to hypocrisy pervade the two practices of talking over human lives to which I turn next: confession and gossip. Both represent efforts at moral deliberation, weighing conduct, and setting standards. As Georg Simmel noted, while secrecy sets barriers between men, it also offers "the Seductive temptation to break through the barriers by gossip and confession." This temptation, he added, accompanies the psychic life of the secret like an overtone.

Endnotes

1. True, the view of the self keeping secrets from itself is not identical to that of its deceiving itself or lying to itself. These can no more be equated than can keeping secrets, deceiving, and lying in their own right. For our purposes, however, of asking whether such views are possible in the first place, and what implications they hold for moral choice, they need not be dealt with one at a time; especially as all self-deception must involve keeping something secret from oneself.
2. Without the simultaneity, the claim loses its paradoxical character, but also much of its explanatory value with respect to what is so unaccountable about human ignorance of the seemingly self-evident. No one doubts that we can hide things and then forget where they are (though, hiding them *in order* to forget is less likely to succeed); or that we can set our watches late or play other tricks on ourselves in order to achieve a change in behavior.

Living Up to One's Word (hsin* 信)

Roger Ames

A final Concept pertinent to this introduction of Confucius' understanding of thinking is closely allied with the notion of *chih*. It is *hsin** 信 "living up to one's word." As we have indicated in a correspondence theory, cognitive knowledge involves the representation of a state of affairs as it really is. Knowing, then, is dependent upon the existence in fact (as opposed to appearance, thought, or language) of an objective reality, and the true correspondence between thought and this reality.

For Confucius, realizing (*chih*) is significantly different from this concept of knowing. Reality is immanent, relative, and contingent. It is something achieved rather than recognized. Since reality is not independent of a realizer, it follows that truth cannot be a consequence of simple correspondence. Rather, truth must involve something like "appropriateness" or "genuineness."

Huston Smith attempts to contrast the dominant Western and Chinese paradigms of truth in the following manner:

> Truth for China is personal in a dual or two-fold sense. Outwardly, it takes into consideration the feelings of the persons an act or utterance will affect.... Meanwhile, inwardly it aligns the speaker to the self he ought to be; invoking a word dear to the correspondence theorists we can say that truth "adequates" its possessor to his normative self. The external and internal referents of the notion are tightly fused, of course, for it is primarily by identifying with the feelings of others (developing *jen*) that one becomes a *chün-tzu* (the self one should be)....

Smith highlights the personal nature of truth as a kind of sincerity in which one brackets his or her own private preferences in favor of "optimizing the feelings of all interested parties." He then goes on to define truth as some-

Chapter VII: Self-Deception and Integrity

thing authored. This definition is quite consistent with our own explication of *chih* as "to realize." Smith describes truth as "a kind of performative."

> It holds an act or utterance to be true to the extent that it "gestalts" (composes, resolves) the ingredients of a situation in a way that furthers a desired outcome—in China's case, social harmony. Truth thus conceived is a kind of performative: it is speech or deed aimed at effecting an intended consequence.

We would want to provide Smith's insight an even stronger performative meaning. Truth is speech and deed that *effects* an intended consequence. In order to trace this understanding of truth back to Confucius and demonstrate its appropriateness, we must begin with the *Chung-yung's* concept of *ch'eng* (誠), commonly rendered "sincerity."

A careful reading of the *Chung-yung* reveals that *ch'eng* 誠 is used in this basically Confucian-oriented text in a manner that would associate it functionally with *tao* in the Taoist texts. That is to say, *ch'eng* is the immanental source not only of man, but of all things:

> *Ch'eng* means self-completing; and *tao* means self-*tao*-ing. *Ch'eng* is the full consequence of all things; to be not-*ch'eng* is to be nothing. It is for this reason that the exemplary person (*chün tzu*) prizes *ch'eng*. *Ch'eng* is not simply "self-completing," but is that whereby one completes things. To complete oneself is to become a "person" (*jen*); to complete things is "to realize" (*chih*).

As one would expect, the major distinction between the Taoist *tao* and this Confucian notion of *ch'eng* derives from the fact that the former interprets man through the structures of his natural environment, while the latter begins from human beings and tends to understand the cosmos through human categories. The focus of the Taoist is to understand humanity from the perspective of the unfolding pattern of existence, while the Confucian direction is to pursue an understanding of all existence from the human perspective. The Taoists, being reluctant to rely exclusively upon the Confucian-laden term, *sheng jen* 聖, "sage," as their comprehensive level of personhood, thus generate their own category, *chen jen* /;;, "authentic person." Similarly, the later interpreters of Confucius represented in the *Chung-yung* employ the term *ch'eng* 誠 "integrity," rather than the Taoist-burdened *tao* 健. *Ch'eng*, then, is the extending of the specifically human activity of actualizing genuine personhood from man himself to all constituents in the process of existence. As Tu Wei-ming remarks: "To say that Heaven is *sincere* [*ch'eng*] seems to transform the idea of an honest person into a general description of the Way of Heaven."

We have above defined "to realize" (*chih* 和) as effective forecasting. Given the interdependent nature of this world and the coextensive nature of realizer and that which is realized, the distinctions entailed in the correspondence between idea and reality are not operative. That is, not only is there no appreciable distinction between truth and reality as such, there is also no distinction among the event encompassing a subjective knower, an objective reality known, and the description of this relationship as truth. Fundamentally, to realize (*chih*) and to be true for oneself (that is, to have integrity) (*ch'eng*) are two ways of saying the same thing, both being open to valuation in qualitative terms.

The character translated "integrity," *ch'eng* (誠) is etymologically constituted by "to speak" (*yen* 言) and "to complete, to realize" (*ch'eng*˙ 成). Its meaning, then, is "to realize that which is spoken." Thus, if would be expected that *ch'eng*, like *chih*, would refer to an accurate, self-fulfilling forecasting. It is so described in the *Chung-yung*:

> The tao of the highest integrity (*ch'eng*) is being able to realize beforehand: when the state is going to prosper, there are certain to be auspicious signs; when the state is going to perish, it is certain to be revealed in portents. It is manifest in the divining stalks and shells, and in the way that things comport themselves. When fortune or misfortune approaches, one is certain to realize beforehand whether it is good or not. Thus, the highest integrity (*ch'eng*) is "god-like."

The *Chung-yung*, in this way similar to the more metaphysical portions of *Mencius*, can be read as an attempt to establish a cosmological vision supportive of Confucius' social and political philosophy. It is not unexpected, therefore, to find *ch'eng* used in *Mencius* in a manner that anticipates its further elaboration in the *Chung-yung*. "Everything is complete here in me. Can there be any greater joy than in plumbing oneself and finding oneself true (*ch'eng*)? In fact *Mencius*, in a passage paralleled in the *Chung-yung*, describes the process of existence in terms of *ch'eng*. We want to look closely at this passage because it provides us with an important insight into the way in which the meaning of *ch'eng* as "integrity," as "truth/reality" may have been derived from the *Analects*:

> If a person in a subordinate position does not have the support of his superiors, he will not be able to govern the people. There is a way of gaining the support of those above him: one who does not live up to his word (*hsin*˙ 信) with his friends will not gain the support of his superiors. There is a way of living up to one's word with friends: if one in serving his relatives does not give them pleasure, he will not live up to his word with friends. There is a way of pleasing one's relatives: if in plumbing oneself, he finds that he is not true (*pu ch'eng* 誠), he will not please his relatives. There is a way of being true to oneself (*ch'eng*); if one is not clearly aware of what is good, he will not be true to himself. Therefore, truth (*ch'eng*) is the process of existence (lit., "the way of Heaven"), and to reflect on truth (*ch'eng*) is the process of being a person.

The *Chung-yung* passage that parallels *Mencius* here continues by describing the appropriate manner in which to cultivate the way of *ch'eng*:

Chapter VII: Self-Deception and Integrity

"Learn about it (the way of *ch'eng*) broadly, question it exhaustively, reflect on it carefully, distinguish it clearly, and practice it with earnestness." Now, the focus of Confucius is on how to realize oneself as a human being in a social and political context rather than on metaphysical speculations about personhood. In fact, the *Analects* reveals on several occasions Confucius' profound disinterest in metaphysical questions.

Confucius limits his concern to the way of the human being (*jen tao* / ;; or better, *jen* tao* /;;) as an achieved social and political "truth/reality," and how it can be effected in the medium of communication through "living up to one's word" (*hsin** h). In this "way of *ch'eng*" described in *Mencius* and the *Chung-yung*, on the other hand; *ch'eng* covers both ontological as well as experiential truth. We would thus argue that the development of *ch'eng* as an ultimately ontological designation for truth in *Mencius* and the *Chung-yung* might best be construed as speculative extension of Confucius' conception of social and political truth. The language of the *Chung-yung* passage cited above which describes the proper manner of cultivating "the way of *ch'eng*" is reminiscent of if not in fact derived from a passage in the *Analects* which describes how to become a person (that is, how to become *jen**). Where the *Mencius* and the *Chung-yung* take a turn towards the fundamental definition of personhood, this turn would still seem to have its origins in the more practical, sociopolitical dynamics of becoming a person emphasized by Confucius.

This intimate relationship between "living up to one's word" (*hsin** h), as an aspect of effecting sociopolitical truth, and *ch'eng* J, as the process of ontological truth, is further suggested by the fact that in the *Shuo-wen* lexicon, these two characters are each defined by the other. The Tuan Yü-ts'ai commentary to the *Shuo-wen* underscores the "person-making" connotations of *hsin** which are so prominent in Confucius: "Since when a 'person' speaks there is nothing that he fails to live up to (*hsin**), this character is constituted of 'person' (*jen* /;;) and 'to speak' (*yen* /;;)." In fact, it is likely that Tuan's commentary is based on an *Analects* passage in which Confucius makes "living up to one's word" a necessary condition for achieving personhood (2/22): "I am not aware that one can become a person without living up to his word (*hsin**)."

Living up to one's word (*hsin**) is a major concept for Confucius, occurring some forty times in the *Analects*. In fact, it is said to be one of the four categories under which Confucius taught: culture (*wen** /;;), conduct (*hsing* /;;), doing one's best as oneself (*chung* /;;), and living up to one's word (*hsin** h). It is integrally related to the notions of "being sparing in one's words" (*chin* /;;) and "doing one's best as oneself" (*chung* /;;). Because living up to one's word is more than simply a willingness or even a promise to accord with what one says, it is perhaps close to the archaic notion of "plighting one's troth": the claim that one has the acquired ability, acumen and resources to enact and make real what one says.

If *hsin** were nothing more than a commitment to try to carry out what one says, the success or failure of one's actions would not be an issue, yet Confucius makes a lack of ability a condition of failing to be *hsin** (8/16): "I do not understand persons who are reckless and not straightforward, who are ignorant and not attentive, and who are lacking in ability and do not live up to their word (*hsin**)." Confucius asserts that "living up to one's word" (*hsin**) is the way to realize or "complete" (*ch'eng** J, cognate with *ch'eng* J, "integrity," "being true for oneself") one's own significance and appropriateness in the world. *Mencius* reiterates this aspect of "living up to ones word" when he claims that "having it in oneself" is called *hsin**. It was because *hsin** is more than simply a commitment that Confucius was pleased when his disciple, Ch'i-tiao K'ai, declined to take an official post, saying (5/6): "I do not think that I am yet able to live up to this (*hsin**)." The disciple was certainly not admitting that he was less than trustworthy, as Arthur Waley's rendering of this same passage might suggest: "I have not yet perfected myself in the virtue of good faith." *Hsin** rather entails as a necessary condition being able to carry out what one says and thus being able to make it true and real. The fact that many of the occurrences of *hsin** in the *Analects* are coupled with "doing one's best as oneself" (*chung* /;;) would suggest that *hsin** is fundamentally performative. *Hsin** h is the doing of what one says with earnestness.

Another feature of Confucius' emphasis on living up to one's word (*hsin**) is that it seems to be a necessary condition for establishing the relationship of "friendship" (*yu* /;;), and for winning the continuing support of the people. That is, living up to one's word is an essential factor in establishing interpersonal credibility which, for Confucius, is a precondition for realizing oneself as a person.

In spite of the fact that living up to one's word is necessary to qualify as a person, it does not follow that it is sufficient. Where living up to one's word is generally regarded as a positive trait, the appropriateness of this characterization really depends upon the "word" that one is living up to. In distinguishing three levels of the gentleman-scholar, Confucius attributes living up to one's word even to the third and lowest. This virtue in and of itself does not, it would seem, prompt an unqualified recommendation for promotion to higher levels. For Confucius, then, it is possible for someone to be morally retarded—to be a "small person" (*hsiao jen* /;;)—and yet still live up to his word (13/20):

> One who is certain to live up to his word and finish what he starts, even though this is no more than a small person being stubborn, can still qualify as a third level of the gentleman-scholar."

Confucius, even in characterizing himself, tends to celebrate his love of learning (*hao hsüeh* /;;) over his concern to live up to his word, regarding the latter as a more common trait.

Chapter VII: Self-Deception and Integrity

Finally, there is an important relationship in Confucius between living up to one's word (*hsin** h) and "signification" (*yi* /;;) which requires brief elaboration. This concept, *yi*, discussed more fully below in the context of the notion of self-articulation, is a categorical notion in Confucius which locates the ultimate source of aesthetic, moral, and rational significance in the human being himself. It is with this capacity to significate that a, person appropriates meaning from his cultural tradition and discloses his own creativity.

*Hsin** requires the articulation; disclosure, and realization of personal significance. If a person is true to his word, he has made himself a source of meaning in the world, meaning that can be realized and transmitted by others. Thus, the *Analects* records (1/13): "Living up to one's word (*hsin** h) comes close to significating (*yi* /;;) in that these words (as articulations of significance) can then be repeated. . . ." Of course, where one's words are not grounded in, and informed by, significance (*yi*) and, as a consequence, are not lived up to, they hardly bear repeating.

The concept, *hsin**, is a necessary although not sufficient condition for the articulation and achievement of personal significance. To the extent that *hsin*˙ is grounded in personal significating, the human being is capable of contributing meaning to his world.

Integrity: Wholeness of Standards and Actions

Charles E. Watson

Often admired and always respected, the person with integrity faces many of the same difficulties and opportunities others do, but somehow negotiates his way through life's bends and snags on a higher plane and above the confusion that engulfs those of less solid character. Where others stumble or fall because of character flaws, this person is able to stride forward freely.

There is wholeness in what the person with integrity says and does. There is consistency between his actions and what he purports to honor. He pursues his aims along the high road and is uninterrupted and undiminished by temptations for quick or easy personal gain. He seems undisturbed by the opinions others hold or express about him and what he honors. His upright conduct is made possible through steadfast adherence to unbending principles and standards, and his character is marked by an undaunted quest for important ends far larger than his own needs, comfort, and interests.

What he did in the past is consistent with who he is now and what he can be expected to be in the future. And because of his steady approach to life along these paths, others recognize him as being incorruptible and worthy of their confidence and respect. "Integrity" and "integer" have the same Latin origin—*integritas,* meaning whole, complete. The person with integrity is undivided. His standards and actions are sound, and they are one. This person is consistent in what he says and does.

The Nature of Integrity

The human creature hungers for many things: for the physiological necessities that sustain and perpetuate life, for security and a sense of well-

Chapter VII: Self-Deception and Integrity

being, for the acceptance and approval of others, for self-esteem, and for self-expression. Much of human behavior is aimed at satisfying these appetites, and each appetite, when pursued within certain bounds, helps advance the human condition.

The pursuit of life's necessities gives rise to improvements in agriculture, manufacturing, and commerce. The pursuit of security and safety gives rise to improvements in planning. The pursuit of social relationships gives rise to the formation of families and communities and the regulation of behavior within these social complexes. The pursuits of self-esteem and self-fulfillment give rise to self-development and creative expression.

Each person has modest appetites that serve him, in a sense, by making him more human as he looks after his own welfare and the welfare of others, thus elevating the quality of living. But these appetites expand if they are fed purely for their own sake. Anytime a person desires something inordinately, it can become an absorbing passion, making him its servant, thereby destroying his likable qualities. The man who can be trusted is the one who can say 'no' to his overexpanding appetites and who knows right from wrong.

We all know of those who have allowed their pursuit for material possessions or food to swell uncontrollably into greed or gluttony, or allowed the pursuit of sexual relations to lead them away from marriage with a lifelong companion and turn into unbridled lust. Overconcern for the approbation of others can turn into a never-ending obsession for praise. Pursuit of a healthy sense of self-worth can go too far and turn into conceit. And the pursuit of self-realization can grow beyond a useful level and turn into an empty pleasure when it is pursued solely for the benefit of one's self. Whenever someone turns his attention primarily to the task of satisfying one of his appetites for its own sake, that task can quickly turn into an obsession destroying his character and also destroying the possibility of ever satisfying the appetite itself. Like an addiction, the obsession becomes the source of more pain than joy. The Romans had a proverb: "Money is like sea water, the more a man drinks it the thirstier he becomes."

When an appetite swells to become an addiction, the person will do anything to feed it, so helpless is he under its domination. The sure footing of reliable standards and worthy aims pursued on a high plane is thereby lost, and his character is diminished if not destroyed. Whenever the satisfaction of one's needs becomes preeminent in one's concerns, the issues of right and wrong are relegated a subordinate level of importance and ethical conduct is at risk.

Integrity requires that we be impervious to the persistent, nagging demands of our appetites for "still more" and to an overconcern about praise and blame coming from others. The belief that just a little bit more of whatever it is a man wants will satisfy his appetites, plus his actions aimed at putting his cravings to rest, invite compulsiveness to take root. The person with integrity is able to ignore the clamoring cries for more from his appetites that promise to bring happiness and pleasure if they are met.

Two essential elements enable a person to escape the cries for "more" coming from within. First, one needs a purpose or cause to follow that he honors more than anything else, including his own comfort and well-being. By following such a cause, outside of the self, the individual becomes able to transcend the cries for "more" coming from his appetites within and is thereby able to neglect his pestering whims. Second, he needs to be loyal to his cause. He must obey its demands.

Popular among many is the belief that one can acquire wealth and approval and recognition first, and then go on to develop the qualities of honesty and dependability. That is to say, after appetites are satisfied, one can work to achieve integrity. This fallacy has disastrously affected many lives, and history is strewn with the wrecks of men who have gambled that it would work. Appetites when fed for their own sake rarely loosen their hold on men's minds but swell larger as they are fed.

The Opinions of Others

As social creatures, humans have a strong need to feel loved, needed, and respected and to enjoy a close and lasting bond with others. It is widely believed that these social needs will be met to the extent that one shapes his behavior so as to be pleasing to others. To a large extent this works, so it isn't surprising that people are deeply concerned with their own standing in the eyes of others and that much of what they do is intended to gain them approval.

Great benefit arises from this. The desire to have a good reputation and to escape criticism serves as a strong deterrent to unwanted behavior. Social forces of this nature maintain civilization to a far greater extent, and surely more effectively, than laws and the policing actions necessary when laws are violated. The need to maintain a good reputation has far more influence on behavior than the fear of punishment. But the need for approval can also become an obsession and destroy both peace of mind and genuine character.

The desire for popularity puts people on the trail of pursuing praise instead of what may be praiseworthy. Here one is on shaky ground; what may be popular today may not be tomorrow, and what may meet with acclaim from one group may bring censure from another.

Integrity rests on neglecting the changing and conflicting opinions of others and faithfully following what one believes to be standards that are worthy of his obedience. Writing to his sister, Benjamin Franklin expressed this same idea. "One's true happiness depends more upon one's own judgment of one's own self, or a consciousness of rectitude in action and inten-

Chapter VII: Self-Deception and Integrity

tion, and the approbation of those few who judge impartially, than upon the applause of the unthinking, undiscerning multitude, who are apt to cry 'Hosanna' today, and tomorrow, 'crucify him.'"

We are left with the sobering conclusion that self-satisfaction of the highest kind has its basis in virtuous and self-approving conduct. A useful question people can consider before taking any action that will guide them toward integrity is not, "Will it be praised?" but "Ought it be praised?" And no amount of favorable responses to the former can justify an action that receives a negative answer to the latter.

Integrity is largely a matter of doing what one believes to be right as his conscience so guides him. The ideal is to be unconcerned with winning the praises of others and impervious to their criticism. The greatness of Abraham Lincoln is revealed by his steadfast adherence to what he believed to be right and good for the nation, despite the bitter attacks against him in the press. When asked why he did not try to defend his actions, Lincoln said that history would be a far better judge of him than contemporary critics and that if he were to respond to every attack it would not be possible for him to attend to the things that really required his attention.

Conscientious people often ask, "How well am I doing on this project?" And it is indeed important that each member of an organization work toward a level of performance that will please higher-ups. After all, people are being paid to perform in the ways their leaders deem appropriate. But beyond the normal concern for solid performance in keeping with their superiors' wishes and expectations there is a point at which a person can become obsessed with pleasing everyone. Frequently this overconcern is tied to something more than just winning the superior's approval; it is motivated by the hope of moving up in the organization. In these situations the concern is not to perform well primarily to help the organization succeed, but to perform well enough to win attention and praise in order to achieve a promotion or an advancement.

Concern for one's own advancement need not be condemned, but self-serving efforts to look good and win something for oneself can easily lead one to try "anything" just to succeed and move ahead. Whenever a person's concern focuses primarily on moving ahead in an organization, it is possible for his integrity to be pushed aside and his actions to become unreliable and treacherous. Douglas D. Danforth, of Westinghouse, warns, "Don't necessarily worry about the third job up. Because if you do every job as best you can and you give it your all, you're going to be recognized, and you're going to succeed, and you're going to go up forward to the limit of your God-given and developed ability."

The willingness of millions of eager men and women to work hard to succeed sustains the vitality of the nation's economic performance. But eagerness to succeed can extend beyond healthy hard work and efforts aimed at excellent performance. We see this with people who resort to the "game" of power and politics. Popular articles and books on this subject suggest ways their readers can move ahead and get what they want.

The idea behind the power game, as it is frequently referred to by these writers, is to gain some advantage for one's self, through any number of innocent looking means. However, these prescriptions unleash enormous opportunities for compromising one's integrity. For by following the advice given on how to acquire and use power for one's own advantage, it is tempting to overlook the difference between a course of action that is right and a course that is merely expedient and self-serving. Playing the power game and worrying over how to gain and use power for one's purposes involves manipulating situations to one's advantage.

One peril that is always associated with gaining and exercising power is collapse of character. This is because in the process of gaining the power needed to do something, one is apt to become engrossed with gaining more power for its own sake. History holds many examples of self-serving people who have become obsessed with power and as a result have destroyed their characters and eventually themselves. Gerald Greenwald, of Chrysler, advises against the power and politics mystique and the advice offered by writers of popular self-help books. He urges dedicated hard work as the only sensible approach to getting ahead. "I've listened to others describe corporate politics. And I have to say I've seen very little of it. I won't say I haven't seen any. . . . Personally. . . . if I want to get ahead, the way for me to get ahead is to do my job so well that my boss gets promoted."

Having One's Own Standards

One keeps his needs from turning into obsessions by ignoring the expanding demands for "more" coming from within. This includes remaining unconcerned with winning praise from others. Self-control alone is insufficient in these matters. Having definite standards and worthwhile aims and the tenacity to choose what is right above all other considerations are also necessary. Clarity of purpose and honesty in thinking are other important dimensions which lead to integrity in a person's character. It is difficult to imagine someone standing up and battling for causes or standards for extended periods of time who is deficient in these areas. One's resolve in defending or advancing causes or standards is made possible by genuinely believing in them. And the depth of a person's belief is enhanced by the amount of careful thought he has given it.

Standards, if they are to count for anything, must be personal. Frequently, the adherence to one's standards will be tested to the point where there is a cost associated with holding to them. The beliefs of Neil Harlan, of McKesson Corporation, serve as an illustration here. "I'm not willing to

Chapter VII: Self-Deception and Integrity

be chairman and chief executive officer of a corporation that ignores the problems in the communities in which it lives. And, we don't. . . . As long as I'm chief executive officer of this company, we are going to do these things [support causes in the community]. Then the stockholders can make up their minds whether they want a chief executive officer who's going to do those things. And if they don't, well, they can get another one."

Organizations, too, can be found that abide by standards their leaders believe to be right and follow honorable paths even though these paths will not necessarily lead to some material advantage. These include anything from equal employment opportunities to quality products.

Just as with an individual, a company may have to bear a terrific price in order to live up to a standard. Douglas Danforth, of Westinghouse, describes one situation that illustrates this idea. "We are in the engineered materials business. I know of cases where we have produced and shipped a batch of material that probably would have functioned. The customer probably would never have found it. But we recalled it and reproduced it because we felt in the long run we were going to be better off and our integrity would not be questioned in any way."

In other cases, sales are lost or at least placed in jeopardy because a company would have to lower its standards to get the business. For instance R. R. Donnelly, the biggest printing company in America, will not print *Playboy* or *Penthouse* or any magazine or material that they believe is not in good taste. And Blockbuster Video will not include X-rated movies in its stores for rental. Any number of business leaders have refused to entertain customers in ways these leaders did not consider proper, despite the fact that refusal might result in loss of sales their companies could otherwise have made.

Doing What One Believes Is Right

In contemplating an action, many among us are prone to ask, "What's in it for me?" There is a tendency in our time to calculate every action with the belief that the intelligent way to live is to maximize what one can get for oneself. The thrust of economic theory and management decision-making tools and techniques embraces this viewpoint. Illegal, harmful, or evil actions, of course, are not to be seriously considered, they are ruled out. But a serious shortcoming to this way of thinking is that it places adherence to standards and pursuit of worthy ends in a subordinate position to that of grasping whatever benefits may be had. Integrity demands thinking on an entirely different plane.

Merely avoiding illegal or improper actions may meet the law, but those who are known for their integrity live to reach higher standards. The notion that the good life is achieved by logically calculating every action so as to maximize what one can gain is one of the popular superstitions of our age. The reasonably perceptive person will quickly outgrow this concept of how to live; he will see that it may achieve some gains but does not deliver integrity. Socrates stated that, "A man who is good for anything ought not to calculate the chance of living or dying; he ought only to consider whether in doing anything he is doing right or wrong—acting the part of a good man or of a bad."

What is "right" from a business standpoint, the textbooks claim, is whatever maximizes profits or the shareholders' wealth; the correct decision, their authors tell us, is the one that produces the greatest return. Were this philosophy to be followed all of the time, integrity in business would be unheard of. There are many business leaders who are guided by a higher standard of conduct than cold calculation of the bottom line. Integrity can only be attained when people struggle with the question, "Am I doing right or wrong?" instead of, "What will I gain by doing things one way or another?" It should not be surprising, therefore, to observe that in practically every situation where integrity manifests itself, we find people struggling with one question only: "What's the right thing to do?" and then having the resolve to do that, as the following examples illustrate.

The Bank Check Order

In the days before checks were personalized, banks would buy them in large quantities—maybe a half a year's supply at one time—with the bank's name printed on them. A newly hired salesman for Deluxe Check Printers, eager to do well, took an order from a West Coast bank—5 million checks! Elated with his huge sales order, this young salesman telephoned company president, George McSweeny, to tell of his windfall. Stunned by the news, Mr. McSweeny asked, "Five million checks? What is the size of the bank?" The salesman told him. "Well, that will be more checks than they'll need for several years. You go back and tell him that's more checks than he'll need," said McSweeny. "He should cut that order way back to less than a million. And give him the reasons why—they could spoil or be damaged or the bank's routing number could be changed." This was done. The bank's president was flabbergasted but thankful for the honesty and fair treatment he received.

The Tylenol Disaster

In 1982, authorities concluded that Johnson & Johnson's Tylenol, manufactured by their McNeil Laboratories unit, was linked to several deaths in the Chicago area. Some person or persons, had laced Tylenol capsules with cyanide. Johnson & Johnson got the report on a Thursday morning. The McNeil management acted immediately, recalling first one lot and then a second without lengthy discussion.

When more information about the poisonings became known a decision to remove all capsules from the market was made at Johnson & Johnson headquarters in New Brunswick the following Tuesday. That decision, which cost $80 million after taxes in loss of profits, was made by the chairman of the board, James Burke, with a consensus of senior management. However, the initial decisions were made by the people from McNeil, without checking through the hierarchy. Their immediate concern was for the public.

What's most revealing about this situation is that neither top management at McNeil, in Fort Washington, Pennsylvania, nor senior Johnson & Johnson executives, in New Brunswick, New Jersey, knew what the economics of their decisions were going to be when they issued the recall notices. In fact, they didn't total the costs until much later, because, in their thinking, that had nothing to do with the decision. Their most urgent concerns were for the public welfare.

The Mexico Earthquake

Historically, Carnation has been an international company. Anywhere in the United States or abroad where Carnation participates, that company has a policy of jumping in immediately when disaster strikes to help people by providing food products and money. In the case of the 1985 Mexico City earthquake, Carnation chairman, Timm F. Crull, notes, "We immediately donated, not thinking about our brand . . . or helping the image of the company. It's not even important. It's our responsibility to help our communities that we do business in. And we will immediately donate money or products or whatever is necessary without hesitation, and we have people who are doing that in almost every operation or unit of our company."

A Moral Obligation

Doing the "right thing" is not something one does if it is convenient or because it returns benefits. It is done because someone believes it should be done—because he believes higher concerns call for it. Levi Strauss & Company, with its genuine commitment to human dignity and fairness, works to make every work environment one of equal opportunity. Once Levi Strauss & Company bought out a plant in Blackstone, Virginia, that was all white. Shortly thereafter Levi's plant's manager, Paul Glasgow, came to top management and said, "I think the time is right to integrate the plant"

Their response was, "Good. We're with you."

He then went to the leaders in that small Southern town, to make his intentions known. Glasgow learned that they wanted to divide the plant into "black" and "white" sections. Levi's management said, "No, we're not going to do that."

The town's leaders then asked for a dividing line to be painted so as to keep blacks on one side and whites on the other. And, again the company refused.

Next, separate drinking fountains and toilet facilities were requested. And again Levi said, "no" to that proposal. The people at Blackstone didn't like Levi's stand; it violated their long-standing customs. An attempt was next made to pressure Levi; the local employment service stopped sending applicants to the plant for available jobs.

Paul Glasgow asked headquarters in San Francisco, "What will we do?" And, Walter Haas, Jr., who was chairman and CEO at the time, said, "Close the plant."

The plant never was closed; it is still operating. And it is operating there on Levi's terms of equal opportunity. Because of this courageous stand, the employment practices in the whole community were altered.

The Apology

Plato

In 399 B.C. Socrates was brought to trial before a court composed of 501 Athenian citizens. In his defense he spoke as follows:

How you, O Athenians, have been affected by my accusers, I cannot tell; but I know that they almost made me forget who I was—so persuasively did they speak; and yet they have hardly uttered a word of truth. But of the many falsehoods told by them, there was one which quite amazed me;—I mean when they said that you should be upon your guard and not allow yourselves to be deceived by the force of my eloquence. To say this, when they were certain to be detected as soon as I opened my lips and proved myself to be anything but a great speaker, did indeed appear to me most shameless—unless by the force of eloquence they mean the force of truth; for if such is their meaning, I admit that I am eloquent. But in how different a way from theirs! Well, as I was saying, they have scarcely spoken the truth at all; but from me you shall hear the whole truth: not, however, delivered after their manner in a set oration duly ornamented with words and phrases. No, by heaven! but I shall use the words and arguments which occur to me at the moment; for I am confident in the justice of my cause: at my time of life I ought not to be appearing before you, O men of Athens, in the character of a juvenile orator—let no one expect it of me. And I must beg of you to grant me a favor:—If I defend myself in my accustomed manner, and you hear me using the words which I have been in the habit of using in the agora, at the tables of the money-changers, or anywhere else, I would ask you not to be surprised, and not to interrupt me on this account. For I am more than seventy years of age, and appearing now for the first time in a court of law, I am quite a stranger to the language of the place; and therefore I would have you regard me as if I were really a stranger, whom you would excuse if he spoke in his native tongue, and after the fashion of his country:—Am I making an unfair request of you? Never mind the manner, which may or may not be good; but think only of the truth of my words, and give heed to that: let the speaker speak truly and the judge decide justly.

And first, I have to reply to the older charges and to my first accusers, and then I will go on to the later ones. For of old I have had many accusers, who have accused me falsely to you during many years; and I am more afraid of them than of Anytus and his associates, who are dangerous, too, in their own way. But far more dangerous are the others, who began when you were children, and took possession of your minds with their falsehoods, telling of one Socrates, a wise man, who speculated about the heaven above, and searched into the earth beneath, and made the worse appear the better cause. The disseminators of this tale are the accusers whom I dread; for their hearers are apt to fancy that such enquirers do not believe in the existence of the gods. And they are many, and their charges against me are of ancient date, and they were made by them in the days when you were more impressible than you are now—in childhood, or it may have been in youth—and the cause when heard went by default, for there was none to answer. And hardest of all, I do not know and cannot tell the names of my accusers; unless in the chance case of a comic poet. All who from envy and malice have persuaded you—some of them having first convinced themselves—all this class of men are most difficult to deal with; for I cannot have them up here, and cross-examine them, and therefore I must simply fight with shadows in my own defence, and argue when there is no one who answers. I will ask you then to assume with me, as I was saying, that my opponents are of two kinds; one recent, the other ancient: and I hope that you will see the propriety of my answering the latter first, for these accusations you heard long before the others, and much oftener.

Well, then, I must make my defence, and endeavour to clear away in a short time, a slander which has lasted a long time. May I succeed, if to succeed be for my good and yours, or likely to avail me in my cause! The task is not an easy one; I quite understand the nature of it. And so leaving the event with God, in obedience to the law I will now make my defence.

I will begin at the beginning, and ask what is the accusation which has given rise to the slander of me, and in fact has encouraged Meletus, to prefer this charge against me. Well, what do the slanderers say? They shall be my prosecutors, and I will sum up their words in an affidavit: "Socrates is an evildoer, and a curious person, who searches into things under the earth and in heaven, and he makes the worse appear the better cause; and he teaches the aforesaid doctrines to others." Such is the nature of the accusation: it is just what you have yourselves seen in the comedy of Aristophanes, who has introduced a man whom he calls Socrates, going about and saying that he walks in air, and talking a deal of nonsense concerning matters of which I do not pretend to know either much or little—not that I mean to speak disparagingly of any one who is a student of natural philosophy. I should be very sorry if Meletus could bring so grave a charge against me. But the simple truth is, O Athenians, that I have nothing to do with physical speculations. Very many of those here present are witnesses to the truth of this, and to them I appeal. Speak then, you who have heard me, and tell your neighbours whether any of you have ever known me hold forth in few words or in many upon such matters. . . . You hear their answer. And from what they say of this part of the charge you will be able to judge of the truth of the rest.

As little foundation is there for the report that I am a teacher, and take money; this accusation has no more truth in it than the other. Although, if a man were really able to instruct mankind, to receive money for giving instruction would, in my opinion, be an honour to him. There is Gorgias of Leontium, and Prodicus of Ceos, and Hippias of Elis, who go the round of the cities, and are able to persuade the young men to leave their own citizens by whom they might be taught for nothing, and come to them whom they not only pay, but are thankful if they may be allowed to pay them. There is at this time a Parian philosopher residing in Athens, of whom I have heard; and I came to hear of him in this way:—I came across a man who has spent a world of money on the Sophists, Callias, the son of Hipponicus, and knowing that he had sons, I asked him: "Callias," I said, "if your two sons were foals or calves, there would be no difficulty in finding some one to put over them; we should hire a trainer of horses, or a farmer, probably, who would improve and perfect them in their own proper virtue and excellence; but as they are human beings, whom are you thinking of placing over them? Is there any one who understands human and political virtue? You must have thought about the matter, for you have sons; is there any one?" "There is," he said. "Who is he?" said I; "and of what country? and what does he charge?" "Evenus the Parian," he replied; "he is the man, and his charge is five minae." Happy is Evenus, I said to myself, if he really has this wisdom, and teaches at such a moderate charge. Had I the same, I should have been very proud and conceited; but the truth is that I have no knowledge of the kind.

I dare say, Athenians, that some one among you will reply, "Yes, Socrates, but what is the origin of these accusations which are brought against you; there must have been something strange which you have been doing? All these rumours and this talk about you would never have arisen if you had been like other men: tell us, then, what is the cause of them, for we should be sorry to judge hastily of you." Now, I regard this as a fair challenge, and I will endeavour to explain to you the reason why I am called wise and have such an evil fame. Please to attend then. And although some of you may think that I am joking, I declare that I will tell you the entire truth. Men of Athens, this reputation of mine has come of a certain sort of wisdom which I possess. If you ask me what kind of wisdom, I reply, wisdom such as may perhaps be attained by man, for to that extent I am inclined to believe that I am wise; whereas the persons of whom I was speaking have a superhuman wisdom, which I may fail to describe, because I have it not myself; and he who says that I have, speaks falsely, and is taking away my character. And here, O men of Athens, I must beg you not to interrupt me, even if I seem to say something extravagant. For the word which I will speak is not mine. I will refer you to a witness who is worthy of credit; that witness shall be the god of Delphi—he will tell you about my wisdom, if I have any, and of what sort it is. You must have known Chaerephon; he was early a friend of mine, and also a friend of yours, for he shared in the recent exile of the people, and returned with you. Well, Chaerephon, as you know, was very impetuous in all his doings, and he went to Delphi and boldly asked the oracle to tell him whether—as I was saying, I must beg you not to interrupt—he asked the oracle to tell him whether any one was wiser than I was, and the Pythian prophetess answered, that there was no man wiser. Chaerephon is dead himself; but his brother, who is in court, will confirm the truth of what I am saying.

Why do I mention this? Because I am going to explain to you why I have such an evil name. When I heard the answer, I said to myself, What can the god mean? and what is the interpretation of his riddle? for I know I have no wisdom, small or great. What then can he mean when he says that I am the wisest of men? And yet he is a god, and cannot lie; that would be against his nature. After long consideration, I thought of a method of trying the question. I reflected that if I could only find a man wiser than myself, then I might go to the god with a refutation in my hand. I should say to him, "Here is a man who is wiser than I am; but you said that I was the wisest." Accordingly I went to one who had the reputation of wisdom, and observed him—his name I need not mention; he was a politician whom I selected for examination—and the result was as follows: When I began to talk with him, I could not help thinking that he was not really wise, although he was thought wise by many, and still wiser by himself; and thereupon I tried to explain to him that he thought himself wise, but was not really wise; and the consequence was that he hated me, and his enmity was shared by several who were present and heard me. So I left him, saying, to myself, as I went away: Well, although I do not suppose that either of us knows anything really beautiful and good, I am better off than he is,—for he knows nothing, and thinks that he knows; I neither know nor think that I know. In this latter particular, then, I seem to have slightly the advantage of him. Then I went to another who had still higher pretensions to wisdom, and my conclusion was exactly the same. Whereupon I made another enemy of him, and many others besides him.

Then I went to one man after another, being not unconscious of the enmity which I provoked, and I lamented and feared this: but necessity was laid upon me,—the word of God, I thought, ought to be considered first. And I said to myself, Go I must to all who appear to know, and find out the meaning of the oracle. And I swear to you, Athenians, by the dog I swear!—for I must tell you the truth—the result of my mission was just this: I found that the men most in repute were all but the most foolish; and that others less esteemed were really wiser and better. I will tell you the

Chapter VII: Self-Deception and Integrity

tale of my wanderings and of the "Herculean" labours, as I may call them, which I endured only to find at last the oracle irrefutable. After the politicians, I went to the poets; tragic, dithyrambic, and all sorts. And there, I said to myself, you will be instantly detected; now you will find out that you are more ignorant than they are. Accordingly I took them some of the most elaborate passages in their own writings, and asked what was the meaning of them—thinking that they would teach me something. Will you believe me? I am almost ashamed to confess the truth, but I must say that there is hardly a person present who would not have talked better about their poetry than they did themselves. Then I knew that not by wisdom do poets write poetry, but by a sort of genius and inspiration; they are like diviners or soothsayers who also say many fine things, but do not understand the meaning of them. The poets appeared to me to be much in the same case; and I further observed that upon the strength of their poetry they believed themselves to be the wisest of men in other things in which they were not wise. So I departed, conceiving myself to be superior to them for the same reason that I was superior to the politicians.

At last I went to the artisans. I was conscious that I knew nothing at all, as I may say, and I was sure that they knew many fine things; and here I was not mistaken, for they did know many things of which I was ignorant, and in this they certainly were wiser than I was. But I observed that even the good artisans fell into the same error as the poets;—because they were good workmen they thought that they also knew all sorts of high matters, and this defect in them overshadowed their wisdom; and therefore I asked myself on behalf of the oracle, whether I would like to be as I was, neither having their knowledge nor their ignorance, or like them in both; and I made answer to myself and to the oracle that I was better off as I was.

This inquisition has led to my having many enemies of the worst and most dangerous kind, and has given occasion also to many calumnies. And I am called wise, for my hearers always imagine that I myself possess the wisdom which I find wanting in others: but the truth is, O men of Athens, that God only is wise; and by his answer he intends to show that the wisdom of men is worth little or nothing; he is not speaking of Socrates, he is only using my name by way of illustration, as if he said, He, O men, is the wisest, who, like Socrates, knows that his wisdom is in truth worth nothing. And so I go about the world obedient to the god, and search and make enquiry into the wisdom of any one, whether citizen or stranger, who appears to be wise; and if he is not wise, then in vindication of the oracle I show him he is not wise; and my occupation quite absorbs me, and I have no time to give either to any public matter of interest or to any concern of my own, but I am in utter poverty by reason of my devotion to the god.

There is another thing:—young men of the richer classes, who have not much to do, come about me of their own accord; they like to hear the pretenders examined, and they often imitate me, and proceed to examine others; there are plenty of persons, as they quickly discover, who think that they know something, but really know little or nothing; and then those who are examined by them instead of being angry with themselves are angry with me: This confounded Socrates, they say; this villainous misleader of youth!—and then if somebody asks them, Why, what evil does he practice or teach? they do not know, and cannot tell; but in order that they may not appear to be at a loss, they repeat the ready-made charges which are used against all philosophers about teaching things up in the clouds and under the earth, and having no gods, and making the worse appear the better cause; for they do not like to confess that their presence of knowledge has been detected—which is the truth; and as they are numerous and ambitious and energetic, and are drawn up in battle array and have persuasive tongues, they have filled your ears with their loud and inveterate calumnies. And this is the reason why my three accusers, Meletus and Anytus and Lycon, have set upon me; Meletus, who has a quarrel with me on behalf of the poets; Anytus, on behalf of the craftsmen and politicians; Lycon, on behalf of the rhetoricians: and, as I said at the beginning, I cannot expect to get rid of such a mass of calumny all in a moment. And this, O men of Athens, is the truth and the whole truth; I have concealed nothing, I have dissembled nothing. And yet, I know that my plainness of speech makes them hate me, and what is their hatred but a proof that I am speaking the truth? Hence has arisen the prejudice against me; and this is the reason of it, as you will find out either in this or in any future enquiry.

I have said enough in my defence against the first class of my accusers; I turn to the second class. They are headed by Meletus, that good man and true lover of his country, as he calls himself. Against these, too, I must try to make a defence:—Let their affidavit be read: it contains something of this kind: It says that Socrates is a doer of evil, who corrupts the youth; and who does not believe in the gods of the State, but has other new divinities of his own. Such is the charge; and now let us examine the particular counts. He says that I am a doer of evil, and corrupt the youth; but I say, O men of Athens, that Meletus is a doer of evil, in that he pretends to be in earnest when he is only in jest, and is so eager to bring men to trial from a pretended zeal and interest about matters in which he really never had the smallest interest. And the truth of this I will endeavour to prove to you.

Come hither, Meletus, and let me ask a question of you. You think a great deal about the improvement of youth?

Yes, I do.

Tell the judges, then, who is their improver, for you must know, as you have taken the pains to discover their corrupter, and are citing and accusing me before them. Speak, then, and tell the judges who their improver is.—Observe, Meletus, that you are silent, and have nothing to say But is not this rather disgraceful, and a very considerable proof of what I was saying, that you have no interest in the matter? Speak up, friend, and tell us who their improver is.

The laws.

But that, my good sir, is not my meaning. I want to know who the person is, who, in the first place, knows the laws.

The judges, Socrates, who are present in court.

What, do you mean to say, Meletus, that they are able to instruct and improve youth?

Certainly they are.

What, all of them, or some only and not others?

All of them.

By the goddess. Here, that is good news! There are plenty of improvers, then. And what do you say of the audience,—do they improve them?

Yes, they do.

And the senators?

Yes, the senators improve them.

But perhaps the members of the assembly corrupt them?—or do they improve them?

They improve them.

Then every Athenian improves and elevates them; all with the exception of myself; and I alone am their corrupter? Is that what you affirm?

That is what I stoutly affirm.

I am very unfortunate if you are right. But suppose I ask you a question: How about horses? Does one man do them harm and all the world good? Is not the exact opposite the truth? One man is able to do them good, or at least not many—the trainer of horses, that is to say, does them good, and others who have to do with them rather injure them? Is not that true, Meletus, of horses, or of any other animals? Most assuredly it is; whether you and Anytus say yes or no. Happy indeed would be the condition of youth if they had one corrupter only, and all the rest of the world were their improvers. But you, Meletus, have sufficiently shown that you never had a thought about the young: your carelessness is seen in your not caring about the very things which you bring against me.

And now, Meletus, I will ask you another question—by Zeus I will: Which is better, to live among bad citizens, or among good ones? Answer, friend, I say; the question is one which may be easily answered. Do not the good do their neighbours good, and the bad do them evil?

Certainly.

And is there any one who would rather be injured than benefited by those who live with him? Answer, my good friend, the law requires you to answer—does any one like to be injured?

Certainly not.

And when you accuse me of corrupting and deteriorating the youth, do you allege that I corrupt them intentionally or unintentionally?

Intentionally, I say.

But you have just admitted that the good do their neighbours good, and the evil do them evil. Now, is that a truth which your superior wisdom has recognized thus early in life, and am I, at my age, in such darkness and ignorance as not to know that if a man with whom I have to live is corrupted by me, I am very likely to be harmed by him; and yet I corrupt him, and intentionally, too—so you say, although neither I nor any other human being is ever likely to be convinced by you. But either I do not corrupt them, or I corrupt them unintentionally; and on either view of the case you lie. If my offence is unintentional, the law has no cognizance of unintentional offences: you ought to have taken me privately, and warned and admonished me; for if I had been better advised, I should have left off doing what I only did unintentionally—no doubt I should; but you would have nothing to say to me and refused to teach me. And now you bring me up in this court, which is a place not of instruction, but of punishment.

It will be very clear to you, Athenians, as I was saying, that Meletus has no care at all, great or small, about the matter. But still I should like to know, Meletus, in what I am affirmed to corrupt the young. I suppose you mean, as I infer from your indictment, that I teach them not to acknowledge the gods which the State acknowledges, but some other new divinities or spiritual agencies in their stead. These are the lessons by which I corrupt the youth, as you say.

Yes, that I say emphatically.

Then, by the gods, Meletus, of whom we are speaking, tell me and the court, in somewhat plainer terms, what you mean! For I do not as yet understand whether you affirm that I teach other men to acknowledge some gods, and therefore that I do believe in gods, and am not an entire atheist—this you do not lay to my charge,—but only you say that they are not the same gods which the city recognizes—the charge is that they are different gods. Or, do you mean that I am an atheist simply, and a teacher of atheism?

I mean the latter—that you are a complete atheist.

What an extraordinary statement! Why do you think so, Meletus? Do you mean that I do not believe in the godhead of the sun or moon, like other men?

I assure you, judges, that he does not: for he says that the sun is stone, and the moon earth.

Friend Meletus, you think that you are accusing Anaxagoras: and you have but a bad opinion of the judges, if you fancy them illiterate to such a degree as not to know that these doctrines are found in the books of Anaxagoras the Clazomenian, which are full of them. And so, forsooth, the youth are said to be taught them by Socrates, when there are not infrequently exhibitions of them at the theatre (price of admission one drachma at the most); and they might pay their money, and laugh at Socrates if he pretends to father these extraordinary views. And so, Meletus, you really think that I do not believe in any god?

Chapter VII: Self-Deception and Integrity

I swear by Zeus that you believe absolutely in none at all.

Nobody will believe you, Meletus, and I am pretty sure that you do not believe yourself. I cannot help thinking, that he has written this indictment in a spirit of mere wantonness and youthful bravado. Has he not compounded a riddle, thinking to try me? He said to himself; I shall see whether the wise Socrates will discover my facetious contradiction, or whether I shall be able to deceive him and the rest of them. For he certainly does appear to me to contradict himself in the indictment as much as if he said that Socrates is guilty of not believing in the gods, and yet of believing in them—but this is not like a person who is in earnest.

I should like you, O men of Athens, to join me in examining what I conceive to be his inconsistency; and do you, Meletus, answer. And I must remind the audience of my request that they would not make a disturbance if I speak in my accustomed manner:

Did ever man, Meletus, believe in the existence of human things, and not of human beings? . . . I wish, men of Athens, that he would answer, and not be always trying to get up an interruption. Did ever any man believe in horsemanship, and not in horses, or in flute-playing, and not in flute-players? No, my friend; I will answer to you and to the court, as you refuse to answer for yourself. There is no man who ever did. But now please to answer the next question: Can a man believe in spiritual and divine agencies, and not in spirits or demigods?

He cannot.

How lucky I am to have extracted that answer, by the assistance of the court! But then you swear in the indictment that I teach and believe in divine or spiritual agencies (new or old, no matter for that); at any rate, I believe in spiritual agencies—so you say and swear in the affidavit; and yet if I believe in divine beings, how can I help believing in spirits or demigods;—must I not? To be sure I must; and therefore I may assume that your silence gives consent. Now what are spirits or demigods? are they not either gods or the sons of gods?

Certainly they are.

But this is what I call the facetious riddle invented by you: the demigods or spirits are gods, and you say first that I do not believe in gods, and then again that I do believe in gods; that is, if I believe in demigods. For if the demigods are the illegitimate sons of gods, whether by the nymphs or by any other mothers, of whom they are said to be the sons—what human being will ever believe that there are no gods if they are the sons of gods? You might as well affirm the existence of mules, and deny that of horses and asses. Such nonsense, Meletus, could only have been intended by you to make trial of me. You have put this into the indictment because you had nothing real of which to accuse me. But no one who has a particle of understanding will ever be convinced by you that the same men can believe in divine and superhuman beings, and yet not believe that there are gods and demigods and heroes.

I have said enough in answer to the charge of Meletus: any elaborate defence is unnecessary; but I know only too well how many are the enmities which I have incurred, and this is what will be my destruction if I am destroyed;—not Meletus, nor yet Anytus, but the envy and detraction of the world, which has been the death of many good men, and will probably be the death of many more; there is no danger of my being the last of them.

Some one will say: And are you not ashamed, Socrates, of a course of life which is likely to bring you to an untimely end? To him I may fairly answer: There you are mistaken: a man who is good for anything ought not to calculate the chance of living or dying; he ought only to consider whether in doing anything he is doing right or wrong—acting the part of a good man or a bad. Whereas, upon your view, the son of Thetis above all, who altogether despised danger in comparison with disgrace; and when he was so eager to slay Hector, his goddess mother said to him, that if he avenged his companion Patroclus, and slew Hector, he would die himself—"Fate," she said, in these or the like words, "waits for you next after Hector"; he, receiving this warning, utterly depised danger and death, and instead of fearing them, feared rather to live in dishonour, and not to avenge his friend. "Let me die forthwith," he replies, "and be avenged of my enemy, rather than abide here by the beaked ships, a laughing stock and a burden of the earth." Had Achilles any thought of death and danger? For wherever a man's place is, whether the place which he has chosen or that in which he has been placed by a commander, there he ought to remain in the hour of danger; he should not think of death or of anything but of disgrace. And this, O men of Athens, is a true saying.

Strange, indeed, would be my conduct, O men of Athens, if I, who, when I was ordered by the generals whom you chose to command me at Potidaea and Amphipolis and Delium, remained where they placed me, like any other man, facing death—if now, when, as I conceive and imagine, God orders me to fulfill the philosopher's mission of searching into myself and other men, I were to desert my post through fear of death, or any other fear; that would indeed be strange, and I might justly be arraigned in court for denying the existence of the gods, if I disobeyed the oracle because I was afraid of death, fancying that I was wise when I was not wise. For the fear is indeed the pretence of wisdom, and not real wisdom, being a pretence of knowing the unknown; and no one knows whether death, which men in their fear apprehend to be the greatest evil, may not be the greatest good. Is not this ignorance of a disgraceful sort, the ignorance which is the conceit that a man knows what he does not know? And in this respect only I believe myself to differ from men in general, and may perhaps claim to be wiser than they are:—that whereas I know but little of the world below, I do not suppose that I know: but I do know that injustice and disobedience to a better, whether God or man, is evil and dishonourable, and I will never fear or avoid a possible good rather than a certain evil. And therefore if you let me go now, and are not convinced by

Anytus, who said that since I had been prosecuted I must be put to death; (or if not that I ought never to have been prosecuted at all); and that if I escape now, your sons will all be utterly ruined by listening to my words— if you say to me, Socrates, this time we will not mind Anytus, and you shall be let off, but upon one condition, that you are not to enquire and speculate in this way any more, and that if you are caught doing so again you shall die;—if this was the condition on which you let me go, I should reply: Men of Athens, I honour and love you; but I shall obey God rather than you, and while I have life and strength I shall never cease from the practice and teaching of philosophy, exhorting any one whom I meet and saying to him after my manner: You, my friend,—a citizen of the great and mighty and wise city of Athens,—are you not ashamed of heaping up the greatest amount of money and honour and reputation, and caring so little about wisdom and truth and the greatest improvement of the soul, which you never regard or heed at all? And if the person with whom I am arguing, says: Yes, but I do care; then I do not leave him or let him go at once; but I proceed to interrogate and examine him, and if I think that he has no virtue in him, but only says that he has, I reproach him with undervaluing the greater, and overvaluing the less. And I shall repeat the same words to every one whom I meet, young and old, citizen and alien, but especially to the citizens, inasmuch as they are my brethren. For know that this is the command of God; and I believe that no greater good has ever happened in the State than my service to the God. For I do nothing but go about persuading you all, old and young alike, not to take thought for your persons or your properties, but first and chiefly to care about the greatest improvement of the soul. I tell you that virtue is not given by money, but that from virtue comes money and every other good of man, public as well as private. This is my teaching, and if this is the doctrine which corrupts the youth, I am a mischievous person. But if any one says that this is not my teaching, he is speaking an untruth. Wherefore, O men of Athens, I say to you, do as Anytus bids or not as Anytus bids, and either acquit me or not; but whichever you do, understand that I shall never alter my ways, not even if I have to die many times.

Men of Athens, do not interrupt, but hear me; there was an understanding between us that you should hear me to the end: I have something more to say, at which you may be inclined to cry out; but I believe that to hear me will be good for you, and therefore I beg that you will not cry out. I would have you know, that if you kill such an one as I am, you will injure yourselves more than you will injure me. Nothing will injure me, not Meletus nor yet Anytus—they cannot, for a bad man is not permitted to injure a better than himself. I do not deny that Anytus may, perhaps, kill him, or drive him into exile, or deprive him of civil rights; and he may imagine, and others may imagine, that he is inflicting a great injury upon him: but there I do not agree. For the evil of doing as he is doing—the evil of unjustly taking away the life of another—is greater far.

And, now, Athenians, I am not going to argue for my own sake, as you may think, but for yours, that you may not sin against the God by condemning me, who am his gift to you. For if you kill me you will not easily find a successor to me, who, if I may use such a ludicrous figure of speech, am a sort of gadfly, given to the State by God; and the State is a great and noble steed who is tardy in his motions owing to his very size, and requires to be stirred into life. I am that gadfly which God has attached to the State, and all day long and in all places am always fastening upon you, and persuading and reproaching you. You will not easily find another like me, and therefore I would advise you to spare me. I dare say that you may feel out of temper (like a person who is suddenly awakened from sleep), and you think that you might easily strike me dead as Anytus advises, and then you would sleep on for the remainder of your lives, unless God in his care of you sent you another gadfly. When I say that I am given to you by God, the proof of my mission is this:—if I had been like other men, I should not have neglected all my own concerns or patiently seen the neglect of them during all these years, and have been doing yours, coming to you individually like a father or elder brother, exhorting you to regard virtue; such conduct, I say, would be unlike human nature. If I had gained anything, or if my exhortations had been paid, there would have been some sense in my doing so; but now, as you will perceive, not even the impudence of my accusers dares to say that I have ever extracted or sought pay of any one; of that they have no witness. And I have a sufficient witness to the truth of what I say—my poverty.

Some one may wonder why I go about in private giving advice and busying myself with the concerns of others, but do not venture to come forward in public and advise the State. I will tell you why. You have heard me speak at sundry times and in divers places of an oracle or sign which comes to me, and this is the divinity which Meletus ridicules in the indictment. This sign, which is a kind of voice, first began to come to me when I was a child; it always forbids but never commands me to do anything which I am going to do. This is what deters me from being a politician. And rightly, as I think. For I am certain, O men of Athens, that if I had engaged in politics, I should have perished long ago, and done no good either to you or to myself And do not be offended at my telling you the truth; for the truth is, that no man who goes to war with you or any other multitude, honestly striving against the many lawless and unrighteous deeds which are done in a State, will save his life; he who will fight for the right, if he would live even for a brief space, must have a private station and not a public one.

I can give you convincing evidence of what I say, not words only, but what you value far more—actions. Let me relate to you a passage of my own life which will prove to you that I should never have yielded to injustice from any fear of death and that "as I should have refused to yield" I must have died at once. I will tell you a tale of the courts, not very

Chapter VII: Self-Deception and Integrity

interesting perhaps, but nevertheless true. The only office of State which I ever held, O men of Athens, was that of senator: the tribe Antiochis, which is my tribe, had, the presidency at the trial of the generals who had not taken up the bodies of the slain after the battle of Arginusae; and you proposed to try them in a body, contrary to law, as you all thought afterwards; but at the time I was the only one of the Prytanes who was opposed to the illegality, and I gave my vote against you; and when the orators threatened to impeach and arrest me, and you called and shouted, I made up my mind that I would run the risk, having law and justice with me, rather than take part in your injustice because I feared imprisonment and death. This happened in the days of the democracy. But when the oligarchy of the Thirty was in power, they sent for me and four others into the rotunda, and bade us bring Leon the Salaminian from Salamis, as they wanted to put him to death. This was a specimen of the sort of commands which they were always giving with the view of implicating as many as possible in their crimes; and then I showed, not in word only but in deed, that, if I may be allowed to use such an expression, I cared not a straw for death, and that my great and only care was lest I should do an unrighteous or unholy thing. For the strong arm of that oppressive power did not frighten me into doing wrong; and when we came out of the rotunda the other four went to Salamis and fetched Leon, but I went quietly home. For which I might have lost my life, had not the power of the Thirty shortly afterwards come to an end. And many will witness to my words.

Now, do you really imagine that I could have survived all these years, if I had led a public life, supposing that like a good man I had always maintained the right and had made justice, as I ought, the first thing? No, indeed, men of Athens, neither I nor any other man. But I have been always the same in all my actions, public as well as private, and never have I yielded any base compliance to those who are slanderously termed my disciples, or to any other. Not that I have any regular disciples. But if any one likes to come and hear me while I am pursuing my mission, whether he be young or old, he is not excluded. Nor do I converse only with those who pay; but any one, whether he be rich or poor, may ask and answer me and listen to my words; and whether he turns out to be a bad man or a good one, neither result can be justly imputed to me; for I never taught or professed to teach him anything. And if any one says that he has ever learned or heard anything from me in private which all the world has not heard, let me tell you that he is lying.

But I shall be asked, Why do people delight in continually conversing with you? I have told you already, Athenians, the whole truth about this matter: they like to hear the cross-examination of the pretenders to wisdom; there is amusement in it. Now, this duty of cross-examining other men has been imposed upon me by God; and has been signified to me by oracles, visions, and in every way in which the will of divine power was ever intimated to any one. This is true, O Athenians; or, if not true, would be soon refuted. If I am or have been corrupting the youth, those of them who are now grown up and have become sensible that I gave them bad advice in the days of their youth should come forward as accusers, and take their revenge; or if they do not like to come themselves, some of their relatives, fathers, brothers, or other kinsmen, should say what evil their families have suffered at my hands. Now is their time. Many of them I see in the court. There is Crito, who is of the same age of the same deme with myself, and there is Critobulus his son, whom I also see. Then again there is Lysanias of Sphettus, who is the father of Aeschines—he is present; and also there is Antiphon of Cephisus, who is the father of Epigenes; and there are the brothers of several who have associated with me. There is Nicostratus the son of Theosdotides, and the brother of Theodotus (now Theodotus himself is dead, and therefore he, at any rate, will not seek to stop him); and there is Paralus the son of Demodocus, who had a brother Theages; and Adeimantus the son of Ariston, whose brother Plato is present; and Aeantodorus, who is the brother of Appollodorus, whom I also see. I might mention a great many others, some of whom Meletus should have produced as witnesses in the course of his speech; and let him still produce them, if he has forgotten—I will make way for him. And let him say, if he has any testimony of the sort which he can produce. Nay, Athenians, the very opposite is the truth. For all these are ready to witness on behalf of the corrupter, of the injurer of their kindred, as Meletus and Anytus call me; not the corrupted youth only—there might have been a motive for that—but their uncorrupted elder relatives. Why should they too support me with their testimony? Why, indeed, except for the sake of truth and justice, and because they know that I am speaking the truth, and that Meletus is a liar.

Well, Athenians, this and the like of this is all the defence which I have to offer. Yet a word more. Perhaps there may be some one who is offended at me, when he calls to mind how he himself on a similar, or even a less serious occasion, prayed and entreated the judges with many tears, and how he produced his children in court, which was a moving spectacle, together with a host of relations and friends; whereas I, who am probably in danger of my life, will do none of these things. The contrast may occur to his mind, and he may be set against me, and vote in anger because he is displeased at me on this account. Now, if there be such a person among you,—mind, I do not say that there is,—to him I may fairly reply: My friend, I am a man, and like other men, a creature of flesh and blood, and not "of wood or stone," as Homer says; and I have a family, yes, and sons, O Athenians, three in number, one almost a man, and two others who are still young; and yet I will not bring any of them hither in order to petition you for an acquittal. And why not? Not from any self-assertion or want of respect for you. Whether I am or am not afraid of death is another question, of which I will not now speak. But, having regard to public opinion,

Chapter VII: Self-Deception and Integrity

I feel that such conduct would be discreditable to myself, and to you, and to the whole State. One who has reached my years, and who has a name for wisdom, ought not to demean himself. Whether this opinion of me be deserved or not, at any rate the world has decided that Socrates is in some way superior to other men. And if those among you who are said to be superior in wisdom and courage, and any other virtue, demean themselves in this way, how shameful is their conduct! I have seen men of reputation, when they have been condemned, behaving in the strangest manner: they seemed to fancy that they were going to suffer something dreadful if they died, and that they could be immortal if you only allowed them to live; and I think that such are a dishonour to the State, and that any stranger coming in would have said to them that the most eminent men of Athens, to whom the Athenians themselves give honour and command, are no better than women. And I say that these things ought not to be done by those of us who have a reputation; and if they are done, you ought not to permit them; you ought rather to show that you are far more disposed to condemn the man who gets up a doleful scene and makes the city ridiculous, than him who holds his peace.

But, setting aside the question of public opinion, there seems to be something wrong in asking a favour of a judge, and thus procuring an acquittal, instead of informing and convincing him. For his duty is, not to make a present of justice, but to give judgment; and he has sworn that he will judge according to the laws, and not according to his own good pleasure; and we ought not to encourage you, nor should you allow yourselves to be encouraged, in this habit of perjury—there can be no piety in that. Do not then require me to do what I consider dishonourable and impious and wrong, especially now, when I am being tried for impiety on the indictment of Meletus. For if, O men of Athens, by force of persuasion and entreaty I could overpower your oaths, then I should be teaching you to believe that there are no gods, and in defending should simply convict myself of the charge of not believing in them. But that is not so—far otherwise. For I do believe that there are gods, and in a sense higher than that in which any of my accusers believe in them. And to you and to God I commit my cause, to be determined by you as is best for you and me. . . .

A majority of the jurors then found Socrates guilty: 281 votes against 220. The condemned man was allowed to propose a penalty in lieu of the death penalty proposed by Meletus. Socrates again spoke:

There are many reasons why I am not grieved, O men of Athens, at the vote of condemnation. I expected it, and am only surprised that the votes are so nearly equal; for I had thought that the majority against me would have been far larger; but now, had thirty votes gone over to the other side, I should have escaped Meletus. I may say more; for without the assistance of Anytus and Lycon, any one may see that he would not have had a fifth part of the votes, as the law requires, in which case he would have incurred a fine of a thousand drachmae.

And so he proposes death as the penalty. And what shall I propose on my part, O men of Athens? Clearly that which is my due. And what is my due? What returns shall be made to the man who has never had the wit to be idle during his whole life; but has been careless of what the many care for—wealth, and family interests, and military offices, and speaking in the assembly, and magistracies, and plots, and parties. Reflecting that I was really too honest a man to be a politician and live, I did not go where I could do no good to you or to myself; but where I could do the greatest good privately to every one of you, thither I went, and sought to persuade every man among you that he must look to himself, and seek virtue and wisdom before he looks to his private interests, and look to the State before he looks to the interests of the State; and that this should be the order which he observes in all his actions. What shall be done to such an one? Doubtless some good thing, O men of Athens, if he has his reward; and the good should be of a kind suitable to him. What would be a reward suitable to a poor man who is your benefactor, and who desires leisure that he may instruct you? There can be no reward so fitting as maintenance in the Prytaneum, O men of Athens, a reward which he deserves far more than the citizen who has won the prize at Olympia in the horse or chariot race, whether the chariots were drawn by two horses or by many. For I am in want, and he has enough; and he only gives you the appearance of happiness, and I give you the reality. And if I am to estimate the penalty fairly, I should say that maintenance in the Prytaneum is the just return.

Perhaps you think that I am braving you in what I am saying now, as in what I said before about the tears and prayers. But this is not so. I speak rather because I am convinced that I never intentionally wronged any one, although I cannot convince you—the time has been too short; if there were a law at Athens, as there is in other cities, that a capital cause should not be decided in one day, then I believe that I should have convinced you. But I cannot in a moment refute great slanders; and, as I am convinced that I never wronged another, I will assuredly not wrong myself. I will not say of myself that I serve any evil, or propose any penalty. Why should I? Because I am afraid of the penalty of death which Meletus proposes? When I do not know whether death is a good or an evil, why should I propose a penalty which would certainly be an evil? Shall I say imprisonment? And why should I live in prison, and be the slave of the magistrate of the year—of the Eleven? Or shall the penalty be a fine, and imprisonment until the fine is paid? There is the same objection. I should have to lie in prison, for money I have none, and cannot pay. And if I say exile (and this may possibly be the penalty which you will affix), I must indeed be blinded by the love of life, if I am so irrational as to expect that when you, who are my own citizens, cannot endure my discourses and words, and have found them so grievous and odious that you will have no more of them, others are likely to endure me. No, indeed, men of Athens, that is not very likely. And what a life should I lead, at my age, wandering from city to city, ever changing my place of exile, and always being driven out! For I am quite sure that wherever I go, there, as here, the young men will flock to me; and if I drive them away, their elders will drive me out at their request; and if I let them come, their fathers and friends will drive me out for their sakes.

Some one will say: Yes, Socrates, but cannot you hold your tongue, and then you may go into a foreign city, and no one will interfere with you? Now, I have great difficulty in making you understand my answer to this. For if I tell you that to do as you say would be a disobedience to the God, and therefore that I cannot hold my tongue, you will not believe that I am serious; and if I say again that daily to discourse about virtue, and of those other things about which you hear me examining myself and others, is the greatest good of man, and that the unexamined life is not worth living, you are still less likely to believe me. Yet I say what is true, although a thing of which it is hard for me to persuade you. Also, I have never been accustomed to think that I deserve to suffer any harm. Had I money I might have estimated the offence at what I was able to pay, and not have been much the worse. But I have none, and therefore I must ask you to proportion the fine to my means. Well, perhaps I could afford a mina, and therefore I propose that penalty: Plato, Crito, Critobulus, and Apollodorus, my friends here, bid me say thirty minae, and they will be the sureties. Let thirty minae be the penalty; for which sum they will be ample security to you. . . .

Another vote was taken and the death penalty was passed. Socrates then made his final statement:

Not much time will be gained, O Athenians, in return for the evil name which you will get from the detractors of the city, who will say that you killed Socrates, a wise man; for they will call me wise, even although I am not wise, when they want to reproach you. If you had waited a little while, your desire would have been fulfilled in the course of nature. For I am far advanced in years, as you may perceive, and not far from death. I am speaking now not to all of you, but only to those who have condemned me to death. And I have another thing to say to them: You think that I was convicted because I had not words of the sort which would have procured my acquittal—I mean, if I had thought fit to leave nothing undone or unsaid. Not so; the deficiency which led to my conviction was not of words—certainly not. But I had not the boldness or impudence or inclination to address you as you would have liked me to do, weeping and wailing and lamenting, and saying and doing many things which you have been accustomed to hear from others, and which, as I maintain, are unworthy of me. I thought at the time that I ought not to do anything common or mean when in danger: nor do I now repent of the style of my defence; I would rather die having spoken after my manner, than speak in your manner and live. For neither in war nor yet at law ought I or any man to use every way of escaping death. Often in battle there can be no doubt that if a man will throw away his arms, and fall on his knees before his pursuers, he may escape death; and in other dangers there are other ways of escaping death, if a man is willing to say and do anything. The difficulty, my friends, is not to avoid death, but to avoid unrighteousness; for that runs faster than death. I am old and move slowly, and the slower runner has overtaken me, and my accusers are keen and quick, and the faster runner, who is unrighteousness, has overtaken them. And now I depart hence condemned by you to suffer the penalty of death,—they too go their ways condemned by the truth to suffer the penalty of villainy and wrong, and I must abide by my award—let them abide by theirs. I suppose that these things may be regarded as fated,—and I think that they are well.

And now, O men who have condemned me, I would fain prophesy to you; for I am about to die, and in the hour of death men are gifted with prophetic power. And I prophesy to you who are my murderers, that punishment far heavier than you have inflicted on me will surely await you. Me you have killed because you wanted to escape the accuser, and not to give an account of your lives. But that will not be as you suppose: far otherwise. For I say that there will be more accusers of you than there are now; accusers whom hitherto I have restrained: and as they are younger they will be more inconsiderate with you, and you will be more offended at them. If you think that by killing men you can prevent some one from censuring your evil lives, you are mistaken; that is not a way of escape which is either possible or honorable; the easiest and the noblest way is not to be disabling others, but to be improving yourselves. This is the prophecy which I utter before my departure to the judges who have condemned me.

Friends, who would have acquitted me, I would like also to talk with you about the thing which has come to pass, while the magistrates are busy, and before I go to the place at which I must die. Stay then a little, for we may as well talk with one another while there is time. You are my friends, and I should like to show you the meaning of this event which has happened to me. O my judges—for you I may truly call judges—I should like to tell you a wonderful circumstance. Hitherto the divine faculty of which the internal oracle is the source has constantly been in the habit of opposing me even about trifles, if I was going to make a slip or error in any matter; and now as you see there has come upon me that which may be thought, and is generally believed to be, the last and worst evil. But the oracle made no sign of opposition, either when I was leaving my house in the morning, or when I was on my way to the court, or while I was speaking, at anything which I was going to say; and yet I have often been stopped in the middle of a speech, but now in nothing I either said or did touching the matter in hand has the oracle opposed me. What do I take to be the explanation of this silence? I will tell you. It is an intimation that what has happened to me is a good, and that those of us who think that death is an evil are in error. For the customary sign would surely have opposed me had I been going to evil and not to good.

Let us reflect in another way, and we shall see that there is great reason to hope that death is a good; for one of two things—either death is a state of nothingness and utter unconsciousness, or, as men say, there is a change and migration of the soul from this world to another. Now, if you suppose that there is no consciousness, but a sleep like the sleep of him who is undisturbed even by dreams, death will be an unspeakable gain. For if a person were to select the night in which his sleep was undisturbed even by dreams, and were to compare with this the other days and nights of his life, and then were to tell us how many days and nights he had passed in the course of his life better and more pleasantly than this one, I think that any man, I will not say a private man, but even the great king will not find many such days or nights, when compared with the others. Now, if death be of such a nature, I say that to die is gain; for eternity is then only a single night. But if death is the journey to another place, and there, as men say, all the dead abide, what good, O my friends and judges, can be greater than this? If, indeed, when the pilgrim arrives in the world below, he is delivered from the professors of justice in this world, and finds the true judges who are said to give judgment there, Minos and Rhadamanthus and Aeacus and Triptolemus, and other sons of God who were righteous in their own life, that pilgrimage will be worth making. What would not a man give if he might converse with Orpheus and Musaeus and Hesiod and Homer? Nay, if this be true, let me die again and again. I myself, too, shall have a wonderful interest in there meeting and conversing with Palamedes, and Ajax the son of Telamon, and any other ancient hero who has suffered death through an unjust judgment; and there will be no small pleasure, as I think, in comparing my own sufferings with theirs. Above all, I shall then be able to continue my search into true and false knowledge; as in this world, so also in the next; and I shall find out who is wise, and who pretends to be wise, and is not. What would not a man give, O judges, to be able to examine the leader of the great Trojan expedition; or Odysseus or Sisyphus, or numberless others, men and women too! What infinite delight would there be in conversing with them and asking them questions! In another world they do not put a man to death for asking questions: assuredly not. For besides being happier than we are, they will be immortal, if what is said is true.

Wherefore, O judges, be of good cheer about death, and know of a certainty, that no evil can happen to a good man, either in life or after death. He and his are not neglected by the gods; nor has my own approaching end happened by mere chance. But I see clearly that the time had arrived when it was better for me to die and be released from trouble; wherefore the oracle gave no sign. For which reason, also, I am not angry with my condemners, or with my accusers; they have done me no harm, although they did not mean to do me any good; and for this I may gently blame them.

Still, I have a favour to ask of them. When my sons are grown up, I would ask you, O my friends, to punish them; and I would have you trouble them, as I have troubled you, if they seem to care about riches, or anything, more than about virtue; or if they pretend to be something when they are really nothing,—then reprove them, as I have reproved you, for not caring about that for which they ought to care, and thinking that they are something when they are really nothing. And if you do this, both I and my sons will have received justice at your hands.

The hour of departure has arrived, and we go our ways—I to die, and you to live. Which is better God only knows.

Integrity

Lynne McFall

Coherence

Integrity is the state of being "undivided; an integral whole." What sort of coherence is at issue here? I think there are several.

One kind of coherence is simple consistency: consistency within one's set of principles or commitments. One cannot maintain one's integrity if one has unconditional commitments that conflict, for example, justice and personal happiness, or conditional commitments that cannot be ranked. For example, truth telling and kindness.

Another kind of coherence is coherence between principle and action. Integrity requires "sticking to one's principles," moral or otherwise, in the face of temptation, including the temptation to redescription.

Take the case of a woman with a commitment to marital fidelity. She is attracted to a man who is not her husband, and she is tempted. Suppose, for the purity of the example, that he wants her too but will do nothing to further the affair; the choice is hers. Now imagine your own favorite scene of seduction.

After the fact, she has two options. (There are always these two options, which makes the distinction between changing one's mind and weakness of the will problematic, but assume that this is a clear case.) She can (1) admit to having lost the courage of her convictions (retaining the courage of her mistakes) or (2) rewrite her principles in various ways (e.g., by making fidelity a general principle, with exceptions, or by retroactively canceling her "subscription"). Suppose she chooses the latter. Whatever she may have gained, she has lost some integrity. Weakness of the will is one contrary of integrity. Self-deception is another. A person who admits to having succumbed to temptation has more integrity than the person who sells out, then fixes the books, but both suffer its loss.

A different sort of incoherence is exhibited in the case where someone does the right thing for (what he takes to be) the wrong reason. For example, in Dostoyevsky's *The Devils*, Stepan Verkhovensky says, "All my life I've been lying. Even when I spoke the truth. I never spoke for the sake of the truth, but for my own sake." Coherence between principle and action is necessary but not sufficient. One's action might *correspond* with one's principle, at some general level of description, but be inconsistent with that principle more fully specified. If one values not just honesty but honesty for its own sake, then honesty motivated by self-interest is not enough for integrity.

So the requirement of coherence is fairly complicated. In addition to simple consistency, it puts constraints on the way in which one's principles may be held (the "first-person" requirement), on how one may act given one's principles (coherence between principle and action), and on how one may be motivated in acting on them (coherence between principle and motivation). Call this *internal coherence*.

To summarize the argument so far: personal integrity requires that an agent (1) subscribe to some consistent set of principles or commitments and (2), in the face of temptation or challenge, (3) uphold these principles or commitments, (4) for what the agent takes to be the right reasons.

These conditions are rather formal. Are there no constraints on the *content* of the principles or commitments a person of integrity may hold?

Integrity and Importance

Consider the following statements.

> Sally is a person of principle: pleasure.

> Harold demonstrates great integrity in his single-minded pursuit of approval.

> John was a man of uncommon integrity. He let nothing—not friendship, not justice, not truth—stand in the way of his amassment of wealth.

That none of these claims can be made with a straight face suggests that integrity is inconsistent with such principles.

A person of integrity is willing to bear the consequences of her convictions, even when this is difficult, that is, when the consequences are unpleasant. A person whose only principle is "Seek my own pleasure" is not a candidate for integrity because there is no possibility of conflict—between pleasure and principle—in which integrity could be lost. Where there is no possibility of its loss, integrity cannot exist.

Chapter VII: Self-Deception and Integrity

Similarly in the case of the approval seeker. The single-minded pursuit of approval is inconsistent with integrity. Someone who is describable as an egg sucker, brownnose, fawning flatterer cannot have integrity, whatever he may think of the merits of such behavior. A commitment to spinelessness does not vitiate its spinelessness—another of integrity's contraries.

The same may he said for the ruthless seeker of wealth. A person whose only aim is to increase his bank balance is a person for whom nothing is ruled out: duplicity, theft, murder. Expedience is *contrasted* to a life of principle, so an ascription of integrity is out of place. Like the pleasure seeker and the approval seeker, he lacks a "core," the kind of commitments that give a person character and that makes a loss of integrity possible. In order to sell one's soul, one must have something to sell. . . .

Most of us, when tempted to "sell out," are tempted by pleasure, approval, money, status, or personal gain of some other sort. The political prisoner under the thumbscrew wants relief, however committed he may be to the revolution. Less dramatically, most of us want the good opinion of others and a decent standard of living. Self-interest in these forms is a legitimate aim against which we weigh our other concerns. But most of us have other "higher," commitments, and so those who honor most what we would resist are especially liable to scorn.

This tendency to objectify our own values in the name of personal integrity can best be seen, I think, in a more neutral case. Consider the following claim:

> The connoisseur showed real integrity in preferring the Montrachet to the Mountain Dew.

Even if he was sorely tempted to guzzle the Mountain Dew and forbore only with the greatest difficulty, the connoisseur, we would say, did not show integrity in preferring the better wine. Why? Resisting temptation is not the only test of integrity; the challenge must be to something *important*. . . .

One may die for beauty, truth, justice, the objection might continue, but not for Montrachet. Wine is not that important. . . .

When we grant integrity to a person, we need not *approve* of his or her principles or commitments, but we must at least recognize them as ones a reasonable person might take to be of great importance and ones that a reasonable person might be tempted to sacrifice to some lesser yet still recognizable goods. It may not be possible to spell out these conditions without circularity, but that this is what underlies our judgments of integrity seems clear enough. Integrity is a personal virtue granted with social strings attached. By definition, it precludes "expediency, artificiality, or shallowness of any kind." The pleasure seeker is guilty of shallowness, the approval seeker of artificiality, and the profit seeker of expedience of the worst sort. . . .

Integrity, Friendship and the Olaf Principle

An attitude essential to the notion of integrity is that there are some things that one is not prepared to do, or some things one *must* do. I shall call this the "Olaf Principle," in honor of e. e. cummings's poem about Olaf, the "conscientious object-or." This principle requires that some of one's commitments be unconditional.

In what sense?

There are, in ordinary moral thought, expressions of the necessity or impossibility of certain actions or types of actions that do not neatly correspond to the notions of necessity and impossibility most often catalogued by moral theorists. "I *must* stand by my friend" (or "I *cannot* let him down") may have no claim to logical, psychological, rational, or moral necessity in any familiar sense. There is nothing logically inconsistent in the betrayal of friendship, or one could never be guilty of it. It is not psychologically impossible, since many have in fact done it and survived to do it again. Rationality does not require unconditional allegiance, without some additional assumptions, for one may have better reason to do a conflicting action, for example, where the choice is between betraying a friend and betraying one's country (although I am sympathetic to E. M. Forster's famous statement to the contrary). Nor is the necessity expressed one that has a claim to universality, for different persons may have different unconditional commitments. Impartiality and absoluteness are not what is at stake, for the choice may be between a friend and ten innocent strangers, and one person may have different unconditional commitments at different times. It is not clear, then, what sense of *unconditional commitment* is at issue.

Unless corrupted by philosophy, we all have things we think we would never do, under any imaginable circumstances, whatever we may give to survival or pleasure, power and the approval of strangers; some part of ourselves beyond which we will not retreat, some weakness however prevalent in others that we will not tolerate in ourselves. And if we do that thing, betray that weakness, we are not the persons we thought; there is nothing left that we may even in spite refer to as *I*.

I think it is in this sense that some commitments must be unconditional: they are conditions of continuing as ourselves. Suppose, for example, that I take both friendship and professional advancement to be great goods, and my best friend and I are candidates for a promotion. Suppose, too, that I know the person who has the final decision has an unreasoned hatred of people who drink more than is socially required, as my friend does. I let this be known, not directly of course, with the predictable result that I am given the promotion.

Now in one sense I have not done anything dishonest. My friend may be the first to admit the pleasure he takes in alcohol. It may even be one of the reasons I value his friendship. (Loyal drinking companions are not easy to come by.) But this is clearly a betrayal of friendship. Is it so obviously a failure of integrity?

In *any* conflict between two great goods, I may argue, one must be "betrayed." And between you and me, I choose me.

What is wrong with this defense?

To beat someone out of a job by spreading vicious truths is proof that I am no friend. It is in the nature of friendship that one cannot intentionally hurt a friend in order to further one's own interests. So if I claim to be this person's friend, then I am guilty of incoherence, and therefore lack integrity.

Why does incoherence seem the wrong charge to make? The answer, I think, is that it is much too weak.

Some of our principles or commitments are more important to us than others. Those that can be sacrificed without remorse may be called *defeasible* commitments. For many of us, professional success is an important but defeasible commitment. I would like to be a successful philosopher, esteemed by my colleagues and widely published, but neither success nor failure will change my sense of personal worth.

Contrasted to defeasible commitments are *identity-conferring* commitments: they reflect what we take to be most important and so determine, to large extent, our (moral) identities. . . .

For many of us, friendship is an identity-conferring commitment. If we betrayed a friend in order to advance our careers, we could not "live with" ourselves; we would not be the persons we thought we were. This is what it means to have a "core": a set of principles or commitments that makes us who we are. Such principles cannot be justified by reference to other values, because they are the most fundamental commitments we have: they determine what, for us, is to *count* as a reason. . . .

Moral Integrity

If integrity is a moral virtue, then it is a special sort of virtue. One cannot be solely concerned with one's own integrity, or there would be no object for one's concern. Thus integrity seems to be a higher-order virtue. To have moral integrity, then, it is natural to suppose that one must have some lower-order moral commitments; that moral integrity adds a moral requirement to personal integrity. . . .

What makes something a moral principle?

One commonly accepted view is that moral principles are characterized by impartiality and universality. Assuming this is true, it follows that moral integrity will require that these conditions be met.

Is this plausible?

Let us return to the principled adulterer and look at it from the husband's point of view. At first he feels betrayed and is hurt. Then he stops to consider what impartiality requires. Perhaps my wife's new lover makes her happier than I can, he reasons, and the affair will certainly make her lover happier, so there is all that happiness to be weighed against my pain. The children are grown, so it is not hurting them. Impartiality seems to require that I grant her this freedom, even encourage it.

Second example. Suppose you are having a bad day. The car breaks down on the way to teach a class in which three students fall asleep and the rest are bored or belligerent. Your latest philosophical masterpiece has come back in the mail with a note from the editor saying that the referees' comments were too abusive to decently pass on to you. During office hours your best student wonders aloud what moral theory has to do with anything that genuinely worries anyone. You have been worrying about that yourself. You wait an hour for a friend who was supposed to meet you at noon but who seems to have forgotten. On the way back from drinking your lunch, just as despair is about to take over for self-pity, you run into K. He sees by your wild eyes that you are in a bad way. He is just going to lunch, he says, and invites you along. You agree, having had nothing to eat since the English muffin your toaster burned for breakfast. While waiting to order, he listens sympathetically to your litany of unrelieved bad luck and real failure. He tries to cheer you up. Feeling better, you express your appreciation, tell him that he is a good friend. He says he is only doing his moral duty. You smile, thinking this philosophical irony. His blank expression suggests you are wrong. Over Caesar salad he tells you about his dear wife, whom he married because no one was more in need of love, nor so unlikely to find it. Somewhere between the main course and the coffee you realize he was not kidding. He is only doing for you what he would do for anyone in your sorry state—his duty.

The fairly simple point of these examples is that impartiality is incompatible with friendship and love, and so incompatible with personal integrity where friendship and love are identity-conferring commitments.

What does moral integrity require?

Any identity-conferring commitment *except* to impartiality will be inconsistent with impartiality. If moral integrity presupposes personal integrity, and personal integrity requires identity-conferring commitments, then moral integrity is, generally, inconsistent with impartiality. . . .

Conclusion

Moral integrity is as much a threat to social morality as personal integrity. The difference is that the attack comes from *within* the moral point of view, and its target is impartiality. Perhaps, then, integrity should be given up, as having a moral cost that is too great.

I think this would be a mistake. The reason is made graphically clear in a story by the science fiction writer Theodore Sturgeon, called "The Dark Room." In this story the narrator, Conway, has a friend named Beck who regularly gives cocktail parties at which everyone who attends is eventually humiliated. A sweet old woman, the author of children's books, tells an obscene story. A man who prides himself on his dignity and decorum urinates on the living room floor. An undercover agent walks up to a CIA man and spills his guts. And at the most recent party, Conway's loyal wife ends up in bed with one of the other guests. This gets his attention; on reflection he sees the pattern of humiliation and resolves to find out what's going on. Breaking into Beck's house while he's out of town Conway comes upon an alien being who has the ability to take on any form, to be whatever people want to see. The alien confesses that he feeds on the humiliation of humans. Without it he will die. He finances the parties for Beck in order to get new victims, whose humiliation he causes. This explanation satisfies Conway except for one thing: why, having attended every party, has *he* never been humiliated? The alien explains that Conway is an "immune": a creature who cannot be humiliated because there is nothing he would not do.

Without integrity, and the identity-conferring commitments it assumes, there would be nothing to fear the loss of, not because we are safe but because we have nothing to lose.

Chapter VIII
Friendship and Love

In order to properly understand friendship and love one must begin with the dilemma of solitude. *Radical solitude,* according to Jean-Louis Servan-Schreiber is the realization on the part of an individual that, "I exist alone." Does rebelling against solitude require that a person deny his or her autonomy as an individual?

Servan-Schreiber explores the threefold solitude of the modern individual: existential solitude, emotional solitude, and social solitude. People need courage in order to take charge of their individual lives, but Servan-Schreiber points out that certain relationships help us bear our existential solitude better.

Bacon's essay, "Of Friendship," begins with a consideration of the theme of solitude. Until one understands solitude (and Bacon believes few people have thought deeply about its meaning and extent), one is not in a position to understand friendship. He states poignantly that "a crowd is not company; and faces are but a gallery of pictures; and talk but a *tinkling symbol,* where there is no love."

According to Bacon, friendship is an important part of what makes us human: *"Whoever is delighted in solitude is either a wild beast or a god."* Furthermore, he states that without true friends "the world is but a wilderness." He proceeds to discuss three fruits of friendship which ennoble the life of a man or woman, namely, peace in the affections, support of the judgment and aid—bearing a part, in all actions, and occasions."

In his work, "On Philosophy and Friendship," Seneca claims that the wise man is self-sufficient. He can, in other words, do without friends. But, even one possessed of wisdom desires friends, neighbors and associates.

The secret of making friendships, Seneca says, is embodied in Hecato's dictum: "If you would be loved, love." The purpose of friendship should not be utility but, rather, the acts of practicing friendship bring forth people with noble qualities. This nobility reaches its highest manifestation in love, for Seneca, "friendship run mad." Seneca states, "Pure love, careless of all other things, kindles the soul with desire for the beautiful object," not for the sake of gain, but, "not without the hope of a return of the affection."

Aristotle tells us that friendship is inextricably related to virtue and that it is "indispensable to life." "Nobody," he claims, "would choose to live without friends, although he were in possession of every other good."

Aristotle distinguishes three types of friendship based on the object of the friendship. He claims that friendships are based either on utility (i.e. usefulness), on pleasure, or on goodness. Only the latter gives the possibility for perfect friendship. It lasts as long as virtue and, Aristotle teaches, ". . . virtue is a permanent quality."

"It is often said," Elizabeth Telfer reminds us, "that friendships are among the most important constituents of a worthwhile life." In her essay "Friendship," Teller attempts to clarify the nature of friendship, to examine the relationship which morality bears to friendship, and to consider the value of friendship to individuals and to society.

Telfer claims there are three conditions which are necessary and sufficient for friendship: "shared activities, the passions of friendship, and acknowledgment of the fulfillment of the first two conditions, constituting an acknowledgment of and consent to the special relationship." She denies that individuals have formal duties to friends and emphasizes the "personal" sense of the relationship. Finally, Telfer concludes, that friendship is life-enhancing, in that it "makes us more alive." It also enhances many of our other activities and it enlarges our knowledge.

Emerson attempts to get to the very heart of the matter concerning the nature and beauty of friendship. His words embody an eloquence worthy of the subject-matter of which he writes. "Friendship," he writes, "like the immortality of the soul, is too good to be believed." Friendships are not to be treated daintily, but with the "roughest courage." In this regard, they must be made of the "tough fibre of the human heart." This type of friendship is "the solidest thing we know."

"A friend," Emerson continues, "is a person with whom I may be sincere. Before him [a friend] I may think aloud." He concludes his essay with a reflection on the essence of friendship. According to Emerson: "The essence of friendship is entireness, a total magnanimity and trust. It must not surmise or provide for infirmity. It treats its object as a god, that it may deify both."

In his letter, "On Grief for Lost Friends," Seneca calls the reader's attention to the human condition. The untimely loss of a close firend not only brings grief but it brings an awareness of one's own mortality:

Chapter VIII: Friendship and Love

Now is the time for you to reflect, not only that all things are mortal, but also that their mortality is subject to no fixed law. Whatever can happen at any time can happen today.

On occasions of such loss there will be tears but Seneca recommended a moderate response, "We may weep, but we must not wail."

In reading Seneca's insights of friendship one is reminded of all the pleasures friendship has provided. Seneca urged that individuals hold onto the sweet thoughts of friends and make new friends. "Fortune," he said, "has robbed us of one friend, but we have robbed ourselves of every friend we have failed to make."

Janice Raymond characterizes friendship as "a thoughtful passion." A thoughtful passion manifests a thinking heart.

In "The Conditions of Female Friendship," Raymond reflects upon the meaning and relationships which hold among three concepts: thoughtfulness, passion and happiness. The thoughtful, self-directed thinking woman is a candidate for female friendship as opposed to "socialized femininity." Furthermore, she can befriend herself and her solitude need no longer be loneliness. Passion links thought and action in a meaningful way.

Raymond relates thoughtful passion to human happiness. To be happy, according to Raymond, is to be "life-glad." That is, ". . . happiness is striving for the full use of one's powers that make one 'life-glad.'"

Stuart Miller sees the modern emphasis on individualism as a serious challenge to male friendship. He writes:

> Valuing personal growth more than consistency in human relations is, of course, a strikingly modern stance. As an idea, it arises from the whole trend toward individualism and self-expression that marks the modern person, particularly the American. Unfortunately, the ideology of growth further helps to corrode human relationships; by putting individual growth over mutual association it helps to destroy the very idea of serious male friendship. . . .

Male friendship, Miller tells us, is as necessary as it is rare. This type of friendship requires four ingredients: intimacy, complicity, engagement, and commitment. In "Men and Friendship" these four ingredients are discussed.

There is a great deal of confusion about what love is. Robert Solomon attempts to give clarity to our understanding of the question, "What is love?" He tells us:

> . . . love is much more than a "feeling" (and) can be understood only "from the inside," as a language can be understood only by someone who has . . . *lived* in it.

521

Love involves the transformation of both the self and the other. It is from only within a created world—a *loveworld*. This world is a changing and dynamic world.

> To understand love is to understand this tension, this dialectic between individuality and the shared ideal. To think that love is to be found at the ends of the spectrum—in that first enthusiastic "discovery" of a shared togetherness or at the end of the road, after a lifetime together—is to miss the loveworld almost entirely, for it is neither an initial flush of feeling nor the retrospective congratulations of old age but a struggle for unity and identity. And in this struggle—neither the ideal of togetherness nor the contrary demand for the individual autonomy and identity alone—that defines the dynamics of that convulsive and tenuous world we call romantic love.

Mo Tzu taught that partisanship was at the base of all political and social chaos and upheaval. At the very heart of the world's trouble, misfortune, and calamity lies partiality. That is, the cause of all human ills was a lack of universal love. Mo Tzu advocated universal love and believed that righteousness was a direct expression of Heaven's active will. He wrote, "If I do what heaven desires, then heaven will do what I desire." In other words, "it is the business of the benevolent man to try to promote what is beneficial to the world and to eliminate what is harmful." Benefit comes from loving others. This type of active, loving comportment to the world is motivated by universality.

Three significant Greek words are all translated "love." An examination of the meanings of these three words and the distinctions they make will help us gain greater clarity in our understanding of the phenomenon of love.

Eros is translated as both "love" and "desire." *Eros* is sensual love and physical passion. The term denotes both romantic love and animal heat. Eros was a Greek deity whose Roman equivalent was the god Cupid.

Phileo is human love. It is conditional and, as such, denotes justice. That is, giving [love] to that one who deserves it. It is often referred to as "brotherly love," (i.e., Philadelphia). The term is closely aligned with *philia*, "friend." Among the secular Greeks, the highest form of this love was manifest in philanthropy—the love of one's fellow human beings.

Agape was not used by profane writers and was basically unknown outside of the New Testament. *Agape* is, literally, "God's love" or "the love of God." It is unconditional. It is that love which springs from deep veneration and which chooses its object by a decision of will and subsequently demonstrates compassionate devotion to it. Because it is unconditional, it is love in its fullest conceivable form. The New Testament declared, "God is love." This love is the nature of God.

I Corinthians 13 speaks of the characteristics of *agape* love as manifest in the life of the believer in God whose heart and thinking are in alignment with God's revealed word and will. The word *agape* has often been translated "charity." It is selfless giving, the kind of love that "seeks not its own" and "is kind." The believer, living in this love, manifests a godly character and "thinks no evil." Of the so-called "Christian Virtues"—faith, hope and love—"the greatest of these is love."

In "Love, the Answer to the Problem of Human Existence," Eric Fromm stated with penetrating insight that "any theory of love must begin with a theory . . . of human existence." That is, it must take into consideration the problematic nature of life in the world. I have claimed in this book, and designed the structure of the book in such a way, that all problems of ethics must first take into account the nature of the world and the nature of human existence in that world. Fromm's description of the problem and human need is powerful. He wrote:

> This desire for interpersonal fusion is the most powerful striving in man. It is the most fundamental passion, it is the force which keeps the human race together, the clan, the family, society. The failure to achieve it means insanity or destruction—self-destruction or destruction of others. Without love, humanity could not exist for a day.

What is the nature of this union or fusion? What is love? "Mature love," according to Fromm,

> . . . is *union under the condition of preserving one's integrity,* one's individuality. *Love is an active power in man;* a power which breaks through the walls which separate man from his fellow men, which unites him with others; love makes him overcome the sense of isolation and separateness, yet it permits him to be himself, to retain his integrity. In love the paradox occurs that two beings become one and yet remain two.

Solitude

Jean-Louis-Servan-Schreiber

We are born and die alone, that we all know. But must we also live alone? Certainly today more than yesterday, and this is probably for the best.

The situation of every human being, enclosed in his sack of skin, is one of radical solitude. Even with close friends or in a lover's embrace, communication with another is only partial and transitory. This truth lends itself to the most poignant appeals, to the greatest poetry. In it art finds inspiration.

But in rebelling against solitude we also deny the definition of our self.

If I exist as an individual, which is what I want, I can't unite with anyone else without losing my uniqueness and my autonomy. Plainly, I only "exist" alone. "Living" sets forth other problems and evokes other, very varied responses.

We seem to bear our existential solitude better when living as a couple, a family, a group. But the price we pay is to be a little less ourselves in order to fit in with others. So great is the fear of solitude that most people find this price small and settle for it readily.

But the *self* does not so easily consent to being put down. And when it rebels, we witness all those misunderstandings, antagonisms, and painful ruptures which mark the history of our relationships. The *self* asserts its resistance by throwing us back into our solitude, like a boxer forced against the ropes.

Our age confronts us with our fundamental solitude in two domains, that of everyday life and that of our existence as individuals. If therefore I must take full responsibility for myself and leave my mark, it is obvious that no one else can do it for me.

An individual must realize and decide that he is not bound to an established group, doctrine, or system by himself. Many people never reach this stage of maturity, either because they have not had the benefit of favorable circumstances or because they have refused to face the implications of the simple fact of being alive.

Chapter VIII: Friendship and Love

For it takes courage to admit that I can escape neither my solitude nor my fear, even if actually being alone turns out to be less negative or painful than I had imagined.

Solitude can be fertile, captivating, exciting. But it is rarely sweet, for it includes a portent of death, which we all fear. And, in order to escape this fear, we are ready for all sorts of compromises and subterfuges, some of them even degrading.

Like death, solitude both terrifies and fascinates us. We feel that it contains something unspeakable, and we wish we had the courage to approach it. But we can spend an entire lifetime in evasion refusing to explore and accept the depths, even the lowest depths, of our being, with all that they contain of both creativity and destruction.

This avoidance becomes impossible, however, once we take on the legacy of our culture and society and choose to be on our own. The solitude of the individual should not disconcert or hurt us. Since history now urges me to become the author of my own life, progress lies in refusing to give up control to anyone else, whether God or Caesar or Shrink.

Besides this philosophical solitude, which is anything but new, there is now, also, the contemporary, solitary life-style which increases our feeling of isolation.

How does society define one of its members? By his physical characteristics (height, weight, the color of his eyes), and by his social positioning, the business that employs him, the person to whom he is married, the city where he lives. It is almost impossible to identify me, in spite of the complexity of my personal make-up, except in terms of my physical characteristics and the groups to which I belong.

But group bonds have lost their strength. Those which have not disappeared have loosened their grip on us, as if the individual were casting off his mooring. Even the institutions we still think of as the most vigorous show signs of decline.

Churches

Generally speaking, few of us still define ourselves by our religion. In Europe, only slightly more than one out of ten people, most beyond a certain age, attend religious services regularly. Only certain sacraments survive; "If it weren't for marriages and funerals, we'd never see the rest of the family."

Sunday church service once had a social function. People talked to one another as they came out of church; they had a chance to show off a new suit or dress and to invite friends to Sunday dinner. Nowadays there is no gathering place or rite that brings families and neighbors together. For something equivalent we must join a community or social group, and few people do so.

Nations

By sheer force of habit we still tell ethnic jokes and cheer for national teams. But the national image has faded considerably, even in the United States, and this is all to the good.

In Europe, what purpose is served by calling oneself French or Dutch when everywhere we drive the same cars, see the same American films, endure the same rates of unemployment?

There is talk of cultural identity. But the few people with sufficient culture to be identified by it are just the very ones who think internationally.

Business Enterprises

Until recently, the workplace, whether private or government, substituted for the village square in providing meetings and exchanges. People spent the greater part of their time at work, and whether they stayed in one place for ten years or, as in Japan, for a lifetime, there came to be almost symbiotic bonds between the individual and his professional surroundings.

But both employers and employees, on the pretext of diversification or renewal, now prefer shorter-term contracts. And, with every new job, bonds have to be reknit. With this as the status quo, companionship among fellow workers is slow to turn into lasting friendship.

Trade Unions

Union leaders everywhere are aware of falling membership, although they cannot fathom the reason. Aside from unemployment and a growing distaste for politicalization, there is an increasing resort to individual rather than collective action. There is a feeling, more instinctive than reasoned, that mass action has reached the limits of its effectiveness. Of this, the weakening of the unions is the most recent and tangible sign.

Chapter VIII: Friendship and Love

Political Parties

Now that, during electoral campaigns, candidates have to hire people to paste up posters instead of relying on the usual party volunteers, and meetings are held more often around a table than in a public square, it is plain that party loyalties belong to the past. Parties have given up ideologies (except for extremists, who are considered laughable for this very reason) and hardly dare publish a platform.

Why should a citizen involve himself when he sees that the most important problems are no longer determined by politics?

The Couple

Now that convention, moral restraint, and legal bonds have been discredited, the bubble is quick to burst forty to fifty percent of the time. Our image of the couple has changed. It no more implies the ancient linkage of production and procreation intended to favor the man's professional development and a budding family. Now we have the chance meeting of two individuals, looking for happiness but impelled, in order to cope with the uncertainties of life, to keep their independence.

The very fact of having to reckon with the risk of the failure of their union introduces a centrifugal force into their relationship. Both partners are on the alert for the signs of a crack. They make much of problems which, in the preceding generation, would have been either solved or nipped in the bud, but never would have torn them apart.

Planned obsolescence seems to be built into the very notion of today's couple.

Other relationships may follow, but while they should obviate solitude, their very number often intensifies its impact on us. The end of the myth of eternal love is today's most powerful spur to awareness of our fundamental solitude.

The Family

If there is any life raft left this should be it. We change our lovers, employers, residences, and opinions, but parents and children remain the same. Even when everything else gives way there is still the biological bond, that is, until the spread of test-tube babies introduces further confusion. But the life raft has shrunk, and aboard it we often tear each other apart.

The family upon which we fall back has no connection with the tribal country family of days gone by. In Europe now as in America, we hardly know when and where our grandparents were born, we no longer visit our cousins, we live with one of our divorced parents and the children of his or her new spouse. Many adults are bound to their parents only by enlisting them as baby-sitters while they go off for a weekend and/or a whole vacation.

Even if parents do not divorce early on, the family's real existence is limited to the twenty to twenty-five years it takes to educate and launch the children. Then the parents find themselves practically alone with one another should they still live together, with a considerable period of life before them.

Add to all that has been said the anonymity of big-city life and we can measure the rapid atrophy of all the systems—large and small—which gave preceding generations a sense of belonging.

Moreover, the spread of graduate studies demanded by increasing specialization combines with the loss of traditional supports, to produce the most modern solitude of all: meritocracy.

Formerly affiliation with a class or clan compensated for the chance elements of birth and education. But now, unless we make a sudden advance in our adult years, the course of our life depends on the baggage we have accumulated before we are twenty-five.

Meritocracy is a worldwide phenomenon. Students are ferociously keen on getting into particular colleges, and more and more we read of parents who start to worry about their children's future success when they are still in the primary grades. Will it soon be that life can be a failure at age seven?

Inequalities still play an important part in the strategy and financing of education, handing out trumps to some children and handicaps to others. But whereas before the family or its influential friends could still provide an underequipped young person with a cushioned career, now advanced studies are what count. So much the worse for those who have not taken advantage of the chance their parents gave them to develop their brains!

Meritocracy, then, adds its weight to the swing of the scales from the collective to the individual. And economic difficulties lead governments to define more narrowly the limits of what social security, insurance, and welfare programs can guarantee to the citizen. But when we call up this financial aspect of the program we must not forget that it is only the outward sign of a deeper change of direction connected with the retreat of ideologies.

A single idea has dominated our century, supported by the two pillars of contemporary thought, the psychology of Freud and Marxist socialism; namely, that the individual does not bear the main responsibility for what he is and does.

Chapter VIII: Friendship and Love

For Freud and for his heirs and successors, by the time we reach the age of taking control of our own life it is already too late; the emotional trials of our earliest years have left us prematurely scarred. For socialists, the educational, political, and economic structures of society dominate and manipulate us; alone we are weak and defeated.

These two a priori conceptions of human experience turn us into vulnerable, powerless individuals, wanting to be taken care of.

Although today these two notions seem outdated, this does not mean that they were of no use in the past. Not too many years ago the majority of people were poor and ignorant. Today's majority is assuredly not rich and sophisticated, but the level has risen to such an extent that most citizens can assume responsibilities for their own lives.

"Make it on your own!" the System will more and more frequently tell us. "You are quite big and old enough and, as for me, I've no longer the means to take care of you."

Such is the threefold solitude of modern man: existential, *because no body of ideas offers him the answers he cannot do without;* emotional, *in that the traditional supports have eroded; and* social, *now that the State's protective structures are crumbling.*

Some may mourn this state of affairs and view the future with discouragement, as the domain of the lonely crowd. But it is possible, as well, to see a long-awaited progress. The ideal of an individual who is self-reliant amid the group to which he chooses to belong has its roots in ancient Greece and was incarnated by men of the Renaissance. The fact that it is no longer limited to the happy few, but is becoming accessible to the many, is to the credit of this era of Western civilization.

It is not by chance that there is a phrase to describe this new situation: *to take charge of oneself.* A little tough, perhaps, like the course of a solitary navigator, but very tempting.

Before embarking, however, we must study the reefs that lie ahead and outfit ourselves to cope with them.

Of Friendship

Bacon

It had been hard for him that spake it, to have put more truth and untruth together, in few words, than in that speech; *whosoever is delighted in solitude, is either a wild beast, or a god.* For it is most true, that a natural and secret hatred, and aversation towards *society,* in any man, hath somewhat of the savage beast; but it is most untrue, that it should have any character, at all, of the divine nature; except it proceed, not out of a pleasure in *solitude,* but out of a love and desire, to sequester a man's self, for a higher conversation: such as is found, to have been falsely and fainedly, in some of the heathen; as *Epimenides* the Candian, *Numa* the Roman, *Empedocles* the Sicilian, and *Apollonius* of Tyana; and truly and really, in divers of the ancient hermits, and holy fathers of the church. But little do men perceive, what *solitude* is, and how far it extendeth. For a crowd is not company; and faces are but a gallery of pictures; and talk but a *tinkling cymbal,* where there is no *love.* The Latin adage meeteth with it a little; *magna civitas, magna solitudo;* because in a great town, *friends* are scattered; so that there is not that fellowship, for the most part, which is in less *neighborhoods.* But we may go further, and affirm most truly; that it is a mere, and miserable *solitude,* to want true *friends;* without which the world is but a wilderness: and even in this sense also of *solitude,* whosoever in the frame of his nature and affections, is unfit for *friendship,* he taketh it of the beast, and not from humanity.

A principal *fruit of friendship,* is the ease and discharge of the fullness and swellings of the heart, which passions of all kinds do cause and induce. We know diseases of stoppings, and suffocations, are the most dangerous in the body; and it is not much otherwise in the mind: you may take *sarsa* to open the liver; *steel* to open the spleen; *flowers of sulphur* for the lungs; *castoreum* for the brain; but no receipt openeth the heart, but a true *friend;* to whom you may impart, griefs, joys, fears, hopes, suspicions, counsels, and whatsoever heth upon the heart, to oppress it, in a kind of civil shrift or confession.

Chapter VIII: Friendship and Love

It is a strange thing to observe, how high a rate, great kings and monarchs, do set upon this *fruit of friendship,* whereof we speak: so great, as they purchase it, many times, at the hazard of their own safety, and greatness. For princes, in regard of the distance of their fortune, from that of their subjects and servants, cannot gather this *fruit;* except (to make themselves capable thereof) they raise some persons, to be as it were companions, and almost equals to themselves, which many times sorteth to inconvenience. The modern languages give unto such persons, the name of *favorites,* or *privadoes;* as if it were matter of grace, or conversation. But the Roman name attaineth the true use, and cause thereof; naming them *participes curarum;* for it is that, which tieth the knot. And we see plainly, that this hath been done, not by weak and passionate *princes* only, but by the wisest, and most politic that ever reigned; who have oftentimes joined to themselves, some of their servants; whom both themselves have called *friends;* and allowed others likewise to call them in the same manner; using the word which is received between private men.

L. Sulla, when he commanded *Rome,* raised *Pompey* (after surnamed the *Great)* to that height, that *Pompey* vaunted himself for *Sulla's* overmatch. For when he had carried the *consulship* for a friend of his, against the pursuit of *Sulla,* and that *Sulla* did a little resent thereat, and began to speak great, *Pompey* turned upon him again, and in effect bade him be quiet; *for that more men adored the sun rising, than the sun setting.* With *Julius Caesar, Decimus Brutus* had obtained that interest, as he set him down, in his testament, for heir in remainder, after his *nephew.* And this was the man, that had power with him, to draw him forth to his death. For when *Caesar* would have discharged the senate, in regard of some ill presages, and specially a dream of *Calpurnia;* this man lifted him gently by the arm, out of his chair, telling him, he hoped he would not dismiss the senate, till his wife had dreamt a better dream. And it seemeth, his favor was so great, as *Antonius* in a letter, which is recited *verbatim,* in one of *Cicero's Philippics,* caueth him *venefica, witch;* as if he had enchanted *Caesar. Augustus* raised *Agrippa* (though of mean birth) to that height, as when he consulted with *Maecenas,* about the marriage of his daughter Julia, *Maecenas* took the liberty to tell him; *that he must either marry his daughter to Agrippa, or take away his life, there was no third way, he had made him so great.* With *Tiberius Caesar, Sejanus* had ascended to that height, as they two were termed and reckoned, as a pair of friends. *Tiberius* in a letter to him saith; *haec pro amicitiâ nostrâ non occultavi:* and the whole Senate, dedicated an altar to *friendship,* as to a *goddess,* in respect of the great dearness of *friendship,* between them two. The like or more was between *Septimius Severus,* and *Plautianus.* For he forced his eldest son to marry the daughter of *Plautianus;* and would often maintain *Plautianus,* in doing affronts to his son: and did write also in a letter to the senate, by these words; *I love the man so well, as I wish he may over-live me.* Now if these princes, had been as a *Trajan,* or a *Marcus Aurelius,* a man might have thought, that this had proceeded of an abundant goodness of nature; but being men so wise, of such strength and severity of mind, and so extreme lovers of themselves, as all these were; it proveth most plainly, that they found their own felicity (though as great as ever happened to mortal men) but as an half piece, except they might have a *friend* to make it entire: and yet, which is more, they were *princes,* that had wives, sons, nephews; and yet all these could not supply the comfort of *friendship.*

It is not to be forgotten, what *Commineus* observeth, of his first master *Duke Charles* the *Hardy;* namely, that he would communicate his secrets with none; and least of all, those secrets, which troubled him most. Whereupon he goeth on, and saith, that towards his latter time; *that closeness did impair, and a little perish his understanding.* Surely *Commineus* might have made the same judgement also, if it had pleased him, of his second master *Lewis* the Eleventh, whose closeness was indeed his tormentor. The parable of *Pythagoras* is dark, but true; *cor ne edito*; *eat not the heart.* Certainly, if a man would give it a hard phrase, those that want *friends* to open themselves unto, are cannibals of their own *hearts.* But one thing is most admirable, (wherewith I will conclude this first *fruit of friendship)* which is, that this communicating of a man's self to his *friend,* works two contrary effects; for it redoubleth *joys,* and cutteth *griefs* in halves. For there is no man, that imparteth his *joys* to his *friend,* but he *joyeth* the more; and no man, that imparteth his *griefs* to his *friend,* but he *grieveth* the less. So that it is, in truth of operation upon a man's mind, of like virtue, as the *alchemists* use to attribute to their stone, for man's body; that it worketh all contrary effects, but still to the good, and benefit of nature. But yet, without praying in aid of *alchemists,* there is a manifest image of this, in the ordinary course of nature. For in bodies, *union* strengtheneth and cherisheth any natural action; and, on the other side, weakeneth and dulleth any violent impression: and even so is it of minds.

The second *fruit of friendship,* is healthful and sovereign for the *understanding,* as the first is for the *affections.* For *friendship* maketh indeed a *fair day* in the *affections,* from storm and tempests: but it maketh *daylight* in the *understanding,* out of darkness and confusion of thoughts. Neither is this to be understood, only of faithful counsel, which a man receiveth from his *friend;* but before you come to that, certain it is, that whosoever hath his mind fraught, with many thoughts, his wits and understanding do clarify and break up, in the communicating and discoursing with another: he tosseth his thoughts, more easily; He marshalleth them more orderly; He seeth how they look when they are turned into. words; finally, he waxeth wiser than himself; and that more by an hour's discourse, than by a day's meditation. It was well said by *Themistocles* to the King of *Persia; that speech was like cloth of arras, opened, and put abroad;*

whereby the imagery doth appear in figure; whereas in thoughts, they lie but as in packs. Neither is this second *fruit* of *friendship,* in opening the *understanding,* restrained only to such *friends,* as are able to give a man counsel: (they indeed are best) but even, without that, a man learneth of himself, and bringeth his own thoughts to light, and whetteth his wits as against a stone, which itself cuts not. In a word, a man were better relate himself, to a statue, or picture, than to suffer his thoughts to pass in smother.

Add now, to make this second *fruit of friendship* complete, that other point, which lieth more open, and falleth within vulgar observation; which is *faithful counsel* from a *friend. Heraclitus* saith well, in one of his enigmas; *dry light is ever the best.* And certain it is, that the light, that a man receiveth, by counsel from another, is drier, and purer, than that which cometh from his own understanding, and judgement; which is ever infused and drenched in his affections and customs. So as, there is as much difference, between the *counsel,* that a *friend* giveth, and that a man giveth himself, as there is between the *counsel* of a *friend,* and of a *flatterer.* For there is no such *flatterer,* as is a man's self; and there is no such remedy, against flattery of a man's self, as the liberty of a *friend. Counsel* is of two sorts; the one concerning *manners*, the other concerning *business.* For the first; the best preservative to keep the mind in health, is the faithful admonition of a *friend.* The calling of a man's self, to a strict account, is a medicine, sometime, too piercing and corrosive. Reading good books of *morality,* is a little flat, and dead. Observing our faults in others, is sometimes unproper for our case. But the best receipt (best (I say) to work, and best to take) is the admonition of a *friend.* It is a strange thing to behold, what gross errors, and extreme absurdities, many (especially of the greater sort) do commit, for want of a *friend,* to tell them of them; to the great damage, both of their fame, and fortune. For, as *S. James* saith, they are as men, *that look sometimes into a glass, and presently forget their own shape, and favor.* As for *business,* a man may think, if he will, that, two eyes see no more than one; or that a gamester seeth always more than a looker on; or that a man in anger, is as wise as he, that hath said over the four and twenty letters; or that a musket may be shot off, as well upon the arm, as upon a rest; and such other fond and high imaginations, to think himself all in all. But when all is done, the help of good *counsel,* is that, which setteth *business* straight. And if any man think, that he will take *counsel,* but it shall be by pieces; asking *counsel* in one business of one man, and in another business of another man; it is well, (that is to say, better perhaps than if he asked none at all;) but he runneth two dangers: one, that he shall not be faithfully counseled; for it is a rare thing, except it be from a perfect and entire *friend,* to have counsel given, but such as shall be bowed and crooked to some ends, which he hath that giveth it. The other, that he shall have counsel given, hurtful, and unsafe, (though with good meaning) and mixed, partly of mischief, and partly of remedy: even as if you would call a physician, that is thought good, for the cure of the disease, you complain of, but is unacquainted with your body; and therefore, may put you in way for a present cure, but overthroweth your health in some other kind; and so cure the disease, and kill the patient. But a *friend*, that is wholly acquainted with a man's estate, will beware by furthering any present *business*, how he dasheth upon other inconvenience. And therefore, rest not upon *scattered* counsels; they will rather distract, and mislead, than settle, and direct.

After these two noble *fruits of friendship; (peace in the affections,* and *support of the judgement,)* followeth the last *fruit;* which is like the *pomegranate*, full of many kernels; I mean *aid*, and *bearing a part*, in all *actions*, and *occasions*. Here, the best way, to represent to life the manifold use of *friendship*, is to cast and see, how many things there are, which a man cannot do himself; and then it will appear, that it was a sparing speech of the ancients, to say, *that a friend is another himself;* for that a *friend* is far more than *himself*. Men have their time, and die many times in desire of some things, which they principally take to heart; the bestowing of a child, the finishing of a work, or the like. If a man have a true *friend*, he may rest almost secure, that the care of those things, will continue after him. So that a man hath as it were two lives in his desires. A man hath a body, and that body is confined to a place; but where *friendship* is, all offices of life, are as it were granted to him, and his deputy. For he may exercise them by his *friend*. How many things are there, which a man cannot, with any face or comeliness, say or do himself? A man can scarce allege his own merits with modesty, much less extol them: a man cannot sometimes brook to supplicate or beg: and a number of the like. But all these things, are graceful in a *friend's* mouth, which are blushing in a man's own. So again, a man's person hath many proper relations, which he cannot put off. A man cannot speak to his son, but as a father; to his wife, but as a husband; to his enemy, but upon terms: whereas a *friend* may speak, as the case requires, and not as it sorteth with the person. But to enumerate these things were endless; I have given the rule, where a man cannot fitly play his own part: if he have not a *friend,* he may quit the stage.

On Philosophy and Friendship

Seneca

You desire to know whether Epicurus is right when, in one of his letters,[1] he rebukes those who hold that the wise man is self-sufficient and for that reason does not stand in need of friendships. This is the objection raised by Epicurus against Stilbo and those who believe[2] that the Supreme Good is a soul which is insensible to feeling.

We are bound to meet with a double meaning if we try to express the Greek term 'lack of feeling' summarily, in a single word, rendering it by the Latin word *impatientia*. For it may be understood in the meaning the opposite to that which we wish it to have. What we mean to express is, a soul which rejects any sensation of evil; but people will interpret the idea as that of a soul which can endure no evil. Consider, therefore, whether it is not better to say "a soul that cannot be harmed," or "a soul entirely beyond the realm of suffering." There is this difference between ourselves and the other school[3]: our ideal wise man feels his troubles, but overcomes them; their wise man does not even feel them. But we and they alike hold this idea, that the wise man is self-sufficient. Nevertheless, he desires friends, neighbours, and associates, no matter how much he is sufficient unto himself. And mark how self-sufficient he is; for on occasion he can be content with a part of himself. If he lose a hand through disease or war, or if some accident puts out one or both of his eyes, he will be satisfied with what is left, taking as much pleasure in his impaired and maimed body as he took when it was sound. But while he does not pine for these parts if they are missing, he prefers not to lose them. In this sense the wise man is self-sufficient, that he can do without friends, not that he desires to do without them. When I say "can," I mean this: he endures the loss of a friend with equanimity.

But he need never lack friends, for it lies in his own control how soon he shall make good a loss. Just as Phidias, if he lose a statue, can straightway carve another, even so our master in the art of making friendships can fill the place of a friend he has lost. If you ask how one can make oneself a friend quickly, I will tell you, provided we are agreed that I may pay my debt[4] at once and square the account, so far as this letter is concerned. Hecato[5] says: "I can show you a philtre, compounded without drugs, herbs, or any witch's incantation: 'If you would be loved, love.'" Now there is great pleasure, not only in maintaining old and established friendships, but also in beginning and acquiring new ones. There is the same difference between winning a new friend and having already won him, as there is between the farmer who sows and the farmer who reaps. The philosopher Attalus used to say: "It is more pleasant to make than to keep a friend, as it is more pleasant to the artist to paint than to have finished painting." When one is busy and absorbed in one's work, the very absorption affords great delight; but when one has withdrawn one's hand from the completed masterpiece, the pleasure is not so keen. Henceforth it is the fruits of his art that he enjoys; it was the art itself that he enjoyed while he was painting. In the case of our children, their young manhood yields the more abundant fruits, but their infancy was sweeter.

Let us now return to the question. The wise man, I say, self-sufficient though he be, nevertheless desires friends if only for the purpose of practising friendship, in order that his noble qualities may not lie dormant. Not, however, for the purpose mentioned by Epicurus[6] in the letter quoted above: "That there may be someone to sit by him when he is ill, to help him when he is in prison or in want;" but that he may have someone by whose sick-bed he himself may sit, someone a prisoner in hostile hands whom he himself may set free. He who regards himself only, and enters upon friendships for this reason, reckons wrongly. The end will be like the beginning: he has made friends with one who might assist him out of bondage; at the first rattle of the chain such a friend will desert him. These are the so-called "fair-weather" friendships; one who is chosen for the sake of utility will be satisfactory only so long as he is useful. Hence prosperous men are blockaded by troops of friends; but those who have failed stand amid vast loneliness, their friends fleeing from the very crisis which is to test their worth. Hence, also, we notice those many shameful cases of persons who, through fear, desert or betray. The beginning and the end cannot but harmonize. He who begins to be your friend because it pays will also cease because it pays. A man will be attracted by some reward offered in exchange for his friendship, if he be attracted by aught in friendship other than friendship itself.

For what purpose, then, do I make a man my friend? In order to have someone for whom I may die, whom I may follow into exile, against whose death I may stake my own life, and pay the pledge, too. The friendship which you portray is a bargain and not a friendship; it regards convenience only, and looks to the results. Beyond question the feeling of a lover has in it something akin to friendship; one might call it friendship run mad. But, though this is true, does anyone love for the sake of gain, or promotion, or renown? Pure[7] love, careless of all other things, kindles the soul with desire for the beautiful object, not without the hope of a return of the affection. What then? Can a cause which is more honourable produce a passion that is base? You may retort: "We are not now discussing the question whether friendship is to be cultivated for its own sake." On the contrary, nothing more urgently requires demonstration; for if friendship is to be sought for its own sake, he may seek it who is self-sufficient. "How, then," you ask, "does he seek it?" Precisely as he seeks an object of great beauty, not attracted to it by desire for gain, nor yet frightened by the instability of Fortune. One who seeks friendship for favourable occasions, strips it of all its nobility.

"The wise man is self-sufficient." This phrase, my dear Lucilius, is incorrectly explained by many; for they withdraw the wise man from the world, and force him to dwell within his own skin. But we must mark with care what this sentence signifies and how far it applies; the wise man is sufficient unto himself for a happy existence, but not for mere existence. For he needs many helps towards mere existence; but for a happy existence he needs only a sound and upright soul, one that despises Fortune.

I should like also to state to you one of the distinctions of Chrysippus,[8] who declares that the wise man is in want of nothing, and yet needs many things.[9] "On the other hand," he says, "nothing is needed by the fool, for he does not understand how to use anything, but he is in want of everything." The wise man needs hands, eyes, and many things that are necessary for his daily use; but he is in want of nothing. For want implies a necessity, and nothing is necessary to the wise man. Therefore, although he is self-sufficient, yet he has need of friends. He craves as many friends as possible, not, however, that he may live happily; for he will live happily even without friends. The Supreme Good calls for no practical aids from outside; it is developed at home, and arises entirely within itself. If the good seeks any portion of itself from without, it begins to be subject to the play of Fortune.

People may say: "But what sort of existence will the wise man have, if he be left friendless when thrown into prison, or when stranded in some foreign nation, or when delayed on a long voyage, or when cast upon a lonely shore? "His life will be like that of Jupiter, who, amid the dissolution of the world, when the gods are confounded together and Nature rests for a space from her work, can retire into himself and give himself over to his own thoughts."[10] In some such way as this the sage will act; he will retreat into himself, and live with himself. As long as he is allowed to order his affairs according to his judgment, he is self-sufficient—and marries a wife; he is self-sufficient—and brings up children; he is self-sufficient—and yet could not live if he had to live without the society of man. Natural promptings, and not his own selfish needs, draw him into friendships. For just as other things have for us an inherent attractiveness, so has friendship.

As we hate solitude and crave society, as nature draws men to each other, so in this matter also there is an attraction which makes us desirous of friendship. Nevertheless, though the sage may love his friends dearly, often comparing them with himself, and putting them ahead of himself, yet all the good will be limited to his own being, and he will speak the words which were spoken by the very Stilbo[11] whom Epicurus criticizes in his letter. For Stilbo, after his country was captured and his children and his wife lost, as he emerged from the general desolation alone and yet happy, spoke as follows to Demetrius, called Sacker of Cities because of the destruction he brought upon them, in answer to the question whether he had lost anything: "I have all my goods with me!" There is a brave and stout-hearted man for you! The enemy conquered, but Stilbo conquered his conqueror. "I have lost nothing!" Aye, he forced Demetrius to wonder whether he himself had conquered after all. "My goods are all with me!" In other words, he deemed nothing that might be taken from him to be a good.

We marvel at certain animals because they can pass through fire and suffer no bodily harm; but how much more marvellous is a man who has marched forth unhurt and unscathed through fire and sword and devastation! Do you understand now how much easier it is to conquer a whole tribe than to conquer one *man?* This saying of Stilbo makes common ground with Stoicism; the Stoic also can carry his goods unimpaired through cities that have been burned to ashes; for he is self-sufficient. Such are the bounds which he sets to his own happiness.

But you must not think that our school alone can utter noble words; Epicurus himself, the reviler of Stilbo, spoke similar language[12]; put it down to my credit, though I have already wiped out my debt for the present day.[13] He says: "Whoever does not regard what he has as most ample wealth, is unhappy, though he be master of the whole world." Or, if the following seems to you a more suitable phrase,—for we must try to render the meaning and not the mere words : "A man may rule the world and still be unhappy, if he does not feel that he is supremely happy." In order, however, that you may know that these sentiments are universal,[14] suggested, of course, by Nature, you will find in one of the comic poets this verse:

> Unblest is he who thinks himself unblest.[15]

For what does your condition matter, if it is bad in your own eyes? You may say: "What then? If yonder man, rich by base means, and yonder man, lord of many but slave of more, shall call themselves happy, will their own opinion make them happy?" It matters not what one says, but what one feels; also, not how one feels on one particular day, but how one feels at all times. There is no reason, however, why you should fear that this great privilege will fall into unworthy hands; only the wise man is pleased with his own. Folly is ever troubled with weariness of itself. Farewell.

Endnotes

1. Frag. 174 Usener.
2. *i.e.*, the Cynics.
3. *i.e.*, the Cynics.
4. *i.e.*, the *diurna mercedula;* see *Ep.* vi. 7.
5. Frag. 27 Fowler.
6. Frag. 175 Usener.
7. "Pure love," *i.e.*, love in its essence, unalloyed with other emotions.
8. *Cf.* his *Frag. moral.* 674 von Arnim.
9. The distinction is based upon the meaning of *egere*, "to be in want of" something indispensable, and *opus esse*, "to have need of" something which one can do without.
10. This refers to the Stoic conflagration; after certain cycles their world was destroyed by fire. *Cf.* E. V. Arnold, *Roman Stoicism,* pp. 192f.; *cf.* also Chrysippus, *Frag. phys.* 1065 von Arnim.
11. *Gnomologici Vaticani* 515^a Sternberg.
12. Frag. 474 Usener.
13. *Cf.* above, § 6.
14. *i.e.*, not confined to the Stoics, etc.
15. Author unknown; perhaps, as Buecheler thinks, adapted from the Greek.

Excerpts from Seneca: *Epistulae Morales,* translated by R. M. Gummere, copyright © 1917 by Harvard University Press. Reprinted by permission of the Loeb Classical Library.

Friendship

Aristotle

It will be natural to discuss friendship or love next, for friendship is a kind of virtue or implies virtue. It is also indispensable to life. For nobody would choose to live without friends, although he were in possession of every other good. Nay, it seems that if people are rich and hold official and authoritative positions, they have the greatest need of friends; for what is the good of having this sort of prosperity if one is denied the opportunity of beneficence, which is never so freely or so admirably exercised as towards friends? Or how can it be maintained in safety and security without friends? For the greater a person's importance, the more liable it is to disaster. In poverty and other misfortunes we regard our friends as our only refuge. Again, friends are helpful to us, when we are young, as guarding us from error, and when we are growing old, as taking care of us, and supplying such deficiencies of action as are the consequences of physical weakness, and when we are in the prime of life, as prompting us to noble actions, according to the adage, "Two come together"; for two people have a greater power both of intelligence and of action *than either of the two by himself.*

It would seem that friendship or love is the natural instinct of a parent towards a child, and of a child towards a parent, not only among men, but among birds and animals generally, and among creatures of the same race towards one another, especially among men. This is the reason why we praise men who are the friends of their fellow-men or philanthropists. We may observe too in travelling how near and dear every man is to his fellow-man.

Again, it seems that friendship or love is the bond which holds states together, and that legislators set more store by it than by justice; for concord is apparently akin to friendship, and it is concord that they especially seek to promote, and faction, as being hostility to the state, that they especially try to expel.

Chapter VIII: Friendship and Love

If people are friends, there is no need of justice between them; but people may be just, and yet need friendship. Indeed it seems that justice, in its supreme form, assumes the character of friendship.

Nor is friendship indispensable only; it is also noble. We praise people who are fond of their friends, and it is thought to be a noble thing to have many friends, and there are some people who hold that to be a friend is the same thing as to be a good man.

But the subject of friendship or love is one that affords scope for a good many differences of opinion. Some people define it as a sort of likeness, and define people who are like each other as friends. Hence the sayings "Like seeks like," "Birds of a feather," and so on. Others on the contrary say that "two of a trade never agree." Upon this subject *some philosophical thinkers* indulge in more profound physical speculations; Euripides asserting that

> "the parched Earth loves the rain, And the great Heaven rain-laden loves to fall Earthwards";

Heraclitus that "the contending tends together," and that "harmony most beautiful is formed of discords," and that "all things are by strife engendered"; others, among whom is Empedocles, taking the opposite view and urging that "like desires like."

The physical questions we may leave aside as not being germane to the present enquiry. But let us investigate all such questions as are of human interest and relate to characters and emotions, e.g. whether friendship can be formed among all people, or it is impossible for people to be friends if they are vicious, and whether there is one kind of friendship or more than one. . . .

It is possible, I think, to elucidate the subject of friendship or love, by determining what it is that is lovable or an object of love. For it seems that it is not everything which is loved, but only that which is lovable, and that this is what is good or pleasant or useful. It would seem too that a thing is useful if it is a means of gaining something good or pleasant, and if so, it follows that what is good and what is pleasant will be lovable in the sense of being ends.

It may be asked then, Is it that which is good *in itself*, or that which is good relatively to us, that we love? For there is sometimes a difference between them; and the same question may be asked in regard to that which is pleasant. It seems then that everybody loves what is good relatively to himself, and that, while it is the good which is lovable in an absolute sense, it is that which is good relatively to each individual that is lovable in his eyes. It may be said that everybody loves not that which is good, but that which appears good relatively to himself. But this is not an objection that will make any difference; for in that case that which is lovable will be that which appears to be lovable.

There being three motives of friendship or love, it must be observed that we do not apply the term "friendship" or "love" to the affection felt for inanimate things. The reason is (1) that they are incapable of reciprocating affection, and (2) that we do not wish their good; for it would, I think, be ridiculous to wish the good e.g. of wine; if we wish it at all, it is only in the sense of wishing the wine to keep well, in the hope of enjoying it ourselves. But it is admitted that we ought to wish our friend's good for his sake, and not for our own. If we wish people good in this sense, we are called well-wishers, unless our good wishes are returned; such reciprocal well-wishing is called friendship or love.

But it is necessary, I think, to add, that the well-wishing must not be unknown. A person often wishes well to people whom he has not seen, but whom he supposes to be virtuous or useful; and it is possible that one of these persons may entertain the same feeling towards him. Such people then, it is clear, wish well to one another; but they cannot be properly called friends, as their disposition is unknown to each other. It follows that, if they are to be friends, they must be well-disposed to each other, and must wish each other's good, from one of the motives which have been assigned, and that each of them must know the fact of the other wishing him well.

But as the motives of friendship are specifically different, there will be a corresponding difference in the affections and friendships.

The kinds of friendship therefore will be three, being equal in number to the things which are lovable, *or are objects of friendship or love*, as every such object admits of a reciprocal affection between two persons, each of whom is aware of the other's love.

People who love each other wish each other's good in the point characteristic of their love. Accordingly those whose mutual love is based upon utility do not love each other for their own sakes, but only in so far as they derive some benefit one from another. It is the same with those whose love is based upon pleasure. Thus we are fond of witty people, not as possessing a certain character, but as being pleasant to ourselves. People then, whose love is based upon utility, are moved to affection by a sense of their own good, and people whose love is based upon pleasure, by a sense of their own pleasure; and they love a person not for being what he is in himself, but for being useful or pleasant to them. These friendships then are only friendships in an accidental sense; for the person loved is not loved as being what he is, but as being a source either of good or of pleasure. Accordingly, such friendships are easily dissolved, if the persons do not continue always the same; for they abandon their love if they cease to be pleasant or useful to each other. But utility is not a permanent quality; it varies at different times. Thus, when the motive of a friendship is done away, the friendship itself is dissolved, as it was dependent upon that motive. A friendship of this kind seems especially to occur among old

Chapter VIII: Friendship and Love

people, as in old age we look to profit rather than pleasure, and among such people in the prime of life or in youth as have an eye to their own interest. Friends of this kind do not generally even live together; for sometimes they are not even pleasant to one another; nor do they need the intercourse of friendship, unless they bring some profit to one another, as the pleasure which they afford goes no further than they entertain hopes of deriving benefit from it. Among these friendships we reckon the friendship of hospitality, *i.e. the friendship which exists between a host and his guests.*

It would seem that the friendship of the young is based upon pleasure; for they live by emotion and are most inclined to pursue what is pleasant to them at the moment. But as their time of life changes, their pleasures are transformed. They are therefore quick at making friendships and quick at abandoning them; for the friendship changes with the object which pleases them, and friendship of this kind is liable to sudden change. Young men are amorous too, amorousness being generally a matter of emotion and pleasure, hence they fall in love and soon afterwards fall out of love, changing from one condition to another many times in the same day. But amorous people wish to spend their days and lives together, as it is thus that they attain the object of their friendship.

The perfect friendship or love is the friendship or love of people who are good and alike in virtue; for these people are alike in wishing each other's good, in so far as they are good, and they are good in themselves. But it is people who wish the good of their friends for their friends' sake that are in the truest sense friends, as their friendship is the consequence of their own character, and is not an accident. Their friendship therefore continues as long as their virtue, and virtue is a permanent quality.

Again, each of them is good in an absolute sense, and good in relation to his friend. For good men are not only good in an absolute sense, but serve each other's interest. They are pleasant too; for the good are pleasant in an absolute sense, and pleasant in relation to one another, as everybody finds pleasure in such actions as are proper to him, and the like, and all good people act alike or nearly alike.

Such a friendship is naturally permanent, as it unites in itself all the proper conditions of friendship. For the motive of all friendship or affection is good or pleasure, whether it be absolute or relative to the person who feels the affection, and it depends upon a certain similarity. In the friendship of good men all these specified conditions belong to the friends in themselves; for other friendships *only* bear a resemblance to the perfect friendship. That which is good in an absolute sense is also in an absolute sense pleasant. These are the principal objects of affection, and it is upon these that affectionate feeling, and affection in the highest and best sense, depend.

Friendships of this kind are likely to be rare; for such people are few. They require time and familiarity too; for, as the adage puts it, it is impossible for people to know one another until they have consumed the proverbial salt together; nor can people admit one another to friendship, or be friends at all, until each has been proved lovable and trustworthy to the other.

People, who are quick to treat one another as friends, wish to be friends but are not so really, unless they are lovable and know each other to be lovable; for the wish to be friends may arise in a minute, but not friendship. . . .

It is the friendship of the good which is friendship in the truest sense, as has been said several times. For it seems that, while that which is good or pleasant in an absolute sense is an object of love and desire, that which is good or pleasant to each individual is an object of love or desire to him; but the love or desire of one good man for another depends upon such goodness and pleasantness as are at once absolute and relative to the good.

Affection resembles a feeling but friendship resembles a moral state. For while affection may be felt for inanimate as much as for animate things, the love of friends for one another implies moral purpose, and such purpose is the outcome of a moral state.

Again, we wish the good of those whom we love for their own sake, and the wish is governed not by feeling but by the moral state. In loving our friend too, we love what is good for ourselves; as when a good man becomes a friend, he becomes a blessing to his friend. Accordingly each of two friends loves what is good for himself, and returns as much as he receives in good wishes and in pleasure; for, as the proverb says, equality is friendship.

Friendship

Elizabeth Telfer

It is often said that friendships are among the most important constituents of a worth-while life. I wish to examine this view by trying to answer three questions about friendship: what it is, how morality bears on it, and why it is thought to be important.

1 *The Nature of Friendship*

We can begin our answer to the first question with the obvious point that there is a certain type of activity which all friends, *qua* friends, engage in: the performing of services of all kinds for some other person. Suppose, however, that a man fetches coal and shopping and clears the snow for the lonely old lady next door. This kind of case would not really be one of friendship, for, while she might say, 'My neighbour's been a real *friend* to me this winter', we would normally distinguish between 'befriending' or 'being a friend to' and 'being friends' or 'being a friend of'. In the situation described we would not speak of the existence of a friendship or say that the pair were friends or that he was a friend of hers (as distinct from a friend to her). His conduct is in some ways like that of a friend, but the situation is not one of *friendship*, and it is the latter concept with which we are concerned.

It might be suggested that what is missing in the example is reciprocity. But the old lady and her neighbour do not become friends simply because in return for his fetching and shovelling she knits him socks. What are missing are two other types of activity, which are not so much reciprocal as actually *shared:* those activities the main point of which is that they involve contact with the friend, such as talking together or exchanging letters; and joint engagement in pursuits which the friends would in any case perform quite apart from the friendship—notably leisure pursuits, but also sometimes work, worship and so on. My thesis, then, is that there are three types of activity which are all necessary conditions of friendship: reciprocal services, mutual contact and joint pursuits. I shall henceforth refer to these necessary conditions collectively, as the 'shared activity' condition for friendship.

The 'shared activity' condition, however, is not a sufficient condition for friendship. This becomes clear if we imagine a case where the condition is fulfilled. Consider, for example, the situation where two neighbours, each living alone, perform services for each other, go to the pictures together, and drop in on each other to chat in the evenings. Would we be able to say that the pair were friends, simply on the strength of this situation? I think it is clear that we would not, on the ground that friendship depends, not only on the performance of certain *actions*, but also on their being performed for certain specific *reasons*—out of friendship, as we say, rather than out of duty or pity or indeed self-interest. These reasons can, I think, be seen as a set of long-term *desires*, which motivate and hence explain actions done out of friendship. My contention is that the existence of the relevant desires is a second necessary condition for friendship. Let us examine these desires—which we may call the *passions* of friendship—in more detail.

The first element in the passions of friendship is affection; friends must have affection for, or be fond of, each other. (This passion is not of course peculiar to friendship; for example, it is also felt by colleagues of long standing, or by members of the same family.) I define 'affection' as a desire for another's welfare and happiness *as a particular individual*. This desire is thus to be distinguished both from sense of duty and from benevolence. For these motives prompt us to seek others' good in general, whereas we want to say that those who feel affection feel a concern for another which they do not feel for everyone. It is this concern which normally motivates services performed out of friendship, whereas befriending is motivated by benevolence, pity or sense of duty. This special concern for friends also gives rise to reactions of special pleasure at their good fortune, pain at their misfortune, anger with those who injure them, and so on.

Two points about affection may be briefly noted before we consider other passions of friendship. The first concerns its relation with benevolence and sense of duty. We have said that benevolence and sense of duty are to be distinguished from affection because affection is for the individual. But surely, it may be argued, the benevolent and the dutiful man also concern themselves with the individual? The answer here is to distinguish between two kinds of concern for the individual. To say that the benevolent or dutiful man concerns himself with the individual is to say that he sees each individual as making separate claims which may not only compete with the majority interest but also differ in content from those of other individuals. But the concern of affection is not for *each* individual, but for *this* individual rather than others.

The second point I wish to make about affection is that it does not seem to have any necessary connection with the particular character of him for whom it is felt. If asked to explain why we are fond of someone, we *may* mention characteristics in him which stimulate affection, but it makes equally good sense to give an historical explanation—'I've known him for a long time' or 'I looked after him when he was ill' or a biological one such as 'He's my brother, after all'. Affection is in this sense *irrational*, and because of this may survive radical changes in the character of its object. Thus we often continue to be fond of someone when we no longer like or respect him, and such a situation is not considered in any way odd.

The second element in the passions which are part of friendship, and one which distinguishes it from many other relationships which involve affection, is a desire on the part of the friends for each others' company as distinct from a desire for company as such. It will normally be this desire which leads friends to seek contact with each other and to share pursuits, and which also gives rise to our pleasure when we see friends, regret at parting, and so on. It is the presence of this desire which distinguishes a case of friendship from those where a man keeps company with another out of loneliness, or pity, or sense of duty.

Is this desire for another's company irrational in the same way as affection is? I think not, at least where it is part of *friendship* and not of being in love, infatuation, *etc*. These latter states also involve a desire for the other's company. But whereas it is characteristic of them that a sufferer from them may intelligibly say 'I don't know what it is about him/her that draws me, but I cannot be without him/her' we would not speak of friendship unless the friends are prepared to *explain* the desire for each other's company, and to do so in terms of two particular attitudes towards each other: liking, and the sense of a bond or of something in common.

Now both these attitudes are rational, in the sense that they are necessarily based on beliefs about the nature of the friend: we *like* a person and feel we *are like* him because of what we think he is *like*. The degree of rationality which this involves, however, is rather limited. For even where we *can* give our reasons for liking someone or feeling a bond with him, we cannot further justify these reasons, or always explain why they operate in one case and not in another apparently similar. And we may find it very difficult to *state* our reasons at all. In such a case the most we might be prepared to say is that there must be qualities in the friend, even if we cannot 'pin them down', such that if he ceased to have them we would cease to like or feel akin to him. Let me say a little more about these two attitudes.

Liking is a difficult phenomenon to analyze. Although it is a *reason* for seeking someone's company, it is not simply *equivalent* to enjoyment of his company, as might at first seem, as we can for a time enjoy the company of people whom we do not basically like—indeed, certain kinds of unpleasant people have their own fascination. It seems rather to be a quasi-aesthetic attitude, roughly specifiable as 'finding a person to one's taste', and depends partly on such things as his physical appearance, mannerisms, voice and speech, and style of life; partly on his traits of character, moral and other. The relative importance of these features as a basis for liking obviously depends on the liker.

This account of liking tends to suggest that before we can like someone we have to tot up items in his nature and strike a balance between the attractive and the unattractive aspects of it. But in reality our reaction, like a reaction to a picture, is to a whole personality seen as a unified thing. This is why we often find it very difficult to say what it is we like about a person. Sometimes what we like is partly the way in which everything about the person seems to 'hang together' and be part of a unified style; sometimes we enjoy a contrast, for example that between a mild unassuming exterior and an iron determination. Of course, the fact that we like a personality as a unity or whole does not rule out the possibility that we may dislike some individual features intensely. But in such a case we characteristically feel that these features are not merely objectionable in themselves, but also somehow mar, or intrude upon, a whole that is otherwise pleasing; and this fact sharpens our vexation.

The sense of a bond, or the sense that we have something in common with another person, is a quite separate reason for seeking his company from the existence of liking. For people can be ill-at-ease with those whom they like, and explain why they are *not* friends with them, contrary to others' expectation, by saying 'I like him, but I can't seem to communicate with him,' or 'We don't talk the same language' or 'We don't seem to have much in common'. The bond may be shared interests or enthusiasms or views, but it may also be a similar style of mind or way of thinking which makes for a high degree of empathy.

In the light of this discussion we can I think reject the notion that we need to think of our friends as good people, as Plato and Aristotle sometimes seem to assume. For there seems no *necessary* incompatibility between fondness, liking, and a sense of a bond, on the one hand, and disapproval of some qualities in a person, on the other. (Indeed, we can even have a kind of admiration or liking for the very qualities of which we at the same time disapprove.) On the other hand, some moral defects arouse distaste as well as disapproval and so prevent liking. And one of the strongest bonds may well be, even if not matched virtue and mutual admiration as in Aristotle, at least similar moral seriousness and shared moral purpose. Again, to say that we need not think of our friends as good people is not to say that friendship with a thoroughly bad person is morally permissible or to deny that some moral defects may make a person incapable of friendship.

One reason why Aristotle insists that friendship (at any rate the truest form of friendship) must be between good men is that he thinks that to care for someone because he is virtuous is to care for him for his own sake, whereas to care for him because he is useful or pleasant is not.[1] Now if Aristotle means merely that it is not true friendship to care for someone for what you can get out of him, we agree. But he seems rather to mean that to care for a man because of his virtue is to care for him 'in himself', rather than because of contingent and changeable facts about him, and that 'caring for him in himself' in this sense is one of the requirements of friendship.

Now it is clear that Aristotle is mistaken in supposing that a man's virtue is not a contingent and changeable fact—as indeed he later admits.[2] But his other assumption—that we care for friends 'in themselves' rather than for any contingent facts about them—has a certain plausibility. How far is it valid? It is false if it means that qualities in the friend cannot be *reasons* for friendship. For liking and the sense of a bond, which are necessary conditions of friendship, both depend on the friend's nature. It follows that if the friends change in such a way that they cease to like each other or to have anything in common, the friendship is at an end—not in the sense that it would be wise or usual to break it off, but by definition. It may be that 'Love is not love which alters when it alteration finds'; but friendship, which is based on and dependent on reasons, is different.

But there are two senses in which Aristotle's requirement is valid, as can be seen in the light of my earlier discussion. First, there is an element in friendship—affection—which does not have the same dependence on the nature of the friend as liking and sense of a bond. It *may* fade if the friend alters, but there is no logical reason why it should do so, and often it in fact does not. Secondly, even liking, although it depends on qualities which others may also have, is nevertheless a reaction to an individual, not a type. Thus if I like James because he is witty, gentle, and good at making things, I like him, not as one example of a witty, gentle and craftsmanlike person, for whom another such might be substituted, but as an individual whose uniqueness defies complete classification.[3]

My account so far of friendship is in terms of two necessary conditions: shared activities and the passions of friendship. But it might well be objected that this account fails to do justice to an important aspect of friendship, that of commitment and choice. Indeed, an objector might go further, and say that to give the status of a necessary condition to the passions of friendship is *incompatible* with the plain fact that we can speak of choosing to be someone's friend. His argument is that since we can speak of choosing to be someone's friend, but cannot choose our feelings, the presence of certain feelings cannot be a necessary condition for friendship. Their rôle, he would maintain, is rather that of *reasons* for friendship, reasons why I might choose to be someone's friend. Similarly, if my inclinations alter, this may be a reason for breaking off the friendship, but it does not *mean* that the friendship is broken off. Such an objector might compare friendship in this respect to marriage, which is normally entered upon on the basis of certain feelings but which exists whether or not these feelings obtain. He might go on to say that in friendship, as in marriage, it makes sense to ask which feelings do justify entering upon the friendship, and again which changes of feelings (if any) justify breaking it off.

My reply to this objection is first of all to recall the case where the usual passions of friendship do not obtain, but the behaviour does—where, for example, A helps B and does things with him, not out of spontaneous inclination, but out of pity or sense of duty. My claim is that if B comes to realize A's real motives he would naturally say, not 'You shouldn't have become my friend', but 'You don't really regard me as a friend at all'. Again, if A ceases to like B or to feel any bond with him, but goes on acting as before 'for auld lang syne', as it were, B on becoming aware of the situation would I think say 'You don't really think of me as a friend any more.'

To some extent, of course, I am stipulating, rather than reporting, that the presence of the inclinations is a necessary part of friendship. I think the word may sometimes be used to describe a relationship analogous to marriage. But perhaps I can make the stipulation more palatable by pointing out that, even on my analysis so far, choice necessarily enters into friendship. For although the right passions are a necessary condition of friendship they are not by themselves a sufficient condition. A man who possesses these passions has still to act on them—actually to help instead of merely wanting to, for example—and insofar as he acts he is necessarily making choices. In this way my two necessary conditions are compatible with, and themselves imply, *choice* in friendship—though they also imply that we cannot choose to be a friend of just anyone, since the relevant passions cannot be summoned up at will.

It might plausibly be maintained, however, that we speak of choosing our friends in a stronger sense than that already covered by the two necessary conditions of shared activities and passions of friendship. For the existence of what I have called shared activities need not imply more than a series of unconnected choices, not seen by the chooser as forming any pattern. But choosing a friend seems to mean forming a long-term *policy* of action: making one decision to act in general in the ways we have described, not making many decisions on particular occasions.

Is it a necessary condition of friendship that we should choose our friends, in this stronger sense? It seems clear that we need not (though we may) make a conscious decision of the kind I have just described; we can speak of people as gradually *becoming* friends, or of friendship as *springing up*, thus suggesting that there need not be any definite beginning to the friendship. But nevertheless I would claim that a weaker version of this condition is necessary: namely, that the existence of the passions of friendship in both parties, and the practice on both sides of acting on them, once established, be *acknowledged* by the parties. This acknowledgement involves, not so much the *formation* of a policy, as endorsement of or consent to a policy which is by then enshrined in practice. This is part of what is meant by *commitment* in friendship.

I have claimed that there are three necessary conditions for friendship: shared activities, the passions of friendship, and acknowledgement of the fulfillment of the first two conditions, constituting an acknowledgement of and consent to the special relationship. I now add that I regard these as not only individually necessary but also jointly sufficient for friendship.

2 *Friendship and Duty*

But friends can also be said to be committed in a quite different sense from that which I have been discussing: friendship is seen as giving rise to *duties* and corresponding rights. Examples of such duties, as commonly conceived, are: to help the friend when under attack (physical or verbal) or in need or trouble of any kind; to proffer advice and criticism, not only when asked for but also when not asked for but needed. The notion of duties to friends, however, is by no means unproblematic, and before I can consider these duties further I must discuss three arguments to the effect that it does not make sense to speak of duties to friends.

The first argument can be dismissed fairly briskly. It is to the effect that friendship is an involuntary relationship, and no duties can be founded on an involuntary relationship. I have already denied that friendship is involuntary in the relevant sense. But in any case we should query the assumption that no duties can arise from an involuntary relationship. Cannot children be said to have duties to their parents, or siblings to each other?

The second reason for rejecting the notion of duties to friends is more problematic. It is that to speak of duty implies the possibility that the action may be against the grain, whereas we spontaneously want to help our friends. We cannot meet this difficulty simply by saying that we can often speak of duties in situations where we also in fact wish to do the actions, as in the case of duties to family. For whether or not we wish to help our families is a contingent matter, whereas I have made it part of the very definition of friendship that we should want to help our friends.

This difficulty about duties to friends can I think be circumvented by stressing two points. First, the existence of friendship, while it implies general goodwill, need not imply that the friends wish each other well at all times and in all respects. Thus it is quite compatible with friendship for a man to lose concern temporarily for a friend—perhaps as the result of a quarrel—or to find that some aspect of his friend's behaviour always tries his patience. In these cases it makes perfectly good sense to say that caring for his friend goes against the grain. Secondly, some of our duties to our friends are extremely disagreeable (such as telling them unpleasant 'home truths'). There is thus a point in speaking of duty in that our natural concern for our friends' welfare, though prompting us in the right direction, is not so strong that all the required actions come easily to us.

The third objection which may be raised to the conception that we have duties to friends is that duties belong to impersonal relationships, whereas friendship is a personal relationship. The force of this objection, however, obviously depends on what sense of 'personal' and 'impersonal' is in question. Let us therefore consider in what senses friendship may be said to be personal, and whether any of them preclude us from speaking of 'duties of friendship'.[4]

First, friendship is personal in that it necessarily involves knowledge by acquaintance. But in this it does not differ from many relationships which obviously involve duties: for example, that of husband and wife.

Secondly, friendship is personal in that it necessarily involves what we may call a 'reactive' attitude: that which regards another human being, not as an object to be manipulated causally, but as a *person, i.e.,* a rational agent capable of self-determination.[5] But our relationships with all adult sane human beings should be, and normally are, personal in this sense; it therefore cannot be incompatible with the existence of duties.

Thirdly, we may say that friendship is personal in that it is 'part of one's private life'. But the notion of private life itself needs elucidation. It may mean anything which is not connected with one's work. In this sense relationships with one's family, friends, fellow-churchmen, fellow-clubmen, mistress, are all part of one's private life. Or one may use the term in a sense relative to one's interlocutor, meaning roughly 'whatever I choose to keep apart from you'. In this sense family life may be private life to one's colleagues, friendships and love affairs to one's family. But 'private life' in both these senses can include relationships in which we normally speak of duties, so we cannot base an argument against the conception of duties to friends on the idea that friendship is part of private life.

Fourthly, we may say that friendship is personal in that it is part of one's 'non-official life', as contrasted with 'official life' in which what to do is in some way fixed or laid down. It might then be argued that the official sphere (which would include not only work, or most forms of it, but also membership of organizations such as clubs, churches and political parties, and of relationships which are governed by law and convention such as marriage and parenthood) is that in which it makes sense to speak of duty. The non-official sphere, on the other hand, to which belong friendships, companionships and acquaintanceships, and love affairs, is outside the scope of duty. This argument from the non-official nature of friendship seems to have a certain plausibility. But it in fact comprises two different claims, which must be considered separately.

First, then, the claim may be that duties belong to conventional or institutional relationships, whereas friendship is a natural relationship. To support the claim examples are adduced of relationships involving duties: for example, that of husband to wife (and *vice versa*), schoolmaster to pupils, treasurer of club to club members, and so on. In all these cases the role is *defined* in terms of a set of duties: one cannot explain what a husband is without explaining the rights and duties of marriage. But friendship can be explained entirely in natural terms (in the kind of way we explained it in our first section). Hence, it may be argued, friendship is not a duty-relationship.

But this argument is confused. For there are cases of *natural* relationships, such as that between parent and child, which give rise to duties just as much as do the conventional relationships. The difference is that, whereas the statement that husbands have duties to wives is analytic, the statement that parents have duties to children is synthetic. If then friendship is a natural relationship, it may well involve duties in the same way as parenthood does—duties whose precise content will depend on the nature of the particular society. We incur these duties as a result of making friends just as we incur the duties of parents as a result of having children.

The second claim based on the non-official nature of friendship may be developed as a criticism of our reply to the first. It may be argued that parenthood, although like friendship in being a natural rather than a conventional relationship, is nevertheless official in a sense in which friendship is not, because society *recognizes* the duties of parenthood. This recognition is shown both by the legal enforcement of some very important duties, and by the more informal sanctions of disapproval which are brought to bear on parents who neglect non-legal duties to their children. Nothing of this kind—the argument goes on—happens in the case of friendship, and therefore we cannot speak of duties to friends.

This second argument assumes that duties are always dependent on the attitudes of society. But this assumption does not seem to be correct. We may grant that the precise content of one's duties may vary from society to society, since people's needs vary in different societies and are met in different ways by different social arrangements. But it does not follow that we have no duties except those recognized by society. For example, it makes sense to say that parents had a duty to educate their daughters as well as their sons, even at the time when society did not recognize this duty, because the daughters had a need which was not being met at all. In the same way we might have duties to friends, which society does not recognize, in view of some need which is not otherwise met.

I conclude then that the personal nature of friendship, however this is interpreted, does not rule out the possibility of our having duties to friends.

It is possible, however, to attack the notion of duties to friends from a quite different point of view. This attack would grant that it *makes sense* to speak of duties to friends, but hold that we are *mistaken* in thinking that we in fact have such duties, because the alleged duties to friends cannot be properly grounded or justified. It might of course be retorted that further defence of the view that friends have special duties to each other is neither possible nor necessary; it is just an ultimate moral principle that we have special duties to friends. But it does not seem to be self-evident that we have special duties to a small group of people, simply because we care about them and seek their company. In any case, those who oppose the idea of duties to friends might well go on to argue that friendship seems *prima facie* to involve a kind of *injustice*, in that it means giving preferential treatment to those who differ neither in need nor in desert—in other words that, so far from being duties, our services to friends might be construed as positively immoral.

Faced with these arguments, the defenders of the duties of friendship will point out first of all that not all services to friends are in any sense exclusive of services to others. Thus we can distinguish between the expenditure on our friends of time or money which might otherwise have been spent on others, and the proffering of advice or criticism which is *not* thereby rendered unavailable for others. It is only in the first type of case that the issue of the morality of preferential treatment for friends arises sharply. And even there the alleged duties to help our friends are acknowledged to be severely restricted in various ways by the demands of other specific duties.

But these restrictions still leave an area in which no duty arising out of another rôle is in question but in which there may be a choice between helping a friend and helping a stranger. Suppose, for example, a man could spend an evening helping to decorate either a friend's flat or that of an old age pensioner, or could spend spare cash either on a loan to friends or on contributions to Oxfam. Most people would say that the friends had, if not a prior claim, at least a competing claim, and our present problem is to defend this view.

A plausible line of defence seems to be an appeal to a Rule-Utilitarian position. Thus it might be argued that many sets of rights and duties which set up special claims not obviously required by justice, are justified by the conduciveness of their observance to the general good. If for example a parent is asked why he should support his child, he will reply that it is one of the duties of a parent. If he is then asked *why* parents should be held to have special duties to their children, instead of their being the responsibility of the State or of grand-parents, he will say that it is best for all concerned that parents should have special responsibility for children. In the same way, then, we may suggest that the general welfare is best served by our regarding friends as having a special claim on us. We may defend this view on the grounds that more happiness overall is produced if each man makes the welfare of a few others his special concern, for two reasons: he will be able to be more effective if he concentrates his energies, and he will be able to know more precisely what the needs of a small group are.

Chapter VIII: Friendship and Love

※ ※ ※

Now the first of these arguments does not by itself support the view that we have special duties to *friends*, but only the view that we should choose *a* small group as special recipients of our benevolence. But if we add the second argument, about the knowledge of needs, we can defend the view that the special group we choose should be that of our friends. It is not only that we have a good deal of contact with our friends and get to know their needs that way, for this fact applies equally to our family or to colleagues at work. But we also have a special understanding of our friends' needs, in virtue not only of the *rapport* which by definition exists between friends but also of a sharpened *awareness*, which results from the special concern friends in any case have for each other.

We can thus advance beyond the point made earlier, that there is nothing self-contradictory in the idea of duties towards those for whom we already feel a special concern, and assert that the existence of this concern is part of the *justification* for the claim that we have special duties to friends. As we have just seen, a special concern, in making us especially aware of others' needs, gives us the duties that are attendant on special knowledge of needs. But it also gives us a special degree of *power* to help, and in this way also gives us special duties. This is because a man can have a duty to do only what he is able to do, and in some cases he is able, as a result of the strength of his concern for a friend, to do for him what he *could* not do (and hence could not have a duty to do) for anyone else.

It might be argued at this point that I have not met the objection that it is *unjust* to view friends as having special claims; for since friendship is, and is bound to be, very unevenly distributed, the rights which it confers will also be unevenly distributed. I think the only possible answer is that this is a case where the utility of a practice is high enough to compensate for the fact that some measure of injustice is involved in it. But in any case when we speak of duties to friends we are clearly speaking of *prima facie* duties, which would be overridden by a stronger claim.

I can now briefly sum up the conclusions of this section. I have tried to show that various arguments, purporting to show that it does not make sense to speak of duties to friends, are not cogent: those from the alleged involuntariness of friendship, from the constraining nature of duty, and from the personalness, in either the 'knowledge by acquaintance' or the 'reactive' or the 'private life' sense, of the relationship of friendship. I considered at more length the notion that friendship is separated from duty by being personal in the sense of 'nonofficial'. I suggested there that we could speak of the duties of friendship even though they are both non-institutional and unsupported by social sanctions. I then raised a new type of problem, that of *grounding* the alleged duties to friends. I have tried to show that this can be done in terms of the general good.

3 The Value of Friendship

It may be said that the train of thought so far has been that, *if* we have friends, *then* we have certain duties to them. But this does not constitute a demonstration of the value of friendship itself, any more than it shows the value of parenthood to say that if people produce children then they have a duty towards them.

Now some people will say that there is no point in raising the question what the *good* of friendship is, since people cannot help having friends in any case. But this is not strictly true, as we have seen; commitment to friendship is a voluntary matter. It may be true that people cannot help forming vaguer and looser associations, and that they cannot help having the *passions* of friendship towards various other people. But this does not amount to the inevitability of friendship itself.

It may be said that if our emotional make-up is such as to incline us to want to make friends, then this in itself constitutes a *prima facie* case for the goodness of friendship. For how can we show something to be good (it may be maintained) except by showing that it meets deep-seated desires?

But this argument is cogent only if the desires in question—the passions of friendship—are unavoidable; whereas it seems clear that, even if we cannot ourselves get rid of them once we have them, we can foster or inhibit their development in children. Certain kinds of early environment make people less inclined to form strong attachments later, and whether this is a good or bad thing depends on whether friendship itself is a good or a bad thing. Nor can we settle the question by saying that a person who cannot make friends is considered psychologically unhealthy. For we would not include a capacity for friendship in our requirement for psychological health unless we already assumed that friendship is a good thing, so we cannot defend friendship in the name of mental health without going round in a circle.

Why, then, is friendship always considered a good thing—perhaps one of the chief blessings of life? Part of the reason has been given already in my previous section. It is true that my account of the duties of friendship did not raise the question of the value of friendship itself, but rather asked whether, given that we have friends, we are to regard ourselves as having duties to them. But we can use the conclusions of the account as part of a justification of friendship itself. Friendship, we may say, promotes the general happiness by providing a degree and kind of consideration for others' welfare which cannot exist outside it, and which compensates by its excellence for the 'unfairness' of the unequal distribution of friendship. For even those who have no friends are (we may suppose) better off than they would be if there were no such thing as friendship, since the understanding developed by it and the mutual criticism involved in it will improve the way friends deal with people outside the relationship.

But we value friendship for reasons other than its general serviceability to society. To see what these are, we may start from Aristotle's account of why the happy man needs friends[6]—though he tends to assume, as we have seen, that friendship worthy of the name must be between good people. He suggests first that friends are *useful* to a man both to help him in his need and to be recipients of his beneficence in his prosperity. These points have both been partially dealt with earlier; but we would say, not that a man must have friends in order to receive or give *any* help (as Aristotle seems to suggest) but rather that there are particular services which a man can receive only from friends and perform only for them.

Secondly, Aristotle suggests friendship is *pleasant*. He sees this pleasure mainly in terms of the *good* man's pleasure at his equally good friend's virtuous actions. But the joys of friendship are many and various. Notably, of course, there is the pleasure of the friend's company and of shared activity with someone of kindred outlook. Nor need the fact that we gain this pleasure mean that the friendship is 'for the sake of pleasure'. We may begin a friendship because we enjoy someone's company, but soon we enjoy his company because he is a friend.

Now an appeal to pleasure as a justification of friendship may not seem to be on very safe ground, for friendship, like any other attachment we may form, increases our potentiality for pain as well as for pleasure. It could well be argued that from the point of view of the balance of pleasure over pain we would do better to play safe by eschewing friendship. But this pessimistic view does not take into account the full range of the pleasures of friendship. It is true that we can set the pleasure of making a new friend against the sorrow of losing an old one, or the pleasure of a friend's company against the pain of his absence, or the pleasure of discovering his excellences against the pain of disillusionment with him. But there are some pleasures of friendship which have no corresponding pains. These are the pleasures which arise from doing things with a friend, as opposed to doing them alone or with others. What we are doing may be in any case enjoyable—playing games, playing music, conversation, philosophy—in which case the presence of the friend enhances the pleasure. Or what we do may in itself be unattractive, but become fun—indeed, be turned into a kind of game—when shared with a friend: for example, spring-cleaning or moving house.

This discussion of the pleasures of friendship points to a third value in friendship, noted indirectly by Aristotle: friendship is *life-enhancing*, it makes us have life 'more abundantly'. This happens in various different ways. First, it increases our stake in the world, and hence our capacity for emotions. We have already noticed this point in terms of the increased capacity for pleasure and pain, but it applies also to the whole range of emotions: hope, fear, anger, pride and so on. Friendship makes us 'more alive' because it makes us *feel* more.

Secondly, friendship enhances many of our *activities*, by intensifying our absorption in them, and hence the quality of our performance of them. The increased absorption is partly a by-product (or rather perhaps an aspect) of the increased pleasure which joint activity with friends produces, since (as Aristotle says) pleasure taken in an activity intensifies it. But I think collaboration with friends may also produce an increased emotional commitment to the activity which is separable from the effects of enhanced pleasure.

Thirdly, friendship enlarges our *knowledge*. I have already spoken of the increased knowledge of human needs and wishes which springs from close association with some one other person. But friendship can enlarge our knowledge throughout the whole gamut of human experience, by enabling us in some measure to adopt the viewpoint of another person through our sympathetic identification with him. Through friendship we can know what it is like to feel or think or do certain things which we do not feel, think or do ourselves. And our knowledge is not merely knowledge by description, but knowledge by acquaintance, derived from our sympathetic sharing of his experience.

We might compare this effect of friendship with that of reading a great work of literature. C. S. Lewis, trying to answer the question 'What is the good of Literature?', says "We want to be more than ourselves . . . we want to see with other eyes, to imagine with other imaginations, to feel with other hearts, as well as with our own.

". . . It is not a question of knowing [in the sense of gratifying our rational curiosity about other people's psychology] at all. It is *connaître* not *savoir*; it is *erleben*: we become these other selves."[7] This empathy with the authors of literature is exactly like the empathy with friends which I have tried to describe, and indeed C. S. Lewis himself compares in this respect the effects of love with those of literature.

Friendship, then, contributes to the well-being of society and to the profit, pleasure and life-enhancement of the friends. But this strong justification of friendship need not show that a particular person is mistaken in deciding it is not for him. He might legitimately do this either because he feels that his temperament makes him unlikely to be a satisfactory friend or because he feels called upon to embark on some absorbing project which will leave no time or energy for friendship.

Perhaps I might conclude by pointing out that too much dwelling on the values of friendship has its own dangers. It may lead people to concentrate on looking for *friendships* rather than friends, and to value the other person as a possible term in a relationship rather than as himself. But it may well be that this attitude, which is wrong in itself and hurtful if detected, is also self-defeating: in other words, that we attain the valuable relationship of friendship only when we cease to think about it and concentrate on the friend himself.

Endnotes

1. Aristotle *Nicomachean Ethics* 1156a 10–19, 1156b 6–12.
2. *Op. cit.* 1165b 12–22.
3. This discussion of liking owes much to W. G. Madagan, "Respect for Persons as a Moral Principle," Part 1 *Philosophy* 1960.
4. This discussion of senses of "personal" and "impersonal" is based on that in R. S. Downie, *Roles and Values*, pp. 134–8 (Methuen 1971).
5. For the notion of a reactive attitude see P. F. Strawson, "Freedom and Resentment," *Proceedings of the British Academy* 1962.
6. Aristotle, *op. cit.* 1169b 3–1170b 19.
7. C. S. Lewis, *An Experiment in Criticism*, pp. 137, 139 (Cambridge University Press 1961).

Meeting of the Aristotelian Society at 5/7, Tavistock Place, London W.C.1, on Monday, 24th May 1971, at 7:30 p.m.

Elizabeth Telfer: "Friendship," first published in *Proceedings of the Aristotelian Society for 1970*, copyright © 1970 by the Aristotelian Society. Reprinted by courtesy of the Editor of the Aristotelian Society.

Friendship

Emerson

We have a great deal more kindness than is ever spoken. Maugre all the selfishness that chills like east winds in the world, the whole human family is bathed with an element of love like a fine ether. How many persons we meet in houses, whom we scarcely speak to, whom yet we honor, and who honor us! How many we see in the street, or sit with in church, whom, though silently, we warmly rejoice to be with! Read the language of these wandering eye-beams. The heart knoweth.

The effect of the indulgence of this human affection is a certain cordial exhilaration. In poetry and in common speech the emotions of benevolence and complacency which are felt towards others are likened to the material effects of fire; so swift, or much more swift, more active, more cheering, are these fine inward irradiations. From the highest degree of passionate love to the lowest degree of good-will, they make the sweetness of life.

Our intellectual and active powers increase with our affection. The scholar sits down to write, and all his years of meditation do not furnish him with one good thought or happy expression; but it is necessary to write a letter to a friend,—and forthwith troops of gentle thoughts invest themselves, on every hand, with chosen words. See, in any house where virtue and self-respect abide, the palpitation which the approach of a stranger causes. A commended stranger is expected and announced, and an uneasiness betwixt pleasure and pain invades all the hearts of a household. His arrival almost brings fear to the good hearts that would welcome him. The house is dusted, all things fly into their places, the old coat is exchanged for the new, and they must get up a dinner if they can. Of a commended stranger, only the good report is told by others, only the good and new is heard by us. He stands to us for humanity. He is what we wish. Having imagined and invested him, we ask how we should stand related in conversation and action with such a man, and are uneasy with fear. The same idea exalts conversation with him. We talk better than we are wont. We have the nimblest fancy, a richer memory, and our dumb devil has

Chapter VIII: Friendship and Love

taken leave for the time. For long hours we can continue a series of sincere, graceful, rich communications, drawn from the oldest, secretest experience, so that they who sit by, of our own kinsfolk and acquaintance, shall feel a lively surprise at our unusual powers. But as soon as the stranger begins to intrude his partialities, his definitions, his defects into the conversation, it is all over. He has heard the first, the last and best he will ever hear from us. He is no stranger now. Vulgarity, ignorance, misapprehension are old acquaintances. Now, when he comes, he may get the order, the dress and the dinner,—but the throbbing of the heart and the communications of the soul, no more.

What is so pleasant as these jets of affection which make a young world for me again? What so delicious as a just and firm encounter of two, in a thought, in a feeling? How beautiful, on their approach to this beating heart, the steps and forms of the gifted and the true! The moment we indulge our affections, the earth is metamorphosed; there is no winter and no night; all tragedies, all ennuis vanish,—all duties even; nothing fills the proceeding eternity but the forms all radiant of beloved persons. Let the soul be assured that somewhere in the universe it should rejoin its friend, and it would be content and cheerful alone for a thousand years.

I awoke this morning with devout thanksgiving for my friends, the old and the new. Shall I not call God the Beautiful, who daily showeth himself so to me in his gifts? I chide society, I embrace solitude, and yet I am not so ungrateful as not to see the wise, the lovely and the noble-minded, as from time to time they pass my gate. Who hears me, who understands me, becomes mine,—a possession for all time. Nor is Nature so poor but she gives me this joy several times, and thus we weave social threads of our own, a new web of relations; and, as many thoughts in succession substantiate themselves, we shall by and by stand in a new world of our own creation, and no longer strangers and pilgrims in a traditional globe. My friends have come to me unsought. The great God gave them to me. By oldest right, by the divine affinity of virtue with itself, I find them, or rather not I, but the Deity in me and in them derides and conceals the thick walls of individual character, relation, age, sex, circumstance, at which he usually connives, and now makes many one. High thanks I owe you, excellent lovers, who carry out the world for me to new and noble depths, and enlarge the meaning of all my thoughts. These are new poetry of the first Bard,—poetry without stop,—hymn, ode and epic, poetry still flowing, Apollo and the Muses chanting still. Will these too separate themselves from me again, or some of them? I know not, but I fear it not; for my relation to them is so pure that we hold by simple affinity, and the Genius of my life being thus social, the same affinity will exert its energy on whomsoever is as noble as these men and women, wherever I may be.

I confess to an extreme tenderness of nature on this point. It is almost dangerous to me to "crush the sweet poison of misused wine" of the affections. A new person is to me a great event and hinders me from sleep. I have often had fine fancies about persons which have given me delicious hours; but the joy ends in the day; it yields no fruit. Thought is not born of it; my action is very little modified. I must feel pride in my friend's accomplishments as if they were mine, and a property in his virtues. I feel as warmly when he is praised, as the lover when he hears applause of his engaged maiden. We over-estimate the conscience of our friend. His goodness seems better than our goodness, his nature finer, his temptations less. Every thing that is his,—his name, his form, his dress, books and instruments,—fancy enhances. Our own thought sounds new and larger from his mouth.

Yet the systole and diastole of the heart are not without their analogy in the ebb and flow of love. Friendship, like the immortality of the soul, is too good to be believed. The lover, beholding his maiden, half knows that she is not verily that which he worships; and in the golden hour of friendship we are surprised with shades of suspicion and unbelief. We doubt that we bestow on our hero the virtues in which he shines, and afterwards worship the form to which we have ascribed this divine inhabitation. In strictness, the soul does not respect men as it respects itself. In strict science all persons underlie the same condition of an infinite remoteness. Shall we fear to cool our love by mining for the metaphysical foundation of this Elysian temple? Shall I not be as real as the things I see? If I am, I shall not fear to know them for what they are. Their essence is not less beautiful than their appearance, though it needs finer organs for its apprehension. The root of the plant is not unsightly to science, though for chaplets and festoons we cut the stem short. And I must hazard the production of the bald fact amidst these pleasing reveries, though it should prove an Egyptian skull at our banquet. A man who stands united with his thought conceives magnificently of himself. He is conscious of a universal success, even though bought by uniform particular failures. No advantages, no powers, no gold or force, can be any match for him. I cannot choose but rely on my own poverty more than on your wealth. I cannot make your consciousness tantamount to mine. Only the star dazzles; the planet has a faint, moonlike ray. I hear what you say of the admirable parts and tried temper of the party you praise, but I see well that, for all his purple cloaks, I shall not like him, unless he is at least a poor Greek like me. I cannot deny it, O friend, that the vast shadow of the Phenomenal includes thee also in its pied and painted immensity,—thee also, compared with whom all else is shadow. Thou art not Being, as Truth is, as Justice is,—thou art not my soul, but a picture and effigy of that. Thou hast come to me lately, and already thou art seizing thy hat and cloak. It is not that the soul puts forth friends as the tree puts forth leaves, and presently, by the germination of new buds, extrudes the old leaf? The law of nature is alternation for evermore. Each electrical state superinduces the opposite. The soul environs itself with friends that it may enter into a grander self-acquaintance or solitude; and it goes alone for a season that it may exalt its conversation or society. This method betrays itself along the whole history of our personal relations. The instinct of affection revives the hope of union with our mates, and the returning sense of insulation recalls us from the chase. Thus every man passes his life in the search after friendship, and if he should record his true sentiment, he might write a letter like this to each new candidate for his love:—

> DEAR FRIEND,
> If I was sure of thee, sure of thy capacity, sure to match my mood with thine, I should never think again of trifles in relation to thy comings and goings. I am not very wise; my moods are quite attainable, and I respect thy genius; it is to me as yet unfathomed; yet dare I not presume in thee a perfect intelligence of me, and so thou art to me a delicious torment. Thine ever, or never.

Yet these uneasy pleasures and fine paints are for curiosity and not for life. They are not to be indulged. This is to weave cobweb, and not cloth. Our friendships hurry to short and poor conclusions, because we have made them a texture of wine and dreams, instead of the tough fibre of the human heart. The laws of friendship are austere and eternal, of one web with the laws of nature and of morals. But we have aimed at a swift and petty benefit, to suck a sudden sweetness. We snatch at the slowest fruit in the whole garden of God, which many summers and many winters must ripen. We seek our friend not sacredly, but with an adulterate passion which would appropriate him to ourselves. In vain. We are armed all over with subtle antagonisms, which, as soon as we meet, begin to play, and translate all poetry into stale prose. Almost all people descend to meet. All association must be a compromise, and, what is worst, the very flower and aroma of the flower of each of the beautiful natures disappears as they approach each other. What a perpetual disappointment is actual society, even of the virtuous and gifted! After interviews have been compassed with long foresight we must be tormented presently by baffled blows, by sudden, unreasonable apathies, by epilepsies of wit and of animal spirits, in the heyday of friendship and thought. Our faculties do not play us true, and both parties are relieved by solitude.

I ought to be equal to every relation. It makes no difference how many friends I have and what content I can find in conversing with each, if there be one to whom I am not equal. If I have shrunk unequal from one contest, the joy I find in all the rest becomes mean and cowardly. I should hate myself, if then I made my other friends my asylum:—

> "The valiant warrior famousèd for fight,
> After a hundred victories, once foiled,
> Is from the book of honor razèd quite
> And all the rest forgot for which he toiled."

Our impatience is thus sharply rebuked. Bashfulness and apathy are a tough husk in which a delicate organization is protected from premature ripening. It would be lost if it knew itself before any of the best souls were yet ripe enough to know and own it. Respect the *naturlangsamkeit* which hardens the ruby in a million years, and works in duration in which Alps and Andes come and go as rainbows. The good spirit of our life has no heaven which is the price of rashness. Love, which is the essence of God, is not for levity, but for the total worth of man. Let us not have this childish luxury in our regards, but the austerest worth; let us approach our friend with an audacious trust in the truth of his heart, in the breadth, impossible to be overturned, of his foundations.

The attractions of this subject are not to be resisted, and I leave, for the time, all account of subordinate social benefit, to speak of that select and sacred relation which is a kind of absolute, and which even leaves the language of love suspicious and common, so much is this purer, and nothing is so much divine.

I do not wish to treat friendships daintily, but with roughest courage. When they are real, they are not glass threads or frostwork, but the solidest thing we know. For now, after so many ages of experience, what do we know of nature or of ourselves? Not one step has man taken toward the solution of the problem of his destiny. In one condemnation of folly stand the whole universe of men. But the sweet sincerity of joy and peace which I draw from this alliance with my brother's soul is the nut itself whereof all nature and all thought is but the husk and shell. Happy is the house that shelters a friend! It might well be built, like a festal bower or arch, to entertain him a single day. Happier, if he know the solemnity of that relation and honor its law! He who offers himself a candidate for that covenant comes up, like an Olympian, to the great games where the first-born of the world are the competitors. He proposes himself for contests where Time, Want, Danger, are in the lists, and he alone is victor who has truth enough in his constitution to preserve the delicacy of his beauty from the wear and tear of all these. The gifts of fortune may be present or absent, but all the speed in that contest depends on intrinsic nobleness and the contempt of trifles. There are two elements that go to the composition of friendship, each so sovereign that I can detect no superiority in either, no reason why either should be first named. One is truth. A friend is a person with whom I may be sincere. Before him I may think aloud. I am arrived at last in the presence of a man so real and equal that I may drop even those undermost garments of dissimulation, courtesy, and second thought, which men never put off, and may deal with him with the simplicity and wholeness with which one chemical atom meets another. Sincerity is the luxury allowed, like diadems and authority, only to the highest rank; *that* being permitted to speak truth, as having none above it to court or conform unto. Every man alone is sincere. At the entrance of a second person, hypocrisy begins. We parry and fend the approach of our fellow-man by compliments, by gossip, by amusements, by affairs. We cover up our thought from him under a hundred folds. I knew a man who under a certain religious frenzy cast off this drapery, and omitting all compliment and commonplace, spoke to the conscience of every person he encountered, and that with great insight and beauty. At first he was resisted, and all men agreed he was mad. But persisting—as indeed he could not help doing—for some time in this course, he attained to the advantage of bringing every man of his acquaintance into true relations with him. No man would think of speaking falsely with him, or of putting him off with any chat of markets or reading-rooms. But every man was constrained by so much sincerity to the like plaindealing, and what love of nature, what poetry, what symbol of truth he had, he did certainly show him. But to most of us society shows not its face and eye, but its side and its back. To stand in true relations with men in a false age is worth a fit of insanity, is it not? We can seldom go erect. Almost every man we meet requires some civility—requires to be humored; he has some fame, some talent, some whim of religion or philanthropy in his head that is not to be questioned, and which spoils all conversation with him. But a friend is a sane man who exercises not my ingenuity, but me. My friend gives me entertainment without requiring any stipulation on my part. A friend therefore is a sort of paradox in nature. I who alone am, I who see nothing in nature whose existence I can affirm with equal evidence to my own, behold now the semblance of my being, in all its height, variety and curiosity, reiterated in a foreign form; so that a friend may well be reckoned the masterpiece of nature.

The other element of friendship is tenderness. We are holden to men by every sort of tie, by blood, by pride, by fear, by hope, by lucre, by lust, by hate, by admiration, by every circumstance and badge and trifle,—but we can scarce believe that so much character can subsist in another as to draw us by love. Can another be so blessed and we so pure that we can offer him tenderness? When a man becomes dear to me I have touched the goal of fortune. I find very little written directly to the heart of this matter in books. And yet I have one text which I cannot choose but remember. My author says,—"I offer myself faintly and bluntly to those whose I effectually am, and tender myself least to him to whom I am the most devoted." I wish that friendship should have feet, as well as eyes and eloquence. It must plant itself on the ground, before it vaults over the moon. I wish it to be a little of a citizen, before it is quite a cherub. We chide the citizen because he makes love a commodity. It is an exchange of gifts, of useful loans; it is good neighborhood; it watches with the sick; it holds the pall at the funeral; and quite loses sight of the delicacies and nobility of the relation. But though we cannot find the good under this disguise of a sutler, yet on the other hand we cannot forgive the poet if he spins his thread too fine and does not substantiate his romance by the municipal virtues of justice, punctuality, fidelity and pity. I hate the prostitution of the name of friendship to signify modish and worldly alliances. I much prefer the company of ploughboys and tin-peddlers to the silken and perfumed amity which celebrates its days of encounter by a frivolous display, by rides in a curricle and dinners at the best taverns. The end of friendship is a commerce the most strict and homely that can be joined; more strict than any of which we have experience. It is for aid and comfort through all the relations and passages of life and death. It is fit for serene days and graceful gifts and country rambles, but also for rough roads and hard fare, shipwreck, poverty and persecution. It keeps company with the sallies of the wit and the trances of religion. We are to dignify to each other the daily needs and offices of man's life, and embellish it by courage, wisdom and unity. It should never fall into something usual and settled, but should be alert and inventive and add rhyme and reason to what was drudgery.

Friendship may be said to require natures so rare and costly, each so well tempered and so happily adapted, and withal so circumstanced (for even in that particular, a poet says, love demands that the parties be altogether paired), that its satisfaction can very seldom be assured. It cannot subsist in its perfection, say some of those who are learned in this warm lore of the heart, betwixt more than two. I am not quite so strict in my terms, perhaps because I have never known so high a fellowship as others. I please my imagination more with a circle of god-like men and women variously related to each other and between whom subsists a lofty intelligence. But I find this law of *one to one* peremptory for conversation, which is the practice and consummation of friendship. Do not mix waters too much. The best mix as ill as good and bad. You shall have very useful and cheering discourse at several times with two several men, but let all three of you come together and you shall not have one new and hearty word. Two may talk and one may hear, but three cannot take part in a conversation of the most sincere and searching sort. In good company there is never such discourse between two, across the table, as takes place when you leave them alone. In good company the individuals merge their egotism into a social soul exactly co-extensive with the several consciousnesses there present. No partialities of friend to friend, no fondnesses of brother to sister, of wife to husband, are there pertinent, but quite otherwise. Only he may then speak who can sail on the common thought of the party, and not poorly limited to his own. Now this convention, which good sense demands, destroys the high freedom of great conversation, which requires an absolute running of two souls into one.

No two men but being left alone with each other enter into simpler relations. Yet it is affinity that determines *which* two shall converse. Unrelated men give little joy to each other, will never suspect the latent powers of each. We talk sometimes of a great talent for conversation, as if it were a permanent property in some individuals. Conversation is an evanescent relation,—no more. A man is reputed to have thought and eloquence; he cannot, for all that, say a word to his cousin or his uncle. They accuse his silence with as much reason as they would blame the insignificance of a dial in the shade. In the sun it will mark the hour. Among those who enjoy his thought he will regain his tongue.

Friendship requires that rare mean betwixt likeness and unlikeness that piques each with the presence of power and of consent in the other party. Let me be alone to the end of the world, rather than that my friend should overstep, by a word or a look, his real sympathy. I am equally balked by antagonism and by compliance. Let him not cease an instant to be himself. The only joy I have in his being mine, is that the *not mine* is *mine*. I hate, where I looked for a manly furtherance or at least a manly resistance, to find a mush of concession. Better be a nettle in the side of your friend than his echo. The condition which high friendship demands is ability to do without it. That high office requires great and sublime parts. There must be very two, before there can be very one. Let it be an alliance of two large, formidable natures, mutually beheld, mutually feared, before yet they recognize the deep identity which, beneath these disparities, unites them.

He only is fit for this society who is magnanimous; who is sure that greatness and goodness are always economy; who is not swift to intermeddle with his fortunes. Let him not intermeddle with this. Leave to the diamond its ages to grow, nor expect to accelerate the births of the eternal. Friendship demands a religious treatment. We talk of choosing our friends, but friends are self-elected. Reverence is a great part of it. Treat your friend as a spectacle. Of course he has merits that are not yours, and that you cannot honor if you must needs hold him close to your person. Stand aside; give those merits room; let them mount and expand. Are you the friend of your friend's buttons, or of his thought? To a great heart he will still be a stranger in a thousand particulars, that he may come near in the holiest ground. Leave it to girls and boys to regard a friend as property, and to suck a short and all-confounding pleasure, instead of the noblest benefit.

Let us buy our entrance to this guild by a long probation. Why should we desecrate noble and beautiful souls by intruding on them? Why insist on rash personal relations with your friend? Why go to his house, or know his mother and brother and sisters? Why be visited by him at your own? Are these things material to our covenant? Leave this touching and clawing. Let him be to me a spirit. A message, a thought, a sincerity, a glance from him, I want, but not news, nor pottage. I can get politics and chat and neighborly conveniences from cheaper companions. Should not the society of my friend be to me poetic, pure, universal and great as nature itself? Ought I to feel that our tie is profane in comparison with yonder bar of cloud that sleeps on the horizon, or that clump of waving grass that divides the brook? Let us not vilify, but raise it to that standard. That great defying eye, that scornful beauty of his mien and action, do not pique yourself on reducing, but rather fortify and enhance. Worship his superiorities; wish him not less by a thought, but hoard and tell them all. Guard him as thy counterpart. Let him be to thee for ever a sort of beautiful enemy, untamable, devoutly revered, and not a trivial conveniency to be soon outgrown and cast aside. The hues of the opal, the light of the diamond, are not to be seen if the eye is too near. To my friend I write a letter and from him I receive a letter. That seems to you a little. It suffices me. It is a spiritual gift, worthy of him to give and of me to receive. It profanes nobody. In these warm lines the heart will trust itself, as it will not to the tongue, and pour out the prophecy of a godlier existence than all the annals of heroism have yet made good.

Respect so far the holy laws of this fellowship as not to prejudice its perfect flower by your impatience for its opening. We must be our own before we can be another's. There is at least this satisfaction in crime, according to the Latin proverb;—you can speak to your accomplice on even terms. *Crimen quos inquinat, æquat.* To those whom we admire and love, at first we cannot. Yet the least defect of self-possession vitiates, in my judgment, the entire relation. There can never be deep peace between two spirits, never mutual respect, until in their dialogue each stands for the whole world.

What is so great as friendship, let us carry with what grandeur of spirit we can. Let us be silent,—so we may hear the whisper of the gods. Let us not interfere. Who set you to cast about what you should say to the select souls, or how to say any thing to such? No matter how ingenious, no matter how graceful and bland. There are innumerable degrees of folly and wisdom, and for you to say aught is to be frivolous. Wait, and thy heart shall speak. Wait until the necessary and everlasting overpowers you, until day and night avail themselves of your lips. The only reward of virtue is virtue; the only way to have a friend is to be one. You shall not come nearer a man by getting into his house. If unlike, his soul only flees the faster from you, and you shall never catch a true glance of his eye. We see the noble afar off and they repel us; why should we intrude? Late,—very late,—we perceive that no arrangements, no introductions, no consuetudes or habits of society would be of any avail to establish us in such relations with them as we desire,—but solely the uprise of nature in us to the same degree it is in them; then shall we meet as water with water; and if we should not meet them then, we shall not want them, for we are already they. In the last analysis, love is only the reflection of a man's own worthiness from other men. Men have sometimes exchanged names with their friends, as if they would signify that in their friend each loved his own soul.

The higher the style we demand of friendship, of course the less easy to establish it with flesh and blood. We walk alone in the world. Friends such as we desire are dreams and fables. But a sublime hope cheers ever the faithful heart, that elsewhere, in other regions of the universal power, souls are now acting, enduring and daring, which can love us and which we can love. We may congratulate ourselves that the period of nonage, of follies, of blunders and of shame, is passed in solitude, and when we are finished men we shall grasp heroic hands in heroic hands. Only be admonished by what you already see, not to strike leagues of friendship with cheap persons, where no friendship can be. Our impatience betrays us into rash and foolish alliances which no god attends. By persisting in your path, though you forfeit the little you gain the great. You demonstrate yourself, so as to put yourself out of the reach of false relations, and you draw to you the first-born of the world,—those rare pilgrims whereof only one or two wander in nature at once, and before whom the vulgar great show as spectres and shadows merely.

It is foolish to be afraid of making our ties too spiritual, as if so we could lose any genuine love. Whatever correction of our popular views we make from insight, nature will be sure to bear us out in, and though it seem to rob us of some joy, will repay us with a greater. Let us feel if we will the absolute insulation of man. We are sure that we have all in us. We go to Europe, or we pursue persons, or we read books, in the instinctive faith that these will call it out and reveal us to ourselves. Beggars all. The persons are such as we; the Europe, an old faded garment of dead persons; the books, their ghosts. Let us drop this idolatry. Let us give over this mendicancy. Let us even bid our dearest friends farewell, and defy them, saying 'Who are you? Unhand me: I will be dependent no more.' Ah! seest thou not, O brother, that thus we part only to meet again on a higher platform, and only be more each other's because we are more our own? A friend is Janus-faced; he looks to the past and the future. He is the child of all my foregoing hours, the prophet of those to come, and the harbinger of a greater friend.

I do then with my friends as I do with my books. I would have them where I can find them, but I seldom use them. We must have society on our own terms, and admit or exclude it on the slightest cause. I cannot afford to speak much with my friend. If he is great he makes me so great that I cannot descend to converse. In the great days, presentiments hover before me in the firmament. I ought then to dedicate myself to them. I go in that I may seize them, I go out that I may seize them. I fear only that I may lose them receding into the sky in which now they are only a patch of brighter light. Then, though I prize my friends, I cannot afford to talk with them and study their visions, lest I lose my own. It would indeed give me a certain household joy to quit this lofty seeking, this spiritual astronomy or search of stars, and come down to warm sympathies with you; but then I know well I shall mourn always the vanishing of my mighty gods. It is true, next week I shall have languid moods, when I can well afford to occupy myself with foreign objects; then I shall regret the lost literature of your mind, and wish you were by my side again. But if you come, perhaps you will fill my mind only with new visions; not with yourself but with your lustres, and I shall not be able any more than now to converse with you. So I will owe to my friends this evanescent intercourse. I will receive from them not what they have but what they are. They shall give me that which properly they cannot give, but which emanates from them. But they shall not hold me by any relations less subtile and pure. We will meet as though we met not, and part as though we parted not.

It has seemed to me lately more possible than I knew, to carry a friendship greatly, on one side, without due correspondence on the other. Why should I cumber myself with regrets that the receiver is not capacious? It never troubles the sun that some of his rays fall wide and vain into ungrateful space, and only a small part on the reflecting planet. Let your greatness educate the crude and cold companion. If he is unequal, he will presently pass away; but thou art enlarged by thy own shining, and no longer a mate for frogs and worms, dost soar and burn with the gods of the empyrean. It is thought a disgrace to love unrequited. But the great will see that true love cannot be unrequited. True love transcends the unworthy object and dwells and broods on the eternal, and when the poor interposed mask crumbles, it is not sad, but feels rid of so much earth and feels its independency the surer. Yet these things may hardly be said without a sort of treachery to the relation. The essence of friendship is entireness, a total magnanimity and trust. It must not surmise or provide for infirmity. It treats its object as a god, that it may deify both.

On Grief for Lost Friends

Seneca

I am grieved to hear that your friend Flaccus is dead, but I would not have you sorrow more than is fitting. That you should not mourn at all I shall hardly dare to insist; and yet I know that it is the better way. But what man will ever be so blessed with that ideal steadfastness of soul, unless he has already risen far above the reach of Fortune? Even such a man will be stung by an event like this, but it will be only a sting. We, however, may be forgiven for bursting into tears, if only our tears have not flowed to excess, and if we have checked them by our own efforts. Let not the eyes be dry when we have lost a friend, nor let them overflow. We may weep, but we must not wail.

Do you think that the law which I lay down for you is harsh, when the greatest of Greek poets has extended the privilege of weeping to one day only, in the lines where he tells us that even Niobe took thought of food?[1] Do you wish to know the reason for lamentations and excessive weeping? It is because we seek the proofs of our bereavement in our tears, and do not give way to sorrow, but merely parade it. No man goes into mourning for his own sake. Shame on our ill-timed folly! There is an element of self-seeking even in our sorrow.

"What," you say, "am I to forget my friend?" It is surely a short-lived memory that you vouchsafe to him, if it is to endure only as long as your grief; presently that brow of yours will be smoothed out in laughter by some circumstance, however casual. It is to a time no more distant than this that I put off the soothing of every regret, the quieting of even the bitterest grief. As soon as you cease to observe yourself, the picture of sorrow which you have contemplated will fade away; at present you are keeping watch over your own suffering. But even while you keep watch it slips away from you, and the sharper it is, the more speedily it comes to an end.

Let us see to it that the recollection of those whom we have lost becomes a pleasant memory to us. No man reverts with pleasure to any subject which he will not be able to reflect upon without pain. So too it cannot but be that the names of those whom we have loved and lost come back to us with a sort of sting; but there is a pleasure even in this sting. For, as my friend Attalus[2] used to say: "The remembrance of lost friends is pleasant in the same way that certain fruits have an agreeably acid taste, or as in extremely old wines it is their very bitterness that pleases us. Indeed, after a certain lapse of time, every thought that gave pain is quenched, and the pleasure comes to us unalloyed." If we take the word of Attalus for it, "to think of friends who are alive and well is like enjoying a meal of cakes and honey; the recollection of friends who have passed away gives a pleasure that is not without a touch of bitterness. Yet who will deny that even these things, which are bitter and contain an element of sourness, do serve to arouse the stomach?" For my part, I do not agree with him. To me, the thought of my dead friends is sweet and appealing. For I have had them as if I should one day lose them; I have lost them as if I have them still.

Therefore, Lucilius, act as befits your own serenity of mind, and cease to put a wrong interpretation on the gifts of Fortune. Fortune has taken away, but Fortune has given. Let us greedily enjoy our friends, because we do not know how long this privilege will be ours. Let us think how often we shall leave them when we go upon distant journeys, and how often we shall fail to see them when we tarry together in the same place; we shall thus understand that we have lost too much of their time while they were alive. But will you tolerate men who are most careless of their friends, and then mourn them most abjectly, and do not love anyone unless they have lost him? The reason why they lament too unrestrainedly at such times is that they are afraid lest men doubt whether they really have loved; all too late they seek for proofs of their emotions. If we have other friends, we surely deserve ill at their hands and think ill of them, if they are of so little account that they fail to console us for the loss of one. If, on the other hand, we have no other friends, we have injured ourselves more than Fortune has injured us; since Fortune has robbed us of one friend, but we have robbed ourselves of every friend whom we have failed to make. Again, he who has been unable to love more than one, has had none too much love even for that one.[3] If a man who has lost his one and only tunic through robbery chooses to bewail his plight rather than look about him for some way to escape the cold, or for something with which to cover his shoulders, would you not think him an utter fool?

You have buried one whom you loved; look about for someone to love. It is better to replace your friend than to weep for him. What I am about to add is, I know, a very hackneyed remark, but I shall not omit it simply because it is a common phrase: A man ends his grief by the mere passing of time, even if he has not ended it of his own accord. But the most shameful cure for sorrow, in the case of a sensible man, is to grow weary of sorrowing. I should prefer you to abandon grief, rather than have grief abandon you; and you should stop grieving as soon as possible, since, even if you wish to do so, it is impossible to keep it up for a long time. Our forefathers[4] have enacted that, in the case of women, a year should be the limit for mourning; not that they needed to mourn for so long, but that they should mourn no longer. In the case of men, no rules are laid down, because to mourn at all is not regarded as honourable. For all that, what woman can you show me, of all the pathetic females that could scarcely be dragged away from the funeral-pile or torn from the corpse, whose tears have lasted a whole month? Nothing becomes offensive so quickly as grief; when fresh, it finds someone to console it and attracts one or another to itself; but after becoming chronic, it is ridiculed, and rightly. For it is either assumed or foolish.

He who writes these words to you is no other than I, who wept so excessively for my dear friend Annaeus Serenus[5] that, in spite of my wishes, I must be included among the examples of men who have been overcome by grief. To-day, however, I condemn this act of mine, and I understand that the reason why I lamented so greatly was chiefly that I had never imagined it possible for his death to precede mine. The only thought which occurred to my mind was that he was the younger, and much younger, too,—as if the Fates kept to the order of our ages!

Therefore let us continually think as much about our own mortality as about that of all those we love. In former days I ought to have said: "My friend Serenus is younger than I; but what does that matter? He would naturally die after me, but he may precede me." It was just because I did not do this that I was unprepared when Fortune dealt me the sudden blow. Now is the time for you to reflect, not only that all things are mortal, but also that their mortality is subject to no fixed law. Whatever can happen at any time can happen to-day. Let us therefore reflect, my beloved Lucilius, that we shall soon come to the goal which this friend, to our own sorrow, has reached. And perhaps, if only the tale told by wise men is true[6] and there is a bourne to welcome us, then he whom we think we have lost has only been sent on ahead. Farewell.

Excerpts from Seneca: *Epistulae Morales*, translated by R. M. Gummere, copyright © 1917 by Harvard University Press. Reprinted by permission of the Loeb Classical Library.

Endnotes

1. Homer, *Iliad*, xix. 229 and xxiv. 602.
2. The teacher of Seneca, often mentioned by him.

3. The reason is, as Lipsius observed, that friendship is essentially a social virtue, and is not confined to one object. The pretended friendship for one and only one is a form of self-love, and is not unselfish love.
4. According to tradition, from the time of Numa Pompilius.
5. An intimate friend of Seneca, probably a relative, who died in the year 63 from eating poisoned mushrooms (Pliny, *N. H.* xxii. 96). Seneca dedicated to Serenus several of his philosophical essays.
6. *Cf.* the closing chapter of the *Agricola* of Tacitus: *si, ut sapientibus placet, non cum corpore exstinguuntur magnae animae*, etc.

The Conditions of Female Friendship

Janice Raymond

Thoughtfulness

Thinking is a necessary condition of female friendship. The thinking I advocate is better described by the word *thoughtfulness*. In my use of it, *thoughtfulness* is characterized on the one hand by ability to reason and on the other by considerateness and caring. It is this kind of thoughtfulness that is necessary for Gyn/affection.

The commonly accepted definition of *thoughtfulness* is concern for others, attentiveness to others' needs, and considerateness for others. However, the word in its primary sense means literally "full of thought." Other meanings are "absorbed in thought," "meditative," or "characterized by careful reasoned thinking." Thus the word thoughtfulness contains a dual meaning and poses another tension. I contend that these two meanings must come together and be expressed in Gyn/affection.

Thoughtfulness has contributed much to the divisions and dissensions among women. . . .

Many women have expressed disappointment and frustration at the lack of thoughtfulness that pervades many women's groups and that women seem to accept as a matter of course in feminist relationships and gatherings.

On the other hand, many women have been socialized to react almost instinctively to other people's needs, mostly those of men and children. Women have been drained by a kind of thoughtfulness that is really lacking in thought to the extent that it is indiscriminately given, without thinking about the conditions under which it is extended and the fact that it is left to women in any context to be thoughtful. Here the thinking is missing from thoughtfulness so that women give and give, extend themselves constantly, and deal and deal with the needs of others in what has at times almost amounted to a feminine compulsion. The thoughtfulness that most women are trained to extend in a hetero-relational context is not born out of Self-directed thinking. Many women "go into robot" performing "emotional labor" to fulfill all sorts of others' needs. For women, the cost of this kind of thoughtfulness has been the obliteration of thinking.

A vision of female friendship restores the thinking to thoughtfulness. At the same time, it restores a thoughtfulness to thinking, that is a respect and considerateness for another's needs. Only thoughtfulness, in its more expanded meaning, can sustain female friendship and give it daily life. A thinking friendship must become a thoughtful friendship in the full sense of the word *thoughtfulness*. Many women may be brilliant thinkers, but that thinking has to be accompanied by a genuine attentiveness and respect for other women if female friendship is to flourish. On the other hand, many women may be caring and considerate of others, but if this thoughtfulness lacks a Self-directed thinking that "prepares us ever anew to meet whatever we must meet in our daily lives," it reinforces socialized femininity rather than female friendship. The word *thoughtfulness* conveys the meaning of a thinking considerateness and a considerate thinking. It is not accidental that it has such a dual meaning. A woman who truly thinks is, more expansively, full of thought in many realms. . . .

"*Intercourse with oneself*" is crucial to both the idea of thinking and that of friendship, for it is where both come together. Thinking is where I keep myself company, where I find my original friend, if you will. It is the solitude, as opposed to loneliness, where I am alone with, but not lonely in, the companionship of myself. Thinking is where I am at home with myself when, for all sorts of reasons, I withdraw from the world. "The partner who comes to life when you are alert and alone is the only one from whom you can never get away—except by ceasing to think." This is one of the major reasons why women have lost their Selves—because they have stopped thinking. By not thinking, an individual loses her original friendship with her Self. Through thinking, a person discovers that she can be her real Self. In discovering this, she also realizes that the conversation that took place in the duality of thinking activity—that is, the duality of "myself with myself," the "two-in-one," or "the one who asks and the one who answers"—enables conversation with others. When I discover, through thinking, that I can converse with my real Self, I have to realize that such a conversation is possible with others. This is the awakening of female friendship in which the search for others like my Self begins. . . .

A woman must be at the same time a friend to her original Self and to others. Which comes first is hard to determine. What is clear is that thinking and friendship go hand in hand. . . .

Chapter VIII: Friendship and Love

Passion

As female friendship is characterized by thoughtfulness, it is also marked by passion. Friendship is a passion but, in my vision, it is a thoughtful passion. It manifests a thinking heart.

The tension between thinking and feeling, as signified in the phrase "thoughtful passion," is evident in the etymology of the word *passion*. *Passion* derives from Old French and Latin roots meaning "suffering, pain or some disorder of body or spirit." It also means being "affected by external agency." However, etymologies are often multidimensional, and so we find another meaning of *passion* defined as "any kind of feeling by which the mind is powerfully affected or moved . . . an eager outreaching of the mind toward something" (*Oxford English Dictionary*).

A passionate friendship upholds the integrity between thought and passion. In passionate friendship, there is no separation between the two. It is not so much that they merge, but that they have not been fractured to begin with. . . .

A thoughtfully passionate friendship is passion at its most active. It keeps passion active and does not allow it to degenerate into its more passive modes. More concretely, it helps two women to become their own person. There is a dynamic integrity of existence in a thoughtful passion that is missing in more sentimental friendship. Friendship that is characterized by thoughtful passion ensures that a friend does not lose her Self in the heightened awareness of and attachment to another woman.

The loss of Self has happened most frequently in lover relationships. And, in fact, passion is generally associated with lovers, not with friends, or not with friends who aren't lovers. There has been much discussion of passion within the lover relationship, but not much talk of friendship within love. It is my opinion that when a lover finds that she is losing her Self in the heightened awareness of and attachment to another woman in a sexually passionate relationship, the friendship is problematic. Either the friendship wasn't strong initially or it got swallowed up in the sexual passion of the lover relationship. Thus passion deteriorates into its more passive mode, engulfing a necessary friendship and eclipsing its ability to generate a needed thoughtfulness about the friendship that is required for passion to survive and thrive.

In any kind of lover relationship that is committed, one's lover should be one's best friend. And if one's best friend is one's lover, she should also be the primary passion of her lover's life. A truly passionate love life, above all, must be pervaded by a thoughtful passion. . . .

When a woman lives as a woman, among women, among men, she at the same time questions the man-made world but does not dissociate from it, assimilate to it, or allow it to define her as a victim in it. She demands her place in it as a woman whose affinities are with women. She takes on the existence of what Mary Daly might refer to as "defiant deviant." Hannah Arendt might have named her a "conscious pariah," and Virginia Woolf would have probably welcomed her into the "Society of Outsiders." I prefer the term *inside outsider* because it helps to make clear the dual tension of women who see the man-made world for what it is and exist in it with worldly integrity, while at the same time seeing beyond it to something different. The term also highlights the reality of women who know that they can never really be insiders yet who recognize the liabilities of the dissociated outsider.

The inside outsider lives in the world with worldly integrity, weaving the strands of feminist wisdom into the texture of the world and paving the way for the entrance of women as women, that is, women on our own terms, into the world. As an inside outsider, a woman's work is characterized by the dual tension between her feminism and her worldliness. Her worldliness is dependent on her feminist vision, yet her feminist vision is actualized in her worldly location. . . .

The practical question, however, is How and where do women participate in the world? The worldliness I am advocating is not necessarily that of joining the antinuclear movement, the state legislature, or any other such worldly activities on their own terms. The terms of such endeavors are rarely woman-defined or woman-oriented. If participation in such worldly activities, or in others, is to be engaged in with worldly integrity, this participation must be on our terms, not in an absolute sense but in a way that enables woman-identified women to work within these worlds with integrity and with the ability to effect change—in other words, to work as inside outsiders.

If integrity means "that from which nothing can be taken," women must learn a few lessons from the feminist political past. Historically, women have been the mainstays of the abolitionist movements, peace movements, and other movements for human rights and social justice worldwide. In all of these movements, the feminist question was rarely highlighted. As a result, women did not participate in such movements on our own terms, and a worldly integrity was lacking. There are, of course, exceptions to this, but I am speaking in general.

On a more particular level, it might be helpful to give some concrete examples of how a woman functions as an inside outsider. Or, in other words, how does a woman live and act with worldly integrity? There are individual women and women's groups explicitly dedicated to women's causes. They may work in organizations specifically devoted to battered women, to the feminist campaign against pornography, or in various service organizations that meet women's needs. Or, as individuals, they may defend women in court, institute legislation against rape or for equal pay, or dismantle discriminatory and oppressive structures in which many women live their domestic and work lives. They may edit feminist journals, provide women-centered health care, and/or teach Women's Studies. All these types of feminist work have made a profound impact on the man-made world, changing, for example, the face of patriarchal legislation, health care, and learning, as well as creating more woman-centered and institutional structures. . . .

In the final analysis, worldliness is a materializing of dual vision, of two sights seeing. Liberation, if it requires "seeing with more than ordinary sight," also requires "seeing with ordinary sight." As vision radically upheaves the existent man-made world, it must at some point give rise to coherent groups, lasting structures, and patterns of worldly activity. As vision disturbs, it must also stabilize. The structures of women living in the world must also be built.

> It is a fact of social/political movements that radicalism does not sustain a movement. For a movement to endure, its broad base and widespread influence must be assured. But radicalism is *essential* for the life of a movement, as it will bring to it the most uncompromising critique of the abusive, exploitative power that the movement seeks to undermine and overcome. It is the presence of radical critique which assures us that the movement will not devolve to simple reform—that is, patchwork on an exploitative, corrupt, and ruthless power structure.

Women must use this radicalism to re-fashion women's existence in the real world. However, without structure and stability, radicalism will be frantic, bursting with energy, but short-lived. In this process, we must keep the tension between movement and stasis. Feminist far-sighted vision is meaningless unless it is accompanied by near-sighted realism which gives it shape and staying power. It is also meaningless unless such dual vision can translate into happiness—a happiness in this world.

Happiness

There has not been much talk or writing about happiness in the women's movement. If is almost as if feminists expected that happiness could come about only in some future life, after the struggle is won and the revolution over. Malraux once noted that in the twentieth century, the so-called intellectuals found in revolution what many others formerly sought in eternal life; that is, the revolution "saves those that make it."

Many women have defined feminism only in political terms, accentuating struggle against male tyranny. They have failed to see that just as feminism is a politics of risk and resistance, it must hold out to women some promise of happiness now. Organized sisterhood against the conditions of female oppression and the feminist fight against all states of atrocities against women serve as a powerful bulwark against the forces and structures of patriarchy. However, a purely political feminism, emphasizing only conflict and resistance, bears too strong a resemblance to religious eschatologies (theologies of the future) that would have women believe that the true happiness is achievable only in some life to come.

What is happiness? We use the term today more in a psychological sense, that is, as a disposition, feeling, or state of being that a person experiences. Originally, however, the term had an ethical meaning. In its earliest philosophical usage, happiness was connected with moral purpose, with teleology. Happiness was found in the fulfillment of some activity, end, or goal of life. Aristotle reminds us that happiness is an activity of the mind, of contemplation. Combining these meanings, happiness has also been defined as the feeling that accompanies the activity of the whole self, or the feeling of self-realization. Along with this, happiness means the harmonious life itself.

My own definition of happiness is an amalgam and rephrasing of these meanings. On the one hand happiness, as I am describing it, is striving for the full use of one's powers. It is attained in fulfilling certain ends or purposes. On the other hand, one must experience happiness. Therefore, it is a state of existence which I think can best be summarized in Nadezhda Mandelstam's translation of the Russian word *zhizneradostny* as "life-glad." Literally, she means to be glad in/about/with life. To be "life-glad" adds a certain depth and substance to the word *happiness*. In short, then, happiness is striving for the full use of one's powers that make one "life-glad."

I do not mean to speak about happiness as if it is an all-or-nothing existence. For example, a woman can be happy in her work but unhappy at home. Happiness implies, however, that one is constantly seeking for the integrity of the Self and that it is a process. It is, as I said, a striving. But the more that endeavor is transformed into existence, the more one is "life-glad." It should not be, as Charlotte Brontë noted, a task. "No mockery in this world ever sounds to me so hollow as that of being told to cultivate happiness. What does such advice mean? Happiness is not a potato, to be planted in mould, and tilled with manure."

Female friendship gives women the context in which to be "life-glad." It creates a private and public sphere where happiness can become a reality. It provides encouragement and environment for the full use of one's powers. And since the profession of friendship means that the one who befriends has a greater interest in her friend's happiness than in that of others in general, female friendship strives for the full use of the friend's powers.

Men and Friendship

Stuart Miller

In the face of such social forces as rationalism, professionalism, economic and physical mobility, and individualism—all tending to destroy intimacy—modern people have attempted to substitute for the old tight fabric of relationships one relationship alone. Over the last two centuries, romantic love has come to be as seen as something to which everybody, not just the rich person, is entitled. Moreover, romantic love, as the social historian Carl Degler has traced its evolution, has come to be seen as something one combines with marriage.

Most people's imaginations have come to be dominated by the idea of a lifelong, exciting intimacy with one person of the opposite sex. That this expectation is not universally realized does not stop people from trying. Despite the high divorce rate, a far greater percentage of the American population marries now than ever before.

In a world that tends to denature the emotional being, the modern man or woman clings to a spouse. It is not surprising, then, that most Americans will tell you their spouses are their best friends, although many more men will so declare than women. As a result, fear and guilt are attached to relationships outside marriage. When a man, for example, wants to go out at night with the boys, he doesn't just go; he tells them that first he must ask his wife whether their social schedule will allow it. There is no implied free social time for him other than that negotiated and granted by his wife.

A similar compact binds the woman, of course, although the women's movement has given women more liberty for outside relationships with their own sex than men now have. In essence, the man has become totally emotionally dependent on his wife. And because of changes in women's legal status and their increasing opportunities for professional work, a husband fears making a mistake. A wife can now afford to walk out on him, after all, and even take the children.

Increasingly, vital masculine energy that might be used to bond with another man is drained away. He may want the particularly adventurous flavor of male companionship, even deep friendship, but he is cautious about asking for it. The problem then arises that, as rich as his relationship with his wife may be, he eventually suffers from claustrophobia, from a sense of being suffocated in the arms of the Great Mother, an archetype he gradually projects on his spouse as his relationships with men become less vital.

Many women are aware of this pattern and occasionally encourage their husbands to seek male friends. But the social forces we have discussed stand in his way. The result, ironically, is that the wife finds her husband less interesting and adventurous than she wants and the husband experiences himself as a male failure, not sufficiently strong or adept enough even to implement his wife's simple, good advice. We are back, then, to the Great Mother and the kind of resentments that turn marital relationships sour.

All this tends directly to undermine the sexual life of the couple. Sexual attraction and excitation depend in part on perceived differences between partners, which are then bridged by the spark of sexual expression. When the sense of male and female difference becomes too diluted, as in many rather close and boring marriages, people get less sexy. The sexologist C. A. Tripp notes that "many women intuitively understand this refueling operation, and although they may miss their men who 'are off with the boys,' they use the time themselves to recuperate, correctly sensing that they are ultimate benefactors of men's diversion from them. Their hunch is right, as is the hunch of other women who feel a pensive disquietude with men who have no close male ties." In sum, if men had deep relationships with other men, their married sex lives would be better.

※ ※ ※

Part of the reason contemporary men attempt to put all their emotional and personal needs into the nest of romantic marriage comes from their deep feelings of hurt, shame, and guilt attendant upon the transitoriness and the failure of their earlier close male friendships. Because of all the historical forces we have noted, impermanence is typical of male friendships, as of all other relationships in our time. Some recent scholars of friendship, like the American psychologists John Reisman and Joel Block, urge us to accept such changes as a simple fact of modern life. They profess to be puzzled that the ancient ideal of "lifelong loyalty" in friendship be so much admired by people when, in fact, most friendships do not last a lifetime. They urge that people become more realistic, acknowledge that different friends serve different needs at different periods of life, and that this procession of more or less temporary relationships is a normal part of personal growth.

Valuing personal growth more than consistency in human relations is, of course, a strikingly modern stance. As an idea, it arises from the whole trend toward individualism and self-expression that marks the modern person, particularly the American. Unfortunately, the ideology of growth further helps to corrode human relationships; by putting individual growth over mutual association it helps to destroy the very idea of serious male friendship. . . .

Our modern mobility, which separates men from one another in the most cruel ways, combines with our individualistic ideology of personal growth to litter our past with dead friendships. We rush to fill a puzzling emptiness with the love of women and with notions of our growth into rational adults.

All men know that these tactics don't entirely work. This changing and tearing up, particularly of masculine relationships, that were supposed to have an enduring strength about them, are corrosive to men's souls. So we come to doubt others and to hate ourselves. We come to doubt life itself. We can try to be "mature." . . . Or we can try to be the way many psychologists say we should be, telling ourselves that life is simply that way and that friends serve different functions at different times. So many tools for our living. But that is not at all, not at all what we had in mind for our male friendships. . . .

I declare that true male friendship, the kind that very, very few adult men in America and Europe have with one another, requires intimacy, complicity, engagement, and commitment. It is a relationship profoundly personal.

Intimacy, being at ease, being understood and understanding, one can find more frequently in modern life than friendship, now that a growing informality of manners and an acceptance of a certain emotional expressiveness have definitely signaled our difference from the more repressive aspects of nineteenth-century social life. Indeed, a dozen modern interests contribute toward moments of intimacy—from psychology, psychotherapy, and encounter groups through nostalgia for the proletarian and the natural or rural, through the cultivated casualness of the modern workplace, to experimentation with drugs and involvement in political and religious movements. The same tendencies promote the increasing occurrence of moments, however fleeting, of complicity, a feeling of secret understanding and even of revolt or secession from society and from wearing our normal social personae.

Friendship between men may be on its way back. Indeed, from younger men one sometimes gets the impression that they are determined to maintain male friendship in their lives. The recent proliferation of popular books on the subject of friendship in general, despite their oversimplifications and lack of feeling, give further evidence that a renewal of male friendship may be preparing itself somewhere in the collective unconscious.

Intimacy and complicity, however, do not by themselves make friendship. Even familiarity—cosiness and trust and occasional supportiveness—

can be mistaken for friendship. True friendship must also be true engagement with the friend—a very frequent mutual holding in the mind and heart. Though the centrifugal pressures of modern life limit the frequency of the physical presence of friends, engagement makes physical proximity less of a problem. Male friendship can thus be thought of as a place in a man's inner being, a space in his life, that is daily occupied by another man, a place that is regularly charged with love, concern, thoughtfulness—and, sometimes, resentment, anger, even deep hurt. *Engagement* means emotional involvement.

True friendship implies commitment, the understanding that a friend will be there, will not let go, that a friend will maintain the engagement in the face of obstacles, misunderstandings, and temptations, that a friend is prepared to undertake inconveniences, even sacrifices.

A true male friendship is personal. The relationship is its own context. Friendship may arise from another relationship—work, for example—but it is not dependent upon it. Male friendship is just one man and another. That so many friendships break up or attenuate into nothing when commonplace, interest, or work are no longer shared means that men have not had the essential friendship.

If a man changes religion or political belief, that does not change an essential friendship. The friends have been truly involved with each other, not just with parties, organizations, or even, extreme as it may seem, with mutual ideas or interests. All these other elements have their own value and importance, but from the point of view of male friendship, they are merely the furnishings, at most a supporting context, tools for the friendship.

A man's high-voltage engagement with another man, each of whom has a daily place in the other's inner being—from such inwardness, all necessary, dignified, and pleasant actions can grow. That's male friendship.

And, yes, it is rare.

I say to others, "If you can stand the quest for a true male friend, it is worthwhile." Each man will find his own way, but I have some brief advice.

In our times, we must first truly accept the necessity for an art of male friendship. Though Willie Morris makes his point about friendship being a grace that one receives, it is not generally sufficient to await the coming of such a gift. Why even those who most strictly speaking seek grace are always busy trying to get what they know can only be given by God. As talented artists who are busy working away at practice and execution, so must friends be diligent. Without deliberately focusing on my need for male friendship, I would have continued to miss Larry—both who he is and his availability for friendship. I have met many people who claim that friendship must be "wholly natural," that it must "just happen to you," and

Chapter VIII: Friendship and Love

that "it can't be meditated or forced—that's too cold-blooded!" Believe me, there is nothing cold-blooded in thinking about love, about those we love, and in giving and seeking love.

This is especially true in our own cool and changing world. While a whole gamut of human relationships were "natural" in some older societies, they are no longer so in modern urban life. No type of human relationship is a given anymore, is seemingly "natural." Morris and others who plead for simple naturalness in relationships are not new voices. But just as couples these days must work at—indeed, continually reinvent—marriage and child-rearing, men must, if they are to have it, work at male friendship.

What makes a deliberate approach to friendship so necessary now is that everything in our culture is against it. Paradoxically, to keep up one's attention and effort, one must remain continually conscious of the formidable obstacles to committed, intimate, engaged, and personal relations. Ferruccio discussed some of the opposing forces: the calls of work and family life, the squeeze of time, the cynicism that comes with aging. There are, as we saw earlier, many others. The list is endless and every person should add to it. It is good to look your enemy in the eye.

Bold acts of consciousness are, I think, the true basis for an art of friendship these days. No gimmicks will work. The arts of friendship we need are inner acts, acts of the depth of the heart, of self-searching, and of decision.

Inwardly accepting the necessity to give friendship one's closest attention and recalling the social obstacles to friendship are the two basic inner acts.

Others are:

Being willing to acknowledge the hurt of your own loneliness. We live in a lonely time when no one is alone. Our mobile conditions give most of us an enormous but shifting and, therefore, superficial acquaintance. Let the reality of your loneliness be a spur to your own authentic quest.

Being shameless in thinking, then talking, about male friendship because it is important. Make room for friendship in your life. Make a federal case out of it.

Being willing to be hurt, repeatedly, by people you befriend.

Being persistent. People will back away from you, frightened because they have been hypnotized by society into believing they haven't the time, the energy, the interest, to be friends. They are simply not used to friendship anymore. Bizarre as it may seem, deep friendship strikes them as bizarre. Keep coming.

Committing time to friendship: time for writing letters, for thinking about friends, for telephoning friends, for disappointments, for generous acts.

Acting forthrightly with your friend and with the courage of your own delicate needs and desires by living the openness, generosity, and commitment you want from him. You thus help create an example, a magnetic field, in which (with luck) a man may respond. Friendship may arise.

A cunning hint: be willing to ask your friend for favors, to take, to sacrifice a part of your independence.

One hope: the art gets easier. Gradually, you give up the shame and embarrassment while still retaining an essential vulnerability.

After all such art, pray for grace.

※ ※ ※

Personal initiatives, however, will not be wholly sufficient. The fact that male friendship is as dead as it is requires collective action. So often in the personal quest for friendship, thinking a lack of a true male friend is a problem to solve alone, a man finds himself feeling crazy. Jung puts it well:

> A collective problem, if not recognized as such, always appears as a personal problem, and in individual cases may give the impression that something is out of order in the realm of the personal psyche. The personal sphere is indeed disturbed, but such disturbances need not be primary; they may well be secondary; the consequences of an insupportable change in the social atmosphere.

The current social atmosphere renders true friendship between men very difficult. When you decide to take male friendship seriously, to make it a real presence in your own life, then you and I both have a better chance of succeeding at our friendships. Our behavior seems, again, more natural, and we take courage from one another.

Let courage then be the word to close upon. A Frenchman, about sixty years old, gray-haired, wiry, and distinguished, one who had ridden his cavalry mount to the front to face the Nazi tanks invading France only to be compelled to retreat in shame, tried to put the whole matter of friendship in brief perspective: "Of course friendship is dead now. There was a time, and I remember my father talking about it, when men had other images in their minds about how to behave. Men were supposed to be steady, to adhere to heroic codes, to keep their word, and to be willing to sacrifice. One learned it by example in many families. My father taught me that one should behave in life with 'honor and elegance.' That was almost all the advice he had to give me. But such talk seems absurd now, doesn't it, because we have become a people of sellers and buyers. Our attitudes toward human relationships are those of supermarket shoppers: we want what is cheap and quick and easy; we want variety; and we want novelty. But friendship requires a whole other set of mind, doesn't it? Commitment, courage. . ."

Recently, as I have become convinced that Larry Alexander is really available for friendship with me, that he is capable of or, at least, that he may be willing to commit himself to our friendship, I have felt a paradoxi-

Chapter VIII: Friendship and Love

cal emotion. I have been seeking a true male friend for so long and, at last, here is a possibility. Yet something in me draws away from Larry.

Puzzled, I attend to this feeling. To my dishonor, I hear within me a seductive whispering, a little inner beast posing the questions that dissolve all manliness: "Are you sure you want to get this involved? Do you think you can afford to take on another person? What if he makes demands of you: he gets sick, he loses his money?"

This reflexive cringing from all true engagement is a curious emotion. Probably it is part of human nature, the instinct of self-preservation asserting itself, a deep suspicion of involvement with others, of involvement with anyone outside myself. A reaction known even to our most ancient poets.

To meet such fears, only courage will do.

> Oh Gods! Let me have the strength and the courage to love my friends!
> —PINDAR'S PRAYER

What Love Is

Robert C. Solomon

The question, What is love? is neither a request for a confession nor an excuse to start moralizing. It is not an invitation to amuse us with some *bon mot* ("Love is the key that opens up the doors of happiness") or to impress us with an author's sensitivity. And love is much more than a "feeling." When a novelist wants us to appreciate his character's emotions, he does not just describe sweaty palms and a moment of panic; he instead describes *a world*, the world as it is experienced—in anger, or in envy, or in love. Theorizing about emotion, too, is like describing an exotic world. It is a kind of conceptual anthropology—identifying a peculiar list of characters—heroes, villains, knaves or lovers—understanding a special set of rules and roles—rituals, fantasies, myths, slogans and fears. But these are not merely empirical observations on the fate of a feeling; none of this will make any sense to anyone who has not [had the emotion.] Love can be understood only "from the inside," as a language can be understood only by someone who speaks it, as a world can be known only by someone who has—even if vicariously—*lived* in it.

To analyze an emotion by looking at the world it defines allows us to cut through the inarticulateness of mere "feelings" and do away once and for all with the idea that emotions in general and love in particular are "ineffable" or beyond description. This might make some sense if describing an emotion were describing something "inside of us." It is not easy, for example, to describe how one feels when nauseous; even describing something so specific as a migraine headache falls back on clumsy metaphors ("as if my head's in a vise," "as if someone were driving a nail through my skull"). But once we see that every emotion defines a world for itself, we can then describe in some detail what that world involves, with its many variations, describe its dimensions and its dynamics. The world defined by love—or what we shall call the *loveworld*—is a world woven around a single relationship with all else pushed to the periphery. To understand love is to understand the specifics of this relationship and the world woven around it.

Chapter VIII: Friendship and Love

Love has been so misunderstood both because so often it has been taken to be *other*-worldly rather than one world of emotion among others, and because it has sometimes been taken to be a "mere emotion"—just a feeling and not a world at all. Because of this, perhaps it would be best to illustrate the theory that every emotion is a world by beginning with a less problematic emotion, namely, *anger*. Anger too defines its world. It is a world in which one defines oneself in the role of "the offended" and defines someone else (or perhaps a group or an institution) as "the offender." The world of anger is very much a courtroom world, a world filled with blame and emotional litigation. It is a world in which everyone else tends to become a co-defendant, a friend of the court, a witness or at least part of the courtroom audience. (But when you're *very* angry, there are no innocent bystanders.) Writes Lewis Carroll in *Alice in Wonderland*: "'I'll be judge, I'll be jury,' said cunning old Fury." It is a world in which one does indeed define oneself as judge and jury, compete with a grim righteousness, with "justice"—one's own vengeance—as the only legitimate concern. It is a *magical* world, which can change a lackadaisical unfocused morning into a piercing, all-consuming day, an orgy of vindictive self-righteousness and excitement. At the slightest provocation it can change an awkward and defensive situation into an aggressive confrontation. To describe the world of anger is therefore to describe its fantasies, for example, the urge to kill, though rarely is this taken seriously or to its logical conclusion. It has its illusions too, for instance, the tendency to exaggerate the importance of some petty grievance to the level of cosmic injustice; in anger we sometimes talk as if "man's inhumanity to man" is perfectly manifested in some minor sleight at the office yesterday. It is a world with a certain fragility; a single laugh can explode the whole pretense of angry self-righteousness. And it is a world with a purpose—for when do we feel more self-righteous than in anger? Getting angry in an otherwise awkward situation may be a way of saving face or providing a quick ego boost; "having a bad temper" may be not so much a "character trait" as an emotional strategy, a way of *using* emotion as a means of controlling other people. To describe anger, in other words, is to describe the way the world is structured—and why—by a person who is angry.

The world of love—the loveworld—can be similarly described as a theatrical scenario, not as a courtroom but rather as "courtly," a romantic drama defined by its sense of elegance (badly interpreted as "spiritual"), in which we also take up a certain role—"the lover"—and cast another person into a complementary role—"the beloved." But where anger casts two antagonistic characters, romantic love sets up an idea of unity, absolute complementary and total mutual support and affection. It is the *rest* of the world that may be the antagonist. [The Russian novelist] Boris Pasternak describes the loveworld beautifully—the world as Adam and Eve, naked, surrounded by chaos.

It is a world we know well, of course—the world of *Casablanca*, *Romeo and Juliet* and a thousand stories and novels. It is a world in which we narrow our vision and our cares to that single duality, all else becoming trifles, obstacles or interruptions. It is a magical world, in which an ordinary evening is transformed into the turning point of a lifetime, the metamorphosis of one's self into a curious kind of double being. It may seem like a sense of "discovery"; in fact it is a step in a long search, a process of creation. . . .

Like every emotional world, the loveworld has its essential rules and rituals, its basic structures and internal dynamics. Some of these rules and structures are so obvious that it is embarrassing to have to spell them out, for example, the fact that the loveworld (typically) includes two people, instead of only one (as in shame) or three (as in jealousy) or indeed an entire class of people (as in national mourning or revolutionary resentment). Or the fact that the loveworld involves extremely "positive" feelings about the person loved, perhaps even the uncritical evaluation that he or she is "the most wonderful person in the world." Or the fact that the loveworld is held together by the mutual desire to be together (to touch, be touched, to caress and make love) no less essentially than the world of Newton and Einstein is held together by the forces of electromagnetism and gravity. Such features are so obvious to us that we fail to think of them as the structures of love; we take them for granted and, when asked to talk about love, consider them not even worth mentioning. Having thus ignored the obvious, love becomes a mystery. But other seemingly equally "obvious" features of love may not be part of the structure of the loveworld at all—for example, the comforting equation between love and trust. Here, indeed, there is some room for "mystery" in love, not the emotion itself but its essential lack of predictability, the fascination with the unknown and the attraction that comes not with trust but with vulnerability, sometimes even suspicion and doubt. . . .

The "Object" Of Love

Talking about the loveworld is not only a way to avoid the hopeless conception of love as a feeling; it is also a way of rejecting an insidious view of love—and emotions in general—which many philosophers have come to accept as "obvious," particularly in this century. The view simply stated, is that love is an attitude *toward* someone, a feeling directed *at* a person, instead of a shared world. The view is often disguised by a piece of professional jargon—an impressive work, "intentionality." It is said that emotions are "intentional," which is a way of saying that they are "about" something. What an emotion is "about" is called its "intentional object" or, simply, its "object." Thus shame is an emotion which is "about" someone else. The language comes from the medieval scholastics, by way of an Austrian philosopher named Franz Brentano, one of whose students in Vienna was the young Sigmund Freud. Thus Freud talks all the time about the "object" of love, not without some discomfort, for though the conception fits his general theories perfectly, he nonetheless sensed correctly that some considerable conceptual damage was being done to the emotion thereby.

The idea—thought not the terminology—of "intentionality" and "intentional objects" was introduced into British philosophy by the Scottish philosopher David Hume. He analyzed a number of emotions in terms of the "objects" with which they were "naturally associated," for example pride and humility, which both took as their "objects" oneself, and hatred and love, which both took as their objects another person. But we can already see what is going to be wrong with this familiar type of analysis. First of all, all such talk about "objects" leaves out the crucial fact that, in love at least, it is the other as a "subject" that is essential. To be in love (even unrequited) is [to wish] to be looked *at*, not just to look. Thus it is the eyes, not the body (nor the soul), that present the so called "beloved," not as object but as subject, not first as beautiful or lovable but always as (potentially) *loving*. It's the eyes that have it, nothing else. . . .

Love is not just an attitude directed toward another person: it is an emotion which, [one hopes], is *shared with* him or her. . . . [A]ny account of love that begins with the idea of an "object" of love is probably going to miss the main point of the emotion, namely, that it is not an emotion "about" another person so much as, in our terms, a world we share. . . .

One obvious misunderstanding is this: the Christian view of love is not alone in teaching us that love is essentially *selfless*. Proponents of romantic love have argued that too. The idea is that love is thoroughly "about" another person, so that any degree of self-love is incompatible with "true" selfless love. But this is impossible. There is no emotion without self-involvement, and no love that is not also "about" oneself. The other side is just as confused, however; La Rochefoucauld, for example, insists that "all love is self-love." But to be self-involved is not yet to be selfish, nor does self-involvement in any way exclude a total concern for the other person as well. The practical consequence of this confusion, in turn, is the readiness with which we can be made to feel guilty at the slightest suggestion that our love is not "pure" but turns on "selfish" motives, and it renders unaskable what is in fact a most intelligible question—namely, "What am I getting out of this?"—to which the answer may well be, "Not enough to make it worth while." But then, love is not just what one "gets out of it" either.

※ ※ ※

So what is love? It is, in a phrase, an emotion through which we create for ourselves a little world—the loveworld, in which we play the roles of lovers and, quite literally, create our selves as well. . . . Even so-called "unrequited" love is shared love and shared identity, if only from one side and thereby woefully incomplete. Of course, occasionally an imagined identity may be far preferable to the actuality, but even when this is the case unrequited love represents at most a hint toward a process and not the process as such. Unrequited love is still love, but love in the sense that a sprout from an acorn is already an oak, no more. . . .

In love we transform ourselves and one another, but the key to this emotion is the understanding that the transformation of selves is not merely reciprocal, a swap of favors like "I'll cook you dinner if you'll wash the car." The self transformed in love is a shared self, and therefore by its very nature at odds with, even contradictory to, the individual autonomous selves that each of us had before. Sometimes our new shared self may be a transformation of a self that I (perhaps we) shared before. Possibly all love is to some extent the transposition of seemingly "natural" bonds which have somehow been abandoned or destroyed, and therefore the less than novel transformation of a self that has always been shared, in one way or another. But the bonds of love are always, to some extent, "unnatural," and our shared identity is always, in some way, uncomfortable. Aristophanes' delightful allegory about the double creatures cleft in two and seeking their other halves is charming but false. Love is never so neat and tidy, antigen and antibody forming the perfect fit. The Christian concept of a couple sanctified as a "union" before God is reassuring, as if one thereby receives some special guarantee, an outside bond of sorts, which will keep two otherwise aimless souls together. But the warranty doesn't apply. What is so special about romantic love, and what makes it so peculiar to our and similar societies, is the fact that it is entirely based on the idea of individuality and freedom, and this means, first of all, that the presupposition of love is a strong sense of individual identity and autonomy which exactly contradicts the ideal of "union" and "yearning to be one" that some of our literature has celebrated so one-sidedly. And, second, the freedom that is built into the loveworld includes not just the freedom to come together but the freedom to go as well. Thus love and the loveworld are always in a state of tension, always changing, dynamic, tenuous and explosive.

. . . To understand love is to understand this tension, this dialectic between individuality and the shared ideal. To think that love is to be found at the ends of the spectrum—in that first enthusiastic "discovery" of a shared togetherness or at the end of the road, after a lifetime together—is to miss the loveworld almost entirely, for it is neither an initial flush of feeling nor the retrospective congratulations of old age but a struggle for unity and identity. And it is this struggle—neither the ideal of togetherness nor the contrary demand for individual autonomy and identity alone—that defines the dynamics of that convulsive and tenuous world we call romantic love.

Universal Love

Mo Tzu

Mo Tzu said: It is the business of the benevolent man to try to promote what is beneficial to the world and to eliminate what is harmful. Now at the present time, what brings the greatest harm to the world? Great states attacking small ones, great families overthrowing small ones, the strong oppressing the weak, the many harrying the few, the cunning deceiving the stupid, the eminent lording it over the humble—these are harmful to the world. So too are rulers who are not generous, ministers who are not loyal, fathers who are without kindness, and sons who are unfilial, as well as those mean men who, with weapons, knives, poison, fire, and water, seek to injure and undo each other.

When we inquire into the cause of these various harms, what do we find has produced them? Do they come about from loving others and trying to benefit them? Surely not! They come rather from hating others and trying to injure them. And when we set out to classify and describe those men who hate and injure others, shall we say that their actions are motivated by universality or partiality? Surely we must answer, by partiality, and it is this partiality in their dealings with one another that gives rise to all the great harms in the world. Therefore we know that partiality is wrong.

Mo Tzu said: Whoever criticizes others must have some alternative to offer them. To criticize and yet offer no alternative is like trying to stop flood with flood or put out fire with fire. It will surely have no effect. Therefore Mo Tzu said: Partiality should be replaced by universality.

But how can partiality be replaced by universality? If men were to regard the states of others as they regard their own, then who would raise up his state to attack the state of another? It would be like attacking his own. If men were to regard the cities of others as they regard their own, then who would raise up his city to attack the city of another? It would be like attacking his own. If men were to regard the families of others as they regard their own, then who would raise up his family to overthrow that of another? It would be like overthrowing his own. Now when states and cities do not attack and make war on each other and families and individuals do not overthrow or injure one another, is this a harm or a benefit to the world? Surely it is a benefit.

When we inquire into the cause of such benefits, what do we find has produced them? Do they come about from hating others and trying to injure them? Surely not! They come rather from loving others and trying to benefit them. And when we set out to classify and describe those men who love and benefit others, shall we say that their actions are motivated by partiality or by universality? Surely we must answer, by universality, and it is this universality in their dealings with one another that gives rise to all the great benefits in the world. Therefore Mo Tzu has said that universality is right.

I have said previously that it is the business of the benevolent man to try to promote what is beneficial to the world and to eliminate what is harmful. Now I have demonstrated that universality is the source of all the great benefits in the world and partiality is the source of all the great harm. It is for this reason that Mo Tzu has said that partiality is wrong and universality is right.

"The Will of Heaven"

Now what does Heaven desire and what does it hate? Heaven desires righteousness and hates unrighteousness. Thus if I lead the people of the world to devote themselves to righteousness, then I am doing what Heaven desires. If I do what Heaven desires, then Heaven will do what I desire. Now what do I desire and what do I hate? I desire good fortune and prosperity and hate misfortune and calamity. If I do not do what Heaven desires and instead do what Heaven does not desire, then I will be leading the people of the world to devote themselves to what will bring misfortune and calamity.

How do I know that Heaven desires righteousness and hates unrighteousness? In the world, where there is righteousness there is life; where there is no righteousness there is death. Where there is righteousness there is wealth; where there is no righteousness there is poverty. Where there is righteousness there is order; where there is no righteousness there is disorder. Now Heaven desires life and hates death, desires wealth and hates poverty, desires order and hates disorder. So I know that Heaven desires righteousness and hates unrighteousness.

Moreover, righteousness is what is right. Subordinates do not decide what is right for their superiors; it is the superiors who decide what is right for their subordinates. Therefore the common people devote their strength to carrying out their tasks, but they cannot decide for themselves what is right. There are gentlemen to do that for them. The gentlemen devote their strength to carrying out their tasks, but they cannot decide for themselves what is right. There are ministers and officials to do that for them. The ministers and officials devote their strength to carrying out their tasks, but they cannot decide for themselves what is right. There are the three high ministers and the feudal lords to do that for them. The three high ministers and the feudal lords devote their strength to managing the affairs of government, but they cannot decide for themselves what is right. There is the Son of Heaven to do that for them. But the Son of Heaven cannot decide for himself what is right. There is Heaven to decide that for him. The gentlemen of the world have no difficulty in perceiving that the Son of Heaven decides what is right for the three high ministers, the feudal lords, the gentlemen, and the common people. But the people of the world are unable to perceive that Heaven decides what is right for the Son of Heaven. Therefore Yü, T'ang, Wen, and Wu, the sage kings of the Three Dynasties of antiquity, wishing to make it clear to the people of the world that it is Heaven that decides what is right for the Son of Heaven, all without exception fed their sacrificial oxen and sheep, fattened their dogs and pigs, prepared clean offerings of millet and wine, and sacrificed to the Lord on High and the spirits in order to seek blessing and good fortune from Heaven. But I have never heard of Heaven seeking blessing and good fortune from the Son of Heaven! So I know that it is Heaven that decides what is right for the Son of Heaven.

  The Son of Heaven is the most eminent person in the world and the richest in the world. He who desires riches and eminence must not fail to obey the will of Heaven. He who obeys the will of Heaven, loving all men universally and working for their benefit, will surely win reward. But he who disobeys the will of Heaven, showing partiality and hatred and working to injure others, will surely incur punishment.

The Love of God

from I Corinthians

13 Though I speak with the tongues of men and of angels, and have not |love|, I am become *as* sounding |bronze|, or a tinkling cymbal.

2 And though I have *the gift of* prophecy, and understand all mysteries, and all knowledge; and though I have all faith, so that I could remove mountains, and have not |love|, I am nothing.

3 And though I bestow all my goods to feed *the poor*, and though I give my body to be burned, and have not |love|, it profiteth me nothing.

4 |Love| suffereth long, *and* is kind; |love| envieth not; |love| vaunteth not itself, is not puffed up,

5 Doth not behave itself unseemly, seeketh not its own, is not easily provoked, thinketh no evil,

6 Rejoiceth not in iniquity, but rejoiceth in the truth;

7 Beareth all things, believeth all things, hopeth all things, endureth all things.

8 |Love| never faileth; but whether *there be* prophecies, they shall |be done away|; whether *there be* tongues, they shall cease; whether *there be* knowledge, it shall vanish away.

9 For we know in part, and we prophesy in part.

10 But when that which is perfect is come, then that which is in part shall be done away.

11 When I was a child, I spoke as a child, I understood as a child, I thought as a child; but when I became a man, I put away childish things.

12 For now we see |in a mirror|, darkly; but then, face to face; now I know in part, but then shall I know even as also I am known.

13 And now abideth faith, hope, |love|, these three; but the greatest of these *is* |love|.

Love, the Answer to the Problem of Human Existence

Erich Fromm

Any theory of love must begin with a theory of man, of human existence. While we find love, or rather, the equivalent of love, in animals, their attachments are mainly a part of their instinctual equipment; only remnants of this instinctual equipment can be seen operating in man. What is essential in the existence of man is the fact that he has emerged from the animal kingdom, from instinctive adaptation, that he has transcended nature—although he never leaves it; he is a part of it—and yet once torn away from nature, he cannot return to it; once thrown out of paradise—a state of original oneness with nature—cherubim with flaming swords block his way, if he should try to return. Man can only go forward by developing his reason, by finding a new harmony, a human one, instead of the prehuman harmony which is irretrievably lost.

When man is born, the human race as well as the individual, he is thrown out of a situation which was definite, as definite as the instincts, into a situation which is indefinite, uncertain and open. There is certainty only about the past—and about the future only as far as that it is death.

Man is gifted with reason; he is *life being aware of itself*; he has awareness of himself, of his fellow man, of his past, and of the possibilities of his future. This awareness of himself as a separate entity, the awareness of his own short life span, of the fact that without his will he is born and against his will he dies, that he will die before those whom he loves, or they before him, the awareness of his aloneness and separateness, of his helplessness before the forces of nature and of society, all this makes his separate, disunited existence an unbearable prison. He would become insane could he not liberate himself from this prison and reach out, unite himself in some form or other with men, with the world outside.

The experience of separateness arouses anxiety; it is, indeed, the source of all anxiety. Being separate means being cut off, without any capacity to use my human powers. Hence to be separate means to be helpless, unable to grasp the world—things and people—actively; it means that the world can invade me without my ability to react. Thus, separateness is the source of intense anxiety. Beyond that, it arouses shame and the feeling of guilt. This experience of guilt and shame in separateness is expressed in the Biblical story of Adam and Eve. After Adam and Eve have eaten of the "tree of knowledge of good and evil," after they have disobeyed (there is no good and evil unless there is freedom to disobey), after they have become human by having emancipated themselves from the original animal harmony with nature, i.e., after their birth as human beings—they saw "that they were naked—and they were ashamed." Should we assume that a myth as old and elementary as this has the prudish morals of the nineteenth-century outlook, and that the important point the story wants to convey to us is the embarrassment that their genitals were visible? This can hardly be so, and by understanding the story in a Victorian spirit, we miss the main point, which seems to be the following: after man and woman have become aware of themselves and of each other, they are aware of their separateness, and of their difference, inasmuch as they belong to different sexes. But while recognizing their separateness they remain strangers, because they have not yet learned to love each other (as is also made very clear by the fact that Adam defends himself by blaming Eve, rather than by trying to defend her). *The awareness of human separation, without reunion by love—is the source of shame. It is at the same time the source of guilt and anxiety.* . . .

Man—of all ages and cultures—is confronted with the solution of one and the same question: the question of how to overcome separateness, how to achieve union, how to transcend one's own individual life and find at-onement. The question is the same for primitive man living in caves, for nomadic man taking care of his flocks, for the peasant in Egypt, the Phoenician trader, the Roman soldier, the medieval monk, the Japanese samurai, the modern clerk and factory hand. The question is the same, for it springs from the same ground: the human situation, the conditions of human existence. . . .

As soon as one ignores smaller differences which belong more to the periphery than to the center, one discovers that there is only a limited number of answers which have been given. . . .

The history of religion and philosophy is the history of these answers, of their diversity, as well as of their limitation in number.

The answers depend, to some extent, on the degree of individuation which an individual has reached. In the infant I-ness has developed but little yet; he still feels one with mother, has no feeling of separateness as long as mother is present. . . .

Similarly, the human race in its infancy still feels one with nature. The soil, the animals, the plants are still man's world. He identifies himself with animals, and this is expressed by the wearing of animal masks, by the worshiping of a totem animal or animal gods. But the more the human race

Chapter VIII: Friendship and Love

emerges from these primary bonds, the more it separates itself from the natural world, the more intense becomes the need to find new ways of escaping separateness.

One way of achieving this aim lies in all kinds of *orgiastic states*. These may have the form of an auto-induced trance, sometimes with the help of drugs. Many rituals of primitive tribes offer a vivid picture of this type of solution. In a transitory state of exaltation the world outside disappears, and with it the feeling of separateness from it. Inasmuch as these rituals are practiced in common, an experience of fusion with the group is added which makes this solution all the more effective. Closely related to, and often blended with this orgiastic solution, is the sexual experience. The sexual orgasm can produce a state similar to the one produced by a trance, or to the effects of certain drugs. Rites of communal sexual orgies were a part of many primitive rituals. It seems that after the orgiastic experience, man can go on for a time without suffering too much from his separateness. Slowly the tension of anxiety mounts, and then is reduced again by the repeated performance of the ritual.

As long as these orgiastic states are a matter of common practice in a tribe, they do not produce anxiety or guilt. To act in this way is right, and even virtuous, because it is a way shared by all, approved and demanded by the medicine men or priests; hence there is no reason to feel guilty or ashamed. It is quite different when the same solution is chosen by an individual in a culture which has left behind these common practices. Alcoholism and drug addiction are the forms which the individual chooses in a non-orgiastic culture. In contrast to those participating in the socially patterned solution, such individuals suffer from guilt feelings and remorse. While they try to escape from separateness by taking refuge in alcohol or drugs, they feel all the more separate after the orgiastic experience is over, and thus are driven to take recourse to it with increasing frequency and intensity. Slightly different from this is the recourse to a sexual orgiastic solution. To some extent it is a natural and normal form of overcoming separateness, and a partial answer to the problem of isolation. But in many individuals in whom separateness is not relieved in other ways, the search for the sexual orgasm assumes a function which makes it not very different from alcoholism and drug addiction. It becomes a desperate attempt to escape the anxiety engendered by separateness, and it results in an ever-increasing sense of separateness, since the sexual act without love never bridges the gap between two human beings, except momentarily.

All forms of orgiastic union have three characteristics: they are intense, even violent; they occur in the total personality, mind *and* body; they are transitory and periodical. Exactly the opposite holds true for that form of union which is by far the most frequent solution chosen by man in the past and in the present: the union based on *conformity* with the group, its customs, practices and beliefs. Here again we find a considerable development.

In a primitive society the group is small; it consists of those with whom one shares blood and soil. With the growing development of culture, the group enlarges; it becomes the citizenry of a *polis*, the citizenry of a large state, the members of a church. Even the poor Roman felt pride because he could say *"civis romanus sum"*; Rome and the Empire were his family, his home, his world. Also in contemporary Western society the union with the group is the prevalent way of overcoming separateness. It is a union in which the individual self disappears to a large extent, and where the aim is to belong to the herd. If I am like everybody else, if I have no feelings or thoughts which make me different, if I conform in custom, dress, ideas, to the pattern of the group, I am saved; saved from the frightening experience of aloneness. . . .

. . . Man becomes a "nine to fiver," he is part of the labor force, or the bureaucratic force of clerks and managers. He has little initiative, his tasks are prescribed by the organization of the work; there is even little difference between those high up on the ladder and those on the bottom. They all perform tasks prescribed by the whole structure of the organization, at a prescribed speed, and in a prescribed manner. Even the feelings are prescribed: cheerfulness, tolerance, reliability, ambition, and an ability to get along with everybody without friction. Fun is routinized in similar, although not quite as drastic ways. Books are selected by the book clubs, movies by the film and theater owners and the advertising slogans paid for by them; the rest is also uniform: the Sunday ride in the car, the television session, the card game, the social parties. From birth to death, from Monday to Monday, from morning to evening—all activities are routinized, and prefabricated. How should a man caught in this net of routine not forget that he is a man, a unique individual, one who is given only this one chance of living, with hopes and disappointments, with sorrow and fear, with the longing for love and the dread of the nothing and of separateness?

A third way of attaining union lies in *creative activity*, be it that of the artist, or of the artisan. In any kind of creative work the creating person unites himself with his material, which represents the world outside of himself. Whether a carpenter makes a table, or a goldsmith a piece of jewelry, whether the peasant grows his corn or the painter paints a picture, in all types of creative work the worker and his object become one, man unites himself with the world in the process of creation. This, however, holds true only for productive work, for work in which *I* plan, produce, see the result of my work. In the modern work process of a clerk, the worker on the endless belt, little is left of this uniting quality of work. The worker becomes an appendix to the machine or to the bureaucratic organization. He has ceased to be he—hence no union takes place beyond that of conformity.

The unity achieved in productive work is not interpersonal; the unity achieved in orgiastic fusion is transitory; the unity achieved by conformity is only pseudo-unity. Hence, they are only partial answers to the problem

Chapter VIII: Friendship and Love

of existence. The full answer lies in the achievement of interpersonal union, of fusion with another person, in *love*.

This desire for interpersonal fusion is the most powerful striving in man. It is the most fundamental passion, it is the force which keeps the human race together, the clan, the family, society. The failure to achieve it means insanity or destruction—self-destruction or destruction of others. Without love, humanity could not exist for a day. Yet, if we call the achievement of interpersonal union "love," we find ourselves in a serious difficulty. Fusion can be achieved in different ways—and the differences are not less significant than what is common to the various forms of love. Should they all be called love? Or should we reserve the word "love" only for a specific kind of union, one which has been the ideal virtue in all great humanistic religions and philosophical systems of the last four thousand years of Western and Eastern history?

As with all semantic difficulties, the answer can only be arbitrary. What matters is that we know what kind of union we are talking about when we speak of love. Do we refer to love as the mature answer to the problem of existence, or do we speak of those immature forms of love which may be called *symbiotic union*? In the following pages I shall call love only the former. I shall begin the discussion of "love" with the latter.

Symbiotic union has its biological pattern in the relationship between the pregnant mother and the foetus. They are two, and yet one. They live "together" (*symbiosis*), they need each other. The foetus is a part of the mother, it receives everything it needs from her; mother is its world, as it were; she feeds it, she protects it, but also her own life is enhanced by it. In the *psychic* symbiotic union, the two bodies are independent, but the same kind of attachment exists psychologically.

The *passive* form of the symbiotic union is that of submission, or if we use a clinical term, of *masochism*. The masochistic person escapes from the unbearable feeling of isolation and separateness by making himself part and parcel of another person who directs him, guides him, protects him; who is his life and his oxygen, as it were. The power of the one to whom one submits is inflated, may he be a person or a god; he is everything, I am nothing, except inasmuch as I am part of him. As a part, I am part of greatness, of power, of certainty. The masochistic person does not have to make decisions, does not have to take any risks; he is never alone—but he is not independent; he has no integrity; he is not yet fully born. . . .

The *active* form of symbiotic fusion is domination or, to use the psychological term corresponding to masochism, *sadism*. The sadistic person wants to escape from his aloneness and his sense of imprisonment by making another person part and parcel of himself. He inflates and enhances himself by incorporating another person, who worships him.

The sadistic person is as dependent on the submissive person as the latter is on the former; neither can live without the other. The difference is only that the sadistic person commands, exploits, hurts, humiliates, and that the masochistic person is commanded, exploited, hurt, humiliated. This is a considerable difference in a realistic sense; in a deeper emotional sense, the difference is not so great as that which they both have in common: fusion without integrity. . . .

In contrast to symbiotic union, mature *love is union under the condition of preserving one's integrity,* one's individuality. *Love is an active power in man;* a power which breaks through the walls which separate man from his fellow men, which unites him with others; love makes him overcome the sense of isolation and separateness, yet it permits him to be himself, to retain his integrity. In love the paradox occurs that two beings become one and yet remain two.

. . . In the most general way, the active character of love can be described by stating that love is primarily *giving,* not receiving.

What is giving? Simple as the answer to this question seems to be, it is actually full of ambiguities and complexities. The most widespread misunderstanding is that which assumes that giving is "giving up" something, being deprived of, sacrificing. The person whose character has not developed beyond the stage of the receptive, exploitative, or hoarding orientation, experiences the act of giving in this way. . . .

For the productive character, giving has an entirely different meaning. Giving is the highest expression of potency. In the very act of giving, I experience my strength, my wealth, my power. This experience of heightened vitality and potency fills me with joy. I experience myself as overflowing, spending, alive, hence as joyous. Giving is more joyous than receiving, not because it is a deprivation, but because in the act of giving lies the expression of my aliveness. . . .

In the sphere of material things giving means being rich. Not he who *has* much is rich, but he who *gives* much. The hoarder who is anxiously worried about losing something is, psychologically speaking, the poor, impoverished man, regardless of how much he has. Whoever is capable of giving of himself is rich. . . .

The most important sphere of giving, however, is not that of material things, but lies in the specifically human realm. What does one person give to another? He gives of himself, of the most precious he has, he gives of his life. This does not necessarily mean that he sacrifices his life for the other—but that he gives him of that which is alive in him; he gives him of his joy, of his interest, of his understanding, of his knowledge, of his humor, of his sadness—of all expressions and manifestations of that which is alive in him. In thus giving of his life, he enriches the other person, he enhances the other's sense of aliveness by enhancing his own sense of aliveness. He does not give in order to receive; giving is in itself exquisite joy. But in giving he cannot help bringing something to life in the other person, and this which is brought to life reflects back to him; in truly giving, he cannot help receiving that which is given back to him. Giving implies to make the

Chapter VIII: Friendship and Love

other person a giver also and they both share in the joy of what they have brought to life. In the act of giving something is born, and both persons involved are grateful for the life that is born for both of them. Specifically with regard to love this means: love is a power which produces love; impotence is the inability to produce love....

Beyond the element of giving, the active character of love becomes evident in the fact that it always implies certain basic elements, common to all forms of love. These are *care, responsibility, respect* and *knowledge*.

That love implies *care* is most evident in a mother's love for her child. No assurance of her love would strike us as sincere if we saw her lacking in care for the infant, if she neglected to feed it, to bathe it, to give it physical comfort; and we are impressed by her love if we see her caring for the child. It is not different even with the love for animals or flowers. If a woman told us that she loved flowers, and we saw that she forgot to water them, we would not believe in her "love" for flowers. *Love is the active concern for the life and the growth of that which we love.* Where this active concern is lacking, there is no love....

Care and concern imply another aspect of love; that of *responsibility*. Today responsibility is often meant to denote duty, something imposed upon one from the outside. But responsibility, in its true sense, is an entirely voluntary act; it is my response to the needs, expressed or unexpressed, of another human being....

Responsibility could easily deteriorate into domination and possessiveness, were it not for a third component of love, *respect*. Respect is not fear and awe; it denotes, in accordance with the root of the word (*respicere* = to look at), the ability to see a person as he is, to be aware of his unique individuality. Respect means the concern that the other person should grow and unfold as he is. Respect, thus, implies the absence of exploitation. I want the loved person to grow and unfold for his own sake, and in his own ways, and not for the purpose of serving me. If I love the other person, I feel one with him or her, but with him *as he is*, not as I need him to be as an object for my use. It is clear that respect is possible only if *I* have achieved independence; if I can stand and walk without needing crutches, without having to dominate and exploit anyone else. Respect exists only on the basis of freedom: "l'amour est l'enfant de la liberté" as an old French song says; love is the child of freedom, never that of domination.

To respect a person is not possible without *knowing* him; care and responsibility would be blind if they were not guided by knowledge. Knowledge would be empty if it were not motivated by concern. There are many layers of knowledge; the knowledge which is an aspect of love is one which does not stay at the periphery, but penetrates to the core. It is possible only when I can transcend the concern for myself and see the other person in his own terms. I may know, for instance, that a person is angry, even if he does not show it overtly; but I may know him more deeply than that; then I know that he is anxious, and worried; that he feels lonely, that he feels guilty. Then I know that his anger is only the manifestation of something deeper, and I see him as anxious and embarrassed, that is, as the suffering person, rather than as the angry one.

Knowledge has one more, and a more fundamental, relation to the problem of love. The basic need to fuse with another person so as to transcend the prison of one's separateness is closely related to another specifically human desire, that to know the "secret of man." While life in its merely biological aspects is a miracle and a secret, man in his human aspects is an unfathomable secret to himself—and to his fellow man. We know ourselves, and yet even with all the efforts we make, we do not know ourselves. We know our fellow man, and yet we do not know him, because we are not a thing, and our fellow man is not a thing. The further we reach into the depth of our being, or someone else's being, the more the goal of knowledge eludes us. Yet we cannot help desiring to penetrate into the secret of man's soul, into the innermost nucleus which is "he."

There is one way, a desperate one, to know the secret: it is that of complete power over another person; the power which makes him do what we want, feel what we want, think what we want; which transforms him into a thing, our thing, our possession. The ultimate degree of this attempt to know lies in the extremes of sadism, the desire and ability to make a human being suffer; to torture him, to force him to betray his secret in his suffering. . . .

In children we often see this path to knowledge quite overtly. The child takes something apart, breaks it up in order to know it; or it takes an animal apart; cruelly tears off the wings of a butterfly in order to know it, to force its secret. The cruelty itself is motivated by something deeper: the wish to know the secret of things and of life.

The other path to knowing "the secret" is love. Love is active penetration of the other person, in which my desire to know is stilled by union. In the act of fusion I know you, I know myself, I know everybody—and I "know" nothing. I know in the only way knowledge of that which is alive is possible for man—by experience of union—not by any knowledge our thought can give. Sadism is motivated by the wish to know the secret, yet I remain as ignorant as I was before. I have torn the other being apart limb from limb, yet all I have done is to destroy him. Love is the only way of knowledge, which in the act of union answers my quest. In the act of loving, of giving myself, in the act of penetrating the other person, I find myself, I discover myself, I discover us both, I discover man.

Erich Fromm, "Love, the Answer to the Problem of Human Existence" from *The Art of Loving*, pp. 6–26. Copyright © 1956 by Erich Fromm. Reprinted with the permission of HarperCollins Publishers, Inc.

Chapter IX
Happiness

Everyone, it seems, desires happiness. But, what exactly are people seeking in their quest for happiness? What is the nature of happiness? How does happiness differ from pleasure? What does it mean to be happy? And, how can an individual become happy? Is happiness the same for everyone? Or, is happiness different for different individuals? Finally, how can men and women engage successfully in the pursuit of happiness over the course of an entire lifetime? The selections in this chapter help us think clearly about the above questions.

Psalm I tells us that the happy individual is that one who "delights in the law of the Lord." The Psalm contrasts the way of the just with the way of the wicked. The happy individual has stability (i.e. is "planted") and "whatsoever he does, prospers (i.e. flourishes)." In contrast, the way of the wicked vanishes.

In the famous story of Solon and Croesus, Herodotus teaches that the correct understanding of human happiness must take into consideration a whole life. One must always, he contends, "look to the end." Solon, one of the wisest men of his day, in the course of his travels went to Sardis to see Croesus. Croesus was the most powerful and wealthy ruler of his time. He believed his happiness consisted in the abundance of his worldly riches and in the magnificence of all that he controlled. He asked Solon, "Who is the happiest man you have ever seen?" He asked, of course, thinking himself to be the happiest. But, Solon refused to flatter Croesus and admonished him with the example of Tellus. Solon stated: "Great wealth can make a man no happier than moderate means, when he has the luck to continue in prosperity to the end." Thus, the happy individual is one of sufficient means and enjoys good luck plus "the blessings of a sound body, health, freedom from trouble, fine children, and good looks." The happy individual must keep these to the end and die peacefully. Until the end Solon tells us that one "is not happy, but only lucky."

Aristotle holds that there is general agreement that "to live well" or "to do well" is the same thing as "to be happy." However, people disagree as to the nature of happiness. Regarding this point, Aristotle sharply points out that "the masses do not give the same account of it (happiness) as the philosophers." The masses are inconsistent in their understanding of happiness and identify it with different things in different circumstances. There can, they believe, be as many views of human happiness as there are individuals. In other words, the masses believe happiness is whatever one thinks it is. Aristotle disagrees.

Aristotle argues that happiness is the highest good. It is the supreme good. Why? Because, "the highest good is clearly something final," and happiness is the only good which ". . . we always desire for its own sake and never as a means to something else." He defines human happiness as "an activity of the soul in accordance with complete or perfect virtue." Like Solon, Aristotle believes human happiness must be understood within the context of a complete life.

Frankl is concerned, among other matters, with how it is possible to have meaning in suffering. Most people assume that the meaning of life is to be found in pleasure. Frankl's denial of this uncritically held point of view is emphatic. He states: "Pleasure is not the goal of our aspirations, but the consequence of attaining them." He continues that ". . . pleasure does not loom up before us as the goal of an ethical act; rather, an ethical act carries pleasure on its back." Life presents each person with unique possibilities and our being consists in being responsible—responsible to actualize values.

St. Augustine, in contrast, does not believe that happiness is the highest good. Rather, he defines happiness as one's enjoyment of the highest good. Augustine sets two conditions for the chief good: first, nothing is better than it and second, it must be something that cannot be lost against the will. Furthermore, he holds that the chief good must be a good of the soul and not the body. It is the possession of virtue and wisdom which come as a result of following God. That one who follows God will "live both well and happily."

The basic ethical teachings of Epictetus, the Stoic philosopher, are summarized in *The Encheiridion* or *Manual*. It is believed that these teachings were intended as instruction for young people aspiring to be Stoic philosophers. The Stoic lifestyle involves strict discipline and indifference to external circumstances. Epictetus himself rejected the pursuit of pleasure. On this point the Stoic philosopher is often contrasted with Epicureanism, the philosophy of pleasure.

In many ways, Epictetus is concerned not with the positive cultivation of happiness but with practical advice which will help an individual to avoid unpleasant experiences and misfortune. The key is to realize that some matters are in our control and some are not. So, disappointment comes in trying to control that which one cannot control. To those things

Chapter IX: Happiness

not within our control Epictetus says that one should confess, "It is nothing to me." It is not things that disturb people and cause trouble but rather improper judgments about those things. Thus, Epictetus offers the following prescription and exhortation: "Do not seek to have everything that happens happen as you wish, but wish for everything to happen as it actually does happen, and your life will be serene."

In his "Letter to Menoeceus," Epicurus exhorts both young and old to study philosophy: "For no one can come too early or too late to secure the health of his soul." Philosophy instructs the individual to "meditate on the things which make for our happiness."

According to Epicurus, pleasure is the basis of all happiness. Happiness is a life lived in tranquility, (Greek: *ataraxia*), that is, a state of freedom from both pain in the body and the mind. To achieve this state one must disregard the religious teachings which instill fear of the gods and fear of death. These fears can be allayed by an accurate understanding of the natural laws (i.e. the *logical atomism* of Democritus). The happy life is essentially the life of rationally mediated pleasures. The Epicurean lifestyle typically involved a withdrawal from the world to a small garden community. There, among the company of a few close friends and, of course, philosophy one could cultivate serenity.

Heinrich Zimmer presents the Buddhist view of enlightenment. He states that "in essence Buddhism is meant only for the happy few." Zimmer begins with the Buddhist truth that *all life is sorrowful* and expands upon its meaning as follows: ". . . members of the human race are spiritually unhealthy, the symptom being that we carry on our shoulders a burden of sorrow; the disease is endemic." Since the illness has been diagnosed and its cause determined, the Buddhist prognostication is that a cure is possible. The end of Buddhism is thus to remove the cause of disease, sickness and sorrow and effect healing: "The Buddha's thoroughgoing treatment is guaranteed to eradicate the cause of the sickly spell and dream of ignorance, and thus to make possible the attainment of a state of serene, awakened perfection."

Zimmer goes on to explicate the imagery and meaning in the ferryboat crossing, he discusses *samsara* and *nirvana*, but concludes the deepest insight in Buddhism, thus enlightenment, rests in nonexistence and denying the reality of things.

True Happiness

Psalm 1

I

Happy the man who follows not
    the counsel of the wicked
Nor walks in the way of sinners,
    nor sits in the company of the
        insolent,
But delights in the law of the Lord
    and meditates on his law day and
        night.
He is like a tree
    planted near running water,
That yields its fruit in due season,
    and whose leaves never fade.
    [Whatever he does, prospers.]

II

Not so the wicked, not so;
    they are like chaff which the wind
        drives away.
Therefore in judgment the wicked
    shall not stand,
    nor shall sinners, in the assembly of
        the just.
For the Lord watches over the way
    of the just,
    but the way of the wicked vanishes.

The Story of Solon and Croesus

Herodotus

In the course of time Croesus subdued all the peoples west of the river Halys, except the Cilicians and Lycians. The rest he kept in subjection—Lydians, Phrygians, Mysians, Mariandynians, Chalybians, Paphlagonians, Thracians (both Thynian and Bithynian), Carians, Ionians, Dorians, Aeolians, and Pamphylians.

When all these nations had been added to the Lydian empire, and Sardis was at the height of her wealth and prosperity, all the great Greek teachers of that epoch, one after another, paid visits to the capital. Much the most distinguished of them was Solon the Athenian, the man who at the request of his countrymen had made a code of laws for Athens. He was on his travels at the time, intending to be away ten years, in order to avoid the necessity of repealing any of the laws he had made. That, at any rate, was the real reason of his absence, though he gave it out that what he wanted was just to see the world. The Athenians could not alter any of Solon's laws without him, because they had solemnly sworn to give them a ten years' trial.

For this reason, then—and also no doubt for the pleasure of foreign travel—Solon left home and, after a visit to the court of Amasis in Egypt, went to Sardis to see Croesus.

Croesus entertained him hospitably in the palace, and three or four days after his arrival instructed some servants to take him on a tour of the royal treasuries and point out the richness and magnificence of everything. When Solon had made as thorough an inspection as opportunity allowed, Croesus said: "Well, my Athenian friend, I have heard a great deal about your wisdom, and how widely you have travelled in the pursuit of knowledge. I cannot resist my desire to ask you a question: who is the happiest man you have ever seen?"

The point of the question was that Croesus supposed himself to be the happiest of men. Solon, however, refused to flatter, and answered in strict accordance with his view of the truth. "An Athenian," he said, "called Tellus."

Croesus was taken aback. "And what," he asked sharply, "is your reason for this choice?"

"There are two good reasons," said Solon, "first, his city was prosperous, and he had fine sons, and lived to see children born to each of them, and all these children surviving; and, secondly, after a life which by our standards was a good one, he had a glorious death. In a battle with the neighbouring town of Eleusis, he fought for his countrymen, routed the enemy, and died like a soldier; and the Athenians paid him the high honour of a public funeral on the spot where he fell."

All these details about the happiness of Tellus, Solon doubtless intended as a moral lesson for the king; Croesus, however, thinking he would at least be awarded second prize, asked who was the next happiest person whom Solon had seen.

"Two young men of Argos," was the reply; "Cleobis and Biton. They had enough to live on comfortably; and their physical strength is proved not merely by their success in athletics, but much more by the following incident. The Argives were celebrating the festival of Hera, and it was most important that the mother of the two young men should drive to the temple in her ox-cart; but it so happened that the oxen were late in coming back from the fields. Her two sons therefore, as there was no time to lose, harnessed themselves to the cart and dragged it along, with their mother inside, for a distance of nearly six miles, until they reached the temple. After this exploit, which was witnessed by the assembled crowd, they had a most enviable death—a heaven-sent proof of how much better it is to be dead than alive. Men kept crowding round them and congratulating them on their strength, and women kept telling the mother how lucky she was to have such sons, when, in sheer pleasure at this public recognition of her sons' act, she prayed the goddess Hera, before whose shrine she stood, to grant Cleobis and Biton, who had brought her such honour, the greatest blessing that can fall to mortal man.

"After her prayer came the ceremonies of sacrifice and feasting; and the two lads, when all was over, fell asleep in the temple—and that was the end of them, for they never woke again.

"The Argives had statues made of them, which they sent to Delphi, as a mark of their particular respect."

Croesus was vexed with Solon for giving the second prize for happiness to the two young Argives, and snapped out: "That's all very well, my Athenian friend; but what of my own happiness? Is it so utterly contemptible that you won't even compare me with mere common folk like those you have mentioned?"

"My lord," replied Solon, "I know God is envious of human prosperity and likes to trouble us; and you question me about the lot of man. Listen

Chapter IX: Happiness

then: as the years lengthen out, there is much both to see and to suffer which one would wish otherwise. Take seventy years as the span of a man's life: those seventy years contain 25,200 days, without counting intercalary months. Add a month every other year, to make the seasons come round with proper regularity, and you will have thirty-five additional months, which will make 1050 additional days. Thus the total of days for your seventy years is 26,250, and not a single one of them is like the next in what it brings. You can see from that, Croesus, what a chancy thing life is. You are very rich, and you rule a numerous people; but the question you asked me I will not answer, until I know that you have died happily. Great wealth can make a man no happier than moderate means, unless he has the luck to continue in prosperity to the end. Many very rich men have been unfortunate, and many with a modest competence have had good luck. The former are better off than the latter in two respects only, whereas the poor but lucky man has the advantage in many ways; for though the rich have the means to satisfy their appetites and to bear calamities, and the poor have not, the poor, if they are lucky, are more likely to keep clear of trouble, and will have besides the blessings of a sound body, health, freedom from trouble, fine children, and good looks.

"Now if a man thus favoured dies as he has lived, he will be just the one you are looking for: the only sort of person who deserves to be called happy. But mark this: until he is dead, keep the word 'happy' in reserve. Till then, he is not happy, but only lucky.

"Nobody of course can have all these advantages, any more than a country can produce everything it needs: whatever it has, it is bound to lack something. The best country is the one which has most. It is the same with people: no man is ever self-sufficient—there is sure to be something missing. But whoever has the greatest number of the good things I have mentioned, and keeps them to the end, and dies a peaceful death, that man, my lord Croesus, deserves in my opinion to be called happy.

"Look to the end, no matter what it is you are considering. Often enough God gives a man a glimpse of happiness, and then utterly ruins him."

These sentiments were not of the sort to give Croesus any pleasure; he let Solon go with cold indifference, firmly convinced that he was a fool. For what could be more stupid than to keep telling him to look at the "end" of everything, without any regard to present prosperity?

After Solon's departure Croesus was dreadfully punished, presumably because God was angry with him for supposing himself the happiest of men. It began with a dream he had about a disaster to one of his sons: a dream which came true. He had two sons: one with a physical disability, being deaf and dumb; the other, named Atys, as fine a young man as one can fancy. Croesus dreamt that Atys would be killed by a blow from an iron weapon. He woke from the dream in horror, and lost no time in getting his son a wife, and seeing to it that he no longer took the field with the Lydian soldiers, whom he used to command. He also removed all the weapons—javelins, spears and so on—from the men's rooms, and had them piled up in the women's quarters, because he was afraid that some blade hanging on the wall might fall on Atys' head.

The arrangements for the wedding were well in hand, when there came to Sardis an unfortunate stranger who had been guilty of manslaughter. He was a Phrygian, and related to the Phrygian royal house. This man presented himself at the palace and begged Croesus to cleanse him from blood-guilt according to the laws of the country (the ceremony is much the same in Lydia as in Greece): and Croesus did as he asked. When the formalities were over, Croesus, wishing to know who he was and where he came from, said: "What is your name, stranger, and what part of Phrygia have you come from, to take refuge with me? What man or woman did you kill?"

"Sire," the stranger replied, "I am the son of Gordias, and Midas was my grandfather. My name is Adrastus. I killed my brother by accident, and here I am, driven from home by my father and stripped of all I possessed."

"Your family and mine," said Croesus, "are friends. You have come to a friendly house. If you stay in my dominions, you shall have all you need. The best thing for you will be not to take your misfortune too much to heart." Adrastus, therefore, took up his residence in the palace.

Now it happened just at this time that Mount Olympus in Mysia was infested by a monstrous boar. This tremendous creature used to issue from his mountain lair and play havoc with the crops, and many times the Mysians had taken the field against him, but to no purpose. The unfortunate hunters received more damage than they were able to inflict. As a last resource the Mysians sent to Croesus.

"Sire," the messengers said, "a huge beast of a boar has appeared amongst us, and is doing fearful damage. We want to catch him, but we can't. Please, my lord, send us your son with a party of young men, and some dogs, so that we can get rid of the brute."

Croesus had not forgotten his dream, and in answer to this request forbade any further mention of his son.

"I could not send him," he said; "he is just married, and that keeps him busy. But I will certainly send picked men, with a complete hunting outfit, and I will urge them to do all they can to help rid you of the animal."

This answer satisfied the Mysians; but at that moment Atys, who had heard of their request, entered the room. The young man, finding that Croesus persisted in his refusal to let him join the hunting party, said to his father: "Once honour demanded that I should win fame as a huntsman and fighter; but now, father, though you cannot accuse me of cowardice or lack of spirit, you won't let me take part in either of these admirable pursuits. Think what a figure I must cut when I walk between here and the place of assembly! What will people take me for? What must my young wife think of me? That she hasn't married much of a husband, I fear! Now, father,

Chapter IX: Happiness

either let me join this hunt, or give me an intelligible reason why what you're doing is good for me."

"My son," said Croesus, "of course you are not a coward or anything unpleasant of that kind. That is not the reason for what I'm doing. The fact is, I dreamt that you had not long to live—that you would be killed by an iron weapon. It was that dream that made me hasten your wedding; and the same thing makes me refuse to let you join in this enterprise. As long as I live, I am determined to protect you, and to rob death of his prize. You are my only son, for I do not count that wretched cripple, your brother."

"No one can blame you, father," Atys replied, "for taking care of me after a dream like that. Nevertheless there is something which you have failed to observe, and it is only right that I should point it out to you. You dreamt that I should be killed by an iron weapon. Very well: has a boar got hands? Can a boar hold this weapon you fear so much? Had you dreamt that I should be killed by a boar's tusk or anything of that sort, your precautions would be justified. But you didn't: it was a weapon which was to kill me. Let me go, then. It is only to hunt an animal, not to fight against men."

"My boy," said Croesus, "I own myself beaten. You interpret the dream better than I did. I cannot but change my mind, and allow you to join the expedition."

The king then sent for Adrastus the Phrygian, and said to him: "Through no fault of your own, Adrastus, you came to me in great distress and with an ugly stain on your character. I gave you ritual purification, welcomed you to my house, and have spared no expense to entertain you. Now I expect a fair return for my generosity: take charge of my son on this boar-hunt; protect him from footpads and cut-throats on the road. In any case it is your duty to go where you can distinguish yourself: your family honour demands it, and you are a stalwart fellow besides."

"Sire," Adrastus answered, "under ordinary circumstances I should have taken no part in this adventure. A man under a cloud has no business to associate with those who are luckier than himself. Indeed I have no heart for it, and there are many reasons to prevent my going. But your wishes make all the difference. It is my duty to gratify you in return for your kindness; so I am ready to do as you ask. So far as it lies in my power to protect your son, you may count on his returning safe and sound."

When Adrastus had given his answer, the party set out, men, dogs, and all. They made their way to Olympus and kept their eyes open for the boar. As soon as they spotted him, they surrounded him and let fly with spears—and then it was that the stranger—Adrastus, the very man whom Croesus had cleansed from the stain of blood—aimed at the boar, missed him, and struck the king's son. Croesus' dream had come true.

A messenger hurried off to Sardis, and Croesus was told of the encounter with the boar and the death of his son. The shock of the news was dreadful; and the horror of it was increased by the fact that the weapon had been thrown by the very man whom the king had cleansed from the guilt of blood. In the violence of his grief Croesus prayed to Zeus, calling on him as God of Purification to witness what he had suffered at the hands of his guest; he invoked him again under his title of Protector of the Hearth, because he has unwittingly entertained his son's murderer in his own house; and yet again as God of Friendship, because the man he had sent to guard his son had turned out to be his bitterest enemy.

Before long the Lydians arrived with the body, followed by the unlucky killer. He took his stand in front of the corpse, and stretching out his hands in an attitude of submission begged the king to cut his throat there and then upon the dead body of his son.

"My former trouble," he said, "was bad enough. But now that I have ruined the man who absolved me of my guilt, I cannot bear to live."

In spite of his grief Croesus was moved to pity by these words. "Friend," he said, "as you condemn yourself to death, there is nothing more I can require of you. Justice is satisfied. This calamity is not your fault; you never meant to strike the blow, though strike it you did. Some God is to blame—some God who long ago warned me of what was to happen."

Croesus buried his son with all proper ceremony; and as soon as everything was quiet after the funeral, Adrastus—the son of Gordias, the grandson of Midas: the man who had killed his brother and ruined the host who gave him purification—convinced that he was the unluckiest of all the men he had ever known, stabbed himself and fell dead upon the tomb.

Sardis was captured by the Persians and Croesus taken prisoner, after a reign of fourteen years and a siege of fourteen days. The oracle was fulfilled; Croesus had destroyed a mighty empire—his own.

The Persians brought their prisoner into the presence of the king, and Cyrus chained Croesus and placed him with fourteen Lydian boys on a great pyre that he had built; perhaps he intended them as a choice offering to some god of his, or perhaps he had made a vow and wished to fulfil it; or it may be that he had heard that Croesus was a godfearing man, and set him on the pyre to see if any divine power would save him from being burnt alive. But whatever the reason, that was what he did; and Croesus, for all his misery, as he stood on the pyre, remembered how Solon had declared that no man could be called happy until he was dead. It was as true as if God had spoken it. Till then Croesus had not uttered a sound; but when he remembered, he sighed bitterly and three times, in anguish of spirit, pronounced Solon's name.

Cyrus heard the name and told his interpreters to ask who Solon was; but for a while Croesus refused to answer the question and kept silent; at last, however, he was forced to speak. "He was a man," he said, "who ought to have talked with every king in the world. I would give a fortune to have had it so." Not understanding what he meant, they renewed their questions and pressed him so urgently to explain, that he could no longer refuse. He then related how Solon the Athenian once came to Sardis, and made light of the splendour which he saw there, and how everything he said—though it applied to all men and especially to those who imagine themselves fortunate—had in his own case proved all too true.

While Croesus was speaking, the fire had been lit and was already burning round the edges. The interpreters told Cyrus what Croesus had said, and the story touched him. He himself was a mortal man, and was burning alive another who had once been as prosperous as he. The thought of that, and the fear of retribution, and the realization of the instability of human things, made him change his mind and give orders that the flames should at once be put out, and Croesus and the boys brought down from the pyre. But the fire had got a hold, and the attempt to extinguish it failed. The Lydians say that when Croesus understood that Cyrus had changed his mind, and saw everyone vainly trying to master the fire, he called loudly upon Apollo with tears to come and save him from his misery, if any of his gifts had been pleasant to him. It was a clear and windless day; but suddenly in answer to Croesus' prayer clouds gathered and a storm broke with such violent rain that the flames were put out.

This was proof enough for Cyrus that Croesus was a good man whom the gods loved; so he brought him down from the pyre and said, "Tell me, Croesus; who was it who persuaded you to march against my country and be my enemy rather than my friend?"

"My lord," Croesus replied, "the luck was yours when I did it, and the loss was mine. The god of the Greeks encouraged me to fight you: the blame is his. No one is fool enough to choose war instead of peace—in peace sons bury fathers, but in war fathers bury sons. It must have been heaven's will that this should happen."

Cyrus had his chains taken off and invited him to sit by his side. He made much of him and looked at him with a sort of wonder, as did everyone else who was near enough to see.

Translated by Aubrey de Sélincourt

Virtue and Happiness

Aristotle

Every art and every scientific inquiry, and similarly every action and purpose, may be said to aim at some good. Hence the good has been well defined as that at which all things aim. But it is clear that there is a difference in ends; for the ends are sometimes activities, and sometimes results beyond the mere activities. Where there are ends beyond the action, the results are naturally superior to the action.

As there are various actions, arts, and sciences, it follows that the ends are also various. Thus health is the end of the medical art, a ship of shipbuilding, victory of strategy, and wealth of economics. It often happens that a number of such arts or sciences combine for a single enterprise, as the art of making bridles and all such other arts as furnish the implements of horsemanship combine for horsemanship, and horsemanship and every military action for strategy; and in the same way, other arts or sciences combine for others. In all these cases, the ends of the master arts or sciences, whatever they may be, are more desirable than those of the subordinate arts or sciences, as it is for the sake of the former that the latter are pursued. It makes no difference to the argument whether the activities themselves are the ends of the action, or something beyond the activities, as in the above-mentioned sciences.

If it is true that in the sphere of action there is some end which we wish for its own sake, and for the sake of which we wish everything else, and if we do not desire everything for the sake of something else (for, if that is so, the process will go on *ad infinitum*, and our desire will be idle and futile), clearly this end will be good and the supreme good. Does it not follow then that the knowledge of this good is of great importance for the conduct of life? Like archers who have a mark at which to aim, shall we not have a better chance of attaining what we want? If this is so, we must endeavor to comprehend, at least in outline, what this good is, and what science of faculty makes it its object. . . .

As every science and undertaking aims at some good, what is in our view the good at which political science aims, and what is the highest of all

Chapter IX: Happiness

practical goods? As to its name there is, I may say, a general agreement. The masses and the cultured classes agree in calling it happiness, and conceive that "to live well" or "to do well" is the same thing as "to be happy." But as to what happiness is they do not agree, nor do the masses give the same account of it as the philosophers. The former take it to be something visible and palpable, such as pleasure, wealth, or honor; different people, however, give different definitions of it, and often even the same man gives different definitions at different times. When he is ill, it is health, when he is poor, it is wealth; if he is conscious of his own ignorance, he envies people who use grand language above his own comprehension. Some philosophers, on the other hand, have held that, besides these various goods, there is an absolute good which is the cause of goodness in them all. [These were members of Plato's school of thought.] It would perhaps be a waste of time to examine all these opinions; it will be enough to examine such as are most popular or as seem to be more or less reasonable.

. . . Men's conception of the good or of happiness may be read in the lives they lead. Ordinary or vulgar people conceive it to be a pleasure, and accordingly choose a life of enjoyment. For there are, we may say, three conspicuous types of life, the sensual, the political, and, thirdly, the life of thought. Now the mass of men present an absolutely slavish appearance, choosing the life of brute beasts, but they have ground for so doing because so many persons in authority share the tastes of Sardanapalus. [A half legendary ruler of ancient Assyria, whose name to the Greeks stood for the extreme of Oriental luxury and extravagance.] Cultivated and energetic people, on the other hand, identify happiness with honor, as honor is the general end of political life. But this seems too superficial an idea for our present purpose; for honor depends more upon the people who pay it than upon the person to whom it is paid, and the good we feel is something which is proper to a man himself and cannot be easily taken away from him. Men too appear to seek honor in order to be assured of their own goodness. Accordingly, they seek it at the hands of the sage and of those who know them well, and they seek it on the ground of their virtue; clearly then, in their judgment at any rate, virtue is better than honor. Perhaps then we might look on virtue rather than honor as the end of political life. Yet even this idea appears not quite complete; for a man may possess virtue and yet be asleep or inactive throughout life, and not only so, but he may experience the greatest calamities and misfortunes. Yet no one would call such a life a life of happiness, unless he were maintaining a paradox. But we need not dwell further on this subject, since it is sufficiently discussed in popular philosophical treatises. The third life is the life of thought, which we will discuss later. [The discussion of the life of thought occurs in Box X.]

The life of money making is a life of constraint; and wealth is obviously not the good of which we are in quest; for it is useful merely as a means to something else. It would be more reasonable to take the things mentioned before—sensual pleasure, honor, and virtue—as ends than wealth, since they are things desired on their own account. Yet these too are evidently not ends, although much argument has been employed to show that they are. . . .

But leaving this subject for the present, let us revert to the good of which we are in quest and consider what it may be. For it seems different in different activities or arts; it is one thing in medicine, another in strategy, and so on. What is the good in each of these instances? It is presumably that for the sake of which all else is done. In medicine this is health, in strategy victory, in architecture a house, and so on. In every activity and undertaking it is the end, since it is for the sake of the end that all people do whatever else they do. If then there is an end for all our activity, this will be the good to be accomplished; and if there are several such ends, it will be these.

Our argument has arrived by a different path at the same point as before; but we must endeavor to make it still plainer. Since there are more ends than one, and some of these ends—for example, wealth, flutes, and instruments generally—we desire as means to something else, it is evident that not all are final ends. But the highest good is clearly something final. Hence if there is only one final end, this will be the object of which we are in search; and if there are more than one, it will be the most final. We call that which is sought after for its own sake more final than that which is sought after as a means to something else; we call that which is never desired as a means to something else more final than things that are desired both for themselves and as means to something else. Therefore, we call absolutely final that which is always desired for itself and never as a means to something else. Now happiness more than anything else answers to this description. For happiness we always desire for its own sake and never as a means to something else, whereas honor, pleasure, intelligence, and every virtue we desire partly for their own sakes (for we should desire them independently of what might result from them), but partly also as means to happiness, because we suppose they will prove instruments of happiness. Happiness, on the other hand, nobody desires for the sake of these things, nor indeed as a means to anything else at all. . . .

Perhaps, however, it seems a commonplace to say that happiness is the supreme good; what is wanted is to define its nature a little more clearly. The best way of arriving at such a definition will probably be to ascertain the function of man. For, as with a flute player, a sculptor, or any artist, or in fact anybody who has a special function or activity, his goodness and excellence seem to lie in his function, so it would seem to be with man, if indeed he has a special function. Can it be said that, while a carpenter and a cobbler have special functions and activities, man, unlike them, is naturally functionless? Or, as the eye, the hand, the foot, and similarly each part of the body has a special function, so may man be regarded as having a special function apart from all these? What, then, can this function be? It is not life; for life is apparently something that man shares with plants; and we are looking for something peculiar to him. We must exclude therefore the life of nutrition and growth. There is next what may be called the life of sensation. But this too, apparently, is shared by man with horses, cattle, and all other animals. There remains what I may call the active life of the rational part of man's being. Now this rational part is twofold; one part is rational in the sense of being obedient to reason, and the other in the sense of possessing and exercising reason and intelligence. The active life too may be conceived of in two ways, [In other words, life may be taken to mean either the mere possession of certain faculties or their active exercise.] either as a state of character, or as an activity; but we mean by it the life of activity, as this seems to be the truer form of the conception.

The function of man then is activity of soul in accordance with reason, or not apart from reason. Now, the function of a man of a certain kind, and of a man who is good of that kind—for example, of a harpist and a good harpist—are in our view the same in kind. This is true of all people of all kinds without exception, the superior excellence being only an addition to the function; for it is the function of a harpist to play the harp, and of a good harpist to play the harp well. This being so, if we define the function of man as a kind of life, and this life as an activity of the soul or a course of action in accordance with reason, and if the function of a good man is such activity of a good and noble kind, and if everything is well done when it is done in accordance with its proper excellence, it follows that the good of man is activity of soul in accordance with virtue, or, if there are more virtues than one, in accordance with the best and most complete virtue. But we must add the words "in a complete life." For as one swallow or one day does not make a spring, so one day or a short time does not make a man blessed or happy. . . .

Our account accords too with the view of those who hold that happiness is virtue or excellence of some sort; for activity in accordance with virtue is virtue. But there is plainly a considerable difference between calling the supreme good possession or use, a state of mind, or an activity. For a state of mind may exist without producing anything good—for example, if a person is asleep, or in any other way inert. Not so with an activity, since activity implies acting and acting well. As in the Olympic games it is not the most beautiful and strongest who receive the crown but those who actually enter the combat, for from those come the victors, so it is those who act that win rightly what is noble and good in life.

Their life too is pleasant in itself. For pleasure is a state of mind, and whatever a man is fond of is pleasant to him, as a horse is to a lover of horses, a show to a lover of spectacles, and, similarly, just acts to a lover of justice, and virtuous acts in general to a lover of virtue. Now most men find a sense of discord in their pleasures, because their pleasures are not all naturally pleasant. But the lovers of nobleness take pleasure in what is naturally pleasant, and virtuous acts are naturally pleasant. Such acts then are pleasant both to these persons and in themselves. Nor does the life of such persons need more pleasure attached to it as a sort of charm; it possesses pleasure in itself. For, it may be added, a man who does not delight in noble acts is not good; as nobody would call a man just who did not enjoy just action, or liberal who did not enjoy liberal action, and so on. If this is so, it follows that acts of virtue are pleasant in themselves. They are also good and noble, and good and noble in the highest degree, for the judgment of the virtuous man on them is right, and his judgment is as we have described. Happiness then is the best and noblest and pleasantest thing in the world. . . .

Still it is clear, as we said, that happiness requires the addition of external goods; for it impossible, or at least difficult, to do noble needs with no outside means. For many things can be done only through the aid of friends or wealth or political power; and there are some things the lack of which spoils our felicity, such as good birth, wholesome children, and personal beauty. For a man who is extremely ugly in appearance or low born or solitary and childless can hardly be happy; perhaps still less so, if he has exceedingly bad children or friends, or has had good children or friends and lost them by death. As we said, then, happiness seems to need prosperity of this kind in addition to virtue. For this reason some persons identify happiness with good fortune, though others do so with virtue. . . .

It is reasonable then not to call an ox or a horse or any other animal happy; for none of them is capable of sharing in this activity. For the same reason no child can be happy, since the youth of a child keeps him for the time being from such activity; if a child is ever called happy, the ground of felicitation is his promise, rather than his actual performance. For happiness demands, as we said, a complete virtue and a complete life. And there are all sorts of changes and chances in life, and the most prosperous of men may in his old age fall into extreme calamities, as Priam did in the heroic legends. [The disastrous fate of Priam, king of Troy, was part of the well-known Homeric tales.] And a person who has experienced such chances and died a miserable death, nobody calls happy. . . .

If it is right to wait for the end, and only when the end has come, to call a man happy, not for being happy then but for having been so before, surely it is an extraordinary thing that, at the time when he is happy, we should not speak the truth about him, because we are unwilling to call the living happy in view of the changes to which they are liable, and because we have formed an idea of happiness as something permanent and exempt from the possibility of change, while every man is liable to many turns of fortune's wheel. . . .

The difficulty we have now discussed proves again the correctness of our definition. For there is no human function so constant as virtuous activities; . . . Among these activities too the most noble are the most permanent, and it is of them that the life of happiness chiefly and most continuously consists. This is apparently the reason why they are not likely to be forgotten. [Aristotle means that it is comparatively easy to forget scientific truths, when they have once been learned, but it is difficult, if not impossible, to love the habit of virtuous activity. In other words, knowledge is less stable, and therefore less valuable, than character.] The element of durability then which is required will be found in the happy man, and he will preserve his happiness through life; for always or chiefly he will pursue such actions and thoughts as accord with virtue; nor will anyone bear the chances of life so nobly, with such a perfect composure, as he who is truly good. . . .

Now the events of chance are numerous and of different magnitudes. Small pieces of good fortune or the reverse do not turn the scale of life in any way, but great and numerous events make life happier if they turn out well, since they naturally give it beauty and the use of them may be noble and good. If, on the other hand, they turn out badly, they mar and mutilate happiness by causing pain and hinderances to many activities. Still, even in these circumstances, nobility shines out when a person bears with calmness the weight of accumulated misfortunes, not from insensibility but from dignity and greatness of spirit.

Then if activities determine the quality of life, as we said, no happy man can become miserable; for he will never do what is hateful and mean. For our idea of the truly good and wise man is that he bears all the chances of life with dignity and always does what is best in the circumstances, as a good general makes the best use of the forces at his command in war, or a good cobbler makes the best shoe with the leather given him, and so on through the whole series of the arts. If this is so, the happy man can never become miserable. I do not say that he will be fortunate if he meets such chances of life as Priam. Yet he will not be variable or constantly changing, for he will not be moved from his happiness easily or by ordinary misfortunes, but only by great and numerous ones; nor after them will he quickly regain his happiness. If he regains it at all, it will be only over a long and complete period of time and after great and notable achievement.

We may safely then define a happy man as one who is active in accord with perfect virtue and adequately furnished with external goods, not for some chance period of time but for his whole lifetime. . . .

Inasmuch as happiness is an activity of soul in accordance with complete or perfect virtue, it is necessary to consider virtue, as this will perhaps be the best way of studying happiness. . . .

Virtue or excellence being twofold, partly intellectual and partly moral, intellectual virtue is both originated and fostered mainly by teaching; it therefore demands experience and time. Moral virtue on the other hand is the outcome of habit, . . . From this fact it is clear that no moral virtue is implanted in us by nature; a law of nature cannot be altered by habituation. . . . It is neither by nature than nor in defiance of nature that virtues are implanted in us. Nature gives us the capacity of receiving them, and that capacity is perfected by habit. . . .

It is not enough to state merely that virtue is a moral state, we must also describe the character of that moral state.

It must be laid down then that every virtue or excellence has the effect of producing a good condition of that of which it is a virtue or excellence, and of enabling it to perform its function well. Thus the excellence of the eye makes the eye good and its function good, as it is by the excellence of the eye that we see well. Similarly, the excellence of the horse makes a horse excellent and good at racing, at carrying its rider and at facing the enemy.

If then this is universally true, the virtue or excellence of man will be such a moral state as makes a man good and able to perform his proper function well. We have already explained how this will be the case, but another way of making it clear will be to study the nature or character of this virtue.

Now in everything, whether it be continuous or discrete, it is possible to take a greater, a smaller, or an equal amount, and this either absolutely or in relation to ourselves, the equal being a mean between excess and deficiency. By the mean in respect of the thing itself, or the absolute mean, I understand that which is equally distinct from both extremes; and this is one and the same thing for everybody. By the mean considered relatively to ourselves I understand that which is neither too much nor too little; but this is not one thing, nor is it the same for everybody. Thus if 10 be too much and 2 too little we take 6 as a mean in respect of the thing itself; for 6 is as much greater than 2 as it is less than 10, and this is a mean in arithmetical proportion. But the mean considered relatively to ourselves must not be ascertained in this way. It does not follow that if 10 pounds of meat be too much and 2 be too little for a man to eat, a trainer will order him 6 pounds, as this may itself be too much or too little for the person who is to take it; it will be too little e.g. for Milo [the famous Crotoniate wrestler], but too much for a beginner in gymnastics. It will be the same with running and wrestling; the right amount will vary with the individual. This being so, everybody who understands his business avoids alike excess and deficiency; he seeks and chooses the mean, not the absolute mean, but the mean considered relatively to ourselves.

Every science then performs its function well, if it regards the mean and refers the works which it produces to the mean. This is the reason why it is usually said of successful works that it is impossible to take anything from them or to add anything to them, which implies that excess or deficiency is fatal to excellence but that the mean state ensures it. Good artists too, as we say, have an eye to the mean in their works. But virtue, like Nature herself, is more accurate and better than any art; virtue therefore will aim at the mean;—I speak of moral virtue, as it is moral virtue which is concerned with emotions and actions, and it is these which admit of excess

Chapter IX: Happiness

and deficiency and the mean. Thus it is possible to go too far, or not to go far enough, in respect of fear, courage, desire, anger, pity, and pleasure and pain generally, and the excess and the deficiency are alike wrong; but to experience these emotions at the right times and on the right occasions and towards the right persons and for the right causes and in the right manner is the mean or the supreme good, which is characteristic of virtue. Similarly there may be excess, deficiency, or the mean, in regard to actions. But virtue is concerned with emotions and actions, and here excess is an error and deficiency a fault, whereas the mean is successful and laudable, and success and merit are both characteristics of virtue.

It appears then that virtue is a mean state, so far at least as it aims at the mean. . . .

Virtue then is a state of deliberate moral purpose consisting in a mean that is relative to ourselves, the mean being determined by reason, or as a prudent man would determine it. . . .

But it is not enough to lay down this as a general rule; it is necessary to apply it to particular cases. As in reasonings upon actions, general statements, although they are broader, are less exact than particular statements. For all action refers to particulars, and it is essential that our theories should harmonize with the particular cases to which they apply.

We must take particular virtues then from the catalogue of virtues.

In regard to feelings of fear and confidence, courage is a mean state. On the side of excess, he whose fearlessness is excessive has no name, as often happens, but he whose confidence is excessive is foolhardy, while he whose timidity is excessive and whose confidence is deficient is a coward.

In respect of pleasures and pains, although not indeed of all pleasures and pains, and to a less extent in respect of pains than of pleasures, the mean state is temperance, the excess is licentiousness. We never find people who are deficient in regard to pleasures; accordingly such people again have not received a name, but we may call them insensible.

As regards the giving and taking of money, the mean state is liberality, the excess and deficiency are prodigality and illiberality. . . .

In respect of honour and dishonour the mean state is highmindedness, the excess is what is called vanity, the deficiency littlemindedness. . . . Let us now discuss the other virtues in accordance with the method which we have followed hitherto.

Anger, like other emotions, has its excess, its deficiency, and its mean state. It may be said that they have no names, but as we call one who observes the mean gentle, we will call the mean state gentleness. Among the extremes, if a person errs on the side of excess, he may be called passionate and his vice passionateness, if on that of deficiency, he may be called impassive and his deficiency impassivity. . . .

It has now been sufficiently shown that moral virtue is a mean state, and in what sense it is a mean state; it is a mean state as lying between two vices, a vice of excess on the one side and a vice of deficiency on the other, and as aiming at the mean in the emotions and actions.

That is the reason why it is so hard to be virtuous; for it is always hard work to find the mean in anything, e.g., it is not everybody, but only a man of science, who can find the mean or centre of a circle. So too anybody can get angry—that is an easy matter—and anybody can give or spend money, but to give it to the right persons, to give the right amount of it and to give it at the right time and for the right cause and in the right way, this is not what anybody can do, nor is it easy. That is the reason why it is rare and laudable and noble to do well. . . .

If happiness consists of virtuous activity, it must be the activity of the highest virtue, or in other words, of the best part of our nature. Whether it is reason or something else that seems to exercise rule and authority over us by natural right and to reach up to things noble and divine—because it is itself either divine or the most divine part of us—the activity of this part in accordance with its proper virtue will be perfect happiness.

This . . . is an activity of thought or contemplation. Such a view would agree with our previous arguments and with the truth itself; for thought is the highest of our activities, as reason is the highest of our faculties, and the objects with which reason is concerned are the highest that can be known. Thought is also the most continuous, for it can more easily be continuous than any kind of action. We consider pleasure too an essential element of happiness; and we know there is no virtuous activity so pleasant as the activity of wisdom or philosophic reflection. Certainly philosophy is thought to offer pleasures of wonderful purity and certainty; and it is reasonable to suppose that people who know pass their time more pleasantly than people who are only searching.

Self-sufficiency too, of which we hear, is particularly a characteristic of thought activity. For while a philosopher, a just man, and everyone else needs the necessaries of life, after they are adequately provided with these things a just man still needs people to whom and with whom he may do justice, and a temperate man, a brave man, and everyone else needs others too. But the philosopher can contemplate truth by himself, and the wiser he is, the better he can do so. It is perhaps better for him to have fellow workers; nevertheless he is of all the most self-sufficient. It would seem too that this activity is the only one loved for its own sake, since it has no result but thinking; whereas from all practical action we gain something more or less besides the action itself. . . .

We conclude then that happiness reaches as far as the power of thought does, and that the greater a person's power of thought, the greater will be his happiness; not as something accidental but in virtue of his thinking, for that is noble in itself. Hence happiness must be a form of contemplation.

Man, nevertheless, being human, needs some external prosperity. His nature alone is not sufficient to support his thinking; it needs bodily health, food, and care of every kind. We must not however suppose that, because one cannot be happy without some external goods, a great variety of such goods is necessary for happiness. For neither self-sufficiency nor moral action demands excess of such things. We can do noble deeds without being lords of land and sea, for moderate means will enable a person to act virtuously. We may readily see this is so; for private persons are known to do good acts not less but actually more than their rulers. It is enough to have just as much as is needed for virtue. The man who lives in the active exercise of virtue will be happy. . . .

Happiness Not the End

Viktor E. Frankl

In the foregoing we have dealt with the question of meaning as it applies to the meaning of the universe. Now we shall take up a consideration of the many cases where patients ask what is the meaning of their individual, their personal lives. There is a characteristic twist a good many patients give to this question, which inexorably leads them to ethical nihilism. The patient will flatly assert that, after all, the whole meaning of life is pleasure. In the course of his argument he will cite it as an indisputable finding that all human activity is governed by the striving for happiness, that all psychic processes are determined exclusively by the pleasure principle. This theory of the dominant role of the pleasure principle in the whole of the psychic life is, as is well known, one of the basic tenets of psychoanalysis; the reality principle is not actually opposed to the pleasure principle, but is a mere extension of the pleasure principle, and serves its purposes.

Now, to our mind the pleasure principle is an artificial creation of psychology. Pleasure is an artificial creation of psychology. Pleasure is not the goal of our aspirations, but the consequence of attaining them. Kant long ago pointed this out. Commenting on the hedonist ethics, eudemonism, Scheler has remarked that pleasure does not loom up before us as the goal of an ethical act; rather, an ethical act carries pleasure on its back. The theory of the pleasure principle overlooks the intentional quality of all psychic activity. In general, men do not want pleasure; they simply want what they want. Human volition has any number of ends, of the most varied sorts, whereas pleasure would always take the same form, whether secured by ethical or unethical behavior. Hence it is evident that adopting the pleasure principle would, on the moral plane, lead to a leveling of all potential-human aims. It would become impossible to differentiate one action from another, since all would have the same purpose in view. A sum of money disbursed on good food or given in alms could be said to have served the same purpose: in either case the money went to remove unpleasurable feelings within the spender.

Chapter IX: Happiness

Define conduct in these terms and you devaluate every genuine moral impulse in man. In reality, an impulse of sympathy is already moral in itself, even before it is embodied in an act which allegedly has only the negative significance of eliminating unpleasure. For the same situation which in one person may arouse sympathy may stimulate a sadistic malicious joy in another, who gloats over someone's misfortune and in this manner experiences positive pleasure. If it were true that, for example, we read a good book only for the sake of the pleasurable sensation we feel during the reading, we might with equal justification spend our money on good cake. In reality, life is little concerned with pleasure or unpleasure. For the spectator in the theater it does not matter so much that he see a comedy or a tragedy; what allures him is the content, the intrinsic value of the play. Certainly no one will maintain that the unpleasure sensations which are aroused in the spectators who behold tragic events upon the stage are the real aim of their attendance at the theater. In that case, all theatergoers would have to be classed as disguised masochists.

But the argument that pleasure is the final goal of all (not merely the final effect of certain isolated) aspirations can be most effectively countered by reversing it. If, for example, it were true that Napoleon fought his battles only in order to experience the pleasure sensations of victory (the same pleasure sensations which the ordinary soldier might obtain by stuffing his belly, swilling, and whoring), then the reverse must also be true; that the "ultimate aim" of Napoleon's last disastrous battles, the "final purpose" of his defeats, could only have been the unpleasurable sensations which followed these defeats as surely as the pleasurable sensations followed the victories.

When we set up pleasure as the whole meaning of life, we insure that in the final analysis life shall inevitably seem meaningless. Pleasure cannot possibly lend meaning to life. For what is pleasure? A condition. The materialist—and hedonism is generally linked up with materialism—would even say pleasure is nothing but a state of the cells of the brain. And for the sake of inducing such a state, is it worth living, experiencing, suffering, and doing deeds? Suppose a man condemned to death is asked, a few hours before his execution, to choose the menu for his last meal. He might then reply: Is there any sense, in the face of death, in enjoying the pleasures of the palate? Since the organism will be a cadaver two hours later, does it matter whether it did or did not have one more opportunity to experience that state of the brain cells which is called pleasure? Yet all life is confronted with death, which should cancel out this element of pleasure. Anyone holding this hapless view of life as nothing but a pursuit of pleasure would have to doubt every moment of such a life, if he were to be consistent. He would be in the same frame of mind as a certain patient who was hospitalized after an attempted suicide. The patient in question described to me the following experience: In order to carry out his plan for suicide, he needed to get to an outlying part of the city. The street-cars were no longer running, and he therefore decided to take a cab. "Then I thought it over," he said, "wondering whether I ought to spend the few marks. Right away I could not help smiling at wanting to save a few marks when I would be dead so soon."

Life itself teaches most people that "we are not here to enjoy ourselves." Those who have not yet learned this lesson might be edified by the statistics of a Russian experimental psychologist who showed that the normal man in an average day experiences incomparably more unpleasure sensations than pleasure sensations. How unsatisfying the pleasure principle is in theory as well as practice is evident from a commonplace experience. If we ask a person why he does not do something that to us seems advisable, and the only "reason" he gives is: "I don't feel like it; it would give me no pleasure," we feel that this reply is distinctly unsatisfactory. It is apparent that the reply is insufficient because we can never admit pleasure or unpleasure as an argument for or against the advisability of any action.

The pleasure principle would remain untenable as a moral maxim even if it were actually what Freud claims it to be in his *Beyond the Pleasure Principle*: namely, a derivative from the general tendency of organic life to return to the peace of the inorganic. Freud thought he could prove the kinship of all pleasure-striving with what he named the death instinct. To our mind it is quite conceivable that all these psychological and biological primary tendencies might be reduced further, perhaps to a universal principle of tension reduction which operates to reduce all tension in every realm of being. Physics recognizes a similar law in its theory of entropy as leading to a final phase of the cosmos. Nirvana might be considered the psychological correlate of entropy; reduction of all psychic tensions by liberation from unpleasure sensations might then be viewed as the microcosmic equivalent of macrocosmic entropy. Nirvana, that is, may be entropy "seen from within." The principle of tension reduction itself, however, would represent the opposite of a principle of individuation which would endeavor to preserve all being as individuated being, as otherness. The very existence of such a polarity suggests that such formulations of universal principles, such findings of cosmic laws lead us up a blind alley, as far as ethics is concerned. For these phenomena have little bearing on our subjective and moral lives. What commands us to identify ourselves with all these principles and tendencies? To what extent is our ethical system to assent to such principles, even if we discover them in our own psychic life? We might equally well take the stand that our moral task is to oppose the rule of such forces with all our strength.

The nature of our education, heavily weighted as it is on the side of materialism, has left most of us with an exaggerated respect for the findings of the so-called exact sciences. We accept without question the picture of the world presented by physics. But how real, for example, is the entropy with which physics threatens us—how real is this universal doom, or this cosmic catastrophe which physics predicts, and in the light of which all the efforts of ourselves and our posterity seem to dwindle to nought? Are we not rather taught by "inner experience," by ordinary living unbiased by theories, that our natural pleasure in a beautiful sunset is in a way "more real" than, say, astronomical calculations of the time when the earth will crash into the sun? Can anything be given to us more directly than our own personal experience, our own deep feeling of our humanity as responsibility? "The most certain science is conscience," someone once remarked, and no theory of the physiological nature of life, nor the assertion that joy is a strictly organized dance of molecules or atoms or electrons within the gray matter of the brain, has ever been so compelling and convincing. Similarly, a man who is enjoying supreme artistic pleasure or the happiness of love never doubts for a moment that his life is meaningful.

Joy, however, may make life meaningful only if it itself has meaning. Its meaning cannot lie within itself. In fact it lies outside of itself. For joy is always directed toward an object. Scheler has already shown that joy is an intentional emotion—in contrast to mere pleasure, which he reckons among non-intentional emotions in a category he calls "conditional" emotions. Pleasure, that is, is an emotional condition. Here we are again reminded of Erwin Straus's concept of the "presentist" mode of life. In that mode a person remains in the conditional state of pleasure (say, in intoxication) without reaching out to the realm of objects—which in this case would be the realm of values. Only when the emotions work in terms of values can the individual feel pure "joy." This is the explanation of why joy can never be an end in itself; it itself, as joy, cannot be purposed as a goal. How well Kierkegaard expressed this in his maxim that the door to happiness opens outward. Anyone who tries to push this door open thereby causes it to close still more. The man who is desperately anxious to be happy thereby cuts off his own path to happiness. Thus in the end all striving for happiness—for the supposed "ultimate" in human life—proves to be in itself impossible. . . .

On The Meaning of Suffering

We have said that man's being consists of being conscious and being responsible. His responsibility is always responsibility for the actualization of values: not only "eternal" values, but also "situational values" (Scheler). Opportunities for the actualization of values change from person to person just as much as they change from hour to hour. The requirement that values be actualized—a requirement that radiates from the world of values into the lives of men—thus becomes a concrete demand for every single hour and a personal summons to every single person. The possibilities that every person has exclusively for himself are just as specific as the possibilities presented by every historical situation in its peculiar singularity. Thus the various values merge to form a concrete task for the individual. That merging gives them the uniqueness whereby every man feels himself personally and validly addressed. Until he learns what constitutes the singularity and uniqueness of his own existence, he cannot experience the fulfillment of his life task as something binding upon him.

In discussing the question of the meaning of life we have set up three categories of values. While the values of the first category are actualized by doing, experiential values are realized by the passive receiving of the world (nature, art) into the ego. Attitudinal values, however, are actualized wherever the individual is faced with something unalterable, something imposed by destiny. From the manner in which a person takes these things upon himself, assimilates these difficulties into his own psyche, there flows an incalculable multitude of value-potentialities. This means that *human life can be fulfilled not only in creating and enjoying, but also in suffering!*

Those who worship the superficial cult of success obviously will not understand such conclusions. But when we pause and consider our everyday judgments upon human existence, we see that we ascribe value and dignity to many things independently of the success or failure which may attend them. Great artists, in particular, have understood and described this phenomenon of inner fulfillment in spite of outward failure. An example that comes readily to mind is Tolstoy's story *The Death of Ivan Ilyich*. The story concerns a respectable government official, the abysmal meaninglessness of whose life only dawns upon him when he is faced with unexpected death. But with insight into this meaninglessness the man grows far beyond himself in the last hours of his life; he attains an inner greatness which retroactively hallows all of his previous life—in spite of its apparent futility—and makes it meaningful. Life, that is, can receive its ultimate meaning not only as the result of death (the man who is a hero), but in the very process of death. Not only the sacrifice of one's life can give life meaning; life can reach nobility even as it founders on the rocks.

The untenability of the cult of success becomes obvious as soon as we consider the moral problem of sacrifice. Insofar as a sacrifice is "calculated," performed after careful reckoning of the prospects of its bringing about a desired end, it loses all ethical significance. Real sacrifice occurs only when we run the risk of having sacrificed in vain. Would anyone maintain that a person who plunges into the water to save someone has acted less ethically, or unethically, because both are drowned? Do we not rather presuppose this risk when we assign a high ethical standing to the rescuer's action? Consider what a high ethical rating we place upon the life of a man who has fought vainly but heroically—and has died heroically but not vainly.

Lack of success does not signify lack of meaning. This also becomes obvious when we look back upon our own past and consider, say, the times we have been in love. Let anyone honestly ask himself whether he would be prepared to strike his unhappy love affairs, with all their self-

Chapter IX: Happiness

doubt and suffering, out of the record of his life. Almost certainly he would not. The fullness of suffering did not seem to him lack of fulfillment. On the contrary, the suffering matured him; he grew as a result of it; his ill-fated love gave him more than many an erotic success might have given him.

In general, people are inclined to overestimate the positive or negative aspects, or the pleasant or unpleasant tone of their experiences. In giving an exaggerated importance to these aspects, they are apt to cultivate an unjustified self-pity in respect to fate. We have already discussed the numerous senses in which man is "not in this world for enjoyment." We have pointed out that pleasure is incapable of giving meaning to man's life. If this is so, lack of pleasure in life does not detract from its meaning. Once again art comes to our aid with examples: we have only to recall how irrelevant with regard to artistic merit is the question of whether a melody is in the major or minor modes. Not only are the unfinished symphonies among the finest, as we have mentioned in another connection; so also are the *"pathétiques."*

We have said that in creating, man actualizes creative values; in experiencing, experiential values; and in suffering, attitudinal values. Beyond that, however, suffering has a meaning in itself. In suffering from something we move inwardly away from it, we establish a distance between our personality and this something. As long as we are still suffering from a condition that ought not to be, we remain in a state of tension between what actually is on the one hand and what ought to be on the other hand. And only while in this state of tension can we continue to envision the ideal. As we have already seen, this even applies to the person who has despaired of himself; by the very fact of his despair he has cast off some of the blame attaching to himself, since he is evaluating his own reality in terms of an ideality and the fact that he can at all envision values (even though unrealized ones) implies a certain value in himself. He could not sit in judgment upon himself if he did not already possess the worth and dignity of a judge—of a man who has perceived what ought to be as against what at the moment is. Suffering therefore establishes a fruitful, one might say a revolutionary, tension in that it makes for emotional awareness of what ought not to be. To the degree that a person identifies himself with things as they are, he eliminates his distance from them and forfeits the fruitful tension between what is and what ought to be.

Thus there is revealed in man's emotions a deep wisdom superior to all reason, which in fact runs counter to the gospel of rationalistic utility. Consider, for instance, the effects of grief and repentance. From the utilitarian point of view both necessarily appear to be meaningless. To mourn for anything irrevocably lost must seem useless and foolish from the point of view of "sound common sense," and this holds also for repenting an irredeemable wrong. But for the inner biography of man, grief and repentance do have meaning. Grieving for a person whom we have loved and lost in a sense continues his life, and repentance permits the culprit to rise again, as it were, freed of guilt. The loved person whom we grieve for has been lost objectively, in empirical time, but he is preserved subjectively, in inner time. Grief brings him into the mind's present. And repentance, as Scheler has shown, has the power to wipe out a wrong; though the wrong cannot be undone, the culprit himself undergoes a moral rebirth. This opportunity to make past events fruitful for one's inner history does not stand in opposition to man's responsibility, but in a dialectical relationship. For guilt presupposes responsibility. Man is responsible in view of the fact that he cannot retrace a single step; the smallest as well as the biggest decision remains a final one. None of his acts of commission or omission can be wiped off the slate as if they had never been. Nevertheless, in repenting man may inwardly break with an act, and in living out this repentance—which is an inner event—he can undo the outer event on a spiritual, moral plane. Only to the most superficial view is there any contradiction between these two statements.

Schopenhauer, as is well known, complained that human life dangles between trouble and boredom. In reality both have their profound meaning. Boredom is a continual reminder. What leads to boredom? Inactivity. But activity does not exist for the purpose of our escaping boredom; rather, boredom exists so that we will escape inactivity and do justice to the meaning of our life. The struggle of life keeps us in "suspense" because the meaning of life depends upon whether or not we fulfill the demands placed upon us by our tasks. This suspense is therefore different in nature from the type engendered by a neurotic passion for sensation or a hysterical hunger for stimulus.

The meaning of "trouble" is also that it is a reminder. On the biological plane, as we know, pain is a meaningful watcher and warder. In the psycho-spiritual realm it has a similar function. Suffering is intended to guard man from apathy, from psychic *rigor mortis*. As long as we suffer we remain psychically alive. In fact, we mature in suffering, grow because of it—it makes us richer and stronger. Repentance, as we have seen, has the power to undo, and the significance of undoing, an outer event in the moral sense, within the biography of the individual; grief has the power to perpetuate, and the significance of perpetuating, the past in the present. Both thus serve to correct the past, so to speak. In so doing they solve a problem—as diversion and narcotization cannot do. The person who tries to "take his mind off" a misfortune or narcotize his feelings solves no problem, comes to no terms with misfortune; all he does is get rid of a mere aftereffect of the misfortune: the sensation of unpleasure. By diversion or narcotization he makes himself "ignore" what has happened—he no longer knows it. He tries to escape reality. He takes refuge, say, in intoxication. But this is to commit a subjectivistic, in fact a psychologistic, error: the error of acting as if "silencing" the feeling by narcotization also makes an end of the object of the emotion; as if what has been banished to

Chapter IX: Happiness

non-consciousness were thereby banished to unreality. But the act of looking at something does not create that thing; neither does the act of looking away annihilate it. And so the suppression of an impulse of grief does not annul the thing that is grieved over. Mourners, in fact, ordinarily rebel against, say, taking a sedative instead of weeping all through the night. To the trite suggestion that he take a sleeping-powder the grief-stricken person commonly retorts that his sleeping better will not awaken the lost one whom he mourns. Death—that paradigm of the irreversible event—is not wiped off the slate by being pushed out of consciousness, any more than when the mourner himself takes refuge in absolute non-consciousness—the non-consciousness and the non-responsibility of his own death.

As contrasted with narcotization, intoxication has positive aspects. The essence of intoxication is a turning away from the objective world and a turning toward a subjective world. Narcotization, on the other hand, leads only to non-consciousness of unhappiness, to "happiness" in Schopenhauer's negative sense, to a nirvana mood. Narcotization is spiritual anesthesia. But just as surgical anesthesia can induce death, so spiritual anesthesia can lead to a kind of spiritual death. Consistent suppression of intrinsically meaningful emotional impulses because of their possible unpleasurable tone ends in the killing of a person's inner life. A sense of the meaning of emotional experiences is deeply rooted in human beings, as the following example indicates. There is a type of melancholia in which sadness is conspicuous by its absence. Instead, the patients complain that they cannot feel sad enough, that they cannot cry out their melancholy, that they are emotionally cold and inwardly dead. Such patients are suffering from what we call *melancholia anæsthetica*. Anyone acquainted with such cases knows that greater despair can scarcely exist than the despair of such persons because they are unable to be sad. This paradox again makes it plain that the pleasure principle is a mere construct but not a phenomenological fact. Out of his emotional *"logique du cœur"* man is actually always striving, whether his emotions be joyful or sad, to remain psychically "alive" and not to sink into apathy. The paradox that the sufferer from *melancholia anæsthetica* should suffer from his incapacity to suffer is therefore only a paradox for psychopathology. For existential analysis it is no paradox at all, since existential analysis recognizes the meaning of suffering, installs suffering in a place of honor in life. Suffering and trouble belong to life as much as fate and death. None of these can be subtracted from life without destroying its meaning. To subtract trouble, death, fate, and suffering from life would mean stripping life of its form and shape. Only under the hammer blows of fate, in the white heat of suffering, does life gain shape and form.

The destiny a person suffers therefore has a twofold meaning: to be shaped where possible, and to be endured where necessary. Let us also remember that "inactive," passive enduring still retains the immanent meaning of all suffering. On the other hand, man must be on his guard against the temptation to lay down his arms prematurely, too soon accepting a state of things as destined and bowing his head before a merely imaginary fate. Only when he no longer has any possibility of actualizing creative values, when there is really no means at hand for shaping fate—then is the time for attitudinal values to be actualized; then alone does it have meaning for him to "take his cross." The very essence of an attitudinal value inheres in the manner in which a person resigns himself to the inevitable; in order therefore for attitudinal values to be truly actualized, it is important that the fate he resigns himself to must be actually inevitable. It must be what Brod has called "noble misfortune" as against the "ignoble misfortune," the latter being something which is either avoidable, or for which the person himself is to blame.[1]

One way or another, then, every situation holds out the opportunity for the actualization of values—either creative or attitudinal values. "There is no predicament that we cannot ennoble either by doing or enduring," says Goethe. We might say that even in enduring there is a kind of doing implicit, provided that the enduring is of the right kind, that what must be endured is a fated situation that cannot be either altered by doing or avoided by not doing. This "right" enduring is the kind which constitutes a moral achievement; only such unavoidable suffering is meaningful suffering. This moral achievement implicit in suffering is something that the ordinary person in his simple, straightforward way knows quite well. He can well understand, for example, the following incident:

Some years ago when prizes were to be awarded to British Boy Scouts for highest accomplishments, the coveted awards went to three boys hospitalized for incurable diseases who nevertheless remained brave and cheerful and steadfastly endured their suffering. Their record of suffering was recognized as greater in accomplishment that the records in athletics, etc., of so many other Boy Scouts.

"Life is not anything; it is only the opportunity for something." This maxim of Hebbel's seems to cover the subject. For the alternatives are either to shape fate (that is, one's unalterable situation) and so realize creative values, or, if this should really prove to be impossible, to take such an attitude toward fate that, in the sense of attitudinal values, there is achievement in suffering. It sounds like a tautology to say that illnesses give people the "opportunity" for "suffering." But if we understand "opportunity" and "suffering" in the above sense, the matter ceases to be obvious. It is above all not obvious because a fundamental distinction must be made between sickness—including psychic illness—and suffering. On the one hand, people can be sick without "suffering" in the proper sense. On the other hand, there is a suffering beyond all sickness, a fundamental human suffering, the suffering which belongs to human life by the very nature and meaning of life. Consequently, cases may arise where existential analysis is called upon to make a person capable of suffering—whereas psychoanaly-

Chapter IX: Happiness

sis, for instance, aims only at making him capable of pleasure or capable of doing. For there are situations in which man can fulfill himself only in genuine suffering, and in no other way. And just as men can miss the "opportunity for something" which life means, so can they miss their opportunity for genuine suffering, with its opening for the actualizing of attitudinal values. In the light of this we can agree with Dostoevsky when he said that he feared only one thing: that he might not be worthy of his torment. And we can now appreciate what an accomplishment there is in the suffering of patients who appear to be struggling—to be worthy of their torment.

An extraordinarily brilliant young man was abruptly forced to give up his active professional life. An abscess of the spinal cord caused by tubercular affection had produced symptoms of paralysis in the legs. An operation (laminectomy) was considered. Friends of the patient consulted one of the foremost neurosurgeons of Europe. He was pessimistic about the prognosis and refused to undertake the operation. This decision was reported in a letter to another of the sick man's friends, who was caring for him at her country house. The unsuspecting servant girl handed the letter to her mistress while the latter was breakfasting with her sick guest. What followed is described by the patient in a letter of his from which we take the following passages: ". . . In the situation Eva could not help letting me read the letter. And so I was informed of my death sentence, which was obvious from the surgeon's remarks.—I recall the movie about the *Titanic*, which I saw many years ago. What I particularly recall is the scene in which the paralyzed cripple, played by Fritz Kortner, reciting the Lord's Prayer, ushers a small group of fellow victims toward death, while the ship sinks and the water rises higher and higher around their bodies. I came out of the movie deeply shaken. What a gift of fate it must be, I thought at the time, consciously to go toward one's death. And now here was fate granting me that! I get this last chance to test my fighting spirit, only this is a fight where the question of victory is ruled out at the start. Rather, it's a last exertion of simple strength, a last gymnastic drill, as it were. . . . I want to bear the pain without narcotics as long as it is at all possible. . . . 'A fight for a lost cause?' In terms of our philosophy, that phrase has to be stricken off the books. The fighting alone is what counts. . . . There cannot be any lost causes. . . . In the evening we played Bruckner's *Fourth*, the *Romantic Symphony*. I was filled with emotion of love for all mankind, a sense of cosmic vastness.—For the rest, I work away at mathematics and don't give way to sentimentality."

At another time illness and the approach of death may draw forth the ultimate capacities from a man who has hitherto wasted his life in "metaphysical frivolity" (Scheler) and let his own potentialities lie fallow. A young woman who had led an utterly pampered existence was one day unexpectedly thrown into a concentration camp. There she fell ill and was visibly wasting away. A few days before she died she said these very words: "Actually I am grateful to my fate for having treated me so harshly. In my former middle-class existence I certainly had things a great deal too easy. I never was very serious about my literary ambitions." She saw death coming and looked it squarely in the eye. From her bed in the infirmary she could catch a glimpse of a chestnut tree in blossom outside the window. She spoke of this tree often, though from where the sick woman's head lay just one twig with two blossoms was visible. "This tree is my only friend in solitude," the woman said. "I converse with it." Was this a hallucination? Was she delirious? Did she think the tree was "answering" her? What strange dialogue was this; what had the flowering tree "said" to the dying woman? "It says: 'I am here, I am here—I am life, eternal life.'"

Viktor von Weizsäcker once remarked that the patient, as the sufferer, is superior to the doctor. Certainly I had that feeling when I left this patient. A doctor who is sensitive to the imponderables of a situation will always feel a kind of shame when attending a patient with an incurable disease, or a dying person. For the doctor himself is helpless, incapable of wresting this victim from death. But the patient has become a hero who is meeting his fate and holding his own by accepting it in tranquil suffering. That is, upon a metaphysical plane, a true achievement—while the doctor in the physical world, in his physician's realm, has his hands tied, is a failure.

From *The Doctor and the Soul: From Psychotherapy to Logotherapy*, by Viktor E. Frankl, translated by Richard and Clara Winston. Copyright © 1955, 1965 by Alfred A. Knopf, Inc. Reprinted by permission of the publisher.

Endnote

1. The difference between evitable or blameworthy destiny ("ignoble misfortune") on the one hand and inevitable, immutable destiny ("noble misfortune") on the other hand (to suffer the latter alone provides opportunities for the realization of attitudinal values) has its parallel in the distinction mountaineers make between subjective and objective dangers. For the mountaineer it is not discreditable to succumb to objective perils (such as a falling rock), while it is considered shameful to be halted by a subjective failure (such as faulty equipment, lack of skill, or inadequate climbing-experience).

Happiness Is Enjoying the Chief Good

Saint Augustine

Happiness is in the enjoyment of man's chief good. Two conditions of the chief good: 1st, Nothing is better than it; 2nd, it cannot be lost against the will.

How then, according to reason, ought man to live? We all certainly desire to live happily; and there is no human being but assents to this statement almost before it is made. But the title happy cannot, in my opinion, belong either to him who has not what he loves, whatever it may be, or to him who has what he loves if it is hurtful, or to him who does not love what he has, although it is good in perfection. For one who seeks what he cannot obtain suffers torture, and one who has got what is not desirable is cheated, and one who does not seek for what is worth seeking for is diseased. Now in all these cases the mind cannot but be unhappy, and happiness and unhappiness cannot reside at the same time in one man; so in none of these cases can the man be happy. I find, then, a fourth case, where the happy life exists,—when that which is man's chief good is both loved and possessed. For what do we call enjoyment but having at hand the object of love? And no one can be happy who does not enjoy what is man's chief good, nor is there any one who enjoys this who is not happy. We must then have at hand our chief good, if we think of living happily.

We must now inquire what is man's chief good, which of course cannot be anything inferior to man himself. For whoever follows after what is inferior to himself, becomes himself inferior. But every man is bound to

637

follow what is best. Wherefore man's chief good is not inferior to man. Is it then something similar to man himself? It must be so, if there is nothing above man which he is capable of enjoying. But if we find something which is both superior to man, and can be possessed by the man who loves it, who can doubt that in seeking for happiness man should endeavour to reach that which is more excellent than the being who makes the endeavour? For if happiness consists in the enjoyment of a good than which there is nothing better, which we call the chief good, how can a man be properly called happy who has not yet attained to his chief good? or how can that be the chief good beyond which something better remains for us to arrive at? Such, then, being the chief good, it must be something which cannot be lost against the will. For no one can feel confident regarding a good which he knows can be taken from him, although he wishes to keep and cherish it. But if a man feels no confidence regarding the good which he enjoys, how can he be happy while in such fear of losing it?

Man—what?

Let us then see what is better than man. This must necessarily be hard to find, unless we first ask and examine what man is. I am not now called upon to give a definition of man. The question here seems to me to be,— since almost all agree, or at least, which is enough, those I have now to do with are of the same opinion with me, that we are made up of soul and body,—What is man? Is he both of these? or is he the body only, or the soul only? For although the things are two, soul and body, and although neither without the other could be called man (for the body would not be man without the soul, nor again would the soul be man if there were not a body animated by it), still it is possible that one of these may be held to be man, and may be called so. What then do we call man? Is he soul and body, as in a double harness, or like a centaur? Or do we mean the body only, as being in the service of the soul which rules it, as the word lamp denotes not the light and the case together, but only the case, though on account of the light? Or do we mean only mind, and that on account of the body which it rules, as horseman means not the man and the horse, but the man only, and that as employed in ruling the horse? This dispute is not easy to settle; or, if the proof is plain, the statement requires time. This is an expenditure of time and strength which we need not incur. For whether the name man belongs to both, or only to the soul, the chief good of man is not the chief good of the body; but what is the chief good either of both soul and body, or of the soul only, that is man's chief good.

Chapter IX: Happiness

Man's chief good is not the chief good of the body only, but the chief good of the soul.

Now if we ask what is the chief good of the body, reason obliges us to admit that it is that by means of which the body comes to be in its best state. But of all the things which invigorate the body, there is nothing better or greater than the soul. The chief good of the body, then, is not bodily pleasure, not absence of pain, not strength, not beauty, not swiftness, or whatever else is usually reckoned among the goods of the body, but simply the soul. For all the things mentioned the soul supplies to the body by its presence, and, what is above them all, life. Hence I conclude that the soul is not the chief good of man, whether we give the name of man to soul and body together, or to the soul alone. For as, according to reason, the chief good of the body is that which is better than the body, and from which the body receives vigour and life, so whether the soul itself is man, or soul and body both, we must discover whether there is anything which goes before the soul itself, in following which the soul comes to the perfection of good of which it is capable in its own kind. If such a thing can be found, all uncertainty must be at an end, and we must pronounce this to be really and truly the chief good of man.

If, again, the body is man, it must be admitted that the soul is the chief good of man. But clearly, when we treat of morals—when we inquire what manner of life must be held in order to obtain happiness—it is not the body to which the precepts are addressed, it is not bodily discipline which we discuss. In short, the observance of good customs belongs to that part of us which inquires and learns, which are the prerogatives of the soul; so, when we speak of attaining to virtue, the question does not regard the body. But if it follows, as it does, that the body which is ruled over by a soul possessed of virtue is ruled both better and more honourably, and is in its greatest perfection in consequence of the perfection of the soul which rightfully governs it, that which gives perfection to the soul will be man's chief good, though we call the body man. For if my coachman, in obedience to me, feeds and drives the horses he has charge of in the most satisfactory manner, himself enjoying the more of my bounty in proportion to his good conduct, can any one deny that the good condition of the horses, as well as that of the coachman, is due to me? So the question seems to me to be not, whether soul and body is man, or the soul only, or body only, but what gives perfection to the soul; for when this is obtained, a man cannot but be either perfect, or at least much better than in the absence of this one thing.

Virtue gives perfection to the soul; the soul obtains virtue by following God; following God is the happy life.

No one will question that virtue gives perfection to the soul. But it is a very proper subject of inquiry whether this virtue can exist by itself or only in the soul. Here again arises a profound discussion, needing lengthy treatment; but perhaps my summary will serve the purpose. God will, I trust, assist me, so that, notwithstanding our feebleness, we may give instruction on these great matters briefly as well as intelligibly. In either case, whether virtue can exist by itself without the soul, or can exist only in the soul, undoubtedly in the pursuit of virtue the soul follows after something, and this must be either the soul itself, or virtue, or something else. But if the soul follows after itself in the pursuit of virtue, it follows after a foolish thing; for before obtaining virtue it is foolish. Now the height of a follower's desire is to reach that which he follows after. So the soul must either not wish to reach what it follows after, which is utterly absurd and unreasonable, or, in following after itself while foolish, it reaches the folly which it flees from. But if it follows after virtue in the desire to reach it, how can it follow what does not exist? or how can it desire to reach what it already possesses? Either, therefore, virtue exists beyond the soul, or if we are not allowed to give the name of virtue except to the habit and disposition of the wise soul, which can exist only in the soul, we must allow that the soul follows after something else in order that virtue may be produced in itself; for neither by following after nothing, nor by following after folly, can the soul, according to my reasoning, attain to wisdom.

This something else, then, by following after which the soul becomes possessed of virtue and wisdom, is either a wise man or God. But we have said already that it must be something that we cannot lose against our will. No one can think it necessary to ask whether a wise man, supposing we are content to follow after him, can be taken from us in spite of our unwillingness or our persistence. God then remains, in following after whom we live well, and in reaching whom we live both well and happily.

OF THE MORALS OF THE CATHOLIC CHURCH From *The Works of Aurelius Augustine.* Edited by M. Dods (T. & T. Clark, Edinburgh, 1892). Reprinted with permission from T. & T. Clark Ltd., Edinburgh, Scotland

The Encheiridion

Epictetus

1. Some things are under our control, while others are not under our control. Under our control are conception, choice, desire, aversion, and, in a word, everything that is our own doing; not under our control are our body, our property, reputation, office, and, in a word, everything that is not our own doing. Furthermore, the things under our control are by nature free, unhindered, and unimpeded; while the things not under our control are weak, servile, subject to hindrance, and not our own. Remember, therefore, that if what is naturally slavish you think to be free, and what is not your own to be your own, you will be hampered, will grieve, will be in turmoil, and will blame both gods and men; while if you think only what is your own to be your own, and what is not your own to be, as it really is, not your own, then no one will ever be able to exert compulsion upon you, no one will hinder you, you will blame no one, will find fault with no one, will do absolutely nothing against your will, you will have no personal enemy, no one will harm you, for neither is there any harm that can touch you.

With such high aims, therefore, remember that you must bestir yourself with no slight effort to lay hold of them, but you will have to give up some things entirely, and defer others for the time being. But if you wish for these things also, and at the same time for both office and wealth, it may be that you will not get even these latter, because you aim also at the former, and certainly you will fail to get the former, which alone bring freedom and happiness.

Make it, therefore, your study at the very outset to say to every harsh external impression, "You are an external impression and not at all what you appear to be." After that examine it and test it by these rules which you have, the first and most important of which is this: Whether the impression has to do with the things which are under our control, or with those which are not under our control; and, if it has to do with some one of the things not under our control, have ready to hand the answer, "It is nothing to me."

2. Remember that the promise of desire is the attainment of what you desire, that of aversion is not to fall into what is avoided, and that he who fails in his desire is unfortunate, while he who falls into what he would avoid experiences misfortune. If, then, you avoid only what is unnatural among those things which are under your control, you will fall into none of the things which you avoid; but if you try to avoid disease, or death, or poverty, you will experience misfortune. Withdraw, therefore, your aversion from all the matters that are not under our control, and transfer it to what is unnatural among those which are under our control. But for the time being remove utterly your desire; for if you desire some one of the things that are not under our control you are bound to be unfortunate; and, at the same time, not one of the things that are under our control, which it would be excellent for you to desire, is within your grasp. But employ only choice and refusal, and these too but lightly, and with reservations, and without straining.

3. With everything which entertains you, is useful, or of which you are fond, remember to say to yourself, beginning with the very least things, "What is its nature?" If you are fond of a jug, say "I am fond of a jug"; for when it is broken you will not be disturbed. If you kiss your own child or wife, say to yourself that you are kissing a human being; for when it dies you will not be disturbed.

4. When you are on the point of putting your hand to some undertaking, remind yourself what the nature of that undertaking is. If you are going out of the house to bathe, put before your mind what happens at a public bath—those who splash you with water, those who jostle against you, those who vilify you and rob you. And thus you will set about your undertaking more securely if at the outset you say to yourself, "I want to take a bath, and, at the same time, to keep my moral purpose in harmony with nature." And so do in every undertaking. For thus, if anything happens to hinder you in your bathing, you will be ready to say, "Oh, well, this was not the only thing that I wanted, but I wanted also to keep my moral purpose in harmony with nature; and I shall not so keep it if I am vexed at what is going on."

5. It is not the things themselves that disturb men, but their judgments about these things. For example, death is nothing dreadful, or else Socrates too would have thought so, but the judgment that death is dreadful, *this* is the dreadful thing. When, therefore, we are hindered, or disturbed, or grieved, let us never blame anyone but ourselves, that means, our own judgments. It is the part of an uneducated person to blame others where he himself fares ill; to blame himself is the part of one whose education has begun; to blame neither another nor his own self is the part of one whose education is already complete.

6. Be not elated at any excellence which is not your own. If the horse in his elation were to say, "I am beautiful," it could be endured; but when you

Chapter IX: Happiness

say in your elation, "I have a beautiful horse," rest assured that you are elated at something good which belongs to a horse. What, then, is your own? The use of external impressions. Therefore, when you are in harmony with nature in the use of external impressions, then be elated; for then it will be some good of your own at which you will be elated.

7. Just as on a voyage, when your ship has anchored, if you should go on shore to get fresh water, you may pick up a small shell-fish or little bulb on the way, but you have to keep your attention fixed on the ship, and turn about frequently for fear lest the captain should call; and if he calls, you must give up all these things, if you would escape being thrown on board all tied up like the sheep. So it is also in life: If there be given you, instead of a little bulb and a small shell-fish, a little wife and child, there will be no objection to that; only, if the Captain calls, give up all these things and run to the ship, without even turning around to look back. And if you are an old man, never even get very far away from the ship, for fear that when He calls you may be missing.

8. Do not seek to have everything that happens happen as you wish, but wish for everything to happen as it actually does happen, and your life will be serene.

9. Disease is an impediment to the body, but not to the moral purpose, unless that consents. Lameness is an impediment to the leg, but not to the moral purpose. And say this to yourself at each thing that befalls you; for you will find the thing to be an impediment to something else, but not to yourself.

10. In the case of everything that befalls you, remember to turn to yourself and see what faculty you have to deal with it. If you see a handsome lad or woman, you will find continence the faculty to employ here; if hard labour is laid upon you, you will find endurance; if reviling, you will find patience to bear evil. And if you habituate yourself in this fashion, your external impressions will not run away with you.

11. Never say about anything, "I have lost it," but only "I have given it back." Is your child dead? It has been given back. Is your wife dead? She has been given back. "I have had my farm taken away." Very well, this too has been given back. "Yet it was a rascal who took it away." But what concern is it of yours by whose instrumentality the Giver called for its return? So long as He gives it to you, take care of it as of a thing that is not your own, as travellers treat their inn.

12. If you wish to make progress, dismiss all reasoning of this sort: "If I neglect my affairs, I shall have nothing to live on." "If I do not punish my slave-boy he will turn out bad." For it is better to die of hunger, but in a state of freedom from grief and fear, than to live in plenty, but troubled in mind. And it is better for your slave-boy to be bad than for you to be unhappy. Begin, therefore, with the little things. Your paltry oil gets spilled, your miserable wine stolen; say to yourself; "This is the price paid

for a calm spirit, this the price for peace of mind." Nothing is got without a price. And when you call your slave-boy, bear in mind that it is possible he may not heed you, and again, that even if he does heed, he may not do what you want done. But he is not in so happy a condition that your peace of mind depends upon him.

13. If you wish to make progress, then be content to appear senseless and foolish in externals, do not make it your wish to give the appearance of knowing anything; and if some people think you to be an important personage, distrust yourself. For be assured that it is no easy matter to keep your moral purpose in a state of conformity with nature, and, at the same time, to keep externals; but the man who devotes his attention to one of these two things must inevitably neglect the other.

14. If you make it your will that your children and your wife and your friends should live for ever, you are silly; for you are making it your will that things not under your control should be under your control, and that what is not your own should be your own. In the same way, too, if you make it your will that your slave-boy be free from faults, you are a fool; for you are making it your will that vice be not vice, but something else. If, however, it is your will not to fail in what you desire, this is in your power. Wherefore, exercise yourself in that which is in your power. Each man's master is the person who has the authority over what the man wishes or does not wish, so as to secure it, or take it away. Whoever, therefore, wants to be free, let him neither wish for anything, nor avoid anything, that is under the control of others; or else he is necessarily a slave.

15. Remember that you ought to behave in life as you would at a banquet. As something is being passed around it comes to you; stretch out your hand and take a portion of it politely. It passes on; do not detain it. Or it has not come to you yet; do not project your desire to meet it, but wait until it comes in front of you. So act toward children, so toward a wife, so toward office, so toward wealth; and then some day you will be worthy of the banquets of the gods. But if you do not take these things even when they are set before you, but despise them, then you will not only share the banquet of the gods, but share also their rule. For it was by so doing that Diogenes and Heracleitus, and men like them, were deservedly divine and deservedly so called.

16. When you see someone weeping in sorrow, either because a child has gone on a journey, or because he has lost his property, beware that you be not carried away by the impression that the man is in the midst of external ills, but straightway keep before you this thought: "It is not what has happened that distresses this man (for it does not distress another), but his judgment about it." Do not, however, hesitate to sympathize with him so far as words go, and, if occasion offers, even to groan with him; but be careful not to groan also in the centre of your being.

17. Remember that you are an actor in a play, the character of which is determined by the Playwright; if He wishes the play to be short, it is short;

Chapter IX: Happiness

if long, it is long; if He wishes you to play the part of a beggar, remember to act even this rôle adroitly; and so if your rôle be that of a cripple, an official, or a layman. For this is your business, to play admirably the rôle assigned you; but the selection of that rôle is Another's.

18. When a raven croaks inauspiciously, let not the external impression carry you away, but straightway draw a distinction in your mind, and say, "None of these portents are for me, but either for my paltry body, or my paltry estate, or my paltry opinion, or my children, or my wife. But for me every portent is favourable, if I so wish; for whatever be the outcome, it is within my power to derive benefit from it."

19. You can be invincible if you never enter a contest in which victory is not under your control. Beware lest, when you see some person preferred to you in honour, or possessing great power, or otherwise enjoying high repute, you are ever carried away by the external impression, and deem him happy. For if the true nature of the good is one of the things that are under our control, there is no place for either envy or jealousy; and you yourself will not wish to be a praetor, or a senator, or a consul, but a free man. Now there is but one way that leads to this, and that is to despise the things that are not under our control.

20. Bear in mind that it is not the man who reviles or strikes you that insults you, but it is your judgment that these men are insulting you. Therefore, when someone irritates you, be assured that it is your own opinion which has irritated you. And so make it your first endeavour not to be carried away by the external impression; for if once you gain time and delay, you will more easily become master of yourself.

21. Keep before your eyes day by day death and exile, and everything that seems terrible, but most of all death; and then you will never have any abject thought, nor will you yearn for anything beyond measure.

22. If you yearn for philosophy, prepare at once to be met with ridicule, to have many people jeer at you, and say, "Here he is again, turned philosopher all of a sudden," and "Where do you suppose he got that high brow?" But do you not put on a high brow, and do you so hold fast to the things which to you seem best, as a man who has been assigned by God to this post; and remember that if you abide by the same principles, those who formerly used to laugh at you will later come to admire you, but if you are worsted by them, you will get the laugh on yourself twice.

23. If it should ever happen to you that you turn to externals with a view to pleasing someone, rest assured that you have lost your plan of life. Be content, therefore, in everything to *be* a philosopher, and if you wish also to be taken for one, show to yourself that you are one, and you will be able to accomplish it.

24. Let not these reflections oppress you: "I shall live without honour, and be nobody anywhere." For, if lack of honour is an evil, you cannot be in evil through the instrumentality of some other person, any more than

you can be in shame. It is not your business, is it, to get office, or to be invited to a dinner-party? Certainly not. How, then, can this be any longer a lack of honour? And how is it that you will be "nobody anywhere," when you ought to be somebody only in those things which are under your control, wherein you are privileged to be a man of the very greatest honour? But your friends will be without assistance? What do you mean by being "without assistance"? They will not have paltry coin from you, and you will not make them Roman citizens. Well, who told you that these are some of the matters under our control, and not rather things which others do? And who is able to give another what he does not himself have? "Get money, then," says some friend, "in order that we too may have it." If I can get money and at the same time keep myself self-respecting, and faithful, and high-minded, show me the way and I will get it. But if you require me to lose the good things that belong to me, in order that you may acquire the things that are not good, you can see for yourselves how unfair and inconsiderate you are. And which do you really prefer? Money, or a faithful and self-respecting friend? Help me, therefore, rather to this end, and do not require me to do those things which will make me lose these qualities.

"But my country," says he, "so far as lies in me, will be without assistance." Again I ask, what kind of assistance do you mean? It will not have loggias or baths of your providing. And what does that signify? For neither does it have shoes provided by the blacksmith, nor has it arms provided by the cobbler; but it is sufficient if each man fulfill his own proper function. And if you secured for it another faithful and self-respecting citizen, would you not be doing it any good? "Yes." Very well, and then you also would not be useless to it. "What place, then, shall I have in the State?" says he. Whatever place you *can* have, and at the same time maintain the man of fidelity and self-respect that is in you. But if, through your desire to help the State, you lose these qualities, of what good would you become to it, when in the end you turned out to be shameless and unfaithful?

25. Has someone been honoured above you at a dinner-party, or in salutation, or in being called in to give advice? Now if these matters are good, you ought to be happy that he got them; but if evil, be not distressed because you did not get them; and bear in mind that, if you do not act the same way that others do, with a view to getting things which are not under our control, you cannot be considered worthy to receive an equal share with others. Why, how is it possible for a person who does not haunt some man's door, to have equal shares with the man who does? For the man who does not do escort duty, with the man who does? For the man who does not praise, with the man who does? You will be unjust, therefore, and insatiable, if, while refusing to pay the price for which such things are bought, you want to obtain them for nothing. Well, what is the price for heads of lettuce? An obol, perhaps. If then, somebody gives up his obol and gets his heads of lettuce, while you do not give your obol, and do not

Chapter IX: Happiness

get them, do not imagine that you are worse off than the man who gets his lettuce. For as he has his heads of lettuce, so you have your obol which you have not given away.

Now it is the same way also in life. You have not been invited to somebody's dinner-party? Of course not; for you didn't give the host the price at which he sells his dinner. He sells it for praise; he sells it for personal attention. Give him the price, then, for which it is sold, if it is to your interest. But if you wish both not to give up the one and yet to get the other, you are insatiable and a simpleton. Have you, then, nothing in place of the dinner? Indeed you have; you have not had to praise the man you did not want to praise; you have not had to put up with the insolence of his doorkeepers.

26. What the will of nature is may be learned from a consideration of the points in which we do not differ from one another. For example, when some other person's slave-boy breaks his drinking-cup, you are instantly ready to say, "That's one of the things which happen." Rest assured, then, that when your own drinking-cup gets broken, you ought to behave in the same way that you do when the other man's cup is broken. Apply now the same principle to the matters of greater importance. Some other person's child or wife has died; no one but would say, "Such is the fate of man." Yet when a man's own child dies, immediately the cry is, "Alas! Woe is me!" But we ought to remember how we feel when we hear of the same misfortune befalling others.

27. Just as a mark is not set up in order to be missed, so neither does the nature of evil arise in the universe.

28. If someone handed over your body to any person who met you, you would be vexed; but that you hand over your mind to any person that comes along, so that, if he reviles you, it is disturbed and troubled—are you not ashamed of that?

29. In each separate thing that you do, consider the matters which come first and those which follow after, and only then approach the thing itself. Otherwise, at the start you will come to it enthusiastically, because you have never reflected upon any of the subsequent steps, but later on, when some difficulties appear, you will give up disgracefully. Do you wish to win an Olympic victory? So do I, by the gods! for it is a fine thing. But consider the matters which come before that, and those which follow after, and only when you have done that, put your hand to the task. You have to submit to discipline, follow a strict diet, give up sweet cakes, train under compulsion, at a fixed hour, in heat or in cold; you must not drink cold water, nor wine just whenever you feel like it; you must have turned yourself over to your trainer precisely as you would to a physician. Then when the contest comes on, you have to "dig in" beside your opponent, and sometimes dislocate your wrist, sprain your ankle, swallow quantities of sand, sometimes take a scourging, and along with all that get beaten. After

you have considered all these points, go on into the games, if you still wish to do so; otherwise, you will be turning back like children. Sometimes they play wrestlers, again gladiators, again they blow trumpets, and then act a play. So you too are now an athlete, now a gladiator, then a rhetorician, then a philosopher, yet with your whole soul nothing; but like an ape you imitate whatever you see, and one thing after another strikes your fancy. For you have never gone out after anything with circumspection, nor after you had examined it all over, but you act at haphazard and half-heartedly.

In the same way, when some people have seen a philosopher and have heard someone speaking like Euphrates (though, indeed, who can speak like him?), they wish to be philosophers themselves. Man, consider first the nature of the business, and then learn your own natural ability, if you are able to bear it. Do you wish to be a contender in the pentathlon, or a wrestler? Look to your arms, your thighs, see what your loins are like. For one man has a natural talent for one thing, another for another. Do you suppose that you can eat in the same fashion, drink in the same fashion, give way to impulse and to irritation, just as you do now? You must keep vigils, work hard, abandon your own people, be despised by a paltry slave, be laughed to scorn by those who meet you, in everything get the worst of it, in honour, in office, in court, in every paltry affair. Look these drawbacks over carefully, if you are willing at the price of these things to secure tranquillity, freedom and calm. Otherwise, do not approach philosophy; don't act like a child—now a philosopher, later on a tax-gatherer, then a rhetorician, then a procurator of Caesar. These things do not go together. You must be one person, either good or bad; you must labour to improve either your own governing principle or externals; you must work hard either on the inner man, or on things outside; that is, play either the role of a philosopher or else that of a layman.

30. Our duties are in general measured by our social relationships. He is a father. One is called upon to take care of him, to give way to him in all things, to submit when he reviles or strikes you. "But he is a bad father." Did nature, then, bring you into relationship with a *good* father? No, but simply with a father. "My brother does me wrong." Very well, then, maintain the relation that you have toward him; and do not consider what he is doing, but what you will have to do, if your moral purpose is to be in harmony with nature. For no one will harm you without your consent; you will have been harmed only when you think you are harmed. In this way, therefore, you will discover what duty to expect of your neighbour, your citizen, your commanding officer, if you acquire the habit of looking at your social relations with them.

31. In piety towards the gods, I would have you know, the chief element is this, to have right opinions about them—as existing and as administering the universe well and justly—and to have set yourself to obey them and to submit to everything that happens, and to follow it voluntarily, in

Chapter IX: Happiness

the belief that it is being fulfilled by the highest intelligence. For if you act in this way, you will never blame the gods, nor find fault with them for neglecting you. But this result cannot be secured in any other way than by withdrawing your idea of the good and the evil from the things which are not under our control, and placing it in those which are under our control, and in those alone. Because, if you think any of those former things to be good or evil, then, when you fail to get what you want and fall into what you do not want, it is altogether inevitable that you will blame and hate those who are responsible for these results. For this is the nature of every living creature, to flee from and to turn aside from the things that appear harmful, and all that produces them, and to pursue after and to admire the things that are helpful, and all that produces them. Therefore, it is impossible for a man who thinks that he is being hurt to take pleasure in that which he thinks is hurting him, just as it is also impossible for him to take pleasure in the hurt itself. Hence it follows that even a father is reviled by a son when he does not give his child some share in the things that seem to be good; and this it was which made Polyneices and Eteocles enemies of one another, the thought that the royal power was a good thing. That is why the farmer reviles the gods, and so also the sailor, and the merchant, and those who have lost their wives and their children. For where a man's interest lies, there is also his piety. Wherefore, whoever is careful to exercise desire and aversion as he should is at the same time careful also about piety. But it is always appropriate to make libations, and sacrifices, and to give of the first fruits after the manner of our fathers, and to do all this with purity, and not in a slovenly or careless fashion, nor, indeed, in a niggardly way, nor yet beyond our means.

32. When you have recourse to divination, remember that you do not know what the issue is going to be, but that you have come in order to find this out from the diviner; yet if you are indeed a philosopher, you know, when you arrive, what the nature of it is. For if it is one of the things which are not under our control, it is altogether necessary that what is going to take place is neither good nor evil. Do not, therefore, bring to the diviner desire or aversion, and do not approach him with trembling, but having first made up your mind that every issue is indifferent and nothing to you, but that, whatever it may be, it will be possible for you to turn it to good use, and that no one will prevent this. Go, then, with confidence to the gods as to counsellors; and after that, when some counsel has been given you, remember whom you have taken as counsellors, and whom you will be disregarding if you disobey. But go to divination as Socrates thought that men should go, that is, in cases where the whole inquiry has reference to the outcome, and where neither from reason nor from any other technical art are means vouchsafed for discovering the matter in question. Hence, when it is your duty to share the danger of a friend or of your country, do not ask the diviner whether you ought to share that danger. For if the diviner forewarns you that the omens of sacrifice have been

unfavourable, it is clear that death is portended, or the injury of some member of your body, or exile; yet reason requires that even at this risk you are to stand by your friend, and share the danger with your country. Wherefore, give heed to the greater diviner, the Pythian Apollo, who cast out of his temple the man who had not helped his friend when he was being murdered.

33. Lay down for yourself, at the outset, a certain stamp and type of character for yourself, which you are to maintain whether you are by yourself or are meeting with people. And be silent for the most part, or else make only the most necessary remarks, and express these in few words. But rarely, and when occasion requires you to talk, talk, indeed, but about no ordinary topics. Do not talk about gladiators, or horse-races, or athletes, or things to eat or drink—topics that arise on all occasions; but above all, do not talk about people, either blaming, or praising, or comparing them. If, then, you can, by your own conversation bring over that of your companions to what is seemly. But if you happen to be left alone in the presence of aliens, keep silence.

Do not laugh much, nor at many things, nor boisterously.

Refuse, if you can, to take an oath at all, but if that is impossible, refuse as far as circumstances allow.

Avoid entertainments given by outsiders and by persons ignorant of philosophy; but if an appropriate occasion arises for you to attend, be on the alert to avoid lapsing into the behavior of such laymen. For you may rest assured, that, if a man's companion be dirty, the person who keeps close company with him must of necessity get a share of his dirt, even though he himself happens to be clean.

In things that pertain to the body take only as much as your bare need requires, I mean such things as food, drink, clothing, shelter, and household slaves; but cut down everything which is for outward show or luxury.

In your sex-life preserve purity, as far as you can, before marriage, and, if you indulge, take only those privileges which are lawful. However, do not make yourself offensive, or censorious, to those who do indulge, and do not make frequent mention of the fact that you do not yourself indulge.

If someone brings you word that So-and-so is speaking ill of you, do not defend yourself against what has been said, but answer, "Yes, indeed, for he did not know the rest of the faults that attach to me; if he had, these would not have been the only ones he mentioned."

It is not necessary, for the most part, to go to the public shows. If, however, a suitable occasion ever arises, show that your principal concern is for none other than yourself, which means, wish only for that to happen which does happen, and for him only to win who does win; for so you will suffer no hindrance. But refrain utterly from shouting, or laughter at anyone, or great excitement. And after you have left, do not talk a great deal about what took place, except in so far as it contributes to your own

Chapter IX: Happiness

improvement; for such behavior indicates that the spectacle has aroused your admiration.

Do not go rashly or readily to people's public readings, but when you do go, maintain your own dignity and gravity, and at the same time be careful not to make yourself disagreeable.

When you are about to meet somebody, in particular when it is one of those men who are held in very high esteem, propose to yourself the question, "What would Socrates or Zeno have done under these circumstances?" and then you will not be at a loss to make proper use of the occasion. When you go to see one of those men who have great power, propose to yourself the thought, that you will not find him at home, that you will be shut out, that the door will be slammed in your face, that he will pay no attention to you. And if, despite all this, it is your duty to go, go and take what comes, and never say to yourself, "It was not worth all the trouble." For this is characteristic of the layman, that is, a man who is vexed at externals.

In your conversation avoid making mention at great length and excessively of your own deeds or dangers, because it is not as pleasant for others to hear about your adventures, as it is for you to call to mind your own dangers.

Avoid also raising a laugh, for this is a kind of behavior that slips easily into vulgarity, and at the same time is calculated to lessen the respect which your neighbours have of you. It is dangerous also to lapse into foul language. When, therefore, anything of the sort occurs, if the occasion be suitable, go even so far as to reprove the person who has made such a lapse; if, however, the occasion does not arise, at all events show by keeping silence, and blushing, and frowning, that you are displeased by what has been said.

34. When you get an external impression of some pleasure, guard yourself, as with impressions in general, against being carried away by it; nay, let the matter wait upon *your* leisure, and give yourself a little delay. Next think of the two periods of time, first, that in which you will enjoy your pleasure, and second, that in which, after the enjoyment is over, you will later repent and revile your own self; and set over against these two periods of time how much joy and self-satisfaction you will get if you refrain. However, if you feel that a suitable occasion has arisen to do the deed, be careful not to allow its enticement, and sweetness, and attractiveness to overcome you; but set over against all this the thought, how much better is the consciousness of having won a victory over it.

35. When you do a thing which you have made up your mind ought to be done, never try not to be seen doing it, even though most people are likely to think unfavourably about it. If, however, what you are doing is not right, avoid the deed itself altogether; but if it is right, why fear those who are going to rebuke you wrongly?

36. Just as the propositions, "It is day," and "It is night," are full of meaning when separated, but meaningless if united; so also, granted that for you to take the larger share at a dinner is good for your body, still, it is bad for the maintenance of the proper kind of social feeling. When, therefore, you are eating with another person, remember to regard, not merely the value for your body of what lies before you, but also to maintain your respect for your host.

37. If you undertake a rôle which is beyond your powers, you both disgrace yourself in that one, and at the same time neglect the rôle which you might have filled with success.

38. Just as you are careful, in walking about, not to step on a nail or to sprain your ankle, so be careful also not to hurt your governing principle. And if we observe this rule in every action, we shall be more secure in setting about it.

39. Each man's body is a measure for his property, just as the foot is a measure for his shoe. If, then, you abide by this principle, you will maintain the proper measure, but if you go beyond it, you cannot help but fall headlong over a precipice, as it were, in the end. So also in the case of your shoe; if once you go beyond the foot, you get first a gilded shoe, then a purple one, then an embroidered one. For once you go beyond the measure there is no limit.

40. Immediately after they are fourteen, women are called "ladies" by men. And so when they see that they have nothing else but only to be the bedfellows of men, they begin to beautify themselves, and put all their hopes in that. It is worth while for us to take pains, therefore, to make them understand that they are honoured for nothing else but only for appearing modest and self-respecting.

41. It is a mark of an ungifted man to spend a great deal of time in what concerns his body, as in much exercise, much eating, much drinking, much evacuating of the bowels, much copulating. But these things are to be done in passing; and let your whole attention be devoted to the mind.

42. When someone treats you ill or speaks ill of you, remember that he acts or speaks thus because he thinks it is incumbent upon him. That being the case, it is impossible for him to follow what appears good to you, but what appears good to himself; whence it follows, that, if he gets a wrong view of things, the man that suffers is the man that has been deceived. For if a person thinks a true composite judgment to be false, the composite judgment does not suffer, but the person who has been deceived. If, therefore, you start from this point of view, you will be gentle with the man who reviles you. For you should say on each occasion, "He thought that way about it."

43. Everything has two handles, by one of which it ought to be carried and by the other not. If your brother wrongs you, do not lay hold of the matter by the handle of the wrong that he is doing, because this is the

handle by which the matter ought not to be carried; but rather by the other handle—that he is your brother, that you were brought up together, and then you will be laying hold of the matter by the handle by which it ought to be carried.

44. The following statements constitute a *non sequitur*: "I am richer than you are, therefore I am superior to you"; or, "I am more eloquent than you are, therefore I am superior to you." But the following conclusions are better: "I am richer than you are, therefore my property is superior to yours"; or, "I am more eloquent than you are, therefore my elocution is superior to yours." But *you* are neither property nor elocution.

45. Somebody is hasty about bathing; do not say that he bathes badly, but that he is hasty about bathing. Somebody drinks a good deal of wine; do not say that he drinks badly, but that he drinks a good deal. For until you have decided what judgment prompts him, how do you know that what he is doing is bad? And thus the final result will not be that you receive convincing sense-impressions of some things, but give your assent to others.

46. On no occasion call yourself a philosopher, and do not, for the most part, talk among laymen about your philosophic principles, but do what follows from your principles. For example, at a banquet do not say how people ought to eat, but eat as a man ought. For remember how Socrates had so completely eliminated the thought of ostentation, that people came to him when they wanted him to introduce them to philosophers, and he used to bring them along. So well did he submit to being overlooked. And if talk about some philosophic principle arises among laymen, keep silence for the most part, for there is great danger that you will spew up immediately what you have not digested. So when a man tells you that you know nothing, and you, like Socrates, are not hurt, then rest assured that you are making a beginning with the business you have undertaken. For sheep too, do not bring their fodder to the shepherds and show how much they have eaten, but they digest their food within them, and on the outside produce wool and milk. And so do you, therefore, make no display to the laymen of your philosophical principles, but let them see the results which come from these principles when digested.

47. When you have become adjusted to simple living in regard to your bodily wants, do not preen yourself about the accomplishment; and so likewise, if you are a water-drinker, do not on every occasion say that you are a water-drinker. And if ever you want to train to develop physical endurance, do it by yourself and not for outsiders to behold; do not throw your arms around statues, but on occasion, when you are very thirsty, take cold water into your mouth, and then spit it out, without telling anybody.

48. This is the position and character of a layman: He never looks for either help or harm from himself, but only from externals. This is the position and character of the philosopher: He looks for all his help or harm from himself.

Signs of one who is making progress are: He censures no one, praises no one, blames no one, finds fault with no one, says nothing about himself as though he were somebody or knew something. When he is hampered or prevented, he blames himself. And if anyone compliments him, he smiles to himself at the person complimenting; while if anyone censures him, he makes no defence. He goes about like an invalid, being careful not to disturb, before it has grown firm, any part which is getting well. He has put away from himself his every desire, and has transferred his aversion to those things only, of what is under our control, which are contrary to nature. He exercises no pronounced choice in regard to anything. If he gives the appearance of being foolish or ignorant he does not care. In a word, he keeps guard against himself as though he were his own enemy lying in wait.

49. When a person gives himself airs because he can understand and interpret the books of Chrysippus,[1] say to yourself, "If Chrysippus had not written obscurely, this man would have nothing about which to give himself airs."

But what is it I want? To learn nature and to follow her. I seek, therefore, someone to interpret her; and having heard that Chrysippus does so, I go to him. But I do not understand what he has written; I seek, therefore, the person who interprets Chrysippus. And down to this point there is nothing to justify pride. But when I find the interpreter, what remains is to put his precepts into practice; this is the only thing to be proud about. If, however, I admire the mere act of interpretation, what have I done but turned into a grammarian instead of a philosopher? The only difference, indeed, is that I interpret Chrysippus instead of Homer. Far from being proud, therefore, when somebody says to me, "Read me Chrysippus," I blush the rather, when I am unable to show him such deeds as match and harmonize with his words.

50. Whatever principles are set before you, stand fast by these like laws, feeling that it would be impiety for you to transgress them. But pay no attention to what somebody says about you, for this is, at length, not under your control.

51. How long will you still wait to think yourself worthy of the best things, and in nothing to transgress against the distinction set up by the reason? You have received the philosophical principles which you ought to accept, and you have accepted them. What sort of a teacher, then, do you still wait for, that you should put off reforming yourself until he arrives? You are no longer a lad, but already a full-grown man. If you are now neglectful and easy-going, and always making one delay after another, and fixing first one day and then another, after which you will pay attention to yourself, then without realizing it you will make no progress, but, living and dying, will continue to be a layman throughout. Make up your mind, therefore, before it is too late, that the fitting thing for you to do is to live as a mature man who is making progress, and let everything which seems to

Chapter IX: Happiness

you to be best be for you a law that must not be transgressed. And if you meet anything that is laborious, or sweet, or held in high repute, or in no repute, remember that *now* is the contest, and here before you are the Olympic games, and that it is impossible to delay any longer, and that it depends on a single day and a single action, whether progress is lost or saved. This is the way Socrates became what he was, by paying attention to nothing but his reason in everything that he encountered. And even if you are not yet a Socrates, still you ought to live as one who wishes to be a Socrates.

52. The first and most necessary division in philosophy is that which has to do with the application of the principles, as, for example, Do not lie. The second deals with the demonstrations, as, for example, How comes it that we ought not to lie? The third confirms and discriminates between these processes, as, for example, How does it come that this is a proof? For what is a proof, what is logical consequence, what contradiction, what truth, what falsehood? Therefore, the third division is necessary because of the second, and the second because of the first; while the most necessary of all, and the one in which we ought to rest, is the first. But we do the opposite; for we spend our time in the third division, and all our zeal is devoted to it, while we utterly neglect the first. Wherefore, we lie, indeed, but are ready with the arguments which prove that one ought not to lie.

53. Upon every occasion we ought to have the following thoughts at our command:

> Lead thou me on, O Zeus, and Destiny.
> To that goal long ago to me assigned.
> I'll follow and not falter; if my will
> Prove weak and craven, still I'll follow on.

> "Who so has rightly with necessity complied,
> We count him wise, and skilled in things divine."

> "Well, O Crito, if so it is pleasing to the gods, so let it be."
> "Anytus and Meletus can kill me, but they cannot hurt me."

Endnote

1. [A Greek Stoic philosopher (c. 279–206 B.C.)—Ed.]

Reprinted from Epictetus, *The Discourses*, Vol. II, translated by W. A. Oldfather, Cambridge, Mass.: Harvard University Press, by Permissions of the publishers and The Loeb Classical Library.

Letter to Menoeceus

Epicurus

Let no one when young delay to study philosophy, nor when he is old grow weary of his study. For no one can come too early or too late to secure the health of his soul. And the man who says that the age for philosophy has either not yet come or has gone by is like the man who says that the age for happiness is not yet come to him, or has passed away. Wherefore both when young and old a man must study philosophy, that as he grows old he may be young in blessings through the grateful recollection of what has been, and that in youth he may be old as well, since he will know no fear of what is to come. We must then meditate on the things that make our happiness, seeing that when that is with us we have all, but when it is absent we do all to win it.

The things which I used unceasingly to commend to you, these do and practise, considering them to be the first principles of the good life. First of all believe that god is a being immortal and blessed, even as the common idea of a god is engraved on men's minds, and do not assign to him anything alien to his immortality or ill-suited to his blessedness: but believe about him everything that can uphold his blessedness and immortality. For gods there are, since the knowledge of them is by clear vision. But they are not such as the many believe them to be: for indeed they do not consistently represent them as they believe them to be. And the impious man is not he who denies the gods of the many, but he who attaches to the gods the beliefs of the many. For the statements of the many about the gods are not conceptions derived from sensation, but false suppositions, according to which the greatest misfortunes befall the wicked and the greatest blessings the good by the gift of the gods. For men being accustomed always to their own virtues welcome those like themselves, but regard all that is not of their nature as alien.

Become accustomed to the belief that death is nothing to us. For all good and evil consists in sensation, but death is deprivation of sensation. And therefore a right understanding that death is nothing to us makes the mortality of life enjoyable, not because it adds to it an infinite span of time, but because it takes away the craving for immortality. For there is nothing terrible in life for the man who has truly comprehended that there is nothing terrible in not living. So that the man speaks but idly who says that he fears death not because it will be painful when it comes, but because it is painful in anticipation. For that which gives no trouble when it comes, is but an empty pain in anticipation. So death, the most terrifying of ills, is nothing to us, since so long as we exist death is not with us; but when death comes, then we do not exist. It does not then concern either the living or the dead, since for the former it is not, and the latter are no more.

But the many at one moment shun death as the greatest of evils, at another yearn for it as a respite from the evils in life. But the wise man neither seeks to escape life nor fears the cessation of life, for neither does life offend him nor does the absence of life seem to be any evil. And just as with food he does not seek simply the larger share and nothing else, but rather the most pleasant, so he seeks to enjoy not the longest period of time, but the most pleasant.

And he who counsels the young man to live well, but the old man to make a good end, is foolish, not merely because of the desirability of life, but also because it is the same training which teaches to live well and to die well. Yet much worse still is the man who says it is good not to be born, but

> once born make haste to pass the gates of Death. [Theognis, 427]

For if he says this from conviction why does he not pass away out of life? For it is open to him to do so, if he had firmly made up his mind to this. But if he speaks in jest, his words are idle among men who cannot receive them.

We must then bear in mind that the future is neither ours, nor yet wholly not ours, so that we may not altogether expect it as sure to come, nor abandon hope of it, as if it will certainly not come.

We must consider that of desires some are natural, others vain, and of the natural some are necessary and others merely natural; and of the necessary some are necessary for happiness, others for the repose of the body, and others for very life. The right understanding of these facts enables us to refer all choice and avoidance to the health of the body and the soul's freedom from disturbance, since this is the aim of the life of blessedness. For it is to obtain this end that we always act, namely, to avoid pain and fear. And when this is once secured for us, all the tempest of the soul is dispersed, since the living creature has not to wander as though in search of something that is missing, and to look for some other thing by which he can fulfill the good of the soul and the good of the body. For it is then that we have need of pleasure, when we feel pain owing to the absence of pleasure; but when we do not feel pain, we no longer need pleasure. And for this cause we call pleasure the beginning and end of the blessed life. For we recognize pleasure as the first good innate in us, and from pleasure we begin every act of choice and avoidance, and to pleasure we return again, using the feeling as the standard by which we judge every good.

And since pleasure is the first good and natural to us, for this very reason we do not choose every pleasure, but sometimes we pass over many pleasures, when greater discomfort accrues to us as the result of them: and similarly we think many pains better than pleasures, since a greater pleasure comes to us when we have endured pains for a long time. Every pleasure then because of its natural kinship to us is good, yet not every pleasure is to be chosen: even as every pain also is an evil, yet not all are always of a nature to be avoided. Yet by a scale of comparison and by the consideration of advantages and disadvantages we must form our judgment on all these matters. For the good on certain occasions we treat as bad, and conversely the bad as good.

And again independence of desire we think a great good—not that we may at all times enjoy but a few things, but that, if we do not possess many, we may enjoy the few in the genuine persuasion that those have the sweetest pleasure in luxury who least need it, and that all that is natural is easy to be obtained, but that which is superfluous is hard. And so plain savours bring us a pleasure equal to a luxurious diet, when all the pain due to want is removed; and bread and water produce the highest pleasure, when one who needs them puts them to his lips. To grow accustomed therefore to simple and not luxurious diet gives us health to the full, and makes a man alert for the needful employments of life, and when after long intervals we approach luxuries, disposes us better towards them, and fits us to be fearless of fortune.

When, therefore, we maintain that pleasure is the end, we do not mean the pleasures of profligates and those that consist in sensuality, as is supposed by some who are either ignorant or disagree with us or do not understand, but freedom from pain in the body and from trouble in the mind. For it is not continuous drinkings and revellings, nor the satisfaction of lusts, nor the enjoyment of fish and other luxuries of the wealthy table, which produce a pleasant life, but sober reasoning, searching out the motives for all choice and avoidance, and banishing mere opinions, to which are due the greatest disturbance of the spirit.

Of all this the beginning and the greatest good is prudence. Wherefore prudence is a more precious thing even than philosophy: for from prudence are sprung all the other virtues, and it teaches us that it is not possible to live pleasantly without living prudently and honourably and justly, nor, again, to live a life of prudence, honour, and justice without living pleasantly. For the virtues are by nature bound up with the pleasant life, and the pleasant life is inseparable from them. For indeed who, think you, is a better man than he who holds reverent opinions concerning the gods, and is at all times free from fear of death, and has reasoned out the end ordained by nature? He understands that the limit of good things is easy to fulfill and easy to attain, whereas the course of ills is either short in time or slight in pain: he laughs at destiny, whom some have introduced as the mistress of all things. He thinks that with us lies the chief power in determining events, some of which happen by necessity and some by chance, and some are within our control; for while necessity cannot be called to account, he sees that chance is inconstant, but that which is in our control is subject to no master, and to it are naturally attached praise and blame. For, indeed, it were better to follow the myths about the gods than to become a slave to the destiny of the natural philosophers: for the former suggests a hope of placating the gods by worship, whereas the latter involves a necessity which knows no placation. As to chance, he does not regard it as a god as most men do (for in a god's acts there is no disorder), nor as an uncertain cause of all things: for he does not believe that good and evil are given by chance to man for the framing of a blessed life, but that opportunities for great good and great evil are afforded by it. He therefore thinks it better to be unfortunate in reasonable action than to prosper in unreason. For it is better in a man's actions that what is well chosen should fail, rather than that what is ill chosen should be successful owing to chance.

Meditate therefore on these things and things akin to them night and day by yourself, and with a companion like to yourself, and never shall you be disturbed waking or asleep, but you shall live like a god among men. For a man who lives among immortal blessings is not like to a mortal being.

Reprinted by permission from Whitney J. Oates, ed. *The Stoic and Epicurean Philosophers* (New York: Modern Library, Random House, 1940), pp. 30–33. Originally printed in *Epicurus, The Extant Remains*, trans. Cyril Bailey, copyright © 1926 by The Clarendon Press. By permission of the Oxford University Press.

Enlightenment

Heinrich Zimmer

Buddhism was the only religious and philosophical message of India to spread far beyond the borders of its homeland. Conquering Asia to the north and east, it became in those vast areas the creed of the masses and shaped the civilization for centuries. This tends to conceal the fact that in essence Buddhism is meant only for the happy few. The philosophical doctrine at the root of the numerous fascinating popular features is not the kind of teaching that one would have expected to see made readily accessible to all. In fact, of the numerous answers that have been offered, during the millenniums, in all quarters of the world, as solutions to life's enigmas, this one must be ranked as the most uncompromising, obscure, and paradoxical.

The Buddhist monks of Ceylon tell us how—according to their tradition—the Order of the Buddha, the "Awakened One," was founded. The great princely yogi, Gautama Sakyamuni, departed in secret from the palace and kingdom of his father and devoted himself to austerities for many years, until he arrived at the threshold of absolute Enlightenment. Sitting then beneath the Bo Tree, he was approached and tempted by the god Kama-Mara ("Desire and Death"), the master magician of the world illusion. Having overcome the tempter by remaining immovable in introversion, the prince experienced the Great Awakening, since which time he has been known as the "Awakened One," the Buddha. Absorbed in the vast experience, he remained beneath the Bo Tree, unmoved, untouched, for seven days and seven nights, "experiencing the bliss of the Awakening," then arose, as though to depart from that place, but could not depart. He placed himself beneath a second tree, and there again, for seven days and nights, remained merged in the stream of the bliss of the awakening. A third time, under a third tree, a spell of seven days and nights again absorbed him. He moved from tree to tree in this way for seven weeks, and during the fifth was protected by the hood of the serpent-king, Mucalinda. Following the blessed period of forty-nine days, his glorious glance opened again to the world. Then he understood that what he had experienced was beyond speech; all endeavor to talk about it would be vain. He determined, consequently, not to attempt to make it known.

But Brahma, the Universal Lord of the fleeting processes of life, in his eternal abode at the summit of the egg-shaped cosmos, looking down on the Awakened One, realized that the decision had been made to withhold the teaching. Brahma, himself a creature, indeed the highest of all creatures, was perturbed to know that the sublime knowledge (knowledge unknown to Brahma) was not to be revealed. He descended from the zenith and with prayer implored the Buddha to become the teacher of mankind, the teacher of the gods, the teacher of the created world. All were enwrapped in the womb of sleep, dreaming a dream known as the waking life of created beings. Brahma implored that the truly Awake should open his path to all. For there might be some, the god urged, some happy few among these deluded beings, whose eyes would not be blinded by the dust of passion, and these would understand. As lotus flowers arising from the dark waters of a lake are to be found in various stages of maturity—some with buds still deep under water, some nearing the surface, some already open, prepared to drink the rays of the sun—just so, there might be among mankind and the gods a few prepared to hear.

The Buddha was moved, thus, to teach the path. Disciples came, an Order assumed shape, and the Buddhist tradition was brought into existence. Nevertheless, from the beginning, by the nature of the problem, the doctrine had been meant only for those prepared to hear. It was never intended to interfere with either the life and habits of the multitude or the course of civilization. In time it might even vanish from the world, becoming incomprehensible and meaningless—for the lack of anyone capable of treading the path to understanding; and this, too, would be right. In contrast, in other words, to the other great teachers of mankind (Zarathustra preaching the religious law of Persia; Confucius commenting on the restored system of early Chinese thought; Jesus announcing Salvation to the world), Gautama, the prince of the royal Sakya clan, is known properly as Sakyamuni: the "silent sage (*muni*) of the Sakyas"; for in spite of all that has been said and taught about him, the Buddha remains the symbol of something beyond what can be said and taught.

In the Buddhist texts there is no word that can be traced with unquestionable authority to Gautama Sakyamuni. We glimpse only the enlightening shadow of his personality; yet this suffices to merge us in a spiritual atmosphere that is unique. For though India in his time, half a millennium before Christ, was a veritable treasure-house of magical-religious lore—to our eyes a jungle of mythological systems—the teaching of the Enlightened One offered no mythological vision, either of the present world or of a world beyond, and no tangible creed. It was presented as a therapy, a treatment or cure for those strong enough to follow it—a method and a process of healing. Apparently Gautama, at least in his terminology, broke from all the popular modes and accepted methods of Indian religious and philosophical instruction. He offered his advice in the practical manner of a spiritual physician, as though, through him, the art of Indian medicine were entering the sphere of spiritual problems—that grand old arena where, for centuries magicians of every kind had been tapping powers by which they and their disciples lifted themselves to the heights of divinity.

Following the procedure of the physician of his day inspecting a patient, the Buddha makes four statements concerning the case of man. These are the so-called "Four Noble Truths" which constitute the heart and kernel of his doctrine. The first, *All life is sorrowful*, announces that we members of the human race are spiritually unhealthy, the symptom being that we carry on our shoulders a burden of sorrow; the disease is endemic. No discussion of any question of guilt goes with this matter-of-fact diagnosis; for the Buddha indulged in no metaphysical or mythological dissertations. He inquired into the cause on the practical, psychological level, however; hence we have, as the second of the "Four Noble Truths," *The cause of suffering is ignorant craving.*

As in the teaching of the Sankhya, an involuntary state of mind common to all creatures is indicated as the root of the world-disease. The craving of nescience, not-knowing-better (*avidya*), is the problem—nothing less and nothing more. Such ignorance is a natural function of the life-process, yet not necessarily ineradicable; no more ineradicable than the innocence of a child. It is simply that we do not know that we are moving in a world of mere conventions and that our feelings, thoughts, and acts are determined by these. We imagine that our ideas about things represent their ultimate reality, and so we are bound in by them as by the meshes of a net. They are rooted in our own consciousness and attitudes; mere creations of the mind; conventional, involuntary patterns of seeing things, judging, and behaving; yet our ignorance accepts them in every detail, without question, regarding them and their contents as the facts of existence. This—this mistake about the true essence of reality—is the cause of all the sufferings that constitute our lives.

The Buddhist analysis goes on to state that our other symptoms (the familiar incidents and situations of our universal condition of non-well being) are derivatives, one and all, of the primary fault. The tragedies and comedies in which we get ourselves involved, which we bring forth from ourselves and in which we act, develop spontaneously from the impetus of our innermost condition of nonknowing. This sends us forth in the world with restricted senses and conceptions. Unconscious wishes and expectations, emanating from us in the shape of subjectively determined decisions and acts, transcend the limits of the present; they precipitate for us the future, being themselves determined from the past. Inherited from former births, they cause future births, the endless stream of life in which we are carried along being greater far than the bounds of individual birth and death. In other words, the ills of the individual cannot be understood in terms of the individual's mistakes; they are rooted in our human way of life, and the whole content of this way of life is a pathological blend of unfulfilled cravings, wrong longings, fears, regrets, and pains. Such a state of suffering is something from which it would be only sensible to be healed.

This radical statement about the problems that most of us take for granted as the natural concomitants of existence, and decide simply to endure, is balanced in the doctrine of the Buddha by the third and fourth of the "Four Noble Truths." Having diagnosed the illness and determined its cause, the physician next inquires whether the disease can be cured. The Buddhist prognostication is that a cure is indeed possible; hence we hear: *The suppression of suffering can be achieved*; and the last of Four Truths prescribes the way: *The way is the Noble Eightfold Path*—Right View, Right Aspiration, Right Speech, Right Conduct, Right Means of Livelihood, Right Endeavor, Right Mindfulness, and Right Contemplation.

The Buddha's thoroughgoing treatment is guaranteed to eradicate the cause of the sickly spell and dream of ignorance, and thus to make possible the attainment of a state of serene, awakened perfection. No philosophical explanation of man or the universe is required, only this spiritual physician's program of psychodietetics. And yet the doctrine can hardly appeal to the multitude; for these are not convinced that their lives are as unwholesome as they obviously are. Only those few who not only would like to try, but actually feel acutely a pressing need to undertake some kind of thoroughgoing treatment, would have the will and stamina to carry to the end such an arduous, self-ordained discipline as that of the Buddhist cure.

The way of Gautama Sakyamuni is called the "middle path"; for it avoids extremes. One pair of extremes is that of the outright pursuit of worldly desires, on the one hand, and the severe, ascetic, bodily discipline of such contemporaries of the Buddha as the Jainas, on the other, whose austerity was designed to culminate in annihilation of the physical frame. Another pair of extremes is that of skepticism, denying the possibility of transcendental knowledge, and the argumentative assertion of undemonstrable metaphysical doctrines. Buddhism eschews the blind alleys to either side and conduces to an attitude that will of itself lead one to the transcendental experience. It rejects explicitly *all* of the contending formulae of the intellect, as inadequate either to lead to or to express the paradoxical truth, which reposes far, far beyond the realm of cerebral conceptions.

A conversation of the Buddha, recorded among the so-called "Long Dialogues," enumerates an extended list of the practical and theoretical disciplines by which people master various skills, crafts, and professions, or seek some understanding of their own nature and the meaning of the universe. All are described and then dismissed without criticism, but with the formula: "Such Knowledge and opinions, if thoroughly mastered, will lead inevitably to certain ends and produce certain results in one's life. The Enlightened One is aware of all these possible consequences, and also of what lies behind them. But he does not attach much importance to this knowledge. For within himself he fosters another knowledge—the knowledge of cessation, of the discontinuance of worldly existence, of utter repose by emancipation. He has perfect insight into the manner of the springing into existence of our sensations and feelings, and into the manner of their vanishing again with all their sweetness and bitterness, and into the way of escape from them altogether, and into the manner in which, by non-attachment to them through right knowledge of their character, he has himself won release from their spell."

Buddhism attaches no serious importance to such knowledge as entangles men more tightly in the net of life, knowledge that adds a comfortable material or interesting spiritual background to existence and thereby only contributes additional substance to the maintenance of the personality. Buddhism teaches that the value attributed to a thing is determined by the particular pattern of life from which it is regarded and the personality concerned. The weight of a fact or idea varies with the unenlightenment of the observer—his spontaneous commitment to certain spheres of phenomena and ranges of human value. The atmosphere, nay the world, surrounding and overpowering him, is continually being produced from his own unconscious nature, and affects him in terms of his commitment to his own imperfections. Its traits are the phenomenal projections of his inner state of ignorance sent out into the realm of sense-perception and there, as it were, discovered by an act of empirical experience. Hence Buddhism denies, finally, the force and validity of everything that can be known.

A Tibetan author—A Buddhist Dalai-Lama—puts it this way: The one substance, which fundamentally is devoid of qualities, appears to be of various, completely differing flavors, according to the kind of being who tastes it. The same beverage which for the gods in their celestial realm will be the delightful drink of immortality, for men on earth will be mere water, and for the tormented inmates of hell a vile, disgusting liquid which they will be loath to swallow even though tortured with intolerable pangs of thirst. The three qualities of, or ways of experiencing, the one substance are here nothing more than the normal effects of three orders of karma. The senses themselves are conditioned by the subjective forces that brought them into being and hold them under strict control. The world without is no mere illusion—it is not to be regarded as nonexistent; yet it derives its enchanting or appalling features from the involuntary inner attitude of the one who sees it. The alluring hues and frightening shadows that form its very tissue are projected reflexes of the tendencies of the psyche.

One lives, in other words, enveloped by the impulses of the various layers of one's own nature, woven in the spell of their specific atmosphere, to which one submits as to an outside world. The goal of the techniques of the Buddhist therapy is to bring this process of self-envelopment to a stop. The living process is likened to a fire burning. Through the involuntary activity of one's nature as it functions in contact with the outer world, life as we know it goes on incessantly. The treatment is the extinction (*nirvana*) of the fire, and Buddha, the Awake, is the one no longer kindled or enflamed. The Buddha is far from having dissolved into nonbeing; it is not He who is extinct but the life illusion—the passions, desires, and normal dynamisms of the physique and psyche. No longer blinded, he no longer feels himself to be conditioned by the false ideas and attendant desires that normally go on shaping individuals and their spheres, life after life. The Buddha realizes himself to be void of the characteristics that constitute an individual subject to a destiny. Thus released from karma, the universal law, he reposes beyond fate, no longer subject to the consequences of personal limitations. What other people behold when they look upon his physical presence is a sort of mirage; for he is intrinsically devoid of the attributes that they venerate and are themselves striving to attain.

Buddhist art has attempted to render this paradoxical experience of the Enlightened One in certain curious works of sculpture, which represent the scene of the temptation of the Buddha. The fierce hosts of Kama-Mara, the tempter, assail the meditation of the one about to be enlightened as he sits beneath the holy tree. They brandish weapons, fling uprooted trees and prodigious rocks against him, and attempt by every means to break the calm of his meditation. By threats they strive to arouse in him some fear of death, the trace of an impulse of self-preservation, a wish to cling to the perishable frame of the body, which they are menacing with destruction. Simultaneously, the charm of life—all its loveliness—in the guise of divine women, is displayed before him; so that the allure of the senses should move him—not literally bring him from his place, but only provoke the least stir of a will to enjoy, which would amount to a step back into the thralldom of life. But both temptations fail. The powers work in vain to discover in his nature some flaw, some last remainder of fear and desire. The menacing and the enticing gestures equally fail to touch him; for he has vanished from the sphere of the currents and cross-currents of delight and despair, which constitute the warp and woof of life. In the works of sculpture in question, this unassailable state of the "one who cannot be reached any more" is expressed by omitting the Buddha-image from the composition. Amid the turmoil of the hosts and the captivating attitudes of the daughters of the tempter, the holy seat beneath the Bo Tree is empty; the Buddha is not to be seen.

The De-spirited One is never depicted through visible or tangible features in the early Buddhist monuments; for anything tangible or visible would amount to a description of him—either as a man or as a god. He would be endowed then with such features as befit beings shaped by the influences of former lives, beings brought by the law of karma into human or celestial forms. Any shape would by its nature communicate a wrong notion of his essence, which is on a nondepictable plane. A shape would show him to be tied by the subtle bonds of karma to the sphere of some set of limiting and transitory qualifications, whereas the whole sense of his being is that he is released from such symptoms of ignorance and desire. In viewing these early works of Buddhist sculpture one is to think of the Buddha as truly there, on the throne of Enlightenment, but as though he were a bubble of emptiness. Footprints on the ground and a slight hollowing of the cushion betray his presence, but no visible trait could possibly render the essence of his nature. Visible traits (beauty and grandeur, for example, or the dazzling charm of a divinity) are the signs of ordinary beings, and reveal their karma. But the Buddha is without karma and therefore must be rendered without determinable form. That is the most consistent, nay the only perfectly adequate way to designate his absolute emancipation from the law that enjoins all to go on assuming the varying transitory garbs of renewed existences.

The Buddha's doctrine is called *yana*. The word means "a vehicle," or, more to the point, "a ferryboat." The "ferryboat" is the principal image employed in Buddhism to render the sense and function of the doctrine. The idea persists through all the differing and variously conflicting teachings of the numerous Buddhist sects that have evolved in many lands, during the long course of the magnificent history of the widely disseminated doctrine. Each sect describes the vehicle in its own way, but no matter how described it remains always the ferry.

To appreciate the full force of this image, and to understand the reason for its persistence, one must begin by realizing that in everyday Hindu life the ferryboat plays an extremely prominent role. It is an indispensable means of transportation in a continent traversed by many mighty rivers and where bridges are practically nonexistent. To reach the goal of almost any journey one will require a ferry, time and time again, the only possible crossing of the broad and rapid streams being by goat or by a ford. The Jainas called their way of salvation the ford (*tirtha*), and the supreme Jaina teachers were *Tirthankaras*, "those making, or providing, a ford." In the same sense, Buddhism, by its doctrine, provides a ferryboat across the rushing river of samsara to the distant bank of liberation. Through enlightenment (*bodhi*) the individual is transported.

The gist of Buddhism can be grasped more readily and adequately by fathoming the main metaphors through which it appeals to our intuition than by a systematic study of the complicated superstructure, and the fine details of the developed teaching. For example, one need only think for a moment about the actual, everyday experience of the process of crossing a river in a ferryboat, to come to the simple idea that inspires and underlies all of the various rationalized systematizations of the doctrine. To enter the Buddhist vehicle—the boat of the discipline—means to begin to cross the

Chapter IX: Happiness

river of life, from the shore of the commonsense experience of non-enlightenment, the shore of spiritual ignorance (*aidya*), desire (*kama*), and death (*mara*), to the yonder bank of transcendental wisdom (*vidya*), which is liberation (*moksa*) from this general bondage. Let us consider, briefly, the actual stages involved in any crossing of a river by ferry, and see if we can experience the passage as a kind of initiation-by-analogy into the purport of the stages of the Buddhist pilgrim's progress to his goal.

Standing on the nearer bank, this side the stream, waiting for the boat to put in, one is a part of its life, sharing in its dangers and opportunities and in whatever may come to pass on it,. One feels the warmth or coolness of its breezes, hears the rustle of its trees, experiences the character of its people, and knows that its earth is underfoot. Meanwhile the other bank, the far bank, is beyond reach—a mere optical image across the broad, flowing waters that divide us from its unknown world of forms. We have really no idea what it will be like to stand in that distant land. How this same scenery of the river and its two shorelines will appear from the other side we cannot imagine. How much of these houses will be visible among the trees? What prospects up and down the river will unfold? Everything over here, so tangible and real to us at present—these real, solid objects, these tangible forms—will be no more than remote, visual patches, inconsequential optical effects, without power to touch us, either to help or to harm. This solid earth itself will be a visual, horizontal line beheld from afar, one detail of an extensive scenic view, beyond our experience, and of no more force for us than a mirage.

The ferryboat arrives; and as it comes to the landing we regard it with a feeling of interest. It brings with it something of the air of that yonder land which will soon be our destination. Yet when we are entering it we still feel like members of the world from which we are departing, and there is still that feeling of unreality about our destination. When we lift our eyes from the boat and boatman, the far bank is still only a remote image, no more substantial than it was before.

Softly the ferryboat pushes off and begins to glide across the moving waters. Presently one realizes that an invisible line has been recently, imperceptibly passed, beyond which the bank left behind is assuming gradually the unsubstantiality of a mere visual impression, a kind of image, while the farther bank, drawing slowly nearer, is beginning to turn into something real. The former dim remoteness is becoming the new reality and soon is solid ground, creaking under keel—real earth—the sand and stone on which we tread in disembarking; whereas the world left behind, recently so tangible, has been transmuted into an optical reflex devoid of substance, out of reach and meaningless, and has forfeited the spell that it laid upon us formerly—with all its features, all its people and events—when we walked upon it and ourselves were a portion of its life. Moreover, the new reality, which now possesses us, provides an utterly new view of the river, the valley, and the two shores, a view very different from the other, and completely unanticipated.

Now while we were in the process of crossing the river in the boat, with the shore left behind becoming gradually vaguer and more meaningless—the streets and homes, the dangers and pleasures, drawing steadily away—there was a period when the shoreline ahead was still rather far off too; and during that time the only tangible reality around us was the boat, contending stoutly with the current and precariously floating on the rapid waters. The only details of life that then seemed quite substantial and that greatly concerned us were the various elements of the ferryboat itself: the contours of the hull and gunwales, the rudder and the sail, the various ropes, and perhaps a smell of tar. The rest of existence, whether out ahead or left behind, signified no more than a hopeful prospect and a fading recollection—two poles of unrealistic sentimental association affiliated with certain clusters of optical effects far out-of-hand.

In the Buddhist texts this situation of the people in a ferryboat is compared to that of the good folk who have taken passage in the vehicle of the doctrine. The boat is the teaching of the Buddha, and the implements of the ferry are the various details of Buddhist discipline: meditation, yoga-exercises, the rules of ascetic life, and the practice of self-abnegation. These are the only things that disciples in the vehicle can regard with deep conviction; such people are engrossed in a fervent belief in the Buddha as the ferryman and the Order as their bounding gunwale (framing, protecting, and defining their perfect ascetic life) and in the guiding power of the doctrine. The shoreline of the world has been left behind but the distant one of release not yet attained. The people in the boat, meanwhile, are involved in a peculiar sort of middle prospect which is all their own.

Among the conversations of the Buddha known as the "Medium-length Dialogues," there appears a discourse on the value of the vehicle of the doctrine. First the Buddha describes a man who, like himself or any of his followers, becomes filled with a loathing of the perils and delights of secular existence. That man decides to quit the world and cross the stream of life to the far land of spiritual safety. Collecting wood and reeds, he builds a raft, and by this means succeeds in attaining the other shore. The Buddha confronts his monks, then, with the question.

"What would be your opinion of this man," asks the Buddha, "would he be a clever man, if, out of gratitude for the raft that has carried him across the stream to safety, he, having reached the other shore, should cling to it, take it on his back, and walk about with the weight of it?"

The monks reply. "No, certainly the man who would do that would not be a clever man."

The Buddha goes on. "Would not the clever man be the one who left the raft (of no use to him any longer) to the current of the stream, and walked ahead without turning back to look at it? Is it not simply a tool to be cast away and forsaken once it has served the purpose for which it was made?"

The disciples agree that this is the proper attitude to take toward the vehicle, once it has served its purpose.

The Buddha then concludes. "In the same way the vehicle of the doctrine is to be cast away and forsaken, once the other shore of Enlightenment (*nirvana*) has been attained."

The rules of the doctrine are intended for beginners and advanced pupils, but become meaningless for the perfect. They can be of no service to the truly enlightened, unless to serve him, in his role of teacher, as a convenient medium by which to communicate some suggestion of the truth to which he has attained. It was by means of the doctrine that the Buddha sought to express what he had realized beneath the tree as inexpressible. He could communicate with the world through his doctrine and thus help his unprepared disciples when they were at the start, or somewhere in the middle, of the way. Talking down to the level of relative or total ignorance, the doctrine can move the still imperfect yet ardent mind; but it can say nothing any more, nothing ultimately real, to the mind that has cast away darkness. Like the raft, it must be left behind, therefore, once the goal has been attained; for it can thenceforth be no more than an inappropriate burden.

Moreover, not the raft only, but the stream too, becomes void of reality for the one who has attained the other shore. When such a one turns around to look again at the land left behind, what does he see? What *can* one see who has crossed the horizon beyond which there is no duality? He looks—and there *is* no "other shore"; there is no torrential separating river; there is no raft; there is no ferryman; there can have been no crossing of the nonexistent stream. The whole scene of the two banks and the river between is simply gone. There can be no such thing for the enlightened eye and mind, because to see or think of anything as something "other" (a distant reality, different from one's own being) would mean that full Enlightenment had not yet been attained. There can be an "other shore" only for people still in the spheres of dualistic perception; those this side the stream or still inside the boat and heading for the "other shore"; those who have not yet disembarked and thrown away the raft. Illumination means that the delusory distinction between the two shores of a worldly and a transcendental existence no longer holds. There *is* no stream of rebirths flowing between two separated shores: no samsara and no nirvana.

Thus the long pilgrimage to perfection through innumerable existences, motivated by the virtues of self-surrender and accomplished at the cost of tremendous sacrifices of ego, disappears like a landscape of dreams when one awakes. The long-continued story of the heroic career, the many lives of increasing self-purification, the picture-book legend of detachment won through the long passion, the saintly epic of the way to become a savior—enlightened and enlightening—vanishes like a rainbow. All becomes void; whereas once, when the dream was coming to pass step by step, with ever-recurrent crises and decisions, the unending series of dramatic sacrifices held the soul completely under its spell. The secret meaning of Enlightenment is that this titan-effort of pure soul-force, this ardent struggle to reach the goal by acts, ever-renewed, of beautiful self-surrender, this supreme, long strife through ages of incarnations to attain release from the universal law of moral causation (*karma*)—is without reality. At the threshold of its own realization it dissolves, together with its background of self-entangled life, like a nightmare at the dawn of day.

For the Buddha, therefore, even the notion of nirvana is without meaning. It is bound to the pairs-of-opposites and can be employed only in opposition to samsara—the vortex where the life-force is spellbound in ignorance by its own polarized passions of fear and desire.

The Buddhist way of ascetic training is designed to conduce to the understanding that there is no substantial ego—nor any object anywhere—that lasts, but only spiritual processes, welling and subsiding: sensations, feelings, visions. These can be suppressed or set in motion and watched at will. The idea of the extinction of the fire of lust, ill will, and ignorance becomes devoid of meaning when this psychological power and point of view has been attained; for the process of life is no longer experienced as a burning fire. To speak seriously, therefore, of nirvana as a goal to be attained is simply to betray the attitude of one still remembering or experiencing the process as the burning of the fire. The Buddha himself adopts such an attitude only for the teaching of those still suffering, who feel that they would like to make the flames extinct. His famous Fire Sermon is an accommodation, not by any means the final word of the sage whose final word is silence. From the perspective of the Awake, the Illumined One, such opposed verbalizations as nirvana and samsara, enlightenment and ignorance, freedom and bondage, are without reference, void of content. That is why the Buddha refused to discuss nirvana. The pointlessness of the connotations that would inevitably seem to be intended by his words would confuse those trying to follow his mysterious way. They being still in the ferryboat framed of these conceptions and requiring them as devices of transport to the shore of understanding, their teacher would not deny before them the practical function of such convenient terms; and yet would not give the terms weight, either, by discussion. Words like "enlightenment," "ignorance," "freedom," and "entanglement" are preliminary helps, referring to no ultimate reality, mere hints or signposts for the traveler, which serve to point him to the goal of an attitude beyond their own suggestions of a contrariety. The raft being finally left behind, and the vision lost of the two banks and the separating river, then there is in truth neither the realm of life and death nor that of release. Moreover, there is no

Chapter IX: Happiness

Buddhism—no boat, since there are neither shores nor waters between. There is no boat, and there is no boatman—no Buddha.

The great paradox of Buddhism, therefore, is that no Buddha has ever come into existence to enlighten the world with Buddhist teachings. The life and mission of Gautama Sakyamuni is only a general misunderstanding by the unenlightened world, helpful and necessary to guide the mind toward illumination, but to be discarded when—and if—enlightenment is to be attained. Any monk failing to get rid of such ideas clings (by clinging to them) to the general mundane delusion which he imagines himself to be striving to leave behind. For, briefly, so long as nirvana is looked upon as something different from samsara, the most elementary error about existence still has to be overcome. These two ideas mirror contrary attitudes of the semiconscious individual toward himself and the outer sphere in which he lives; but beyond this subjective range they have no substantiation.

Buddhism—this popular creed which has won the reverence of all Eastern Asia—contains this boldest paradox at its very root; the most startling reading of reality ever whispered into human ear. All good Buddhists tend to avoid, therefore, statements about existence and nonexistence. Their "Middle Path" goes between by simply pointing out that the validity of a conception is always relative to one's position along the road of progress from Ignorance to Buddhahood. Attitudes of assertion and negation belong to worldly beings on the hither bank of ignorance, and to pious people making headway in the crowded ferryboat of the doctrine. Such a conception as Voidness (*sunyata*) can have meaning only for an ego clinging to the reality of things; one who has lost the feeling that things are real can make no sense of such a word. And yet words of this kind remain in all the texts and teachings. Indeed, the great *practical* miracle of Buddhism is that terms of this kind, used successfully as steppingstones, do not become rocks on which to found and build a creed.

The greater portion of the Buddhist literature that has become available and familiar to us in translation is adjusted in this way, pedagogically, to the general human attitude of partial ignorance. It is intended for the teaching and guidance of disciples. It outlines and points the way along the path of the Buddhas (*buddha-marga*), depicting the career of the hero "going to enlightenment" (*bodhicarya*). Its position, therefore, is comparable to that of the ferryman inviting people on our hither bank to enter his boat and cross the waters, or guiding his crew in their handling of the craft during the passage. The yonder bank is represented only in a preliminary, very sketchy way; only hinted at and attractively suggested, for the captivation and continued inspiration of those still spellbound by the notions of this dualistic shore—men and women trying to make up their minds to leave, or else in the toilsome stages of crossing to an absolute contrary point of view, which they will perceive presently to be utterly inconsistent with their expectation.

This pedagogical interest of Buddhism entails, unavoidably, a screening of the ultimate essence of the doctrine. The introductory statements, graded as they are, lead right up to the goal—but then have to be put behind, or the goal itself will never be attained. Anyone wishing to gain some inkling of the transformation of perspective intended will have to turn from the great volumes of initiatory conversations, questions, analyses, and codifications to a somewhat less conspicuous, curious, special branch of Buddhist writings, in which an attempt is made actually to state something of the supreme experience.

One may well marvel at the bold experiment—an effort to represent the ultimate essence of an incommunicable intuition through words and conceptions familiar to the usual philosophical and pious understanding. But, wonderful to relate, a vivid sense of the ineffable reality known in "extinction" (*nirvana*) is actually conveyed in this unexampled body of strange, esoteric texts. They are named *Prajna-paramita*: "The Accomplishment of Transcendental Wisdom," or "The Wisdom (*prajna*) Gone to the Other Shore (*param-ita*)." And they are a series of the most curious dialogues, conducted in a sort of conversation-circle of Buddhas and Bodhisattvas—mostly legendary beings, superhuman saviors, without a single merely human, still half-bewildered aspirant-to-enlightenment among them.

The Illumined Ones behave in a way that should be rather shocking and confusing to any sound thinker, who, from habit and firm determination, is resolved to keep his feet on the ground. In a sort of mocking conversation, these Buddhas and Bodhisattvas entertain themselves with enigmatical statements of the unstatable truth. They delight in declaring, time and again, that there is no such thing as Buddhism, no such thing as Enlightenment, nothing remotely resembling the extinction of nirvana, setting traps for each other and trying to trick each other into assertions that might imply—even remotely—the reality of such conceptions. Then, most artfully, they always elude the cleverly placed hazards and hidden pitfalls—and all engage in a glorious, transolympian laugh; for the merest hint of a notion of nirvana would have betrayed a trace of the vestige of the opposite attitude, samsara, and the clinging to individual existence.

For example, in one of the texts the Buddha makes the following declaration to his pupil Subhuti. "Whosoever stands in the ferryboat of the saviors-who-lead-to-the-far-bank shall bear in mind the rescue of all living beings, conducting them to release-and-extinction in the pure and perfect nirvana. And when, by virtue of this attitude, he has rescued all living beings, no being whatsoever has been made to reach nirvana."

Following this paradoxical remark, the Buddha supplies his explanation. "Why, O Subhuti, is this so? Because, if this savior had the notion of the actual existence of any being, he could not be called a perfect Enlightened One. If there could occur to him the conception of a living being donning the garb of various bodies and migrating through numerous existences, or the idea of an individual personality, then he could not be called a Bodhisattva, 'a being whose essence is Enlightenment." And why is this so? Because there is no such thing as anything or anybody standing in the vehicle of the Enlightened Ones."

Another text states that on a certain day, when myriads of gods had flocked together to celebrate with a great feast the solemn occasion of the Buddha's preaching of s sermon, they were all saying joyfully: "Forsooth, this is the second time that the wheel of the true law has been set in motion on Indian soil, let us go and watch!" But the Buddha, turning stealthily to Subhuti, whispered something that he would not tell the gods; for it was beyond their power of understanding. "This is not the second time that the wheel of the true law has been set in motion; there is no setting in motion of anything, nor any stopping of the motion of anything. Knowing just that, is the perfection of wisdom (*prajna-paramita*), which is characteristic of the beings whose essence is enlightenment."

These bewildering texts, with their explicit teaching of the Wisdom of the Far Bank (*prajna-paramita*), belong to a later period of the Buddhist tradition, the stage of the so-called "Great Ferryboat," or Mahayana, which teaches that the secret meaning and goal for the doctrine is the universal Buddahood of *all* beings. This is in contrast to the earlier doctrine of the so-called "Little Ferryboat," the Hinayana, where, though an effective way to *individual release* is disclosed, the accomplishment of *Buddhahood* is regarded as a goal attained only by very few throughout the cycling ages. The *Prajna-paramita* texts of the Mahayana were intended to counteract what their authors regarded as a basic misunderstanding, in the Hinayana, of the very essence of the wisdom of the Buddha, a misunderstanding caused by thinking that the preliminary teaching was an expression of the Buddha's transcendental realization. The emphasis on the means, the path, the rules of the order, and the ethical disciplines of the ferry-ride was stifling the essence of the tradition within the very fold of Buddhism itself. The Mahayana way, on the other hand, was to reassert this essence by means of a bold and stunning paradox.

"The Enlightened One," we read, "sets forth in the Great Ferryboat; but there is nothing from which he sets forth. He starts from the universe; but in truth he starts from nowhere. His boat is manned with all the perfections; and is manned by no one. It will find its support on nothing whatsoever and will find its support on the state of all-knowing, which will serve it as a non-support. Moreover, no one has ever set forth in the Great Ferryboat; no one will ever set forth in it, and no one is setting forth in it now. And why is this? Because neither the one setting forth nor the goal for which he sets forth is to be found: therefore, who should be setting forth, and whither?"

The conceptions that go to make up the communicated doctrine are, from the point of view of the Enlightened One, without corresponding ultimate realities. They are part of a raft, which is good and helpful for the crossing of a stream of ignorance and indispensable for disciples on the way, but they are devoid of meaning for the finished master whose crossing is accomplished. They mirror shapes of the transitory process of life, and so have no lasting substance. They lead to enlightenment, and yet are fallacious, broken reflections of its truth. Indeed, they are different from what is known to the enlightened; just as the boat, or raft, is different from the farther shore. Such helpful concepts emerge, together with all the rest of these visible and thinkable things round about us, from an infinitely pure reality, which is beyond conceptions, void of limiting qualities, undifferentiated, and untouched by the dialectic of the pairs-of-opposites, of which it is the ground—just as the heavens and the atmosphere, which are visible, stand as apparitions on the fundamentally pure void of ether.

"Just as, in the vast ethereal sphere, stars and darkness, light and mirage, dew, foam, lightning, and clouds emerge, become visible, and vanish again, like the features of a dream—so everything endowed with an individual shape is to be regarded," Thus we read in one of the most celebrated of these Mahayana texts of meditation. From the intangible matter that pervades the universe, tangible shapes emerge as its ephemeral transformations. But their breaking into existence and their vanishing away does not affect the limpid, profound serenity of the basic element, the space of which they fill for their short spell of being. Comparably, the Enlightened Ones, with unruffled self-composure, watch their own sensations, feelings, and other experiences of the outer world and their inner life, remaining untouched by them, beyond the changes continually coming to pass in them, like the reposeful ether beyond the changes of the forms within its infinite space.

So far as the Awakened One is concerned, the notion of Awakening is at bottom as devoid of meaning as the notion that there is a dreamlike state that precedes it (the state of ordinary life—our own attitude and atmosphere). It is unreal. It does not exist. It is the sail of the nonexistent raft. The Buddhist yogi is taught, by means of the disciplines, to realize, within, such a peace as one perceives looking outward into the vast ethereal realm with its sublime display of transient forms. He is taught to experience, gazing inward, through successive stages of self-control and meditation, an ethereal essence of his own—sheer voidness, unsullied by any process of the mind and not changed by any effect of the senses in their contact with the outer world. By imbuing himself completely with an utter aloofness comparable to that of the celestial atmosphere in relation to the various luminous and darkening phenomena that pass through it, he realizes the real meaning of the Buddhist transcendental wisdom, the nature of the view from the yonder shore. He comes to know that fundamentally nothing whatsoever is happening to the true essence of his nature, nothing to give cause for either distress or joy.

The disciple Subhuti said: "Profound, O Venerable One, is the perfect Transcendental Wisdom."

Chapter IX: Happiness

Quoth the Venerable One: "Abysmally profound, like the space of the universe, O Subhuti, is the perfect Transcendental Wisdom."

The disciple Subhuti said again: "Difficult to be attained through Awakening is the perfect Transcendental Wisdom, O Venerable One."

Quoth the Venerable One: "That is the reason, O Subhuti, why no one ever attains it through Awakening."

And the two—we may imagine—roared with laughter. Here is metaphysics as the intellect's greatest game.

FROM *Philosophies of India*, by Heinrich Zimmer, copyright 1951 Princeton University Press, © 1979 renewed by Princeton University Press, reprinted by permission of Princeton University Press. It is a violation of the law to reproduce this selection by any means whatsoever without the written permission of the copyright holder.

Chapter X
The Individual and Society

Quest for Goodness began with a consideration of the individual in the world—a world of trouble. But, the individual lives in a world with others and so the topic of responding to others was taken up next. This was followed by a consideration of moral theories and ethical perspectives as well as discussion concerning the grounds of moral obligation. In addition, a detailed examination of the challenges of relativism was included. Then, in order, followed a collection of writings on vice and virtue, lying and veracity, and self-deception and integrity.

Philosophical writings on the relationships of friendship and love were placed immediately prior to the chapter on happiness. Finally, *Quest for Goodness* closes with a treatment concerning the more formal relationships between the individual and society.

Reinhold Niebuhr, in his "realistic analysis," of the problems which beset human society sees a "seemingly irreconcilable conflict between the needs of society and the imperatives of a sensitive conscience." He continues:

> This conflict, which could be most briefly defined as the conflict between ethics and politics, is made inevitable by the double focus of the moral life. The focus is in the inner life of the individual, and the others in the necessities of man's social life.

The highest moral ideal from the perspective of society is justice. In what ways does a just society enhance an individual's potential for happiness? What constitutes legitimate use of force by a society over a given individual? What, if anything, does the individual owe to society? What are possible ways by which the conflict between individual morality and societal ethics can be resolved?

Niebuhr's essay, "The Conflict Between Individual and a Social Morality," gives structure to this fundamental problem and offers insights with regard to possible approaches to this basic problem. He cautions that any approach must consider seriously the problem of social and technological change and the restlessness this situation creates:

> Our age is, for good or ill, immersed in the social problem. A technological civilization makes stability impossible. It changes the circumstances of life too rapidly to incline anyone to a reverent acceptance of an ancestral order. Its rapid developments and its almost daily changes in the physical circumstances of life destroy the physical symbols of stability and therefore make for restlessness, even if these movements were not in a direction which imperil the whole human enterprise.

He continues to the conclusion that, in a world dominated by technology, ". . . we are therefore bound to feel harassed and disillusioned." Hopefully, a dynamic personal ethic can make it possible to harmonize, at some level, individual and societal ends.

Confucius was concerned to bring about the Chinese ideal of a grand harmony. In *The Analects,* he discusses personal growth and interpersonal relationships. There are, he asserts, three kinds of friends which will help an individual bring about personal growth and improvement, namely, ". . . friends who are straight, who are true to their word, and who are well-informed."

In Chinese thought, no sharp distinction can be made between the individual and the community. In one sense, the individual is the sum of his or her relationships. To be an individual is precisely to be a part of a "ritually constituted" community. Confucius says: "To discipline oneself through ritual practice is to become authoritatively human." Likewise, good government must be instituted according to the cosmic order of things and a government thus constituted rules effectively only by the power of moral force.

In "The Republic" Book IV, Plato writes what is, perhaps, the single most influential treatise on the relationship of the individual to the state in the Western world. The ideal state, for Plato, aims at justice and is "ordered with a view to the good of the whole." The individual soul is a microcosm of the state—the state being essentially the individual soul "writ large."

In this dialogue Plato discusses the four great virtues which govern both the individual and the state: wisdom, courage, temperance, and justice. The soul has three main divisions or functions according to Plato. The rational element is the highest and rules the soul best with wisdom. The spirited part of the soul ought to be governed by courage and the desires and appetites are, ideally, moderated by temperance. A state of justice

Chapter X: The Individual and Society

obtains in the human soul when each of its parts is functioning in accordance with its proper work.

So, too, the ideal state has three main classes: guardians, auxiliaries, and traders. Each class, ideally, is to carry out its own proper work in accordance with the appropriate virtue. The ideal state, like the ideal individual, will be the master of itself. For Plato, ". . . the words 'temperance' and 'self-mastery' truly express the rule of the better part over the worse."

The best state is a state where individual citizens are nurtured and well-educated by the state. These people are expert in their work and, essentially, mind their own business. If the design of the state is sound, it will insure happiness to all, in proportion to their proper station.

John Stuart Mill's *On Liberty* is a classic statement regarding the importance of individual liberty. Mill declares that the whole object of his essay is to put forth one very simple principle:

> The principle is the sole end for which mankind are warranted, individually or collectively, in interfering with the liberty of action of any of their number in self-protection. That the only purpose for which power can be rightfully exercised over any member of civilized community, against his will, is to prevent harm to others. His own good, either physical or moral, is not a sufficient warrant.

Mill goes on to state that his ultimate ethical principle is the principle of utility in its "largest sense." He then goes on to discuss the principles of individual liberty. "No society," Mill argues, "in which these liberties are not, on the whole, respected is free . . ."

In the remainder of the excerpts from *On Liberty* reprinted here, Mill writes on the liberty of thought and discussion, argues that individuality is one of the elements of human well-being and discusses the limits to the authority of society over the individual. This later important problem is structured by three questions: What is the rightful limit to sovereignty of the individual over himself? Where does the authority of society begin? How much of human life should be assigned to individuality, and how much to society?

Law and jurisprudence, in its best sense, is an extension of ethics. Patrick Devlin, a contemporary British judge, takes up the problem of "The Enforcement of Morals." He asks three fundamental questions to which he formulates reasoned responses. The questions are:

1. Has society the right to pass judgment at all on matters of morals? Ought there, in other words, to be a public morality, or are morals always a matter for private judgment?

2. If society has the right to pass judgment, has it also the right to use the weapon of law to enforce it?

3. If so, ought it to use the weapon in all cases or only in some; and, if only in some, on what principle should it distinguish?

Devlin's arguments center around his understanding of the meaning and structure of human societies. Devlin states that "society means a community of ideas; without shared ideas on politics, morals, and ethics no society can exist." Like Niebuhr, Devlin differentiates a moral structure and a political structure. However, he views it as a mistake to regard them as two mutually exclusive, independent systems. He says:

> Every society has a moral structure as well as a political one: or rather, since that might suggest two independent systems, I should say that the structure of every society is made up of both politics and morals.

Devlin's essay helps the reader to think clearly about the important questions which concern the individual and the power of society. He argues that the state does indeed have the right to enforce morality. However, he urges society to use both caution and prudence in making these judgments. He advocates the criteria for these judgments be the standard of the "reasonable man" or the "right-minded" individual and that "elastic principles" be employed.

Ronald Dworkin takes a deontological approach to rights. Dworkin insists that rights are extraordinarily important moral concerns, "trump cards," and must be taken seriously. One view of rights centers on the metaphor of balancing. Dworkin states:

> The metaphor of balancing the public interest against personal claims is established in our political and judicial rhetoric, and this metaphor gives the model both familiarity and appeal. Nevertheless, the first model is a false one, certainly in the case of rights generally regarded as important, and the metaphor is the heart of its error.

Dworkin advocates an alternative model to the balancing view. He holds that "anyone who professes to take rights seriously . . . must accept, at minimum, one or both of two important ideas." First, the powerful idea" of human dignity. This idea is generally associated with Kant and was presented in Chapter II of this volume. The second idea which Dworkin considers vital is the idea of political liberty. Rights need and deserve strong protection from government because they are necessary for the respect and dignity of individual human beings. This view of rights, Dworkin insists, is especially important in the cases of minority individuals.

Both Malcolm X and Charlotte Bunch address the problem of rights from the point of view of minorities. In the selection which follows, Malcolm X makes an important distinction between human rights and civil rights.

Civil rights are determined by a particular government. They are instituted via laws. "On the other hand," Malcolm X claims that:

> human rights go beyond the jurisdiction of this government. Human rights are international. Human rights are something that a man has by dint of his having been born.

Chapter X: The Individual and Society

The struggle for the rights of African-Americans in the United States was unable to get outside help, according to Malcolm X, because they erroneously labeled it a civil rights movement. This categorization places the struggle within the realm of American domestic policy. The problem, when viewed properly, is a *human* rights problem. If one is respected as a human being, Malcolm X contends, then that individual will also be respected as a citizen.

Bunch contends that important rights for women have been systematically excluded from the Western conception of human rights. "The human rights community," Bunch insists, "must move beyond its male defined norms in order to respond to the brutal and systematic violation of women globally." She offers four approaches, with emphasis on practical applications, that will help revise the current conception of human rights to include women's rights.

According to John Rawls, "Justice is the first virtue of social institutions." Rawls' aim in "Justice as Fairness" is to present a conception of justice. He states:

> . . . the guiding idea is that the principles of justice for the basic structure of society are the object of the original agreement. They are the principles that free and rational persons concerned to further their own interests would accept in an initial position of equality as defining the fundamental terms of their relationship.

Rawls is an egalitarian. That is, he favors the principle of equality. He holds that free and rational people, stripped of bias, would favor this position too. He uses a hypothetical example, which includes the "veil of ignorance" to illustrate this point. His theory also contains justification for inequalities.

John Hospers is a libertarian. On this view, the guiding principle is liberty or freedom as manifest in human choices. Hospers lays down three fundamental principles of his libertarian thesis. First, *no one is anyone else's master, and no one is anyone else's slave.* Second, *other men's lives are not yours to dispose of.* Third, *no human being should be a nonvoluntary mortgage on the life of another.*

On the basis of the above principles, Hospers lays out a doctrine which honors the right to make and act upon free choices in such a way that other human beings also have an equal right to act in accordance with their choices. He defends rights to life, liberty and individual property. He also believes that government is the greatest violator of basic rights. Hospers claims that, "Government is the most dangerous institution known to man."

Karl Marx's writings on alienation are penetrating and profound. Many claim that his essay, "Alienated Man," is prophetic. For Marx, political economies transform the world, including human beings, into commodities. He wrote:

> On the basis of political economy itself, in its own words, we have shown that the worker sinks to the level of a commodity and becomes indeed the most wretched of commodities, . . .

Furthermore, Marx asserts:

> With the *increasing value* of the world of things proceeds in direct proportion the *devaluation* of the world of men. Labor produces not only commodities: it produces itself and the worker as a *commodity* . . . .

The modern political economy results in four forms of alienation or *estrangement*. It alienates the laborer from the *product of his/her labor;* it alienates the laborer from his/her life (proper) activity and thus changes the entire *act of production*. Also, it alienates the laborer from his/her essential being or species of being and, finally, it alienates people from each other.

Kwame N. Krumah was one of the most revered and respected political and social theorists/activists in post-colonial Africa. "Consciencism" traces out three heritages of African society: pre-colonial, traditional African heritage, Islam, and Euro-Christianity. He attempts to harmonize these three heritages in a combined presence which is "in tune with the original humanist principles underlying African society." He calls this theoretical point of view *philosophical consciencism* and believes that it can function as a basis which will embody the distinctively African experience.

The Declaration of Independence is the single most powerful statement of fundamental American ideals. Jefferson's writing declares that "all men are created equal" and further, "that they are endowed by their Creator with certain unalienable Rights, that among these are Life, Liberty and the pursuit of Happiness." He goes on to say that the purpose of good government is not to grant these rights but to help individuals secure them. Finally, he declares that governments derive "their just powers from the consent of the governed."

In "I Have A Dream," Martin Luther King, Jr. revived and breathed new life into the American ideal. He delivered, on the steps of the Lincoln Memorial, a stinging indictment of the lack of equality for black Americans almost two hundred years after the Declaration was written. He closed his address with a powerful, passionate, hopeful, and inspiring vision for the future of all Americans. King presented a vision in which America will be transformed from a nation of discord "into a beautiful symphony of brotherhood" where "all of God's children" will be free.

The Conflict Between Individual and Social Morality

Reinhold Niebuhr

A realistic analysis of the problems of human society reveals a constant and seemingly irreconcilable conflict between the needs of society and the imperatives of a sensitive conscience. This conflict, which could be most briefly defined as the conflict between ethics and politics, is made inevitable by the double focus of the moral life. One focus is in the inner life of the individual, and the other in the necessities of man's social life. From the perspective of society the highest moral ideal is justice. From the perspective of the individual the highest ideal is unselfishness. Society must strive for justice even if it is forced to use means, such as self-assertion, resistance, coercion and perhaps resentment, which cannot gain the moral sanction of the most sensitive moral spirit. The individual must strive to realise his life by losing and finding himself in something greater than himself.

These two moral perspectives are not mutually exclusive and the contradiction between them is not absolute. But neither are they easily harmonised. Efforts to harmonise them were analysed in the previous chapter. It was revealed that the highest moral insights and achievements of the individual conscience are both relevant and necessary to the life of society. The most perfect justice cannot be established if the moral imagination of the individual does not seek to comprehend the needs and interests of his fellows. Nor can any non-rational instrument of justice be used without great peril to society, if it is not brought under the control of moral goodwill. Any justice which is only justice soon degenerates into something less than justice. It must be saved by something which is more than justice. The realistic wisdom of the statesman is reduced to foolishness if it is not under the influence of the foolishness of the moral seer. The latter's idealism results in political futility and sometimes in moral confusion, if it is not brought into commerce and communication with the realities of man's collective life. This necessity and possibility of fusing moral and political insights does not, however, completely eliminate certain irreconcilable elements in the two types of morality, internal and external, individual and social. These elements make for constant confusion but they also add to the richness of human life. We may best bring our study of ethics and politics to a close by giving them some further consideration.

From the internal perspective the most moral act is one which is actuated by disinterested motives. The external observer may find good in selfishness. He may value it as natural to the constitution of human nature and as necessary to society. But from the viewpoint of the author of an action, unselfishness must remain the criterion of the highest morality. For only the agent of an action knows to what degree self-seeking corrupts his socially approved actions. Society, on the other hand, makes justice rather than unselfishness its highest moral ideal. Its aim must be to seek equality of opportunity for all life. If this equality and justice cannot be achieved without the assertion of interest against interest, and without restraint upon the self-assertion of those who infringe upon the rights of their neighbors, then society is compelled to sanction self-assertion and restraint. It may even, as we have seen, be forced to sanction social conflict and violence.

Historically the internal perspective has usually been cultivated by religion. For religion proceeds from profound introspection and naturally makes good motives the criteria of good conduct. It may define good motives either in terms of love or of duty, but the emphasis is upon the inner springs of action. Rationalised forms of religion usually choose duty rather than love as the expression of highest virtue (as in Kantian and Stoic morality), because it seems more virtuous to them to bring all impulse under the dominion of reason than to give any impulses, even altruistic ones, moral pre-eminence. The social viewpoint stands in sharpest contrast to religious morality when it views the behavior of collective rather than individual man, and when it deals with the necessities of political life. Political morality, in other words, is in the most uncompromising antithesis to religious morality.

Rational morality usually holds an intermediary position between the two. Sometimes it tries to do justice to the inner moral necessities of the human spirit rather than to the needs of society. If it emphasises the former it may develop an ethic of duty rather than the religious ethic of disinterestedness. But usually rationalism in morals tends to some kind of utilitarianism. It views human conduct from the social perspective and finds its ultimate standards in some general good and total social harmony. From that viewpoint it gives moral sanction to egoistic as well as to altruistic impulses, justifying them because they are natural to human nature and necessary to society. It asks only that egoism be reasonably expressed. Upon that subject Aristotle said the final as well as the first authoritative word. Reason, according to his theory, establishes control over all the impulses, egoistic and altruistic, and justifies them both if excesses are avoided and the golden mean is observed.

Chapter X: The Individual and Society

The social justification for self-assertion is given a typical expression by the Earl of Shaftesbury, who believed that the highest morality represented a harmony between "self-affections" and "natural affections." "If," said Shaftesbury, "a creature be self-neglectful and insensible to danger, or if he want such a degree of passion of any kind, as is useful to preserve, sustain and defend himself, this must certainly be esteemed vicious in regard of the end and design of nature."[1]

It is interesting that a rational morality which gives egoism equality of moral standing with altruism, provided both are reasonably expressed and observe the "law of measure," should again and again find difficulty in coming to terms with the natural moral preference which all unreflective moral thought gives to altruism. Thus Bishop Butler begins his moral theorising by making conscience the balancing force between "self-love" and "benevolence." But gradually conscience gives such a preference to benevolence that it becomes practically identified with it. Butler is therefore forced to draw in reason (originally identified with conscience) as a force higher than conscience to establish harmony between self-love and conscience.[2]

The utilitarian attempt to harmonise the inner and outer perspectives of morality is inevitable and, within limits, possible. It avoids the excesses, absurdities and perils into which both religious and political morality may fall. By placing a larger measure of moral approval upon egoistic impulses than does religious morality and by disapproving coercion, conflict and violence more unqualifiedly than politically oriented morality, it manages to resolve the conflict between them. But it is not as realistic as either. It easily assumes a premature identity between self-interest and social interest and establishes a spurious harmony between egoism and altruism. With Bishop Butler most utilitarian rationalists in morals believe "that though benevolence and self-love are different . . . yet they are so perfectly coincident that the greatest satisfaction to ourselves depends upon having benevolence in due degree, and that self-love is one chief security of our right behavior to society."[3] Rationalism in morals therefore insists on less inner restraint upon self-assertion than does religion, and believes less social restraint to be necessary than political realism demands.

The dangers of religion's inner restraint upon self-assertion, and of its effort to achieve complete disinterestedness, are that such a policy easily becomes morbid, and that it may make for injustice by encouraging and permitting undue self-assertion in others. Its value lies in its check upon egoistic impulses, always more powerful than altruistic ones. If the moral enterprise is begun with the complacent assumption that selfish and social impulses are nicely balanced and equally justified, even a minimum equilibrium between them becomes impossible.

The more the moral problem is shifted from the relations of individuals to the relations of groups and collectives, the more the preponderance of the egoistic impulses over the social ones is established. It is therefore revealed that no inner checks are powerful enough to bring them under complete control. Social control must consequently be attempted; and it cannot be established without social conflict. The moral perils attending such a political strategy have been previously considered. They are diametrically opposite to the perils of religious morality. The latter tend to perpetuate injustice by discouraging self-assertion against the inordinate claims of others. The former justify not only self-assertion but the use of non-rational power in reinforcing claims. They may therefore substitute new forms of injustice for old ones and enthrone a new tyranny on the throne of the old. A rational compromise between these two types of restraint easily leads to a premature complacency toward self-assertion. It is therefore better for society to suffer the uneasy harmony between the two types of restraint than to run the danger of inadequate checks upon egoistic impulses. Tolstoi and Lenin both present perils to the life of society; but they are probably no more dangerous than the compromises with human selfishness effected by modern disciples of Aristotle.

If we contemplate the conflict between religious and political morality it may be well to recall that the religious ideal in its purest form has nothing to do with the problem of social justice. It makes disinterestedness an absolute ideal without reference to social consequences. It justifies the ideal in terms of the integrity and beauty of the human spirit. While religion may involve itself in absurdities in the effort to achieve the ideal by purely internal discipline, and while it may run the peril of deleterious social consequences, it does do justice to inner needs of the human spirit. The veneration in which a Tolstoi, a St. Francis, a crucified Christ, and the saints of all ages have been held, proves that, in the inner sanctuary of their souls, selfish men know that they ought not be selfish, and venerate what they feel they ought to be and cannot be.

Pure religious idealism does not concern itself with the social problem. It does not give itself to the illusion that material and mundane advantages can be gained by the refusal to assert your claims to them. It may believe, as Jesus did, that self-realisation is the inevitable consequence of self-abnegation. But this self-realisation is not attained on the level of physical life or mundane advantages. It is achieved in spiritual terms, such as the martyr's immortality and the Saviour's exaltation in the hearts of his disciples. Jesus did not counsel his disciples to forgive seventy times seven in order that they might convert their enemies or make them more favorably disposed. He counselled it as an effort to approximate complete moral perfection, the perfection of God. He did not ask his followers to go the second mile in the hope that those who had impressed them into service would relent and give them freedom. He did not say that the enemy ought to be loved so that he would cease to be an enemy. He did not dwell upon the social consequences of these moral actions, because he viewed them from an inner and a transcendent perspective.

Chapter X: The Individual and Society

Nothing is clearer than that a pure religious idealism must issue in a policy of non-resistance which makes no claims to be socially efficacious. It submits to any demands, however unjust, and yields to any claims, however inordinate, rather than assert self-interest against another. "You will meekly bear," declared Epictetus, "for you will say on every occasion 'It seemed so to him.'" This type of moral idealism leads either to asceticism, as in the case of Francis and other Catholic saints, or at least to the complete disavowal of any political responsibility, as in the case of Protestant sects practicing consistent non-resistance, as, for instance, the Anabaptists, Mennonites, Dunkers and Doukhobors. The Quakers assumed political responsibilities, but they were never consistent non-resisters. They disavowed violence but not resistance.

While social consequences are not considered in such a moral strategy, it would be shortsighted to deny that it may result in redemptive social consequences, at least within the area of individual and personal relationships. Forgiveness may not always prompt the wrongdoer to repentance; but yet it may. Loving the enemy may not soften the enemy's heart; but there are possibilities that it will. Refusal to assert your own interests against another may not shame him into unselfishness; but on occasion it has done so. Love and benevolence may not lead to complete mutuality; but it does have that tendency, particularly within the area of intimate relationships. Human life would, in fact, be intolerable if justice could be established in all relationships only by self-assertion and counter-assertion, or only by a shrewd calculation of claims and counter-claims. The fact is that love, disinterestedness and benevolence do have a strong social and utilitarian value, and the place they hold in the hierarchy of virtues is really established by that value, though religion may view them finally from an inner or transcendent perspective. "The social virtues," declares David Hume, "are never regarded without their beneficial tendencies nor viewed as barren and unfruitful. The happiness of mankind, the order of society, the harmony of families, the mutual support of friends, are always considered as a result of their gentle domination over the breasts of men."[4] The utilitarian and social emphasis is a little too absolute in the words of Hume, but it is true within limits. Even the teachings of Jesus reveal a prudential strain in which the wholesome social consequences of generous attitudes are emphasised. "With what measure you mete, it shall be measured to you again." The paradox of the moral life consists in this: that the highest mutuality is achieved where mutual advantages are not consciously sought as the fruit of love. For love is purest where it desires no returns for itself; and it is most potent where it is purest. Complete mutuality, with its advantages to each party to the relationship, is therefore most perfectly realised where it is not intended, but love is poured out without seeking returns. That is how the madness of religious morality, with its trans-social ideal, becomes the wisdom which achieves wholesome social consequences. For the same reason a purely prudential morality must be satisfied with something less than the best.

Where human relations are intimate (and love is fully effective only in intimate and personal relations), the way of love may be the only way to justice. Where rights and interests are closely interwoven, it is impossible to engage in a shrewd and prudent calculation of comparative rights. Where lives are closely intertwined, happiness is destroyed if it is not shared. Justice by assertion and counter-assertion therefore becomes impossible. The friction involved in the process destroys mutual happiness. Justice by a careful calculation of competing rights is equally difficult, if not impossible. Interests and rights are too mutual to allow for their precise definition in individual terms. The very effort to do so is a proof of the destruction of the spirit of mutuality by which alone intimate relations may be adjusted. The spirit of mutuality can be maintained only by a passion which does not estimate the personal advantages which are derived from mutuality too carefully. Love must strive for something purer than justice if it would attain justice. Egoistic impulses are so much more powerful than altruistic ones that if the latter are not given stronger than ordinary support, the justice which even good men design is partial to those who design it.

This social validity of a moral ideal which transcends social considerations in its purest heights, is progressively weakened as it is applied to more and more intricate, indirect and collective human relations. It is not only unthinkable that a group should be able to attain a sufficiently consistent unselfish attitude toward other groups to give it a very potent redemptive power, but it is improbable that any competing group would have the imagination to appreciate the moral calibre of the achievement. Furthermore a high type of unselfishness, even if it brings ultimate rewards, demands immediate sacrifices. An individual may sacrifice his own interests, either without hope of reward or in the hope of an ultimate compensation. But how is an individual, who is responsible for the interests of his group, to justify the sacrifice of interests other than his own? "It follows," declares Hugh Cecil, "that all that department of morality which requires an individual to sacrifice his interests to others, everything which falls under the heading of unselfishness, is inappropriate to the action of a state. No one has a right to be unselfish with other people's interests."[5]

This judgment is not sufficiently qualified. A wise statesman is hardly justified in insisting on the interests of his group when they are obviously in unjust relation to the total interests of the community of mankind. Nor is he wrong in sacrificing immediate advantages for the sake of higher mutual advantages. His unwillingness to do this is precisely what makes nations so imprudent in holding to immediate advantages and losing ultimate values of mutuality. Nevertheless it is obvious that fewer risks can be taken with community interests than with individual interests. The inability to take risks naturally results in a benevolence in which selfish advantages

Chapter X: The Individual and Society

must be quite apparent, and in which therefore the moral and redemptive quality is lost.

Every effort to transfer a pure morality of disinterestedness to group relations has resulted in failure. The Negroes of America have practiced it quite consistently since the Civil War. They did not rise against their masters during the war and remained remarkably loyal to them. Their social attitudes since that time, until a very recent date, have been compounded of genuine religious virtues of forgiveness and forbearance, and a certain social inertia which was derived not from religious virtue but from racial weakness. Yet they did not soften the hearts of their oppressors by their social policy.

During the early triumphs of fascism in Italy the socialist leaders suddenly adopted pacifist principles. One of the socialist papers counselled the workers to meet the terror of fascism with the following strategy: "(1) Create a void around fascism. (2) Do not provoke; suffer any provocation with serenity. (3) To win, be better than your adversary. (4) Do not use the weapons of your enemy. Do not follow in his footsteps. (5) Remember that the blood of guerilla warfare falls upon those who shed it. (6) Remember that in a struggle between brothers those are victors who conquer themselves. (7) Be convinced that it is better to suffer wrong than to commit it. (8) Don't be impatient. Impatience is extremely egoistical; it is instinct; it is yielding to one's ego urge. (9) Do not forget that socialism wins the more when it suffers, because it was born in pain and lives on its hopes. (10) Listen to the mind and to the heart which advises you that the working people should be nearer to sacrifice than to vengeance."[6] A nobler decalogue of virtues could hardly have been prescribed. But the Italian socialists were annihilated by the fascists, their organisations destroyed, and the rights of the workers subordinated to a state which is governed by their enemies. The workers may live "on their hopes," but there is no prospect of realising their hopes under the present regime by practicing the pure moral principles which the socialistic journal advocated. Some of them are not incompatible with the use of coercion against their foes. But inasfar as they exclude coercive means they are ineffectual before the brutal will-to-power of fascism.

The effort to apply the doctrines of Tolstoi to the political situation of Russia had a very similar effect. Tolstoi and his disciples felt that the Russian peasants would have the best opportunity for victory over their oppressors if they did not become stained with the guilt of the same violence which the czarist regime used against them. The peasants were to return good for evil, and win their battles by non-resistance. Unlike the policies of Gandhi, the political programme of Tolstoi remained altogether unrealistic. No effort was made to relate the religious ideal of love to the political necessity of coercion. Its total effect was therefore socially and politically deleterious. It helped to destroy a rising protest against political and economic oppression and to confirm the Russian in his pessimistic passivity. The excesses of the terrorists seemed to give point to the Tolstoian opposition to violence and resistance. But the terrorists and the pacifists finally ended in the same futility. And their common futility seemed to justify the pessimism which saw no escape from the traditional injustices of the Russian political and economic system. The real fact was that both sprang from a romantic middle-class or aristocratic idealism, too individualistic in each instance to achieve political effectiveness. The terrorists were diseased idealists, so morbidly oppressed by the guilt of violence resting upon their class, that they imagined it possible to atone for that guilt by deliberately incurring guilt in championing the oppressed. Their ideas were ethical and, to a degree, religious, though they regarded themselves as irreligious. The political effectiveness of their violence was a secondary consideration. The Tolstoian pacifists attempted the solution of the social problem by diametrically opposite policies. But, in common with the terrorists, their attitudes sprang from the conscience of disquieted individuals. Neither of them understood the realities of political life because neither had an appreciation for the significant characteristics of collective behavior. The romantic terrorists failed to relate their isolated acts of terror to any consistent political plan. The pacifists, on the other hand, erroneously attributed political potency to pure non-resistance.

Whenever religious idealism brings forth its purest fruits and places the strongest check upon selfish desire it results in policies which, from the political perspective, are quite impossible. There is, in other words, no possibility of harmonising the two strategists designed to bring the strongest inner and the most effective social restraint upon egoistic impulse. It would therefore seem better to accept a frank dualism in morals than to attempt a harmony between the two methods which threatens the effectiveness of both. Such a dualism would have two aspects. It would make a distinction between the moral judgments applied to the self and to others; and it would distinguish between what we expect of individuals and of groups. The first distinction is obvious and is explicitly or implicitly accepted whenever the moral problem is taken seriously. To disapprove your own selfishness more severely than the egoism of others is a necessary discipline if the natural complacency toward the self and severity in the judgment of others is to be corrected. Such a course is, furthermore, demanded by the logic of the whole moral situation. One can view the actions of others only from an external perspective; and from that perspective the social justification of self-assertion becomes inevitable. Only the actions of the self can be viewed from the internal perspective; and from that viewpoint all egoism must be morally disapproved. If such disapproval should occasionally destroy self-assertion to such a degree as to invite the aggression of others, the instances will be insignificant in comparison with the number of cases in which the moral disapproval of egoism merely tends to reduce the inordinate self-assertion of the average man. Even in those few cases in which egoism is reduced by religious discipline to such proportions that it invites injustice in an immediate situation, it will have social usefulness in glorifying the moral principle and setting an example for future generations.

The distinction between individual and group morality is a sharper and more perplexing one. The moral obtuseness of human collectives makes a morality of pure disinterestedness impossible. There is not enough imagination in any social group to render it amenable to the influence of pure love. Nor is there a possibility of persuading any social group to make a venture in pure love, except, as in the case of the Russian peasants, the recently liberated Negroes and other similar groups, a morally dubious social inertia should be compounded with the ideal. The selfishness of human communities must be regarded as an inevitability. Where it is inordinate it can be checked only by competing assertions of interest; and these can be effective only if coercive methods are added to moral and rational persuasion. Moral factors may qualify, but they will not eliminate, the resulting social contest and conflict. Moral goodwill may seek to relate the peculiar interests of the group to the ideal of a total and final harmony of all life. It may thereby qualify the self-assertion of the privileged, and support the interests of the disinherited, but it will never be so impartial as to persuade any group to subject its interests completely to an inclusive social ideal. The spirit of love may preserve a certain degree of appreciation for the common weaknesses and common aspirations which bind men together above the areas of social conflict. But again it cannot prevent the conflict. It may avail itself of instruments of restraint and coercion, through which a measure of trust in the moral capacities of an opponent may be expressed and the expansion rather than contraction of those capacities is encouraged. But it cannot hide the moral distrust expressed by the very use of the instruments of coercion. To some degree the conflict between the purest individual morality and an adequate political policy must therefore remain.

The needs of an adequate political strategy do not obviate the necessity of cultivating the strictest individual moral discipline and the most uncompromising idealism. Individuals, even when involved in their communities, will always have the opportunity of loyalty to the highest canons of personal morality. Sometimes, when their group is obviously bent upon evil, they may have to express their individual ideals by disassociating themselves from their group. Such a policy may easily lead to political irresponsibility, as in the case of the more extreme sects of non-resisters. But it may also be socially useful. Religiously inspired pacifists who protest against the violence of their state in the name of a sensitive individual conscience may never lame the will-to-power of a state as much as a class-conscious labor group. But if their numbers grew to large proportions, they might affect the policy of the government. It is possible, too, that their example may encourage similar non-conformity among individuals in the enemy nation and thus mitigate the impact of the conflict without weakening the comparative strength of their own community.

The ideals of a high individual morality are just as necessary when loyalty to the group is maintained and its general course in relation to other groups is approved. There are possibilities for individual unselfishness, even when the group is asserting its interests and rights against other communities. The interests of the individual are related to those of the group, and he may therefore seek advantages for himself when he seeks them for his group. But this indirect egoism is comparatively insignificant beside the possibilities of expressing or disciplining his egoism in relation to his group. If he is a leader in the group, it is necessary to restrain his ambitions. A leadership, free of self-seeking, improves the morale of the whole group. The leaders of disinherited groups, even when they are avowed economic determinists and scorn the language of personal idealism, are frequently actuated by high moral ideals. If they sought their own personal advantage they could gain it more easily by using their abilities to rise from their group to a more privileged one. The temptation to do this among the abler members of disinherited groups is precisely what has retarded the progress of their class or race.

The progress of the Negro race, for instance, is retarded by the inclination of many able and educated Negroes to strive for identification and assimilation with the more privileged white race and to minimise their relation to a subject race as much as possible. The American Labor Movement has failed to develop its full power for the same reason. Under the influence of American individualism, able labor men have been more ambitious to rise into the class of owners and their agents than to solidify the laboring class in its struggle for freedom. There is, furthermore, always the possibility that an intelligent member of a social group will begin his career in unselfish devotion to the interests of his community, only to be tempted by the personal prizes to be gained, either within the group or by shifting his loyalty to a more privileged group. The interests of individuals are, in other words, never exactly identical with those of their communities. The possibility and necessity of individual moral discipline is therefore never absent, no matter what importance the social struggle between various human communities achieves. Nor can any community achieve unity and harmony within its life, if the sentiments of goodwill and attitudes of mutuality are not cultivated. No political realism which emphasises the inevitability and necessity of a social struggle, can absolve individuals of the obligation to check their own egoism, to comprehend the interests of others and thus to enlarge the areas of co-operation.

Whether the co-operative and moral aspects of human life, or the necessities of the social struggle, gain the largest significance, depends upon time and circumstance. There are periods of social stability, when the general equilibrium of social forces is taken for granted, and men give themselves to the task of making life more beautiful and tender within the limits

Chapter X: The Individual and Society

of the established social system. The Middle Ages were such a period. While they took injustices for granted, such as would affront the conscience of our day, it cannot be denied that they elaborated amenities, urbanities and delicate refinements of life and art which must make our age seem, in comparison, like the recrudescence of barbarism.

Our age is, for good or ill, immersed in the social problem. A technological civilisation makes stability impossible. It changes the circumstances of life too rapidly to incline any one to a reverent acceptance of an ancestral order. Its rapid developments and its almost daily changes in the physical circumstances of life destroy the physical symbols of stability and therefore make for restlessness, even if these movements were not in a direction which imperil the whole human enterprise. But the tendencies of an industrial era are in a definite direction. They tend to aggravate the injustices from which men have perennially suffered; and they tend to unite the whole of humanity in a system of economic interdependence. They make us more conscious of the relations of human communities to each other, than of the relations of individuals within their communities. They obsess us therefore with the brutal aspects of man's collective behavior. They, furthermore, cumulate the evil consequences of these brutalities so rapidly that we feel under a tremendous urgency to solve our social problem before it is too late. As a generation we are therefore bound to feel harassed as well as disillusioned.

In such a situation all the highest ideals and tenderest emotions which men have felt all through the ages, when they became fully conscious of their heritage and possible destiny as human beings, will seem from our perspective to be something of a luxury. They will be under a moral disadvantage, because they appear as a luxury which only those are able to indulge who are comfortable enough to be comparatively oblivious to the desperate character of our contemporary social situation. We live in an age in which personal moral idealism is easily accused of hypocrisy and frequently deserves it. It is an age in which honesty is possible only when it skirts the edges of cynicism. All this is rather tragic. For what the individual conscience feels when it lifts itself above the world of nature and the system of collective relationships in which the human spirit remains under the power of nature, is not a luxury but a necessity of the soul. Yet there is beauty in our tragedy. We are, at least, rid of some of our illusions. We can no longer buy the highest satisfactions of the individual life at the expense of social injustice. We cannot build our individual ladders to heaven and leave the total human enterprise unredeemed of its excesses and corruptions.

In the task of that redemption the most effective agents will be men who have substituted some new illusions for the abandoned ones. The most important of these illusions is that the collective life of mankind can achieve perfect justice. It is a very valuable illusion for the moment; for justice cannot be approximated if the hope of its perfect realization does not generate a sublime madness in the soul. Nothing but such madness will do battle with malignant power and "spiritual wickedness in high places." The illusion is dangerous because it encourages terrible fanaticisms. It must therefore be brought under the control of reason. One can only hope that reason will not destroy it before its work is done.

Endnotes

1. Third Earl of Shaftesbury, *An Inquiry Concerning Virtue or Merit*, Bk. II, Part I, sec. III.
2. *Cf.* Joseph Butler, *Fifteen Sermons on Human Nature.*
3. Butler, *op. cit.,* Sermon I.
4. David Hume, *An Enquiry Concerning the Principles of Morals*, Part 2, sec. II.
5. Hugh Cecil, *Conservatism*, p. 182.
6. Quoted by Max Nomad, *Rebels and Renegades,* p. 294.

from The Analects

Confucius

On Personal Growth

Confucius said, "At 15 my heart-and-mind were set upon learning; at 30 I took my stance; at 40 I was no longer of two minds; at 50 I realized the order prevailing in the world; at 60 my ear was attuned; at 70 I could give my heart-and-mind free rein without overstepping the mark." (2/4)

Kung-sun Ch'ao of Wei asked Tzu-kung, "Who did Confucius learn from?" Tzu-kung replied, "The culture [*tao*] of King Wen and Wu has not yet fallen to the ground. It resides in people. While none remain unaffected by it, those who are worthy have got it in great measure, while those who are not still have a modicum of it. Who then did Confucius not learn from? Again, how could there be a single, constant teacher for him?" (19/22)

Learn broadly yet be determined in your own dispositions; enquire with urgency yet reflect closely on the question at hand: becoming authoritative in your person lies in this. (19/6)

If someone can recite the three hundred *Songs* but yet when you give him official responsibility, he fails you, or when you send him to distant quarters he is not able to act on his own initiative, then although he knows so much, what good is it to him? (13/5)

To realize that you know something when you do, and to realize that you do not when you do not—this then is knowing. (2.17)

The wise—those who realize the world—enjoy water; the authoritatively human enjoy mountains. The wise are active; the authoritatively human are still. Those wise find enjoyment; the authoritatively human are long-lived. (6/23)

Having a sense of propriety as one's raw stuff, to practice it in ritual relations, to express it with humility, and to complete it in living up to one's word: this, then, is the exemplary person. (15/18)

Since the exemplary person will be deemed wise or not because of one word, how could one be but careful about what one has to say? (19/25)

The Master said, "My, but I am in a state of decline. How long has it been since I have visited with the Duke of Chou in my dreams!" (7/5)

On Interpersonal Relations

The exemplary person seeks harmony rather than agreement; the small person does the opposite. (13/23)

Tzu-kung asked, "Is there one expression that one can act on to the end of one's days?"

The Master replied, "There is deference: do not impose on other people what you yourself do not desire." (15/24)

Confucius said, "Having three kinds of friends will bring personal improvement; three kinds will bring injury. To have friends who are straight, who are true to their word, and who are well-informed is to be improved; to have friends who are ingratiating, foppish, and superficial is to be injured." (16/4)

The disciples of Tzu-hsia asked Tzu-chang about friendship. Tzu-chang queried, "What has Tzu-hsia told you?" They replied, "Join together with those from whom you can learn; spurn those from whom you can't." Tzu-chang says, "This is different from what I have heard. The exemplary person exalts the worthy and is tolerant of the common, praises those who are capable and is sympathetic to those who are not. If in comparison with others I am truly worthy, who am I unable to tolerate? If I am not worthy in the comparison, and people are going to spurn me, on what basis do I spurn them?" (19/3)

On Ritually Constituted Community

Confucius said, "To discipline oneself through ritual practice is to become authoritatively human. If for the space of one day one were able to accomplish this, the world would turn to one as a model of humanity. However, becoming truly human emerges out of oneself; how could it emerge out of others?" (12/1)

What does one who is not authoritatively human have to do with ritual practice or with music? (3/3)

On Government

Lead the people with administrative injunctions and organize them with penal law, and they will avoid punishments but will be without a sense of shame. Lead them with excellence and organize them through roles and ritual practices, and they will develop a sense of shame, and moreover, will order themselves harmoniously. (2/3)

Someone asked Confucius, "Why are you not in government?" Confucius replied, "The *Book of Documents* says: 'Filiality! Simply extend filiality and fraternity into government.' This 'filiality' then, is also taking part in government. Why must one take part in formal government?" (2/21)

Fan Ch'ih asked about becoming authoritatively human, and the Master replied, "Love others." He asked about realization and the Master said, "Realize others." Fan Ch'ih did not understand and so the Master explained, 'If you promote the straight over the crooked you can make the crooked straight." (12/22)

On Cosmic Order

It is the human being who broadens natural and moral order [*tao*], not natural and moral order that broadens the human being. (15/29)

The Master did not converse on strange omens, the use of force, the problem of disorder, or the gods. (7/21)

Chi-lu asked about serving the gods and the spirits of the dead, but the Master replied, "If you are not yet able to serve other people, how can you serve the spirits of the dead?" Chi-lu then asked about death, but the Master replied, "If you do not yet understand life, how can you understand death?" (11/12)

Confucius was the sun and moon which no one can climb beyond. Even if someone wanted to cut himself off from the sun and moon, what damage could one do to him? (19/24)

The exemplary person holds three things in awe: the natural order of things, the distinguished person, and the words of the sage. (16/8)

Translated by Roger T. Ames.

The Ideal State

Plato

Here Adeimantus interposed a question: How would you answer, Socrates, said he, if a person were to say that you are not making these men very happy, and that they are themselves to blame; the city in fact belongs to them, but they reap no advantage from it; whereas other men acquire lands, and build large and handsome houses, and have everything handsome about them, offering sacrifices to the gods on their own account, and practicing hospitality; moreover, they have the gold and silver which you have just mentioned, and all that is usual among the favorites of fortune; but our poor citizens are no better than mercenaries who are quartered in the city and are always mounting guard?

Yes, I said; and you may add that they are only fed, and not paid in addition to their food like other men; and therefore they cannot, if they would, take a private journey abroad; they have no money to spend on a mistress or any other luxurious fancy, which, as the world goes, is thought to be happiness; and many other accusations of the same nature might be added.

But, said he, let us suppose all this to be included in the charge.

You mean to ask, I said, what will be our answer?

Yes.

If we proceed along the old path, my belief, I said, is that we shall find the answer. And our answer will be that, even as they are, our guardians may very likely be the happiest of men; but that our aim in founding the State was not the disproportionate happiness of any one class, but the greatest happiness of the whole; we thought that in a State which is ordered with a view to the good of the whole we should be most likely to find justice, and in the worst-ordered State injustice; and, having found them, we might then decide upon the answer to our first question. At present, I take it, we are fashioning the happy State, not piecemeal, or with a view of making a few happy citizens, but as a whole; and by-and-by we will proceed to view the opposite kind of State. Suppose that we were painting a statue, and someone came up to us and said, Why do you not

Chapter X: The Individual and Society

put the most beautiful colors on the most beautiful parts of the body—the eyes ought to be purple, but you have made them black—to him we might fairly answer, "Sir, you would not surely have us beautify the eyes to such a degree that they are no longer eyes; consider rather whether, by giving this and the other features their due proportion, we make the whole beautiful." And so I say to you, do not compel us to assign to the guardians a sort of happiness which will make them no guardians at all; for we too can clothe our husbandmen in royal apparel, and set crowns of gold on their heads, and bid them till the ground as much as they like, and no more. Our potters also might be allowed to repose on couches, and feast by the fireside, passing round the winecup, while their wheel is conveniently at hand, so that they may make a few pots when they feel inclined; in this way we might make every class happy—and then, as you imagine, the whole State would be happy. But do not put this idea into our heads; for, if we listen to you, the husbandman will be no longer a husbandman, the potter will cease to be a potter, and no one will have the character of any distinct class in the State. Now this is not of much consequence where the corruption of society, and pretension to be what you are not, is confined to cobblers; but when the guardians of the laws and of the government are only seeming and not real guardians, then see how they turn the State upside down; and on the other hand they alone have the power of giving order and happiness to the State. We mean our guardians to be true saviors and not the destroyers of the State, whereas our opponent is thinking of peasants at a festival, who are enjoying a life of revelry, not of citizens who are doing their duty to the State. But, if so, we mean different things, and he is speaking of something which is not a State. And therefore we must consider whether in appointing our guardians we look to their greatest happiness individually, or whether our aim is not to ensure that happiness appears in the State as a whole. What these guardians or auxiliaries must be compelled or induced to do (and the same may be said of every other trade), is to become as expert as possible in their professional work. And thus the whole State will grow up in a noble order, and the several classes will receive the proportion of happiness which nature assigns to them.

I think that you are quite right.

I wonder whether you will agree with another remark which occurs to me.

What may that be?

There seem to be two causes of the deterioration of the arts.

What are they?

Wealth, I said, and poverty.

How do they act?

The process is as follows: When a potter becomes rich, will he, think you, any longer take the same pains with his art?

Certainly not.

He will grow more and more indolent and careless?

Very true.

And the result will be that he becomes a worse potter?

Yes; he greatly deteriorates.

But, on the other hand, if he has no money and cannot provide himself with tools or other requirements of his craft, his own work will not be equally good, and he will not teach his sons or apprentices to work equally well.

Certainly not.

Then, under the influence either of poverty or of wealth, workmen and their work are equally liable to degenerate?

That is evident.

Here then is a discovery of new evils, I said, against which the guardians will have to watch, or they will creep into the city unobserved.

What evils?

Wealth, I said, and poverty; the one is the parent of luxury and indolence, and the other of meanness and viciousness, and both of a revolutionary spirit.

That is very true, he replied; but still I should like to know, Socrates, how our city will be able to go to war, especially against an enemy who is rich and powerful, if deprived of the sinews of war.

Evidently it would be difficult, I replied, to wage war with one such enemy; but it will be easier where there are two of them.

How so? he asked.

In the first place, I said, if we have to fight, our side will be trained warriors fighting against an army of rich men.

That is true, he said.

And do you not suppose, Adeimantus, that a single boxer who was perfect in his art would easily be a match for two stout and well-to-do gentlemen who were not boxers?

Hardly, if they came upon him at once.

What, not, I said, if he were able to run away and then turn and strike at the one who first came up? And supposing he were to do this several times under the heat of a scorching sun, might he not, being an expert, overturn more than one stout personage?

Certainly, he said, there would be nothing wonderful in that.

And yet rich men probably have more instruction in the science and practice of boxing than they have in military science.

Likely enough.

Then we may assume that our athletes will be able to fight with two or three times their own number?

I will accept that, for I think you right.

And suppose that, before engaging, our citizens send an embassy to one of the two cities, telling them what is the truth: "Silver and gold we neither have nor are permitted to have, but you may; do you therefore

Chapter X: The Individual and Society

come and help us in war, and take the spoils of the other city." Who, on hearing these words; would choose to fight against lean wiry dogs, rather than, with the dogs on their side, against fat and tender sheep?

That is not likely; and yet there might be a danger to the poor State if the wealth of many States were to be gathered into one.

But how simple of you to think that the term State is applicable at all to any but our own!

Why so?

You ought to speak of other States in the plural number; not one of them is a city, but many cities, as they say in the game. Each will contain not less than two divisions, one the city of the poor, the other of the rich, which are at war with one another; and within each there are many smaller divisions. You would be altogether beside the mark if you treated these as a single State; but if you deal with them as many, and give the wealth or power or persons of the one to the others, you will always have a great many friends and not many enemies. And your State, while the wise order which has now been prescribed continues to prevail in her, will be the greatest of States, I do not mean to say in reputation or appearance, but in deed and truth, though she number not more than a thousand defenders. A single State of that size you will hardly find, either among Hellenes or barbarians, though many that appear to be as great and many times greater.

That is most true, he said.

Hence, I said, it can be seen what will be the best limit for our rulers to fix when they are considering the size of the State and the amount of territory which they are to include, and beyond which they will not go.

What limit would you propose?

I would allow the State to increase so far as is consistent with unity; that, I think, is the proper limit.

Very good, he said.

Here then, I said, is another order which will have to be conveyed to our guardians: Let them guard against our city becoming small, or great only in appearance. It must attain an adequate size, but it must remain one.

And perhaps, said he, you do not think this is a very severe order?

And here is another, said I, which is lighter still—I mean the duty, of which some mention was made before, of degrading the offspring of the guardians when inferior, and of elevating into the rank of guardians the offspring of the lower classes, when naturally superior. The intention was that, in the case of the citizens generally, each individual should be put to the use for which nature intended him, one to one work, and then every man would do his own business, and become one and not many; and so the whole city would be one and not many.

Yes, he said; that is not so difficult.

The regulations which we are prescribing, my good Adeimantus, are not, as might be supposed, a number of great principles, but trifles all, if care be taken, as the saying is, of the one great thing—a thing, however, which I would rather call, not great, but sufficient for our purpose.

What may that be? he asked.

Education, I said, and nurture: if our citizens are well educated, and grow into sensible men, they will easily see their way through all these, as well as other matters which I omit; such, for example, as marriage, the possession of women and the procreation of children, which will all follow the general principle that friends have all things in common, as the proverb says.

That will be the best way of settling them.

Also, I said, the State, if once started well, moves with accumulating force like a wheel. For where good nurture and education are maintained, they implant good constitutions, and these good constitutions taking root in a good education improve more and more, and this improvement affects the breed in man as in other animals.

Very possibly, he said.

Then to sum up: This is the principle to which our rulers should cling throughout, taking care that neglect does not creep in—that music and gymnastic be preserved in their original form, and no innovation made. They must do their utmost to maintain them intact. And when anyone says that

> Mankind most regard the newest song which the singers have

they will be afraid that he may be praising, not new songs, but a new kind of song; and this ought not to be praised, or conceived to be the meaning of the poet; for any musical innovation is to be shunned, as likely to bring danger to the whole State. So Damon tells me, and I can quite believe him—he says that when modes of music change, the fundamental laws of the State always change with them.

Yes, said Adeimantus; and you may add my suffrage to Damon's and your own.

Then, I said, our guardians must lay the foundations of their fortress in music?

Yes, he said; the lawlessness of which you speak too easily steals in.

Yes, I replied, in the form of amusement, and as though it were harmless.

Why, yes, he said, and harmless it would be; were it not that little by little this spirit of license, finding a home, imperceptibly penetrates into manners and customs; whence issuing with greater force it invades contracts between man and man, and from contracts goes on to laws and constitutions, in utter recklessness, ending at last, Socrates, by an overthrow of all rights, private as well as public.

Is that true? I said.

That is my belief, he replied.

Chapter X: The Individual and Society

Then, as I was saying, our boys should be trained from the first in a stricter system, for if childish amusement becomes lawless, it will produce lawless children, who can never grow up into well-conducted and virtuous citizens.

Very true, he said.

And when boys who have made a good beginning in play, have later gained the habit of good order through music, then this habit accompanies them in all their actions and is a principle of growth to them, and is able to correct anything in the State which had been allowed to lapse. It is the reverse of the picture I have just drawn.

Very true, he said.

Thus educated, they will discover for themselves any lesser rules which their predecessors have altogether neglected.

What do you mean?

I mean such things as these—when the young are to be silent before their elders; how they are to show respect to them by standing and making them sit; what honor is due to parents; what garments or shoes are to be worn; the mode of dressing the hair; deportment and manners in general. You would agree with me?

Yes.

But there is, I think, small wisdom in legislating about such matters—precise written enactments cannot create these observances, and are not likely to make them lasting.

Impossible.

It would seem, Adeimantus, that the direction in which education starts a man will determine his future life. Does not like always attract like?

To be sure.

Until some one grand result is reached which may be good, and may be the reverse of good?

That is not to be denied.

And for this reason, I said, I, for my part, should not attempt to extend legislation to such details.

Naturally enough, he replied.

Well, and about the business of the agora, and the ordinary dealings between man and man, or again about agreements with artisans; about insult and injury, or the commencement of actions, and the appointment of juries, what would you say? there may also arise questions about any impositions and exactions of market and harbor dues which may be required, and in general about the regulations of markets, police, harbors, and the like. But, oh heavens! shall we condescend to legislate on any of these particulars?

No, he said, it is unseemly to impose laws about them on good men; what regulations are necessary they will find out soon enough for themselves.

Yes, I said, my friend, if God will only preserve to them the laws which we have given them.

And without divine help, said Adeimantus, they will go on for ever making and mending their laws and their lives in the hope of attaining perfection.

You would compare them, I said, to those invalids who, having no self-restraint, will not leave off their habits of intemperance?

Exactly.

Yes, I said; and what a delightful life they lead! they are always doctoring their disorders, with no result except to increase and complicate them, and always fancying that they will be cured by any nostrum which anybody advises them to try.

Such cases are very common, he said, with invalids of this sort.

Yes, I replied; and the charming thing is that they deem him their worst enemy who tells them the truth, which is simply that, unless they give up gorging and drinking and wenching and idling, neither drug nor cautery nor amputation nor spell nor amulet nor any other remedy will avail.

Charming? he replied. I see nothing charming in going into a passion with a man who tells you what is right.

These gentlemen, I said, do not seem to be in your good graces.

Asuredly not.

Nor would you approve if a whole State behaves in this way, and that brings me back to my point. For when, in certain ill-ordered States, the citizens are forbidden under pain of death to alter the constitution; and yet he who most sweetly courts those who live under this regime and indulges them and fawns upon them and is skillful in anticipating and gratifying their humors is honored as a great and good statesman—do not these States resemble the persons whom I was describing?

Yes, he said; the fault is the same; and I am very far from approving it.

But what of these ready and eager ministers of political corruption? I said. Do you not admire their coolness and dexterity?

Yes, he said, I do; but not of all of them, for there are some whom the applause of the multitude has deluded into the belief that they are really statesmen.

What do you mean? I said; you should have more feeling for them. When a man cannot measure, and a great many others who cannot measure declare that he is four cubits high, can he help believing what they say?

Nay, he said, certainly not in that case.

Well, then, do not be angry with them; for are they not as good as a play, trying their hand at paltry reforms such as I was describing; they are always fancying that by legislation they will make an end of frauds in contracts, and the other rascalities which I was mentioning, not knowing that they are in reality cutting off the heads of a hydra?

Yes, he said; that is just what they are doing.

Chapter X: The Individual and Society

I conceive, I said, that the true legislator will not trouble himself with this class of enactments whether concerning laws or the constitution either in an ill-ordered or in a well-ordered State; for in the former they are quite useless, and in the latter they will either be of a kind which anyone can devise, or will naturally flow out of our previous regulations.

What, then, he said, is still remaining to us of the work of legislation?

Nothing to us, I replied; but to Apollo, the god of Delphi, there remains the ordering of the greatest and noblest and chiefest things of all.

Which are they? he said.

The institution of temples and sacrifices, and the entire service of gods, demigods, and heroes; also the ordering of the repositories of the dead, and the rites which have to be observed by him who would propitiate the inhabitants of the world below. These are matters of which we are ignorant ourselves, and as founders of a city we should be unwise in trusting them to any interpreter but the ancestral one. For it is Apollo who, sitting at the navel of the earth, is the ancestral interpreter of such observances to all mankind.

You are right, and we will do as you propose.

So now the foundation of your city, son of Ariston, is finished. What comes next? Provide yourself with a bright light and search, and get your brother and Polemarchus and the rest of our friends to help, and let us see where in it we can discover justice and where injustice, and in what they differ from one another, and which of them the man who would be happy should have for his portion, whether seen or unseen by gods and men.

Nonsense, said Glaucon: did you not promise to search yourself, saying that for you not to help justice in her need would be an impiety?

Your reminder is true, and I will be as good as my word; but you must join.

We will, he replied.

Well, then, I hope to make the discovery in this way; I mean to begin with the assumption that our State, if rightly ordered, is perfect.

That is most certain.

And being perfect, is therefore wise and valiant and temperate and just.

That is likewise clear.

And whichever of these qualities we first find in the State, the one which is not yet found will be the residue?

Very good.

If in some other instance there were four things, in one of which we were most interested, the one sought for might come to light first, and there would be no further trouble; or if we came to know the other three first, we should thereby attain the object of our search, for it must clearly be the part remaining.

Very true, he said.

And is not a similar method to be pursued about the virtues, which are also four in number?

Clearly.

First among the virtues found in the State, wisdom comes into view, and in this I detect a certain peculiarity.

What is that?

The State which we have been describing has, I think, true wisdom. You would agree that it is good in counsel?

Yes.

And this good counsel is clearly a kind of knowledge, for not by ignorance, but by knowledge, do men counsel well?

Clearly.

And the kinds of knowledge in a State are many and diverse?

Of course.

There is the knowledge of the carpenter; but is that the sort of knowledge which gives a city the title of wise and good in counsel?

Certainly not; that would only give a city the reputation of skill in carpentering.

Then a city is not to be called wise because possessing a knowledge which counsels for the best about wooden implements?

Certainly not.

Nor by reason of a knowledge which advises about brazen pots, he said, nor as possessing any other similar knowledge?

Not by reason of any of them, he said.

Nor yet by reason of a knowledge which cultivates the earth; that would give the city the name of agricultural?

Yes.

Well, I said, and is there any knowledge in our recently founded State among any of the citizens which advises not about any particular thing in the State, but about the whole, and considers how it can best conduct itself in relation with itself and with other States?

There certainly is.

And what is this knowledge, and among whom is it found? I asked.

It is the knowledge of guarding, he replied, and is found in those rulers whom we were just now describing as perfect guardians.

And what is the name which the city derives from the possession of this sort of knowledge?

The name of good in counsel and truly wise.

And will there be in our city more of these true guardians or more smiths?

The smiths, he replied, will be far more numerous.

Will not the guardians probably be the smallest of all the classes who receive a name from the profession of some kind of knowledge?

Much the smallest.

Chapter X: The Individual and Society

And so by reason of the smallest part or class, and of the knowledge which resides in this presiding and ruling part of itself, the whole State, being thus constituted according to nature, will be wise; and this, which can claim a share in the only knowledge worthy to be called wisdom, has been ordained by nature to be of all classes the least.

Most true.

Thus, then, I said, the nature and place in the State of one of the four virtues has somehow or other been discovered.

And, in my humble opinion, very satisfactorily discovered, he replied.

Again, I said, there is no difficulty in seeing the nature of courage, and in what part that quality resides which gives the name of courageous to the State.

How do you mean?

Why, I said, everyone who calls any State courageous or cowardly, will be thinking of the part which fights and goes out to war on the State's behalf.

No one, he replied, would ever think of any other.

The rest of the citizens may be courageous or may be cowardly, but their courage or cowardice will not, as I conceive, have the effect of making the city either the one or the other.

No.

The city will be courageous also by one part of herself, in which resides the power to preserve under all circumstances that opinion about the nature and description of things to be feared in which our legislator educated them; and this is what you term courage.

I should like to hear what you are saying once more, for I do not think that I perfectly understand you.

I mean that courage is a kind of preservation.

Preservation of what kind?

Of the opinion respecting things to be feared, what they are and of what nature, which the law implants through education; and I mean by the words "under all circumstances" to intimate that in pleasure or in pain, or under the influence of desire or fear, a man preserves and does not lose this opinion. Shall I give you an illustration?

If you please.

You know, I said, that dyers, when they want to dye wool for making the true sea-purple, begin by choosing the white from among all the colors available; this they prepare and dress with much care and pains, in order that the white ground may take the purple hue in full perfection. The dyeing then proceeds; and whatever is dyed in this manner becomes a fast color, and no washing either with lyes or without them can take away the bloom. But, when the ground has not been duly prepared, you will have noticed how poor is the look either of purple or of any other color.

Yes, he said; I know that they have a washed-out and ridiculous appearance.

Then now, I said, you will understand that our object in selecting our soldiers, and educating them in music and gymnastic, was very similar; we were contriving influences which would prepare them to take the dye of the laws in perfection, and the color of their opinion about dangers and of every other opinion was to be indelibly fixed by their nurture and training, not to be washed away by such potent lyes as pleasure—mightier agent far in washing the soul than any soda or lye—or by sorrow, fear, and desire, the mightiest of all other solvents. And this sort of universal saving power of true opinion in conformity with law about real and false dangers I call and maintain to be courage, unless you disagree.

But I agree, he replied; for I suppose that you mean to exclude mere right belief about dangers when it has grown up without instruction, such as that of a wild beast or of a slave—this, in your opinion, is something not quite in accordance with law, which in any case should have another name than courage.

Most certainly.

Then I concede courage to be such as you describe.

Excellent, said I, and if you add the words "of a citizen," you will not be far wrong—hereafter, if you agree, we will carry the examination of courage further, but at present we are seeking not for courage but justice; and for the purpose of our inquiry we have said enough.

You are right, he replied.

Two virtues remain to be discovered in the State—first, temperance, and then justice which is the end of our search.

Very true.

Now, can we find justice without troubling ourselves about temperance?

I do not know how that can be accomplished, he said, nor do I desire that justice should be brought to light and temperance lost sight of; and therefore I wish that you would do me the favor of considering temperance first.

Certainly, I replied, I should not be justified in refusing your request.

Then consider, he said.

Yes, I replied; I will; and as far as I can at present see, temperance has more of the nature of harmony and symphony than have the preceding virtues.

How so? he asked.

Temperance, I replied, is the ordering or controlling of certain pleasures and desires; this is curiously enough implied in the saying of "a man being his own master"; and other traces of the same notion may be found in language, may they not?

No doubt, he said.

Chapter X: The Individual and Society

There is something ridiculous in the expression "master of himself"; for the master must also be the servant and the servant the master, since in all these modes of speaking the same person is denoted.

Certainly.

The meaning of this expression is, I believe, that there is within the man's own soul a better and also a worse principle; and when the better has the worse under control, then he is said to be master of himself; and this is a term of praise; but when, owing to evil education or association, the better principle, which is also the smaller, is overwhelmed by the greater mass of the worse—in this case he is blamed and is called the slave of self and dissolute.

Yes, there is reason in that.

And now, I said, look at our newly created State, and there you will find one of these two conditions realized; for the State, as you will acknowledge, may be justly called master of itself, if the words "temperance" and "self-mastery" truly express the rule of the better part over the worse.

On looking, he said, I see that what you say is true.

Let me further note that the manifold and complex pleasures and desires and pains are generally found in children and women and servants, and in the freemen so called who are of the lowest and more numerous class.

Certainly, he said.

Whereas the simple and moderate desires, which follow reason and are under the guidance of mind and true opinion, are to be found only in a few, and those the best born and best educated.

Very true.

These too, as you may perceive, have a place in your State; and the meaner desires of the many are held down by the desires and wisdom of the more virtuous few.

That I perceive, he said.

Then if there be any city which may be described as master of its own pleasures and desires, and master of itself, ours may claim such a designation?

Certainly, he replied.

It may also for all these reasons be called temperate?

Yes.

And if there be any State in which rulers and subjects will be agreed as to the question who are to rule, that again will be our State? Do you think so?

I do, emphatically.

And the citizens being thus agreed among themselves, in which class will temperance be found—in the rulers or in the subjects?

In both, as I should imagine, he replied.

Do you observe that we were not badly inspired in our guess that temperance bore some resemblance to harmony?

709

Why so?

Why, because temperance is unlike courage and wisdom, each of which resides in a part only, the one making the State wise and the other valiant; not so temperance, which extends to the whole, and runs through all the notes of the scale, and produces a unison of the weaker and the stronger and the middle class, whether you suppose them to be stronger or weaker in wisdom or power or numbers or wealth, or anything else you please. Most truly then may we deem this unity of mind to be temperance, an agreement of the naturally superior and inferior as to the right of rule of either both in states and individuals.

I entirely agree with you.

And so, I said, we may consider three out of the four virtues to have been discovered in our State. What remainder is there of qualities which make a state virtuous? For this, it is evident, must be justice.

The inference is obvious.

The time then has arrived, Glaucon, when, like huntsmen, we should surround the cover, and look sharp that justice does not steal away, and pass out of sight and escape us; for beyond a doubt she is somewhere in this country: watch therefore and strive to catch a sight of her, and if you see her first, let me know.

Would that I could! but you will do right to regard me rather as a follower who has just eyes enough to see what you show him.

Offer up a prayer with me and follow.

I will, but you must show me the way.

Here is no path, I said, and the wood is dark and perplexing; still we must push on.

Let us push on.

Here I saw something: Halloo! I said, I begin to perceive a track, and I believe that the quarry will not escape.

Good news, he said.

Truly, I said, we are stupid fellows.

Why so?

Why, my dear friend, far back from the beginning of our inquiry, justice has been lying at our feet, and we never saw her; nothing could be more ridiculous. Like people who go about looking for what they have in their hands, we looked not at what we were seeking, but at what was far off in the distance; and that, I suppose, was how we missed her.

What do you mean?

I mean to say that for a long time past we have been talking or hearing of justice, and yet have failed to recognize that we were in some sense actually describing it.

I grow impatient at the length of your exordium.

Well then, tell me, I said, whether I am right or not: You remember the original principle which we laid down at the foundation of the State; we decided, and more than once insisted, that one man should practice one

Chapter X: The Individual and Society

occupation only, that to which his nature was best adapted—now justice, in my view, either is this principle or is some form of it.

Yes, we did.

Further, we affirmed that justice was doing one's own business, and not being a busybody; we said so again and again, and many others have said the same to us.

Yes, we said so.

Then to attend to one's own business, in some form or another, may be assumed to be justice. Do you know my evidence for this?

No, but I should like to be told.

Because I think that this is the virtuous quality which remains in the State when the other virtues of temperance and courage and wisdom are abstracted; and that this not only made it possible for them to appear, but is also their preservative as long as they remain; and we were saying that if the three were discovered by us, justice would be the fourth or remaining one.

That follows of necessity.

If we were asked to determine which of these four qualities by its presence will contribute most to the excellence of our State, whether the agreement of rulers and subjects, or the preservation in the soldiers of the opinion which the law ordains about the true nature of dangers, or wisdom and watchfulness in the rulers, or this other which is found in children and women, slave and freeman, artisan, ruler, subject (I mean the quality of every one doing his own work, and not being a busybody), the decision is not so easy.

Certainly, he replied, there would be a difficulty in saying which.

Then the attention of each individual to his own work appears to be a quality rivaling wisdom, temperance, and courage, with reference to the excellence of the State.

Yes, he said.

And the only virtue which, from that point of view, is of equal importance with them, is justice?

Exactly.

Let us look at the question also in this way: Are not the rulers in a State those to whom you would entrust the office of determining suits at law?

Certainly.

In the decision of such suits will any principle be prior to this, that a man may neither take what is another's nor be deprived of what is his own?

No.

Because it is a just principle?

Yes.

Then on this view also justice will be admitted to be the having and doing what is a man's own, and belongs to him?

Very true.

Think, now, and say whether you agree with me or not. Suppose a carpenter sets out to do the business of a cobbler, or a cobbler that of a carpenter; and suppose them to exchange their implements or social position, or the same person to try to undertake the work of both, or whatever be the change; do you think that any great harm would result to the State?

Not much.

But when the cobbler or any other man whom nature designed to be a trader, having his heart lifted up by wealth or strength or the number of his followers or any like advantage, attempts to force his way into the class of warriors, or a warrior into that of legislators and guardians, to which he ought not to aspire, and when these exchange their implements and their social position with those above them; or when one man would be trader, legislator, and warrior all in one, then I think you will agree with me in saying that this interchange and this meddling of one with another is the ruin of the State.

Most true.

Seeing then, I said, that there are three distinct classes, any meddling of one with another, or the change of one into another, is the greatest harm to the State, and may be most justly termed evil-doing?

Precisely.

And the greatest degree of evil-doing to one's own city would be termed by you injustice?

Certainly.

This then is injustice; and on the other hand when the three main classes, traders, auxiliaries, and guardians, each do their own business, that is justice, and will make the city just.

I agree with you.

We will not, I said, be over-positive as yet; but if, on trial, this conception of justice be verified in the individual as well as in the State, there will be no longer any room for doubt; if it be not verified, we must have a fresh inquiry. First let us complete the old investigation, which we began, as you remember, under the impression that, if we could previously examine justice on the larger scale, there would be less difficulty in discerning her in the individual. That larger example appeared to be the State, and accordingly we constructed as good a one as we could, knowing well that in the good State justice would be found. Let the discovery which we made be now applied to the individual—if they agree, we shall be satisfied; or, if there be a difference in the individual, we will come back to the State and have another trial of the theory. The friction of the two when rubbed together may possibly strike the light of justice, from which we can kindle a steady flame in our souls.

That will be in regular course; let us do as you say.

I proceeded to ask: When two things, a greater and less, are called by the same name, are they like or unlike in so far as they are called the same?

Like, he replied.

Chapter X: The Individual and Society

The just man then, if we regard the idea of justice only, will be like the just State?

He will.

And a State was thought by us to be just when the three classes in the State severally did their own business; and also thought to be temperate and valiant and wise by reason of certain other affections and qualities of these same classes?

True, he said.

And so of the individual: we may assume that he has the same three principles in his own soul which are found in the State; and he may be rightly described in the same terms, because he is affected in the same manner?

Certainly, he said.

Once more then, O my friend, we have alighted upon an easy question—whether the soul has these three principles or not?

An easy question? Nay, rather, Socrates, the proverb holds that hard is the good.

Very true, I said; and I must impress upon you, Glaucon, that in my opinion our present methods of argument are not at all adequate to the accurate solution of this question; the true method is another and a longer one. Still we may arrive at a solution not below the level of the previous inquiry.

May we not be satisfied with that? he said—under the circumstances, I am quite content.

I too, I replied, shall be extremely well satisfied.

Then faint not in pursuing the speculation, he said.

Must we not perforce acknowledge, I said, that in each of us there are the same principles and habits which there are in the State; for it is from the individual that the State derives them. Take the quality of passion or spirit—it would be ridiculous to imagine that this quality, when found in States, is not derived from the individuals who are supposed to possess it, e.g., the Thracians, Scythians, and in general the northern nations; and the same may be said of the love of knowledge, which may be claimed as the special characteristic of our part of the world, or of the love of money, which may, with equal truth, be attributed to the Phoenicians and Egyptians.

Exactly so, he said.

This is a fact, and there is no difficulty in perceiving it.

None whatever.

But the question is not quite so easy when we proceed to ask whether these principles are three or one; whether, that is to say, we learn with one part of our nature, are angry with another, and with a third part desire the satisfaction of our natural appetites; or whether the whole soul comes into play in each sort of action—to determine that is the difficulty.

Yes, he said; there lies the difficulty.

Then let us now try and determine whether they are the same or different.

How?

Clearly the same thing cannot act or be acted upon in the same part or in relation to the same thing at the same time, in contrary ways; and therefore whenever this contradiction occurs in things apparently the same, we know that they are really not the same, but different.

Good.

For example, I said, can the same thing be at rest and in motion at the same time in the same part?

Impossible.

Now, I said, let us have still more precise understanding, lest we should hereafter fall out by the way. Imagine the case of a man who is standing and also moving his hands and his head, and suppose a person to say that one and the same person is in motion and at rest at the same moment—to such a mode of speech we should object, and should rather say that one part of him is in motion while another is at rest.

Very true.

And suppose the objector to refine still further, and to draw the nice distinction that not only parts of tops, but whole tops, when they spin round with their pegs fixed on the spot, are at rest and in motion at the same time (and he may say the same of anything which revolves in the same spot), his objection would not be admitted by us, because in such cases things are not at rest and in motion in the same parts of themselves; we should rather say that they have both an axis and a circumference; and that the axis stands still, for there is no deviation from the perpendicular; and that the circumference goes round. But if, while revolving, the axis inclines either to the right or left, forwards or backwards, then in no point of view can they be at rest.

That is the correct mode of describing them, he replied.

Then none of these objections will confuse us, or incline us to believe that the same thing at the same time, in the same part or in relation to the same thing, can be contrary or act or be acted upon in contrary ways.

Certainly not, according to my way of thinking.

Yet, I said, that we may not be compelled to examine all such objections, and prove at length that they are untrue, let us assume their absurdity, and go forward on the understanding that hereafter, if this assumption turn out to be untrue, all the consequences which follow from it shall be withdrawn.

Yes, he said, that will be the best way.

Well, I said, would you not allow that assent and dissent, desire and aversion, attraction and repulsion, are all of them opposites, whether they are regarded as active or passive (for that makes no difference in the fact of their opposition)?

Yes, he said, they are opposites.

Chapter X: The Individual and Society

Well, I said, and hunger and thirst, and the desires in general, and again willing and wishing—all these you would refer to the classes already mentioned. You would say—would you not—that the soul of him who desires is either seeking after the object of desire; or is drawing toward herself the thing which she wishes to possess; or again—for she may merely consent that something should be offered to her—intimates her wish to have it by a nod of assent, as if she had been asked a question?

Very true.

And what would you say of unwillingness and dislike and the absence of desire; should not these be referred to the opposite class of repulsion and rejection?

Certainly.

Admitting this to be true of desire generally, let us suppose a particular class of desires, and out of these we will select hunger and thirst, as they are termed, which are the most obvious of them?

Let us take that class, he said.

The object of one is food, and of the other drink?

Yes.

And here comes the point: is not thirst the desire which the soul has of drink, and of drink only, not of drink qualified by anything else; for example, warm or cold, or much or little, or, in a word, drink of any particular sort? But if there is heat additional to the thirst, it will bring with it the desire of cold drink; or, if cold, then that of warm drink. And again, if the thirst is qualified by abundance or by smallness, it will become a desire for much or little drink, as the case may be: but thirst pure and simple will desire drink pure and simple, which is the natural satisfaction of thirst, as food is of hunger?

Yes, he said; the simple desire is, as you say, in every case of the simple object, and the qualified desire of the qualified object.

But here a confusion may arise; and I should wish to guard against an opponent starting up and saying that no man desires drink only, but good drink, or food only, but good food; for good is the universal object of desire, and if thirst be a desire, it will necessarily be thirst after good drink (or whatever its object is); and the same is true of every other desire.

Yes, he replied, the opponent might seem to be talking sense.

Nevertheless I should still maintain that of relatives some have a quality attached to either term of the relation; others are simple and have their correlatives simple.

I do not know what you mean.

Well, you know of course that the greater is relative to the less?

Certainly.

And the much greater to the much less?

Yes.

And the sometime greater to the sometime less, and the greater that is to be to the less that is to be?

Certainly, he said.

And so of more and less, and of other correlative terms, such as the double and the half, or again, the heavier and the lighter, the swifter and the slower; and of hot and cold, and of any other relatives—is not this true of all of them?

Yes.

And does not the same principle hold in the sciences? The object of science is knowledge (assuming that to be the true definition), but the object of a particular science is a particular kind of knowledge; I mean, for example, that the science of house-building is a kind of knowledge which is defined and distinguished from other kinds and is therefore termed architecture.

Certainly.

Because it has a particular quality which no other has?

Yes.

And it has this particular quality because it has an object of a particular kind; and this is true of the other arts and sciences?

Yes.

Now, then, if I have made myself clear, you will understand my original meaning in what I said about relatives. My meaning was, that if one term of a relation is taken alone, the other is taken alone; if one term is qualified, the other is also qualified. I do not mean to say that relative terms must possess all the same qualities as their correlates; that the science of health is healthy, or that of disease necessarily diseased, or that the sciences of good and evil are therefore good and evil; but only that, when the term science is no longer used absolutely, but has a qualified object which in this case is the nature of health and disease, it becomes defined, and is hence called not merely science, but the science of medicine.

I quite understand, and I think as you do.

Would you not say that thirst is one of these essentially relative terms, having clearly a relation—

Yes, thirst is relative to drink.

And a certain kind of thirst is relative to a certain kind of drink; but thirst taken alone is neither of much nor little, nor of good nor bad, nor of any particular kind of drink, but of drink only?

Certainly.

Then the soul of the thirsty one, in so far as he is thirsty, desires only drink; for this she yearns, and for this she strives?

That is plain.

And if you suppose something which pulls a thirsty soul away from drink, that must be different from the thirsty principle which draws him like a beast to drink; for, as we were saying, the same thing cannot at the same time with the same part of itself act in contrary ways about the same.

Impossible.

Chapter X: The Individual and Society

No more than you can say that the hands of the archer push and pull the bow at the same time, but what you say is that one hand pushes and the other pulls.

Exactly so, he replied.

Now are there times when men are thirsty, and yet unwilling to drink?

Yes, he said, it constantly happens.

And in such a case what is one to say? Would you not say that there was something in the soul bidding a man to drink, and something else forbidding him, which is other and stronger than the principle which bids him?

I should say so.

And the prohibition in such cases is derived from reasoning, whereas the motives which lead and attract proceed from passions and diseases?

Clearly.

Then we may fairly assume that they are two, and that they differ from one another; the one with which a man reasons, we may call the rational principle of the soul, the other, with which he loves and hungers and thirsts and feels the flutterings of any other desire, may be termed the irrational or appetitive, the ally of sundry pleasures and satisfactions?

Yes, he said, we may fairly assume them to be different.

So much, then, for the definition of two of the principles existing in the soul. And what now of passion, or spirit? Is it a third, or akin to one of the preceding?

I should be inclined to say—akin to desire.

Well, I said, there is a story which I remember to have heard, and in which I put faith. The story is, that Leontius, the son of Aglaion, coming up one day from the Piraeus, under the north wall on the outside, observed some dead bodies lying on the ground at the place of execution. He felt a desire to see them, and also a dread and abhorrence of them; for a time he struggled and covered his eyes, but at length the desire got the better of him; and forcing them open, he ran up to the dead bodies, saying, Look, ye wretches, take your fill of the fair sight.

I have heard the story myself, he said.

The moral of the tale is that anger at times goes to war with desire, as though they were two distinct things.

Yes; that is the meaning, he said.

And are there not many other cases in which we observe that when a man's desires violently prevail over his reason, he reviles himself, and is angry at the violence within him, and that in this struggle, which is like the struggle of factions in a State, his spirit is on the side of his reason—but for the passionate or spirited element to take part with the desires when reason decides that she should not be opposed, is a sort of thing which I believe that you never observed occurring in yourself, nor, as I should imagine, in anyone else?

Certainly not.

Suppose that a man thinks he has done a wrong to another, the nobler he is the less able is he to feel indignant at any suffering, such as hunger, or cold, or any other pain which the injured person may inflict upon him—these he deems to be just, and, as I say, his spirit refuses to be excited by them.

True, he said.

But when a man thinks that he is the sufferer of the wrong, then the spirit within him boils and chafes, and is on the side of what it believes to be justice; and though it suffers hunger of cold or other pain, it is only the more determined to persevere and conquer. Such a noble spirit will not be quelled until it has achieved its object or been slain, or until it has been recalled by the reason within, like a dog by the shepherd?

The illustration is perfect, he replied; and in our State, as we were saying, the auxiliaries were to be dogs, and to hear the voice of the rulers, who are their shepherds.

Yes, I said, you understand me admirably; there is, however, a further point which I wish you to consider.

What point?

You remember that passion or spirit appeared at first sight to be a kind of desire, but now we should say quite the contrary; for in the conflict of the soul spirit is arrayed on the side of the rational principle.

Most assuredly.

But a further question arises: Is passion different from reason also, or only a kind of reason; in which latter case, instead of three principles in the soul, there will only be two, the rational and the concupiscent? or rather, as the State was composed of three classes, traders, auxiliaries, counsellors, so may there not be in the individual soul a third element which is passion or spirit, and when not corrupted by bad education is the natural auxiliary of reason?

Yes, he said, there must be a third.

Yes, I replied, if passion, which has already been shown to be different from desire, turn out also to be different from reason.

But that is easily proved—We may observe even in young children that they are full of spirit almost as soon as they are born, whereas some of them never seem to attain to the use of reason, and most of them late enough.

Excellent, I said, and you may see passion equally in brute animals, which is a further proof of the truth of what you are saying. And we may once more appeal to the words of Homer, which have been already quoted by us,

> He smote his breast, and thus rebuked his heart

for in this verse Homer has clearly supposed the power which reasons about the better and worse to be different from the unreasoning anger which is rebuked by it.

Chapter X: The Individual and Society

Very true, he said.

And so, after much tossing, we have reached land, and are fairly agreed that the same principles which exist in the State exist also in the individual, and that they are three in number.

Exactly.

Must we not then infer that the individual is wise in the same way and in virtue of the same quality which makes the State wise?

Certainly.

Also that the State is brave in the same way and by the same quality as an individual is brave, and that there is the same correspondence in regard to the other virtues?

Assuredly.

Therefore the individual will be acknowledged by us to be just in the same way in which the State has been found just?

That follows of course.

We cannot but remember that the justice of the State consisted in each of the three classes doing the work of its own class?

I do not think we have forgotten, he said.

We must now record in our memory that the individual in whom the several components of his nature do their own work will be just, and will do his own work?

Yes, he said, we must record that important fact.

First, it is proper for the rational principle, which is wise, and has the care of the whole soul, to rule, and for the spirit to be the subject and ally?

Certainly.

And, as we were saying, the blending of music and gymnastic will bring them into accord, nerving and sustaining the reason with noble words and lessons, and moderating and soothing and civilizing the wildness of passion by harmony and rhythm?

Quite true, he said.

And these two, thus nurtured and educated, and having learned truly to know their own functions, will rule over the concupiscent, which in each of us is the largest part of the soul and by nature most insatiable of gain; over this they will keep guard, lest, waxing great and strong with the fullness of bodily pleasures, as they are termed, the concupiscent soul, no longer confined to her own sphere, should attempt to enslave and rule those who are not her natural-born subjects, and overturn the whole life of man?

Very true, he said.

Both together will they not be the best defenders of the whole soul and the whole body against attacks from without; the one counseling, and the other going out to fight as the leader directs, and courageously executing his commands and counsels?

True.

719

Likewise it is by reference to spirit that an individual man is deemed courageous, because his spirit retains in pleasure and in pain the commands of reason about what he ought or ought not to fear?

Right, he replied.

And we call him wise on account of that little part which rules, and which proclaims these commands; the part in which is situated the knowledge of what is for the interest of each of the three parts and of the whole?

Assuredly.

And would you not say that he is temperate who has these same elements in friendly harmony, in whom the one ruling principle of reason, and the two subject ones of spirit and desire, are equally agreed that reason ought to rule, and do not rebel?

Certainly, he said, that is a precise account of temperance whether in the State or individual.

And, finally, I said, a man will be just in that way and by that quality which we have often mentioned.

That is very certain.

And is justice dimmer in the individual, and is her form different, or is she the same which we found her to be in the State?

There is no difference in my opinion, he said.

Because, if any doubt is still lingering in our minds, a few commonplace instances will satisfy us of the truth of what I am saying.

What sort of instances do you mean?

If the case is put to us, must we not admit that the just State, or the man of similar nature who has been trained in the principles of such a State, will be less likely than the unjust to make away with a deposit of gold or silver? Would any one deny this?

No one, he replied.

Will such a man ever be involved in sacrilege or theft, or treachery either to his friends or to his country?

Never.

Neither will he ever, for any reason, break faith where there have been oaths or agreements?

Impossible.

No one will be less likely to commit adultery, neglect his father and mother, or fail in his religious duties?

No one.

And the reason for all this is that each part of him is doing its own business, whether in ruling or being ruled?

Exactly so.

Are you satisfied then that the quality which makes such men and such states is justice, or do you hope to discover some other?

Not I, indeed.

Then our dream has been realized, and the suspicion which we expressed that, at the beginning of our work of construction, some divine power must have conducted us to a primary form of justice, has now been verified?

Yes, certainly.

And the division of labor which required the carpenter and the shoemaker and the rest of them to devote himself to the work for which he is naturally fitted, and to do nothing else, was a shadow of justice, and for that reason it was of use?

Clearly.

And in reality justice was such as we were describing, being concerned however, not with a man's external affairs, but with an inner relationship in which he himself is more truly concerned; for the just man does not permit the several elements within him to interfere with one another, or any of them to do the work of others—he sets in order his own inner life, and is his own master and his own law, and at peace with himself; and when he has bound together the three principles within him, which may be compared to the higher, lower, and middle notes of the scale, and any that are intermediate between them—when he has bound all these together, and is no longer many, but has become one entirely temperate and perfectly adjusted nature, then he proceeds to act, if he has to act, whether in a matter of property, or in the treatment of the body, or in some affair of politics or private business; always thinking and calling that which preserves and cooperates with this harmonious condition, just and good action, and the knowledge which presides over it, wisdom, and that which at any time impairs this condition, he will call unjust action, and the opinion which presides over it ignorance.

You have said the exact truth, Socrates.

Very good; and if we were to affirm that we had discovered the just man and the just State, and the nature of justice in each of them, we should not be far from the truth?

Most certainly not.

May we say so, then?

Let us say so.

And now, I said, injustice has to be considered.

Clearly.

Must not injustice be a strife which arises among the same three principles—a meddlesomeness, and interference, and rising up of a part of the soul against the whole, an assertion of unlawful authority, which is made by a rebellious subject against a true prince, of whom he is the natural vassal—what is all this confusion and delusion but injustice and intemperance and cowardice and ignorance, and, in short, every form of vice?

Exactly so.

And if the nature of justice and injustice is known, then the meaning of acting unjustly and being unjust, or again of acting justly, is now also perfectly clear?

How so? he said.

Why, I said, they are like disease and health; being in the soul just what disease and health are in the body.

How so? he said.

Why, I said, that which is healthy causes health, and that which is unhealthy causes disease.

Yes.

And just actions cause justice, and unjust actions cause injustice?

That is certain.

And the creation of health is the institution of a natural order and government of one by another in the parts of the body; and the creation of disease is the production of a state of things at variance with this natural order?

True.

And is not the creation of justice the institution of a natural order and government of one by another in the parts of the soul, and the creation of injustice the production of a state of things at variance with the natural order?

Exactly so, he said.

Then virtue is the health and beauty and well-being of the soul, and vice the disease and weakness and deformity of the same?

True.

And how are virtue and vice acquired—is it not by good and evil practices?

Assuredly.

The time has come, then, to answer the final question of the comparative advantage of justice and injustice: Which is the more profitable, to be just and act justly and honorably, whether one's character is or is not known, or to be unjust and act unjustly, if one is unpunished, that is to say unreformed?

In my judgment, Socrates, the question has now become ridiculous. We know that, when the bodily constitution is gone, life is no longer endurable, though pampered with all kinds of meats and drinks, and having all wealth and all power; and shall we be told that when the natural health of our vital principle is undermined and corrupted, life is still worth having to a man, if only he be allowed to do whatever he likes, except to take steps to acquire justice and virtue and escape from injustice and vice; assuming them both to be such as we have described?

Yes, I said, the question is, as you say, ridiculous. Still, as we are near the spot at which we may see the truth in the clearest manner with our eyes, let us not faint by the way.

Certainly not, he replied.

Come here, then, I said, and behold the various forms of vice, those of them, I mean, which are worth looking at.

I am following you, he replied: proceed.

Chapter X: The Individual and Society

I said, The argument seems to have reached a height from which, as from some tower of speculation, a man may look down and see that virtue is one, but that the forms of vice are innumerable; there being four special ones which are deserving of note.

What do you mean? he said.

I mean, I replied, that there appear to be as many forms of the soul as there are distinct forms of the State.

How many?

There are five of the State, and five of the soul, I said.

What are they?

The first, I said, is that which we have been describing, and which may be given either of two names, monarchy or aristocracy, according as rule is exercised by one man distinguished among the ruling class or by more.

True, he replied.

But I regard the two names as describing one form only; for whether the government is in the hands of one or many, if the governors have been bred and trained in the manner which we have supposed, the fundamental laws of the State will not be disturbed.

Probably not, he replied.

From "The Republic," Book IV, in *The Dialogues of Plato*, translated by Benjamin Jowett (1892).

from On Liberty (1859)

John Stuart Mill

Chapter 1 / Introductory

. . . The object of this essay is to assert one very simple principle, as entitled to govern absolutely the dealings of society with the individual in the way of compulsion and control, whether the means used be physical force in the form of legal penalties or the moral coercion of public opinion. That principle is that the sole end for which mankind are warranted, individually or collectively, in interfering with the liberty of action of any of their number is self-protection. That the only purpose for which power can be rightfully exercised over any member of a civilized community, against his will, is to prevent harm to others. His own good either physical or moral, is not a sufficient warrant. He cannot rightfully be compelled to do or forbear because it will be better for him to do so, because it will make him happier, because, in the opinions of others, to do so would be wise or even right. These are good reasons for remonstrating with him, or reasoning with him, or persuading him, or entreating him, but not for compelling him or visiting him with any evil in case he do otherwise. To justify that, the conduct from which it is desired to deter him must be calculated to produce evil to someone else. The only part of the conduct of anyone for which he is amenable to society is that which concerns others. In the part which merely concerns himself, his independence is, of right, absolute. Over himself, over his own body and mind, the individual is sovereign.

It is, perhaps, hardly necessary to say that this doctrine is meant to apply only to human beings in the maturity of their faculties. We are not speaking of children or of young persons below the age which the law may fix as that of manhood or womanhood. Those who are still in a state to require being taken care of by others must be protected against their own actions as well as against external injury. . . . But as soon as mankind

Chapter X: The Individual and Society

have attained the capacity of being guided to their own improvement by conviction or persuasion (a period long since reached in all nations with whom we need here concern ourselves), compulsion, either in the direct form or in that of pains and penalties for noncompliance, is no longer admissible as a means to their own good, and justifiable only for the security of others.

It is proper to state that I forego any advantage which could be derived to my argument from the idea of abstract right as a thing independent of utility. I regard utility as the ultimate appeal on all ethical questions; but it must be utility in the largest sense, grounded on the permanent interests of man as a progressive being. Those interests, I contend, authorize the subjection of individual spontaneity to external control only in respect to those actions of each which concern the interest of other people. If anyone does an act hurtful to others, there is a *prima facie* case for punishing him by law or, where legal penalties are not safely applicable, by general disapprobation. There are also many positive acts for the benefit of others which he may rightfully be compelled to perform, such as to give evidence in a court of justice, to bear his fair share in the common defense or in any other joint work necessary to the interest of the society of which he enjoys the protection, and to perform certain acts of individual beneficence, such as saving a fellow creature's life or interposing to protect the defenseless against ill usage—things which whenever it is obviously a man's duty to do he may rightfully be made responsible to society for not doing. A person may cause evil to others not only by his actions but by his inaction, and in either case he is justly accountable to them for the injury. The latter case, it is true, requires a much more cautious exercise of compulsion than the former. To make anyone answerable for doing evil to others is the rule; to make him answerable for not preventing evil is, comparatively speaking, the exception. Yet there are many cases clear enough and grave enough to justify that exception. In all things which regard the external relations of the individual, he is *de jure* amenable to those whose interests are concerned, and, if need be, to society as their protector. There are often good reasons for not holding him to the responsibility; but these reasons must arise from the special expediences of the case: either because it is a kind of case in which he is on the whole likely to act better when left to his own discretion than when controlled in any way in which society have it in their power to control him; or because the attempt to exercise control would produce other evils, greater than those which it would prevent. When such reasons as these preclude the enforcement of responsibility, the conscience of the agent himself should step into the vacant judgment seat and protect those interests of others which have no external protection; judging himself all the more rigidly, because the case does not admit of his being made accountable to the judgment of his fellow creatures.

But there is a sphere of action in which society, as distinguished from the individual, has, if any, only an indirect interest: comprehending all that portion of a person's life and conduct which affects only himself or, if it also affects others, only with their free, voluntary, and undeceived consent and participation. When I say only himself, I mean directly and in the first instance; for whatever affects himself may affect others through himself: and the objection which may be grounded on this contingency will receive consideration in the sequel. This, then, is the appropriate region of human liberty. It comprises, first, the inward domain of consciousness, demanding liberty of conscience in the most comprehensive sense, liberty of thought and feeling, absolute freedom of opinion and sentiment on all subjects, practical or speculative, scientific, moral, or theological. The liberty of expressing and publishing opinions may seem to fall under a different principle, since it belongs to that part of the conduct of an individual which concerns other people, but, being almost of as much importance as the liberty of thought itself and resting in great part on the same reasons, is practically inseparable from it. Secondly, the principle requires liberty of tastes and pursuits, of framing the plan of our life to suit our own character, of doing as we like, subject to such consequences as may follow, without impediment from our fellow creatures, so long as what we do does not harm them, even though they should think our conduct foolish, perverse, or wrong. Thirdly, from this liberty of each individual follows the liberty, within the same limits, of combination among individuals; freedom to unite for any purpose not involving harm to others; the persons combining being supposed to be of full age and not forced or deceived.

No society in which these liberties are not, on the whole, respected is free, whatever may be its form of government; and none is completely free in which they do not exist absolute and unqualified. The only freedom which deserves the name is that of pursuing our own good in our own way, so long as we do not attempt to deprive others of theirs or impede their efforts to obtain it. Each is the proper guardian of his own health, whether bodily *or* mental and spiritual. Mankind are greater gainers by suffering each other to live as seems good to themselves than by compelling each to live as seems good to the rest. . . .

Chapter II / Of the Liberty of Thought and Discussion

. . . Let us suppose . . . that the government is entirely at one with the people, and never thinks of exerting any power of coercion unless in agreement with what it conceives to be their voice. But I deny the right of the people to exercise such coercion, either by themselves or by their government. The power itself is illegitimate. The best government has no more title to it than the worst. It is as noxious, or more noxious, when exerted in accordance with public opinion than when in opposition to it. If

Chapter X: The Individual and Society

all mankind minus one were of one opinion, mankind would be no more justified in silencing that one person than he, if he had the power, would be justified in silencing mankind. Were an opinion a personal possession of no value except to the owner, if to be obstructed in the enjoyment of it were simply a private injury, it would make some difference whether the injury was inflicted only on a few persons or on many. But the peculiar evil of silencing the expression of an opinion is that it is robbing the human race, posterity as well as the existing generation—those who dissent from the opinion, still more than those who hold it. If the opinion is right, they are deprived of the opportunity of exchanging error for truth; if wrong, they lose, what is almost as great a benefit, the clearer perception and livelier impression of truth produced by its collision with error.

It is necessary to consider separately these two hypotheses, each of which has a distinct branch of the argument corresponding to it. We can never be sure that the opinion we are endeavoring to stifle is a false opinion; and if we were sure, stifling it would be an evil still.

First, the opinion which it is attempted to suppress by authority may possibly be true. Those who desire to suppress it, of course, deny its truth; but they are not infallible. They have no authority to decide the question for all mankind and exclude every other person from the means of judging. To refuse a hearing to an opinion because they are sure that it is false is to assume that *their* certainty is the same thing as *absolute* certainty. All silencing of discussion is an assumption of infallibility. . . .

The objection likely to be made to this argument would probably take some such form as the following. There is no greater assumption of infallibility in forbidding the propagation of error than in any other thing which is done by public authority on its own judgment and responsibility. Judgment is given to men that they may use it. Because it may be used erroneously, are men to be told that they ought not to use it at all? To prohibit what they think pernicious is not claiming exemption from error, but fulfilling the duty incumbent on them, although fallible, of acting on their conscientious conviction. If we were never to act on our opinions, because those opinions may be wrong, we should leave all our interests uncared for, and all our duties unperformed. An objection which applies to all conduct can be no valid objection to any conduct in particular. It is the duty of governments, and of individuals, to form the truest opinions they can; to form them carefully, and never impose them upon others unless they are quite sure of being right. But when they are sure (such reasoners may say), it is not conscientiousness but cowardice to shrink from acting on their opinions and allow doctrines which they honestly think dangerous to the welfare of mankind, either in this life or in another, to be scattered abroad without restraint, because other people, in less enlightened times, have persecuted opinions now believed to be true. Let us take care, it may be said, not to make the same mistake; but governments and nations have made mistakes in other things which are not denied to be fit subjects for the exercise of authority: they have laid on bad taxes, made unjust wars. Ought we therefore to lay on no taxes and, under whatever provocation, make no wars? Men and governments must act to the best of their ability. There is no such thing as absolute certainty, but there is assurance sufficient for the purposes of human life. We may, and must, assume our opinion to be true for the guidance of our own conduct; and it is assuming no more when we forbid bad men to pervert society by the propagation of opinions which we regard as false and pernicious.

I answer, that it is assuming very much more. There is the greatest difference between presuming an opinion to be true because, with every opportunity for contesting it, it has not been refuted, and assuming its truth for the purpose of not permitting its refutation. Complete liberty of contradicting and disproving our opinion is the very condition which justifies us in assuming its truth for purposes of action; and on no other terms can a being with human faculties have any rational assurance of being right.

When we consider either the history of opinion or the ordinary conduct of human life, to what is it to be ascribed that the one and the other are no worse than they are? Not certainly to the inherent force of the human understanding, for on any matter not self-evident there are ninety-nine persons totally incapable of judging of it for one who is capable; and the capacity of the hundredth person is only comparative, for the majority of the eminent men of every past generation held many opinions now know to be erroneous, and did or approved numerous things which no one will now justify. Why is it, then, that there is on the whole a preponderance among mankind of rational opinions and rational conduct? If there really is this preponderance—which there must be unless human affairs are, and have always been, in an almost desperate state—it is owing to a quality of the human mind, the source of everything respectable in man either as an intellectual or as a moral being, namely, that his errors are corrigible. He is capable of rectifying his mistakes by discussion and experience. Not by experience alone. There must be discussion to show how experience is to be interpreted. Wrong opinions and practices gradually yield to fact and argument; but facts and arguments, to produce any effect on the mind, must be brought before it. Very few facts are able to tell their own story, without comments to bring out their meaning. The whole strength and value, then, of human judgment depending on the one property, that it can be set right when it is wrong, reliance can be placed on it only when the means of setting it right are kept constantly at hand. In the case of any person whose judgment is really deserving of confidence, how has it become so? Because he has kept his mind open to criticism of his opinions and conduct. Because it has been his practice to listen to all that could be said against him; to profit by as much of it as was just, and to expound to himself, and upon occasion to others, the fallacy of what was fallacious. Because he has felt that the only way in which a human being can make some approach to knowing the whole of a subject is by hearing

Chapter X: The Individual and Society

what can be said about it by persons of every variety of opinion, and studying all modes in which it can be looked at by every character of mind. No wise man ever acquired his wisdom in any mode but this; nor is it in the nature of human intellect to become wise in any other manner. The steady habit of correcting and completing his own opinion by collating it with those of others, so far from causing doubt and hesitation in carrying it into practice, is the only stable foundation for a just reliance on it; for being cognizant of all that can, at least obviously be said against him and having taken up his position against all gainsayers—knowing that he has sought for objections and difficulties instead of avoiding them, and has shut out no light which can be thrown upon the subject from any quarter—he has a right to think his judgment better than that of any person, or any multitude, who have not gone through a similar process. . . .

Let us now pass to the second division of the argument, and dismissing the supposition that any of the received opinions may be false, let us assume them to be true and examine into the worth of the manner in which they are likely to be held when their truth is not freely and openly canvassed. However unwillingly a person who has a strong opinion may admit the possibility that his opinion may be false, he ought to be moved by the consideration that, however true it may be, if it is not fully, frequently, and fearlessly discussed, it will be held as a dead dogma, not a living truth.

There is a class of persons (happily not quite so numerous as formerly) who think it enough if a person assents undoubtingly to what they think true, though he has no knowledge whatever of the grounds of the opinion and could not make a tenable defense of it against the most superficial objections. Such persons, if they can once get their creed taught from authority, naturally think that no good, and some harm, comes of its being allowed to be questioned. Where their influence prevails, they make it nearly impossible for the received opinion to be rejected wisely and considerately, though it may still be rejected rashly and ignorantly; for to shut out discussion entirely is seldom possible, and when it once gets in, beliefs not grounded on conviction are apt to give way before the slightest semblance of an argument. Waiving, however, this possibility—assuming that the true opinion abides in the mind, but abides as a prejudice, a belief independent of, and proof against, argument—this is not the way in which truth ought to be held by a rational being. This is not knowing the truth. Truth, thus held, is but one superstition the more, accidentally clinging to the words which enunciate a truth. . . .

If, however, the mischievous operation of the absence of free discussion, when the received opinions are true, were confined to leaving men ignorant of the grounds of those opinions, it might be thought that this, if an intellectual, is no moral evil and does not affect the worth of the opinions, regarded in their influence on the character. The fact, however, is that not only the grounds of the opinion are forgotten in the absence of discussion, but too often the meaning of the opinion itself. The words which convey it cease to suggest ideas, or suggest only a small portion of those they were originally employed to communicate. Instead of a vivid conception and a living belief, there remain only a few phrases retained by rote; or, if any part, the shell and husk only of the meaning is retained, the finer essence being lost. The great chapter in human history which this fact occupies and fills cannot be too earnestly studied and meditated on.

It is illustrated in the experience of almost all ethical doctrines and religious creeds:; They are all full of meaning and vitality to those who originate them, and to the direct disciples of the originators. Their meaning continues to be felt in undiminished strength, and is perhaps brought out into even fuller consciousness, so long as the struggle lasts to give the doctrine or creed an ascendancy over other creeds. At last it either prevails and becomes the general opinion, or its progress stops; it keeps possession of the ground it has gained, but ceases to spread further. When either of these results has become apparent, controversy on the subject flags, and gradually dies away. The doctrine has taken its place, if not as a received opinion, as one of the admitted sects or divisions of opinion; those who hold it have generally inherited, not adopted it; and conversion from one of these doctrines to another, being now an exceptional fact, occupies little place in the thought of their professors. Instead of being, as at first, constantly on the alert either to defend themselves against the world or to bring the world over to them, they have subsided into acquiescence and neither listen, when they can help it, to arguments against their creed, nor trouble dissentients (if there be such) with arguments in its favor. From this time may usually be dated the decline in the living power of the doctrine. . . .

. . . There are many reasons, doubtless, why doctrines which are the badge of a sect retain more of their vitality than those common to all recognized sects, and why more pains are taken by teachers to keep their meaning alive; but one reason certainly is that the peculiar doctrines are more questioned and have to be oftener defended against open gainsayers. Both teachers and learners go to sleep at their post as soon as there is no enemy in the field. . . .

It still remains to speak of one of the principal causes which make diversity of opinion advantageous, and will continue to do so until mankind shall have entered a stage of intellectual advancement which at present seems at an incalculable distance. We have hitherto considered only two possibilities: that the received opinion may be false, and some other opinion, consequently, true; or that, the received opinion being true, a conflict with the opposite error is essential to a clear apprehension and deep feeling of its truth. But there is a commoner case than either of these: when the conflicting doctrines, instead of being one true and the other false, share the truth between them, and the nonconforming opinion is needed to supply the remainder of the truth of which the received doctrine embodies only a part. Popular opinions, on subjects not palpable to sense, are often true, but seldom or never the whole truth. They are a part of the truth, sometimes a greater, sometimes a smaller part, but exaggerated, distorted, and disjointed from the truths by which they ought to be accompanied and limited. Heretical opinions, on the other hand, are generally some of these suppressed and neglected truths, bursting the bonds which kept them down, and either seeking reconciliation with the truth contained in the common opinion, or fronting it as enemies, and setting themselves up, with similar exclusiveness, as the whole truth. The latter case is hitherto the most frequent, as, in the human mind, one-sidedness has always been the rule, and many-sidedness the exception. Hence, even in revolutions of opinion, one part of the truth usually sets while another rises. Even progress, which ought to superadd, for the most part only substitutes one partial and incomplete truth for another; improvement consisting chiefly in this, that the new fragment of truth is more wanted, more adapted to the needs of the time than that which it displaces. Such being the partial character of prevailing opinions, even when resting on a true foundation, every opinion which embodies somewhat of the portion of truth which the common opinion omits, ought to be considered precious, with whatever amount of error and confusion that truth may be blended. No sober judge of human affairs will feel bound to be indignant because those who force on our notice truths which we should otherwise have overlooked, overlook some of those which we see. Rather, he will think that so long as popular truth is one-sided, it is more desirable than otherwise that unpopular truth should have one-sided assertors, too, such being usually the most energetic and the most likely to compel reluctant attention to the fragment of wisdom which they proclaim as if it were the whole. . . .

. . . only through diversity of opinion is there, in the existing state of human intellect, a chance of fair play to all sides of the truth. When there are persons to be found who form an exception to the apparent unanimity of the world on any subject, even if the world is in the right, it is always probable that dissentients have something worth hearing to say for themselves, and that truth would lose something by their silence. . . .

We have now recognized the necessity to the mental well-being of mankind (on which all their other well-being depends) of freedom of opinion, and freedom of the expression of opinion, on four distinct grounds, which we will now briefly recapitulate:

First, if any opinion is compelled to silence, that opinion may, for aught we can certainly know, be true. To deny this is to assume our own infallibility.

Secondly, though the silenced opinion be an error, it may, and very commonly does, contain a portion of truth; and since the general or prevailing opinion on any subject is rarely or never the whole truth, it is only by the collision of adverse opinions that the remainder of the truth has any chance of being supplied.

Thirdly, even if the received opinion be not only true, but the whole truth; unless it is suffered to be, and actually is, vigorously and earnestly contested, it will, by most of those who receive it, be held in the manner of a prejudice, with little comprehension or feeling of its rational grounds. And not only this, but, fourthly, the meaning of the doctrine itself will be in danger of being lost or enfeebled, and deprived of its vital effect on the character and conduct: the dogma becoming a mere formal profession, inefficacious for good, but cumbering the ground and preventing the growth of any real and heartfelt conviction from reason or personal experience....

Chapter III / Of Individuality, as One of The Elements of Well-Being

... No one pretends that actions should be as free as opinions. On the contrary, even opinions lose their immunity when the circumstances in which they are expressed are such as to constitute their expression a positive instigation to some mischievous act. An opinion that corn dealers are starvers of the poor, or that private property is robbery, ought to be unmolested when simply circulated through the press, but may justly incur punishment when delivered orally to an excited mob assembled before the house of a corn dealer, or when handed about among the same mob in the form of a placard. Acts of whatever kind, which without justifiable cause do harm to others may be, and in the more important cases absolutely require to be, controlled by the unfavorable sentiments, and, when needful, by the active interference of mankind. The liberty of the individual must be thus far limited; he must not make himself a nuisance to other people. But if he refrains from molesting others in what concerns them, and merely acts according to his own inclination and judgment in things which concern himself, the same reasons which show that opinion should be free prove also that he should be allowed, without molestation, to carry his opinions into practice at his own cost....

Chapter IV / Of the Limits to the Authority of Society Over the Individual

What, then, is the rightful limit to the sovereignty of the individual over himself? Where does the authority of society begin? How much of human life should be assigned to individuality, and how much to society?

Each will receive its proper share if each has that which more particularly concerns it. To individuality should belong the part of life in which it is chiefly the individual that is interested; to society, the part which chiefly interests society.

Though society is not founded on a contract, and though no good purpose is answered by inventing a contract in order to deduce social obligations from it, everyone who receives the protection of society owes a return for the benefit, and the fact of living in society renders it indispensable that each should be bound to observe a certain line of conduct toward the rest. This conduct consists, first, in not injuring the interests of one another, or rather certain interests which, either by express legal provision or by tacit understanding, ought to be considered as rights; and secondly, in each person's bearing his share (to be fixed on some equitable principle) of the labors and sacrifices incurred for defending the society or its members from injury and molestation. These conditions society is justified in enforcing at all costs to those who endeavor to withhold fulfillment. Nor is this all that society may do. The acts of an individual may be hurtful to others or wanting in due consideration for their welfare, without going to the length of violating any of their constituted rights. The offender may then be justly punished by opinion, though not by law. As soon as any part of a person's conduct affects prejudicially the interests of others, society has jurisdiction over it, and the question whether the general welfare will or will not be promoted by interfering with it becomes open to discussion. But there is no room for entertaining any such question when a person's conduct affects the interests of no persons besides himself, or needs not affect them unless they like (all the persons concerned being of full age and the ordinary amount of understanding). In all such cases, there should be perfect freedom, legal and social, to do the action and stand the consequences. . . .

The distinction here pointed out between the part of a person's life which concerns only himself and that which concerns others, many persons will refuse to admit. How (it may be asked) can any part of the conduct of a member of society be a matter of indifference to the other members? No person is an entirely isolated being; it is impossible for a person to do anything seriously or permanently hurtful to himself without mischief reaching at least to his near connections, and often far beyond them. If he injures his property, he does harm to those who directly or indirectly derived support from it, and usually diminishes, by a greater or less amount, the general resources of the community. If he deteriorates his bodily or mental faculties, he not only brings evil upon all who depended upon him for any portion of their happiness, but disqualifies himself for rendering the services which he owes to his fellow creatures generally, perhaps becomes a burden on their affection or benevolence; and if such conduct were very frequent hardly any offense that is committed would detract more from the general sum of good. Finally, if by his vices or follies a person does no direct harm to others, he is nevertheless (it may be said) injurious by his example, and ought to be compelled to control himself for the sake of those whom the sight or knowledge of his conduct might corrupt or mislead.

And even (it will be added) if the consequences of misconduct could be confined to the vicious or thoughtless individual, ought society to abandon to their own guidance those who are manifestly unfit for it? If protection against themselves is confessedly due to children and persons under age, is not society equally bound to afford it to persons of mature years who are equally incapable of self-government? If gambling, or drunkenness, or incontinence, or idleness, or uncleanliness are as injurious to happiness, and as great a hindrance to improvement, as many or most of the acts prohibited by law, why (it may be asked) should not law, so far as is consistent with practicability and social convenience, endeavor to repress these also? And as a supplement to the unavoidable imperfections of law, ought not opinion at least to organize a powerful police against these vices and visit rigidly with social penalties those who are known to practice them? There is no question here (it may be said) about restricting individuality, or impeding the trial of new and original experiments in living. The only things it is sought to prevent are things which have been tried and condemned from the beginning of the world until now—things which experience has shown not to be useful or suitable to any person's individuality. There must be some length of time and amount of experience after which a moral or prudential truth may be regarded as established; and it is merely desired to prevent generation after generation from falling over the same precipice which has been fatal to their predecessors.

I fully admit that the mischief which a person does to himself may seriously affect, both through their sympathies and their interests, those nearly connected with him and, in a minor degree, society at large. When, by conduct of this sort, a person is led to violate a distinct and assignable obligation to any other person or persons, the case is taken out of the self-regarding class and becomes amenable to moral disapprobation in the proper sense of the term. If, for example, a man, through intemperance or extravagance, becomes unable to pay his debts, or, having undertaken the moral responsibility of a family, becomes from the same cause incapable of supporting or educating them, he is deservedly reprobated and might be justly punished; but it is for the breach of duty to his family or creditors, not for the extravagance. If the resources which ought to have been devoted to them had been diverted from them for the most prudent investment, the moral culpability would have been the same. George Barnwell murdered his uncle to get money for his mistress, but if he had done it to set himself up in business, he would equally have been hanged. Again, in the frequent case of a man who causes grief to his family by addiction to bad habits, he deserves reproach for his unkindness or ingratitude; but so he may for cultivating habits not in themselves vicious, if they are painful to those with whom he passes his life, or who from personal ties are dependent on him for their comfort. Whoever fails in the consideration generally due to the interests and feelings of others, not being compelled by some more imperative duty, or justified by allowable self-preference, is a subject of moral disapprobation for that failure, but not for the cause of it, nor for the errors, merely personal to himself, which may have remotely led to it. In like manner, when a person disables himself, by conduct purely self-regarding, from the performance of some definite duty incumbent on him to the public, he is guilty of a social offense. No person ought to be punished simply for being drunk; but a soldier or policeman should be punished for being drunk on duty. Whenever, in short, there is a definite damage, or a definite risk of damage, either to an individual or to the public, the case is taken out of the province of liberty and placed in that of morality or law.

But with regard to the merely contingent or, as it may be called, constructive injury which a person causes to society by conduct which neither violates any specific duty to the public, nor occasions perceptible hurt to any assignable individual except himself, the inconvenience is one which society can afford to bear, for the sake of the greater good of human freedom. . . .

But the strongest of all the arguments against the interference of the public with purely personal conduct is that, when it does interfere, the odds are that it interferes wrongly and in the wrong place. On questions of social morality, of duty to others, the opinion of the public, that is, of an overruling majority, though often wrong, is likely to be still oftener right, because on such questions they are only required to judge of their own interests, of the manner in which some mode of conduct, if allowed to be practiced, would affect themselves. But the opinion of a similar majority, imposed as a law on the minority, on questions of self-regarding conduct is quite as likely to be wrong as right, for in these cases public opinion means, at the best, some people's opinion of what is good or bad for other people, while very often it does not even mean that—the public, with the most perfect indifference, passing over the pleasure or convenience of those whose conduct they censure and considering only their own preference. There are many who consider as an injury to themselves any conduct which they have a distaste for, and resent it as an outrage to their feelings; as a religious bigot, when charged with disregarding the religious feelings of others, has been known to retort that they disregard his feelings by persisting in their abominable worship or creed. But there is no parity between the feeling of a person for his own opinion and the feeling of another who is offended at his holding it, no more than between the desire of a thief to take a purse and the desire of the right owner to keep it. And a person's taste is as much his own peculiar concern as his opinion or his purse. It is easy for anyone to imagine an ideal public which leaves the freedom and choice of individuals in all uncertain matters undisturbed and only requires them to abstain from modes of conduct which universal experience has condemned. But where has there been seen a public which set any such limit to its censorship? Or when does the public trouble itself about universal experience? In its interferences with personal conduct it is seldom thinking of anything but the enormity of acting or feeling differently from itself; and this standard of judgment, thinly disguised, is held up to mankind as the dictate of religion and philosophy by nine-tenths of all moralists and speculative writers. These teach that things are right because they are right; because we feel them to be so. They tell us to search in our own minds and hearts for laws of conduct binding on ourselves and on all others. What can the poor public do but apply these instructions and make their own personal feelings of good and evil, if they are tolerably unanimous in them, obligatory on all the world? . . .

The Enforcement of Morals

Lord Patrick Devlin

... In jurisprudence, as I have said, everything is thrown open to discussion and, in the belief that they cover the whole field, I have framed three interrogatories addressed to myself to answer:

1. Has society the right to pass judgement at all on matters of morals? Ought there, in other words, to be a public morality, or are morals always a matter for private judgement?
2. If society has the right to pass judgement, has it also the right to use the weapon of the law to enforce it?
3. If so, ought it to use that weapon in all cases or only in some; and if only in some, on what principles should it distinguish?

I shall begin with the first interrogatory and consider what is meant by the right of society to pass a moral judgement, that is, a judgement about what is good and what is evil. . . . What makes a society of any sort is community of ideas, not only political ideas but also ideas about the way its members should behave and govern their lives; these latter ideas are its morals. Every society has a moral structure as well as a political one: or rather, since that might suggest two independent systems, I should say that the structure of every society is made up both of politics and morals. Take, for example, the institution of marriage. Whether a man should be allowed to take more than one wife is something about which every society has to make up its mind one way or the other. In England we believe in the Christian idea of marriage and therefore adopt monogamy as a moral principle. Consequently the Christian institution of marriage has become the basis of family life and so part of the structure of our society. It is there not because it is Christian. It has got there because it is Christian, but it remains there because it is built into the house in which we live and could not be removed without bringing it down. The great majority of those who live in this country accept it because it is the Christian idea of marriage and for them the only true one. But a non-Christian is bound by it, not because it is part of Christianity but because, rightly or wrongly, it has been adopted by the society in which he lives. It would be useless for him to stage a debate designed to prove that polygamy was theologically more correct and socially preferable; if he wants to live in the house, he must accept it as built in the way in which it is.

We see this more clearly if we think of ideas or institutions that are purely political. Society cannot tolerate rebellion; it will not allow argument about the rightness of the cause. Historians a century later may say that the rebels were right and the Government was wrong and a percipient and conscientious subject of the State may think so at the time. But it is not a matter which can be left to individual judgement.

The institution of marriage is a good example for my purpose because it bridges the division, if there is one, between politics and morals. Marriage is part of the structure of our society and it is also the basis of a moral code which condemns fornication and adultery. The institution of marriage would be gravely threatened if individual judgements were permitted about the morality of adultery; on these points there must be a public morality. But public morality is not to be confined to those moral principles which support institutions such as marriage. People do not think of monogamy as something which has to be supported because our society has chosen to organize itself upon it; they think of it as something that is good in itself and offering a good way of life and that it is for that reason that our society has adopted it. I return to the statement that I have already made, that society means a community of ideas; without shared ideas on politics, morals, and ethics no society can exist. Each one of us has ideas about what is good and what is evil; they cannot be kept private from the society in which we live. If men and women try to create a society in which there is no fundamental agreement abut good and evil they will fail; if, having based it on common agreement, the agreement goes, the society will disintegrate. For society is not something that is kept together physically; it is held by the invisible bonds of common thought. If the bonds were too far relaxed the members would drift apart. A common morality is part of the bondage. The bondage is part of the price of society; and mankind, which needs society, must pay its price. . . .

You may think that I have taken far too long in contending that there is such a thing as public morality, a proposition which most people would readily accept, and may have left myself too little time to discuss the next question which to many minds may cause greater difficulty: to what extent should society use the law to enforce its moral judgements? But I believe that the answer to the first question determines the way in which the second should be approached and may indeed very nearly dictate the answer to the second question. If society has no right to make judgements on morals, the law must find some special justification for entering the field of morality: if homosexuality and prostitution are not in themselves wrong, then the onus is very clearly on the lawgiver who wants to frame a law against certain aspects of them to justify the exceptional treatment. But if society has the right to make a judgement and has it on the basis that a recognized morality is as necessary to society as, say, a recognized government, then society may use the law to preserve morality in the same way as it uses it to safeguard anything else that is essential to its existence. If therefore the first proposition is securely established with all its implications, society has a prima facie right to legislate against immorality as such. . . .

    I think, . . . that it is not possible to set theoretical limits to the power of the State to legislate against immorality. It is not possible to settle in advance exceptions to the general rule or to define inflexibly areas of morality into which the law is in no circumstances to be allowed to enter. Society is entitled by means of its law to protect itself from dangers, whether from within or without. Here again I think that the political parallel is legitimate. The law of treason is directed against aiding the king's enemies and against sedition from within. The justification of this is that established government is necessary for the existence of society and therefore its safety against violent overthrow must be secured. But an established morality is as necessary as good government to the welfare of society. Societies disintegrate from within more frequently than they are broken up by external pressures. There is disintegration when no common morality is observed and history shows that the loosening of moral bonds is often the first stage of disintegration, so that society is justified in taking the same steps to preserve its moral code as it does to preserve its government and other essential institutions. The suppression of vice is as much the law's business as the suppression of subversive activities; it is no more possible to define a sphere of private morality than it is to define one of private subversive activity. It is wrong to talk of private morality or of the law not being concerned with immorality as such or to try to set rigid bounds to the part which the law may play in the suppression of vice. There are no theoretical limits to the power of the State to legislate against treason and sedition, and likewise I think there can be no theoretical limits to legislation against immorality. You may argue that if a man's sins affect only himself it cannot be the concern of society. If he chooses to get drunk every night in the privacy of his own home, is any one except himself the worse for it? But suppose a quarter or a half of the population got drunk every night, what sort of society would it be? You cannot set a theoretical limit to the number of people who can get drunk before society is entitled to legislate against drunkenness. The same may be said of gambling. . . .

    In what circumstances the State should exercise its power is the third of the interrogatories I have framed. But before I get to it I must raise a point which might have been brought up in any one of the three. How are the moral judgements of society to be ascertained? By leaving it until now, I can ask it in the more limited form that is now sufficient for my purpose. How is the law-maker to ascertain the moral judgements of society. It is surely not enough that they should be reached by the opinion of the majority; it would be too much to require the individual assent of every citizen. English law has evolved and regularly uses a standard which does not depend on the counting of heads. It is that of the reasonable man. He is not to be confused with the rational man. He is not expected to reason about anything and his judgement may be largely a matter of feeling. It is the viewpoint of the man in the street—or to use an archaism familiar to all lawyers—the man in the Clapham omnibus. He might also be called the right-minded man. For my purpose I should like to call him the man in the jury box, for the moral judgement of society must be something about which any twelve men or women drawn at random might after discussion be expected to be unanimous. This was the standard the judges applied in the days before Parliament was as active as it is now and when they laid down rules of public policy. They did not think of themselves as making law but simply as stating principles which every right-minded person would accept as valid. It is what Pollock called 'practical morality,' which is based not on theological or philosophical foundations but 'in the mass of continuous experience half-consciously or unconsciously accumulated and embodied in the morality of common sense.' He called it also 'a certain way of thinking on questions of morality which we expect to find in a reasonable civilized man or a reasonable Englishman, taken at random.'[1]

Immorality then, for the purpose of the law, is what every right-minded person is presumed to consider to be immoral. Any immorality is capable of affecting society injuriously and in effect to a greater or lesser extent it usually does; this is what gives the law its *locus standi*. It cannot be shut out. But—and this brings me to the third question—the individual has a *locus standi* too; he cannot be expected to surrender to the judgement of society the whole conduct of his life. It is the old and familiar question of striking a balance between the rights and interests of society and those of the individual. This is something which the law is constantly doing in matters large and small. To take a very down-to-earth example, let me consider the right of the individual whose house adjoins the highway to have access to it; that means in these days the right to have vehicles stationary in the highway, sometimes for a considerable time if there is a lot of loading or unloading. There are many cases in which the courts have had to balance the private right of access against the public right to use the highway without obstruction. It cannot be done by carving up the highway into public and private areas. It is done by recognizing that each have rights over the whole, that if each were to exercise their rights to the full, they would come into conflict; and therefore that the rights of each must be curtailed so as to ensure as far as possible that the essential needs of each are safeguarded.

I do not think that one can talk sensibly of a public and private morality any more than one can of a public or private highway. Morality is a sphere in which there is a public interest and a private interest, often in conflict, and the problem is to reconcile the two. This does not mean that it is impossible to put forward any general statements about how in our society the balance ought to be struck. Such statements cannot of their nature be rigid or precise; they would not be designed to circumscribe the operation of the law-making power but to guide those who have to apply it. While every decision which a court of law makes when it balances the public against the private interest is an *ad hoc* decision, the cases contain statements of principle to which the court should have regard when it reaches it decision. In the same way it is possible to make general statements of principle which it may be thought the legislature should bear in mind when it is considering the enactment of laws enforcing morals.

I believe that most people would agree upon the chief of these elastic principles. There must be toleration of the maximum individual freedom that is consistent with the integrity of society. . . . The principle appears to me to be peculiarly appropriate to all questions of morals. Nothing should be punished by the law that does not lie beyond the limits of tolerance. It is not nearly enough to say that a majority dislike a practice; there must be a real feeling of reprobation. . . . We should ask ourselves in the first instance whether, looking at it calmly and dispassionately, we regard it as a vice so abominable that its mere presence is an offense. If that is the genuine feeling of the society in which we live, I do not see how society can be denied the right to eradicate it. Our feeling may not be so intense as that. We may feel about it that, if confined, it is tolerable, but that if spread it might be gravely injurious; it is in this way that most societies look upon fornication, seeing it as a natural weakness which must be kept within bounds but which cannot be rooted out. It becomes then a question of balance, the danger to society in one scale and the extent of the restriction in the other. . . .

The limits of tolerance shift. This is supplementary to what I have been saying but of sufficient importance in itself to deserve statement as a separate principle which law-makers have to bear in mind. . . . It may be that over-all tolerance is always increasing. The pressure of the human mind, always seeking greater freedom of thought, is outwards against the bonds of society forcing their gradual relaxation. It may be that history is a tale of contraction and expansion and that all developed societies are on their way to dissolution. I must not speak of things I do not know; and anyway as a practical matter no society is willing to make provision for its own decay. I return therefore to the simple and observable fact that in matters of morals the limits of tolerance shift. Laws, especially those which are based on morals, are less easily moved. It follows as another good working principle that in any new matter of morals the law should be slow to act. By the next generation the swell of indignation may have abated and the law be left without the strong backing which it needs. But it is then difficult to alter the law without giving the impression that moral judgement is being weakened. . . .

A third elastic principle must be advanced more tentatively. It is that as far as possible privacy should be respected. This is not an idea that has ever been made explicit in the criminal law. Acts or words done or said in public or in private are all brought within its scope without distinction in principle. But there goes with this a strong reluctance on the part of judges and legislators to sanction invasions of privacy in the detection of crime. The police have no more right to trespass than the ordinary citizen has; there is no general right of search; to this extent an Englishman's home is still his castle. The Government is extremely careful in the exercise even of those powers which it claims to be undisputed. Telephone tapping and interference with the mails afford a good illustration of this. . . .

This indicates a general sentiment that the right to privacy is something to be put in the balance against the enforcement of the law. Ought the same sort of consideration to play any part in the formation of the law? Clearly only in a very limited number of cases. When the help of the law is invoked by an injured citizen, privacy must be irrelevant; the individual cannot ask that his right to privacy should be measured against injury criminally done to another. But when all who are involved in the deed are consenting parties and the injury is done to morals, the public interest in the moral order can be balanced against the claims of privacy. . . .

Endnote

1. *Essays in Jurisprudence and Ethics* (1882), Macmillan, pp. 278 and 353.

© Oxford University Press 1965. From *The Enforcement of Morals* by Patrick Devlin. Reprinted by permission of Oxford University Press.

Taking Rights Seriously

Ronald Dworkin

The Rights of Citizens

The language of rights now dominates political debate in the United States. Does the Government respect the moral and political rights of its citizens? Or does the Government's foreign policy, or its race policy, fly in the face of these rights? Do the minorities whose rights have been violated have the right to violate the law in return? Or does the silent majority itself have rights, including the right that those who break the law be punished? It is not surprising that these questions are now prominent. The concept of rights, and particularly the concept of rights against the Government, has its most natural use when a political society is divided, and appeals to cooperation or a common goal are pointless.

The debate does not include the issue of whether citizens have *some* moral rights against their Government. It seems accepted on all sides that they do. Conventional lawyers and politicians take it as a point of pride that our legal system recognizes, for example, individual rights of free speech, equality, and due process. They base their claim that our law deserves respect, at least in part, on that fact, for they would not claim that totalitarian systems deserve the same loyalty.

Some philosophers, of course, reject the idea that citizens have rights apart from what the law happens to give them. Bentham thought that the idea of moral rights was "nonsense on stilts." But that view has never been part of our orthodox political theory, and politicians of both parties appeal to the rights of the people to justify a great part of what they want to do. I shall not be concerned, in this essay, to defend the thesis that citizens have moral rights against their governments; I want instead to explore the implications of that thesis for those, including the present United States Government, who profess to accept it.

It is much in dispute, of course, what *particular* rights citizens have. Does the acknowledged right to free speech, for example, include the right to participate in nuisance demonstrations? In practice the Government will have the last word on what an individual's rights are, because its police will do what its officials and courts say. But that does not mean that the Government's view is necessarily the correct view; anyone who thinks it does must believe that men and women have only such moral rights as Government chooses to grant, which means that they have no moral rights at all.

All this si sometimes obscured in the United States by the constitutional system. The American Constitution provides a set of individual *legal* rights in the First Amendment, and in the due process, equal protection, and similar clauses. Under present legal practice the Supreme Court has the power to declare an act of Congress or of a state legislature void if the Court finds that the act offends these provisions. This practice has led some commentators to suppose that individual moral rights are fully protected by this system, but that is hardly so, nor could it be so.

The Constitution fuses legal and moral issues, by making the validity of a law depend on the answer to complex moral problems, like the problem of whether a particular statute respects the inherent equality of all men. This fusion has important consequences for the debates about civil disobedience; I have described these elsewhere[1] and I shall refer to them later. But it leaves open two prominent questions. It does not tell us whether the Constitution, even properly interpreted, recognizes all the moral rights that citizens have, and it does not tell us whether, as many suppose, citizens would have a duty to obey the law even if it did invade their moral rights.

Both questions become crucial when some minority claims moral rights which the law denies, like the right to run its local school system, and which lawyers agree are not protected by the Constitution. The second question becomes crucial when, as now, the majority is sufficiently aroused so that Constitutional amendments to eliminate rights, like the right against self-incrimination, are seriously proposed. It is also crucial in nations, like the United Kingdom, that have no constitution of a comparable nature.

Even if the Constitution were perfect, of course, and the majority left it alone, it would not follow that the Supreme Court could guarantee the individual rights of citizens. A Supreme Court decision is still a legal decision, and it must take into account precedent and institutional considerations like relations between the Court and Congress, as well as morality. And no judicial decision is necessarily the right decision. Judges stand for different positions on controversial issues of law and morals and, as the fights over Nixon's Supreme Court nominations showed, a President is entitled to appoint judges of his own persuasion, provided that they are honest and capable.

So, though the constitutional system adds something to the protection of moral rights against the Government, it falls far short of guaranteeing these rights, or even establishing what they are. It means that, on some occasions, a department other than the legislature has the last word on these issues, which can hardly satisfy someone who thinks such a department profoundly wrong.

It is of course inevitable that some department of government will have the final say on what law will be enforced. When men disagree about moral rights, there will be no way for either side to prove its case, and some decision must stand if there is not to be anarchy. But that piece of orthodox wisdom must be the beginning and not the end of a philosophy of legislation and enforcement. If we cannot insist that the Government reach the right answers about the rights of its citizens, we can insist at least that it try. We can insist that it take rights seriously, follow a coherent theory of what these rights are, and act consistently with its own professions. I shall try to show what that means, and how it bears on the present political debates. . . .

Controversial Rights

The argument so far has been hypothetical: if a man has a particular moral right against the Government, that right survives contrary legislation or adjudication. But this does not tell us what rights he has, and it is notorious that reasonable men disagree about that. There is wide agreement on certain clearcut cases; almost everyone who believes in rights at all would admit, for example, that a man has a moral right to speak his mind in a nonprovocative way on matters of political concern, and that this is an important right that the State must go to great pains to protect. But there is great controversy as to the limits of such paradigm rights, and the so-called "anti-riot" law involved in the famous Chicago Seven trial of the last decade is a case in point.

The defendants were accused of conspiring to cross state lines with the intention of causing a riot. This charge is vague—perhaps unconstitutionally vague—but the law apparently defines as criminal emotional speeches which argue that violence is justified in order to secure political equality. Does the right of free speech protect this sort of speech? That, of course, is a legal issue, because it invokes the free-speech clause of the First Amendment of the Constitution. But it is also a moral issue, because, as I said, we must treat the First Amendment as an attempt to protect a moral right. It is part of the job of governing to "define" moral rights through statutes and judicial decisions, that is, to declare officially the extent that moral rights will be taken to have in law. Congress faced this task in voting on the anti-riot bill, and the Supreme Court has faced it in countless cases. How should the different departments of government go about defining moral rights?

They should begin with a sense that whatever they decide might be wrong. History and their descendants may judge that they acted unjustly when they thought they were right. If they take their duty seriously, they must try to limit their mistakes, and they must therefore try to discover where the dangers of mistake lie.

They might choose one of two very different models for this purpose. The first model recommends striking a balance between the rights of the individual and the demands of society at large. If the Government *infringes* on a moral right (for example, by defining the right of free speech more narrowly than justice requires), then it has done the individual a wrong. On the other hand, if the Government *inflates* a right (by defining it more broadly than justice requires) then it cheats society of some general benefit, like safe streets, that there is no reason it should not have. So a mistake on one side is as serious as a mistake on the other. The course of government is to steer to the middle, to balance the general good and personal rights, giving to each its due.

When the Government, or any of its branches, defines a right, it must bear in mind, according to the first model, the social cost of different proposals and make the necessary adjustments. It must not grant the same freedom to noisy demonstrations as it grants to calm political discussion, for example, because the former causes much more trouble than the latter. Once it decides how much of a right to recognize, it must enforce its decision to the full. That means permitting an individual to act within his rights, as the Government has defined them, but not beyond, so that if anyone breaks the law, even on grounds of conscience, he must be punished. No doubt any government will make mistakes, and will regret decisions once taken. That is inevitable. But this middle policy will ensure that errors on one side will balance out errors on the other over the long run.

The first model described in this way, has great plausibility, and most laymen and lawyers, I think, would respond to it warmly. The metaphor of balancing the public interest against personal claims is established in our political and judicial rhetoric, and this metaphor gives the model both familiarity and appeal. Nevertheless, the first model is a false one, certainly in the case of rights generally regarded as important and the metaphor is the heart of its error.

The institution of rights against the Government is not a gift of God, or an ancient ritual, or a national sport. It is a complex and troublesome practice that makes the Government's job of securing the general benefit more difficult and more expensive, and it would be a frivolous and wrongful practice unless it served some point. Anyone who professes to take rights seriously, and who praises our Government for respecting them, must have some sense of what that point is. He must accept, at the minimum, one or both of two important ideas. The first is the vague but powerful idea of human dignity. This idea, associated with Kant, but defended by philosophers of different schools, supposes that there are ways of treating a man that are inconsistent with recognizing him as a full member of the human community, and holds that such treatment is profoundly unjust.

The second is the more familiar idea of political equality. This supposes that the weaker members of a political community are entitled to the same concern and respect of their government as the more powerful members have secured for themselves, so that if some men have freedom of decision whatever the effect on the general good, then all men must have the same freedom. I do not want to defend or elaborate these ideas here, but only to insist that anyone who claims that citizens have rights must accept ideas very close to these.[2]

It makes sense to say that a man has a fundamental right against the Government, in the strong sense, like free speech, if that right is necessary to protect his dignity, or his standing as equally entitled to concern and respect, or some other personal value of like consequence. It does not make sense otherwise.

So if rights make sense at all, then the invasion of a relatively important right must be a serious matter. It means treating a man as less than a man, or as less worthy of concern than other men. The institution of rights rests on the conviction that this is a grave injustice, and that it is worth paying the incremental cost in social policy or efficiency that is necessary to prevent it. But then it must be wrong to say that inflating rights is as serious as invading them. If the Government errs on the side of the individual, then it simply pays a little more in social efficiency than it has to pay; it pays a little more, that is, of the same coin that it has already decided must be spent. But if it errs against the individual it inflicts an insult upon him that, on its own reckoning, it is worth a great deal of that coin to avoid.

So the first model is indefensible. It rests, in fact, on a mistake I discussed earlier, namely the confusion of society's rights with the rights of members of society. "Balancing" is appropriate when the Government must choose between competing claims of right—between the Southerner's claim to freedom of association, for example, and the black man's claim to an equal education. Then the Government can do nothing but estimate the merits of the competing claims, and act on its estimate. The first model assumes that the "right" of the majority is a competing right that must be balanced in this way; but that, as I argued before, is a confusion that threatens to destroy the concept of individual rights. It is worth noticing that the community rejects the first model in that area where the stakes for the individual are highest, the criminal process. We say that it is better that one innocent man be punished, and that homily rests on the choice of the second model for government.

The second model treats abridging a right as much more serious than inflating one, and its recommendations follow from that judgment. It stipulates that once a right is recognized in clear-cut cases, then the Government should act to cut off that right only when some compelling reason is presented, some reason that is consistent with the suppositions on which the original right must be based. It cannot be an argument for curtailing a right, once granted, simply that society would pay a further price for extending it. There must be something special about that further cost, or there must be some other feature of the case, that makes it sensible to say that although great social cost is warranted to protect the original right, this particular cost is not necessary. Otherwise, the Government's failure to extend the right will show that its recognition of the right in the original case is a sham, a promise that it intends to keep only until that becomes inconvenient.

How can we show that a particular cost is not worth paying without taking back the initial recognition of a right? I can think of only three sorts of grounds that can consistently be used to limit the definition of a particular right. First, the Government might show that the values protected by the original right are not really at stake in the marginal case, or are at stake only in some attenuated form. Second, it might show that if the right is defined to include the marginal case, then some competing right, in the strong sense I described earlier, would be abridged. Third, it might show that if the right were so defined, then the cost to society would not be simply incremental, but would be of a degree far beyond the cost paid to grant the original right, a degree great enough to justify whatever assault on dignity or equality might be involved.

It is fairly easy to apply these grounds to one group of problems the Supreme Court faced, imbedded in constitutional issues. The draft law provided an exemption for conscientious objectors, but this exemption, as interpreted by the draft boards, has been limited to those who object to *all* wars on *religious* grounds. If we suppose that the exemption is justified on the ground that an individual has a moral right not to kill in violation of his own principles, then the question is raised whether it is proper to exclude those whose morality is sufficiently complex to distinguish among wars. The Supreme Court held, as a matter of Constitutional law, that the draft boards were wrong to exclude the former, but competent to exclude the latter.

None of the three grounds I listed can justify either of these exclusions as a matter of political morality. The invasion of personality in forcing men to kill when they believe killing immoral is just as great when these beliefs are based on secular grounds, or take account of the fact that wars differ in morally relevant ways, and there is no pertinent difference in competing rights or in national emergency. There are differences among the cases, of course, but they are insufficient to justify the distinction. A government that is secular on principle cannot prefer a religious to a nonreligious morality as such. There are utilitarian arguments in favor of limiting the exception to religious or universal grounds—an exemption so limited may be less ex-

Chapter X: The Individual and Society

pensive to administer, and may allow easier discrimination between sincere and insincere applicants. But these utilitarian reasons are irrelevant, because they cannot count as grounds for limiting a right.

What about the anti-riot law, as applied in the Chicago trial? Does the law represent an improper limitation of the right to free speech, supposedly protected by the First Amendment? If we were to apply the first model for government to this issue, the argument for the anti-riot law would look strong. But if we set aside talk of balancing as inappropriate, and turn to the proper grounds for limiting a right, then the argument becomes a great deal weaker. The original right of free speech must suppose that it is an assault on human personality to stop a man from expressing what he honestly believes, particularly on issues affecting how he is governed. Surely the assault is greater, and not less, when he is stopped from expressing those principles of political morality that he holds most passionately, in the face of what he takes to be outrageous violations of these principles.

It may be said that the anti-riot law leaves him free to express these principles in a non-provocative way. But that misses the point of the connection between expression and dignity. A man cannot express himself freely when he cannot match his rhetoric to his outrage, or when he must trim his sails to protect values he counts as nothing next to those he is trying to vindicate. It is true that some political dissenters speak in ways that shock the majority, but it is arrogant for the majority to suppose that the orthodox methods of expression are the proper ways to speak, for this is a denial of equal concern and respect. If the point of the right is to protect the dignity of dissenters, then we must make judgments about appropriate speech with the personalities of the dissenters in mind, not the personality of the "silent" majority for whom the anti-riot law is no restraint at all.

So the argument fails, that the personal values protected by the original right are less at stake in this marginal case. We must consider whether competing rights, or some grave threat to society, nevertheless justify the anti-riot law. We can consider these two grounds together, because the only plausible competing rights are rights to be free from violence, and violence is the only plausible threat to society that the context provides.

I have no right to burn your house, or stone you or your car, or swing a bicycle chain against your skull, even if I find these to be natural means of expression. But the defendants in the Chicago trial were not accused of direct violence; the argument runs that the acts of speech they planned made it likely that others would do acts of violence, either in support of or out of hostility to what they said. Does this provide a justification?

The question would be different if we could say with any confidence how much and what sort of violence the anti-riot law might be expected to prevent. Will it save two lives a year, or two hundred, or two thousand? Two thousand dollars of property, or two hundred thousand, or two million? No one can say, not simply because prediction is next to impossible, but because we have no firm understanding of the process by which demonstration disintegrates into riot, and in particular of the part played by inflammatory speech, as distinct from poverty, police brutality, blood lust, and all the rest of human and economic failure. The Government must try, of course, to reduce the violent waste of lives and property, but it must recognize that any attempt to locate and remove a cause of riot, short of a reorganization of society, must be an exercise in speculation, trial, and error. It must make its decisions under conditions of high uncertainty, and the institution of rights, taken seriously, limits its freedom to experiment under such conditions.

It forces the Government to bear in mind that preventing a man from speaking or demonstrating offers him a certain and profound insult, in return for a speculative benefit that may in any event be achieved in other if more expensive ways. When lawyers say that rights may be limited to protect other rights, or to prevent catastrophe, they have in mind cases in which cause and effect are relatively clear, like the familiar example of a man falsely crying "Fire!" in a crowded theater.

But the Chicago story shows how obscure the causal connections can become. Were the speeches of Hoffman or Rubin necessary conditions of the riot? Or had thousands of people come to Chicago for the purposes of rioting anyway, as the Government also argues? Were they in any case sufficient conditions? Or could the police have contained the violence if they had not been so busy contributing to it, as the staff of the President's Commission on Violence said they were?

These are not easy questions, but if rights mean anything, then the Government cannot simply assume answers that justify its conduct. If a man has a right to speak, if the reasons that support that right extend to provocative political speech, and if the effects of such speech on violence are unclear, then the Government is not entitled to make its first attack on that problem by denying that right. It may be that abridging the right to speak is the least expensive course, or the least damaging to police morale, or the most popular politically. But these are utilitarian arguments in favor of starting one place rather than another, and such arguments are ruled out by the concept of rights.

This point may be obscured by the popular belief that political activists look forward to violence and "ask for trouble" in what they say. They can hardly complain, in the general view, if they are taken to be the authors of the violence they expect, and treated accordingly. But this repeats the confusion I tried to explain earlier between having a right and doing the right thing. The speaker's motives may be relevant in deciding whether he does the right thing in speaking passionately about issues that may inflame or enrage the audience. But if he has a right to speak, because the danger in allowing him to speak is speculative, his motives cannot count as independent evidence in the argument that justifies stopping him.

But what of the individual rights of those who will be destroyed by a riot, of the passer-by who will be killed by a sniper's bullet or the shopkeeper who will be ruined by looting? To put the issue in this way, as a question of competing rights, suggests a principle that would undercut the effect of uncertainty. Shall we say that some rights to protection are so important that the Government is justified in doing all it can to maintain them? Shall we therefore say that the Government may abridge the rights of others to act when their acts might simply increase the risk, by however slight or speculative a margin, that some person's right to life or property will be violated?

Some such principle is relied on by those who oppose the Supreme Court's recent liberal rulings on police procedure. These rulings increase the chance that a guilty man will go free, and therefore marginally increase the risk that any particular member of the community will be murdered, raped, or robbed. Some critics believe that the Court's decisions must therefore be wrong.

But no society that purports to recognize a variety of rights, on the ground that a man's dignity or equality may be invaded in a variety of ways, can accept such a principle. If forcing a man to testify against himself, or forbidding him to speak, does the damage that the rights against self-incrimination and the right of free speech assume, then it would be contemptuous for the State to tell a man that he must suffer this damage against the possibility that other men's risk of loss may be marginally reduced. If rights make sense, then the degrees of their importance cannot be so different that some count not at all when others are mentioned.

Of course the Government may discriminate and may stop a man from exercising his right to speak when there is a clear and substantial risk that his speech will do great damage to the person or property of others, and no other means of preventing this are at hand, as in the case of the man shouting "Fire!" in a theater. But we must reject the suggested principle that the Government can simply ignore rights to speak when life and property are in question. So long as the impact of speech on these other rights remains speculative and marginal, it must look elsewhere for levers to pull.

Why Take Rights Seriously?

I said at the beginning of this essay that I wanted to show what a government must do that professes to recognize individual rights. It must dispense with the claim that citizens never have a right to break its law, and it must not define citizens' rights so that these are cut off for supposed reasons of the general good. Any Government's harsh treatment of civil disobedience, or campaign against vocal protest, may therefore be thought to count against its sincerity.

One might well ask, however, whether it is wise to take rights all that seriously after all. America's genius, at least in her own legend, lies in not taking any abstract doctrine to its logical extreme. It may be time to ignore abstractions, and concentrate instead on giving the majority of our citizens a new sense of their Government's concern for their welfare, and of their title to rule.

That, in any event, is what former Vice-President Agnew seemed to believe. In a policy statement on the issue of "weirdos" and social misfits, he said that the liberals' concern for individual rights was a headwind blowing in the face of the ship of state. That is a poor metaphor, but the philosophical point it expresses is very well taken. He recognized, as many liberals do not, that the majority cannot travel as fast or as far as it would like if it recognizes the rights of individuals to do what, in the majority's terms, is the wrong thing to do.

Spiro Agnew supposed that rights are divisive, and that national unity and a new respect for law may be developed by taking them more skeptically. But he is wrong. America will continue to be divided by its social and foreign policy, and if the economy grows weaker again the divisions will become more bitter. If we want our laws and our legal institutions to provide the ground rules within which these issues will be contested then these ground rules must not be the conqueror's law that the dominant class imposes on the weaker, as Marx supposed the law of a capitalist society must be. The bulk of the law—that part which defines and implements social, economic, and foreign policy—cannot be neutral. It must state, in its greatest part, the majority's view of the common good. The institution of rights is therefore crucial, because it represents the majority's promise to the minorities that their dignity and equality will be respected. When the divisions among the groups are most violent, then this gesture, if law is to work, must be most sincere.

The institution requires an act of faith on the part of the minorities, because the scope of their rights will be controversial whenever they are important, and because the officers of the majority will act on their own notions of what these rights really are. Of course these officials will disagree with many of the claims that a minority makes. That makes it all the more important that they take their decisions gravely. They must show that they understand what rights are, and they must not cheat on the full implications of the doctrine. The Government will not re-establish respect for law without giving the law some claim to respect. It cannot do that if it neglects the one feature that distinguishes law from ordered brutality. If the Government does not take rights seriously, then it does not take law seriously either.

Endnotes

1. See Chapter 8.
2. He need not consider these ideas to be axiomatic. He may, that is, have reasons for insisting that dignity or equality are important values, and these reasons may be utilitarian. He may believe, for example, that the general good will be advanced, *in the long run*, only if we treat indignity or inequality as very great injustices, and never allow our *opinions* about the general good to justify them. I do not know of any good arguments for or against this sort of "institutional" utilitarianism, but it is consistent with my point, because it argues that we must treat violations of dignity and equality as special moral crimes, beyond the reach of ordinary utilitarian justification.

Reprinted with permission of Ronald Dworkin, from *Taking Rights Seriously*, by Ronald Dworkin, Harvard University Press, 1977. [Edited]

Human Rights, Civil Rights

Malcolm X

[INTERVIEWER]
One question that I've wondered about—in several of your lectures you've stressed the idea that the struggle of your people is for human rights rather than civil rights. Can you explain a bit what you mean by that?

MALCOLM X:
Civil rights actually keeps the struggle within the domestic confines of America. It keeps it under the jurisdiction of the American government, which means that as long as our struggle for what we're seeking is labeled civil rights, we can only go to Washington, D.C., and then we rely upon either the Supreme Court, the President or the Congress or the senators. These senators—many of them are racists. Many of the congressmen are racists. Many of the judges are racists and oftentimes the president himself is a very shrewdly camouflaged racist. And so we really can't get meaningful redress for our grievances when we are depending upon these grievances being redressed just within the jurisdiction of the United States government.

On the other hand, human rights go beyond the jurisdiction of this government. Human rights are international. Human rights are something that a man has by dint of his having been born. The labeling of our struggle in this country under the title civil rights of the past 12 years has actually made it impossible for us to get outside help. Many foreign nations, many of our brothers and sisters on the African continent who have gotten their independence, have restrained themselves, have refrained from becoming vocally or actively involved in our struggle for fear that they would be violating U.S. protocol, that they would be accused of getting involved in America's domestic affairs.

On the other hand, when we label it human rights, it internationalizes the problem and puts it at a level that makes it possible for any nation or any people anywhere on this earth to speak out in behalf of our human rights struggle.

So we feel that by calling it civil rights for the past 12 years, we've actually been barking up the wrong tree, that ours is a problem of *human* rights.

Plus, if we have our human rights, our civil rights are automatic. If we're respected as a human being, we'll be respected as a citizen; and in this country the black man not only is not respected as a citizen, he is not even respected as a human being.

And the proof is that you find in many instances people can come to this country from other countries—they can come to this country from behind the Iron Curtain—and despite the fact that they come here from these other places, they don't have to have civil-rights legislation passed in order for their rights to be safeguarded.

No new legislation is necessary for foreigners who come here to have their rights safeguarded. The Constitution is sufficient, but when it comes to the black men who were born here—whenever we are asking for our rights, they tell us that new legislation is necessary.

Well, we don't believe that. The Organization of Afro-American Unity feels that as long as our people in this country confine their struggle within the limitations and under the jurisdiction of the United States government, we remain within the confines of the vicious system that has done nothing but exploit and oppress us ever since we've been here. So we feel that our only real hope is to make known that our problem is not a Negro problem or an American problem but rather, it has become a human problem, a world problem, and it has to be attacked at the world level, at a level at which all segments of humanity can intervene in our behalf.

Women's Rights as Human Rights: Toward a Re-Vision of Human Rights

Charlotte Bunch

Significant numbers of the world's population are routinely subject to torture, starvation, terrorism, humiliation, mutilation, and even murder simply because they are female. Crimes such as these against any group other than women would be recognized as a civil and political emergency as well as a gross violation of the victims' humanity. Yet, despite a clear record of deaths and demonstrable abuse, women's rights are not commonly classified as human rights. This is problematic both theoretically and practically, because it has grave consequences for the way society views and treats the fundamental issues of women's lives. This paper questions why women's rights and human rights are viewed as distinct, looks at the policy implications of this schism, and discusses different approaches to changing it.

Women's human rights are violated in a variety of ways. Of course, women sometimes suffer abuses such as political repression that are similar to abuses suffered by men. In these situations, female victims are often invisible, because the dominant image of the political actor in our world is male. However, many violations of women's human rights are distinctly connected to being female—that is, women are discriminated against and abused on the basis of gender. Women also experience sexual abuse in situations where their other human rights are being violated, as political prisoners or members of persecuted ethnic groups, for example. In this paper I address those abuses in which gender is a primary or related factor because gender-related abuse has been most neglected and offers the greatest challenge to the field of human rights today.

The concept of human rights is one of the few moral visions ascribed to internationally. Although its scope is not universally agreed upon, it strikes deep chords of response among many. Promotion of human rights is a widely accepted goal and thus provides a useful framework for seeking redress of gender abuse. Further it is one of the few concepts that speaks to the need for transnational activism and concern about the lives of people globally. The Universal Declaration of Human Rights,[1] adopted in 1948, symbolizes this world vision and defines human rights broadly. While not much is said about women, Article 2 entitles all to "the rights and freedoms set forth in this Declaration, without distinction of any kind, such as race, colour, sex, language, religion, political or other opinion, national or social origin, property, birth or other status." Eleanor Roosevelt and the Latin American women who fought for the inclusion of sex in the Declaration and for its passage clearly intended that it would address the problem of women's subordination.[2]

Since 1948 the world community has continuously debated varying interpretations of human rights in response to global developments. Little of this discussion, however, has addressed questions of gender, and only recently have significant challenges been made to a vision of human rights which excludes much of women's experiences. The concept of human rights, like all vibrant visions, is not static or the property of any one group; rather, its meaning expands as people reconceive of their needs and hopes in relation to it. In this spirit, feminists redefine human rights abuses to include the degradation and violation of women. The specific experiences of women must be added to traditional approaches to human rights in order to make women more visible and to transform the concept and practice of human rights in our culture so that it takes better account of women's lives.

In the next part of this article, I will explore both the importance and the difficulty of connecting women's rights to human rights, and then I will outline four basic approaches that have been used in the effort to make this connection.

Beyond Rhetoric: Political Implications

Few governments exhibit more than token commitment to women's equality as a basic human right in domestic or foreign policy. No government determines its policies toward other countries on the basis of their treatment of women, even when some aid and trade decisions are said to be based on a country's human rights record. Among nongovernmental organizations, women are rarely a priority, and Human Rights Day programs on 10 December seldom include discussion of issues like violence against women or reproductive rights. When it is suggested that governments and human rights organizations should respond to women's rights as concerns that deserve such attention, a number of excuses are offered for why this cannot be done. The responses tend to follow one or more of these lines: (1) sex discrimination is too trivial, or not as important, or will come after larger issues of survival that require more serious attention; (2) abuse of women, while regrettable, is a cultural, private, or individual issue and not a political matter requiring state action; (3) while appropriate for other action, women's rights are not human rights per se; or (4) when the abuse of women is recognized, it is considered inevitable or so pervasive that any consideration of it is futile or will overwhelm other human rights questions. It is important to challenge these responses.

The narrow definition of human rights, recognized by many in the West as solely a matter of state violation of civil and political liberties, impedes consideration of women's rights. In the United States the concept has been further limited by some who have used it as a weapon in the cold war almost exclusively to challenge human rights abuses perpetrated in communist countries. Even then, many abuses that affected women, such as forced pregnancy in Romania, were ignored.

Some important aspects of women's rights do fit into a civil liberties framework, but much of the abuse against women is part of a larger socioeconomic web that entraps women, making them vulnerable to abuses which cannot be delineated as exclusively political or solely caused by states. The inclusion of "second generation" or socio-economic human rights to food, shelter, and work—which are clearly delineated as part of the Universal Declaration of Human Rights—is vital to addressing women's concerns fully. Further, the assumption that states are not responsible for most violations of women's rights ignores the fact that such abuses, although committed perhaps by private citizens, are often condoned or even sanctioned by states. I will return to the question of state responsibility after responding to other instances of resistance to women's rights as human rights.

The most insidious myth about women's rights is that they are trivial or secondary to the concerns of life and death. Nothing could be farther from the truth: sexism kills. There is increasing documentation of the many ways in which being female is life-threatening. The following are a few examples:

- Before birth: Amniocentesis is used for sex selection leading to the abortion of more female fetuses at rates as high as 99 percent in Bombay, India; in China and India, the two most populous nations, more males than females are born even though natural birth ratios would produce more females.[3]
- During childhood: The World Health Organization reports that in many countries, girls are fed less, breast fed for shorter periods of time, taken to doctors less frequently, and die or are physically and mentally maimed by malnutrition at higher rates than boys.[4]

- In adulthood: the denial of women's rights to control their bodies in reproduction threatens women's lives, especially where this is combined with poverty and poor health services. In Latin America, complications from illegal abortions are the leading cause of death for women between the ages of fifteen and thirty-nine.[5]

Sex discrimination kills women daily. When combined with race, class, and other forms of oppression, it constitutes a deadly denial of women's right to life and liberty on a large scale throughout the world. The most pervasive violation of females is violence against women in all its manifestations, from wife battery, incest, and rape, to dowry deaths, genital mutilation, and female sexual slavery. These abuses occur in every country and are found in the home and in the workplace, on streets, on campuses, and in prisons and refugee camps. They cross class, race, age, and national lines; and at the same time, the forms this violence takes often reinforce other oppressions such as racism, "able-bodyism," and imperialism. Case in point: in order to feed their families, poor women in brothels around U.S. military bases in places like the Philippines bear the burden of sexual, racial, and national imperialism in repeated and often brutal violation of their bodies.

Even a short review of random statistics reveals that the extent of violence against women globally is staggering:

- In the United States, battery is the leading cause of injury to adult women, and a rape is committed every six minutes.
- In Peru, 70 percent of all crimes reported to police involve women who are beaten by their partners; and in Lima (a city of seven million people), 168,970 rapes were reported in 1987 alone.
- In India, eight out of ten wives are victims of violence, either domestic battery, dowry-related abuse, or among the least fortunate, murder.
- In France, 95 percent of the victims of violence are women; 51 percent at the hands of a spouse or lover. Similar statistics form places as diverse as Bangladesh, Canada, Kenya, and Thailand demonstrate that more than 50 percent of female homicides were committed by family members.

Where recorded, domestic battery figures range from 40 percent to 80 percent of women beaten, usually repeatedly, indicating that the home is the most dangerous place for women and frequently the site of cruelty and torture. As the Carol Stuart murder in Boston demonstrated, sexist and racist attitudes in the United States often cover up the real threat to women; a woman is murdered in Massachusetts by a husband or lover every 22 days.

Such numbers do not reflect the full extent of the problem of violence against women, much of which remains hidden. Yet rather than receiving recognition as a major world conflict, this violence is accepted as normal or even dismissed as an individual or cultural matter. Georgina Ashworth notes that:

> The greatest restriction of liberty, dignity and movement and at the same time, direct violation of the person is the threat and realization of violence. . . . However violence against the female sex, on a scale which far exceeds the list of Amnesty International victims, is tolerated publicly; indeed some acts of violation are not crimes in law, others are legitimized in custom or court opinion, and most are blamed on the victims themselves.

Violence against women is a touchstone that illustrates the limited concept of human rights and highlights the political nature of the abuse of women. As Lori Heise states: "This is not random violence. . . . [T]he risk factor is being female." Victims are chosen because of their gender. The message is domination: stay in your place or be afraid. Contrary to the argument that such violence is only personal or cultural, it is profoundly political. It results from the structural relationships of power, domination, and privilege between men and women in society. Violence against women is central to maintaining those political relations at home, at work, and in all public spheres.

Failure to see the oppression of women as political also results in the exclusion of sex discrimination and violence against women from the human rights agenda. Female subordination runs so deep that it is still viewed as inevitable or natural, rather than seen as a politically constructed reality maintained by patriarchal interests, ideology, and institutions. But I do not believe that male violation of women is inevitable or natural. Such a belief requires a narrow and pessimistic view of men. If violence and domination are understood as a politically constructed reality, it is possible to imagine deconstructing that system and building more just interactions between the sexes.

The physical territory of this political struggle over what constitutes women's human rights is women's bodies. The importance of control over women can be seen in the intensity of resistance to laws and social changes that put control of women's bodies in women's hands: reproductive rights, freedom of sexuality whether heterosexual or lesbian, laws that criminalize rape in marriage, etc. Denial of reproductive rights and homophobia are also political means of maintaining control over women and perpetuating sex roles and thus have human rights implications. The physical abuse of women is a reminder of this territorial domination and is sometimes accompanied by other forms of human rights abuse such as slavery (forced prostitution), sexual terrorism (rape), imprisonment (confinement to the home), and torture (systematic battery). Some cases are extreme, such as the women in Thailand who died in a brothel fire because they were chained to their beds. Most situations are more ordinary like denying women decent educations or jobs which leaves them prey to abusive marriages, exploitative work, and prostitution.

This raises once again the question of the state's responsibility for protecting women's human rights. Feminists have shown how the distinction between private and public abuse is a dichotomy often used to justify female subordination in the home. Governments regulate many matters in the family and individual spheres. For example, human rights activists pressure states to prevent slavery or racial discrimination and segregation even when these are conducted by nongovernmental forces in private or proclaimed as cultural traditions as they have been in both the southern United States and in South Africa. The real questions are: (1) who decides what are legitimate human rights; and (2) when should the state become involved and for what purposes. Riane Eisler argues that:

> the issue is what types of private acts are and are not protected by the right to privacy and/or the principle of family autonomy. Even more specifically, the issue is whether violations of human rights within the family such as genital mutilation, wife beating, and other forms of violence designed to maintain patriarchal control should be within the purview of human rights theory and action. . . . [T]he underlying problem for human rights theory, as for most other fields of theory, is that the yardstick that has been developed for defining and measuring human rights has been based on the male as the norm.

The human rights community must move beyond its male defined norms in order to respond to the brutal and systematic violation of women globally. This does not mean that every human rights group must alter the focus of its work. However it does require examining patriarchal biases and acknowledging the rights of women as human rights. Governments must seek to end the politically and culturally constructed war on women rather than continue to perpetuate it. Every state has the responsibility to intervene in the abuse of women's rights within its borders and to end its collusion with the forces that perpetuate such violations in other countries.

Toward Action: Practical Approaches

The classification of human rights is more than just a semantics problem because it has practical policy consequences. Human rights are still considered to be more important than women's rights. The distinction perpetuates the idea that the rights of women are of a lesser order than the "rights of man," and, as Eisler describes it, "serves to justify practices that do not accord women full and equal status." In the United Nations, the Human Rights Commission has more power to hear and investigate cases than the Commission on the Status of Women, more staff and budget, and better mechanisms for implementing its findings. Thus it makes a difference in what can be done if a case is deemed a violation of women's rights and not of human rights.

The determination of refugee status illustrates how the definition of human rights affects people's lives. The Dutch Refugee Association, in its pioneering efforts to convince other nations to recognize sexual persecution and violence against women as justifications for granting refugee status, found that some European governments would take sexual persecution into account as an aspect of other forms of political repression, but none would make it the grounds for refugee status per se. The implications of such a distinction are clear when examining a situation like that of the Bangladeshi women, who having been raped during the Pakistan-Bangladesh war, subsequently faced death at the hands of male relatives to preserve "family honor." Western powers professed outrage but did not offer asylum to these victims of human rights abuse.

I have observed four basic approaches to linking women's rights to human rights. These approaches are presented separately here in order to identify each more clearly. In practice, these approaches often overlap, and while each raises questions about the others, I see them as complementary. These approaches can be applied to many issues, but I will illustrate them primarily in terms of how they address violence against women in order to show the implications of their differences on a concrete issue.

1. Women's Rights as Political and Civil Rights. Taking women's specific needs into consideration as part of the already recognized "first generation" political and civil liberties is the first approach. This involves both raising the visibility of women who suffer general human rights violations as well as calling attention to particular abuses women encounter because they are female. Thus, issues of violence against women are raised when they connect to other forms of violation such as the sexual torture of women political prisoners in South America. Groups like the Women's Task Force of Amnesty International have taken this approach in pushing for Amnesty to launch a campaign on behalf of women political prisoners which would address the sexual abuse and rape of women in custody, their lack of maternal care in detention, and the resulting human rights abuse of their children.

Documenting the problems of women refugees and developing responsive policies are other illustrations of this approach. Women and children make up more than 80 percent of those in refugee camps, yet few refugee policies are specifically shaped to meet the needs of these vulnerable populations who face considerable sexual abuse. For example, in one camp where men were allocated the community's rations, some gave food to women and their children in exchange for sex. Revealing this abuse led to new policies that allocated food directly to the women.

The political and civil rights approach is a useful starting point for many human rights groups; by considering women's experiences, these groups can expand their efforts in areas where they are already working. This approach also raises contradictions that reveal the limits of a narrow civil liberties view. One contradiction is to define rape as a human rights abuse only when it occurs in state custody but not on the streets or in the home. Another is to say that a violation of the right to free speech occurs when someone is jailed for defending gay rights, but not when someone is jailed or even tortured and killed for homosexuality. Thus while this approach of adding women and stirring them into existing first generation human rights categories is useful, it is not enough by itself.

2. Women's Rights as Socioeconomic Rights. The second approach includes the particular plight of women with regard to "second generation" human rights such as the rights to food, shelter, health care, and employment. This is an approach favored by those who see the dominant Western human rights tradition and international law as too individualistic and identify women's oppression as primarily economic.

This tendency has its origins among socialists and labor activists who have long argued that political human rights are meaningless to many without economic rights as well. It focuses on the primacy of the need to end women's economic subordination as the key to other issues including women's vulnerability to violence. This particular focus has led to work on issues like women's right to organize as workers and opposition to violence in the workplace, especially in situations like the free trade zones which have targeted women as cheap, nonorganized labor. Another focus of this approach has been highlighting the feminization of poverty or what might better be called the increasing impoverishment of females. Poverty has not become strictly female, but females now comprise a higher percentage of the poor.

Looking at women's rights in the context of socioeconomic development is another example of this approach. Third world peoples have called for an understanding of socioeconomic development as a human rights issue. Within this demand, some have sought to integrate women's rights into development and have examined women's specific needs in relation to areas like land ownership or access to credit. Among those working on women in development, there is growing interest in violence against women as both a health and development issue. If violence is seen as having negative consequences for social productivity, it may get more attention. This type of narrow economic measure, however, should not determine whether such violence is seen as a human rights concern. Violence as a development issue is linked to the need to understand development not just as an economic issue but also as a question of empowerment and human growth.

One of the limitations of this second approach has been its tendency to reduce women's needs to the economic sphere which implies that women's rights will follow automatically with third world development, which may involve socialism. This has not proven to be the case. Many working from this approach are no longer trying to add women into either the Western capitalist or socialist development models, but rather seek a transformative development process that links women's political, economic, and cultural empowerment.

3. Women's Rights and the Law. The creation of new legal mechanisms to counter sex discrimination characterizes the third approach to women's rights as human rights. These efforts seek to make existing legal and political institutions work for women and to expand the state's responsibility for the violation of women's human rights. National and local laws which address sex discrimination and violence against women are examples of this approach. These measures allow women to fight for their rights within the legal system. The primary international illustration is the Convention on the Elimination of All Forms of Discrimination Against Women.

The Convention has been described as "essentially an international bill of rights for women and a framework for women's participation in the development process . . . [which] spells out internationally accepted principles and standards for achieving equality between women and men." Adopted by the UN General Assembly in 1979, the Convention has been ratified or acceded to by 104 countries as of January 1990. In theory these countries are obligated to pursue policies in accordance with it and to report on their compliance to the Committee on the Elimination of Discrimination Against Women (CEDAW).

While the Convention addresses many issues of sex discrimination, one of its shortcomings is failure to directly address the question of violence against women. CEDAW passed a resolution at its eighth session in Vienna in 1989 expressing concern that this issue be on its agenda and instructing states to include in their periodic reports information about statistics, legislation, and support services in this area. The Commonwealth Secretariat in its manual on the reporting process for the convention also interprets the issue of violence against women as "clearly fundamental to the spirit of the Convention," especially in Article 5 which calls for the modification of social and cultural patterns, sex roles, and stereotyping that are based on the idea of the inferiority or the superiority of either sex.

The Convention outlines a clear human rights agenda for women which, if accepted by governments, would mark an enormous step forward. It also carries the limitations of all such international documents in that there is little power to demand its implementation. Within the United Nations, it is not generally regarded as a convention with teeth, as illustrated by the difficulty that CEDAW has had in getting countries to report on compliance with its provisions. Further, it is still treated by governments and most nongovernmental organizations as a document dealing with women's (read "secondary") rights, not human rights. Nevertheless, it is a useful statement of principles endorsed by the United Nations around which women can organize to achieve legal and political change in their regions.

4. Feminist Transformation of Human Rights. Transforming the human rights concept from a feminist perspective, so that it will take greater account of women's lives, is the fourth approach. This approach relates women's rights and human rights, looking first at the violations of women's lives and then asking how the human rights concept can change to be more responsive to women. For example, the GABRIELA women's coalition in the Philippines simply stated that "Women's Rights are Human Rights" in launching a campaign last year. As Ninotchka Rosca explained, coalition members saw that "human rights are not reducible to a question of legal and due process. . . . In the case of women, human rights are affected by the entire society's traditional perception of what is proper or not proper for women." Similarly, a panel at the 1990 International Women's Rights Action Watch conference asserted that "Violence Against Women is a Human Rights Issue." While work in the three previous approaches is often done from a feminist perspective, this last view is the most distinctly feminist with its woman-centered stance and its refusal to wait for permission from some authority to determine what is or is not a human rights issue.

This transformative approach can be taken toward any issue, but those working from this approach have tended to focus most on abuses that arise specifically out of gender, such as reproductive rights, female sexual slavery, violence against women, and "family crimes" like forced marriage, compulsory heterosexuality, and female mutilation. There are also the issues most often dismissed as not really human rights questions. This is therefore the most hotly contested area and requires that barriers be broken down between public and private, state and nongovernmental responsibilities.

Those working to transform the human rights vision from this perspective can draw on the work of others who have expanded the understanding of human rights previously. For example, two decades ago there was no concept of "disappearances" as a human rights abuse. However, the women of the Plaza de Mayo in Argentina did not wait for an official declaration but stood up to demand state accountability for these crimes. In so doing, they helped to create a context for expanding the concept of responsibility for deaths at the hands of paramilitary or right-wing death squads which, even if not carried out by the state, were allowed by it to happen. Another example is the developing concept that civil rights violations include "hate crimes," violence that is racially motivated or directed against homosexuals, Jews or other minority groups. Many accept that states have an obligation to work to prevent such rights abuses, and getting violence against women seen as a hate crime is being pursued by some.

The practical applications of transforming the human rights concept from feminist perspectives need to be explored further. The danger in pursuing only this approach is the tendency to become isolated from and competitive with other human rights groups because they have been so reluctant to address gender violence and discrimination. Yet most women experience abuse on the grounds of sex, race, class, nation, age, sexual preference. and politics as interrelated, and little benefit comes from separating them as competing claims. The human rights community need not abandon other issues but should incorporate gender perspectives into them and see how these expand the terms of their work. By recognizing issues like violence against women as human rights concerns, human rights scholars and activists do not have to take these up as their primary tasks. However, they do have to stop gatekeeping and guarding their prerogative to determine what is considered a "legitimate" human rights issue.

As mentioned before, these four approaches are overlapping and many strategies for change involve elements of more than one. All of these approaches contain aspects of what is necessary to achieve women's rights. At the time when dualist ways of thinking and views of competing economic systems are in question, the creative task is to look for ways to connect these approaches and to see how we can go beyond exclusive views of what people need in their lives. In the words of an early feminist group, we need bread and roses, too. Women want food and liberty and the possibility of living lives of dignity free from domination and violence. In this struggle, the recognition of women's rights as human rights can play an important role.

Notes

1. Universal Declaration of Human Rights, *adopted* 10 December 1948, G.A. Res. 217A (III), U.N. Doc. A/810 (1948).
2. Blanche Wiesen Cook, "Eleanor Roosevelt and Human Rights: The Battle for Peace and Planetary Decency," Edward P. Crapol, ed. *Women and American Foreign Policy: Lobbyists, Critics, and Insiders* (New York: Greenwood Press, 1987), 98–118; Georgina Ashworth, "Of Violence and Violation: Women and Human Rights, " *Change Thinkbook II* (London, 1986).
3. Vibhuti Patel, *In Search of Our Bodies: A Feminist Look at Women, Health, and Reproduction in India* (Shakti, Bombay, 1987); Lori Heise, "International Dimensions of Violence Against Women," *Response*, vol. 12, no 1 (1989): 3.

4. Sundari Ravindran, *Health Implications of Sex Discrimination in Childhood* (Geneva: World Health Organization, 1986). These problems and proposed social programs to counter them in India are discussed in detail in "Gender Violence: Gender Discrimination Between Boy and Girl in Parental Family," paper published by CHETNA (Child Health Education Training and Nutrition Awareness), Ahmedabad, 1989.
5. Debbie Taylor, ed., *Women: A World Report. A New Internationalist Book* (Oxford: Oxford University Press, 1985), 10. See Joni Seager and Ann Olson, eds., *Women In The World: An International Atlas* (London: Pluto Press, 1986) for more statistics on the effects of sex discrimination.

Reprinted by permission of *Human Rights Quarterly, Volume 12*, Number 4, November 1990.

Justice as Fairness

John Rawls

1. It might seem at first sight that the concepts of justice and fairness are the same, and that there is no reason to distinguish them, or to say that one is more fundamental than the other. I think that this impression is mistaken. In this paper I wish to show that the fundamental idea in the concept of justice is fairness; and I wish to offer an analysis of the concept of justice from this point of view. To bring out the force of this claim, and the analysis based upon it, I shall then argue that it is this aspect of justice for which utilitarianism, in its classical form, is unable to account, but which is expressed, even if misleadingly, by the idea of the social contract.

To start with I shall develop a particular conception of justice by stating and commenting upon two principles which specify it, and by considering the circumstances and conditions under which they may be thought to arise. The principles defining this conception itself, are, of course, familiar. It may be possible, however, by using the notion of fairness as a framework, to assemble and to look at them in a new way. Before stating this conception, however, the following preliminary matters should be kept in mind.

Throughout I consider justice only as a virtue of social institutions, or what I shall call practices. The principles of justice are regarded as formulating restrictions as to how practices may define positions and offices, and assign thereto powers and liabilities, rights and duties. Justice as a virtue of particular actions or of persons I do not take up at all. It is important to distinguish these various subjects of justice, since the meaning of the concept varies according to whether it is applied to practices, particular actions, or persons. These meanings are, indeed, connected, but they are not identical. I shall confine my discussion to the sense of justice as applied to practices, since this sense is the basic one. Once it is understood, the other senses should go quite easily.

Justice is to be understood in its customary sense as representing but *one* of the many virtues of social institutions, for these may be antiquated, inefficient, degrading, or any number of other things, without being unjust. Justice is not to be confused with an all-inclusive vision of a good society;

Chapter X: The Individual and Society

it is only one part of any such conception. It is important, for example, to distinguish that sense of equality which is an aspect of the concept of justice from that sense of equality which belongs to a more comprehensive social ideal. There may well be inequalities which one concedes are just, or at least not unjust, but which, nevertheless, one wishes on other grounds, to do away with. I shall focus attention, then, on the usual sense of justice in which it is essentially the elimination of arbitrary distinctions and the establishment, within the structure of a practice, of a proper balance between competing claims.

Finally, there is no need to consider the principles discussed below as *the* principles of justice. For the moment it is sufficient that they are typical of a family of principles normally associated with the concept of justice. The way in which the principles of this family resemble one another, as shown by the background against which they may be thought to arise, will be made clear by the whole of the subsequent argument.

2. The conception of justice which I want to develop may be stated in the form of two principles as follows: first, each person participating in a practice, or affected by it, has an equal right to the most extensive liberty compatible with a like liberty for all; and second, inequalities are arbitrary unless it is reasonable to expect that they will work out for everyone's advantage, and provided the positions and offices to which they attach, or from which they may be gained, are open to all. These principles express justice as a complex of three ideas: liberty, equality, and reward for services contributing to the common good.

※ ※ ※

The first principle holds, of course, only if other things are equal; that is, while there must always be a justification for departing from the initial position of equal liberty (which is defined by the pattern of rights and duties, powers and liabilities, established by a practice), and the burden of proof is placed on him who would depart from it, nevertheless, there can be, and often there is, a justification for doing so. Now, that similar particular cases, as defined by a practice, should be treated similarly as they arise, is part of the very concept of a practice; it is involved in the notion of an activity in accordance with rules. The first principle expresses an analogous conception, but as applied to the structure of practices themselves. It holds, for example, that there is a presumption against the distinctions and classifications made by legal systems and other practices to the extent that they infringe on the original and equal liberty of the persons participating in them. The second principle defines how this presumption may be rebutted.

It might be argued at this point that justice requires only an equal liberty. If, however, a greater liberty were possible for all without loss or conflict, then it would be irrational to settle on a lesser liberty. There is no reason for circumscribing rights unless their exercise would be incompatible, or would render the practice defining them less effective. Therefore no serious distortion of the concept of justice is likely to follow from including within it the concept of the greatest equal liberty.

The second principle defines what sorts of inequalities are permissible; it specifies how the presumption laid down by the first principle may be put aside. Now by inequalities it is best to understand not *any* differences between offices and positions, but differences in the benefits and burdens attached to them either directly or indirectly, such as prestige and wealth, or liability to taxation and compulsory services. Players in a game do not protest against there being different positions, such as batter, pitcher, catcher, and the like, not to there being various privileges and powers as specified by the rules; nor do the citizens of a country object to there being the different offices of government such as president, senator, governor, judge, and so on, each with their special rights and duties. It is not differences of this kind that are normally thought of as inequalities, but differences in the resulting distribution established by a practice, or made possible by it, of the things men strive to attain or avoid. Thus they may complain about the pattern of honors and rewards set up by a practice (e.g., the privileges and salaries of government officials) or they may object to the distribution of power and wealth which results from the various ways in which men avail themselves of the opportunities allowed by it (e.g., the concentration of wealth which may develop in a free price system allowing large entrepreneurial or speculative gains).

It should be noted that the second principle holds that an inequality is allowed only if there is reason to believe that the practice with the inequality, or resulting in it, will work for the advantage of *every* party engaging in it. Here it is important to stress that *every* party must gain from the inequality. Since the principle applies to practices, it implies that the representative man in every office or position defined by a practice, when he views it as a going concern, must find it reasonable to prefer his condition and prospects with the inequality to what they would be under the practice without it. The principle excludes, therefore, the justification of inequalities on the grounds that the disadvantages of those in one position are outweighed by the greater advantages of those in another position. This rather simple restriction is the main modification I wish to make in the utilitarian principle as usually understood.

※ ※ ※

3. Given these principles one might try to derive them from a priori principles of reason, or claim that they were known by intuition. These are familiar enough steps and, at least in the case of the first principle, might be made with some success. Usually, however, such arguments, made at this point, are unconvincing. They are not likely to lead to an understanding of the basis of the principles of justice, not at least as principles of justice. I wish, therefore, to look at the principles in a different way.

Chapter X: The Individual and Society

Imagine a society of persons amongst whom a certain system of practices is *already* well established. Now suppose that by and large they are mutually self-interested; their allegiance to their established practices is normally founded on the prospect of self-advantage. One need not assume that, in all senses of the term "person," the persons in this society are mutually self-interested. If the characterization as mutually self-interested applies when the line of division is the family, it may still be true that members of families are bound by ties of sentiment and affection and willingly acknowledge duties in contradiction to self-interest. Mutual self-interestedness in the relations between families, nations, churches, and the like, is commonly associated with intense loyalty and devotion on the part of individual members. Therefore, one can form a more realistic conception of this society if one thinks of it as consisting of mutually self-interested families, or some other association. Further, it is not necessary to suppose that these persons are mutually self-interested under all circumstances, but only in the usual situations in which they participate in their common practice.

Now suppose also that these persons are rational: they know their own interests more or less accurately; they are capable of tracing out the likely consequences of adopting one practice rather than another; they are capable of adhering to a course of action once they have decided upon it; they can resist present temptations and the enticements of immediate gain; and the bare knowledge or perception of the difference between their condition and that of others is not, within certain limits and in itself, a source of great dissatisfaction. Only the last point adds anything to the usual definition of rationality. This definition should allow, I think for the idea that a rational man would not be greatly downcast from knowing, or seeing, that others are in a better position than himself, unless he thought their being so was the result of injustice, or the consequence of letting chance work itself out for no useful common purpose, and so on. So if these persons strike us as unpleasantly egoistic, they are at least free in some degree from the fault of envy.

Finally, assume that these persons have roughly similar needs and interests, or needs and interests in various ways complementary, so that fruitful cooperation amongst them is possible; and suppose that they are sufficiently equal in power and ability to guarantee that in normal circumstances none is able to dominate the others. This condition (as well as the others) may seem excessively vague; but in view of the conception of justice to which the argument leads, there seems no reason for making it more exact here.

Since these persons are conceived as engaging in their common practices, which are already established, there is no question of our supposing them to come together to deliberate as to how they will set these practices up for the first time. Yet we can imagine that from time to time they discuss with one another whether any of them has a legitimate complaint against their established institutions. Such discussions are perfectly natural in any normal society. Now suppose that they have settled on doing this in the following way. They first try to arrive at the principles by which complaints, and so practices themselves, are to be judged. Their procedure for this is to let each person propose the principles upon which he wishes his complaints to be tried with the understanding that, if acknowledged, the complaints of others will be similarly tried, and that no complaints will be heard at all until everyone is roughly of one mind as to how complaints are to be judged. They each understand further that the principles proposed and acknowledged on this occasion are binding on future occasions. Thus each will be wary of proposing a principle which would give him a peculiar advantage, in his present circumstances, supposing it to be accepted. Each person knows that he will be bound by it in future circumstances the peculiarities of which cannot be known, and which might well be such that the principle is then to his disadvantage. The idea is that everyone should be required to make *in advance* a firm commitment, which others also may reasonably be expected to make, and that no one be given the opportunity to tailor the canons of a legitimate complaint to fit his own special condition, and then to discard them when they no longer suit his purpose. Hence each person will propose principles of a general kind which will, to a large degree, gain their sense from the various applications to be made of them, the particular circumstances of which being as yet unknown. These principles will express the conditions in accordance with which each is the least unwilling to have his interests limited in the design of practices, given the competing interests of the others, on the supposition that the interests of the others will be limited likewise. The restrictions which would so arise might be thought of as those a person would keep in mind if he were designing a practice in which his enemy were to assign him his place.

The two main parts of this conjectural account have a definite significance. The character and respective situations of the parties reflect the typical circumstances in which questions of justice arise. The procedure whereby principles are proposed and acknowledged represents constraints, analogous to those of having a morality, whereby rational and mutually self-interested persons are brought to act reasonably. Thus the first part reflects the fact that questions of justice arise when conflicting claims are made upon the design of a practice and where it is taken for granted that each person will insist, as far as possible, on what he considers his rights. It is typical of cases of justice to involve persons who are pressing on one another their claims, between which a fair balance or equilibrium must be found. On the other hand, as expressed by the second part, having a morality must at least imply the acknowledgment of principles as impartially applying to one's own conduct as well as to another's, and moreover principles which may constitute a constraint, or limitation, upon the pursuit of one's own interests. There are, of course, other aspects of having a morality: the acknowledgment of moral principles must show itself in accepting a reference to them as reasons for limiting one's claims, in acknowledging the burden of providing a special explanation, or excuse, when one acts contrary to them, or else in showing shame and remorse and a desire to make amends, and so on. It is sufficient to remark here that having a morality is analogous to having made a firm commitment in advance; for one must acknowledge the principles of morality even when to one's disadvantage. A man whose moral judgments always coincided with his interests could be suspected of having no morality at all.

Thus the two parts of the foregoing account are intended to mirror the kinds of circumstances in which questions of justice arise and the constraints which having a morality would impose upon persons so situated. In this way one can see how the acceptance of the principles of justice might come about, for given all these conditions as described, it would be natural if the two principles of justice were to be acknowledged. Since there is no way for anyone to win special advantage for himself, each might consider it reasonable to acknowledge equality as an initial principle. There is, however, no reason why they should regard this position as final; for if there are inequalities which satisfy the second principle, the immediate gain which equality would allow can be considered as intelligently invested in view of its future return. If, as is quite likely, these inequalities work as incentives to draw out better efforts, the members of this society may look upon them as concessions to human nature: they, like us, may think that people ideally should want to serve one another. But as they are mutually self-interested, their acceptance of these inequalities is merely the acceptance of the relations in which they actually stand, and a recognition of the motives which lead them to engage in their common practices. *They* have no title to complain of one another. And, so provided that the conditions of the principle are met, there is no reason why they should not allow such inequalities. Indeed, it would be shortsighted of them to do so, and could result, in most cases, only from their being dejected by the bare knowledge, or perception, that others are better situated. Each person will, however, insist on an advantage to himself, and so on a common advantage, for none is willing to sacrifice anything for the others.

John Rawls *is a professor of philosophy at Harvard University and the author of* A Theory of Justice. *In the following essay, he discusses some of the main ideas of his theory "justice as fairness."*

What Libertarianism Is

John Hospers

The political philosophy that is called libertarianism (from the Latin *libertas*, liberty) is the doctrine that every person is the owner of his own life, and that no one is the owner of anyone else's life; and that consequently every human being has the right to act in accordance with his own choices, unless those actions infringe on the equal liberty of other human beings to act in accordance with *their* choices.

There are several other ways of stating the same libertarian thesis:

1. *No one is anyone else's master, and no one is anyone else's slave.* Since I am the one to decide how my life is to be conducted, just as you decide about yours, I have no right (even if I had the power) to make you my slave and be your master, nor have you the right to become the master by enslaving me. Slavery is *forced* servitude, and since no one owns the life of anyone else, no one has the right to enslave another. Political theories past and present have traditionally been concerned with who should be the master (usually the king, the dictator, or government bureaucracy) and who should be the slaves, and what the extent of the slavery should be. Libertarianism holds that no one has the right to use force to enslave the life of another, or any portion or aspect of that life.

2. *Other men's lives are not yours to dispose of.* I enjoy seeing operas; but operas are expensive to produce. Opera-lovers often say, "The state (or the city, etc.) should subsidize opera, so that we can all see it. Also it would be for people's betterment, cultural benefit, etc." But what they are advocating is nothing more or less than legalized plunder. They can't pay for the productions themselves, and yet they want to see opera, which involves a large number of people and their labor; so what they are saying in effect is, "Get the money through legalized force. Take a little bit more out of every worker's paycheck every week to pay for the operas we want to see." But I have no right to take by force from the workers' pockets to pay for what I want.

Chapter X: The Individual and Society

Perhaps it would be better if he *did* go to see opera—then I should try to convince him to go voluntarily. But to take the money from him forcibly, because in my opinion it would be good for *him*, is still seizure of his earnings, which is plunder.

Besides, if I have the right to force him to help pay for my pet projects, hasn't he equally the right to force me to help pay for his? Perhaps he in turn wants the government to subsidize rock-and-roll, or his new car, or a house in the country? If I have the right to milk him, why hasn't he the right to milk me? If I can be a moral cannibal, why can't he too?

We should beware of the inventors of utopias. They would remake the world according to their vision—with the lives and fruits of the labor of *other* human beings. Is it someone's utopian vision that others should build pyramids to beautify the landscape? Very well, then other men should provide the labor; and if he is in a position of political power, and he can't get men to do it voluntarily, then he must *compel* them to "cooperate"—i.e. he must enslave them.

A hundred men might gain great pleasure from beating up or killing just one insignificant human being; but other men's lives are not theirs to dispose of. "In order to achieve the worthy goals of the next five-year-plan, we must forcibly collectivize the peasants . . ."; but other men's lives are not theirs to dispose of. Do you want to occupy, rent-free, the mansion that another man has worked for twenty years to buy? But other men's lives are not yours to dispose of. Do you want operas so badly that everyone is forced to work harder to pay for their subsidization through taxes? But other men's lives are not yours to dispose of. Do you want to have free medical care at the expense of other people, whether they wish to provide it or not? But this would require them to work longer for you whether they want to or not, and other men's lives are not yours to dispose of.

> The freedom to engage in any type of enterprise, to produce, to own and control property, to buy and sell on the free market, is derived from the rights to life, liberty, and property . . . which are stated in the Declaration of Independence. . . . [but] when the government guarantees a "right" to an education or parity on farm products or a guaranteed annual income, it is staking a claim on the property of one group of citizens for the sake of another group. In short, it is violating one of the fundamental rights it was instituted to protect.[1]

3. *No human being should be a nonvoluntary mortgage on the life of another.* I cannot claim your life, your work, or the products of your effort as mine. The fruit of one man's labor should not be fair game for every freeloader who comes along and demands it as his own. The orchard that has been carefully grown, nurtured, and harvested by its owner should not be ripe for the plucking for any bypasser who has a yen for the ripe fruit. The wealth that some men have produced should not be fair game for

looting by government, to be used for whatever purposes its representatives determine, no matter what their motives in so doing may be. The theft of your money by a robber is not justified by the fact that he used it to help his injured mother.

It will already be evident that libertarian doctrine is embedded in a view of the rights of man. Each human being has the right to live his life as he chooses, compatibly with the equal right of all other human beings to live their lives as they choose.

All man's rights are implicit in the above statement. Each man has the right to life: any attempt by others to take it away from him, or even to injure him, violates this right, through the use of coercion against him. Each man has the right to liberty: to conduct his life in accordance with the alternatives open to him without coercive action by others. And every man has the right to property: to work to sustain his life (and the lives of whichever others he chooses to sustain, such as his family) and to retain the fruits of his labor.

People often defend the rights of life and liberty but denigrate property rights, and yet the right to property is as basic as the other two; indeed, without property rights no other rights are possible. Depriving you of property is depriving you of the means by which you live.

> ... All that which an individual possesses by right (including his life and property) are morally his to use, dispose of and even destroy, as he sees fit. If I own my life, then it follows that I am free to associate with whom I please and not to associate with whom I please. If I own my knowledge and services it follows that I may ask any compensation I wish for providing them for another, or I may abstain from providing them at all, if I so choose. If I own my house, it follows that I may decorate it as I please and live in it with whom I please. If I control my own business, it follows that I may charge what I please for my products or services, hire whom I please and not hire whom I please. All that which I own in fact, I may dispose of as I choose to in reality. For anyone to attempt to limit my freedom to do so is to violate my rights.
>
> Where do my rights end? Where yours begin. I may do anything I wish with my own life, liberty and property without your consent; but I may do nothing with your life, liberty and property without your consent. If we recognize the principle of man's rights, it follows that the individual is sovereign of the domain of his own life and property, and is sovereign of no other domain. To attempt to interfere forcibly with another's use, disposal or destruction of his own property is to initiate force against him and to violate his rights.

I have no right to decide how *you* should spend your time or your money. I can make that decision for myself, but not for you, my neighbor. I may deplore your choice of life-style, and I may talk with you about it provided you are willing to listen to me. But I have no right to use force to change it. Nor have I the right to decide how you should spend the money you have earned. I may appeal to you to give it to the Red Cross, and you may prefer to go to prizefights. But that is your decision, and however much I may chafe about it I do not have the right to interfere forcibly with it, for example by robbing you in order to use the money in accordance with *my* choices. (If I have the right to rob you, have you also the right to rob me?)

When I claim a right, I carve out a niche, as it were, in my life, saying in effect, "This activity I must be able to perform without interference from others. For you and everyone else, this is off limits." And so I put up a "no trespassing" sign, which marks off the area of my right. Each individual's right is his "no trespassing" sign in relation to me and others. I may not encroach upon his domain any more than he upon mine, without my consent. Every right entails a duty, true—but the duty is only that of *forbearance*—that is, of *refraining* from violating the other person's right. If you have a right to life, I have no right to take your life; if you have a right to the products of your labor (property), I have no right to take it from you without your consent. The non-violation of these rights will not guarantee you protection against natural catastrophes such as floods and earthquakes, but it will protect you against the aggressive activities of *other men*. And rights, after all, have to do with one's relations to other human beings, not with one's relations to physical nature.

Nor were these rights created by government; governments—some governments, obviously not all—*recognize* and *protect* the rights that individuals already have. Governments regularly forbid homicide and theft; and, at a more advanced stage, protect individuals against such things as libel and breach of contract.

> It cannot be by chance that they thus agree. They agree because the alleged creating of rights [by government] was nothing else than giving formal sanction and better definition to those assertions of claims and recognitions of claims which naturally originate from the individual desires of men who have to live in presence of one another.
>
> ... Those who hold that life is valuable, hold, by implication, that men ought not to be prevented from carrying on life-sustaining activities. ... Clearly the conception of "natural rights" originates in recognition of the truth that if life is justifiable, there must be a justification for the performance of acts essential to its preservation; and, therefore, a justification of those liberties and claims which make such acts possible.
>
> ... To recognize and enforce the rights of individuals, is at the same time to recognize and enforce the conditions to a normal social life.[2]

The *right to property* is the most misunderstood and unappreciated of human rights, and it is one most constantly violated by governments. "Property" of course does not mean only real estate; it includes anything you can call your own—your clothing, your car, your jewelry, your books and papers.

The right of property is not the right to just *take* it from others, for this would interfere with *their* property rights. It is rather the right to work for it, to obtain non-coercively the money or services which you can present in voluntary exchange.

The right to property is consistently underplayed by intellectuals today, sometimes even frowned upon, as if we should feel guilty for upholding such a right in view of all the poverty in the world. But the right to property is absolutely basic. It is your hedge against the future. It is your assurance that what you have worked to earn will still be there, and be yours, when you wish or need to use it, especially when you are too old to work any longer. . . .

Indeed, only if property rights are respected is there any point to planning for the future and working to achieve one's goals. *Property rights are what makes long-range planning possible*—the kind of planning which is a distinctively human endeavor, as opposed to the day-by-day activity of the lion who hunts, who depends on the supply of game tomorrow but has no real insurance against starvation in a day or a week. Without the right to property, the right to life itself amounts to little: how can you sustain your life if you cannot plan ahead? and how can you plan ahead if the fruits of your labor can at any moment be confiscated by government? . . .

"But why have *individual* property rights? Why not have lands and houses owned by everybody together?" Yes, this involves no violation of individual rights, as long as everybody consents to this arrangement and no one is forced to join it. The parties to it may enjoy the communal living enough (at least for a time) to overcome certain inevitable problems: that some will work and some not, that some will achieve more in an hour than others can do in a day, and still they will all get the same income. The few who do the most will in the end consider themselves "workhorses" who do the work of two or three or twelve, while the others will be "freeloaders" on the efforts of these few. But as long as they can get out of the arrangement if they no longer like it, no violation of rights is involved. They got in voluntarily, and they can get out voluntarily; no one has used force.

"But why not say that everybody owns everything? That we *all* own everything there is?"

To some this may have a pleasant ring—but let us try to analyze what it means. If everybody owns everything, then everyone has an equal right to go everywhere, do what he pleases, take what he likes, destroy if he wishes, grow crops or burn them, trample them under, and so on. Consider what it would be like in practice. Suppose you have saved money to buy a house for yourself and your family. Now suppose that the principle, "everybody owns everything," becomes adopted. Well then, why shouldn't every itinerant hippie just come in and take over, sleeping in your beds and eating in your kitchen and not bothering to replace the food supply or clean up the mess? After all, it belongs to all of us, doesn't it? So we have just as much right to it as you, the buyer, have. What happens if we *all* want to sleep in the bedroom and there's not room for all of us? Is it the strongest who wins?

What would be the result? Since no one would be responsible for anything, the property would soon be destroyed, the food used up, the facilities nonfunctional. Beginning as a house that *one* family could use, it would end up as a house that *no one* could use. And if the principle continued to be adopted, no one would build houses any more—or anything else. What for? They would only be occupied and used by others, without remuneration. . . .

Government

Government is the most dangerous institution known to man. Throughout history it has violated the rights of men more than any individual or group of individuals could do: it has killed people, enslaved them, sent them to forced labor and concentration camps, and regularly robbed and pillaged them of the fruits of their expended labor. Unlike individual criminals, government has the power to arrest and try; unlike individual criminals, it can surround and encompass a person totally, dominating every aspect of one's life, so that one has no recourse from it but to leave the country (and in totalitarian nations even that is prohibited). Government throughout history has a much sorrier record than any individual, even that of a ruthless mass murderer. The signs we see on bumper stickers are chillingly accurate: "Beware: the Government is Armed and Dangerous."

The only proper role of government, according to libertarians, is that of the protector of the citizen against aggression by other individuals. The government, of course, should never initiate aggression; its proper role is as the embodiment of the *retaliatory* use of force against anyone who initiates its use.

If each individual had constantly to defend himself against possible aggressors, he would have to spend a considerable portion of his life in target practice, karate exercises, and other means of self-defenses, and even so he would probably be helpless against groups of individuals who might try to kill, maim, or rob him. He would have little time for cultivating those qualities which are essential to civilized life, nor would improvements in science, medicine, and the arts be likely to occur. The function of government is to take this responsibility off his shoulders: the government undertakes to defend him against aggressors and to punish them if they attack him. When the government is effective in doing this, it enables the citizen to go about his business unmolested and without constant fear for his life. To do this, of course, government must have physical power—the police, to protect the citizen from aggression within its borders, and the armed forces, to protect him from aggressors outside. Beyond that, the government should not intrude upon his life, either to run his business, or adjust his daily activities, or prescribe his personal moral code.

Government, then, undertakes to be the individual's protector; but historically governments have gone far beyond this function. Since they already have the physical power, they have not hesitated to use it for purposes far beyond that which was entrusted to them in the first place. Undertaking initially to protect its citizens against aggression, it has often itself become an aggressor—a far greater aggressor, indeed, than the criminals against whom it was supposed to protect its citizens. Governments have done what no private citizens can do: arrest and imprison individuals without a trial and send them to slave labor camps. Government must have power in order to be effective—and yet the very means by which alone it can be effective make it vulnerable to the abuse of power, leading to managing the lives of individuals and even inflicting terror upon them.

What then should be the function of government? In a word, the *protection of human rights*.

1. *The right to life:* libertarians support all such legislation as will protect human beings against the use of force by others, for example, laws against killing, attempted killing, maiming, beating, and all kinds of physical violence.
2. *The right to liberty:* there should be no laws compromising in any way freedom of speech, of the press, and of peaceable assembly. There should be no censorship of ideas, books, films, or of anything else by government.
3. *The right to property:* libertarians support legislation that protects the property rights of individuals against confiscation, nationalization, eminent domain, robbery, trespass, fraud and misrepresentation, patent and copyright, libel and slander.

Someone has violently assaulted you. Should he be legally liable? Of course. He has violated one of your rights. He has knowingly injured you, and since he has initiated aggression against you he should be made to expiate.

Someone has negligently left his bicycle on the sidewalk where you trip over it in the dark and injure yourself. He didn't to it intentionally; he didn't mean you any harm. Should he be legally liable? Of course, he has, however unwittingly, injured you, and since the injury is caused by him and you are the victim, he should pay.

Someone across the street is unemployed. Should you be taxed to pay for his expenses? Not at all. You have not injured him, you are not respon-

Chapter X: The Individual and Society

sible for the fact that he is unemployed (unless you are a senator or bureaucrat who agitated for further curtailing of business, which legislation passed, with the result that your neighbor was laid off by the curtailed business). You may voluntarily wish to help him out, or better still, try to get him a job to put him on his feet again; but since you have initiated no aggressive act against him, and neither purposely nor accidentally injured him in any way, you should not be legally penalized for the fact of his unemployment. (Actually, it is just such penalties that increase unemployment.)

One man, A, works hard for years and finally earns a high salary as a professional man. A second man, B, prefers not to work at all, and to spend wastefully what money he has (through inheritance), so that after a year or two he has nothing left. At the end of this time he has a long siege of illness and lots of medical bills to pay. He demands that the bills be paid by the government—that is, by the taxpayers of the land, including Mr. A.

But of course B has no such right. He chose to lead his life in a certain way—that was his voluntary decision. One consequence of that choice is that he must depend on charity in case of later need. Mr. A chose not to live that way. (And if everyone lived like Mr. B, on whom would he depend in case of later need?) Each has a right to live in the way he pleases, but each must live with the consequences of his own decision (which, as always, fall primarily on himself). He cannot, in time of need, claim A's beneficence as his right. . . .

Laws may be classified into three types: (1) laws protecting individuals against themselves, such as laws against fornication and other sexual behavior, alcohol, and drugs; (2) laws protecting individuals against aggressions by other individuals, such as laws against murder, robbery, and fraud; (3) laws requiring people to help one another; for example, all laws which rob Peter to pay Paul, such as welfare.

Libertarians reject the first class of laws totally. Behavior which harms no one else is strictly the individual's own affair. Thus, there should be no laws against becoming intoxicated, since whether or not to become intoxicated is the individual's own decision; but there should be laws against driving while intoxicated, since the drunken driver is a threat to every other motorist on the highway (drunken driving falls into type 2). Similarly, there should be no laws against drugs (except the prohibition of sale of drugs to minors) as long as the taking of these drugs poses no threat to anyone else. Drug addiction is a psychological problem to which no present solution exists. Most of the social harm caused by addicts, other than to themselves, is the result of thefts which they perform in order to continue their habit—and then the *legal* crime is the theft, not the addiction. The actual cost of heroin is about ten cents a shot; if it were legalized, the enormous traffic in illegal sale and purchase of it would stop, as well as the accompanying proselytization to get new addicts (to make more money for the pusher) and the thefts performed by addicts who often require eighty dollars a day just to keep up the habit. Addiction would not stop, but the crimes would: it is estimated that 75 percent of the burglaries in New York City today are performed by addicts, and all these crimes could be wiped out at one stroke through the legalization of drugs. (Only when the taking of drugs could be shown to constitute a threat to *others*, should it be prohibited by law. It is only laws protecting people against *themselves* that libertarians oppose.)

Laws should be limited to the second class only: aggression by individuals against other individuals. These are laws whose function is to protect human beings against encroachment by others; and this, as we have seen, is (according to libertarianism) the sole function of government.

Libertarians also reject the third class of laws totally: no one should be forced by law to help others, not even to tell them the time of day if requested, and certainly not to give them a portion of one's weekly paycheck. Governments, in the guise of humanitarianism, have given to some by taking from others (charging a "handling fee" in the process, which, because of the government's waste and inefficiency, sometimes is several hundred percent). And in so doing they have decreased incentive, violated the rights of individuals, and lowered the standard of living of almost everyone.

All such laws constitute what libertarians call *moral cannibalism*. A cannibal in the physical sense is a person who lives off the flesh of other human beings. A *moral* cannibal is one who believes he has a right to live off the "spirit" of other human beings—who believes that he has a moral claim on the productive capacity, time, and effort expended by others.

It has become fashionable to claim virtually everything that one needs or desires as one's *right*. Thus, many people claim that they have a right to a job, the right to free medical care, to free food and clothing, to a decent home, and so on. Now if one asks, apart from any specific context, whether it would be desirable if everyone had these things, one might well say yes. But there is a gimmick attached to each of them: *At whose expense?* Jobs, medical care, education, and so on, don't grow on trees. These are goods and services *produced only by men*. Who, then, is to provide them, and under what conditions?

If you have a right to a job, who is to supply it? Must an employer supply it even if he doesn't want to hire you? What if you are unemployable, or incurably lazy? (If you say "the government must supply it," does that mean that a job must be created for you which no employer needs done, and that you must be kept in it regardless of how much or little you work?) If the employer is forced to supply it at his expense even if he doesn't need you, then isn't *he* being enslaved to that extent? What ever happened to *his* right to conduct his life and his affairs in accordance with his choices?

Chapter X: The Individual and Society

If you have a right to free medical care, then, since medical care doesn't exist in nature as wild apples do, some people will have to supply it to you for free: that is, they will have to spend their time and money and energy taking care of you whether they want to or not. What ever happened to *their* right to conduct their lives as they see fit? Or do you have a right to violate theirs? Can there be a right to violate rights?

All those who demand this or that as a "free service" are consciously or unconsciously evading the fact that there is in reality no such thing as free services. All man-made goods and services are the result of human expenditure of time and effort. There is no such thing as "something for nothing" in this world. If you demand something free, you are demanding that other men give their time and effort to you without compensation. If they voluntarily choose to do this, there is no problem; but if you demand that they be *forced* to do it, you are interfering with their right not to do it if they so choose. "Swimming in this pool ought to be free!" says the indignant passerby. What he means is that others should build a pool, others should provide the materials, and still others should run it and keep it in functioning order, so that *he* can use it without fee. But what right has he to the expenditure of *their* time and effort? To expect something "for free" is to expect it *to be paid for by others* whether they choose to or not.

Many questions, particularly about economic matters, will be generated by the libertarian account of human rights and the role of government. Should government have no role in assisting the needy, in providing social security, in legislating minimum wages, in fixing prices and putting a ceiling on rents, in curbing monopolies, in erecting tariffs, in guaranteeing jobs, in managing the money supply? To these and all similar questions the libertarian answers with an unequivocal no.

"But then you'd let people go hungry!" comes the rejoinder. This, the libertarian insists, is precisely what would not happen; with the restrictions removed, the economy would flourish as never before. With the controls taken off business, existing enterprises would expand and new ones would spring into existence satisfying more and more consumer needs; millions more people would be gainfully employed instead of subsisting on welfare, and all kinds of research and production, released from the stranglehold of government, would proliferate, fulfilling man's needs and desires as never before. It has always been so whenever government has permitted men to be free traders on a free market. But *why* this is so, and how the free market is the best solution to all problems relating to the material aspect of man's life, is another and far longer story. It is told in detail in chapters 3 to 9 of my book, *Libertarianism*.

Notes

1. William W. Bayes, "What Is Property?" *The Freeman*, July 1970, p. 348.
2. Herbert Spencer, *The Man vs. the State* (1884; reprint ed.; Caldwell, Id.: Caxton Printers, 1940), p. 191.

From John Hospers, "What Libertarianism Is," in *The Libertarian Alternative*, ed. by Tibor R. Machan. © 1974 by Tibor R. Machan. Reprinted by permission of Nelson-Hall, Inc., Publishers.

Alienated Man

Karl Marx

We have proceeded from the premises of political economy. We have accepted its language and its laws. We presupposed private property, the separation of labor, capital and land, and of wages, profit of capital and rent of land—likewise division of labor, competition, the concept of exchange-value, etc. On the basis of political economy itself, in its own words, we have shown that the worker sinks to the level of a commodity and becomes indeed the most wretched of commodities; that the wretchedness of the worker is in inverse proportion to the power and magnitude of his production; that the necessary result of competition is the accumulation of capital in a few hands, and thus the restoration of monopoly in a more terrible form; and that finally the distinction between capitalist and land rentier, like that between the tiller of the soil and the factory worker, disappears and that the whole of society must fall apart into the two classes—the property *owners* and the propertyless *workers*.

Political economy starts with the fact of private property, but it does not explain it to us. It expresses in general, abstract formulas the *material* process through which private property actually passes, and these formulas it then takes for *laws*. It does not *comprehend* these laws, i.e., it does not demonstrate how they arise from the very nature of private property. Political economy does not disclose the source of the division between labor and capital, and between capital and land. When, for example, it defines the relationship of wages to profit, it takes the interest of the capitalists to be the ultimate cause, i.e., it takes for granted what it is supposed to explain. Similarly, competition comes in everywhere. It is explained from external circumstances. As to how far these external and apparently accidental circumstances are but the expression of a necessary course of development, political economy teaches us nothing. We have seen how exchange itself appears to it as an accidental fact. The only wheels which political economy sets in motion are *greed* and the war *amongst the greedy—competition*.

Precisely because political economy does not grasp the way the movement is connected, it was possible to oppose, for instance, the doctrine of competition to the doctrine of monopoly, the doctrine of the freedom of the crafts to the doctrine of the guild, the doctrine of the division of landed property to the doctrine of the big estate—for competition, freedom of the crafts and the division of landed property were explained and comprehended only as accidental, premeditated and violent consequences of monopoly, of the guild system, and of feudal property, not as their necessary, inevitable and natural consequences.

Now, therefore, we have to grasp the essential connection between private property, greed, and the separation of labor, capital and landed property; between exchange and competition, value and the devaluation of men, monopoly and competition, etc.—the connection between this whole estrangement and the *money* system.

Do not let us go back to a fictitious primordial condition as the political economist does, when he tries to explain. Such a primordial condition explains nothing; it merely pushes the question away into a gray nebulous distance. It assumes in the form of a fact, of an event, what the economist is supposed to deduce—namely, the necessary relationship between two things—between, for example, division of labor and exchange. Theology in the same way explains the origin of evil by the fall of man; that is, it assumes as a fact, in historical form, what has to be explained.

We proceed from an economic fact *of the present*.

The worker becomes all the poorer the more wealth he produces, the more his production increases in power and size. The worker becomes an ever cheaper commodity the more commodities he creates. With the *increasing value* of the world of things proceeds in direct proportion the *devaluation* of the world of men. Labor produces not only commodities: it produces itself and the worker as a *commodity*—and this in the same general proportion in which it produces commodities.

This fact expresses merely that the object which labor produces—labor's product—confronts it as *something alien*, as a *power independent* of the producer. The product of labor is labor which has been embodied in an object, which has become material: it is the *objectifications* of labor. Labor's realization is its objectification. In the sphere of political economy this realization of labor appears as *loss of realization* for the workers; objectification as *loss of the object* and *bondage to it;* appropriation as *estrangement*, as *alienation*.

So much does labor's realization appear as loss of realization that the worker loses realization to the point of starving to death. So much does objectification appear as loss of the object that the worker is robbed of the objects most necessary not only for his life but for his work. Indeed, labor itself becomes an object which he can obtain only with the greatest effort and with the most irregular interruptions. So much does the appropriation

Chapter X: The Individual and Society

of the object appear as estrangement that the more objects the worker produces the less he can possess and the more he falls under the sway of his product, capital.

All these consequences result from the fact that the worker is related to the *product of his labor* as to an *alien* object. For on this premise it is clear that the more the worker spends himself, the more powerful becomes the alien world of objects which he creates over and against himself, the poorer he himself—his inner world—becomes, the less belongs to him as his own. It is the same in religion. The more man puts into God, the less he retains in himself. The worker puts his life into the object; but now his life no longer belongs to him but to the object. Hence, the greater this activity, the greater is the worker's lack of objects. Whatever the product of his labor is, he is not. Therefore the greater this product, the less is he himself. The *alienation* of the worker in his product means not only that this labor becomes an object, an *external existence*, but that it exists *outside him*, independently, as something alien to him, and that it becomes a power on its own confronting him. It means that the life which he has conferred on the object confronts him as something hostile and alien.

Let us now look more closely at the *objectification*, at the production of the worker; and in it at the *estrangement*, the *loss* of the object, of his product.

The worker can create nothing without *nature*, without the *sensuous external world*. It is the material on which his labor is realized, in which it is active, from which and by means of which it produces.

But just as nature provides labor with the *means of life* in the sense that labor cannot *live* without objects on which to operate, on the other hand, it also provides the *means of life* in the more restricted sense, i.e., the means for the physical subsistence of the *worker* himself.

Thus the more the worker by his labor *appropriates* the external world, hence sensuous nature, the more he deprives himself of *means of life* in a double manner: first, in that the sensuous external world more and more ceases to be an object belonging to his labor—to be his labor's *means of life;* and secondly, in that it more and more ceases to be *means of life* in the immediate sense, means for the physical subsistence of the worker.

In both respects, therefore, the worker becomes a slave of his object, first, in that he receives an *object of labor*, i.e., in that he receives *work;* and secondly, in that he receives *means of subsistence*. Therefore, it enables him to exist, first, as a *worker;* and second as a *physical subject*. The height of this bondage is that it is only as a *worker* that he continues to maintain himself as a *physical subject*, and that it is only as a *physical subject* that he is a *worker*.

(The laws of political economy express the estrangement of the worker in his object thus: the more the worker produces, the less he has to consume; the more values he creates, the more valueless, the more unworthy he becomes; the better formed his product, the more deformed becomes the worker; the more civilized his object, the more barbarous becomes the worker; the more powerful labor becomes, the more powerless becomes the worker; the more ingenious labor becomes, the less ingenious becomes the worker and the more he becomes nature's bondsman.)

Political economy conceals the estrangement inherent in the nature of labor by not considering the direct relationship between the worker (labor) *and production.* It is true that labor produces for the rich wonderful things—but for the worker it produces privation. It produces palaces—but for the worker, hovels. It produces beauty—but for the worker, deformity. It replaces labor by machines, but it throws a section of the workers back to a barbarous type of labor, and it turns the other workers into machines. It produces intelligence—but for the worker stupidity, cretinism.

The direct relationship of labor to its products is the relationship of the worker to the objects of his production. The relationship of the man of means to the objects of production and to production itself is only a *consequence* of this first relationship—and confirms it. We shall consider this other aspect later.

When we ask, then, what is the essential relationship of labor we are asking about the relationship of the *worker* to production.

Till now we have been considering the estrangement, the alienation of the worker only in one of its aspects, i.e., the worker's *relationship to the products of his labor.* But the estrangement is manifested not only in the result but in the *act of production*, within the *producing activity*, itself. How could the worker come to face the product of his activity as a stranger, were it not that in the very act of production he was estranging himself from himself? The product is after all but the summary of the activity, of production. If then the product of labor is alienation, production itself must be active alienation, the alienation of activity, the activity of alienation. In the estrangement of the object of labor is merely summarized the estrangement, the alienation, in the activity of labor itself.

What, then, constitutes the alienation of labor?

First, the fact that labor is *external* to the worker, i.e., it does not belong to his essential being; that in his work, therefore, he does not affirm himself but denies himself, does not feel content but unhappy, does not develop freely his physical and mental energy but mortifies his body and ruins his mind. The worker therefore only feels himself outside his work, and in his work feels outside himself. He is at home when he is not working, and when he is working he is not at home. His labor is therefore not voluntary, but coerced; it is *forced labor*. It is therefore not the satisfaction of a need; it is merely a *means* to satisfy needs external to it. Its alien character emerges clearly in the fact that as soon as no physical or other compulsion exists, labor is shunned like the plague. External labor, labor

Chapter X: The Individual and Society

in which man alienates himself, is a labor of self-sacrifice, of mortification. Lastly, the external character of labor for the worker appears in the fact that it is not his own, but someone else's, that it does not belong to him, that in it he belongs, not to himself, but to another. Just as in religion the spontaneous activity of the human imagination, of the human brain and the human heart, operates independently of the individual—that is, operates on him as an alien, divine or diabolical activity—so is the worker's activity not his spontaneous activity. It belongs to another; it is the loss of his self.

As a result, therefore, man (the worker) only feels himself freely active in his animal functions—eating, drinking, procreating, or at most in his dwelling and in dressing-up, etc.; and in his human functions he no longer feels himself to be anything but an animal. What is animal becomes human and what is human becomes animal.

Certainly eating, drinking, procreating, etc., are also genuinely human functions. But abstractly taken, separated from the sphere of all other human activity and turned into sole and ultimate ends, they are animal functions.

We have considered the act of estranging practical human activity, labor, in two of its aspects. (1) The relation of the worker to the *product of labor* as an alien object exercising power over him. This relation is at the same time the relation to the sensuous external world, to the objects of nature, as an alien world inimically opposed to him. (2) The relation of labor to the *act of production* within the *labor* process. This relation is the relation of the worker to his own activity as an alien activity not belonging to him; it is activity as suffering, strength as weakness, begetting as emasculating, the worker's *own* physical and mental energy, his personal life indeed, what is life but activity?—as an activity which is turned against him, independent of him and not belonging to him. Here we have *self-estrangement*, as previously we had estrangement of the *thing*.

We have still a third aspect of *estranged labor* to deduce from the two already considered.

Man is a species being, not only because in practice and in theory he adopts the species as his object (his own as well as those of other things), but—and this is only another way of expressing it—also because he treats himself as the actual, living species; because he treats himself as a *universal* and therefore a free being.

The life of the species, both in man and in animals, consists physically in the fact that man (like the animal) lives on inorganic nature; and the more universal man is compared with an animal, the more universal is the sphere of inorganic nature on which he lives. Just as plants, animals, stones, air, light, etc., constitute theoretically a part of human consciousness, partly as objects of natural science, partly as objects of art—his spiritual inorganic nature, spiritual nourishment which he must first prepare to make palatable and digestible—so also in the realm of practice they constitute a part of human life and human activity. Physically man lives only on these products of nature, whether they appear in the form of food, heating, clothes, a dwelling, etc. The universality of man appears in practice precisely in the universality which makes all nature his *inorganic* body—both inasmuch as nature is (1) his direct means of life, and (2) the material, the object, and the instrument of his life activity. Nature is man's *inorganic body*—nature, that is, in so far as it is not itself the human body. Man *lives* on nature—means that nature is his *body*, with which he must remain in continuous interchange if he is not to die. That man's physical and spiritual life is linked to nature means simply that nature is linked to itself, for man is a part of nature.

In estranging from man (1) nature, and (2) himself, his own active functions, his life activity, estranged labor estranges the *species* from man. It changes for him the *life of the species* into a means of individual life. First it estranges the life of the species and individual life, and secondly it makes individual life in its abstract form the purpose of the life of the species, likewise in its abstract and estranged form.

Indeed, labor, *life-activity, productive life* itself, appears in the first place merely as a *means* of satisfying a need—the need to maintain physical existence. Yet the productive life is the life of the species. It is life-engendering life. The whole character of a species—its species character—is contained in the character of its life activity; and free, conscious activity is man's species character. Life itself appears only as a *means to life*.

The animal is immediately one with its life activity. It does not distinguish itself from it. It is *its life activity*. Man makes his life activity itself the object of his will and of his consciousness. He has conscious life activity. It is not a determination with which he directly merges. Conscious life activity distinguishes man immediately from animal life activity. It is just because of this that he is a species being. Or rather, it is only because he is a species being that he is a conscious being, i.e., that his own life is an object for him. Only because of that is his activity free activity. Estranged labor reverses this relationship, so that it is just because man is a conscious being that he makes his life activity, his *essential* being, a mere means of his *existence*.

In creating a *world of objects* by his practical activity, in *his work upon* inorganic nature, man proves himself a conscious species being, i.e., as a being that treats the species as its own essential being, or that treats itself as a species being. Admittedly animals also produce. They build themselves nests, dwellings, like the bees, beavers, ants, etc. But an animal only produces what it immediately needs for itself or its young. It produces onesidedly, whilst man produces universally. It produces only under the dominion of immediate physical need, whilst man produces even when he is free from physical need and only truly produces in freedom therefrom. An animal produces only itself, whilst man reproduces the whole of nature. An animal's product belongs immediately to its physical body, whilst man freely confronts his product. An animal forms things in accordance with the standard and the need of the species to which it belongs, whilst man knows how to produce in accordance with the standard of every species, and knows how to apply everywhere the inherent standard to the object. Man therefore also forms things in accordance with the laws of beauty.

It is just in his work upon the objective world, therefore, that man first really proves himself to be a *species being*. This production is his active species life. Through and because of this production, nature appears as *his* work and his reality. The object of labor is, therefore, the *objectifiction of man's species life:* for he duplicates himself not only, as in consciousness, intellectually, but also actively, in reality, and therefore he contemplates himself in a world that he has created. In tearing away from man the object of his production, therefore, estranged labor tears from him his *species life*, his real objectivity as a member of the species and transforms his advantage over animals into the disadvantage that his inorganic body, nature, is taken away from him.

Similarly, in degrading spontaneous, free, activity, to a means, estranged labor makes man's species life a means to his physical existence.

The consciousness which man has of his species is thus transformed by estrangement in such a way that species life becomes for him a means.

Estranged labor turns thus:

(3) *Man's species being,* both nature and his spiritual species property, into a being *alien* to him, into a *means* to his *individual existence*. It estranges from man his own body, as well as external nature and his spiritual essence, his *human* being.

(4) *An* immediate consequence of the fact that man is estranged from the product of his labor, from his life activity, from his species being is the *estrangement of man* from *man*. When man confronts himself, he confronts the *other* man. What applies to a man's relation to his work, to the product of his labor and to himself, also holds of a man's relation to the other man, and to the other man's labor and object of labor.

In fact, the proposition that man's species nature is estranged from him means that one man is estranged from the other, as each of them is from man's essential nature.

The estrangement of man, and in fact every relationship in which man stands to himself, is first realized and expressed in the relationship in which a man stands to other men.

Hence within the relationship of estranged labor each man views the other in accordance with the standard and the relationship in which he finds himself as a worker.

We took our departure from a fact of political economy—the estrangement of the worker and his production. We have formulated this fact in conceptual terms as *estranged, alienated* labor. We have analyzed this concept—hence analyzing merely a fact of political economy.

Let us now see, further, how the concept of estranged, alienated labor must express and present itself in real life.

If the product of labor is alien to me, if it confronts me as an alien power, to whom, then, does it belong?

If my own activity does not belong to me, if it is an alien, a coerced activity, to whom, then, does it belong?

To a being *other* than myself.

Who is this being?

The *gods?* To be sure, in the earliest times the principal production (for example, the building of temples, etc., in Egypt, India and Mexico) appears to be in the service of the gods, and the product belongs to the gods. However, the gods on their own were never the lords of labor. No more was *nature*. And what a contradiction it would be if, the more man subjugated nature by his labor and the more the miracles of the gods were rendered superfluous by the miracles of industry, the more man were to renounce the joy of production and the enjoyment of the product in favor of these powers.

The *alien* being, to whom labor and the product of labor belongs, in whose service labor is done and for whose benefit the product of labor is provided, can only be *man* himself.

If the product of labor does not belong to the worker, if it confronts him as an alien power, then this can only be because it belongs to some *other man than the worker*. If the worker's activity is a torment to him, to another it must be *delight* and his life's joy. Not the gods, not nature, but only man himself can be this alien power over man.

We must bear in mind the previous proposition that man's relation to himself only becomes for him *objective* and *actual* through his relation to the other man. Thus, if the product of his labor, his labor *objectified*, is for him an *alien*, hostile, powerful object independent of him, then his position towards it is such that someone else is master of this object, someone who is alien, hostile, powerful, and independent of him. If his own activity is to him related as an unfree activity, then he is related to it as an activity performed in the service, under the dominion, the coercion, and the yoke of another man.

Every self-estrangement of man, from himself and from nature, appears in the relation in which he places himself and nature to men other than and differentiated from himself. For this reason religious self-estrangement necessarily appears in the relationship of the layman to the priest, or again to a mediator, etc., since we are here dealing with the intellectual world. In the real practical world self-estrangement can only become manifest through the real practical relationship to other men. The medium through which estrangement takes place is itself *practical*. Thus through estranged labor man not only creates his relationship to the object and to the act of production as to men that are alien and hostile to him; he also creates the relationship in which other men stand to his production and to his product, and the relationship in which he stands to these other men. Just as he creates his own production as the loss of his reality, as his punishment; his own product as a loss, as a product not belonging to him; so he creates the domination of the person who does not produce over production and over the product. Just as he estranges his own activity from himself, so he confers to the stranger an activity which is not his own.

We have until now only considered this relationship from the standpoint of the worker and later we shall be considering it also from the standpoint of the non-worker.

Through *estranged, alienated labor*, then, the worker produces the relationship to this labor of a man alien to labor and standing outside it. The relationship of the worker to labor creates the relation to it of the capitalist (or whatever one chooses to call the master of labor). *Private property* is thus the product, the result, the necessary consequence, of *alienated labor*, of the external relation of the worker to nature and to himself.

Private property thus results by analysis from the concept of *alienated labor*, i.e., of *alienated man*, of estranged labor, of estranged life, of *estranged* man.

True, it is as a result of the *movement of private property* that we have obtained the concept of *alienated labor* (of *alienated life*) from political economy. But on analysis of this concept it becomes clear that though private property appears to be the source, the cause of alienated labor, it is rather its consequence, just as the gods are *originally* not the cause but the effect of man's intellectual confusion. Later this relationship becomes reciprocal.

Only at the last culmination of the development of private property does this, its secret, appear again, namely, that on the one hand it is the *product* of alienated labor, and that on the other it is the *means* by which labor alienates itself, the *realization of this alienation*.

This exposition immediately sheds light on various hitherto unsolved conflicts.

1. Political economy starts from labor as the real soul of production; yet to labor it gives nothing, and to private property everything. Confronting this contradiction, Proudhon has decided in favor of labor against private property. We understand, however, that this apparent contradiction is the contradiction of *estranged labor* with itself, and that political economy has merely formulated the laws of estranged labor.

We also understand, therefore, that *wages* and *private property* are identical: since the product, as the object of labor, pays for labor itself, therefore the wage is but a necessary consequence of labor's estrangement. After all, in the wage of labor, labor does not appear as an end in itself but as the servant of the wage. We shall develop this point later, and meanwhile will only derive some conclusions.

An enforced increase of wages (disregarding all other difficulties, including the fact that it would only be by force, too, that higher wages, being an anomaly, could be maintained) would therefore be nothing but *better payment for the slave*, and would not win either for the worker or for labor their human status and dignity.

Indeed, even the *equality of wages* demanded by Proudhon only transforms the relationship of the present-day worker to his labor into the relationship of all men to labor. Society is then conceived as an abstract capitalist.

Wages are a direct consequence of estranged labor, and estranged labor is the direct cause of private property. The downfall of the one must involve the downfall of the other.

2. From the relationship of estranged labor to private property it follows further that the emancipation of society from private property, etc., from servitude, is expressed in the *political* form of the *emancipation of the workers*; not that *their* emancipation alone is at stake, but because the emancipation of the workers contains universal human emancipation—and it contains this, because the whole of human servitude is involved in the relation of the worker to production, and every relation of servitude is but a modification and consequence of this relation.

Just as we have derived the concept of *private property* from the concept of *estranged, alienated labor* by *analysis*, so we can develop every *category* of political economy with the help of these two factors; and we shall find again in each category, e.g., trade, competition, capital, money, only a *definite* and *developed expression* of these first elements.

Before considering this aspect, however, let us try to solve two problems.

1. To define the general *nature of private property*, as it has arisen as a result of estranged labor, in its relation to *truly human* and *social property*.
2. We have accepted the *estrangement of labor*, its *alienation*, as a fact, and we have analyzed this fact. How, we now ask, does *man* come to *alienate*, to estrange, *his labor*? How is this estrangement rooted in the nature of human development? We have already gone a long way to the solution of this problem by *transforming* the question of the *origin of private property* into the question of the relation of *alienated labor* to the course of humanity's development. For when one speaks of *private property*, one thinks of dealing with something external to man. When one speaks of labor, one is directly dealing with man himself. This new formulation of the question already contains its solution.

As to (1): The general nature of private property and its relation to truly human property.

Alienated labor has resolved itself for us into two elements which mutually condition one another, or which are but different expressions of one and the same relationship. *Appropriation* appears as *estrangement*, as *alienation*; and *alienation* appears as *appropriation, estrangement* as true introduction into society.

We have considered the one side—*alienated* labor in relation to the *worker* himself, i.e., the *relation of alienated labor to itself.* The *property relation of the non-worker to the worker and to labor* we have found as the product, the necessary outcome of this relationship. *Private property*, as the material, summary expression of alienated labor, embraces both relations— the *relation of the worker to work and to the produce of his labor and to the non-worker,* and the relation of the *non-worker to the worker and to the product of his labor.*

Having seen that in relation to the worker who *appropriates* nature by means of his labor, this appropriation appears as estrangement, his own spontaneous activity as activity for another and as activity of another, vitality as a sacrifice of life, production of the object as loss of the object to an alien power, to an *alien* person—we shall now consider the relation to the worker, to labor and its object of this person who is *alien*, to labor and the worker.

First it has to be noted that everything which appears in the worker as an *activity of alienation, of estrangement,* appears in the non-worker as a *state of alienation, of estrangement.*

Secondly, that the workers' *real, practical attitude* in production and to the product (as a state of mind) appears in the non-worker confronting him as a *theoretical* attitude.

Thirdly, the non-worker does everything against the worker which the worker does against himself; but he does not do against himself what he does against the worker.

Let us look more closely at these three relations.

[*At this point the first manuscript breaks off unfinished.*]

Source: Karl Marx, *Economic and Philosophic Manuscripts of 1844*, trans. by Martin Milligan (Moscow: Progress Publishers, 1959).

Consciencism

Kwame Nkrumah

The need for subtle means of social cohesion lies in the fact that there is a large portion of life which is outside direct central intervention. In order that this portion of life should be filled with order, non-statutory methods are required. These non-statutory methods, by the large, are the subtle means of social cohesion. But different societies lay different emphases on these subtle means even if the range of conformity which they seek is the same. The emphasis which a particular society lays on a given means depends on the experience, social-economic circumstances and the philosophical foundation of that society.

In Africa, this kind of emphasis must take objective account of our present situation at the return of political independence. From this point of view, there are three broad features to be distinguished here. African society has one segment which comprises our traditional way of life; it has a second segment which is filled by the presence of the Islamic tradition in Africa; it has a final segment which represents the infiltration of the Christian tradition and culture of Western Europe into Africa, using colonialism and neo-colonialism as its primary vehicles. These different segments are animated by competing ideologies. But since society implies a certain dynamic unity, there needs to emerge an ideology which, genuinely catering for the needs of all, will take the place of the competing ideologies, and so reflect the dynamic unity of society, and be the guide to society's continual progress.

The traditional face of Africa includes an attitude towards man which can only be described, in its social manifestation, as being socialist. This arises from the fact that man is regarded in Africa as primarily a spiritual being, a being endowed originally with a certain inward dignity, integrity and value. It stands refreshingly opposed to the Christian idea of the original sin and degradation of man.

This idea of the original value of man imposes duties of a socialist kind upon us. Herein lies the theoretical basis of African communalism. This theoretical basis expressed itself on the social level in terms of institutions such as the clan, underlining the initial equality of all and the responsibility of many for one. In this social situation, it was impossible for classes of a Marxian kind to arise. By a Marxian kind of class, I mean one which has a place in horizontal social stratification. Here classes are related in such a way that there is a disproportion of economic and political power between them. In such a society there exist classes which are crushed, lacerated and ground down by the encumbrance of exploitation. One class sits upon the neck of another. In this sense, there were no classes in traditional African society.

In the traditional African society, no sectional interest could be regarded as supreme; nor did legislative and executive power aid the interests of any particular group. The welfare of the people was supreme.

But colonialism came and changed all this. First, there were the necessities of the colonial administration. . . . For its success, the colonial administration needed a cadre of Africans, who, by being introduced to a certain minimum of European education, became infected with European ideals, which they tacitly accepted as being valid for African societies. Because these African instruments of the colonial administration were seen by all to be closely associated with the new sources of power, they acquired a certain prestige and rank to which they were not entitled by the demands of the harmonious development of their own society.

In addition to them, groups of merchants and traders, lawyers, doctors, politicians and trade unionists emerged, who, armed with skills and levels of affluence which were gratifying to the colonial administration, initiated something parallel to the European middle class. There were also certain feudal-minded elements who became imbued with European ideals either through direct European education or through hobnobbing with the local colonial administration. They gave the impression that they could be relied upon implicitly as repositories of all those staid and conservative virtues indispensable to any exploiter administration. They, as it were, paid the registration fee for membership of a class which was now associated with social power and authority.

Such education as we were all given put before us right from our infancy ideals of the metropolitan countries, ideals which could seldom be seen as representing the scheme, the harmony and progress of African society. The scale and type of economic activity, the idea of the accountability of the individual conscience introduced by the Christian religion, countless other silent influences, these have all made an indelible impression upon African society.

But neither economic nor political subjugation could be considered as being in tune with the traditional African egalitarian view of man and society. Colonialism had in any case to be done away with. The African Hercules has his club poised ready to smite any new head which the colonialist hydra may care to put out.

With true independence regained, however, a new harmony needs to be forged, a harmony that will allow the combined presence of traditional Africa, Islamic Africa and Euro-Christian Africa, so that this presence is in tune with the original humanist principles underlying African society. Our society is not the old society, but a new society enlarged by Islamic and Euro-Christian influences. A new ideology which can solidify in a philosophical statement, but at the same time an ideology which will not abandon the original humanist principles of Africa.

Such a philosophical statement will be born out of the crisis of the African conscience confronted with the three strands of present African society. Such a philosophical statement I propose to name *philosophical consciencism*, for it will give the theoretical basis for an ideology whose aim shall be to contain the African experience of Islamic and Euro-Christian presence as well as the experience of the traditional African society, and, by gestation, employ them for the harmonious growth and development of that society.

Slavery and feudalism represent social-political theories in which the deployment of forces is not a problematic question. In both slavery and feudalism, workers, the people whose toil transforms nature for the development of society, are dissociated from any say in rule. By a vicious division of labour, one class of citizen toils and another reaps where it has not sown. In the slave society, as in the feudal society, that part of society whose labours transform nature is not the same as the part which is better fulfilled as a result of this transformation. If by their fruits we shall know them, they must first grow the fruits. In slave and feudal society, the fruit-eaters are not the fruit-growers. This is the cardinal factor in exploitation, that the section of a society whose labours transform nature is not the same as the section which is better fulfilled as a result of this transformation.

In every non-socialist society, there can be found two strata which correspond to that of the oppressor and the oppressed, the exploiter and exploited. In all such societies, the essential relation between the two strata is the same as that between masters and slaves, lords and serfs. In capitalism, which is only a social-political theory in which the important aspects of slavery and feudalism are refined, a stratified society is required for its proper functioning, a society is required in which the working class is oppressed by the ruling class; for, under capitalism, that portion of society whose labours transform nature and produce goods is not the portion of society which enjoys the fruits of this transformation and productivity. Nor is it the whole of society which is so enhanced.

This might indeed be termed a contradiction. It is a social contradiction in so far as it is contrary to genuine principles of social equity and social justice. It is also an economic contradiction in so far as it is contrary to a harmonious and unlimited economic development.

Capitalism is a development by refinement from feudalism, just as feudalism is a development by refinement from slavery. The essence of reform is to combine a continuity of fundamental principle, with a tactical change in the manner of expression of the fundamental principle. Reform is not a change in the thought, but one in its manner of expression, not a change in what is said but one in idiom. In capitalism, feudalism suffers, or rather enjoys reform, and the fundamental principle of feudalism merely strikes new levels of subtlety. In slavery, it is thought that exploitation, the alienation of the fruits of the labour of others, requires a certain degree of political and forcible subjection. In feudalism, it is thought that a lesser degree of the same kind of subjection is adequate to the same purpose. In capitalism, it is thought that a still lesser degree is adequate. In this way, psychological irritants to revolution are appeased, and exploitation finds a new lease of life, until the people should discover the *opposition* between reform and revolution.

In this way, capitalism continues with its characteristic pompous plans for niggardly reforms, while it coerces one section of a society somehow into making itself available to another section, which battens on it. That development which capitalism marks over slavery and feudalism consists as much in the methods by means of which labour is coerced as in the mode of production. Capitalism is but the gentleman's method of slavery.

Indeed, a standard ruse of capitalism today is to imitate some of the proposals of socialism, and turn its imitation to its own use. Running with the hare and hunting with the hounds is much more than a pastime to capitalism; it is the hub of a complete strategy. In socialism, we seek an increase in levels of production in order solely that the people, by whose exertions production is possible, shall raise their standard of living and attain a new consciousness and level of life. Capitalism does this too, but not for the same purpose. Increased productivity under capitalism does indeed lead to a rise in the standard of living; but when the proportion of distribution of value between exploited and exploiter is kept constant, then any increase in levels of production must mean a greater *quantity*, but not *proportion*, of value accruing to the exploited. Capitalism thus discovers a new way of seeming to implement reform, while really genuinely avoiding it.

If one seeks the social-political ancestor of socialism, one must go to communalism. Socialism stands to communalism as capitalism stands to slavery. In socialism, the principles underlying communalism are given expression in modern circumstances. Thus, whereas communalism in an untechnical society can be *laissez faire*, in a technical society where sophisticated means of production are at hand, if the underlying principles of communalism are not given centralized and correlated expression, class cleavages will arise, which are connected with economic disparities, and thereby with political inequalities. Socialism, therefore, can be and is the defence of the principles of communalism in a modern setting. Socialism is a form of social organization which, guided by the principles underlying communism, adopts procedures and measures made necessary by demographic and technological developments.

These considerations throw great light on the bearing of revolution and reform on socialism. The passage from the ancestral line of slavery via feudalism and capitalism to socialism can only lie through revolution: it cannot lie through reform. For in reform, fundamental principles are held constant and the details of their expression modified. In the words of Marx, it leaves the pillars of the building intact. Indeed, sometimes, reform itself may be initiated by the necessities of preserving identical fundamental principles. Reform is a tactic of self-preservation.

Revolution is thus an indispensable avenue to socialism, where the antecedent social-political structure is animated by principles which are a negation of those of socialism, as in a capitalist structure (and therefore also in a colonialist structure, for a colonialist structure is essentially ancillary to capitalism). Indeed, I distinguish between two colonialisms, between a domestic one, and an external one. Capitalism at home is a domestic colonialism.

But from the ancestral line of communalism, the passage to socialism lies in reform, because the underlying principles are the same. But when this passage carries one through colonialism the reform is revolutionary since the passage from colonialism to genuine independence is an act of revolution. But because of the continuity of communalism with socialism, in communalistic societies, socialism is not a revolutionary creed, but a restatement in contemporary idiom of the principles underlying communalism. The passage from a noncommunalistic society to socialism is a revolutionary one which is guided by the principles underlying communism.

In my autobiography, I said that capitalism might prove too complicated a system for a newly independent country. I wish to add to this the fact that the presuppositions and purposes of capitalism are contrary to those of African society. Capitalism would be a betrayal of the personality and conscience of Africa.

Kwame Nkrumah. *Consciencism: Philosophy and Ideology for Decolonization and Development with Particular Reference to the African Revolution.* London: Heinemann Educational Books, 1964.

The Declaration of Independence

Thomas Jefferson

In Congress, July 4, 1776: The Unanimous Declaration of the Thirteen United States of America

When in the Course of human events it becomes necessary for one people to dissolve the political bands which have connected them with another, and to assume among the powers of the earth, the separate and equal station to which the Laws of Nature and of Nature's God entitle them, a decent respect to the opinions of mankind requires that they should declare the causes which impel them to the separation.

We hold these truths to be self-evident, that all men are created equal, that they are endowed by their Creator with certain unalienable Rights, that among these are Life, Liberty and the pursuit of Happiness. That to secure these rights, Governments are instituted among Men, deriving their just powers from the consent of the governed. That whenever any Form of Government becomes destructive of these ends, it is the Right of the People to alter or to abolish it, and to institute new Government, laying its foundation on such principles and organizing its powers in such form, as to them shall seem most likely to affect their Safety and Happiness. Prudence, indeed, will dictate that Governments long established should not be changed for light and transient causes; and accordingly all experience hath shewn that mankind are more disposed to suffer, while evils are sufferable, than to right themselves by abolishing the forms to which they are accustomed. But when a long train of abuses and usurpations, pursuing invariably the same Object evinces a design to reduce them under absolute Despotism, it is their right, it is their duty, to throw off such Government, and to provide new Guards for their future security. Such has been the patient sufferance of these Colonies; and such is now the necessity which constrains them to alter their former Systems of Government. The history of the present King of Great Britain is a history of repeated injuries and usurpations, all having in direct object the establishment of an absolute Tyranny over these States. To prove this, let Facts be submitted to a candid world.

He has refused his Assent to Laws, the most wholesome and necessary for the public good.

He has forbidden his Government to pass laws of immediate and pressing importance, unless suspended in their operation till his Assent should be obtained; and when so suspended, he has utterly neglected to attend to them.

He has refused to pass other Laws for the accommodation of large districts of people, unless those people would relinquish the right of Representation in the Legislature, a right inestimable to them and formidable to tyrants only.

He has called together legislative bodies at places unusual, uncomfortable, and distant from the depository of their Public Records, for the sole purpose of fatiguing them into compliance with his measures.

He has dissolved Representative Houses repeatedly, for opposing with manly firmness his invasions on the rights of the people.

He has refused for a long time, after such dissolutions, to cause others to be elected; whereby the Legislative Powers, incapable of Annihilation, have returned to the People at large for their exercise; the State remaining in the mean time exposed to all the dangers of invasion from without, and convulsions within.

He has endeavored to prevent the population of these States; for that purpose obstructing the Laws for Naturalization of Foreigners; refusing to pass others to encourage their migration hither, and raising the conditions of new Appropriations of Lands.

He has obstructed the Administration of Justice, by refusing his Assent to Laws for establishing Judiciary Powers.

He has made Judges dependent on his Will alone, for the tenure of their offices, and the amount and payment of their salaries.

He has erected a multitude of New Offices, and sent hither swarms of Officers to harass our people, and eat out their substance.

He has kept among us, in times of peace, Standing Armies without the Consent of our legislatures.

He has affected to render the Military independent of and superior to the Civil Power.

He has combined with others to subject us to a jurisdiction foreign to our constitution, and unacknowledged by our laws; giving his Assent to their Acts of pretended Legislation: For quartering large bodies of armed troops among us: For protecting them, by a mock Trial, from punishment for any Murders which they should commit on the Inhabitants of these States: For cutting off our Trade with all parts of the world: For imposing

Taxes on us without our Consent: For depriving us in many cases, of the benefits of Trial by Jury; For transporting us beyond Seas to be tried for pretended offenses: for abolishing the free System of English Laws in a neighboring Province, establishing therein an Arbitrary government, and enlarging its Boundaries so as to render it at once an example and fit instrument for introducing the same absolute rule into these Colonies: For taking away our Charters, abolishing our most valuable Laws and altering fundamentally and Forms of our Governments: For suspending our own Legislatures, and declaring themselves invested with power to legislate for us in all cases whatsoever.

He has abdicated Government here, by declaring us out of his Protection and waging War against us.

He has plundered our seas, ravaged our Coasts, burnt our towns, and destroyed the lives of our people.

He is at this time transporting large Armies of foreign Mercenaries to complete the works of death, desolation and tyranny, already begun with circumstances of Cruelty & Perfidy scarcely paralleled in the most barbarous ages, and totally unworthy the Head of a civilized nation.

He has constrained our fellow Citizens taken Captive on the high Seas to bear Arms against their Country, to become the executioners of their friends and Brethren, or to fall themselves by their Hands.

He has excited domestic insurrections amongst us, and has endeavored to bring on the inhabitants of our frontiers, the merciless Indian Savages, whose known rule of warfare, is an undistinguished destruction of all ages, sexes, and conditions.

In every state of these Oppressions We have Petitioned for Redress in the most humble terms: Our repeated Petitions have been answered only by repeated injury. A Prince, whose character is thus marked by every act which may define a Tyrant, is unfit to be the ruler of a free people.

Nor have We been wanting in attention to our British brethren. We have warned them from time to time of attempts by their legislature to extend an unwarrantable jurisdiction over us. We have reminded them of the circumstances of our emigration and settlement here. We have appealed to their native justice and magnanimity, and we have conjured them by the ties of our common kindred to disavow these usurpations, which would inevitably interrupt our connections and correspondence. They too have been deaf to the voice of justice and of consanguinity. We must, therefore, acquiesce in the necessity, which denounces our Separation, and hold them, as we hold the rest of mankind, Enemies in War, in Peace Friends.

We, THEREFORE the Representatives of the UNITED STATES OF AMERICA, in General Congress, Assembled, appealing to the Supreme Judge of the world for the rectitude of our intentions, do, in the Name, and by Authority of the good People of these Colonies, solemnly publish and declare, That these United Colonies are, and of Right ought to be FREE AND INDEPENDENT STATES; that they are Absolved from all Allegiance to the British Crown, and that all political connection between them and the State of Great Britain, is and ought to be totally dissolved; and that as Free and Independent States, they have full Power to levy War, conclude Peace, contract Alliances, establish Commerce, and to do all other Acts and Things which Independent States may of right do. And for the support of this Declaration, with a firm reliance on the protection of Divine Providence, we mutually pledge to each other our Lives, our Fortunes, and our sacred Honor.

I Have a Dream

Martin Luther King, Jr.

I am happy to join with you today in what will go down in history as the greatest demonstration for freedom in the history of our nation.

Fivescore years ago, a great American, in whose symbolic shadow we stand today, signed the Emancipation Proclamation. This momentous decree came as a great beacon light of hope to millions of Negro slaves who had been seared in the flames of withering injustice. It came as a joyous daybreak to end the long night of their captivity.

But one hundred years later, the Negro still is not free; one hundred years later, the life of the Negro is still sadly crippled by the manacles of segregation and the chains of discrimination; one hundred years later, the Negro lives on a lonely island of poverty in the midst of a vast ocean of material prosperity; one hundred years later, the Negro is still languishing in the corners of American society and finds himself in exile in his own land.

So we've come here today to dramatize a shameful condition. In a sense we've come to our nation's capital to cash a check. When the architects of our republic wrote the magnificent words of the Constitution and the Declaration of Independence, they were signing a promissory note to which every American was to fall heir. This note was the promise that all men, yes, black men as well as white men, would be guaranteed the unalienable rights of life, liberty, and the pursuit of happiness.

It is obvious today that America has defaulted on this promissory note in so far as her citizens of color are concerned. Instead of honoring this sacred obligation, America has given the Negro people a bad check; a check which has come back marked "insufficient funds." We refuse to believe that there are insufficient funds in the great vaults of opportunity of this nation. And so we've come to cash this check, a check that will give us upon demand the riches of freedom and the security of justice.

We have also come to this hallowed spot to remind America of the fierce urgency of now. This is no time to engage in the luxury of cooling off or to take the tranquilizing drug of gradualism. Now is the time to make real the promises of democracy; now is the time to rise from the dark and desolate valley of segregation to the sunlit path of racial justice; now is the time to lift our nation from the quicksands of racial injustice to the solid rock of brotherhood; now is the time to make justice a reality for all God's children. It would be fatal for the nation to overlook the urgency of the moment. This sweltering summer of the Negro's legitimate discontent will not pass until there is an invigorating autumn of freedom and equality.

Nineteen sixty-three is not an end, but a beginning. And those who hope that the Negro needed to blow off steam and will now be content, will have a rude awakening if the nation returns to business as usual.

There will be neither rest nor tranquility in America until the Negro is granted his citizenship rights. The whirlwinds of revolt will continue to shake the foundations of our nation until the bright day of justice emerges.

But there is something that I must say to my people who stand on the warm threshold which leads into the palace of justice. In the process of gaining our rightful place we must not be guilty of wrongful deeds.

Let us not seek to satisfy our thirst for freedom by drinking from the cup of bitterness and hatred. We must forever conduct our struggle on the high plane of dignity and discipline. We must not allow our creative protest to degenerate into physical violence. Again and again we must rise to the majestic heights of meeting physical force with soul force.

The marvelous new militancy which has engulfed the Negro community must not lead us to a distrust of all white people for many of our white brothers, as evidenced by their presence here today, have come to realize that their destiny is tied up with our destiny and they have come to realize that their freedom is inextricably bound to our freedom. This offense we share mounted to storm the battlements of injustice must be carried forth by a biracial army. We cannot walk alone.

And as we walk, we must make the pledge that we shall always march ahead. We cannot turn back. There are those who are asking the devotees of civil rights, "When will you be satisfied?" We can never be satisfied as long as the Negro is the victim of the unspeakable horrors of police brutality.

We can never be satisfied as long as our bodies, heavy with fatigue of travel, cannot gain lodging in the motels of the highways and the hotels of the cities. We cannot be satisfied as long as the Negro's basic mobility is from a smaller ghetto to a larger one.

We can never be satisfied as long as our children are stripped of their selfhood and robbed of their dignity by signs stating "for whites only." We cannot be satisfied as long as a Negro in Mississippi cannot vote and a Negro in New York believes he has nothing for which to vote. No, we are not satisfied, and we will not be satisfied until justice rolls down like waters and righteousness like a mighty stream.

I am not unmindful that some of you have come here out of excessive trials and tribulation. Some of you have come fresh from narrow jail cells.

Chapter X: The Individual and Society

Some of you have come from areas where your quest for freedom left you battered by the storms of persecution and staggered by the winds of police brutality. You have been the veterans of creative suffering. Continue to work with the faith that unearned suffering is redemptive.

Go back to Mississippi; go back to Alabama; go back to South Carolina; go back to Georgia; go back to Louisiana; go back to the slums and ghettos of the northern cities, knowing that somehow this situation can, and will be changed. Let us not wallow in the valley of despair.

So I say to you, my friends, that even though we must face the difficulties of today and tomorrow, I still have a dream. It is a dream deeply rooted in the American dream that one day this nation will rise up and live out the true meaning of its creed—we hold these truths to be self-evident, that all men are created equal.

I have a dream that one day on the red hills of Georgia, sons of former slaves and sons of former slave-owners will be able to sit down together at the table of brotherhood.

I have a dream that one day, even the state of Mississippi, a state sweltering with the heat of injustice, sweltering with the heat of oppression, will be transformed into an oasis of freedom and justice.

I have a dream my four little children will one day live in a nation where they will not be judged by the color of their skin but by content of their character. I have a dream today!

I have a dream that one day, down in Alabama, with its vicious racists, with its governor having his lips dripping with the words of interposition and nullification, that one day, right there in Alabama, little black boys and black girls will be able to join hands with little white boys and white girls as sisters and brothers. I have a dream today!

I have a dream that one day every valley shall be exalted, every hill and mountain shall be made low, the rough places shall be made plain, and the crooked places shall be made straight and the glory of the lord will be revealed and all flesh shall see it together.

This is our hope. This is the faith that I go back to the South with.

With this faith we will be able to hew out of the mountain of despair a stone of hope. With this faith we will be able to transform the jangling discords of our nation into a beautiful symphony of brotherhood.

With this faith we will be able to work together, to pray together, to struggle together, to go to jail together, to stand up for freedom together, knowing that we will be free one day. This will be the day when all of God's children will be able to sing with new meaning—"my country 'tis of thee; sweet land of liberty; of thee I sing; land where my fathers died, land of the pilgrim's pride; from every mountain side, let freedom ring"—and if America is to be a great nation, this must become true.

So let freedom ring from the prodigious hilltops of New Hampshire.

Let freedom ring from the mighty mountains of New York.

Let freedom ring from the heightening Alleghenies of Pennsylvania.

Let freedom ring from the snow-capped Rockies of Colorado.
Let freedom ring from the curvaceous slopes of California.
But not only that.
Let freedom ring from Stone Mountain of Georgia.
Let freedom ring from Lookout Mountain of Tennessee.
Let freedom ring from every hill and molehill of Mississippi, from every mountainside, let freedom ring.

And when we allow freedom to ring, when we let it ring from every village and hamlet, from every state and city, we will be able to speed up that day when all of God's children—black men and white men, Jews and Gentiles, Catholics and Protestants—will be able to join hands and to sing in the words of the old Negro spiritual, "Free at last, free at last; thank God Almighty, we are free at last."